GLOBALLY HARMONIZED SYSTEM OF CLASSIFICATION AND LABELLING OF CHEMICALS (GHS)

Fifth revised edition

UNITED NATIONS
New York and Geneva, 2013

NOTE

The designations employed and the presentation of the material in this publication do not imply the expression of any opinion whatsoever on the part of the Secretariat of the United Nations concerning the legal status of any country, territory, city or area, or of its authorities, or concerning the delimitation of its frontiers or boundaries.

ST/SG/AC.10/30/Rev.5

UNITED NATIONS
Sales No. E.13.II.E.1
Print ISBN 978- 92-1-117067-2
eISBN 978-92-1-056080-1

FOREWORD

1.   The Globally Harmonized System of Classification and Labelling of Chemicals (GHS) is the culmination of more than a decade of work. There were many individuals involved, from a multitude of countries, international organizations, and stakeholder organizations. Their work spanned a wide range of expertise, from toxicology to fire protection, and ultimately required extensive goodwill and the willingness to compromise, in order to achieve this system.

2.   The work began with the premise that existing systems should be harmonized in order to develop a single, globally harmonized system to address classification of chemicals, labels, and safety data sheets. This was not a totally novel concept since harmonization of classification and labelling was already largely in place for physical hazards and acute toxicity in the transport sector, based on the work of the United Nations Economic and Social Council's Committee of Experts on the Transport of Dangerous Goods . Harmonization had not been achieved in the workplace or consumer sectors, however, and transport requirements in countries were often not harmonized with those of other sectors.

3.   The international mandate that provided the impetus for completing this work was adopted at the 1992 United Nations Conference on Environment and Development (UNCED), as reflected in Agenda 21, para.19.27:

> "A globally harmonized hazard classification and compatible labelling system, including material safety data sheets and easily understandable symbols, should be available, if feasible, by the year 2000".

4.   The work was coordinated and managed under the auspices of the Interorganization Programme for the Sound Management of Chemicals (IOMC) Coordinating Group for the Harmonization of Chemical Classification Systems (CG/HCCS). The technical focal points for completing the work were the International Labour Organization (ILO); the Organisation for Economic Co-operation and Development (OECD); and the United Nations Economic and Social Council's Sub-Committee of Experts on the Transport of Dangerous Goods.

5.   Once completed in 2001, the work was transmitted by the IOMC to the new United Nations Economic and Social Council's Sub-Committee of Experts on the Globally Harmonized System of Classification and Labelling of Chemicals (GHS Sub-Committee). The Sub-Committee was established by Council resolution 1999/65 of 26 October 1999 as a subsidiary body of the former Committee of Experts on the Transport of Dangerous Goods, which was reconfigured and renamed on the same occasion "Committee of Experts on the Transport of Dangerous Goods and on the Globally Harmonized System of Classification and Labelling of Chemicals" (hereafter referred to as "the Committee"). The Committee and its sub-committees work on a biennial basis. Secretariat services are provided by the Transport Division of the United Nations Economic Commission for Europe (UNECE).

6.   The GHS Sub-Committee is responsible for maintaining the GHS, promoting its implementation and providing additional guidance as needs arise, while maintaining stability in the system to encourage its adoption. Under its auspices, the document is regularly revised and updated to reflect national, regional and international experiences in implementing its requirements into national, regional and international laws, as well as the experiences of those doing the classification and labelling.

7.   The first task of the GHS Sub-Committee was to make the GHS available for worldwide use and application. The first version of the document, which was intended to serve as the initial basis for the global implementation of the system, was approved by the Committee at its first session (11-13 December 2002) and published in 2003 under the symbol ST/SG/AC.10/30. Since then, the GHS has been updated every two years.

8.   At its sixth session (14 December 2012), the Committee adopted a set of amendments to the fourth revised edition of the GHS which include, *inter alia,* a new test method for oxidizing solids, miscellaneous provisions intended to further clarify the criteria for some hazard classes (skin corrosion/irritation, severe eye

damage/irritation, and aerosols) and to complement the information to be included in the Safety Data Sheet; revised and simplified classification and labelling summary tables; a new codification system for hazard pictograms, and revised and further rationalized precautionary statements. The fifth revised edition of the GHS takes account of these amendments which were circulated as document ST/SG/AC.10/40/Add.3.

9.   While Governments, regional institutions and international organizations are the primary audiences for the GHS, it also contains sufficient context and guidance for those in industry who will ultimately be implementing the national requirements which are adopted. Availability of information about chemicals, their hazards, and ways to protect people, will provide the foundation for national programmes for the safe management of chemicals. Widespread management of chemicals in countries around the world will lead to safer conditions for the global population and the environment, while allowing the benefits of chemical use to continue. Harmonization will also have benefits in terms of facilitating international trade, by promoting greater consistency in the national requirements for chemical hazard classification and communication that companies engaged in international trade must meet.

10.   In paragraph 23 (c) of its Plan of Implementation adopted in Johannesburg on 4 September 2002, the World Summit on Sustainable Development (WSSD) encouraged countries to implement the GHS as soon as possible with a view to having the system fully operational by 2008. Subsequently, in its resolutions 2003/64 of 25 July 2003, 2005/53 of 27 July 2005, 2007/6 of 23 July 2007, 2009/19 of 29 July 2009 and 2011/25 of 27 July 2011, the United Nations Economic and Social Council invited Governments that had not yet done so, to take the necessary steps, through appropriate national procedures and/or legislation, to implement the GHS as recommended in the WSSD Plan of Implementation. It also reiterated its invitation to the regional commissions, United Nations programmes, specialized agencies and other organizations concerned, to promote the implementation of the GHS and, where relevant, to amend their international legal instruments addressing transport safety, workplace safety, consumer protection or the protection of the environment so as to give effect to the GHS through such instruments. Information about the status of implementation may be found on the UNECE Transport Division website[1].

11.   This publication has been prepared by the secretariat of the United Nations Economic Commission for Europe (UNECE).

12.   Additional information on the work of the Committee and its two sub-committees, as well as corrigenda (if any) which may be issued after publication of this document, can be found on the UNECE Transport Division website[2].

---

[1]   _www.unece.org/trans/danger/publi/ghs/implementation_e.html_.

[2]   _www.unece.org/trans/danger/danger.htm_ and _www.unece.org/trans/danger/publi/ghs/ghs_welcome_e.html_.

TABLE OF CONTENTS

TABLE OF CONTENTS (cont'd)

Page

PART 1

INTRODUCTION

CHAPTER 1.1

PURPOSE, SCOPE AND APPLICATION OF THE GLOBALLY HARMONIZED SYSTEM OF CLASSIFICATION AND LABELLING OF CHEMICALS (GHS)

1.1.1 Purpose

1.1.1.1 The use of chemicals to enhance and improve life is a widespread practice worldwide. But alongside the benefits of these products, there is also the potential for adverse effects to people or the environment. As a result, a number of countries or organizations have developed laws or regulations over the years that require information to be prepared and transmitted to those using chemicals, through labels or safety data sheets (SDS). Given the large number of chemicals available, individual regulation of all of them is simply not possible for any entity. Provision of information gives those using chemicals the identities and hazards of these chemicals, and allows the appropriate protective measures to be implemented in the local use settings.

1.1.1.2 While these existing laws or regulations are similar in many respects, their differences are significant enough to result in different labels or SDS for the same chemical in different countries. Through variations in definitions of hazards, a chemical may be considered flammable in one country, but not another. Or it may be considered to cause cancer in one country, but not another. Decisions on when or how to communicate hazards on a label or SDS thus vary around the world, and companies wishing to be involved in international trade must have large staffs of experts who can follow the changes in these laws and regulations and prepare different labels and SDS. In addition, given the complexity of developing and maintaining a comprehensive system for classifying and labelling chemicals, many countries have no system at all.

1.1.1.3 Given the reality of the extensive global trade in chemicals, and the need to develop national programs to ensure their safe use, transport, and disposal, it was recognized that an internationally-harmonized approach to classification and labelling would provide the foundation for such programs. Once countries have consistent and appropriate information on the chemicals they import or produce in their own countries, the infrastructure to control chemical exposures and protect people and the environment can be established in a comprehensive manner.

1.1.1.4 Thus the reasons for setting the objective of harmonization were many. It is anticipated that, when implemented, the GHS will:

(a) enhance the protection of human health and the environment by providing an internationally comprehensible system for hazard communication;

(b) provide a recognized framework for those countries without an existing system;

(c) reduce the need for testing and evaluation of chemicals; and

(d) facilitate international trade in chemicals whose hazards have been properly assessed and identified on an international basis.

1.1.1.5 The work began with examination of existing systems, and determination of the scope of the work. While many countries had some requirements, the following systems were deemed to be the "major" existing systems and were used as the primary basis for the elaboration of the GHS:

(a) Requirements of systems in the United States of America for the workplace, consumers and pesticides;

(b)   Requirements of Canada for the workplace, consumers and pesticides;

(c)   European Union directives for classification and labelling of substances and preparations;

(d)   The United Nations Recommendations on the Transport of Dangerous Goods.

1.1.1.6   The requirements of other countries were also examined as the work developed, but the primary task was to find ways to adopt the best aspects of these existing systems and develop a harmonized approach. This work was done based on agreed principles of harmonization that were adopted early in the process:

(a)   the level of protection offered to workers, consumers, the general public and the environment should not be reduced as a result of harmonizing the classification and labelling systems;

(b)   the hazard classification process refers principally to the hazards arising from the intrinsic properties of substances and mixtures, whether natural or synthetic[1];

(c)   harmonization means establishing a common and coherent basis for chemical hazard classification and communication, from which the appropriate elements relevant to means of transport, consumer, worker and environment protection can be selected;

(d)   the scope of harmonization includes both hazard classification criteria and hazard communication tools, e.g. labelling and safety data sheets, taking into account especially the four existing systems identified in the ILO report[2];

(e)   changes in all these systems will be required to achieve a single globally harmonized system; transitional measures should be included in the process of moving to the new system;

(f)   the involvement of concerned international organizations of employers, workers, consumers, and other relevant organizations in the process of harmonization should be ensured;

(g)   the comprehension of chemical hazard information, by the target audience, e.g. workers, consumers and the general public should be addressed;

(h)   validated data already generated for the classification of chemicals under the existing systems should be accepted when reclassifying these chemicals under the harmonized system;

(i)   a new harmonized classification system may require adaptation of existing methods for testing of chemicals;

(j)   in relation to chemical hazard communication, the safety and health of workers, consumers and the public in general, as well as the protection of the environment, should be ensured while protecting confidential business information, as prescribed by the competent authorities.

---

[1]   *In some cases it is necessary also to take into account hazards arising from other properties, such as the physical state of the substance or mixture (e.g. pressure and temperature) or properties of substances produced by certain chemical reactions (e.g. flammability of gases produced by contact with water).*

[2]   *1992 ILO Report on the size of the task of harmonizing existing systems of classification and labelling for hazardous chemicals.*

1.1.2   **Scope**

1.1.2.1   The GHS includes the following elements:

       (a)   harmonized criteria for classifying substances and mixtures according to their health, environmental and physical hazards; and

       (b)   harmonized hazard communication elements, including requirements for labelling and safety data sheets.

1.1.2.2   This document describes the classification criteria and the hazard communication elements by type of hazard (e.g. acute toxicity; flammability). In addition, decision logics for each hazard have been developed. Some examples of classification of chemicals in the text, as well as in Annex 8, illustrate how to apply the criteria. There is also some discussion about issues that were raised during the development of the system where additional guidance was thought to be necessary to implement the system.

1.1.2.3   The scope of the GHS is based on the mandate from the 1992 United Nations Conference on Environment and Development (UNCED) for development of such a system as stated in paragraphs 26 and 27 of the Agenda 21, Chapter 19, Programme Area B, reproduced below:

> *"26.   Globally harmonized hazard classification and labelling systems are not yet available to promote the safe use of chemicals, inter alia, at the workplace or in the home. Classification of chemicals can be made for different purposes and is a particularly important tool in establishing labelling systems. There is a need to develop harmonized hazard classification and labelling systems, building on ongoing work;*
>
> *27.   A globally harmonized hazard classification and compatible labelling system, including material safety data sheets and easily understandable symbols, should be available, if feasible, by the year 2000."*

1.1.2.4   This mandate was later analysed and refined in the harmonization process to identify the parameters of the GHS. As a result, the following clarification was adopted by the Interorganization Programme for the Sound Management of Chemicals (IOMC) Coordinating Group to ensure that participants were aware of the scope of the effort:

> *"The work on harmonization of hazard classification and labelling focuses on a harmonized system for all chemicals, and mixtures of chemicals. The application of the components of the system may vary by type of product or stage of the life cycle. Once a chemical is classified, the likelihood of adverse effects may be considered in deciding what informational or other steps should be taken for a given product or use setting. Pharmaceuticals, food additives, cosmetics, and pesticide residues in food will not be covered by the GHS in terms of labelling at the point of intentional intake. However, these types of chemicals would be covered where workers may be exposed, and, in transport if potential exposure warrants. The Coordinating Group for the Harmonization of Chemical Classification Systems (CG/HCCS) recognizes that further discussion will be required to address specific application issues for some product use categories which may require the use of specialized expertise."*[3]

1.1.2.5   In developing this clarification, the CG/HCCS carefully considered many different issues with regard to the possible application of the GHS. There were concerns raised about whether certain sectors or products should be exempted, for example, or about whether or not the system would be applied at all stages of the life cycle of a chemical. Three parameters were agreed in this discussion, and are critical to application of the system in a country or region. These are described below:

---

[3]   *IOMC Description and further clarification of the anticipated application of the Globally Harmonized System (GHS), IFCS/ISG3/98.32B.*

(a) Parameter 1:	The GHS covers all hazardous chemicals. The mode of application of the hazard communication elements of the GHS (e.g. labels, safety data sheets) may vary by product category or stage in the life cycle. Target audiences for the GHS include consumers, workers, transport workers, and emergency responders.

(i) Existing hazard classification and labelling systems address potential exposures to all potentially hazardous chemicals in all types of use situations, including production, storage, transport, workplace use, consumer use, and presence in the environment. They are intended to protect people, facilities, and the environment. The most widely applied requirements in terms of chemicals covered are generally found in the parts of existing systems that apply to the workplace or transport. It should be noted that the term chemical is used broadly in the UNCED agreements and subsequent documents to include substances, products, mixtures, preparations, or any other terms that may be used in existing systems to denote coverage.

(ii) Since all chemicals in commerce are made in a workplace (including consumer products), handled during shipment and transport by workers, and often used by workers, there are no complete exemptions from the scope of the GHS for any particular type of chemical or product. In some countries, for example, pharmaceuticals are currently covered by workplace and transport requirements in the manufacturing, storage, and transport stages of the life cycle. Workplace requirements may also be applied to employees involved in the administration of some drugs, or clean-up of spills and other types of potential exposures in health care settings. SDS's and training must be available for these employees under some systems. It is anticipated that the GHS would be applied to pharmaceuticals in a similar fashion.

(iii) At other stages of the life cycle for these same chemicals, the GHS may not be applied at all. For example, at the point of intentional human intake or ingestion, or intentional application to animals, products such as human or veterinary pharmaceuticals are generally not subject to hazard labelling under existing systems. Such requirements would not normally be applied to these products as a result of the GHS. (It should be noted that the risks to subjects associated with the medical use of human or veterinary pharmaceuticals are generally addressed in package inserts and are not part of this harmonization process.) Similarly, products such as foods that may have trace amounts of food additives or pesticides in them are not currently labelled to indicate the presence or hazard of those materials. It is anticipated that application of the GHS would not require them to be labelled as such.

(b) Parameter 2:	The mandate for development of a GHS does not include establishment of uniform test methods or promotion of further testing to address adverse health outcomes.

(i) Tests that determine hazardous properties, which are conducted according to internationally recognized scientific principles, can be used for purposes of a hazard determination for health and environmental hazards. The GHS criteria for determining health and environmental hazards are test method neutral, allowing different approaches as long as they are scientifically sound and validated according to international procedures and criteria already referred to in existing systems for the hazard class of concern and produce mutually acceptable data. While the OECD is the lead organization for development of harmonized health hazard criteria, the GHS is not tied to the OECD Test Guidelines Program. For example, drugs are tested according to agreed criteria developed under the auspices of the World Health Organization (WHO). Data generated in accordance with these tests would be acceptable under the GHS. Criteria for physical hazards under the UNSCETDG are linked to specific test methods for hazard classes such as flammability and explosivity.

(ii)   The GHS is based on currently available data. Since the harmonized classification criteria are developed on the basis of existing data, compliance with these criteria will not require retesting of chemicals for which accepted test data already exists.

<table>
<tr><td>(c) Parameter 3:</td><td>In addition to animal data and valid in vitro testing, human experience, epidemiological data, and clinical testing provide important information that should be considered in application of the GHS.</td></tr>
</table>

(i)   Most of the current systems acknowledge and make use of ethically obtained human data or available human experience. Application of the GHS should not prevent the use of such data, and the GHS explicitly acknowledges the existence and use of all appropriate and relevant information concerning hazards or the likelihood of harmful effects (i.e. risk).

1.1.2.6   *Other scope limitations*

1.1.2.6.1   The GHS is not intended to harmonize risk assessment procedures or risk management decisions (such as establishment of a permissible exposure limit for employee exposure), which generally require some risk assessment in addition to hazard classification. In addition, chemical inventory requirements in various countries are not related to the GHS [3].

1.1.2.6.2   *Hazard vs. risk*

1.1.2.6.2.1   Each hazard classification and communication system (workplace, consumer, transport) begins coverage with an assessment of the hazards posed by the chemical involved. The degree of its capacity to harm depends on its intrinsic properties, i.e. its capacity to interfere with normal biological processes, and its capacity to burn, explode, corrode, etc. This is based primarily on a review of the scientific studies available. The concept of risk or the likelihood of harm occurring, and subsequently communication of that information, is introduced when exposure is considered in conjunction with the data regarding potential hazards. The basic approach to risk assessment is characterized by the simple formula:

$$\text{hazard} \times \text{exposure} = \text{risk}$$

1.1.2.6.2.2   Thus if you can minimize either hazard or exposure, you minimize the risk or likelihood of harm. Successful hazard communication alerts the user to the presence of a hazard and the need to minimize exposures and the resulting risks.

1.1.2.6.2.3   All of the systems for conveying information (workplace, consumer, transport) include both hazard and risk in some form. They vary in where and how they provide the information, and the level of detail they have regarding potential exposures. For example, exposure of the consumer to pharmaceuticals comprises a specific dose that is prescribed by the physician to address a certain condition. The exposure is intentional. Therefore, a determination has been made by a drug regulatory agency that for the consumer, an acceptable level of risk accompanies the specific dosage provided. Information that is provided to the person taking the pharmaceutical conveys the risks assessed by the drug regulatory agency rather than addressing the intrinsic hazards of the pharmaceutical or its components.

---

[3]   *IOMC Description and further clarification of the anticipated application of the Globally Harmonized System (GHS), IFCS/ISC3/98.32B.*

1.1.3 Application of the GHS

1.1.3.1 *Harmonization of the application of the GHS*

1.1.3.1.1 The goal of the GHS is to identify the intrinsic hazards found in substances and mixtures and to convey hazard information about these hazards. The criteria for hazard classification are harmonized. Hazard statements, symbols and signal words have been standardized and harmonized and now form an integrated hazard communication system. The GHS will allow the hazard communication elements of the existing systems to converge. Competent authorities will decide how to apply the various elements of the GHS based on the needs of the competent authority and the target audience. (See also Chapter 1.4, *Hazard Communication: Labelling,* (paragraph 1.4.10.5.4.2) and Annex 5 *Consumer Product Labelling Based on the Likelihood of Injury).*

1.1.3.1.2 For transport, it is expected that application of the GHS will be similar to application of current transport requirements. Containers of dangerous goods will be marked with pictograms that address acute toxicity, physical hazards, and environmental hazards. As is true for workers in other sectors, workers in the transport sector will be trained. The elements of the GHS that address such elements as signal words and hazard statements are not expected to be adopted in the transport sector.

1.1.3.1.3 In the workplace, it is expected that all of the GHS elements will be adopted, including labels that have the harmonized core information under the GHS, and safety data sheets. It is also anticipated that this will be supplemented by employee training to help ensure effective communication.

1.1.3.1.4 For the consumer sector, it is expected that labels will be the primary focus of GHS application. These labels will include the core elements of the GHS, subject to some sector-specific considerations in certain systems. (See also Chapter 1.4 *Hazard Communication: Labelling* (paragraph 1.4.10.5.4.2) and Annex 5 *Consumer Product Labelling Based on the Likelihood of Injury).*

1.1.3.1.5 *Building block approach*

1.1.3.1.5.1 Consistent with the building block approach, countries are free to determine which of the *building blocks* will be applied in different parts of their systems. However, where a system covers something that is in the GHS, and implements the GHS, that coverage should be consistent. For example, if a system covers the carcinogenicity of a chemical, it should follow the harmonized classification scheme and the harmonized label elements.

1.1.3.1.5.2 In examining the requirements of existing systems, it was noted that coverage of hazards may vary by the perceived needs of the target audience for information. In particular, the transport sector focuses on acute health effects and physical hazards, but has not to date covered chronic effects due to the types of exposures expected to be encountered in that setting. But there may be other differences as well, with countries choosing not to cover all of the effects addressed by the GHS in each use setting.

1.1.3.1.5.3 The harmonized elements of the GHS may thus be seen as a collection of building blocks from which to form a regulatory approach. While the full range is available to everyone, and should be used if a country or organization chooses to cover a certain effect when it adopts the GHS, the full range does not have to be adopted. While physical hazards are important in the workplace and transport sectors, consumers may not need to know some of the specific physical hazards in the type of use they have for a product. As long as the hazards covered by a sector or system are covered consistently with the GHS criteria and requirements, it will be considered appropriate implementation of the GHS. Notwithstanding the fact that an exporter needs to comply with importing countries' requirements for GHS implementation, it is hoped that the application of the GHS worldwide will eventually lead to a fully harmonized situation.

1.1.3.1.5.4   Guidance on the interpretation of the building block approach

(a)   Hazard classes are building blocks:

Within their jurisdiction and keeping in mind the goal of full harmonization as well as international conventions, competent authorities may decide which hazard classes they apply;

(b)   Within a hazard class, each hazard category can be seen as a building block:

For a given hazard class, competent authorities have the possibility not to apply all categories. Nevertheless, in order to preserve consistency, some restrictions to this principle should be set, as follows:

(i)   The classification criteria such as the cut-off values or concentration limits for adopted hazard categories should not be altered. However, adjacent sub-categories (e.g. carcinogenicity Categories 1A and 1B) may be merged into one category. Nevertheless, adjacent hazard categories should not be merged if it results in renumbering the remaining hazard categories. Furthermore, where sub-categories are merged, the names or numbers of the original GHS sub-categories should be retained (e.g. carcinogenicity Category 1 or 1A/B) to facilitate hazard communication;

(ii)   Where a competent authority adopts a hazard category, it should also adopt all the categories for higher hazard levels in that class. As a consequence, when a competent authority adopts a hazard class, it will always adopt at least the highest hazard category (Category 1), and, where more than one hazard category is adopted, these hazard categories will form an unbroken sequence.

NOTE 1:   Some hazard classes contain additional categories that can be considered on a stand alone basis, for example, Category 3 "transient target organ effects" for the hazard class "Specific target organ toxicity" (Chapter 3.8), and hazard category "Effects on or via lactation" for the hazard class "reproductive toxicity" (Chapter 3.7).

NOTE 2:   It is noted, however, that the goal of the GHS is to achieve worldwide harmonization (see 1.1.2.3). Therefore, while differences between sectors may persist, the use of an identical set of categories at a worldwide level within each sector should be encouraged.

1.1.3.2   *Implementation and maintenance of the GHS*

1.1.3.2.1   For the purposes of implementing the GHS, the United Nations Economic and Social Council (ECOSOC) reconfigured the UN Committee of Experts on the Transport of Dangerous Goods by resolution 1999/65 of 26 October 1999. The new Committee of Experts on the Transport of Dangerous Goods and the Globally Harmonized System of Classification and Labelling of Chemicals (UNCETDG/GHS), maintains its Sub-Committee of Experts on the Transport of Dangerous Goods (UNSCETDG) and a new subsidiary body, the Sub-Committee of Experts on the Globally Harmonized System of Classification and Labelling of Chemicals (UNSCEGHS), has been created. The UNSCEGHS has the following functions:

(a)   To act as custodian of the GHS, managing and giving direction to the harmonization process;

(b)   To keep the GHS system up-to-date as necessary, considering the need to introduce changes, ensure its continued relevance and practical utility, and determining the need for and timing of the updating of technical criteria, working with existing bodies as appropriate;

(c)   To promote understanding and use of the GHS and to encourage feedback;

(d)   To make the GHS available for worldwide use and application;

(e)   To make guidance available on the application of the GHS, and on the interpretation and use of technical criteria to support consistency of application; and

(f)   To prepare work programmes and submit recommendations to the committee.

1.1.3.2.2   The UNSCEGHS and the UNSCETDG, both operate under the parent committee with responsibility for these two areas. The Committee is responsible for strategic issues rather than technical issues. It is not envisaged that it would review, change or revisit technical recommendations of the sub-committees. Accordingly, its main functions are:

(a)   To approve the work programmes for the sub-committees in the light of available resources;

(b)   To coordinate strategic and policy directions in areas of shared interests and overlap;

(c)   To give formal endorsement to the recommendations of the sub-committees and provide the mechanism for channelling these to ECOSOC; and

(d)   To facilitate and coordinate the smooth running of the sub-committees.

1.1.4   The GHS document

1.1.4.1   This document describes the GHS. It contains harmonized classification criteria and hazard communication elements. In addition, guidance is included in the document to assist countries and organizations in the development of tools for implementation of the GHS. The GHS is designed to permit self-classification. The provisions for implementation of the GHS allow the uniform development of national policies, while remaining flexible enough to accommodate any special requirements that might have to be met. Furthermore, the GHS is intended to create user-friendly approach, to facilitate the work of enforcement bodies and to reduce the administrative burden.

1.1.4.2   While this document provides the primary basis for the description of the GHS, it is anticipated that technical assistance tools will be made available as well to assist and promote implementation.

CHAPTER 1.2

DEFINITIONS AND ABBREVIATIONS

For the purposes of the GHS:

ADR means the "European Agreement concerning the International Carriage of Dangerous Goods by Road", as amended;

Alloy means a metallic material, homogeneous on a macroscopic scale, consisting of two or more elements so combined that they cannot be readily separated by mechanical means. Alloys are considered to be mixtures for the purpose of classification under the GHS;

Aspiration means the entry of a liquid or solid chemical into the trachea and lower respiratory system directly through the oral or nasal cavity, or indirectly from vomiting;

ASTM means the "American Society of Testing and Materials";

BCF means "bioconcentration factor";

BOD/COD means "biochemical oxygen demand/chemical oxygen demand";

CA means "competent authority";

Carcinogen means a substance or a mixture which induce cancer or increase its incidence;

CAS means "Chemical Abstract Service";

CBI means "confidential business information";

Chemical identity means a name that will uniquely identify a chemical. This can be a name that is in accordance with the nomenclature systems of the International Union of Pure and Applied Chemistry (IUPAC) or the Chemical Abstracts Service (CAS), or a technical name;

Chemically unstable gas means a flammable gas that is able to react explosively even in the absence of air or oxygen;

Competent authority means any national body(ies) or authority(ies) designated or otherwise recognized as such in connection with the Globally Harmonized System of Classification and Labelling of Chemicals (GHS);

Compressed gas means a gas which when packaged under pressure is entirely gaseous at -50 °C; including all gases with a critical temperature ≤ -50 °C;

Corrosive to metal means a substance or a mixture which by chemical action will materially damage, or even destroy, metals;

Critical temperature means the temperature above which a pure gas cannot be liquefied, regardless of the degree of compression;

Dermal corrosion: see *skin corrosion*;

Dermal irritation: see *skin irritation*;

Dissolved gas means a gas which when packaged under pressure is dissolved in a liquid phase solvent;

Dust means solid particles of a substance or mixture suspended in a gas (usually air);

EC_{50} means the effective concentration of substance that causes 50% of the maximum response;

EC Number or (ECN) is a reference number used by the European Communities to identify dangerous substances, in particular those registered under EINECS;

ECOSOC means the Economic and Social Council of the United Nations;

ECx means the concentration associated with x% response;

EINECS means "European Inventory of Existing Commercial Chemical Substances";

ErC_{50} means EC_{50} in terms of reduction of growth rate;

EU means the "European Union";

Explosive article means an article containing one or more explosive substances;

Explosive substance means a solid or liquid substance (or mixture of substances) which is in itself capable by chemical reaction of producing gas at such a temperature and pressure and at such a speed as to cause damage to the surroundings. Pyrotechnic substances are included even when they do not evolve gases;

Eye irritation means the production of changes in the eye following the application of test substance to the anterior surface of the eye, which are fully reversible within 21 days of application;

Flammable gas means a gas having a flammable range with air at 20 °C and a standard pressure of 101.3 kPa;

Flammable liquid means a liquid having a flash point of not more than 93 °C;

Flammable solid means a solid which is readily combustible, or may cause or contribute to fire through friction;

Flash point means the lowest temperature (corrected to a standard pressure of 101.3 kPa) at which the application of an ignition source causes the vapours of a liquid to ignite under specified test conditions;

FAO means the "Food and Agriculture Organization of the United Nations";

Gas means a substance which (i) at 50 °C has a vapour pressure greater than 300 kPa (absolute); or (ii) is completely gaseous at 20 °C at a standard pressure of 101.3 kPa;

GESAMP means the "Joint Group of Experts on the Scientific Aspects of Marine Environmental Protection of IMO/FAO/UNESCO/WMO/WHO/IAEA/UN/UNEP";

GHS means the "Globally Harmonized System of Classification and Labelling of Chemicals";

Hazard category means the division of criteria within each hazard class, e.g. oral acute toxicity includes five hazard categories and flammable liquids includes four hazard categories. These categories compare hazard severity within a hazard class and should not be taken as a comparison of hazard categories more generally;

Hazard class means the nature of the physical, health or environmental hazard, e.g. flammable solid, carcinogen, oral acute toxicity;

Hazard statement means a statement assigned to a hazard class and category that describes the nature of the hazards of a hazardous product, including, where appropriate, the degree of hazard;

IAEA means the "International Atomic Energy Agency";

IARC means the "International Agency for the Research on Cancer";

ILO means the "International Labour Organization";

IMO means the "International Maritime Organization";

Initial boiling point means the temperature of a liquid at which its vapour pressure is equal to the standard pressure (101.3 kPa), i.e. the first gas bubble appears;

IOMC means the "Inter-organization Programme on the Sound Management of Chemicals";

IPCS means the "International Programme on Chemical Safety";

ISO means the "International Organization for Standardization";

IUPAC means the "International Union of Pure and Applied Chemistry";

Label means an appropriate group of written, printed or graphic information elements concerning a hazardous product, selected as relevant to the target sector(s), that is affixed to, printed on, or attached to the immediate container of a hazardous product, or to the outside packaging of a hazardous product;

Label element means one type of information that has been harmonized for use in a label, e.g. pictogram, signal word;

LC_{50} (50% lethal concentration) means the concentration of a chemical in air or of a chemical in water which causes the death of 50% (one half) of a group of test animals;

LD_{50} means the amount of a chemical, given all at once, which causes the death of 50% (one half) of a group of test animals;

$L(E)C_{50}$ means LC_{50} or EC_{50};

Liquefied gas means a gas which when packaged under pressure, is partially liquid at temperatures above - 50 °C. A distinction is made between:

> (i) High pressure liquefied gas: a gas with a critical temperature between -50 °C and +65 °C; and

> (ii) Low pressure liquefied gas: a gas with a critical temperature above +65 °C;

Liquid means a substance or mixture which at 50 °C has a vapour pressure of not more than 300 kPa (3 bar), which is not completely gaseous at 20 °C and at a standard pressure of 101.3 kPa, and which has a melting point or initial melting point of 20 °C or less at a standard pressure of 101.3 kPa. A viscous substance or mixture for which a specific melting point cannot be determined shall be subjected to the ASTM D 4359-90 test; or to the test for determining fluidity (penetrometer test) prescribed in section 2.3.4 of Annex A of the European Agreement concerning the International Carriage of Dangerous Goods by Road (ADR);

MARPOL means the "International Convention for the Prevention of Pollution from Ships";

Mist means liquid droplets of a substance or mixture suspended in a gas (usually air);

Mixture means a mixture or a solution composed of two or more substances in which they do not react;

Montreal Protocol means the Montreal Protocol on Substances that Deplete the Ozone Layer as either adjusted and/or amended by the Parties to the Protocol.

Mutagen means an agent giving rise to an increased occurrence of mutations in populations of cells and /or organisms;

Mutation means a permanent change in the amount or structure of the genetic material in a cell;

NGO means "non-governmental organization";

NOEC (no observed effect concentration) means the test concentration immediately below the lowest tested concentration with statistically significant adverse effect. The NOEC has no statistically significant adverse effect compared to the control;

OECD means the "Organization for Economic Cooperation and Development";

Organic peroxide means a liquid or solid organic substance which contains the bivalent -O-O- structure and may be considered a derivative of hydrogen peroxide, where one or both of the hydrogen atoms have been replaced by organic radicals. The term also includes organic peroxide formulations (mixtures);

Oxidizing gas means any gas which may, generally by providing oxygen, cause or contribute to the combustion of other material more than air does;

> *NOTE: "Gases which cause or contribute to the combustion of other material more than air does" means pure gases or gas mixtures with an oxidizing power greater than 23.5% as determined by a method specified in ISO 10156:2010.*

Oxidizing liquid means a liquid which, while in itself not necessarily combustible, may, generally by yielding oxygen, cause, or contribute to, the combustion of other material;

Oxidizing solid means a solid which, while in itself not necessarily combustible, may, generally by yielding oxygen, cause, or contribute to, the combustion of other material;

Ozone Depleting Potential (ODP) means an integrative quantity, distinct for each halocarbon source species, that represents the extent of ozone depletion in the stratosphere expected from the halocarbon on a mass-for-mass basis relative to CFC-11. The formal definition of ODP is the ratio of integrated perturbations to total ozone, for a differential mass emission of a particular compound relative to an equal emission of CFC-11.

QSAR means "quantitative structure-activity relationship";

Pictogram means a graphical composition that may include a symbol plus other graphic elements, such as a border, background pattern or colour that is intended to convey specific information;

Precautionary statement means a phrase (and/or pictogram) that describes recommended measures that should be taken to minimize or prevent adverse effects resulting from exposure to a hazardous product, or improper storage or handling of a hazardous product;

Product identifier means the name or number used for a hazardous product on a label or in the SDS. It provides a unique means by which the product user can identify the substance or mixture within the particular use setting e.g. transport, consumer or workplace;

Pyrophoric liquid means a liquid which, even in small quantities, is liable of igniting within five minutes after coming into contact with air;

Pyrophoric solid means a solid which, even in small quantities, is liable of igniting within five minutes after coming into contact with air;

Pyrotechnic article means an article containing one or more pyrotechnic substances;

Pyrotechnic substance means a substance or mixture of substances designed to produce an effect by heat, light, sound, gas or smoke or a combination of these as the result of non-detonative self-sustaining exothermic chemical reactions;

Readily combustible solid means powdered, granular, or pasty substance or mixture which is dangerous if it can be easily ignited by brief contact with an ignition source, such as a burning match, and if the flame spreads rapidly;

Recommendations on the Transport of Dangerous Goods, Manual of Tests and Criteria means the latest revised edition of the United Nations publication bearing this title, and any published amendment thereto;

Recommendations on the Transport of Dangerous Goods, Model Regulations means the latest revised edition of the United Nations publication bearing this title, and any published amendment thereto;

Refrigerated liquefied gas means a gas which when packaged is made partially liquid because of its low temperature;

Respiratory sensitizer means a substance that induces hypersensitivity of the airways following inhalation of the substance;

RID means The Regulations concerning the International Carriage of Dangerous Goods by Rail [Annex 1 to Appendix B (Uniform Rules concerning the Contract for International Carriage of Goods by Rail) (CIM) of COTIF (Convention concerning international carriage by rail)], as amended;

SAR means "Structure Activity Relationship";

SDS means "Safety Data Sheet";

Self-accelerating decomposition temperature (SADT) means the lowest temperature at which self-accelerating decomposition may occur with substance as packaged;

Self-heating substance means a solid or liquid substance, other than a pyrophoric substance, which, by reaction with air and without energy supply, is liable to self-heat; this substance differs from a pyrophoric substance in that it will ignite only when in large amounts (kilograms) and after long periods of time (hours or days);

Self-reactive substance means a thermally unstable liquid or solid substance liable to undergo a strongly exothermic decomposition even without participation of oxygen (air). This definition excludes substances or mixtures classified under the GHS as explosive, organic peroxides or as oxidizing;

Serious eye damage means the production of tissue damage in the eye, or serious physical decay of vision, following application of a test substance to the anterior surface of the eye, which is not fully reversible within 21 days of application;

Signal word means a word used to indicate the relative level of severity of hazard and alert the reader to a potential hazard on the label. The GHS uses "Danger" and "Warning" as signal words;

Skin corrosion means the production of irreversible damage to the skin following the application of a test substance for up to 4 hours;

Skin irritation means the production of reversible damage to the skin following the application of a test substance for up to 4 hours;

Skin sensitizer means a substance that will induce an allergic response following skin contact;

Solid means a substance or mixture which does not meet the definitions of liquid or gas;

Substance means chemical elements and their compounds in the natural state or obtained by any production process, including any additive necessary to preserve the stability of the product and any impurities deriving from the process used, but excluding any solvent which may be separated without affecting the stability of the substance or changing its composition;

Substance which, in contact with water, emits flammable gases means a solid or liquid substance or mixture which, by interaction with water, is liable to become spontaneously flammable or to give off flammable gases in dangerous quantities;

Supplemental label element means any additional non-harmonized type of information supplied on the container of a hazardous product that is not required or specified under the GHS. In some cases this information may be required by other competent authorities or it may be additional information provided at the discretion of the manufacturer/distributor;

Symbol means a graphical element intended to succinctly convey information;

Technical name means a name that is generally used in commerce, regulations and codes to identify a substance or mixture, other than the IUPAC or CAS name, and that is recognized by the scientific community. Examples of technical names include those used for complex mixtures (e.g., petroleum fractions or natural products), pesticides (e.g., ISO or ANSI systems), dyestuffs (Colour Index system) and minerals;

UNCED means the "United Nations Conference on Environment and Development";

UNCETDG/GHS means the "United Nations Committee of Experts on the Transport of Dangerous Goods and on the Globally Harmonized System of Classification and Labelling of Chemicals";

UN means the "United Nations";

UNEP means the "United Nations Environment Programme";

UNESCO means the "United Nations Educational, Scientific and Cultural Organization";

UNITAR means the "United Nations Institute for Training and Research";

UNSCEGHS means the "United Nations Sub-Committee of Experts on the Globally Harmonized System of Classification and Labelling of Chemicals";

UNSCETDG means the "United Nations Sub-Committee of Experts on the Transport of Dangerous Goods";

Vapour means the gaseous form of a substance or mixture released from its liquid or solid state.

WHO means the "World Health Organization";

WMO means the "World Meteorological Organization".

CHAPTER 1.3

CLASSIFICATION OF HAZARDOUS SUBSTANCES AND MIXTURES

1.3.1 Introduction

Development of the GHS began with the work on classification criteria by the OECD Task Force on Harmonization of Classification and Labelling (Task Force on HCL) for health and environmental hazards, and by the UNCETDG/ILO Working Group for Physical Hazards.

1.3.1.1 *Health and environmental hazard classes: OECD Task Force on Harmonization of Classification and Labelling (OECD Task Force on HCL)*

1.3.1.1.1 The work of the OECD Task Force on HCL was generally of three related kinds:

(a) Comparison of the major classification systems, identification of similar or identical elements and, for the elements which were dissimilar, development of a consensus on a compromise;

(b) Examination of the scientific basis for the criteria which define the hazard class of concern (e.g. acute toxicity, carcinogenicity), gaining expert consensus on the test methods, data interpretation and level of concern, and then seeking consensus on the criteria. For some hazard classes, the existing schemes had no criteria and the relevant criteria were developed by the Task Force;

(c) Where there was a decision-tree approach (e.g. irritation) or where there were dependent criteria in the classification scheme (acute aquatic toxicity), development of consensus on the process or the scheme for using the criteria.

1.3.1.1.2 The OECD Task Force on HCL proceeded stepwise in developing its harmonized classification criteria. For each hazard class the following steps were undertaken:

(a) Step 1: A thorough analysis of existing classification systems, including the scientific basis for the system and its criteria, its rationale and an explanation of how it is used. Step 1 documents were prepared and amended as required after discussion by the OECD Task Force on HCL for the following hazard classes: eye irritation/serious eye damage, skin irritation/corrosion, sensitizing substances, germ cell mutagenicity, reproductive toxicity, specific target organ toxicity, and chemical mixtures;

(b) Step 2: A proposal for a harmonized classification system and criteria for each hazard class and category was developed. A Step 2 document was prepared and amended as required after discussion by the OECD Task Force on HCL;

(c) Step 3:

(i) OECD Task Force on HCL reached consensus on the revised Step 2 proposal; or

(ii) If attempts at consensus building failed, the OECD Task Force on HCL identified specific "non-consensus" items as alternatives in a revised Step 2 proposal for further discussion and resolution.

(d) Step 4: Final proposals were submitted to the OECD Joint Meeting of the Chemicals Committee and the Working Party on Chemicals, Pesticides and Biotechnology for approval and subsequently to the IOMC CG-HCCS for incorporation into the GHS.

1.3.1.2   *UNCETDG/ILO working group on physical hazards*

The UNCETDG/ILO working group on physical hazards used a similar process to the OECD Task Force on HCL. The work involved a comparison of the major classification systems, identification of similar or identical elements, and for the elements which were dissimilar, development of a consensus on a compromise. For physical hazards, however, the transport definitions, test methods and classification criteria were used as a basis for the work since they were already substantially harmonized. The work proceeded through examination of the scientific basis for the criteria, gaining consensus on the test methods, data interpretation and on the criteria. For most hazard classes, the existing schemes were already in place and being used by the transport sector. On this basis, a portion of the work focused on ensuring that workplace, environment and consumer safety issues were adequately addressed.

1.3.2   **General considerations on the GHS**

1.3.2.1   *Scope of the system*

1.3.2.1.1   The GHS applies to pure substances and their dilute solutions and to mixtures. "Articles" as defined in the Hazard Communication Standard (29 CFR 1910.1200) of the Occupational Safety and Health Administration of the United States of America, or by similar definition, are outside the scope of the system.

1.3.2.1.2   One objective of the GHS is for it to be simple and transparent with a clear distinction between classes and categories in order to allow for "self-classification" as far as possible. For many hazard classes the criteria are semi-quantitative or qualitative and expert judgement is required to interpret the data for classification purposes. Furthermore, for some hazard classes (e.g. eye irritation, explosives or self-reactive substances) a decision tree approach is provided to enhance ease of use.

1.3.2.2   *Concept of "classification"*

1.3.2.2.1   The GHS uses the term "hazard classification" to indicate that only the intrinsic hazardous properties of substances or mixtures are considered.

1.3.2.2.2   Hazard classification incorporates only three steps, i.e.:

(a)   identification of relevant data regarding the hazards of a substance or mixture;

(b)   subsequent review of those data to ascertain the hazards associated with the substance or mixture; and

(c)   a decision on whether the substance or mixture will be classified as a hazardous substance or mixture and the degree of hazard, where appropriate, by comparison of the data with agreed hazard classification criteria.

1.3.2.2.3   As noted in IOMC Description and further clarification of the anticipated application of the GHS in the *Purpose, scope and application* (Chapter 1.1, paragraph 1.1.2.4), it is recognized that once a chemical is classified, the likelihood of adverse effects may be considered in deciding what informational or other steps should be taken for a given product or use setting.

1.3.2.3   *Classification criteria*

1.3.2.3.1   The classification criteria for substances and mixtures are presented in Parts 2, 3 and 4 of this document, each of which is for a specific hazard class or a group of closely related hazard classes. For most hazard classes, the recommended process of classification of mixtures is based on the following sequence:

(a)   Where test data are available for the complete mixture, the classification of the mixture will always be based on that data;

(b)   Where test data are not available for the mixture itself, then bridging principles included and explained in each specific chapter should be considered to see whether they permit classification of the mixture;

In addition, for health and environmental hazards,

(c)   If (i) test data are not available for the mixture itself, and (ii) the available information is not sufficient to allow application of the above mentioned bridging principles, then the agreed method(s) described in each chapter for estimating the hazards based on the information known will be applied to classify the mixture.

1.3.2.3.2   In most cases, it is not anticipated that reliable data for complete mixtures will be available for germ cell mutagenicity, carcinogenicity, and reproductive toxicity hazard classes. Therefore, for these hazard classes, mixtures will generally be classified based on the available information for the individual ingredients of the mixtures, using the cut-off values/concentration limit methods in each chapter. The classification may be modified on a case-by-case basis based on available test data for the complete mixture, if such data are conclusive as described in each chapter.

1.3.2.4   *Available data, test methods and test data quality*

1.3.2.4.1   The GHS itself does not include requirements for testing substances or mixtures. Therefore, there is no requirement under the GHS to generate test data for any hazard class. It is recognized that some parts of regulatory systems do require data to be generated (e.g. pesticides), but these requirements are not related specifically to the GHS. The criteria established for classifying a mixture will allow the use of available data for the mixture itself and/or similar mixtures and/or data for ingredients of the mixture.

1.3.2.4.2   The classification of a substance or mixture depends both on the criteria and on the reliability of the test methods underpinning the criteria. In some cases the classification is determined by a pass or fail of a specific test, (e.g. the ready biodegradation test for substances or ingredients of mixtures), while in other cases, interpretations are made from dose/response curves and observations during testing. In all cases, the test conditions need to be standardized so that the results are reproducible with a given substance and the standardized test yields "valid" data for defining the hazard class of concern. In this context, validation is the process by which the reliability and the relevance of a procedure are established for a particular purpose.

1.3.2.4.3   Tests that determine hazardous properties, which are conducted according to internationally recognized scientific principles, can be used for purposes of a hazard determination for health and environmental hazards. The GHS criteria for determining health and environmental hazards are test method neutral, allowing different approaches as long as they are scientifically sound and validated according to international procedures and criteria already referred to in existing systems for the hazard of concern and produce mutually acceptable data. Test methods for determining physical hazards are generally more clear-cut, and are specified in the GHS.

1.3.2.4.4   *Previously classified chemicals*

One of the general principles established by the IOMC-CG-HCCS states that test data already generated for the classification of chemicals under the existing systems should be accepted when classifying these chemicals under the harmonized system thereby avoiding duplicative testing and the unnecessary use of test animals. This policy has important implications in those cases where the criteria in the GHS are different from those in an existing system. In some cases, it may be difficult to determine the quality of existing data from older studies. In such cases, expert judgement will be needed.

1.3.2.4.5   *Substances/mixtures posing special problems*

1.3.2.4.5.1   The effect of a substance or mixture on biological and environmental systems is influenced, among other factors, by the physico-chemical properties of the substance or mixture and/or ingredients of the mixture and the way in which ingredient substances are biologically available. Some groups of substances may present special problems in this respect, for example, some polymers and metals. A substance or mixture need not be classified when it can be shown by conclusive experimental data from internationally acceptable test methods that the substance or mixture is not biologically available. Similarly, bioavailability data on ingredients of a mixture should be used where appropriate in conjunction with the harmonized classification criteria when classifying mixtures.

1.3.2.4.5.2   Certain physical hazards (e.g. due to explosive or oxidizing properties) may be altered by dilution, as is the case for desensitized explosives, by inclusion in a mixture or article, packaging or other factors. Classification procedures for specific sectors (e.g. storage) should take experience and expertise into account.

1.3.2.4.6   *Animal welfare*

The welfare of experimental animals is a concern. This ethical concern includes not only the alleviation of stress and suffering but also, in some countries, the use and consumption of test animals. Where possible and appropriate, tests and experiments that do not require the use of live animals are preferred to those using sentient live experimental animals. To that end, for certain hazards non-animal observations/measurements are included as part of the classification system. Additionally, alternative animal tests, using fewer animals or causing less suffering are internationally accepted and should be preferred.

1.3.2.4.7   *Evidence from humans*

For classification purposes, reliable epidemiological data and experience on the effects of chemicals on humans (e.g. occupational data, data from accident databases) should be taken into account in the evaluation of human health hazards of a chemical. Testing on humans solely for hazard identification purposes is generally not acceptable.

1.3.2.4.8   *Expert judgement*

The approach to classifying mixtures includes the application of expert judgement in a number of areas in order to ensure existing information can be used for as many mixtures as possible to provide protection for human health and the environment. Expert judgement may also be required in interpreting data for hazard classification of substances, especially where weight of evidence determinations are needed.

1.3.2.4.9   *Weight of evidence*

1.3.2.4.9.1   For some hazard classes, classification results directly when the data satisfy the criteria. For others, classification of a substance or a mixture is made on the basis of the total weight of evidence. This means that all available information bearing on the determination of toxicity is considered together, including the results of valid *in vitro* tests, relevant animal data, and human experience such as epidemiological and clinical studies and well-documented case reports and observations.

1.3.2.4.9.2   The quality and consistency of the data are important. Evaluation of substances or mixtures related to the material being classified should be included, as should site of action and mechanism or mode of action study results. Both positive and negative results are assembled together in a single weight of evidence determination.

1.3.2.4.9.3   Positive effects which are consistent with the criteria for classification in each chapter, whether seen in humans or animals, will normally justify classification. Where evidence is available from both sources and there is a conflict between the findings, the quality and reliability of the evidence from both sources must be assessed in order to resolve the question of classification. Generally, data of good quality and reliability in humans will have precedence over other data. However, even well-designed and conducted epidemiological studies may lack sufficient numbers of subjects to detect relatively rare but still significant effects, or to assess potentially confounding factors. Positive results from well-conducted animal studies are not necessarily negated by the lack of positive human experience but require an assessment of the robustness and quality of both the human and animal data relative to the expected frequency of occurrence of effects and the impact of potentially confounding factors.

1.3.2.4.9.4　　Route of exposure, mechanistic information and metabolism studies are pertinent to determining the relevance of an effect in humans. When such information raises doubt about relevance in humans, a lower classification may be warranted. When it is clear that the mechanism or mode of action is not relevant to humans, the substance or mixture should not be classified.

1.3.2.4.9.5　　Both positive and negative results are assembled together in the weight of evidence determination. However, a single positive study performed according to good scientific principles and with statistically and biologically significant positive results may justify classification.

1.3.3　　Specific considerations for the classification of mixtures

1.3.3.1　　*Definitions*

1.3.3.1.1　　In order to ensure a full understanding of the provisions for classifying mixtures, definitions of certain terms are required. These definitions are for the purpose of evaluating or determining the hazards of a product for classification and labelling, and are not intended to be applied in other situations such as inventory reporting. The intent of the definitions as drawn is to ensure that:

(a)　　all products within the scope of the Globally Harmonized System are evaluated to determine their hazards, and are subsequently classified according to the GHS criteria as appropriate; and

(b)　　the evaluation is based on the actual product involved, i.e. on a stable product. If a reaction occurs during manufacture and a new product results, a new hazard evaluation and classification must take place to apply the GHS to the new product.

1.3.3.1.2　　Working definitions have been accepted for the following terms: substance, mixture, alloy (see Chapter 1.2 for other definitions and abbreviations used in the GHS).

Substance: Chemical elements and their compounds in the natural state or obtained by any production process, including any additive necessary to preserve the stability of the product and any impurities deriving from the process used, but excluding any solvent which may be separated without affecting the stability of the substance or changing its composition.

Mixture: Mixtures or solutions composed of two or more substances in which they do not react.

Alloy: An alloy is a metallic material, homogeneous on a macroscopic scale, consisting of two or more elements so combined that they cannot be readily separated by mechanical means. Alloys are considered to be mixtures for the purpose of classification under the GHS.

1.3.3.1.3　　These definitions should be used to maintain consistency when classifying substances and mixtures in the GHS. Note also that where impurities, additives or individual constituents of a substance or mixture have been identified and are themselves classified, they should be taken into account during classification if they exceed the cut-off value/concentration limit for a given hazard class.

1.3.3.1.4　　It is recognized, as a practical matter, that some substances may react slowly with atmospheric gases, e.g. oxygen, carbon dioxide, water vapour, to form different substances; or they may react very slowly with other ingredients of a mixture to form different substances; or they may self-polymerise to form oligomers or polymers. However, the concentrations of different substances produced by such reactions are typically considered to be sufficiently low that they do not affect the hazard classification of the mixture.

1.3.3.2 *Use of cut-off values/concentration limits*

1.3.3.2.1 When classifying an untested mixture based on the hazards of its ingredients, generic cut-off values or concentration limits for the classified ingredients of the mixture are used for several hazard classes in the GHS[1]. While the adopted cut-off values/concentration limits adequately identify the hazard for most mixtures, there may be some that contain hazardous ingredients at lower concentrations than the harmonized cut-off value/concentration limit that still pose an identifiable hazard. There may also be cases where the harmonized cut-off value/concentration limit is considerably lower than could be expected on the basis of an established non-hazardous level for an ingredient.

1.3.3.2.2 Normally, the generic cut-off values/concentration limits adopted in the GHS should be applied uniformly in all jurisdictions and for all sectors. However, if the classifier has information that the hazard of an ingredient will be evident below the generic cut-off values/concentration limits, the mixture containing that ingredient should be classified accordingly.

1.3.3.2.3 On occasion, conclusive data may show that the hazard of an ingredient will not be evident when present at a level above the generic GHS cut-off value(s)/concentration limit(s). In these cases the mixture could be classified according to those data. The data should exclude the possibility that the ingredient would behave in the mixture in a manner that would increase the hazard over that of the pure substance. Furthermore, the mixture should not contain ingredients that would affect that determination.

1.3.3.2.4 Adequate documentation supporting the use of any values other than the generic cut-off values/concentration limits should be retained and made available for review on request.

1.3.3.3 *Synergistic or antagonistic effects*

When performing an assessment in accordance with the GHS requirements, the evaluator must take into account all available information about the potential occurrence of synergistic effects among the ingredients of the mixture. Lowering classification of a mixture to a less hazardous category on the basis of antagonistic effects may be done only if the determination is supported by sufficient data.

---

[1] *For the purposes of the GHS, the terms "cut-off value" and "concentration limit" are equivalent and are meant to be used interchangeably. Competent authorities may choose whether to use either term to define thresholds that trigger classification.*

CHAPTER 1.4

HAZARD COMMUNICATION: LABELLING

1.4.1   Objectives, scope and application

1.4.1.1   One of the objectives of the work on the Globally Harmonized System (GHS) has been the development of a harmonized hazard communication system, including labelling, safety data sheets and easily understandable symbols, based on the classification criteria developed for the GHS. This work was carried out under the auspices of the ILO, by the ILO working group on hazard communication using the same 3-step procedure outlined for the harmonization of classification in *Classification of hazardous substances and mixtures* (Chapter 1.3, paragraph 1.3.1.1.2).

1.4.1.2   The harmonized system for hazard communication includes the appropriate labelling tools to convey information about each of the hazard classes and categories in the GHS. The use of symbols, signal words or hazard statements other than those which have been assigned to each of the GHS hazard classes and categories, would be contrary to harmonization.

1.4.1.3   The ILO working group considered the application of the general principles described in the IOMC CG/HCCS terms of reference[1] as they apply to hazard communication and recognized that there will be circumstances where the demands and rationale of systems may warrant some flexibility in whether to incorporate certain hazard classes and categories for certain target audiences.

1.4.1.4   For example, the scope of the *UN Recommendations on the Transport of Dangerous Goods, Model Regulations*, encompasses only the most severe hazard categories of the acute toxicity hazard class. This system would not label substances or mixtures falling within the scope of the less severe hazard categories (e.g. those falling within the oral range > 300 mg/kg). However, should the scope of that system be amended to incorporate substances and mixtures falling in these less severe hazard categories, they should be labelled with the appropriate GHS labelling tools. The use of different cut-off values to determine which products are labelled in a hazard category would be contrary to harmonization.

1.4.1.5   It is recognized that the *UN Recommendations on the Transport of Dangerous Goods, Model Regulations* provide label information primarily in a graphic form because of the needs of the target audiences. Therefore the UN Sub-Committee of Experts on the Transport of Dangerous Goods may choose not to include signal words and hazard statements as part of the information provided on the label under the Model Regulations.

1.4.2   Terminology

1.4.2.1   A description of common terms and definitions related to hazard communication is included in Chapter 1.2 *Definitions and abbreviations*.

1.4.3   Target audiences

1.4.3.1   The needs of the target audiences that will be the primary end-users of the harmonized hazard communication scheme have been identified. Particular attention was given to a discussion of the manner in which these target audiences will receive and use the information conveyed about hazardous chemicals. Factors discussed include the potential use of products, availability of information other than the label and the availability of training.

1.4.3.2   It was recognized that it is difficult to completely separate the needs of different target audiences. For example, both workers and emergency responders use labels in storage facilities, and products such as paints and solvents are used both by consumers and in workplaces. In addition, pesticides can be

---

[1]   *IOMC, Coordinating group for the harmonization of chemical classification systems, revised terms of reference and work programme (IOMC/HCS/95 – 14 January 1996).*

used in consumer settings (e.g. lawn and garden products) and workplaces (e.g. pesticides used to treat seed in seed treatment plants). That said, there are certain characteristics which are particular to the different target audiences. The following paragraphs in this section consider the target audiences and the type of information they need.

1.4.3.3   *Workplace*: Employers and workers need to know the hazards specific to the chemicals used and or handled in the workplace, as well as information about the specific protective measures required to avoid the adverse effects that might be caused by those hazards. In the case of storage of chemicals, potential hazards are minimized by the containment (packaging) of the chemical, but in the case of an accident, workers and emergency responders need to know what mitigation measures are appropriate. Here they may require information which can be read at a distance. The label, however, is not the sole source of this information, which is also available through the SDS and workplace risk management system. The latter should also provide for training in hazard identification and prevention. The nature of training provided and the accuracy, comprehensibility and completeness of the information provided on the SDS may vary. However, compared to consumers for example, workers can develop a more in depth understanding of symbols and other types of information.

1.4.3.4   *Consumers:* The label in most cases is likely to be the sole source of information readily available to the consumer. The label, therefore, will need to be sufficiently detailed and relevant to the use of the product. There are considerable philosophical differences on the approach to providing information to consumers. Labelling based on the likelihood of injury (i.e. risk communication) is considered to be an effective approach in this respect by some consumer labelling systems, whilst others take account of the "right to know" principle in providing information to consumers which is solely based on the product's hazards. Consumer education is more difficult and less efficient than education for other audiences. Providing sufficient information to consumers in the simplest and most easily understandable terms presents a considerable challenge. The issue of comprehensibility is of particular importance for this target audience, since consumers may rely solely on label information.

1.4.3.5   *Emergency responders*: Emergency responders need information on a range of levels. To facilitate immediate responses, they need accurate, detailed and sufficiently clear information. This applies in the event of an accident during transportation, in storage facilities or at workplaces. Fire fighters and those first at the scene of an accident for example, need information that can be distinguished and interpreted at a distance. Such personnel are highly trained in the use of graphical and coded information. However, emergency responders also require more detailed information about hazards and response techniques, which they obtain from a range of sources. The information needs of medical personnel responsible for treating the victims of an accident or emergency may differ from those of fire fighters.

1.4.3.6   *Transport*: The *UN Recommendations on the Transport of Dangerous Goods, Model Regulations*, cater for a wide range of target audiences although transport workers and emergency responders are the principal ones. Others include employers, those who offer or accept dangerous goods for transport or load or unload packages of dangerous goods into or from transport vehicles, or freight containers. All need information concerning general safe practices that are appropriate for all transport situations. For example, a driver will have to know what has to be done in case of an accident irrespective of the substance transported: (e.g. report the accident to authorities, keep the shipping documents in a given place, etc.). Drivers may only require limited information concerning specific hazards, unless they also load and unload packages or fill tanks, etc. Workers who might come into direct contact with dangerous goods, for example on board ships, require more detailed information.

1.4.4   Comprehensibility

1.4.4.1   Comprehensibility of the information provided has been one of the most important issues addressed in the development of the hazard communication system (see Annex 6, *Comprehensibility testing methodology*). The aim of the harmonized system is to present the information in a manner that the intended audience can easily understand. The GHS identifies some guiding principles to assist this process:

(a)   Information should be conveyed in more than one way;

(b)   The comprehensibility of the components of the system should take account of existing studies and literature as well as any evidence gained from testing;

(c)   The phrases used to indicate degree (severity) of hazard should be consistent across different hazard types.

1.4.4.2   The latter point was subject to some debate concerning the comparison of severity between long-term effects such as carcinogenicity and physical hazards such as flammability. Whilst it might not be possible to directly compare physical hazards to health hazards, it may be possible to provide target audiences with a means of putting the degree of hazard into context and therefore convey the same degree of concern about the hazard.

1.4.4.3   *Comprehensibility testing methodology*

A preliminary review of the literature undertaken by the University of Maryland indicated that common principles related to comprehensibility could be applied to the development of the harmonized hazard communication scheme. The University of Cape Town developed these into a comprehensive testing methodology to assess the comprehensibility of the hazard communication system (see Annex 6). In addition to testing individual label components, this methodology considers the comprehensibility of label components in combination. This was considered particularly important to assess the comprehensibility of warning messages for consumers where there is less reliance on training to aid understandability. The testing methodology also includes a means of assessing SDS comprehensibility. A summary description of this methodology is provided in Annex 6.

1.4.5   Translation

Options for the use of textual information present an additional challenge for comprehensibility. Clearly words and phrases need to retain their comprehensibility when translated, whilst conveying the same meaning. The IPCS chemical safety card programme has gained experience of this in translating standard phrases in a wide variety of languages. The EU also has experience of translating terms to ensure the same message is conveyed in multiple languages e.g. hazard, risk etc. Similar experience has been gained in North America where the North American Emergency Response Guidebook, which uses key phrases, is available in a number of languages.

1.4.6   Standardization

1.4.6.1   To fulfil the goal of having as many countries as possible adopt the system, much of the GHS is based on standardized approaches to make it easier for companies to comply with and for countries to implement the system. Standardisation can be applied to certain label elements (symbols, signal words, statements of hazard, precautionary statements) and to label format and colour and to SDS format.

1.4.6.2   *Application of standardization in the harmonized system*

For labels, the hazard symbols, signal words and hazard statements have all been standardized and assigned to each of the hazard categories. These standardized elements should not be subject to variation, and should appear on the GHS label as indicated in the Chapters for each hazard class in this document. For safety data sheets, Chapter 1.5 *Hazard communication: Safety Data Sheets* provides a standardized format for the presentation of information. Although precautionary statements have not been fully harmonized in the current GHS, Annex 3 provides guidance to aid in the selection of appropriate statements. Additional work to achieve greater standardization in this area may be undertaken in the future, once countries have gained experience with the system.

1.4.6.3   *Use of non-standardized or supplemental information*

1.4.6.3.1   There are many other label elements which may appear on a label which have not been standardized in the harmonized system. Some of these clearly need to be included on the label, for example precautionary statements. Competent authorities may require additional information, or suppliers may choose to add supplementary information on their own initiative. In order to ensure that the use of non-standardized information does not lead to unnecessarily wide variation in information or undermine GHS information, the use of supplementary information should be limited to the following circumstances:

> (a)   the supplementary information provides further detail and does not contradict or cast doubt on the validity of the standardized hazard information; or

> (b)   the supplementary information provides information about hazards not yet incorporated into the GHS.

> In either instance, the supplementary information should not lower standards of protection.

1.4.6.3.2   The labeller should have the option of providing supplementary information related to the hazard, such as physical state or route of exposure, with the hazard statement rather than in the supplementary information section on the label, see also 1.4.10.5.4.1.

1.4.7   **Updating information**

1.4.7.1   All systems should specify a means of responding in an appropriate and timely manner to new information and updating labels and SDS information accordingly. The following are examples of how this could be achieved.

1.4.7.2   *General guidance on updating of information*

1.4.7.2.1   Suppliers should respond to "new and significant" information they receive about a chemical hazard by updating the label and safety data sheet for that chemical. New and significant information is any information that changes the GHS classification of the substance or mixture and leads to a resulting change in the information provided on the label or any information concerning the chemical and appropriate control measures that may affect the SDS. This could include, for example, new information on the potential adverse chronic health effects of exposure as a result of recently published documentation or test results, even if a change in classification may not yet be triggered.

1.4.7.2.2   Updating should be carried out promptly on receipt of the information that necessitates the revision. The competent authority may choose to specify a time limit within which the information should be revised. This applies only to labels and SDS for products that are not subject to an approval mechanism such as pesticides. In pesticide labelling systems, where the label is part of the product approval mechanism, suppliers cannot update the supply label on their own initiative. However when the products are subject to the transport of dangerous goods requirements, the label used should be updated on receipt of the new information, as above.

1.4.7.2.3   Suppliers should also periodically review the information on which the label and safety data sheet for a substance or mixture is based, even if no new and significant information has been provided to them in respect of that substance or mixture. This will require e.g. a search of chemical hazard databases for new information. The competent authority may choose to specify a time (typically 3 – 5 years) from the date of original preparation, within which suppliers should review the labels and SDS information.

1.4.8   *Confidential business information*

1.4.8.1   Systems adopting the GHS should consider what provisions may be appropriate for the protection of confidential business information (CBI). Such provisions should not compromise the health and safety of workers or consumers, or the protection of the environment. As with other parts of the GHS, the rules of the importing country should apply with respect to CBI claims for imported substances and mixtures.

1.4.8.2   Where a system chooses to provide for protection of confidential business information, competent authorities should establish appropriate mechanisms, in accordance with national law and practice, and consider:

(a)   whether the inclusion of certain chemicals or classes of chemicals in the arrangements is appropriate to the needs of the system;

(b)   what definition of "confidential business information" should apply, taking account of factors such as the accessibility of the information by competitors, intellectual property rights and the potential harm disclosure would cause to the employer or supplier's business; and

(c)   appropriate procedures for the disclosure of confidential business information, where necessary to protect the health and safety of workers or consumers, or to protect the environment, and measures to prevent further disclosure.

1.4.8.3   Specific provisions for the protection of confidential business information may differ among systems in accordance with national law and practice. However, they should be consistent with the following general principles:

(a)   For information otherwise required on labels or safety data sheets, CBI claims should be limited to the names of substances, and their concentrations in mixtures. All other information should be disclosed on the label and/or safety data sheet, as required;

(b)   Where CBI has been withheld, the label or safety data sheet should so indicate;

(c)   CBI should be disclosed to the competent authority upon request. The competent authority should protect the confidentiality of the information in accordance with applicable law and practice;

(d)   Where a medical professional determines that a medical emergency exists due to exposure to a hazardous substance or mixture, mechanisms should be in place to ensure timely disclosure by the supplier or employer or competent authority of any specific confidential information necessary for treatment. The medical professional should maintain the confidentiality of the information;

(e)   For non-emergency situations, the supplier or employer should ensure disclosure of confidential information to a safety or health professional providing medical or other safety and health services to exposed workers or consumers, and to workers or workers' representatives. Persons requesting the information should provide specific reasons for the disclosure, and should agree to use the information only for the purpose of consumer or worker protection, and to otherwise maintain its confidentiality;

(f)   Where non-disclosure of CBI is challenged, the competent authority should address such challenges or provide for an alternative process for challenges. The supplier or employer should be responsible for supporting the assertion that the withheld information qualifies for CBI protection.

1.4.9   Training

Training users of hazard information is an integral part of hazard communication. Systems should identify the appropriate education and training for GHS target audiences who are required to interpret label and/or SDS information and to take appropriate action in response to chemical hazards. Training requirements should be appropriate for and commensurate with the nature of the work or exposure. Key target audiences for training include workers, emergency responders, and those involved in the preparation of labels, SDS and hazard communication strategies as part of risk management systems. Others involved in the transport and supply of hazardous chemicals also require training to varying degrees. In addition, systems should consider strategies required for educating consumers in interpreting label information on products that they use.

1.4.10   Labelling procedures

1.4.10.1   *Scope*

The following sections describe the procedures for preparing labels in the GHS, comprising the following:

(a)   Allocation of label elements;

(b)   Reproduction of the symbol;

(c)   Reproduction of the hazard pictogram;

(d)   Signal words;

(e)   Hazard statements;

(f)   Precautionary statements and pictograms;

(g)   Product and supplier identification;

(h)   Multiple hazards and precedence of information;

(i)   Arrangements for presenting the GHS label elements;

(j)   Special labelling arrangements.

1.4.10.2   *Label elements*

The tables in the individual chapters for each hazard class detail the label elements (symbol, signal word, hazard statement) that have been assigned to each of the hazard categories of the GHS. Hazard categories reflect the harmonized classification criteria. A summary of the allocation of label elements is provided in Annex 1. Special arrangements to take into account the information needs of different target audiences are further described in 1.4.10.5.4.

1.4.10.3   *Reproduction of the symbol*

The following hazard symbols are the standard symbols which should be used in the GHS. With the exception of the new symbol which will be used for certain health hazards and the exclamation mark, they are part of the standard symbol set used in the *UN Recommendations on the Transport of Dangerous Goods, Model Regulations*.

Flame	Flame over circle	Exploding bomb
Corrosion	Gas cylinder	Skull and crossbones
Exclamation mark	Environment	Health Hazard

1.4.10.4   *Pictograms and reproduction of the hazard pictograms*

1.4.10.4.1   A pictogram means a graphical composition that may include a symbol plus other graphic elements, such as a border, background pattern or colour that is intended to convey specific information.

1.4.10.4.2   *Shape and colour*

1.4.10.4.2.1   All hazard pictograms used in the GHS should be in the shape of a square set at a point.

1.4.10.4.2.2   For transport, the pictograms (commonly referred to as labels in transport regulations) prescribed by the *UN Model Regulations on the Transport of Dangerous Goods* should be used. The UN Model Regulations prescribe transport pictogram specifications including colour, symbols, size, background contrast, additional safety information (e.g. hazard class) and general format. Transport pictograms are required to have minimum dimensions of 100 mm by 100 mm, with some exceptions for allowing smaller pictograms for very small packagings and for gas cylinders. Transport pictograms include the symbol in the upper half of the label. The UN Model Regulations require that transport pictograms be printed or affixed to a packaging on a background of contrasting colour. An example showing a typical label for a flammable liquid hazard according to the UN Model Regulations is provided below:

Pictogram for flammable liquid in the UN Model Regulations (Symbol: Flame: black or white;
Background: red; Figure 3 in bottom corner; minimum dimensions 100 mm × 100 mm)

1.4.10.4.2.3   Pictograms prescribed by the GHS but not the *UN Recommendations on the Transport of Dangerous Goods, Model Regulations*, should have a black symbol on a white background with a red frame sufficiently wide to be clearly visible. However, when such a pictogram appears on a label for a package which will not be exported, the competent authority may choose to give suppliers and employers discretion to use a black border. In addition, competent authorities may allow the use of *UN Recommendations on the Transport of Dangerous Goods, Model Regulations* pictograms in other use settings where the package is not covered by the Model Regulations. An example of a GHS pictogram used for a skin irritant is provided below.

Pictogram for skin irritant

1.4.10.4.3   *Codification*

Pictograms prescribed by the GHS for sectors other than transport, and a code uniquely identifying each one, are listed in Section 4 of Annex 3. The pictogram code is intended to be used for reference purposes only. It is not part of the pictogram, and should not appear on labels or in section 2 of the safety data sheet.

1.4.10.5   *Allocation of label elements*

1.4.10.5.1   *Information required for packages covered by the UN Model Regulations on the Transport of Dangerous Goods*

Where a *UN Model Regulations on the Transport of Dangerous Goods* pictogram appears on a label, a GHS pictogram for the same hazard should not appear. The GHS pictograms not required for the transport of dangerous goods should not be displayed on freight containers, road vehicles or railway wagons/tanks.

1.4.10.5.2   *Information required on a GHS label*

    (a)   Signal words

A signal word means a word used to indicate the relative level of severity of hazard and alert the reader to a potential hazard on the label. The signal words used in the GHS are "Danger" and "Warning". "Danger" is mostly used for the more severe hazard categories (i.e. in the main for hazard categories 1 and 2), while "Warning" is mostly used for the less severe. The tables in the individual chapters for each hazard class detail the signal words that have been assigned to each of the hazard categories of the GHS.

    (b)   Hazard statements

        (i)   A hazard statement means a phrase assigned to a hazard class and category that describes the nature of the hazards of a hazardous product, including, where appropriate, the degree of hazard. The tables of label elements in the individual chapters for each hazard class detail the hazard statements that have been assigned to each of the hazard categories of the GHS;

(ii)   Hazard statements and a code uniquely identifying each one are listed in section 1 of Annex 3. The hazard statement code is intended to be used for reference purposes. It is not part of the hazard statement text and should not be used to replace it.

(c)   <u>Precautionary statements and pictograms</u>

(i)   A precautionary statement means a phrase (and/or pictogram) that describes recommended measures that should be taken to minimise or prevent adverse effects resulting from exposure to a hazardous product, or improper storage or handling of a hazardous product. The GHS label should include appropriate precautionary information, the choice of which is with the labeller or the competent authority. Annex 3 contains examples of precautionary statements, which can be used, and also examples of precautionary pictograms, which can be used where allowed by the competent authority;

(ii)   Precautionary statements and a code uniquely identifying each one are listed in section 2 of annex 3. The precautionary statement code is intended to be used for reference purposes. It is not part of the precautionary statement text and should not be used to replace it.

(d)   <u>Product identifier</u>

(i)   A product identifier should be used on a GHS label and it should match the product identifier used on the SDS. Where a substance or mixture is covered by the *UN Model Regulations on the Transport of Dangerous Goods*, the UN proper shipping name should also be used on the package;

(ii)   The label for a substance should include the chemical identity of the substance. For mixtures or alloys, the label should include the chemical identities of all ingredients or alloying elements that contribute to acute toxicity, skin corrosion or serious eye damage, germ cell mutagenicity, carcinogenicity, reproductive toxicity, skin or respiratory sensitization, or specific target organ toxicity (STOT), when these hazards appear on the label. Alternatively, the competent authority may require the inclusion of all ingredients or alloying elements that contribute to the hazard of the mixture or alloy;

(iii)   Where a substance or mixture is supplied exclusively for workplace use, the competent authority may choose to give suppliers discretion to include chemical identities on the SDS, in lieu of including them on labels;

(iv)   The competent authority rules for CBI take priority over the rules for product identification. This means that where an ingredient would normally be included on the label, if it meets the competent authority criteria for CBI, its identity does not have to be included on the label.

(e)   <u>Supplier identification</u>

The name, address and telephone number of the manufacturer or supplier of the substance or mixture should be provided on the label.

1.4.10.5.3   *Multiple hazards and precedence of hazard information*

The following arrangements apply where a substance or mixture presents more than one GHS hazard. It is without prejudice to the building block principle described in the *Purpose, scope and application* (Chapter 1.1). Therefore where a system does not provide information on the label for a particular hazard, the application of the arrangements should be modified accordingly.

1.4.10.5.3.1   Precedence for the allocation of symbols

For substances and mixtures covered by the *UN Recommendations on the Transport of Dangerous Goods, Model Regulations*, the precedence of symbols for physical hazards should follow the rules of the UN Model Regulations. In workplace situations, the competent authority may require all symbols for physical hazards to be used. For health hazards the following principles of precedence apply:

(a)   if the skull and crossbones applies, the exclamation mark should not appear;

(b)   if the corrosive symbol applies, the exclamation mark should not appear where it is used for skin or eye irritation;

(c)   if the health hazard symbol appears for respiratory sensitisation, the exclamation mark should not appear where it is used for skin sensitisation or for skin or eye irritation.

1.4.10.5.3.2   Precedence for allocation of signal words

If the signal word "Danger" applies, the signal word "Warning" should not appear.

1.4.10.5.3.3   Precedence for allocation of hazard statements

All assigned hazard statements should appear on the label, except where otherwise provided in this sub-section. The competent authority may specify the order in which they appear.

However, to avoid evident duplication or redundancy in the information conveyed by hazard statements, the following precedence rules may be applied:

(a)   If the statement H410 "Very toxic to aquatic life with long lasting effects" is assigned, the statement H400 "Very toxic to aquatic life" may be omitted;

(b)   If the statement H411 "Toxic to aquatic life with long lasting effects" is assigned, the statement H401 "Toxic to aquatic life" may be omitted;

(c)   If the statement H412 "Harmful to aquatic life with long lasting effects" is assigned, the statement H402 "Harmful to aquatic life" may be omitted;

(d)   If the statement H314 "Causes severe skin burns and eye damage" is assigned, the statement H318 "Causes serious eye damage" may be omitted.

Competent authorities may decide whether to require use of the above precedence rules, or to leave the choice to the manufacturer/supplier.

Table A3.1.2 in Annex 3 includes specified combinations of hazard statements. Where a combined hazard statement is indicated, the competent authority may specify whether the combined hazard statement or the corresponding individual statements should appear on the label, or may leave the choice to the manufacturer/supplier.

1.4.10.5.4   *Arrangements for presenting the GHS label elements*

1.4.10.5.4.1   Location of GHS information on the label

The GHS hazard pictograms, signal word and hazard statements should be located together on the label. The competent authority may choose to provide a specified layout for the presentation of these and for the presentation of precautionary information, or allow supplier discretion. Specific guidance and examples are provided in the chapters on individual hazard classes.

There have been some concerns about how the label elements should appear on different packagings. Specific examples are provided in Annex 7.

1.4.10.5.4.2   Supplemental information

The competent authority has the discretion to allow the use of supplemental information subject to the parameters outlined in 1.4.6.3. The competent authority may choose to specify where this information should appear on the label or allow supplier discretion. In either approach, the placement of supplemental information should not impede identification of GHS information.

1.4.10.5.4.3   Use of colour outside pictograms

In addition to its use in pictograms, colour can be used on other areas of the label to implement special labelling requirements such as the use of the pesticide bands in the FAO Labelling Guide, for signal words and hazard statements or as background to them, or as otherwise provided for by the competent authority.

1.4.10.5.4.4   Labelling of small packagings

The general principles that should underpin labelling of small packagings are:

(a)   All the applicable GHS label elements should appear on the immediate container of a hazardous substance or mixture where possible;

(b)   Where it is impossible to put all the applicable label elements on the immediate container itself, other methods of providing the full hazard information should be used in accordance with the definition of "Label" in the GHS. Factors influencing this include inter alia:

(i)   the shape, form or size of the immediate container;

(ii)   the number of label elements to be included, particularly where the substance or mixture meets the classification criteria for multiple hazard classes;

(iii)   the need for label elements to appear in more than one official language.

(c)   Where the volume of a hazardous substance or mixture is so low and the supplier has data demonstrating, and the competent authority has determined, that there is no likelihood of harm to human health and/or the environment, then the label elements may be omitted from the immediate container;

(d)   Competent authorities may allow certain label elements to be omitted from the immediate container for certain hazard classes/categories where the volume of the substance or mixture is below a certain amount;

(e)   Some labelling elements on the immediate container may need to be accessible throughout the life of the product, e.g. for continuous use by workers or consumers.

1.4.10.5.5   *Special labelling arrangements*

The competent authority may choose to allow communication of certain hazard information for carcinogens, reproductive toxicity and specific target organ toxicity through repeated exposure on the label and on the SDS, or through the SDS alone (see specific chapters for details of relevant cut-offs for these classes).

Similarly, for metals and alloys, the competent authority may choose to allow communication of the hazard information through the SDS alone when they are supplied in the massive, non-dispersible, form.

Where a substance or mixture is classified as corrosive to metals but not corrosive to skin and/or eyes, the competent authority may choose to allow the hazard pictogram linked to "corrosive to metals" to be omitted from the label of such substances or mixtures which are in the finished state as packaged for consumer use.

1.4.10.5.5.1   Workplace labelling

Products falling within the scope of the GHS will carry the GHS label at the point where they are supplied to the workplace, and that label should be maintained on the supplied container in the workplace. The GHS label or label elements should also be used for workplace containers. However, the competent authority can allow employers to use alternative means of giving workers the same information in a different written or displayed format when such a format is more appropriate to the workplace and communicates the information as effectively as the GHS label. For example, label information could be displayed in the work area, rather than on the individual containers.

Alternative means of providing workers with the information contained in GHS labels are needed usually where hazardous chemicals are transferred from an original supplier container into a workplace container or system, or where chemicals are produced in a workplace but are not packaged in containers intended for sale or supply. Chemicals that are produced in a workplace may be contained or stored in many different ways such as: small samples collected for testing or analysis, piping systems including valves, process or reaction vessels, ore cars, conveyer systems or free-standing bulk storage of solids. In batch manufacturing processes, one mixing vessel may be used to contain a number of different mixtures.

In many situations, it is impractical to produce a complete GHS label and attach it to the container, due, for example, to container size limitations or lack of access to a process container. Some examples of workplace situations where chemicals may be transferred from supplier containers include: containers for laboratory testing or analysis, storage vessels, piping or process reaction systems or temporary containers where the chemical will be used by one worker within a short timeframe. Decanted chemicals intended for immediate use could be labelled with the main components and directly refer the user to the supplier label information and SDS.

All such systems should ensure that there is clear hazard communication. Workers should be trained to understand the specific communication methods used in a workplace. Examples of alternative methods include: use of product identifiers together with GHS symbols and other pictograms to describe precautionary measures; use of process flow charts for complex systems to identify chemicals contained in pipes and vessels with links to the appropriate SDS; use of displays with GHS symbols, colour and signal words in piping systems and processing equipment; use of permanent placarding for fixed piping; use of batch tickets or recipes for labelling batch mixing vessels and use of piping bands with hazard symbols and product identifiers.

1.4.10.5.5.2   Consumer product labelling based on the likelihood of injury

All systems should use the GHS classification criteria based on hazard, however competent authorities may authorize consumer labelling systems providing information based on the likelihood of harm (risk-based labelling). In the latter case the competent authority would establish procedures for determining the potential exposure and risk for the use of the product. Labels based on this approach provide targeted information on identified risks but may not include certain information on chronic health effects (e.g. specific target organ toxicity (STOT)) following repeated exposure, reproductive toxicity and carcinogenicity), that would appear on a label based on hazard alone. A general explanation of the broad principles of risk-based labelling is contained in Annex 5.

1.4.10.5.5.3   Tactile warnings

If tactile warnings are used, the technical specifications should conform with ISO 11683:1997 "Tactile warnings of danger: Requirements".

CHAPTER 1.5

HAZARD COMMUNICATION: SAFETY DATA SHEETS (SDS)

1.5.1 The role of the safety data sheet (SDS) in the harmonized system

1.5.1.1 The SDS should provide comprehensive information about a substance or mixture for use in workplace chemical control regulatory frameworks. Both employers and workers use it as a source of information about hazards, including environmental hazards, and to obtain advice on safety precautions. The information acts as a reference source for the management of hazardous chemicals in the workplace. The SDS is product related and, usually, is not able to provide specific information that is relevant for any given workplace where the product may finally be used, although where products have specialized end uses the SDS information may be more workplace-specific. The information therefore enables the employer (a) to develop an active programme of worker protection measures, including training, which is specific to the individual workplace; and (b) to consider any measures which may be necessary to protect the environment.

1.5.1.2 In addition, the SDS provides an important source of information for other target audiences in the GHS. So certain elements of information may be used by those involved with the transport of dangerous goods, emergency responders (including poison centers), those involved in the professional use of pesticides and consumers. However, these audiences receive additional information from a variety of other sources such as the *UN Recommendations on the Transport of Dangerous Goods, Model Regulations* document and package inserts for consumers and will continue to do so. The introduction of a harmonized labelling system therefore, is not intended to affect the primary use of the SDS which is for workplace users.

1.5.2 Criteria for determining whether an SDS should be produced

An SDS should be produced for all substances and mixtures which meet the harmonized criteria for physical, health or environmental hazards under the GHS and for all mixtures which contain ingredients that meet the criteria for carcinogenic, toxic to reproduction or specific target organ toxicity in concentrations exceeding the cut-off limits for SDS specified by the criteria for mixtures (see 1.5.3.1). The competent authority may also require SDS's for mixtures not meeting the criteria for classification as hazardous but which contain hazardous ingredients in certain concentrations (see 1.5.3.1).

1.5.3 General guidance for compiling a safety data sheet

1.5.3.1 *Cut-off values/concentration limits*

1.5.3.1.1 An SDS should be provided based on the generic cut-off values/concentration limits indicated in Table 1.5.1:

Table 1.5.1: Cut-off values/concentration limits for each health and environmental hazard class

Hazard class	Cut-off value/concentration limit
Acute toxicity	$\geq 1.0\%$
Skin corrosion/Irritation	$\geq 1.0\%$
Serious eye damage/eye irritation	$\geq 1.0\%$
Respiratory/Skin sensitization	$\geq 0.1\%$
Germ cell mutagenicity (Category 1)	$\geq 0.1\%$
Germ cell mutagenicity (Category 2)	$\geq 1.0\%$
Carcinogenicity	$\geq 0.1\%$
Reproductive toxicity	$\geq 0.1\%$
Specific target organ toxicity (single exposure)	$\geq 1.0\%$
Specific target organ toxicity (repeated exposure)	$\geq 1.0\%$
Aspiration hazard (Category 1)	$\geq 10\%$ of Category 1 ingredient(s) and kinematic viscosity ≤ 20.5 mm^2/s at 40°C
Aspiration hazard (Category 2)	$\geq 10\%$ of Category 2 ingredient(s) and kinematic viscosity ≤ 14 mm^2/s at 40°C
Hazardous to the aquatic environment	$\geq 1.0\%$

1.5.3.1.2   As noted in the *Classification of hazardous substances and mixtures* (see Chapter 1.3), there may be some cases when the available hazard data may justify classification on the basis of other cut-off values/concentration limits than the generic ones specified in the health and environment hazard class chapters (chapters 3.2 to 3.10 and 4.1). When such specific cut-off values are used for classification, they should also apply to the obligation to compile an SDS.

1.5.3.1.3   Some competent authorities (CA) may require SDS's to be compiled for mixtures which are not classified for acute toxicity or aquatic toxicity as a result of application of the additivity formula, but which contain acutely toxic or toxic to the aquatic environment ingredients in concentrations equal to or greater than 1%[1].

1.5.3.1.4   In accordance with the building block approach, some competent authorities may choose not to regulate certain categories within a hazard class. In such situations, there would be no obligation to compile an SDS.

1.5.3.1.5   Once it is clear that an SDS is required for a substance or a mixture then the information required to be included in the SDS should in all cases be provided in accordance with GHS requirements.

---

[1]   *The cut-off values for classification of mixtures are normally specified by concentrations expressed as % of the ingredients. In some cases, for example acute toxicity (human health), the cut-off values are expressed as acute toxicity values (ATE). The classification of a mixture is determined by additivity calculation based on acute toxicity values (see Chapter 3.1) and concentrations of ingredients. Similarly acute aquatic toxicity classification may be calculated on the basis of acute aquatic toxicity values (see Chapter 4.1) and where appropriate, corrosion/irritation by adding up concentrations of ingredients (see Chapters 3.2 and 3.3). Ingredients are taken into consideration for application of the formula when the concentration is equal to or greater than 1 %. Some competent authorities (CA) may use this cut-off as a basis of obligation to compile an SDS.*

1.5.3.2   *SDS format*

1.5.3.2.1   The information in the SDS should be presented using the following 16 headings in the order given below:

1. Identification
2. Hazard(s) identification
3. Composition/information on ingredients
4. First-aid measures
5. Fire-fighting measures
6. Accidental release measures
7. Handling and storage
8. Exposure controls/personal protection
9. Physical and chemical properties
10. Stability and reactivity
11. Toxicological information
12. Ecological information
13. Disposal considerations
14. Transport information
15. Regulatory information
16. Other information.

1.5.3.3   *SDS content*

1.5.3.3.1   The SDS should provide a clear description of the data used to identify the hazards. The minimum information in Table 1.5.2 should be included, where applicable and available, on the SDS under the relevant headings[2]. If specific information is not applicable or not available under a particular subheading, the SDS should clearly state this. Additional information may be required by competent authorities.

1.5.3.3.2   Some subheadings relate to information that is national or regional in nature, for example "EC number" and "occupational exposure limits". Suppliers or employers should include information under such SDS subheadings that is appropriate and relevant to the countries or regions for which the SDS is intended and into which the product is being supplied.

1.5.3.3.3   Guidance on the preparation of SDS's under the requirements of the GHS can be found in Annex 4. It has been developed by the GHS Sub-Committee after consideration of the main internationally-recognized standards which provided guidance in the preparation of an SDS, including the ILO Standard under the Recommendation 177 on "Safety in the use of chemicals at work", ISO 11014 of the International Standard Organization (ISO), the European Union Safety Data Sheet Directive 91/155/EEC and the American National Standard Institute (ANSI) standard Z 400.1.

1.5.3.3.4   Additional safety and environmental information is required to address the needs of seafarers and other transport workers in the bulk transport of dangerous goods in sea-going or inland navigation bulk carriers or tank-vessels subject to IMO or national regulations. Paragraph A4.3.14.7 of Annex 4 recommends the inclusion of basic classification information when such cargoes are transported as liquids in bulk according to Annex II of MARPOL and the IBC Code. In addition, ships carrying oil or oil fuel, as defined in Annex I of MARPOL, in bulk or bunkering oil fuel are required before loading to be provided with a "material safety data sheet" in accordance with the IMO's Maritime Safety Committee (MSC) resolution "Recommendations for Material Safety Data Sheets (MSDS) for MARPOL Annex I Oil Cargo and Oil Fuel" (MSC.286(86)). Therefore, in order to have one harmonized SDS for maritime and non-maritime use, the additional provisions of Resolution MSC.286(86) may be included in the GHS SDS, where appropriate, for marine transport of MARPOL Annex I cargoes and marine fuel oils.

---

[2]   *Where "applicable" means where the information is applicable to the specific product covered by the SDS. Where "available" means where the information is available to the supplier or other entity that is preparing the SDS.*

Table 1.5.2   Minimum information for an SDS

1.	Identification of the substance or mixture and of the supplier	(a) GHS product identifier; (b) Other means of identification; (c) Recommended use of the chemical and restrictions on use; (d) Supplier's details (including name, address, phone number etc.); (e) Emergency phone number.
2.	Hazards identification	(a) GHS classification of the substance/mixture and any national or regional information; (b) GHS label elements, including precautionary statements. (Hazard symbols may be provided as a graphical reproduction of the symbols in black and white or the name of the symbol e.g. "flame", "skull and crossbones"); (c) Other hazards which do not result in classification (e.g. "dust explosion hazard") or are not covered by the GHS.
3.	Composition/ information on ingredients	**Substance** (a) Chemical identity; (b) Common name, synonyms, etc.; (c) CAS number and other unique identifiers; (d) Impurities and stabilizing additives which are themselves classified and which contribute to the classification of the substance. **Mixture** The chemical identity and concentration or concentration ranges of all ingredients which are hazardous within the meaning of the GHS and are present above their cut-off levels. *NOTE: For information on ingredients, the competent authority rules for CBI take priority over the rules for product identification.*
4.	First-aid measures	(a) Description of necessary measures, subdivided according to the different routes of exposure, i.e. inhalation, skin and eye contact and ingestion; (b) Most important symptoms/effects, acute and delayed. (c) Indication of immediate medical attention and special treatment needed, if necessary.
5.	Fire-fighting measures	(a) Suitable (and unsuitable) extinguishing media. (b) Specific hazards arising from the chemical (e.g. nature of any hazardous combustion products). (c) Special protective equipment and precautions for fire-fighters.
6.	Accidental release measures	(a) Personal precautions, protective equipment and emergency procedures. (b) Environmental precautions. (c) Methods and materials for containment and cleaning up.
7.	Handling and storage	(a) Precautions for safe handling. (b) Conditions for safe storage, including any incompatibilities.
8.	Exposure controls/personal protection	(a) Control parameters e.g. occupational exposure limit values or biological limit values. (b) Appropriate engineering controls. (c) Individual protection measures, such as personal protective equipment.
9.	Physical and chemical properties	(a) Appearance (physical state, colour etc); (b) Odour; (c) Odour threshold; (d) pH; (e) Melting point/freezing point; (f) Initial boiling point and boiling range; (g) Flash point; (h) Evaporation rate; (i) Flammability (solid, gas); (j) Upper/lower flammability or explosive limits; (k) Vapour pressure;

(Cont'd on next page)

Table 1.5.2   Minimum information for an SDS *(cont'd)*

9.	*Physical and chemical properties (cont'd)*	(l) Vapour density; (m) Relative density; (n) Solubility(ies); (o) Partition coefficient: n-octanol/water; (p) Auto-ignition temperature; (q) Decomposition temperature; (r) Viscosity.
10.	**Stability and reactivity**	(a) Reactivity (b) Chemical stability; (c) Possibility of hazardous reactions; (d) Conditions to avoid (e.g. static discharge, shock or vibration); (e) Incompatible materials; (f) Hazardous decomposition products.
11.	**Toxicological information**	Concise but complete and comprehensible description of the various toxicological (health) effects and the available data used to identify those effects, including: (a) information on the likely routes of exposure (inhalation, ingestion, skin and eye contact); (b) Symptoms related to the physical, chemical and toxicological characteristics; (c) Delayed and immediate effects and also chronic effects from short and long term exposure; (d) Numerical measures of toxicity (such as acute toxicity estimates).
12.	**Ecological information**	(a) Ecotoxicity (aquatic and terrestrial, where available); (b) Persistence and degradability; (c) Bioaccumulative potential; (d) Mobility in soil; (e) Other adverse effects.
13.	**Disposal considerations**	Description of waste residues and information on their safe handling and methods of disposal, including the disposal of any contaminated packaging.
14.	**Transport information**	(a) UN number; (b) UN proper shipping name; (c) Transport hazard class(es); (d) Packing group, if applicable; (e) Environmental hazards (e.g.: Marine pollutant (Yes/No)); (f) Transport in bulk (according to Annex II of MARPOL 73/78 and the IBC Code); (g) Special precautions which a user needs to be aware of, or needs to comply with, in connection with transport or conveyance either within or outside their premises.
15.	**Regulatory information**	Safety, health and environmental regulations specific for the product in question.
16.	**Other information including information on preparation and revision of the SDS**	

PART 2

PHYSICAL HAZARDS

CHAPTER 2.1

EXPLOSIVES

2.1.1　Definitions and general considerations

2.1.1.1　An *explosive substance (or mixture)* is a solid or liquid substance (or mixture of substances) which is in itself capable by chemical reaction of producing gas at such a temperature and pressure and at such a speed as to cause damage to the surroundings. Pyrotechnic substances are included even when they do not evolve gases.

A *pyrotechnic substance (or mixture)* is a substance or mixture of substances designed to produce an effect by heat, light, sound, gas or smoke or a combination of these as the result of non-detonative self-sustaining exothermic chemical reactions.

An *explosive article* is an article containing one or more explosive substances or mixtures.

A *pyrotechnic article* is an article containing one or more pyrotechnic substances or mixtures.

2.1.1.2　The class of explosives comprises:

(a)　Explosive substances and mixtures;

(b)　Explosive articles, except devices containing explosive substances or mixtures in such quantity or of such a character that their inadvertent or accidental ignition or initiation shall not cause any effect external to the device either by projection, fire, smoke, heat or loud noise; and

(c)　Substances, mixtures and articles not mentioned under (a) and (b) above which are manufactured with the view to producing a practical, explosive or pyrotechnic effect.

2.1.2　Classification criteria

2.1.2.1　Substances, mixtures and articles of this class, which are not classified as an unstable explosive, are assigned to one of the following six divisions depending on the type of hazard they present:

(a)　Division 1.1:　Substances, mixtures and articles which have a mass explosion hazard (a mass explosion is one which affects almost the entire quantity present virtually instantaneously);

(b)　Division 1.2:　Substances, mixtures and articles which have a projection hazard but not a mass explosion hazard;

(c)　Division 1.3:　Substances, mixtures and articles which have a fire hazard and either a minor blast hazard or a minor projection hazard or both, but not a mass explosion hazard:

(i)　combustion of which gives rise to considerable radiant heat; or

(ii)　which burn one after another, producing minor blast or projection effects or both;

(d)　Division 1.4:　Substances, mixtures and articles which present no significant hazard: substances, mixtures and articles which present only a small hazard in the event of ignition or initiation. The effects are largely confined to the package and no projection of fragments of appreciable size or range is to be expected. An external fire shall not cause virtually instantaneous explosion of almost the entire contents of the package;

(e) Division 1.5: Very insensitive substances or mixtures which have a mass explosion hazard: substances and mixtures which have a mass explosion hazard but are so insensitive that there is very little probability of initiation or of transition from burning to detonation under normal conditions;

(f) Division 1.6: Extremely insensitive articles which do not have a mass explosion hazard: articles which contain only extremely insensitive substances or mixtures and which demonstrate a negligible probability of accidental initiation or propagation.

2.1.2.2 Explosives, which are not classified as an unstable explosive, are classified in one of the six divisions above based on Test Series 2 to 8 in Part I of the *UN Recommendations on the Transport of Dangerous Goods, Manual of Tests and Criteria* according to the following table:

Table 2.1.1: Criteria for explosives

Category	Criteria
Unstable[a] explosives or explosives of Division 1.1 to 1.6	For explosives of Divisions 1.1 to 1.6, the following are the core set of tests that need to be performed:
	Explosibility: according to UN Test Series 2 (Section 12 of the *UN Recommendations on the Transport of Dangerous Goods, Manual of Tests and Criteria*). Intentional explosives[b] are not subject to UN Test Series 2.
	Sensitiveness: according to UN Test Series 3 (Section 13 of the *UN Recommendations on the Transport of Dangerous Goods, Manual of Tests and Criteria*).
	Thermal stability: according to UN Test 3(c) (Sub-section 13.6.1 of the *UN Recommendations on the Transport of Dangerous Goods, Manual of Tests and Criteria*).
	Further tests are necessary to allocate the correct Division.

[a] *Unstable explosives are those which are thermally unstable and/or too sensitive for normal handling, transport and use. Special precautions are necessary.*

[b] *This comprises substances, mixtures and articles which are manufactured with a view to producing a practical, explosive or pyrotechnic effect.*

NOTE 1: *Explosive substances or mixtures in packaged form and articles may be classified under divisions 1.1 to 1.6 and, for some regulatory purposes, are further subdivided into compatibility groups A to S to distinguish technical requirements (see UN Recommendations on the Transport of Dangerous Goods, Model Regulations, Chapter 2.1).*

NOTE 2: *Some explosive substances and mixtures are wetted with water or alcohols or diluted with other substances to suppress their explosives properties. They may be treated differently from explosive substances and mixtures (as desensitized explosives) for some regulatory purposes (e.g. transport), see 1.3.2.4.5.2.*

NOTE 3: *For classification tests on solid substances or mixtures, the tests should be performed on the substance or mixture as presented. If for example, for the purposes of supply or transport, the same chemical is to be presented in a physical form different from that which was tested and which is considered likely to materially alter its performance in a classification test, the substance or mixture must also be tested in the new form.*

2.1.3 Hazard communication

General and specific considerations concerning labelling requirements are provided in *Hazard communication: Labelling* (Chapter 1.4). Annex 1 contains summary tables about classification and labelling. Annex 3 contains examples of precautionary statements and pictograms which can be used where allowed by the competent authority.

Table 2.1.2: Label elements for explosives

	Unstable Explosive	Division 1.1	Division 1.2	Division 1.3	Division 1.4	Division 1.5	Division 1.6
Symbol	Exploding bomb	Exploding bomb	Exploding bomb	Exploding bomb	Exploding bomb; *or* 1.4 on orange background[a]	1.5 on orange background[a]	1.6 on orange background[a]
Signal word	Danger	Danger	Danger	Danger	Warning	Danger	*No signal word*
Hazard statement	Unstable Explosive	Explosive; mass explosion hazard	Explosive; severe projection hazard	Explosive; fire, blast or projection hazard.	Fire or projection hazard	May mass explode in fire	*No hazard statement*

[a]   *Applies to substances, mixtures and articles subject to some regulatory purposes (e.g. transport).*

NOTE 1:   *Unpackaged explosives or explosives repacked in packagings other than the original or similar packaging shall have the following label elements:*

 (a) *Symbol: exploding bomb;*
 (b) *Signal word: "Danger"; and*
 (c) *Hazard statement: "explosive; mass explosion hazard"*

 unless the hazard is shown to correspond to one of the hazard categories in table 2.1.2, in which case the corresponding symbol, signal word and/or the hazard statement shall be assigned.

NOTE 2:   *Substances and mixtures, as supplied, with a positive result in Test Series 2 in Part I, Section 12, of the UN Recommendations on the Transport of Dangerous Goods, Manual of Tests and Criteria, which are exempted from classification as explosives (based on a negative result in Test Series 6 in Part I, Section 16 of the UN Recommendations on the Transport of Dangerous Goods, Manual of Tests and Criteria,) still have explosive properties. The user should be informed of these intrinsic explosive properties because they have to be considered for handling – especially if the substance or mixture is removed from its packaging or is repackaged – and for storage. For this reason, the explosive properties of the substance or mixture should be communicated in Section 2 (Hazard identification) and Section 9 (Physical and chemical properties) of the Safety Data Sheet in accordance with Table 1.5.2, and other sections of the Safety Data Sheet, as appropriate.*

2.1.4 Decision logic and guidance

The decision logic and guidance, which follow, are not part of the harmonized classification system, but have been provided here as additional guidance. It is strongly recommended that the person responsible for classification studies the criteria before and during use of the decision logic.

2.1.4.1   *Decision logic*

The classification of substances, mixtures and articles in the class of explosives and further allocation to a division is a very complex, three step procedure. Reference to Part I *of the UN Recommendations on the Transport of Dangerous Goods, Manual of Tests and Criteria,* is necessary. The first step is to ascertain whether the substance or mixture has explosive effects (Test Series 1). The second step is the acceptance procedure (Test Series 2 to 4) and the third step is the assignment to a hazard division (Test Series 5 to 7). The assessment whether a candidate for "ammonium nitrate emulsion or suspension or gel, intermediate for blasting explosives (ANE)" is insensitive enough for inclusion as an oxidizing liquid (Chapter 2.13) or an oxidizing solid (Chapter 2.14) is answered by Test Series 8 tests. The classification procedure is according to the following decision logics (see Figures 2.1.1 to 2.1.4).

Figure 2.1.1: **Overall scheme of the procedure for classifying a substance, mixture or article in the class of explosives (Class 1 for transport)**

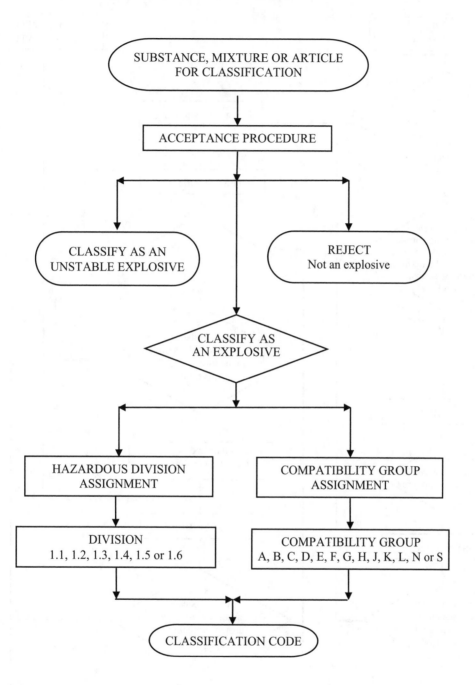

Figure 2.1.2: **Procedure for provisional acceptance of a substance, mixture or article in the class of explosives (Class 1 for transport)**

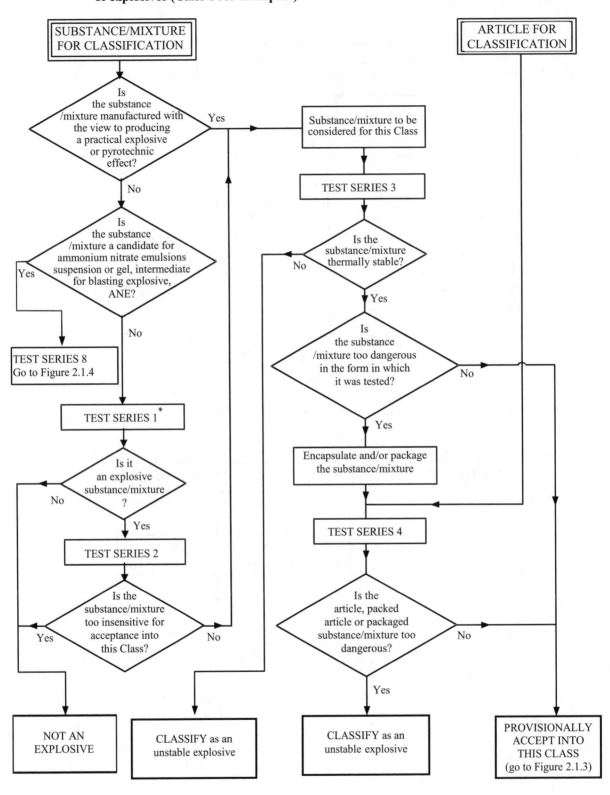

---

* *For classification purposes start with test series 2.*

Figure 2.1.3: Procedure for assignment to a division in the class of explosives (Class 1 for transport)

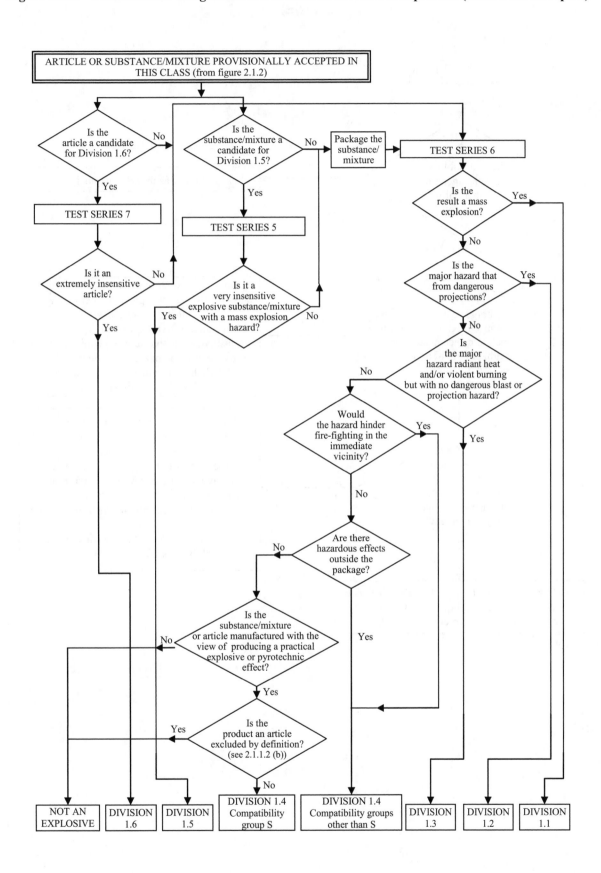

Figure 2.1.4:   Procedure for the classification of ammonium nitrate emulsion, suspension or gel (ANE)

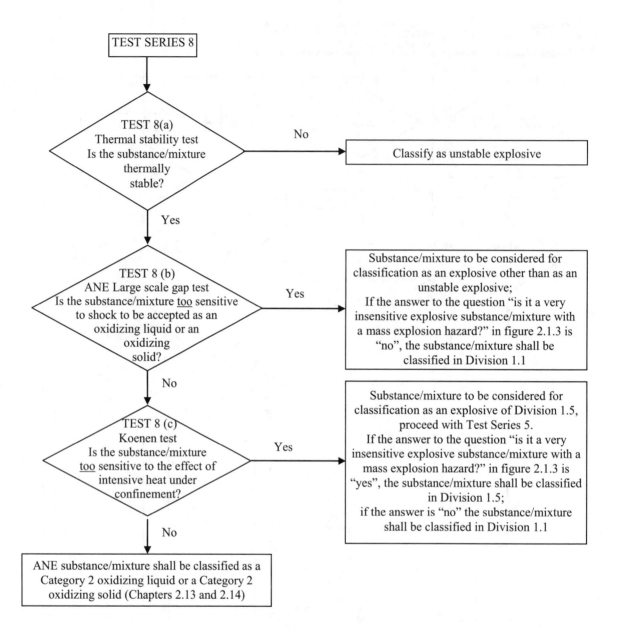

TEST SERIES 8

TEST 8(a)
Thermal stability test
Is the substance/mixture thermally stable?

No → Classify as unstable explosive

Yes

TEST 8 (b)
ANE Large scale gap test
Is the substance/mixture <u>too</u> sensitive to shock to be accepted as an oxidizing liquid or an oxidizing solid?

Yes → Substance/mixture to be considered for classification as an explosive other than as an unstable explosive;
If the answer to the question "is it a very insensitive explosive substance/mixture with a mass explosion hazard?" in figure 2.1.3 is "no", the substance/mixture shall be classified in Division 1.1

No

TEST 8 (c)
Koenen test
Is the substance/mixture <u>too</u> sensitive to the effect of intensive heat under confinement?

Yes → Substance/mixture to be considered for classification as an explosive of Division 1.5, proceed with Test Series 5.
If the answer to the question "is it a very insensitive explosive substance/mixture with a mass explosion hazard?" in figure 2.1.3 is "yes", the substance/mixture shall be classified in Division 1.5;
if the answer is "no" the substance/mixture shall be classified in Division 1.1

No

ANE substance/mixture shall be classified as a Category 2 oxidizing liquid or a Category 2 oxidizing solid (Chapters 2.13 and 2.14)

2.1.4.2 *Guidance*

2.1.4.2.1   Explosive properties are associated with the presence of certain chemical groups in a molecule which can react to produce very rapid increases in temperature or pressure. The screening procedure is aimed at identifying the presence of such reactive groups and the potential for rapid energy release. If the screening procedure identifies the substance or mixture to be a potential explosive, the acceptance procedure (see section 10.3 of the *UN Recommendations on the Transport of Dangerous Goods, Manual of Tests and Criteria*) has to be performed.

NOTE: *Neither a Series 1 type (a) propagation of detonation test nor a Series 2 type (a) test of sensitivity to detonative shock is required if the exothermic decomposition energy of organic materials is less than 800 J/g. For organic substances and mixtures of organic substances with a decomposition energy of 800 J/g or more, tests 1 (a) and 2 (a) need not be performed if the outcome of the ballistic mortar Mk.IIId test (F.1), or the ballistic mortar test (F.2) or the BAM Trauzl test (F.3) with initiation by a standard No.8 detonator (see Appendix 1 to the Manual of Tests and Criteria) is "no". In this case, the results of test 1 (a) and 2 (a) are deemed to be "-".*

2.1.4.2.2   A substance or mixture is not classified as explosive if:

(a)   There are no chemical groups associated with explosive properties present in the molecule. Examples of groups which may indicate explosive properties are given in Table A6.1 in Appendix 6 of the *UN Recommendations on the Transport of Dangerous Goods, Manual of Tests and Criteria*; or

(b)   The substance contains chemical groups associated with explosive properties which include oxygen and the calculated oxygen balance is less than -200.

The oxygen balance is calculated for the chemical reaction:

$$C_xH_yO_z + [x + (y/4)-(z/2)]\ O_2 \rightarrow x.\ CO_2 + (y/2)\ H_2O$$

using the formula:

oxygen balance = -1600 [2x +(y/2) -z]/molecular weight;

(c)   When the organic substance or a homogenous mixture of organic substances contain chemical groups associated with explosive properties but the exothermic decomposition energy is less than 500 J/g and the onset of exothermic decomposition is below 500 °C. (The temperature limit is to prevent the procedure being applied to a large number of organic materials which are not explosive but which will decompose slowly above 500 °C to release more than 500 J/g.) The exothermic decomposition energy may be determined using a suitable calorimetric technique; or

(d)   For mixtures of inorganic oxidizing substances with organic material(s), the concentration of the inorganic oxidizing substance is:

less than 15%, by mass, if the oxidizing substance is assigned to Category 1 or 2;
less than 30%, by mass, if the oxidizing substance is assigned to Category 3.

2.1.4.2.3   In the case of mixtures containing any known explosives, the acceptance procedure has to be performed.

CHAPTER 2.2

FLAMMABLE GASES (INCLUDING CHEMICALLY UNSTABLE GASES)

2.2.1 Definitions

2.2.1.1 A *flammable gas* is a gas having a flammable range with air at 20 °C and a standard pressure of 101.3 kPa.

2.2.1.2 A *chemically unstable gas* is a flammable gas that is able to react explosively even in the absence of air or oxygen.

2.2.2 Classification criteria

2.2.2.1 A flammable gas is classified in one of the two categories for this class according to the following table:

Table 2.2.1: Criteria for flammable gases

Category	Criteria
1	Gases, which at 20 °C and a standard pressure of 101.3 kPa: (a) are ignitable when in a mixture of 13% or less by volume in air; or (b) have a flammable range with air of at least 12 percentage points regardless of the lower flammable limit.
2	Gases, other than those of Category 1, which, at 20 °C and a standard pressure of 101.3 kPa, have a flammable range while mixed in air.

NOTE 1: *Ammonia and methyl bromide may be regarded as special cases for some regulatory purposes.*

NOTE 2: *Aerosols should not be classified as flammable gases. See Chapter 2.3.*

2.2.2.2 A flammable gas that is also chemically unstable is additionally classified in one of the two categories for chemically unstable gases using the methods described in Part III of the Manual of Tests and Criteria according to the following table:

Table 2.2.2: Criteria for chemically unstable gases

Category	Criteria
A	Flammable gases which are chemically unstable at 20°C and a standard pressure of 101.3 kPa
B	Flammable gases which are chemically unstable at a temperature greater than 20°C and/or a pressure greater than 101.3 kPa

2.2.3 Hazard communication

General and specific considerations concerning labelling requirements are provided in *Hazard communication: Labelling* (Chapter 1.4). Annex 1 contains summary tables about classification and labelling. Annex 3 contains examples of precautionary statements and pictograms which can be used where allowed by the competent authority.

Table 2.2.3: Label elements for flammable gases (including chemical unstable gases)

	Flammable gas		Chemically unstable gas	
	Category 1	**Category 2**	**Category A**	**Category B**
Symbol	Flame	*No symbol*	*No additional symbol*	*No additional symbol*
Signal word	Danger	Warning	*No additional signal word*	*No additional signal word*
Hazard statement	Extremely flammable gas	Flammable gas	May react explosively even in the absence of air	May react explosively even in the absence of air at elevated pressure and/or temperature

2.2.4   Decision logic and guidance

The decision logic and guidance, which follow, are not part of the harmonized classification system, but have been provided here as additional guidance. It is strongly recommended that the person responsible for classification studies the criteria before and during use of the decision logic.

2.2.4.1   *Decision logic for flammable gases*

To classify a flammable gas, data on its flammability are required. The classification is according to decision logic 2.2 (a).

Decision logic 2.2 (a)

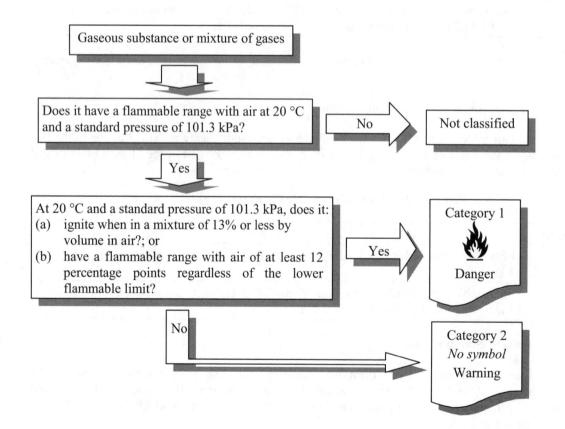

2.2.4.2 *Decision logic for chemically unstable gases*

To classify a flammable gas as chemically unstable, data on its chemical instability are required. The classification is according to decision logic 2.2 (b).

Decision logic 2.2 (b)

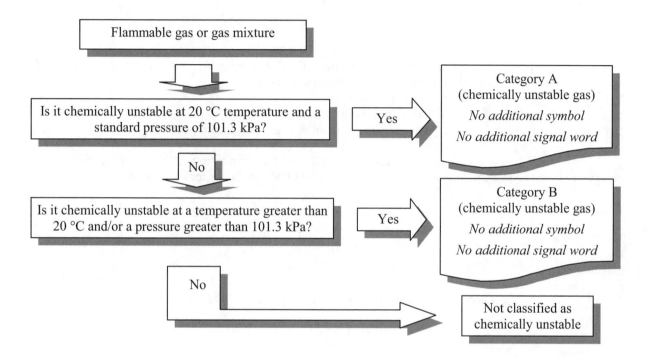

2.2.4.3 *Guidance*

2.2.4.3.1   Flammability should be determined by tests or by calculation in accordance with methods adopted by ISO (see ISO 10156:2010 "Gases and gas mixtures – Determination of fire potential and oxidizing ability for the selection of cylinder valve outlets"). Where insufficient data are available to use these methods, tests by a comparable method recognized by the competent authority may be used.

2.2.4.3.2   Chemical instability should be determined in accordance with the method described in Part III of the Manual of Tests and Criteria. If the calculations in accordance with ISO 10156:2010 show that a gas mixture is not flammable it is not necessary to carry out the tests for determining chemical instability for classification purposes.

2.2.5   Example: Classification of a flammable gas mixture by calculation according to ISO 10156:2010

<u>Formula</u>

$$\sum_{i}^{n} \frac{V_i\%}{T_{ci}}$$

where:

$V_i\%$ = the equivalent flammable gas content;

T_{ci} = the maximum concentration of a flammable gas in nitrogen at which the mixture is still not flammable in air;

i = the first gas in the mixture;

n = the nth gas in the mixture;

K_i = the equivalency factor for an inert gas versus nitrogen;

Where a gas mixture contains an inert diluent other than nitrogen, the volume of this diluent is adjusted to the equivalent volume of nitrogen using the equivalency factor for the inert gas (K_i).

<u>Criterion:</u>

$$\sum_{i}^{n} \frac{V_i\%}{T_{ci}} > 1$$

<u>Gas mixture</u>

For the purpose of this example the following is the gas mixture to be used

$$2\% (H_2) + 6\%(CH_4) + 27\%(Ar) + 65\%(He)$$

<u>Calculation</u>

1.   Ascertain the equivalency factors (Ki) for the inert gases versus nitrogen:

   Ki (Ar) = 0.5
   Ki (He) = 0.5

2.   Calculate the equivalent mixture with nitrogen as balance gas using the Ki figures for the inert gases:

   $2\%(H_2) + 6\%(CH_4) + [27\% \times 0.5 + 65\% \times 0.5](N_2) = 2\%(H_2) + 6\%(CH_4) + 46\%(N_2) = 54\%$

3.   Adjust the sum of the contents to 100%:

   $$\frac{100}{54} \times [2\%(H_2) + 6\%(CH_4) + 46\%(N_2)] = 3.7\%(H_2) + 11.1\%(CH_4) + 85.2\%(N_2)$$

4.   Ascertain the Tci coefficients for the flammable gases:

   Tci H_2 = 5.7%
   Tci CH_4 = 14.3%

5.   Calculate the flammability of the equivalent mixture using the formula:

   $$\sum_{i}^{n} \frac{V_i\%}{T_{ci}} = \frac{3.7}{5.7} + \frac{11.1}{14.3} = 1.42 \qquad\qquad \mathbf{1.42 > 1}$$

Therefore the mixture is <u>flammable</u> in air.

CHAPTER 2.3

AEROSOLS

2.3.1   Definition

Aerosols, this means aerosol dispensers, are any non-refillable receptacles made of metal, glass or plastics and containing a gas compressed, liquefied or dissolved under pressure, with or without a liquid, paste or powder, and fitted with a release device allowing the contents to be ejected as solid or liquid particles in suspension in a gas, as a foam, paste or powder or in a liquid state or in a gaseous state.

2.3.2   Classification criteria

2.3.2.1   Aerosols are classified in one of the three categories of this hazard class, depending on their flammable properties and their heat of combustion. They should be considered for classification in Category 1 or 2 if they contain more than 1% components (by mass) which are classified as flammable according to the GHS criteria, i.e.:

–   Flammable gases (see Chapter 2.2);

–   Flammable liquids (see Chapter 2.6);

–   Flammable solids (see Chapter 2.7);

or if their heat of combustion is at least 20 kJ/g.

NOTE 1:   Flammable components do not cover pyrophoric, self-heating or water-reactive substances and mixtures because such components are never used as aerosol contents.

NOTE 2:   Aerosols do not fall additionally within the scope of chapters 2.2 (flammable gases), 2.5 (gases under pressure), 2.6 (flammable liquids) and 2.7 (flammable solids). Depending on their contents, aerosols may however fall within the scope of other hazard classes, including their labelling elements.

2.3.2.2   An aerosol is classified in one of the three categories for this Class on the basis of its components, of its chemical heat of combustion and, if applicable, of the results of the foam test (for foam aerosols) and of the ignition distance test and enclosed space test (for spray aerosols). See decision logic in 2.3.4.1. Aerosols which do not meet the criteria for inclusion in Category 1 or Category 2 (extremely flammable or flammable aerosols) should be classified in Category 3 (non-flammable aerosols).

NOTE: Aerosols containing more than 1% flammable components or with a heat of combustion of at least 20 kJ/g, which are not submitted to the flammability classification procedures in this chapter should be classified as aerosols, Category 1.

2.3.3   Hazard communication

General and specific considerations concerning labelling requirements are provided in *Hazard communication: Labelling* (Chapter 1.4). Annex 1 contains summary tables about classification and labelling. Annex 3 contains examples of precautionary statements and pictograms which can be used where allowed by the competent authority.

Table 2.3.1: Label elements for aerosols

	Category 1	Category 2	Category 3
Symbol	Flame	Flame	*No symbol*
Signal word	Danger	Warning	Warning
Hazard statement	Extremely flammable aerosol Pressurized container: May burst if heated	Flammable aerosol Pressurized container: May burst if heated	Pressurized container: May burst if heated

2.3.4   Decision logic and guidance

The decision logic and guidance, which follow, are not part of the harmonized classification system, but have been provided here as additional guidance. It is strongly recommended that the person responsible for classification studies the criteria before and during use of the decision logic.

2.3.4.1   *Decision logic*

To classify an aerosol data on its flammable components, on its chemical heat of combustion and, if applicable, the results of the foam test (for foam aerosols) and of the ignition distance test and enclosed space test (for spray aerosols) are required. Classification should be made according to decision logics 2.3 (a) to 2.3 (c).

Decision logic 2.3 (a) for aerosols

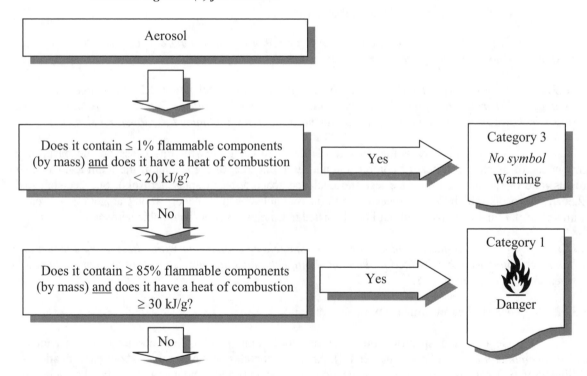

For spray aerosols, go to decision logic 2.3 (b);
For foam aerosols, go to decision logic 2.3 (c);

Decision logic 2.3 (b) for spray aerosols

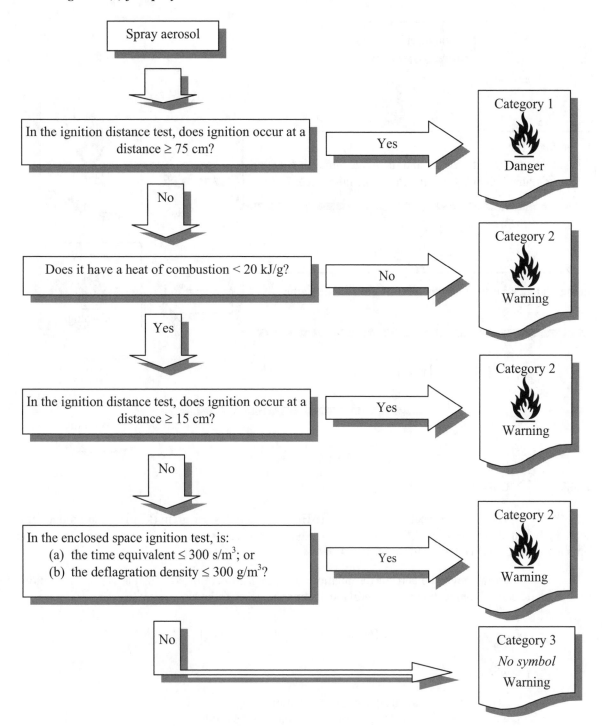

Decision logic 2.3 (c) for foam aerosols

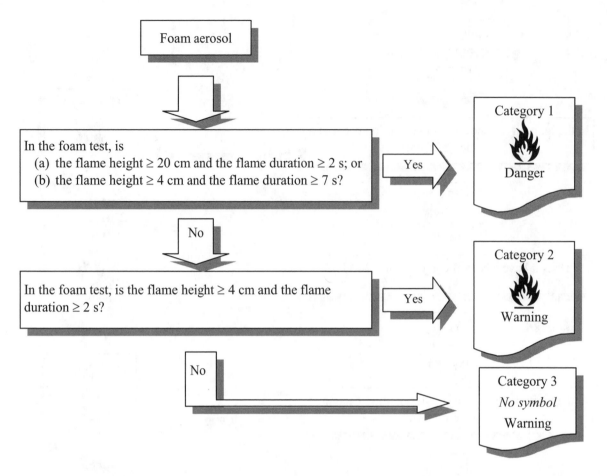

2.3.4.2   *Guidance*

2.3.4.2.1   The chemical heat of combustion (ΔHc), in kilojoules per gram (kJ/g), is the product of the theoretical heat of combustion ($\Delta Hcomb$), and a combustion efficiency, usually less than 1.0 (a typical combustion efficiency is 0.95 or 95%).

For a composite aerosol formulation, the chemical heat of combustion is the summation of the weighted heats of combustion for the individual components, as follows:

$$\Delta Hc \text{ (product)} = \sum_{i}^{n} [\ wi\% \times \Delta Hc(i)]$$

where:

ΔHc	=	chemical heat of combustion (kJ/g);
$wi\%$	=	mass fraction of component i in the product;
$\Delta Hc(i)$	=	specific heat of combustion (kJ/g)of component i in the product;

The chemical heats of combustion can be found in literature, calculated or determined by tests (see ASTM D 240, ISO/FDIS 13943:1999 (E/F) 86.1 to 86.3 and NFPA 30B).

2.3.4.2.2   See sub-sections 31.4, 31.5 and 31.6 of the *UN Recommendations on the Transport of Dangerous Goods, Manual of Tests and Criteria,* for Ignition distance test, Enclosed space ignition test and Aerosol foam flammability test.

CHAPTER 2.4

OXIDIZING GASES

2.4.1 Definition

An *oxidizing gas* is any gas which may, generally by providing oxygen, cause or contribute to the combustion of other material more than air does.

NOTE: *"Gases which cause or contribute to the combustion of other material more than air does" means pure gases or gas mixtures with an oxidizing power greater than 23.5% as determined by a method specified in ISO 10156:2010.*

2.4.2 Classification criteria

An oxidizing gas is classified in a single category for this class according to the following table:

Table 2.4.1: Criteria for oxidizing gases

Category	Criteria
1	Any gas which may, generally by providing oxygen, cause or contribute to the combustion of other material more than air does.

2.4.3 Hazard communication

General and specific considerations concerning labelling requirements are provided in *Hazard communication: Labelling* (Chapter 1.4). Annex 1 contains summary tables about classification and labelling. Annex 3 contains examples of precautionary statements and pictograms which can be used where allowed by the competent authority.

Table 2.4.2: Label elements for oxidizing gases

	Category 1
Symbol	Flame over circle
Signal word	Danger
Hazard statement	May cause or intensify fire; oxidizer

2.4.4 Decision logic and guidance

The decision logic and guidance, which follow, are not part of the harmonized classification system, but have been provided here as additional guidance. It is strongly recommended that the person responsible for classification studies the criteria before and during use of the decision logic.

2.4.4.1 *Decision logic*

To classify an oxidizing gas, tests or calculation methods as described in ISO 10156:2010 "Gases and gas mixtures – Determination of fire potential and oxidizing ability for the selection of cylinder valve outlets" should be performed.

Decision logic 2.4 for oxidizing gases

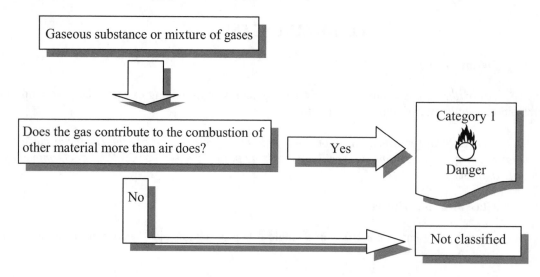

2.4.4.2 Guidance

Example of the classification of an oxidizing gas mixture by calculation according to ISO 10156:2010.

The classification method described in ISO 10156 uses the criterion that a gas mixture should be considered as more oxidising than air if the oxidising power of the gas mixture is higher than 0.235 (23.5%).

The oxidizing power (OP) is calculated as follows:

$$OP = \frac{\sum_{i=1}^{n} x_i C_i}{\sum_{i=1}^{n} x_i + \sum_{k=1}^{p} K_k B_k}$$

Where:

x_i = molar fraction of the i:th oxidising gas in the mixture;

C_i = coefficient of oxygen equivalency of the i:th oxidising gas in the mixture;

K_k = coefficient of equivalency of the inert gas k compared to nitrogen;

B_k = molar fraction of the k:th inert gas in the mixture;

n = total number of oxidising gases in the mixture;

p = total number of inert gases in the mixture;

Example mixture: 9% (O_2) + 16% (N_2O) + 75% (He)

Calculation steps

Step 1:

Ascertain the coefficient of oxygen equivalency (C_i) for the oxidising gases in the mixture and the nitrogen equivalency factors (K_k) for the non-flammable, non-oxidising gases.

C_i (N_2O) = 0.6 (nitrous oxide)

C_i (O_2) = 1 (oxygen)

K_k (He) = 0.9 (helium)

<u>Step 2:</u>

Calculate the oxidising power of the gas mixture

$$OP = \frac{\sum_{i=1}^{n} x_i C_i}{\sum_{i=1}^{n} x_i + \sum_{k=1}^{p} K_k B_k} = \frac{0.09 \times 1 + 0.16 \times 0.6}{0.09 + 0.16 + 0.75 \times 0.9} = 0.201 \qquad \mathbf{20.1 < 23.5}$$

Therefore the mixture is <u>not</u> considered as <u>an oxidising gas.</u>

CHAPTER 2.5

GASES UNDER PRESSURE

2.5.1 Definition

Gases under pressure are gases which are contained in a receptacle at a pressure of 200 kPa (gauge) or more at 20 °C, or which are liquefied or liquefied and refrigerated.

They comprise compressed gases, liquefied gases, dissolved gases and refrigerated liquefied gases.

2.5.2 Classification criteria

2.5.2.1   Gases under pressure are classified, according to their physical state when packaged, in one of four groups in the following table:

Table 2.5.1: Criteria for gases under pressure

Group	Criteria
Compressed gas	A gas which when packaged under pressure is entirely gaseous at -50 °C; including all gases with a critical temperature ≤ -50 °C.
Liquefied gas	A gas which when packaged under pressure, is partially liquid at temperatures above -50 °C. A distinction is made between: (a) High pressure liquefied gas: a gas with a critical temperature between -50°C and +65°C; and (b) Low pressure liquefied gas: a gas with a critical temperature above +65°C.
Refrigerated liquefied gas	A gas which when packaged is made partially liquid because of its low temperature.
Dissolved gas	A gas which when packaged under pressure is dissolved in a liquid phase solvent.

The critical temperature is the temperature above which a pure gas cannot be liquefied, regardless of the degree of compression.

NOTE: Aerosols should not be classified as gases under pressure. See Chapter 2.3.

2.5.3 Hazard communication

General and specific considerations concerning labelling requirements are provided in *Hazard communication: Labelling* (Chapter 1.4). Annex 1 contains summary tables about classification and labelling. Annex 3 contains examples of precautionary statements and pictograms which can be used where allowed by the competent authority.

Table 2.5.2: Label elements for gases under pressure

	Compressed gas	Liquefied gas	Refrigerated liquefied gas	Dissolved gas
Symbol	Gas cylinder	Gas cylinder	Gas cylinder	Gas cylinder
Signal word	Warning	Warning	Warning	Warning
Hazard statement	Contains gas under pressure; may explode if heated	Contains gas under pressure; may explode if heated	Contains refrigerated gas; may cause cryogenic burns or injury	Contains gas under pressure; may explode if heated

2.5.4 Decision logic and guidance

The decision logic and guidance, which follow, are not part of the harmonized classification system, but have been provided here as additional guidance. It is strongly recommended that the person responsible for classification studies the criteria before and during use of the decision logic.

2.5.4.1 *Decision logic*

Classification can be made according to decision logic 2.5.

Decision logic 2.5 for gases under pressure

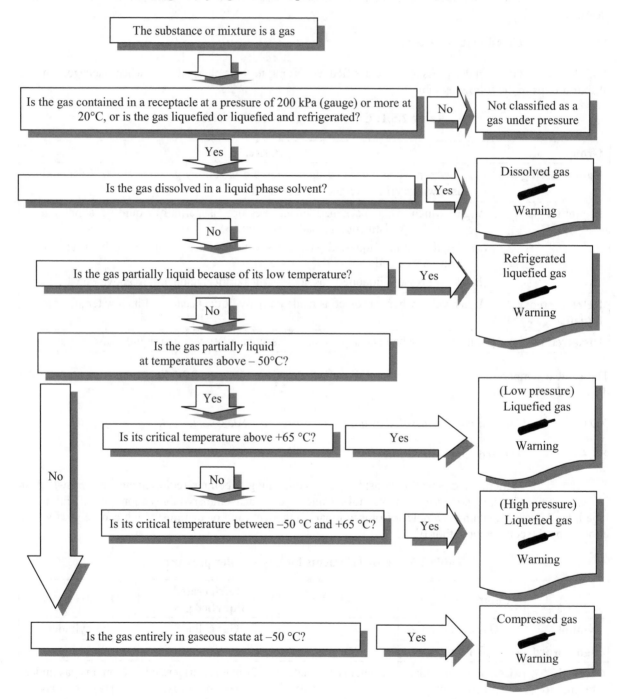

2.5.4.2   *Guidance*

For this group of gases, the following information is required to be known:

(a)   The vapour pressure at 50 °C;

(b)   The physical state at 20 °C at standard ambient pressure;

(c)   The critical temperature.

In order to classify a gas, the above data are needed. Data can be found in literature, calculated or determined by testing. Most pure gases are already classified in the *UN Recommendations on the Transport of Dangerous Goods, Model Regulations*. Most one off mixtures require additional calculations that can be very complex.

CHAPTER 2.6

FLAMMABLE LIQUIDS

2.6.1 Definition

A *flammable liquid* means a liquid having a flash point of not more than 93 °C.

2.6.2 Classification criteria

A flammable liquid is classified in one of the four categories for this class according to the following table:

Table 2.6.1: Criteria for flammable liquids

Category	Criteria
1	Flash point < 23 °C and initial boiling point ≤ 35 °C
2	Flash point < 23 °C and initial boiling point > 35 °C
3	Flash point ≥ 23 °C and ≤ 60 °C
4	Flash point > 60 °C and ≤ 93 °C

NOTE 1: *Gas oils, diesel and light heating oils in the flash point range of 55 °C to 75 °C may be regarded as a special group for some regulatory purposes.*

NOTE 2: *Liquids with a flash point of more than 35 °C and not more than 60 °C may be regarded as non-flammable liquids for some regulatory purposes (e.g. transport) if negative results have been obtained in the sustained combustibility test L.2 of Part III, section 32 of the UN Recommendations on the Transport of Dangerous Goods, Manual of Tests and Criteria.*

NOTE 3: *Viscous flammable liquids such as paints, enamels, lacquers, varnishes, adhesives and polishes may be regarded as a special group for some regulatory purposes (e.g. transport). The classification or the decision to consider these liquids as non-flammable may be determined by the pertinent regulation or competent authority.*

NOTE 4: *Aerosols should not be classified as flammable liquids. See Chapter 2.3.*

2.6.3 Hazard communication

General and specific considerations concerning labelling requirements are provided in *Hazard communication: Labelling* (Chapter 1.4). Annex 1 contains summary tables about classification and labelling. Annex 3 contains examples of precautionary statements and pictograms which can be used where allowed by the competent authority.

Table 2.6.2: Label elements for flammable liquids

	Category 1	Category 2	Category 3	Category 4
Symbol	Flame	Flame	Flame	*No symbol*
Signal word	Danger	Danger	Warning	Warning
Hazard statement	Extremely flammable liquid and vapour	Highly flammable liquid and vapour	Flammable liquid and vapour	Combustible liquid

2.6.4   Decision logic and guidance

The decision logic and guidance, which follow, are not part of the harmonized classification system, but have been provided here as additional guidance. It is strongly recommended that the person responsible for classification studies the criteria before and during use of the decision logic.

2.6.4.1   *Decision logic*

Once the flash point and the initial boiling point are known, the classification of the substance or mixture and the relevant harmonized label information can be obtained according to decision logic 2.6.

Decision logic 2.6 for flammable liquids

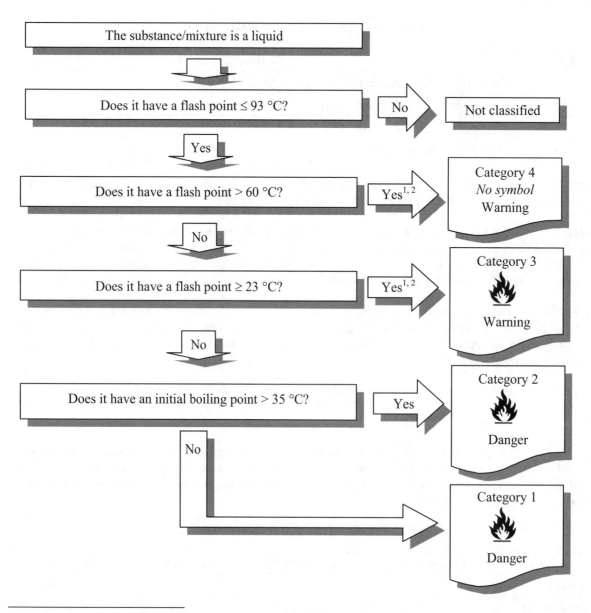

---

[1]   *Gas oils, diesel and light heating oils in the flash point range of 55 °C to 75 °C may be regarded as a special group for some regulatory purposes as these hydrocarbons mixtures have varying flash point in that range. Thus classification of these products in Category 3 or 4 may be determined by the pertinent regulation or competent authority.*

[2]   *Liquids with a flash point of more than 35 °C and not more than 60 °C may be regarded as non-flammable liquids for some regulatory purposes (e.g. transport) if negative results have been obtained in the sustained combustibility test L.2 of Part III, section 32 of the UN Recommendations on the Transport of Dangerous Goods, Manual of Tests and Criteria.*

2.6.4.2 *Guidance*

2.6.4.2.1 In order to classify a flammable liquid, data on its flash point and initial boiling point are needed. Data can be determined by testing, found in literature or calculated.

2.6.4.2.2 In the case of mixtures[3] containing known flammable liquids in defined concentrations, although they may contain non-volatile ingredients e.g. polymers, additives, the flash point need not be determined experimentally if the calculated flash point of the mixture, using the method given in 2.6.4.2.3 below, is at least 5 °C[4] greater than the relevant classification criterion (23 °C and 60 °C, respectively) and provided that:

(a) The composition of the mixture is accurately known (if the material has a specified range of composition, the composition with the lowest calculated flash point should be selected for assessment);

(b) The lower explosion limit of each ingredient is known (an appropriate correlation has to be applied when these data are extrapolated to other temperatures than test conditions) as well as a method for calculating the lower explosion limit of the mixture;

(c) The temperature dependence of the saturated vapour pressure and of the activity coefficient is known for each ingredient as present in the mixture;

(d) The liquid phase is homogeneous.

2.6.4.2.3 A suitable method is described in Gmehling and Rasmussen (Ind. Eng. Chem. Fundament, 21, 186, (1982)). For a mixture containing non-volatile ingredients, e.g. polymers or additives, the flash point is calculated from the volatile ingredients. It is considered that a non-volatile ingredient only slightly decreases the partial pressure of the solvents and the calculated flash point is only slightly below the measured value.

2.6.4.2.4 If data are not available, the flash point and the initial boiling point shall be determined through testing. The flash point shall be determined by closed-cup test method. Open-cup tests are acceptable only in special cases.

2.6.4.2.5 The following methods for determining the flash point of flammable liquids should be used:

International standards:

ISO 1516
ISO 1523
ISO 2719
ISO 13736
ISO 3679
ISO 3680

---

[3] *Up to now, the calculation method is validated for mixtures containing up to six volatile components. These components may be flammable liquids like hydrocarbons, ethers, alcohols, esters (except acrylates), and water. It is however not yet validated for mixtures containing halogenated, sulphurous, and/or phosphoric compounds as well as reactive acrylates.*

[4] *If the calculated flash point is less than 5°C greater than the relevant classification criterion, the calculation method may not be used and the flash point should be determined experimentally.*

National standards:

American Society for Testing Materials International, 100Barr Harbor Drive, PO Box C 700, West Conshohocken, Pennsylvania, USA 19428-2959:

>   ASTM D3828-07a, "Standard Test Methods for Flash Point by Small Scale Closed Cup Tester"
>   ASTM D56-05, "Standard Test Method for Flash Point by Tag Closed Cup Tester"
>   ASTM D3278-96(2004)e1, "Standard Test Methods for Flash Point of Liquids by Small Scale Closed Cup Apparatus"
>   ASTM D93-08, "Standard Test Methods for Flash Point by Pensky-Martens Closed Cup Tester"

Association française de normalisation, AFNOR, 11, rue de Pressensé. 93571 La Plaine Saint-Denis Cedex":

>   French Standard NF M 07 - 019
>   French Standards NF M 07 - 011 / NF T 30 - 050 / NF T 66 - 009
>   French Standard NF M 07 - 036

Deutsches Institut für Normung, Burggrafenstr. 6, D-10787 Berlin:

>   Standard DIN 51755 (flash points below 65 °C)

State Committee of the Council of Ministers for Standardization, 113813, GSP, Moscow, M-49 Leninsky Prospect, 9:

>   GOST 12.1.044-84

2.6.4.2.6   The following methods for determining the initial boiling point of flammable liquids should be used:

International standards:

>   ISO 3924
>   ISO 4626
>   ISO 3405

National standards:

American Society for Testing Materials International, 100 Barr Harbor Drive, PO Box C700, West Conshohocken, Pennsylvania, USA 19428-2959:

>   ASTM D86-07a, "Standard Test Method for Distillation of Petroleum Products at Atmospheric Pressure"
>   ASTM D1078-05, "Standard Test Method for Distillation Range of Volatile Organic Liquids"

Further acceptable methods:

Method A.2 as described in Part A of the Annex to Commission Regulation (EC) No.440/2008[5].

---

[5] *Commission Regulation (EC) No 440/2008 of 30 May 2008 laying down test methods pursuant to Regulation (EC) No 1907/2006 of the European Parliament and of the Council on the Registration, Evaluation, Authorisation and Restriction of Chemicals (REACH) (Official Journal of the European Union, No. L142 of 31.05.2008, p1-739 and No. L143 of 03.06.2008, p.55).*

CHAPTER 2.7

FLAMMABLE SOLIDS

2.7.1 Definitions

A *flammable solid* is a solid which is readily combustible, or may cause or contribute to fire through friction.

Readily combustible solids are powdered, granular, or pasty substances which are dangerous if they can be easily ignited by brief contact with an ignition source, such as a burning match, and if the flame spreads rapidly.

2.7.2 Classification criteria

2.7.2.1   Powdered, granular or pasty substances or mixtures shall be classified as readily combustible solids when the time of burning of one or more of the test runs, performed in accordance with the test method described in the *UN Recommendations on the Transport of Dangerous Goods, Manual of Tests and Criteria*, Part III, sub-section 33.2.1, is less than 45 s or the rate of burning is more than 2.2 mm/s.

2.7.2.2   Powders of metals or metal alloys shall be classified as flammable solids when they can be ignited and the reaction spreads over the whole length of the sample in 10 min or less.

2.7.2.3   Solids which may cause fire through friction shall be classified in this class by analogy with existing entries (e.g. matches) until definitive criteria are established.

2.7.2.4   A flammable solid is classified in one of the two categories for this class using Method N.1 as described in Part III, sub-section 33.2.1 of the *UN Recommendations on the Transport of Dangerous Goods, Manual of Tests and Criteria*, according to the following table:

Table 2.7.1: Criteria for flammable solids

Category	Criteria
1	Burning rate test: Substances or mixtures other than metal powders: (a) wetted zone does not stop fire; and (b) burning time < 45 s or burning rate > 2.2 mm/s Metal powders: burning time ≤ 5 min
2	Burning rate test: Substances or mixtures other than metal powders: (a) wetted zone stops the fire for at least 4 min; and (b) burning time < 45 s or burning rate > 2.2 mm/s Metal powders: burning time > 5 min and ≤ 10 min

NOTE 1:   *For classification tests on solid substances or mixtures, the tests should be performed on the substance or mixture as presented. If for example, for the purposes of supply or transport, the same chemical is to be presented in a physical form different from that which was tested and which is considered likely to materially alter its performance in a classification test, the substance must also be tested in the new form.*

NOTE 2:   *Aerosols should not be classified as flammable solids. See Chapter 2.3.*

2.7.3   Hazard communication

General and specific considerations concerning labelling requirements are provided in *Hazard communication: Labelling* (Chapter 1.4). Annex 1 contains summary tables about classification and labelling. Annex 3 contains examples of precautionary statements and pictograms which can be used where allowed by the competent authority.

Table 2.7.2: Label elements for flammable solids

	Category 1	Category 2
Symbol	Flame	Flame
Signal word	Danger	Warning
Hazard statement	Flammable solid	Flammable solid

2.7.4   Decision logic

The decision logic which follows, is not part of the harmonized classification system, but has been provided here as additional guidance. It is strongly recommended that the person responsible for classification studies the criteria before and during use of the decision logic.

To classify a flammable solid, the test method N.1 as described in Part III, sub-section 33.2.1 of the *UN Recommendations on the Transport of Dangerous Goods, Manual of Tests and Criteria* should be performed. The procedure consists of two tests: a preliminary screening test and a burning rate test. Classification is according to decision logic 2.7.

Decision logic 2.7 for flammable solids

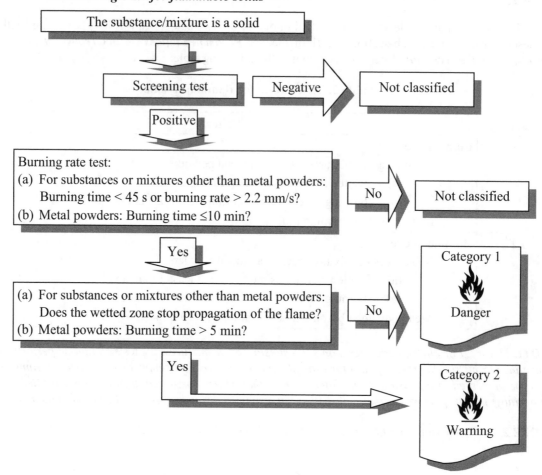

CHAPTER 2.8

SELF-REACTIVE SUBSTANCES AND MIXTURES

2.8.1 Definitions

2.8.1.1   *Self-reactive substances or mixtures* are thermally unstable liquid or solid substances or mixtures liable to undergo a strongly exothermic decomposition even without participation of oxygen (air). This definition excludes substances and mixtures classified under the GHS as explosives, organic peroxides or as oxidizing.

2.8.1.2   A self-reactive substance or mixture is regarded as possessing explosive properties when in laboratory testing the formulation is liable to detonate, to deflagrate rapidly or to show a violent effect when heated under confinement.

2.8.2 Classification criteria

2.8.2.1   Any self-reactive substance or mixture should be considered for classification in this class unless:

(a)   They are explosives, according to the GHS criteria of Chapter 2.1;

(b)   They are oxidizing liquids or solids, according to the criteria of Chapters 2.13 or 2.14, except that mixtures of oxidizing substances which contain 5% or more of combustible organic substances shall be classified as self-reactive substances according to the procedure defined in the note below;

(c)   They are organic peroxides, according to the GHS criteria of Chapter 2.15;

(d)   Their heat of decomposition is less than 300 J/g; or

(e)   Their self-accelerating decomposition temperature (SADT) is greater than 75 °C for a 50 kg package.

NOTE: Mixtures of oxidizing substances, meeting the criteria for classification as oxidizing substances, which contain 5.0% or more of combustible organic substances and which do not meet the criteria mentioned in (a), (c), (d) or (e) above, shall be subjected to the self-reactive substances classification procedure;

Such a mixture showing the properties of a self-reactive substance type B to F (see 2.8.2.2) shall be classified as a self-reactive substance.

2.8.2.2   Self-reactive substances and mixtures are classified in one of the seven categories of "types A to G" for this class, according to the following principles:

(a)   Any self-reactive substance or mixture which can detonate or deflagrate rapidly, as packaged, will be defined as **self-reactive substance TYPE A**;

(b)   Any self-reactive substance or mixture possessing explosive properties and which, as packaged, neither detonates nor deflagrates rapidly, but is liable to undergo a thermal explosion in that package will be defined as **self-reactive substance TYPE B**;

(c)   Any self-reactive substance or mixture possessing explosive properties when the substance or mixture as packaged cannot detonate or deflagrate rapidly or undergo a thermal explosion will be defined as **self-reactive substance TYPE C**;

(d) Any self-reactive substance or mixture which in laboratory testing:

   (i)   detonates partially, does not deflagrate rapidly and shows no violent effect when heated under confinement; or

   (ii) does not detonate at all, deflagrates slowly and shows no violent effect when heated under confinement; or

   (iii) does not detonate or deflagrate at all and shows a medium effect when heated under confinement;

   will be defined as **self-reactive substance TYPE D**;

(e) Any self-reactive substance or mixture which, in laboratory testing, neither detonates nor deflagrates at all and shows low or no effect when heated under confinement will be defined as **self-reactive substance TYPE E**;

(f) Any self-reactive substance or mixture which, in laboratory testing, neither detonates in the cavitated state nor deflagrates at all and shows only a low or no effect when heated under confinement as well as low or no explosive power will be defined as **self-reactive substance TYPE F**;

(g) Any self-reactive substance or mixture which, in laboratory testing, neither detonates in the cavitated state nor deflagrates at all and shows no effect when heated under confinement nor any explosive power, provided that it is thermally stable (self-accelerating decomposition temperature is 60 °C to 75 °C for a 50 kg package), and, for liquid mixtures, a diluent having a boiling point greater than or equal to 150 °C is used for desensitization will be defined as **self-reactive substance TYPE G**. If the mixture is not thermally stable or a diluent having a boiling point less than 150 °C is used for desensitization, the mixture shall be defined as self-reactive substance TYPE F.

NOTE 1:   *Type G has no hazard communication elements assigned but should be considered for properties belonging to other hazard classes.*

NOTE 2:   Types A to G may not be necessary for all systems.

2.8.2.3   *Criteria for temperature control*

Self-reactive substances need to be subjected to temperature control if their self-accelerating decomposition temperature (SADT) is less than or equal to 55 °C. Test methods for determining the SADT as well as the derivation of control and emergency temperatures are given in the *UN Recommendations for the Transport of Dangerous Goods, Manual of Tests and Criteria*, Part II, section 28. The test selected shall be conducted in a manner which is representative, both in size and material, of the package.

2.8.3   Hazard communication

General and specific considerations concerning labelling requirements are provided in *Hazard communication: Labelling* (Chapter 1.4). Annex 1 contains summary tables about classification and labelling. Annex 3 contains examples of precautionary statements and pictograms which can be used where allowed by the competent authority.

Table 2.8.1: Label elements for self-reactive substances and mixtures

	Type A	Type B	Type C and D	Type E and F	Type G[a]
Symbol	Exploding bomb	Exploding bomb and flame	Flame	Flame	*There are no label elements allocated to this hazard category*
Signal word	Danger	Danger	Danger	Warning	
Hazard statement	Heating may cause an explosion	Heating may cause a fire or explosion	Heating may cause a fire	Heating may cause a fire	

[a] *Type G has no hazard communication elements assigned but should be considered for properties belonging to other hazard classes.*

2.8.4   Decision logic and guidance

The decision logic and guidance which follow, are not part of the harmonized classification system, but have been provided here as additional guidance. It is strongly recommended that the person responsible for classification studies the criteria before and during use of the decision logic.

2.8.4.1   *Decision logic*

To classify a self-reactive substance or mixture test series A to H as described in Part II of the *UN Recommendations on the Transport of Dangerous Goods, Manual of Tests and Criteria* should be performed. Classification is according to decision logic 2.8.

The properties of self-reactive substances or mixtures which are decisive for their classification should be determined experimentally. Test methods with pertinent evaluation criteria are given in the *UN Recommendations on the Transport of Dangerous Goods, Manual of Tests and Criteria*, Part II (test series A to H).

Decision logic 2.8 for self-reactive substances and mixtures

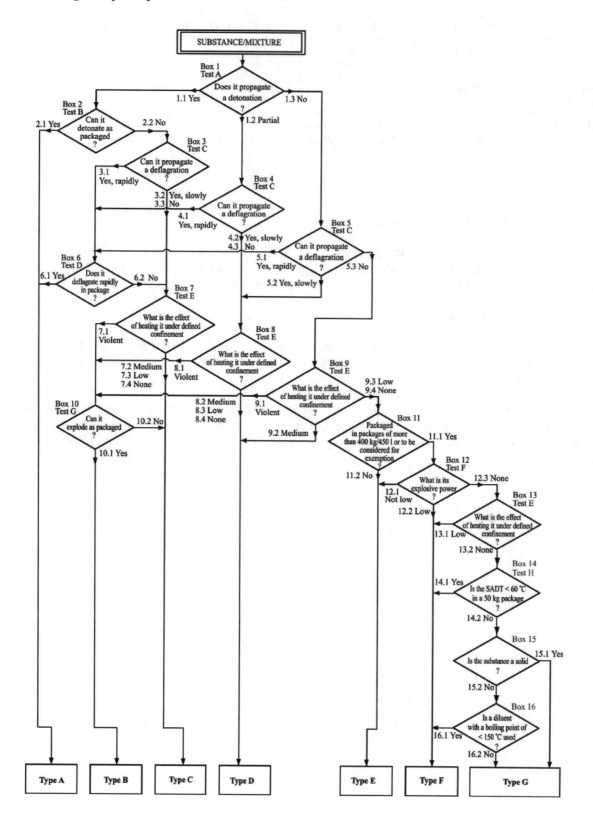

2.8.4.2   *Guidance*

The classification procedures for self-reactive substances and mixtures need not be applied if:

(a)   There are no chemical groups present in the molecule associated with explosive or self-reactive properties; examples of such groups are given in Tables A6.1 and A6.2 in the Appendix 6 of the *UN Recommendations on the Transport of Dangerous Goods, Manual of Tests and Criteria*; or

(b)   For a single organic substance or a homogeneous mixture of organic substances, the estimated SADT is greater than 75 °C or the exothermic decomposition energy is less than 300 J/g. The onset temperature and decomposition energy may be estimated using a suitable calorimetric technique (see 20.3.3.3 in Part II of the *UN Recommendations on the Transport of Dangerous Goods, Manual of Tests and Criteria*).

CHAPTER 2.9

PYROPHORIC LIQUIDS

2.9.1 Definition

A *pyrophoric liquid* is a liquid which, even in small quantities, is liable to ignite within five minutes after coming into contact with air.

2.9.2 Classification criteria

A pyrophoric liquid is classified in a single category for this class using test N.3 in Part III, sub-section 33.3.1.5 of the *UN Recommendations on the Transport of Dangerous Goods, Manual of Tests and Criteria,* according to the following table:

Table 2.9.1: Criteria for pyrophoric liquids

Category	Criteria
1	The liquid ignites within 5 min when added to an inert carrier and exposed to air, or it ignites or chars a filter paper on contact with air within 5 min.

2.9.3 Hazard communication

General and specific considerations concerning labelling requirements are provided in *Hazard communication: Labelling* (Chapter 1.4). Annex 1 contains summary tables about classification and labelling. Annex 3 contains examples of precautionary statements and pictograms which can be used where allowed by the competent authority.

Table 2.9.2: Label elements for pyrophoric liquids

	Category 1
Symbol	Flame
Signal word	Danger
Hazard statement	Catches fire spontaneously if exposed to air

2.9.4 Decision logic and guidance

The decision logic and guidance which follow, are not part of the harmonized classification system, but have been provided here as additional guidance. It is strongly recommended that the person responsible for classification studies the criteria before and during use of the decision logic.

2.9.4.1 *Decision logic*

To classify a pyrophoric liquid, the test method N.3 as described in Part III, sub-section 33.3.1.5 of the *UN Recommendations on the Transport of Dangerous Goods, Manual of Tests and Criteria* should be performed. The procedure consists of two steps. Classification is according to decision logic 2.9.

Decision logic 2.9 for pyrophoric liquids

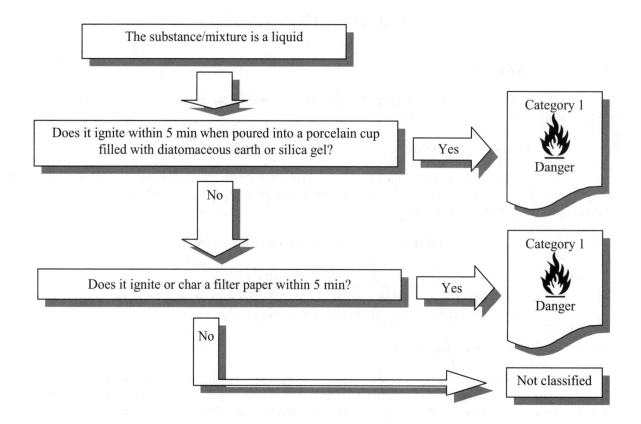

2.9.4.2   *Guidance*

The classification procedure for pyrophoric liquids need not be applied when experience in production or handling shows that the substance or mixture does not ignite spontaneously on coming into contact with air at normal temperatures (i.e. the substance is known to be stable at room temperature for prolonged periods of time (days)).

CHAPTER 2.10

PYROPHORIC SOLIDS

2.10.1 Definition

A *pyrophoric solid* is a solid which, even in small quantities, is liable to ignite within five minutes after coming into contact with air.

2.10.2 Classification criteria

A pyrophoric solid is classified in a single category for this class using test N.2 in Part III, sub-section 33.3.1.4 of the *UN Recommendations on the Transport of Dangerous Goods, Manual of Tests and Criteria* according to the following table:

Table 2.10.1: Criteria for pyrophoric solids

Category	Criteria
1	The solid ignites within 5 min of coming into contact with air.

NOTE: *For classification tests on solid substances or mixtures, the tests should be performed on the substance or mixture as presented. If for example, for the purposes of supply or transport, the same chemical is to be presented in a physical form different from that which was tested and which is considered likely to materially alter its performance in a classification test, the substance or mixture must also be tested in the new form.*

2.10.3 Hazard communication

General and specific considerations concerning labelling requirements are provided in *Hazard communication: Labelling* (Chapter 1.4). Annex 1 contains summary tables about classification and labelling. Annex 3 contains examples of precautionary statements and pictograms which can be used where allowed by the competent authority.

Table 2.10.2: Label elements for pyrophoric solids

	Category 1
Symbol	Flame
Signal word	Danger
Hazard statement	Catches fire spontaneously if exposed to air

2.10.4 Decision logic and guidance

The decision logic and guidance which follow, are not part of the harmonized classification system, but have been provided here as additional guidance. It is strongly recommended that the person responsible for classification studies the criteria before and during use of the decision logic.

2.10.4.1 *Decision logic*

To classify a pyrophoric solid, the test method N.2 as described in Part III, sub-section 33.3.1.4 of *the UN Recommendations on the Transport of Dangerous Goods, Manual of Tests and Criteria* should be performed. Classification is according to decision logic 2.10.

Decision logic 2.10 for pyrophoric solids

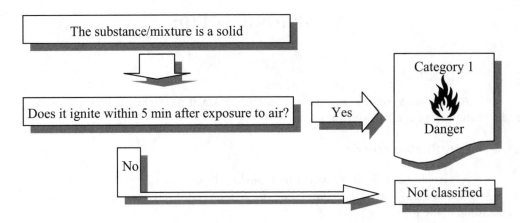

2.10.4.2   *Guidance*

The classification procedure for pyrophoric solids need not be applied when experience in production or handling shows that the substance or mixture does not ignite spontaneously on coming into contact with air at normal temperatures (i.e. the substance or mixture is known to be stable at room temperature for prolonged periods of time (days)).

CHAPTER 2.11

SELF-HEATING SUBSTANCES AND MIXTURES

2.11.1 Definition

A *self-heating substance or mixture* is a solid or liquid substance or mixture, other than a pyrophoric liquid or solid, which, by reaction with air and without energy supply, is liable to self-heat; this substance or mixture differs from a pyrophoric liquid or solid in that it will ignite only when in large amounts (kilograms) and after long periods of time (hours or days).

NOTE: *Self-heating of a substance or mixtures is a process where the gradual reaction of that substance or mixture with oxygen (in air) generates heat. If the rate of heat production exceeds the rate of heat loss, then the temperature of the substance or mixture will rise which, after an induction time, may lead to self-ignition and combustion.*

2.11.2 Classification criteria

2.11.2.1 A substance or mixture shall be classified as a self-heating substance of this class, if in tests performed in accordance with the test method given in the *UN Recommendations on the Transport of Dangerous Goods, Manual of Tests and Criteria*, Part III, sub-section 33.3.1.6:

(a) A positive result is obtained using a 25 mm cube sample at 140 °C;

(b) A positive result is obtained in a test using a 100 mm sample cube at 140 °C and a negative result is obtained in a test using a 100 mm cube sample at 120 °C and the substance or mixture is to be packed in packages with a volume of more than 3 m^3;

(c) A positive result is obtained in a test using a 100 mm sample cube at 140 °C and a negative result is obtained in a test using a 100 mm cube sample at 100 °C and the substance or mixture is to be packed in packages with a volume of more than 450 litres;

(d) A positive result is obtained in a test using a 100 mm sample cube at 140 °C and a positive result is obtained using a 100 mm cube sample at 100 °C.

2.11.2.2 A self-heating substance or mixture is classified in one of the two categories for this class if, in test performed in accordance with test method N.4 in Part III, sub-section 33.3.1.6 of the *UN Recommendations on the Transport of Dangerous Goods, Manual of Tests and Criteria*, the result meets the criteria shown in Table 2.11.1.

Table 2.11.1: Criteria for self-heating substances and mixtures

Category	Criteria
1	A positive result is obtained in a test using a 25 mm sample cube at 140 °C
2	(a) A positive result is obtained in a test using a 100 mm sample cube at 140 °C and a negative result is obtained in a test using a 25 mm cube sample at 140 °C <u>and</u> the substance or mixture is to be packed in packages with a volume of more than 3 m³; or (b) A positive result is obtained in a test using a 100 mm sample cube at 140 °C and a negative result is obtained in a test using a 25 mm cube sample at 140 °C, a positive result is obtained in a test using a 100 mm cube sample at 120 °C <u>and</u> the substance or mixture is to be packed in packages with a volume of more than 450 litres; or (c) A positive result is obtained in a test using a 100 mm sample cube at 140 °C and a negative result is obtained in a test using a 25 mm cube sample at 140 °C <u>and</u> a positive result is obtained in a test using a 100 mm cube sample at 100 °C.

NOTE 1: *For classification tests on solid substances or mixtures, the tests should be performed on the substance or mixture as presented. If for example, for the purposes of supply or transport, the same chemical is to be presented in a physical form different from that which was tested and which is considered likely to materially alter its performance in a classification test, the substance or mixture must also be tested in the new form.*

NOTE 2: *The criteria are based on the self-ignition temperature of charcoal, which is 50 °C for a sample cube of 27 m³. Substances and mixtures with a temperature of spontaneous combustion higher than 50 °C for a volume of 27 m³ should not be assigned to this hazard class. Substances and mixtures with a self-ignition temperature higher than 50 °C for a volume of 450 litres should not be assigned to hazard Category 1 of this hazard class.*

2.11.3   Hazard communication

General and specific considerations concerning labelling requirements are provided in *Hazard communication: Labelling* (Chapter 1.4). Annex 1 contains summary tables about classification and labelling. Annex 3 contains examples of precautionary statements and pictograms which can be used where allowed by the competent authority.

Table 2.11.2: Label elements for self-heating substances and mixtures

	Category 1	**Category 2**
Symbol	Flame	Flame
Signal word	Danger	Warning
Hazard statement	Self-heating; may catch fire	Self-heating in large quantities; may catch fire

2.11.4   Decision logic and guidance

The decision logic and guidance which follow, are not part of the harmonized classification system, but have been provided here as additional guidance. It is strongly recommended that the person responsible for classification studies the criteria before and during use of the decision logic.

2.11.4.1   *Decision logic*

To classify a self-heating substance or mixture, test method N.4, as described in Part III, sub-section 33.3.1.6 of the *UN Recommendations on the Transport of Dangerous Goods, Manual of Tests and Criteria*, should be performed. Classification is according to decision logic 2.11.

Decision logic 2.11 for self-heating substances and mixtures

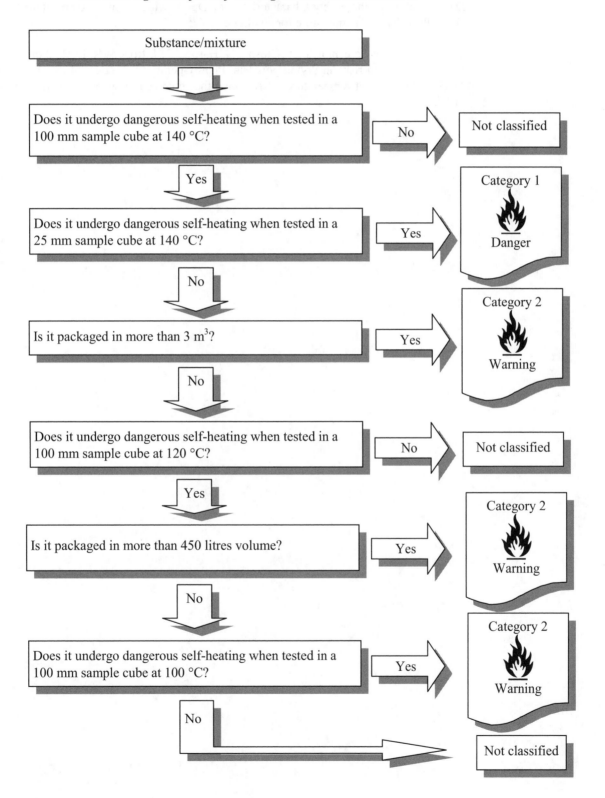

2.11.4.2   *Guidance*

The classification procedure for self-heating substances or mixtures need not be applied if the results of a screening test can be adequately correlated with the classification test and an appropriate safety margin is applied. Examples of screening tests are:

(a)   The Grewer Oven test (VDI guideline 2263, part 1, 1990, Test methods for the Determination of the Safety Characteristics of Dusts) with an onset temperature 80 K above the reference temperature for a volume of 1 *l*;

(b)   The Bulk Powder Screening Test (Gibson, N. Harper, D. J. Rogers, R. Evaluation of the fire and explosion risks in drying powders, Plant Operations Progress, 4 (3), 181-189, 1985) with an onset temperature 60 K above the reference temperature for a volume of 1 *l*.

CHAPTER 2.12

SUBSTANCES AND MIXTURES WHICH, IN CONTACT WITH WATER, EMIT FLAMMABLE GASES

2.12.1 Definition

Substances or mixtures which, in contact with water, emit flammable gases are solid or liquid substances or mixtures which, by interaction with water, are liable to become spontaneously flammable or to give off flammable gases in dangerous quantities.

2.12.2 Classification criteria

A substance or mixture which, in contact with water, emit flammable gases is classified in one of the three categories for this class, using test N.5 in Part III, sub-section 33.4.1.4 of the *UN Recommendations on the Transport of Dangerous Goods, Manual of Tests and Criteria*, according to the following table:

Table 2.12.1: Criteria for substances and mixtures which, in contact with water, emit flammable gases

Category	Criteria
1	Any substance or mixture which reacts vigorously with water at ambient temperatures and demonstrates generally a tendency for the gas produced to ignite spontaneously, or which reacts readily with water at ambient temperatures such that the rate of evolution of flammable gas is equal to or greater than 10 litres per kilogram of substance over any one minute.
2	Any substance or mixture which reacts readily with water at ambient temperatures such that the maximum rate of evolution of flammable gas is equal to or greater than 20 litres per kilogram of substance per hour, and which does not meet the criteria for Category 1.
3	Any substance or mixture which reacts slowly with water at ambient temperatures such that the maximum rate of evolution of flammable gas is equal to or greater than 1 litre per kilogram of substance per hour, and which does not meet the criteria for Categories 1 and 2.

NOTE 1:   *A substance or mixture is classified as a substance which, in contact with water, emits flammable gases if spontaneous ignition takes place in any step of the test procedure.*

NOTE 2:   *For classification tests on solid substances or mixtures, the tests should be performed on the substance or mixture as presented. If for example, for the purposes of supply or transport, the same chemical is to be presented in a physical form different from that which was tested and which is considered likely to materially alter its performance in a classification test, the substance or mixture must also be tested in the new form.*

2.12.3 Hazard communication

General and specific considerations concerning labelling requirements are provided in *Hazard communication: Labelling* (Chapter 1.4). Annex 1 contains summary tables about classification and labelling. Annex 3 contains examples of precautionary statements and pictograms which can be used where allowed by the competent authority.

Table 2.12.2: Label elements for substances and mixtures, which in contact with water, emit flammable gases

	Category 1	Category 2	Category 3
Symbol	Flame	Flame	Flame
Signal word	Danger	Danger	Warning
Hazard statement	In contact with water releases flammable gases which may ignite spontaneously	In contact with water releases flammable gases	In contact with water releases flammable gases

2.12.4   Decision logic and guidance

The decision logic and guidance which follow, are not part of the harmonized classification system, but have been provided here as additional guidance. It is strongly recommended that the person responsible for classification studies the criteria before and during use of the decision logic.

2.12.4.1   *Decision logic*

To classify a substance or mixture which, in contact with water emits flammable gases, test N.5 as described in Part III, sub-section 33.4.1.4 of the *UN Recommendations on the Transport of Dangerous Goods, Manual of Tests and Criteria,* should be performed. Classification is according to decision logic 2.12.

Decision logic 2.12 for substances and mixtures which, in contact with water, emit flammable gases

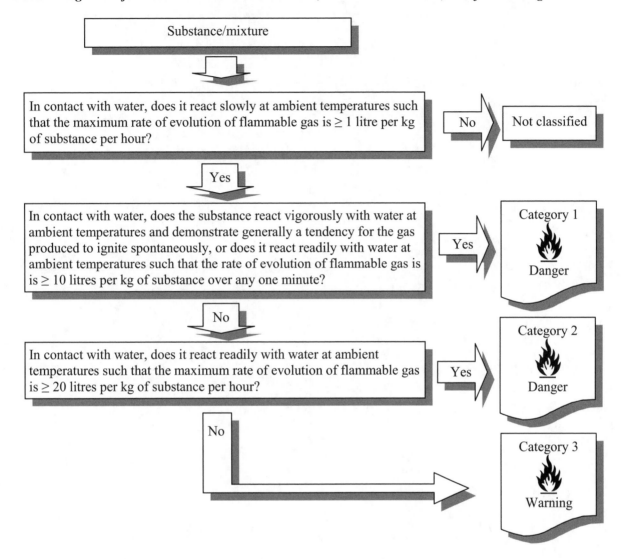

2.12.4.2   *Guidance*

The classification procedure for this class need not be applied if:

(a)   The chemical structure of the substance or mixture does not contain metals or metalloids;

(b)   Experience in production or handling shows that the substance or mixture does not react with water, e.g. the substance is manufactured with water or washed with water; or

(c)   The substance or mixture is known to be soluble in water to form a stable mixture.

CHAPTER 2.13

OXIDIZING LIQUIDS

2.13.1 Definition

An *oxidizing liquid* is a liquid which, while in itself not necessarily combustible, may, generally by yielding oxygen, cause, or contribute to, the combustion of other material.

2.13.2 Classification criteria

An oxidizing liquid is classified in one of the three categories for this class using test O.2 in Part III, sub-section 34.4.2 of the *UN Recommendations on the Transport of Dangerous Goods, Manual of Tests and Criteria,* according to the following table:

Table 2.13.1: Criteria for oxidizing liquids

Category	Criteria
1	Any substance or mixture which, in the 1:1 mixture, by mass, of substance (or mixture) and cellulose tested, spontaneously ignites; or the mean pressure rise time of a 1:1 mixture, by mass, of substance and cellulose is less than that of a 1:1 mixture, by mass, of 50% perchloric acid and cellulose;
2	Any substance or mixture which, in the 1:1 mixture, by mass, of substance (or mixture) and cellulose tested, exhibits a mean pressure rise time less than or equal to the mean pressure rise time of a 1:1 mixture, by mass, of 40% aqueous sodium chlorate solution and cellulose; and the criteria for Category 1 are not met;
3	Any substance or mixture which, in the 1:1 mixture, by mass, of substance (or mixture) and cellulose tested, exhibits a mean pressure rise time less than or equal to the mean pressure rise time of a 1:1 mixture, by mass, of 65% aqueous nitric acid and cellulose; and the criteria for Categories 1 and 2 are not met.

2.13.3 Hazard communication

General and specific considerations concerning labelling requirements are provided in *Hazard communication: Labelling* (Chapter 1.4). Annex 1 contains summary tables about classification and labelling. Annex 3 contains examples of precautionary statements and pictograms which can be used where allowed by the competent authority.

Table 2.13.2: Label elements for oxidizing liquids

	Category 1	Category 2	Category 3
Symbol	Flame over circle	Flame over circle	Flame over circle
Signal word	Danger	Danger	Warning
Hazard statement	May cause fire or explosion; strong oxidizer	May intensify fire; oxidizer	May intensify fire; oxidizer

2.13.4   **Decision logic and guidance**

The decision logic and guidance which follow, are not part of the harmonized classification system, but have been provided here as additional guidance. It is strongly recommended that the person responsible for classification studies the criteria before and during use of the decision logic.

2.13.4.1   *Decision logic*

To classify an oxidizing liquid test method O.2 as described in Part III, sub-section 34.4.2 of the *UN Recommendations on the Transport of Dangerous Goods, Manual of Tests and Criteria* should be performed. Classification is according to decision logic 2.13.

Decision logic 2.13 for oxidizing liquids

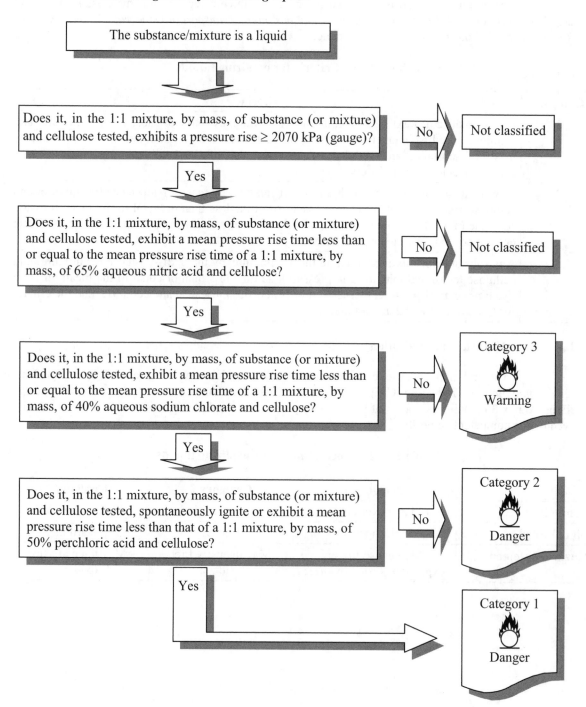

2.13.4.2   *Guidance*

2.13.4.2.1   Experience in the handling and use of substances or mixtures which shows them to be oxidizing is an important additional factor in considering classification in this class. In the event of divergence between tests results and known experience, judgement based on known experience should take precedence over test results.

2.13.4.2.2   In some cases, substances or mixtures may generate a pressure rise (too high or too low), caused by chemical reactions not characterising the oxidizing properties of the substance or mixture. In these cases, it may be necessary to repeat the test described in Part III, sub-section 34.4.2 of the *UN Recommendations on the Transport of Dangerous Goods, Manual of Tests and Criteria* with an inert substance, e.g. diatomite (kieselguhr), in place of the cellulose in order to clarify the nature of the reaction.

2.13.4.2.3   For organic substances or mixtures the classification procedure for this class need not be applied if:

(a)   The substance or mixture does not contain oxygen, fluorine or chlorine; or

(b)   The substance or mixture contains oxygen, fluorine or chlorine and these elements are chemically bonded only to carbon or hydrogen.

2.13.4.2.4   For inorganic substances or mixtures, the classification procedure for this class need not be applied if they do not contain oxygen or halogen atoms.

CHAPTER 2.14

OXIDIZING SOLIDS

2.14.1 Definition

An *oxidizing solid* is a solid which, while in itself is not necessarily combustible, may, generally by yielding oxygen, cause, or contribute to, the combustion of other material.

2.14.2 Classification criteria

An oxidizing solid is classified in one of the three categories for this class using test O.1 in Part III, sub-section 34.4.1 or test O.3 in Part III, sub-section 34.4.3, of the *UN Recommendations on the Transport of Dangerous Goods, Manual of Tests and Criteria,* according to the following table:

Table 2.14.1: Criteria for oxidizing solids

Category	Criteria using test O.1	Criteria using test O.1
1	Any substance or mixture which, in the 4:1 or 1:1 sample-to-cellulose ratio (by mass) tested, exhibits a mean burning time less than the mean burning time of a 3:2 mixture, (by mass), of potassium bromate and cellulose.	Any substance or mixture which, in the 4:1 or 1:1 sample-to-cellulose ratio (by mass) tested, exhibits a mean burning rate greater than the mean burning rate of a 3:1 mixture (by mass) of calcium peroxide and cellulose.
2	Any substance or mixture which, in the 4:1 or 1:1 sample-to-cellulose ratio (by mass) tested, exhibits a mean burning time equal to or less than the mean burning time of a 2:3 mixture (by mass) of potassium bromate and cellulose and the criteria for Category 1 are not met.	Any substance or mixture which, in the 4:1 or 1:1 sample-to-cellulose ratio (by mass) tested, exhibits a mean burning rate equal to or greater than the mean burning rate of a 1:1 mixture (by mass) of calcium peroxide and cellulose and the criteria for Category 1 are not met.
3	Any substance or mixture which, in the 4:1 or 1:1 sample-to-cellulose ratio (by mass) tested, exhibits a mean burning time equal to or less than the mean burning time of a 3:7 mixture (by mass) of potassium bromate and cellulose and the criteria for Categories 1 and 2 are not met.	Any substance or mixture which, in the 4:1 or 1:1 sample-to-cellulose ratio (by mass) tested, exhibits a mean burning rate equal to or greater than the mean burning rate of a 1:2 mixture (by mass) of calcium peroxide and cellulose and the criteria for Categories 1 and 2 are not met.

NOTE 1: *Some oxidizing solids may also present explosion hazards under certain conditions (e.g. when stored in large quantities). For example, some types of ammonium nitrate may give rise to an explosion hazard under extreme conditions and the "Resistance to detonation test" (IMSBC Code[1], Appendix 2, Section 5) may be used to assess this hazard. Appropriate comments should be made in the Safety Data Sheet.*

NOTE 2: *For classification tests on solid substances or mixtures, the tests should be performed on the substance or mixture as presented. If for example, for the purposes of supply or transport, the same chemical is to be presented in a physical form different from that which was tested and which is considered likely to materially alter its performance in a classification test, the substance or mixture must also be tested in the new form.*

---

[1] *International Maritime Solid Bulk Cargoes Code, IMO.*

2.14.3 Hazard communication

General and specific considerations concerning labelling requirements are provided in *Hazard communication: Labelling* (Chapter 1.4). Annex 1 contains summary tables about classification and labelling. Annex 3 contains examples of precautionary statements and pictograms which can be used where allowed by the competent authority.

Table 2.14.2: Label elements for oxidizing solids

	Category 1	Category 2	Category 3
Symbol	Flame over circle	Flame over circle	Flame over circle
Signal word	Danger	Danger	Warning
Hazard statement	May cause fire or explosion; strong oxidizer	May intensify fire; oxidizer	May intensify fire; oxidizer

2.14.4 Decision logic and guidance

The decision logic and guidance which follow, are not part of the harmonized classification system, but have been provided here as additional guidance. It is strongly recommended that the person responsible for classification studies the criteria before and during use of the decision logic.

2.14.4.1 *Decision logic*

To classify an oxidizing solid test method O.1 as described in Part III, sub-section 34.4.1 or test method O.3 as described in Part III, sub-section 34.4.3 of *the UN Recommendations on the Transport of Dangerous Goods, Manual of Tests and Criteria,* should be performed. Classification is according to decision logic 2.14.

Decision logic 2.14 for oxidizing solids

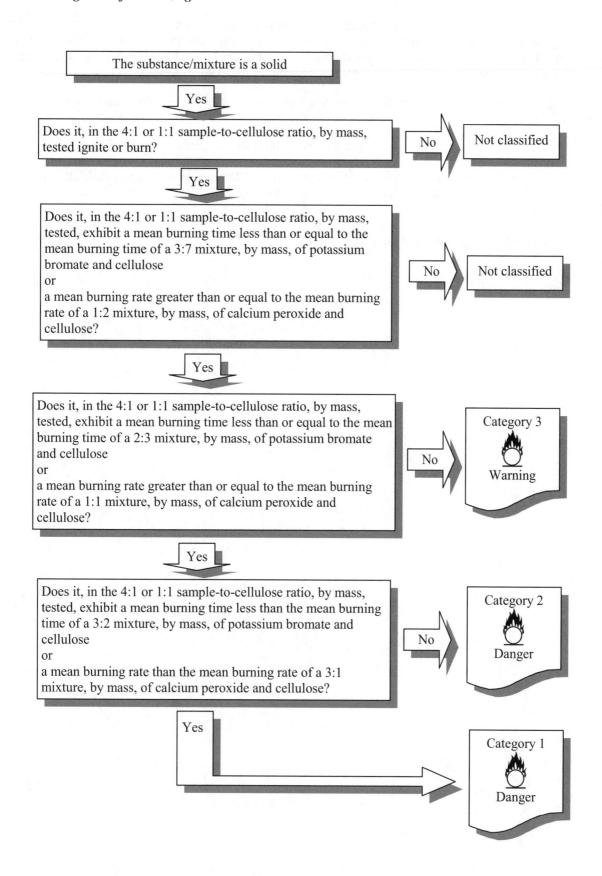

2.14.4.2   *Guidance*

2.14.4.2.1   Experience in the handling and use of substances or mixtures which shows them to be oxidizing is an important additional factor in considering classification in this class. In the event of divergence between tests results and known experience, judgement based on known experience should take precedence over test results.

2.14.4.2.2   The classification procedure for this class need not be applied to organic substances or mixtures if:

(a)   The substance or mixture does not contain oxygen, fluorine or chlorine; or

(b)   The substance or mixture contains oxygen, fluorine or chlorine and these elements are chemically bonded only to carbon or hydrogen.

2.14.4.2.3   The classification procedure for this class need not be applied to inorganic substances or mixtures if they do not contain oxygen or halogen atoms.

CHAPTER 2.15

ORGANIC PEROXIDES

2.15.1   Definition

2.15.1.1   *Organic peroxides* are liquid or solid organic substances which contain the bivalent -O-O- structure and may be considered derivatives of hydrogen peroxide, where one or both of the hydrogen atoms have been replaced by organic radicals. The term also includes organic peroxide formulations (mixtures). Organic peroxides are thermally unstable substances or mixtures, which may undergo exothermic self-accelerating decomposition. In addition, they may have one or more of the following properties:

   (a)   be liable to explosive decomposition;

   (b)   burn rapidly;

   (c)   be sensitive to impact or friction;

   (d)   react dangerously with other substances.

2.15.1.2   An organic peroxide is regarded as possessing explosive properties when in laboratory testing the formulation is liable to detonate, to deflagrate rapidly or to show a violent effect when heated under confinement.

2.15.2   Classification criteria

2.15.2.1   Any organic peroxide shall be considered for classification in this class, unless it contains:

   (a)   not more than 1.0% available oxygen from the organic peroxides when containing not more than 1.0% hydrogen peroxide; or

   (b)   not more than 0.5% available oxygen from the organic peroxides when containing more than 1.0% but not more than 7.0% hydrogen peroxide.

   NOTE: *The available oxygen content (%) of an organic peroxide mixture is given by the formula:*

$$16 \times \sum_{i}^{n} \left(\frac{n_i \times c_i}{m_i} \right)$$

   where:

   n_i =   *number of peroxygen groups per molecule of organic peroxide i;*

   c_i =   *concentration (mass %) of organic peroxide i;*

   m_i =   *molecular mass of organic peroxide i.*

2.15.2.2   Organic peroxides are classified in one of the seven categories of "Types A to G" for this class, according to the following principles:

   (a)   Any organic peroxide which, as packaged, can detonate or deflagrate rapidly will be defined as **organic peroxide TYPE A**;

   (b)   Any organic peroxide possessing explosive properties and which, as packaged, neither detonates nor deflagrates rapidly, but is liable to undergo a thermal explosion in that package will be defined as **organic peroxide TYPE B**;

(c)   Any organic peroxide possessing explosive properties when the substance or mixture as packaged cannot detonate or deflagrate rapidly or undergo a thermal explosion will be defined as **organic peroxide TYPE C**;

(d)   Any organic peroxide which in laboratory testing:

   (i)   detonates partially, does not deflagrate rapidly and shows no violent effect when heated under confinement; or

   (ii)   does not detonate at all, deflagrates slowly and shows no violent effect when heated under confinement; or

   (iii)   does not detonate or deflagrate at all and shows a medium effect when heated under confinement;

will be defined as **organic peroxide TYPE D**;

(e)   Any organic peroxide which, in laboratory testing, neither detonates nor deflagrates at all and shows low or no effect when heated under confinement will be defined as **organic peroxide TYPE E**;

(f)   Any organic peroxide which, in laboratory testing, neither detonates in the cavitated state nor deflagrates at all and shows only a low or no effect when heated under confinement as well as low or no explosive power will be defined as **organic peroxide TYPE F**;

(g)   Any organic peroxide which, in laboratory testing, neither detonates in the cavitated state nor deflagrates at all and shows no effect when heated under confinement nor any explosive power, provided that it is thermally stable (self-accelerating decomposition temperature is 60°C or higher for a 50 kg package), and, for liquid mixtures, a diluent having a boiling point of not less than 150 °C is used for desensitization, will be defined as **organic peroxide TYPE G**. If the organic peroxide is not thermally stable or a diluent having a boiling point less than 150 °C is used for desensitization, it shall be defined as organic peroxide TYPE F.

NOTE 1:   *Type G has no hazard communication elements assigned but should be considered for properties belonging to other hazard classes.*

NOTE 2:   *Types A to G may not be necessary for all systems.*

2.15.2.3   ***Criteria for temperature control***

The following organic peroxides need to be subjected to temperature control:

(a)   Organic peroxide types B and C with an SADT $\leq$ 50 °C;

(b)   Organic peroxide type D showing a medium effect when heated under confinement[1] with an SADT $\leq$ 50 °C or showing a low or no effect when heated under confinement with an SADT $\leq$ 45 °C; and

(c)   Organic peroxide types E and F with an SADT $\leq$ 45 °C.

Test methods for determining the SADT as well as the derivation of control and emergency temperatures are given in the *UN Recommendations on the Transport of Dangerous Goods, Manual of Tests and Criteria*, Part II, section 28. The test selected shall be conducted in a manner which is representative, both in size and material, of the package.

---

[1]   *As determined by test series E as prescribed in the Manual of Tests and Criteria, Part II.*

2.15.3 Hazard communication

General and specific considerations concerning labelling requirements are provided in *Hazard communication: Labelling* (Chapter 1.4). Annex 1 contains summary tables about classification and labelling. Annex 3 contains examples of precautionary statements and pictograms which can be used where allowed by the competent authority.

Table 2.15.1: Label elements for organic peroxides

	Type A	Type B	Type C and D	Type E and F	Type G [a]
Symbol	Exploding bomb	Exploding bomb and flame	Flame	Flame	*There are no label elements allocated to this hazard category.*
Signal word	Danger	Danger	Danger	Warning	
Hazard statement	Heating may cause an explosion	Heating may cause a fire or explosion	Heating may cause a fire	Heating may cause a fire	

[a] *Type G has no hazard communication elements assigned but should be considered for properties belonging to other hazard classes.*

2.15.4 Decision logic and guidance

The decision logic and guidance which follow, are not part of the harmonized classification system, but have been provided here as additional guidance. It is strongly recommended that the person responsible for classification studies the criteria before and during use of the decision logic.

2.15.4.1 Decision logic

To classify an organic peroxide test series A to H as described in Part II of the *UN Recommendations on the Transport of Dangerous Goods, Manual of Tests and Criteria,* should be performed. Classification is according to decision logic 2.15.

Decision logic 2.15 for organic peroxides

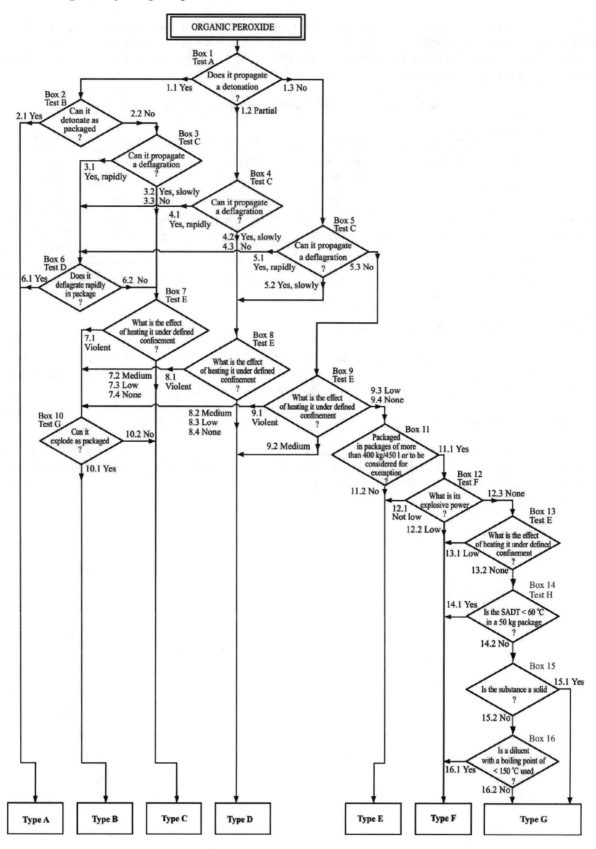

2.15.4.2   *Guidance*

2.15.4.2.1   Organic peroxides are classified by definition based on their chemical structure and on the available oxygen and hydrogen peroxide contents of the mixture (see 2.15.2.1).

2.15.4.2.2   The properties of organic peroxides which are decisive for their classification should be determined experimentally. Test methods with pertinent evaluation criteria are given in the *UN Recommendations on the Transport of Dangerous Goods, Manual of Tests and Criteria*, Part II (Test Series A to H).

2.15.4.2.3   Mixtures of organic peroxides may be classified as the same type of organic peroxide as that of the most dangerous ingredient. However, as two stable ingredients can form a thermally less stable mixture, the self-accelerating decomposition temperature (SADT) of the mixture shall be determined.

CHAPTER 2.16

CORROSIVE TO METALS

2.16.1 Definition

A *substance or a mixture which is corrosive to metals* is a substance or a mixture which by chemical action will materially damage, or even destroy, metals.

2.16.2 Classification criteria

A substance or a mixture which is corrosive to metals is classified in a single category for this class, using the test in Part III, sub-section 37.4 of the *UN Recommendations on the Transport of Dangerous Goods, Manual of Tests and Criteria*, according to the following table:

Table 2.16.1: Criteria for substances and mixtures corrosive to metal

Category	Criteria
1	Corrosion rate on either steel or aluminium surfaces exceeding 6.25 mm per year at a test temperature of 55 °C when tested on both materials.

NOTE: *Where an initial test on either steel or aluminium indicates the substance or mixture being tested is corrosive the follow-up test on the other metal is not required.*

2.16.3 Hazard communication

General and specific considerations concerning labelling requirements are provided in *Hazard communication: Labelling* (Chapter 1.4). Annex 1 contains summary tables about classification and labelling. Annex 3 contains examples of precautionary statements and pictograms which can be used where allowed by the competent authority.

Table 2.16.2: Label elements for substances and mixtures corrosive to metals

	Category 1
Symbol	Corrosion
Signal word	Warning
Hazard statement	May be corrosive to metals

NOTE: *Where a substance or mixture is classified as corrosive to metals but not corrosive to skin and/or eyes, some competent authorities may allow the labelling provisions described in 1.4.10.5.5.*

2.16.4 Decision logic and guidance

The decision logic and guidance which follow, are not part of the harmonized classification system but have been provided here as additional guidance. It is strongly recommended that the person responsible for classification studies the criteria before and during use of the decision logic.

2.16.4.1   *Decision logic*

Decision logic 2.16 for substances and mixtures corrosive to metals

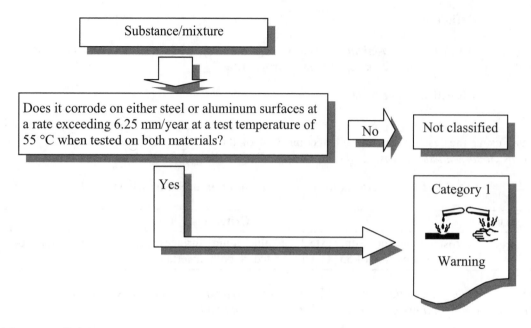

2.16.4.2   *Guidance*

The corrosion rate can be measured according to the test method of Part III, sub-section 37.4 of the *UN Recommendations on the Transport of Dangerous Goods, Manual of Tests and Criteria*. The specimen to be used for the test should be made of the following materials:

(a)   For the purposes of testing steel, steel types S235JR+CR (1.0037 resp.St 37-2), S275J2G3+CR (1.0144 resp.St 44-3), ISO 3574, Unified Numbering System (UNS) G 10200, or SAE 1020;

(b)   For the purposes of testing aluminium: non-clad types 7075-T6 or AZ5GU-T6.

PART 3

HEALTH HAZARDS

CHAPTER 3.1

ACUTE TOXICITY

3.1.1 Definition

Acute toxicity refers to those adverse effects occurring following oral or dermal administration of a single dose of a substance, or multiple doses given within 24 hours, or an inhalation exposure of 4 hours.

3.1.2 Classification criteria for substances

3.1.2.1 Substances can be allocated to one of five hazard categories based on acute toxicity by the oral, dermal or inhalation route according to the numeric cut-off criteria as shown in the table below. Acute toxicity values are expressed as (approximate) LD_{50} (oral, dermal) or LC_{50} (inhalation) values or as acute toxicity estimates (ATE). Explanatory notes are shown following Table 3.1.1.

Table 3.1.1: Acute toxicity hazard categories and acute toxicity estimate (ATE) values defining the respective categories

Exposure route	Category 1	Category 2	Category 3	Category 4	Category 5
Oral (mg/kg bodyweight) *See notes (a) and (b)*	5	50	300	2000	5000 *See detailed criteria in Note (g)*
Dermal (mg/kg bodyweight) *See notes (a) and (b)*	50	200	1000	2000	
Gases (ppmV) *See notes (a), (b) and (c)*	100	500	2500	20000	*See detailed criteria in Note (g)*
Vapours (mg/l) *See notes (a), (b), (c), (d) and (e)*	0.5	2.0	10	20	
Dusts and Mists (mg/l) *See notes (a), (b), (c) and (f)*	0.05	0.5	1.0	5	

Note: *Gases concentration are expressed in parts per million per volume (ppmV).*

Notes to Table 3.1.1:

(a) *The acute toxicity estimate (ATE) for the classification of a substance is derived using the LD_{50}/LC_{50} where available;*

(b) *The acute toxicity estimate (ATE) for a substance in a mixture is derived using:*

   (i) *the LD_{50}/LC_{50} where available; otherwise,*

   (ii) *the appropriate conversion value from Table 3.1.2 that relates to the results of a range test; or*

   (iii) *the appropriate conversion value from Table 3.1.2 that relates to a classification category;*

(c) *Inhalation cut-off values in the table are based on 4 hour testing exposures. Conversion of existing inhalation toxicity data which has been generated according to 1 hour exposures should be by dividing by a factor of 2 for gases and vapours and 4 for dusts and mists;*

(d) *It is recognized that saturated vapour concentration may be used as an additional element by some regulatory systems to provide for specific health and safety protection (e.g. UN Recommendations for the Transport of Dangerous Goods);*

(e) *For some substances the test atmosphere will not just be a vapour but will consist of a mixture of liquid and vapour phases. For other substances the test atmosphere may consist of a vapour which is near the gaseous phase. In these latter cases, classification should be based on ppmV as follows: Category 1 (100 ppmV), Category 2 (500 ppmV), Category 3 (2500 ppmV), Category 4 (20000 ppmV).*

The terms "dust", "mist" and "vapour" are defined as follows:

(i) *Dust: solid particles of a substance or mixture suspended in a gas (usually air);*

(ii *Mist: liquid droplets of a substance or mixture suspended in a gas (usually air);*

(iii) *Vapour: the gaseous form of a substance or mixture released from its liquid or solid state.*

Dust is generally formed by mechanical processes. Mist is generally formed by condensation of supersatured vapours or by physical shearing of liquids. Dusts and mists generally have sizes ranging from less than 1 to about 100 μm;

(f) *The values for dusts and mists should be reviewed to adapt to any future changes to OECD Test Guidelines with respect to technical limitation in generating, maintaining and measuring dust and mist concentrations in respirable form;*

(g) *Criteria for Category 5 are intended to enable the identification of substances which are of relatively low acute toxicity hazard but which under certain circumstances may present a danger to vulnerable populations. These substances are anticipated to have an oral or dermal LD_{50} in the range of 2000-5000 mg/kg bodyweight and equivalent doses for inhalation. The specific criteria for Category 5 are:*

(i) *The substance is classified in this category if reliable evidence is already available that indicates the LD_{50} (or LC_{50}) to be in the range of Category 5 values or other animal studies or toxic effects in humans indicate a concern for human health of an acute nature.*

(ii) *The substance is classified in this category, through extrapolation, estimation or measurement of data, if assignment to a more hazardous category is not warranted, and:*

- *reliable information is available indicating significant toxic effects in humans; or*

- *any mortality is observed when tested up to Category 4 values by the oral, inhalation, or dermal routes; or*

- *where expert judgement confirms significant clinical signs of toxicity, when tested up to Category 4 values, except for diarrhoea, piloerection or an ungroomed appearance; or*

- *where expert judgement confirms reliable information indicating the potential for significant acute effects from other animal studies.*

Recognizing the need to protect animal welfare, testing in animals in Category 5 ranges is discouraged and should only be considered when there is a strong likelihood that results of such a test would have a direct relevance for protecting human health.

3.1.2.2   The harmonized classification system for acute toxicity has been developed in such a way as to accommodate the needs of existing systems. A basic principle set by the IOMC Coordinating Group/Harmonization of Chemical Classification Systems (CG/HCCS) is that "harmonization means establishing a common and coherent basis for chemical hazard classification and communication from which the appropriate elements relevant to means of transport, consumer, worker and environment protection can be selected". To that end, five categories have been included in the acute toxicity scheme.

3.1.2.3   The preferred test species for evaluation of acute toxicity by the oral and inhalation routes is the rat, while the rat or rabbit are preferred for evaluation of acute dermal toxicity. Test data already generated for the classification of chemicals under existing systems should be accepted when reclassifying these chemicals under the harmonized system. When experimental data for acute toxicity are available in several animal species, scientific judgement should be used in selecting the most appropriate LD_{50} value from among valid, well-performed tests.

3.1.2.4   Category 1, the highest hazard category, has cut-off values (see Table 3.1.1) currently used primarily by the transport sector for classification for packing groups.

3.1.2.5   Category 5 is for substances which are of relatively low acute toxicity but which, under certain circumstances, may pose a hazard to vulnerable populations. Criteria for identifying substances in Category 5 are provided in addition to the table. These substances are anticipated to have an oral or dermal LD_{50} value in the range 2000 - 5000 mg/kg bodyweight and equivalent doses for inhalation exposure[1]. In light of animal welfare considerations, testing in animals in Category 5 ranges is discouraged and should only be considered when there is a strong likelihood that results of such testing would have a direct relevance to the protection of human health.

3.1.2.6   *Specific considerations for inhalation toxicity*

3.1.2.6.1   Values for *inhalation toxicity* are based on 4 hours tests in laboratory animals. When experimental values are taken from tests using a 1 hour exposure, they can be converted to a 4 hour equivalent by dividing the 1 hour value by a factor of 2 for gases and vapours and 4 for dusts and mists.

3.1.2.6.2   Units for inhalation toxicity are a function of the form of the inhaled material. Values for dusts and mists are expressed in mg/l. Values for gases are expressed in ppmV. Acknowledging the difficulties in testing vapours, some of which consist of mixtures of liquid and vapour phases, the table provides values in units of mg/l. However, for those vapours which are near the gaseous phase, classification should be based on ppmV. As inhalation test methods are updated, the OECD and other test guideline programs will need to define vapours in relation to mists for greater clarity.

3.1.2.6.3   Vapour inhalation values are intended for use in classification of acute toxicity for all sectors. It is also recognized that the saturated vapour concentration of a chemical is used by the transport sector as an additional element in classifying chemicals for packing groups.

3.1.2.6.4   Of particular importance is the use of well articulated values in the highest hazard categories for dusts and mists. Inhaled particles between 1 and 4 microns mean mass aerodynamic diameter (MMAD) will deposit in all regions of the rat respiratory tract. This particle size range corresponds to a maximum dose of about 2 mg/l. In order to achieve applicability of animal experiments to human exposure, dusts and mists would ideally be tested in this range in rats. The cut-off values in the table for dusts and mists allow clear distinctions to be made for materials with a wide range of toxicities measured under varying test conditions. The values for dusts and mists should be reviewed in the future to adapt to any future changes in OECD or other test guidelines with respect to technical limitations in generating, maintaining, and measuring dust and mist concentrations in respirable form.

---

[1]   *Guidance on Category 5 inhalation values: The OECD Task Force on Harmonization of Classification and Labelling (HCL) did not include numerical values in Table 3.1.1 above for acute inhalation toxicity Category 5 but instead specified doses "equivalent" to the range of 2000-5000 mg/kg bodyweight by the oral or dermal route (see Note (g) to Table 3.1.1). In some systems, the competent authority may prescribe values.*

3.1.2.6.5   In addition to classification for inhalation toxicity, if data are available that indicates that the mechanism of toxicity was corrosivity of the substance or mixture, certain authorities may also choose to label it as *corrosive to the respiratory tract*. Corrosion of the respiratory tract is defined by destruction of the respiratory tract tissue after a single, limited period of exposure analogous to skin corrosion; this includes destruction of the mucosa. The corrosivity evaluation could be based on expert judgment using such evidence as: human and animal experience, existing (*in vitro*) data, pH values, information from similar substances or any other pertinent data.

3.1.3   Classification criteria for mixtures

3.1.3.1   The criteria for substances classify acute toxicity by use of lethal dose data (tested or derived). For mixtures, it is necessary to obtain or derive information that allows the criteria to be applied to the mixture for the purpose of classification. The approach to classification for acute toxicity is tiered, and is dependent upon the amount of information available for the mixture itself and for its ingredients. The flow chart of Figure 3.1.1 below outlines the process to be followed:

Figure 3.1.1: Tiered approach to classification of mixtures for acute toxicity

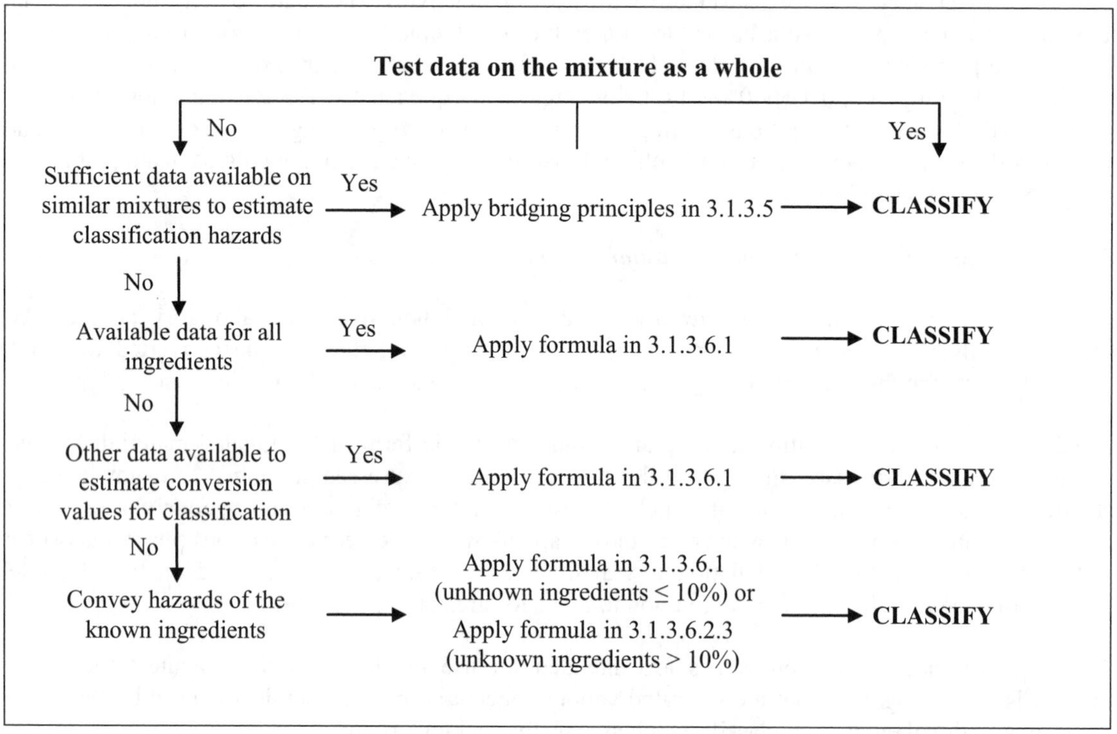

3.1.3.2   Classification of mixtures for acute toxicity can be carried out for each route of exposure, but is only needed for one route of exposure as long as this route is followed (estimated or tested) for all ingredients and there is no relevant evidence to suggest acute toxicity by multiple routes. When there is relevant evidence of toxicity by multiple routes of exposure, classification is to be conducted for all appropriate routes of exposure. All available information should be considered. The pictogram and signal word used should reflect the most severe hazard category and all relevant hazard statements should be used.

3.1.3.3   In order to make use of all available data for purposes of classifying the hazards of mixtures, certain assumptions have been made and are applied where appropriate in the tiered approach:

(a)   The "relevant ingredients" of a mixture are those which are present in concentrations ≥ 1% (w/w for solids, liquids, dusts, mists and vapours and v/v for gases), unless there is a reason to suspect that an ingredient present at a concentration < 1% is still relevant for classifying the mixture for acute toxicity. This point is particularly relevant when classifying untested mixtures which contain ingredients that are classified in Category 1 and Category 2;

(b)   Where a classified mixture is used as an ingredient of another mixture, the actual or derived acute toxicity estimate (ATE) for that mixture may be used when calculating the classification of the new mixture using the formulas in 3.1.3.6.1 and 3.1.3.6.2.3;

(c)   If the converted acute toxicity point estimates for all ingredients of a mixture are within the same category, then the mixture should be classified in that category;

(d)   When only range data (or acute toxicity hazard category information) are available for ingredients in a mixture, they may be converted to point estimates in accordance with Table 3.1.2 when calculating the classification of the new mixture using the formulas in 3.1.3.6.1 and 3.1.3.6.2.3.

Table 3.1.2: Conversion from experimentally obtained acute toxicity range values (or acute toxicity hazard categories) to acute toxicity point estimates for use in the formulas for the classification of mixtures

Exposure routes	Classification category or experimentally obtained acute toxicity range estimate (*see Note 1*)	Converted acute toxicity point estimate (*see Note 2*)
Oral (mg/kg bodyweight)	0 < Category 1 ≤ 5	0.5
	5 < Category 2 ≤ 50	5
	50 < Category 3 ≤ 300	100
	300 < Category 4 ≤ 2000	500
	2000 < Category 5 ≤ 5000	2500
Dermal (mg/kg bodyweight)	0 < Category 1 ≤ 50	5
	50 < Category 2 ≤ 200	50
	200 < Category 3 ≤ 1000	300
	1000 < Category 4 ≤ 2000	1100
	2000 < Category 5 ≤ 5000	2500
Gases (ppmV)	0 < Category 1 ≤ 100	10
	100 < Category 2 ≤ 500	100
	500 < Category 3 ≤ 2500	700
	2500 < Category 4 ≤ 20000	4500
	Category 5 - See footnote to 3.1.2.5.	
Vapours (mg/l)	0 < Category 1 ≤ 0.5	0.05
	0.5 < Category 2 ≤ 2.0	0.5
	2.0 < Category 3 ≤ 10.0	3
	10.0 < Category 4 ≤ 20.0	11
	Category 5 - See footnote to 3.1.2.5.	
Dust/mist (mg/l)	0 < Category 1 ≤ 0.05	0.005
	0.05 < Category 2 ≤ 0.5	0.05
	0.5 < Category 3 ≤ 1.0	0.5
	1.0 < Category 4 ≤ 5.0	1.5
	Category 5 - See footnote to 3.1.2.5.	

Note: *Gases concentration are expressed in parts per million per volume (ppmV).*

NOTE 1:   *Category 5 is for mixtures which are of relatively low acute toxicity but which under certain circumstances may pose a hazard to vulnerable populations. These mixtures are anticipated to have an oral or dermal LD$_{50}$ value in the range of 2000-5000 mg/kg bodyweight or equivalent dose for other routes of exposure. In light of animal welfare considerations, testing in animals in Category 5 ranges is discouraged and should only be considered when there is a strong likelihood that results of such testing would have a direct relevance for protecting human health.*

NOTE 2:   *These values are designed to be used in the calculation of the ATE for classification of a mixture based on its ingredients and do not represent test results. The values are conservatively set at the* *lower end of the range of Categories 1 and 2, and at a point approximately 1/10th from the lower end of the range for Categories 3 – 5.*

3.1.3.4 *Classification of mixtures where acute toxicity test data are available for the complete mixture*

Where the mixture itself has been tested to determine its acute toxicity, it will be classified according to the same criteria as those used for substances presented in Table 3.1.1. If test data for the mixture are not available, the procedures presented below should be followed.

3.1.3.5 *Classification of mixtures where acute toxicity test data are not available for the complete mixture: bridging principles*

3.1.3.5.1   Where the mixture itself has not been tested to determine its acute toxicity, but there are sufficient data on both the individual ingredients and similar tested mixtures to adequately characterize the hazards of the mixture, these data will be used in accordance with the following agreed bridging principles. This ensures that the classification process uses the available data to the greatest extent possible in characterizing the hazards of the mixture without the necessity for additional testing in animals.

3.1.3.5.2   *Dilution*

If a tested mixture is diluted with a diluent that has an equivalent or lower toxicity classification than the least toxic original ingredient, and which is not expected to affect the toxicity of other ingredients, then the new diluted mixture may be classified as equivalent to the original tested mixture. Alternatively, the formula explained in 3.1.3.6.1 could be applied.

3.1.3.5.3   *Batching*

The toxicity of a tested production batch of a mixture can be assumed to be substantially equivalent to that of another untested production batch of the same commercial product, when produced by or under the control of the same manufacturer, unless there is reason to believe there is significant variation such that the toxicity of the untested batch has changed. If the latter occurs, a new classification is necessary.

3.1.3.5.4   *Concentration of highly toxic mixtures*

If a tested mixture is classified in Category 1, and the concentration of the ingredients of the tested mixture that are in Category 1 is increased, the resulting untested mixture should be classified in Category 1 without additional testing.

3.1.3.5.5   *Interpolation within one hazard category*

For three mixtures (A, B and C) with identical ingredients, where mixtures A and B have been tested and are in the same hazard category, and where untested mixture C has the same toxicologically active ingredients as mixtures A and B but has concentrations of toxicologically active ingredients intermediate to the concentrations in mixtures A and B, then mixture C is assumed to be in the same hazard category as A and B.

3.1.3.5.6   *Substantially similar mixtures*

Given the following:

(a)   Two mixtures: (i)   A + B;

(ii)   C + B;

(b)   The concentration of ingredient B is essentially the same in both mixtures;

(c)   The concentration of ingredient A in mixture (i) equals that of ingredient C in mixture (ii);

(d)   Data on toxicity for A and C are available and substantially equivalent, i.e. they are in the same hazard category and are not expected to affect the toxicity of B;

If mixture (i) or (ii) is already classified based on test data, then the other mixture can be assigned the same hazard category.

3.1.3.5.7   *Aerosols*

An aerosol form of a mixture may be classified in the same hazard category as the tested, non-aerosolized form of the mixture for oral and dermal toxicity provided the added propellant does not affect the toxicity of the mixture on spraying. Classification of aerosolized mixtures for inhalation toxicity should be considered separately.

3.1.3.6   Classification of mixtures based on ingredients of the mixture (additivity formula)

3.1.3.6.1   *Data available for all ingredients*

In order to ensure that classification of the mixture is accurate, and that the calculation need only be performed once for all systems, sectors, and categories, the acute toxicity estimate (ATE) of ingredients should be considered as follows:

(a)   Include ingredients with a known acute toxicity, which fall into any of the GHS acute toxicity hazard categories;

(b)   Ignore ingredients that are presumed not acutely toxic (e.g. water, sugar);

(c)   Ignore ingredients if the data available are from a limit dose test (at the upper threshold for Category 4 for the appropriate route of exposure as provided in Table 3.1.1) and do not show acute toxicity.

Ingredients that fall within the scope of this paragraph are considered to be ingredients with a known acute toxicity estimate (ATE). See note (b) to Table 3.1.1 and paragraph 3.1.3.3 for appropriate application of available data to the equation below, and paragraph 3.1.3.6.2.3.

The ATE of the mixture is determined by calculation from the ATE values for all relevant ingredients according to the following formula below for oral, dermal or inhalation toxicity:

$$\frac{100}{ATEmix} = \sum_{n} \frac{C_i}{ATE_i}$$

where:

C_i =   concentration of ingredient i;

n ingredients and i is running from 1 to n;

ATE_i =   Acute toxicity estimate of ingredient i;

3.1.3.6.2   *Data are not available for one or more ingredients of the mixture*

3.1.3.6.2.1   Where an ATE is not available for an individual ingredient of the mixture, but available information such as listed below can provide a derived conversion value, the formula in 3.1.3.6.1 may be applied.

This may include evaluation of:

(a)   Extrapolation between oral, dermal and inhalation acute toxicity estimates[2]. Such an evaluation could require appropriate pharmacodynamic and pharmacokinetic data;

(b)   Evidence from human exposure that indicates toxic effects but does not provide lethal dose data;

(c)   Evidence from any other toxicity tests/assays available on the substance that indicates toxic acute effects but does not necessarily provide lethal dose data; or

(d)   Data from closely analogous substances using structure-activity relationships.

This approach generally requires substantial supplemental technical information, and a highly trained and experienced expert, to reliably estimate acute toxicity. If such information is not available, proceed to the provisions of 3.1.3.6.2.3.

3.1.3.6.2.2   In the event that an ingredient without any useable information for classification is used in a mixture at a concentration ≥ 1%, it is concluded that the mixture cannot be attributed a definitive acute toxicity estimate. In this situation the mixture should be classified based on the known ingredients only, with the additional statement that × percent of the mixture consists of ingredient(s) of unknown acute (oral/dermal/inhalation) toxicity. The competent authority can decide to specify that the additional statement(s) be communicated on the label or on the SDS or both, or to leave the choice of where to place the statement to the manufacturer/supplier.

3.1.3.6.2.3   If the total concentration of the relevant ingredient(s) with unknown acute toxicity is ≤ 10% then the formula presented in 3.1.3.6.1 should be used. If the total concentration of the relevant ingredient(s) with unknown toxicity is > 10%, the formula presented in 3.1.3.6.1 should be corrected to adjust for the percentage of the unknown ingredient(s) as follows:

$$\frac{100 - \left(\sum C_{unknown} \text{ if} > 10\%\right)}{ATE_{mix}} = \sum_n \frac{C_i}{ATE_i}$$

---

[2]   *When mixtures contain ingredients that do not have acute toxicity data for each route of exposure, acute toxicity estimates may be extrapolated from the available data and applied to the appropriate routes (see 3.1.3.2). However, competent authorities may require testing for a specific route. In those cases, classification should be performed for that route based upon the competent authority's requirement.*

3.1.4 **Hazard communication**

3.1.4.1   General and specific considerations concerning labelling requirements are provided in *Hazard communication: Labelling* (Chapter 1.4). Annex 1 contains summary tables about classification and labelling. Annex 3 contains examples of precautionary statements and pictograms which can be used where allowed by the competent authority. The table below presents specific label elements for substances and mixtures that are classified into acute toxicity hazard categories 1 to 5 based on the criteria set forth in this chapter.

Table 3.1.3: Label elements for acute toxicity

	Category 1	**Category 2**	**Category 3**	**Category 4**	**Category 5**
Symbol	Skull and crossbones	Skull and crossbones	Skull and crossbones	Exclamation mark	*No symbol*
Signal word	Danger	Danger	Danger	Warning	Warning
Hazard statement: **--Oral**	Fatal if swallowed	Fatal if swallowed	Toxic if swallowed	Harmful if swallowed	May be harmful if swallowed
--Dermal	Fatal in contact with skin	Fatal in contact with skin	Toxic in contact with skin	Harmful in contact with skin	May be harmful in contact with skin
--Inhalation *see Note*	Fatal if inhaled	Fatal if inhaled	Toxic if inhaled	Harmful if inhaled	May be harmful if inhaled

NOTE: *If a substance/mixture is also determined to be corrosive (based on data such as skin or eye data), corrosivity hazard may also be communicated by some authorities as symbol and/or hazard statement. That is, in addition to an appropriate acute toxicity symbol, a corrosivity symbol (used for skin and eye corrosivity) may be added along with a corrosivity hazard statement such as "corrosive" or "corrosive to the respiratory tract".*

3.1.4.2   The acute toxicity hazard statements differentiate the hazard based on the route of exposure. Communication of acute toxicity classification should also reflect this differentiation. For example, acute oral toxicity Category 1, acute dermal toxicity Category 1 and acute inhalation toxicity Category 1. If a substance or mixture is classified for more than one route of exposure then all relevant classifications should be communicated on the safety data sheet as specified in Annex 4 and the relevant hazard communication elements included on the label as prescribed in 3.1.3.2. If the statement "x % of the mixture consists of ingredient(s) of unknown acute (oral/dermal/inhalation) toxicity" is communicated, as prescribed in 3.1.3.6.2.2, then it can also be differentiated based on the route of exposure. For example, "x % of the mixture consists of ingredient(s) of unknown acute oral toxicity" and "x % of the mixture consists of ingredient(s) of unknown acute dermal toxicity".

3.1.5   **Decision logic**

The decision logic which follows, is not part of the harmonized classification system but is provided here as additional guidance. It is strongly recommended that the person responsible for classification study the criteria before and during use of the decision logic.

3.1.5.1   *Decision logic 3.1.1 for acute toxicity*

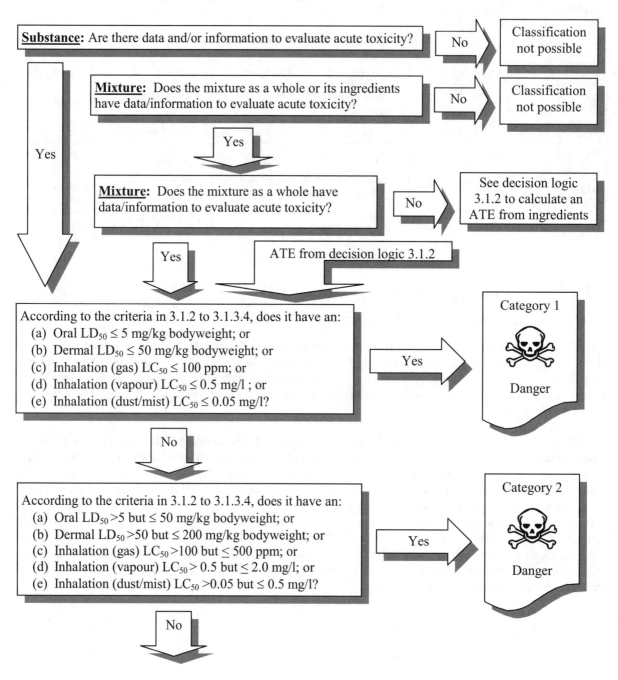

According to the criteria in 3.1.2 to 3.1.3.4, does it have an:
(a) Oral LD$_{50}$ ≤ 5 mg/kg bodyweight; or
(b) Dermal LD$_{50}$ ≤ 50 mg/kg bodyweight; or
(c) Inhalation (gas) LC$_{50}$ ≤ 100 ppm; or
(d) Inhalation (vapour) LC$_{50}$ ≤ 0.5 mg/l ; or
(e) Inhalation (dust/mist) LC$_{50}$ ≤ 0.05 mg/l?

According to the criteria in 3.1.2 to 3.1.3.4, does it have an:
(a) Oral LD$_{50}$ >5 but ≤ 50 mg/kg bodyweight; or
(b) Dermal LD$_{50}$ >50 but ≤ 200 mg/kg bodyweight; or
(c) Inhalation (gas) LC$_{50}$ >100 but ≤ 500 ppm; or
(d) Inhalation (vapour) LC$_{50}$ > 0.5 but ≤ 2.0 mg/l; or
(e) Inhalation (dust/mist) LC$_{50}$ >0.05 but ≤ 0.5 mg/l?

(Cont'd on next page)

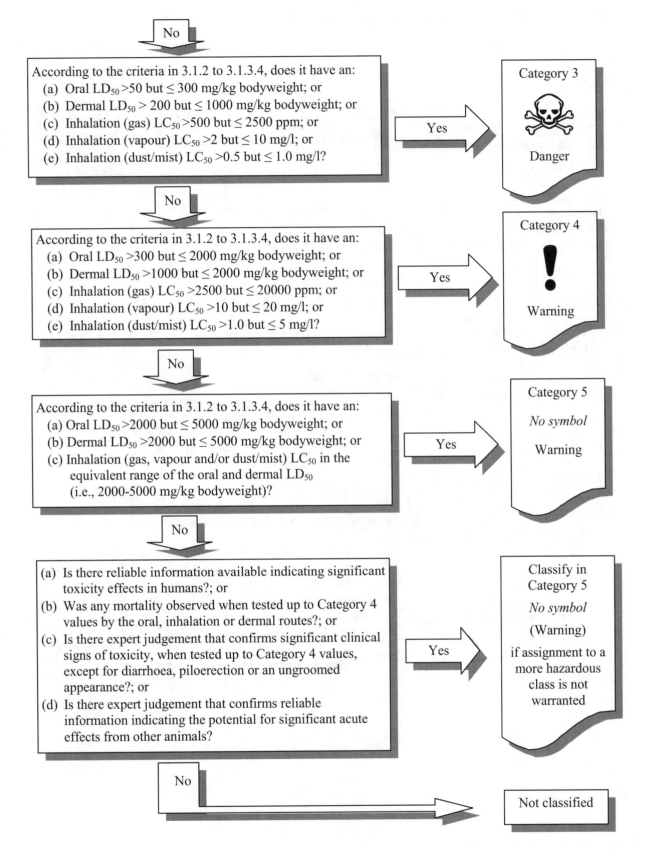

No

According to the criteria in 3.1.2 to 3.1.3.4, does it have an:
  (a) Oral LD_{50} >50 but ≤ 300 mg/kg bodyweight; or
  (b) Dermal LD_{50} > 200 but ≤ 1000 mg/kg bodyweight; or
  (c) Inhalation (gas) LC_{50} >500 but ≤ 2500 ppm; or
  (d) Inhalation (vapour) LC_{50} >2 but ≤ 10 mg/l; or
  (e) Inhalation (dust/mist) LC_{50} >0.5 but ≤ 1.0 mg/l?

Yes →

Category 3

Danger

No

According to the criteria in 3.1.2 to 3.1.3.4, does it have an:
  (a) Oral LD_{50} >300 but ≤ 2000 mg/kg bodyweight; or
  (b) Dermal LD_{50} >1000 but ≤ 2000 mg/kg bodyweight; or
  (c) Inhalation (gas) LC_{50} >2500 but ≤ 20000 ppm; or
  (d) Inhalation (vapour) LC_{50} >10 but ≤ 20 mg/l; or
  (e) Inhalation (dust/mist) LC_{50} >1.0 but ≤ 5 mg/l?

Yes →

Category 4

!

Warning

No

According to the criteria in 3.1.2 to 3.1.3.4, does it have an:
  (a) Oral LD_{50} >2000 but ≤ 5000 mg/kg bodyweight; or
  (b) Dermal LD_{50} >2000 but ≤ 5000 mg/kg bodyweight; or
  (c) Inhalation (gas, vapour and/or dust/mist) LC_{50} in the
      equivalent range of the oral and dermal LD_{50}
      (i.e., 2000-5000 mg/kg bodyweight)?

Yes →

Category 5

No symbol

Warning

No

  (a) Is there reliable information available indicating significant
      toxicity effects in humans?; or
  (b) Was any mortality observed when tested up to Category 4
      values by the oral, inhalation or dermal routes?; or
  (c) Is there expert judgement that confirms significant clinical
      signs of toxicity, when tested up to Category 4 values,
      except for diarrhoea, piloerection or an ungroomed
      appearance?; or
  (d) Is there expert judgement that confirms reliable
      information indicating the potential for significant acute
      effects from other animals?

Yes →

Classify in
Category 5

No symbol

(Warning)

if assignment to a
more hazardous
class is not
warranted

No →

Not classified

3.1.5.2 *Decision logic 3.1.2 for acute toxicity (see criteria in 3.1.3.5 and 3.1.3.6)*

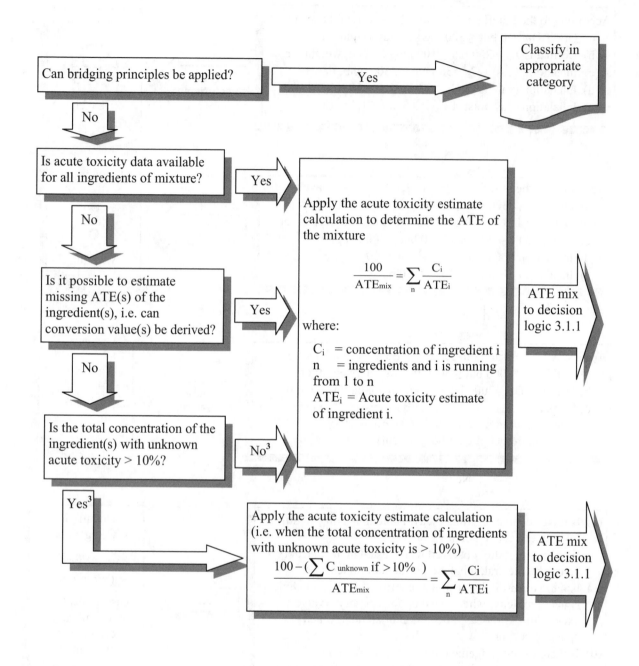

---

[3] *In the event that an ingredient without any useable information is used in a mixture at a concentration ≥ 1%, the classification should be based on the ingredients with the known acute toxicity only, and additional statement(s) should identify the fact that x % of the mixture consists of ingredient(s) of unknown acute (oral/dermal/inhalation) toxicity. The competent authority can decide to specify that the additional statement(s) be communicated on the label or on the SDS or both, or to leave the choice of where to place the statement to the manufacturer/supplier.*

CHAPTER 3.2

SKIN CORROSION/IRRITATION

3.2.1 Definitions and general considerations

3.2.1.1   *Skin corrosion* is the production of irreversible damage to the skin; namely, visible necrosis through the epidermis and into the dermis, following the application of a test substance for up to 4 hours[1]. Corrosive reactions are typified by ulcers, bleeding, bloody scabs, and, by the end of observation at 14 days, by discolouration due to blanching of the skin, complete areas of alopecia, and scars. Histopathology should be considered to evaluate questionable lesions.

Skin irritation is the production of reversible damage to the skin following the application of a test substance for up to 4 hours[1].

3.2.1.2   In a tiered approach, emphasis should be placed upon existing human data, followed by existing animal data, followed by *in vitro* data and then other sources of information. Classification results directly when the data satisfy the criteria. In some cases, classification of a substance or a mixture is made on the basis of the weight of evidence within a tier. In a total weight of evidence approach all available information bearing on the determination of skin corrosion/irritation is considered together, including the results of appropriate validated *in vitro* tests, relevant animal data, and human data such as epidemiological and clinical studies and well-documented case reports and observations (see Chapter 1.3, para. 1.3.2.4.9).

3.2.2 Classification criteria for substances

Substances can be allocated to one of the following three categories within this hazard class:

(a)   Category 1 (skin corrosion)

This category may be further divided into up to three sub-categories (1A, 1B and 1C) which can be used by those authorities requiring more than one designation for corrosivity (see Table 3.2.1)

(b)   Category 2 (skin irritation) (see Table 3.2.2)

(c)   Category 3 (mild skin irritation)

This category is available for those authorities (e.g. pesticides) that want to have more than one skin irritation category (see Table 3.2.2).

3.2.2.1 *Classification based on standard animal test data*

3.2.2.1.1   *Skin corrosion*

3.2.2.1.1.1   A substance is corrosive to skin when it produces destruction of skin tissue, namely, visible necrosis through the epidermis and into the dermis, in at least one tested animal after exposure for up to 4 hours.

3.2.2.1.1.2   Corrosive substances should be classified in Category 1 where sub-categorization is not required by a competent authority or where data are not sufficient for sub-categorization.

3.2.2.1.1.3   When data are sufficient and where required by a competent authority substances may be classified in one of the three sub-categories 1A, 1B or 1C in accordance with the criteria in Table 3.2.1.

---

[1]   *This is a working definition for the purpose of this document.*

3.2.2.1.1.4   For those authorities wanting more than one designation for skin corrosion, up to three sub-categories are provided within the corrosion category (Category 1, see Table 3.2.1): sub-category 1A, where corrosive responses are noted following up to 3 minutes exposure and up to 1 hour observation; sub-category 1B, where corrosive responses are described following exposure greater than 3 minutes and up to 1 hour and observations up to 14 days; and sub-category 1C, where corrosive responses occur after exposures greater than 1 hour and up to 4 hours and observations up to 14 days.

Table 3.2.1: Skin corrosion category and sub-categories[a]

	Criteria
Category 1	Destruction of skin tissue, namely, visible necrosis through the epidermis and into the dermis, in at least one tested animal after exposure ≤ 4 h
Sub-category 1A	Corrosive responses in at least one animal following exposure ≤ 3 min during an observation period ≤ 1 h
Sub-category 1B	Corrosive responses in at least one animal following exposure > 3 min and ≤ 1 h and observations ≤ 14 days
Sub-category 1C	Corrosive responses in at least one animal after exposures > 1 h and ≤ 4 h and observations ≤ 14 days

[a]   *The use of human data is discussed in 3.2.2.2 and in chapters 1.1 (par. 1.1.2.5 (c)) and 1.3 (par. 1.3.2.4.7).*

3.2.2.1.2   *Skin irritation*

3.2.2.1.2.1   A substance is irritant to skin when it produces reversible damage to the skin following its application for up to 4 hours.

3.2.2.1.2.2   An irritation category (Category 2) is provided that:

(a)   recognizes that some test materials may lead to effects which persist throughout the length of the test; and

(b)   acknowledges that animal responses in a test may be variable.

An additional mild irritation category (Category 3) is available for those authorities that want to have more than one skin irritation category.

3.2.2.1.2.3   Reversibility of skin lesions is another consideration in evaluating irritant responses. When inflammation persists to the end of the observation period in 2 or more test animals, taking into consideration alopecia (limited area), hyperkeratosis, hyperplasia and scaling, then a material should be considered to be an irritant.

3.2.2.1.2.4   Animal irritant responses within a test can be variable, as they are with corrosion. A separate irritant criterion accommodates cases when there is a significant irritant response but less than the mean score criterion for a positive test. For example, a test material might be designated as an irritant if at least 1 of 3 tested animals shows a very elevated mean score throughout the study, including lesions persisting at the end of an observation period of normally 14 days. Other responses could also fulfil this criterion. However, it should be ascertained that the responses are the result of chemical exposure. Addition of this criterion increases the sensitivity of the classification system.

3.2.2.1.2.5   An irritation category (Category 2) is presented in Table 3.2.2 using the results of animal testing. Authorities (e.g. for pesticides) also have available a less severe mild irritation category (Category 3). Several criteria distinguish the two categories (Table 3.2.2). They mainly differ in the severity of skin reactions. The major criterion for the irritation category is that at least 2 of 3 tested animals have a mean score of ≥ 2.3 and ≤ 4.0. For the mild irritation category, the mean score cut-off values are ≥ 1.5 and < 2.3 for at least 2 of 3 tested animals. Test materials in the irritation category are excluded from the mild irritation category.

Table 3.2.2: Skin irritation categories [a,b,c]

Categories	Criteria
Irritation (Category 2) (applies to all authorities)	(1) Mean score of ≥ 2.3 and ≤ 4.0 for erythema/eschar or for oedema in at least 2 of 3 tested animals from gradings at 24, 48 and 72 hours after patch removal or, if reactions are delayed, from grades on 3 consecutive days after the onset of skin reactions; or (2) Inflammation that persists to the end of the observation period normally 14 days in at least 2 animals, particularly taking into account alopecia (limited area), hyperkeratosis, hyperplasia, and scaling; or (3) In some cases where there is pronounced variability of response among animals, with very definite positive effects related to chemical exposure in a single animal but less than the criteria above.
Mild irritation (Category 3) (applies to only some authorities)	Mean score of ≥ 1.5 and < 2.3 for erythema/eschar or for oedema from gradings in at least 2 of 3 tested animals from grades at 24, 48 and 72 hours or, if reactions are delayed, from grades on 3 consecutive days after the onset of skin reactions (when not included in the irritant category above).

[a] *The use of human data is addressed in 3.2.2.2 and in chapters 1.1 (para. 1.1.2.5 (c)) and 1.3 (para. 1.3.2.4.7).*

[b] *Grading criteria are understood as described in OECD Test Guideline 404.*

[c] *Evaluation of a 4, 5 or 6-animal study should follow the criteria given in 3.2.5.3.*

3.2.2.2   *Classification in a tiered approach*

3.2.2.2.1   A *tiered approach* to the evaluation of initial information should be considered, where applicable (Figure 3.2.1), recognizing that not all elements may be relevant.

3.2.2.2.2   Existing human and animal data including information from single or repeated exposure should be the first line of evaluation, as they give information directly relevant to effects on the skin.

3.2.2.2.3   Acute dermal toxicity data may be used for classification. If a substance is highly toxic by the dermal route, a skin corrosion/irritation study may not be practicable since the amount of test substance to be applied would considerably exceed the toxic dose and, consequently, would result in the death of the animals. When observations are made of skin corrosion/irritation in acute toxicity studies and are observed up through the limit dose, these data may be used for classification, provided that the dilutions used and species tested are equivalent. Solid substances (powders) may become corrosive or irritant when moistened or in contact with moist skin or mucous membranes.

3.2.2.2.4   *In vitro* alternatives that have been validated and accepted should be used to make classification decisions.

3.2.2.2.5   Likewise, pH extremes like ≤ 2 and ≥ 11.5 may indicate skin effects, especially when associated with significant acid/alkaline reserve (buffering capacity). Generally, such substances are expected to produce significant effects on the skin. In the absence of any other information, a substance is considered corrosive (Skin Category 1) if it has a pH ≤ 2 or a pH ≥ 11.5. However, if consideration of acid/alkaline reserve suggests the substance may not be corrosive despite the low or high pH value, this needs to be confirmed by other data, preferably by data from an appropriate validated in vitro test.

3.2.2.2.6   In some cases sufficient information may be available from structurally related substances to make classification decisions.

3.2.2.2.7   The tiered approach provides guidance on how to organize existing information on a substance and to make a weight of evidence decision about hazard assessment and hazard classification (ideally without conducting new animal tests). Although information might be gained from the evaluation of single parameters within a tier (see 3.2.2.2.1), consideration should be given to the totality of existing information and making an overall weight of evidence determination. This is especially true when there is conflict in information available on some parameters.

Figure 3.2.1: Tiered evaluation for skin corrosion and irritation

Step	Parameter	Finding	Conclusion
1a:	Existing human or animal skin corrosion/irritation data [a] → ↓ Not corrosive/No data ↓	Skin corrosive →	Classify as **skin corrosive** [b]
1b:	Existing human or animal skin corrosion/irritation data [a] → ↓ Not irritant/No data ↓	Skin irritant →	Classify as **skin irritant** [b]
1c:	Existing human or animal skin corrosion/irritation data [a] → ↓ No/Insufficient data ↓	Not a skin corrosive or skin irritant →	**Not classified**
2:	Other, existing skin data in animals [c] → ↓ No/Insufficient data ↓	Yes; other existing data showing that substance may cause skin corrosion or skin irritation →	May be deemed to be a **skin corrosive** [b] or a **skin irritant** [b]
3:	Existing *ex vivo/in vitro* data [d] → ↓ ↘ No/Insufficient data/Negative response ↓	Positive: Skin corrosive → Positive: Skin irritant →	Classify as **skin corrosive** [b] Classify as **skin irritant** [b]
4:	pH-based assessment (with consideration of acid/alkaline reserve of the chemical) [e] → ↓ Not pH extreme, no pH data or extreme pH with data showing low/no acid/alkaline reserve ↓	pH ≤ 2 or ≥ 11.5 with high acid/alkaline reserve or no data for acid/alkaline reserve →	Classify as **skin corrosive**
5:	Validated Structure Activity Relationship (SAR) methods → ↓ ↘ No/Insufficient data ↓	Skin corrosive → Skin irritant →	Deemed to be **skin corrosive** [b] Deemed to be **skin irritant** [b]
6:	Consideration of the total weight of evidence [f] → ↓ ↘	Skin corrosive → Skin irritant →	Deemed to be **skin corrosive** [b] Deemed to be **skin irritant** [b]
7:	**Not classified**		

(a) *Existing human or animal data could be derived from single or repeated exposure(s), for example in occupational, consumer, transport or emergency response scenarios; or from purposely-generated data from animal studies conducted according to validated and internationally accepted test methods. Although human data from accident or poison centre databases can provide evidence for classification, absence of incidents is not itself evidence for no classification as exposures are generally unknown or uncertain;*

(b) *Classify in the appropriate category/sub-category, as applicable;*

(c) *All existing animal data should be carefully reviewed to determine if sufficient skin corrosion/irritation evidence is available. In evaluating such data, however, the reviewer should bear in mind that the reporting of dermal lesions may be incomplete, testing and observations may be made on a species other than the rabbit, and species may differ in sensitivity in their responses;*

(d) *Evidence from studies using validated protocols with isolated human/animal tissues or other, non-tissue-based, though validated, protocols should be assessed. Examples of internationally accepted validated test methods for skin corrosion include OECD Test Guidelines 430 (Transcutaneous*

Electrical Resistance Test (TER)), 431(Human Skin Model Test), and 435 (Membrane Barrier Test Method). An example of a validated internationally accepted in vitro test method for skin irritation is OECD Test Guideline 439 (Reconstructed Human Epidermis Test Method);

(e) *Measurement of pH alone may be adequate, but assessment of acid or alkali reserve (buffering capacity) would be preferable. Presently there is no validated and internationally accepted method for assessing this parameter;*

(f) *All information that is available should be considered and an overall determination made on the total weight of evidence. This is especially true when there is conflict in information available on some parameters. Expert judgment should be exercised prior to making such a determination. Negative results from applicable validated skin corrosion/irritation in vitro tests are considered in the total weight of evidence evaluation.*

3.2.3   Classification criteria for mixtures

3.2.3.1   *Classification of mixtures when data are available for the complete mixture*

3.2.3.1.1   The mixture should be classified using the criteria for substances, taking into account the tiered approach to evaluate data for this hazard class (as illustrated in Figure 3.2.1).

3.2.3.1.2   When considering testing of the mixture, classifiers are encouraged to use a tiered weight of evidence approach as included in the criteria for classification of substances for skin corrosion and irritation to help ensure an accurate classification, as well as to avoid unnecessary animal testing. In the absence of any other information, a mixture is considered corrosive (Skin Category 1) if it has a pH ≤ 2 or a pH ≥ 11.5. However, if consideration of acid/alkaline reserve suggests the mixture may not be corrosive despite the low or high pH value, this needs to be confirmed by other data, preferably by data from an appropriate validated *in vitro* test.

3.2.3.2   *Classification of mixtures when data are not available for the complete mixture: bridging principles*

3.2.3.2.1   Where the mixture itself has not been tested to determine its skin corrosion/ irritation potential, but there are sufficient data on both the individual ingredients and similar tested mixtures to adequately characterize the hazards of the mixture, these data will be used in accordance with the following agreed bridging principles. This ensures that the classification process uses the available data to the greatest extent possible in characterizing the hazards of the mixture without the necessity for additional testing in animals.

3.2.3.2.2   *Dilution*

If a tested mixture is diluted with a diluent which has an equivalent or lower skin corrosivity/irritancy classification than the least skin corrosive/irritant original ingredient and which is not expected to affect the skin corrosivity/irritancy of other ingredients, then the new diluted mixture may be classified as equivalent to the original tested mixture. Alternatively, the method explained in 3.2.3.3 could be applied.

3.2.3.2.3   *Batching*

The skin corrosion/irritation potential of a tested production batch of a mixture can be assumed to be substantially equivalent to that of another untested production batch of the same commercial product when produced by or under the control of the same manufacturer, unless there is reason to believe there is significant variation such that the skin corrosion/irritation potential of the untested batch has changed. If the latter occurs, a new classification is necessary.

3.2.3.2.4   *Concentration of mixtures of the highest corrosion/irritation category*

If a tested mixture classified in the highest sub-category for skin corrosion is concentrated, the more concentrated untested mixture should be classified in the highest corrosion sub-category without additional testing. If a tested mixture classified for skin irritation (Category 2) is concentrated and does not contain skin corrosive ingredients, the more concentrated untested mixture should be classified for skin irritation (Category 2) without additional testing.

3.2.3.2.5   Interpolation within one hazard

For three mixtures (A, B and C) with identical ingredients, where mixtures A and B have been tested and are in the same skin corrosion/irritation hazard category, and where untested mixture C has the same toxicologically active ingredients as mixtures A and B but has concentrations of toxicologically active ingredients intermediate to the concentrations in mixtures A and B, then mixture C is assumed to be in the same skin corrosion/irritation category as A and B.

3.2.3.2.6   *Substantially similar mixtures*

Given the following:

(a)   Two mixtures: (i) A + B;
                        (ii) C + B;

(b)   The concentration of ingredient B is essentially the same in both mixtures;

(c)   The concentration of ingredient A in mixture (i) equals that of ingredient C in mixture (ii);

(d)   Data on skin corrosion/irritation for A and C are available and substantially equivalent, i.e. they are in the same hazard category and are not expected to affect the skin corrosion/irritation potential of B.

If mixture (i) or (ii) is already classified based on test data, then the other mixture can be classified in the same hazard category.

3.2.3.2.7   *Aerosols*

An aerosol form of a mixture may be classified in the same hazard category as the tested non-aerosolized form of the mixture provided that the added propellant does not affect the skin corrosion/irritation properties of the mixture upon spraying.

3.2.3.3   *Classification of mixtures when data are available for all ingredients or only for some ingredients of the mixture*

3.2.3.3.1   In order to make use of all available data for purposes of classifying the skin corrosion/irritation hazards of mixtures, the following assumption has been made and is applied where appropriate in the tiered approach:

The "relevant ingredients" of a mixture are those which are present in concentrations ≥ 1% (w/w for solids, liquids, dusts, mists and vapours and v/v for gases), unless there is a presumption (e.g. in the case of corrosive ingredients) that an ingredient present at a concentration < 1% can still be relevant for classifying the mixture for skin corrosion/irritation.

3.2.3.3.2   In general, the approach to classification of mixtures as corrosive or irritant to skin when data are available on the ingredients, but not on the mixture as a whole, is based on the theory of additivity, such that each skin corrosive or irritant ingredient contributes to the overall corrosive or irritant properties of the mixture in proportion to its potency and concentration. A weighting factor of 10 is used for corrosive ingredients when they are present at a concentration below the concentration limit for classification with Category 1, but are at a concentration that will contribute to the classification of the mixture as an irritant.

The mixture is classified as corrosive or irritant to skin when the sum of the concentrations of such ingredients exceeds a cut-off value/concentration limit.

3.2.3.3.3   Table 3.2.3 below provides the cut-off value/concentration limits to be used to determine if the mixture is considered to be corrosive or irritant to the skin.

3.2.3.3.4   Particular care must be taken when classifying certain types of chemicals such as acids and bases, inorganic salts, aldehydes, phenols, and surfactants. The approach explained in 3.2.3.3.1 and 3.2.3.3.2 might not work given that many such substances are corrosive or irritant at concentrations < 1%. For mixtures containing strong acids or bases the pH should be used as classification criteria (see 3.2.3.1.2) since pH will be a better indicator of corrosion than the concentration limits in Table 3.2.3. A mixture containing corrosive or irritant ingredients that cannot be classified based on the additivity approach shown in Table 3.2.3, due to chemical characteristics that make this approach unworkable, should be classified as skin corrosion Category 1 if it contains ≥ 1% of a corrosive ingredient and as skin irritation Category 2 or Category 3 when it contains ≥ 3% of an irritant ingredient. Classification of mixtures with ingredients for which the approach in Table 3.2.3 does not apply is summarized in Table 3.2.4 below.

3.2.3.3.5   On occasion, reliable data may show that the skin corrosion/irritation of an ingredient will not be evident when present at a level above the generic concentration limits/cut-off values mentioned in Tables 3.2.3 and 3.2.4. In these cases the mixture could be classified according to those data (see also *Classification of hazardous substances and mixtures – Use of cut-off values/Concentration limits* (1.3.3.2)). On occasion, when it is expected that the skin corrosion/irritation of an ingredient will not be evident when present at a level above the generic concentration cut-off values mentioned in Tables 3.2.3 and 3.2.4, testing of the mixture may be considered. In those cases the tiered weight of evidence approach should be applied as described in 3.2.3 and illustrated in Figure 3.2.1.

3.2.3.3.6   If there are data showing that (an) ingredient(s) may be corrosive or irritant to skin at a concentration of < 1% (corrosive) or < 3% (irritant), the mixture should be classified accordingly (see also *Classification of hazardous substances and mixtures – Use of cut-off values/Concentration limits* (1.3.3.2)).

Table 3.2.3: Concentration of ingredients of a mixture classified as skin Category 1, 2 or 3 that would trigger classification of the mixture as hazardous to skin (Category 1, 2 or 3)

Sum of ingredients classified as:	Concentration triggering classification of a mixture as:		
	Skin corrosive	Skin irritant	
	Category 1 (see note below)	Category 2	Category 3
Skin Category 1	≥ 5%	≥ 1% but < 5%	
Skin Category 2		≥ 10%	≥ 1% but < 10%
Skin Category 3			≥ 10%
(10 × Skin Category 1) + Skin Category 2		≥ 10%	≥ 1% but < 10%
(10 × Skin Category 1) + Skin Category 2 + Skin Category 3			≥ 10%

NOTE: *Where the sub-categories of skin Category 1 (corrosive) are used, the sum of all ingredients of a mixture classified as sub-category 1A, 1B or 1C respectively, should each be ≥ 5% in order to classify the mixture as either skin sub-category 1A, 1B or 1C. Where the sum of 1A ingredients is < 5% but the sum of 1A+1B ingredients is ≥ 5%, the mixture should be classified as sub-category 1B. Similarly, where the sum of 1A + 1B ingredients is < 5% but the sum of 1A + 1B + 1C ingredients is ≥ 5% the mixture should be classified as sub-category 1C. Where at least one relevant ingredient in a mixture is classified as Category 1 without sub-categorisation, the mixture should be classified as Category 1 without sub-categorisation if the sum of all ingredients corrosive to skin is ≥ 5%.*

Table 3.2.4: Concentration of ingredients of a mixture when the additivity approach does not apply, that would trigger classification of the mixture as hazardous to skin

Ingredient:	Concentration:	Mixture classified as: Skin
Acid with pH ≤ 2	$\geq 1\%$	Category 1
Base with pH ≥ 11.5	$\geq 1\%$	Category 1
Other corrosive (Category 1) ingredient	$\geq 1\%$	Category 1
Other irritant (Category 2/3) ingredient, including acids and bases	$\geq 3\%$	Category 2/3

3.2.4   Hazard communication

General and specific considerations concerning labelling requirements are provided in *Hazard communication: Labelling* (Chapter 1.4). Annex 1 contains summary tables about classification and labelling. Annex 3 contains examples of precautionary statements and pictograms which can be used where allowed by the competent authority. The table below presents specific label elements for substances and mixtures that are classified as irritating or corrosive to the skin based on the criteria set forth in this chapter.

Table 3.2.5: Label elements for skin corrosion/irritation

	Category 1			Category 2	Category 3
	1 A	**1 B**	**1 C**		
Symbol	Corrosion	Corrosion	Corrosion	Exclamation mark	*No symbol*
Signal word	Danger	Danger	Danger	Warning	Warning
Hazard statement	Causes severe skin burns and eye damage	Causes severe skin burns and eye damage	Causes severe skin burns and eye damage	Causes skin irritation	Causes mild skin irritation

3.2.5   Decision logics and guidance

The decision logics which follow are not part of the harmonized classification system but are provided here as additional guidance. It is strongly recommended that the person responsible for classification study the criteria before and during use of the decision logics.

3.2.5.1 *Decision logic 3.2.1 for skin corrosion/irritation*

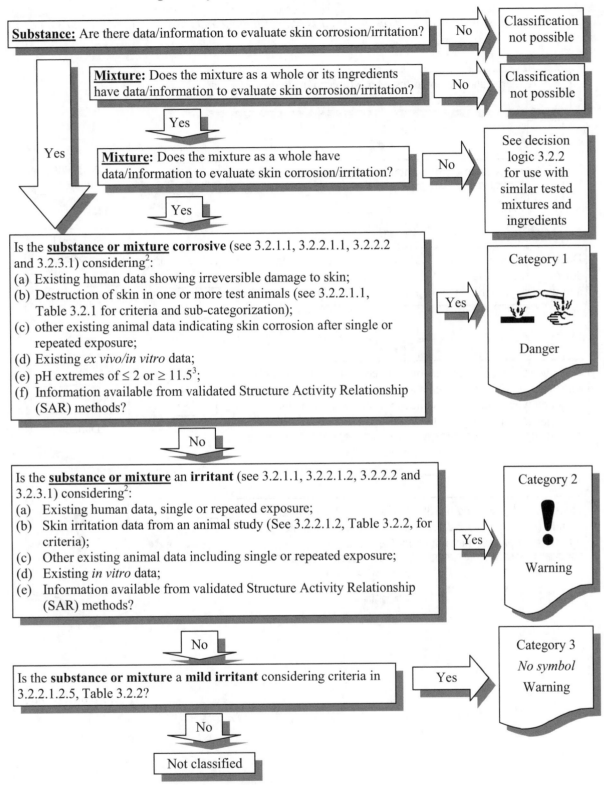

Is the **substance or mixture corrosive** (see 3.2.1.1, 3.2.2.1.1, 3.2.2.2 and 3.2.3.1) considering[2]:
(a) Existing human data showing irreversible damage to skin;
(b) Destruction of skin in one or more test animals (see 3.2.2.1.1, Table 3.2.1 for criteria and sub-categorization);
(c) other existing animal data indicating skin corrosion after single or repeated exposure;
(d) Existing *ex vivo/in vitro* data;
(e) pH extremes of ≤ 2 or ≥ 11.5[3];
(f) Information available from validated Structure Activity Relationship (SAR) methods?

Is the **substance or mixture** an **irritant** (see 3.2.1.1, 3.2.2.1.2, 3.2.2.2 and 3.2.3.1) considering[2]:
(a) Existing human data, single or repeated exposure;
(b) Skin irritation data from an animal study (See 3.2.2.1.2, Table 3.2.2, for criteria);
(c) Other existing animal data including single or repeated exposure;
(d) Existing *in vitro* data;
(e) Information available from validated Structure Activity Relationship (SAR) methods?

Is the **substance or mixture** a **mild irritant** considering criteria in 3.2.2.1.2.5, Table 3.2.2?

---

[2] *Taking into account consideration of the total weight of evidence as needed.*

[3] *Not applicable if consideration of pH and acid/alkaline reserve indicates substance or mixture may not be corrosive and confirmed by other data, preferably by data from an appropriate validated in vitro test.*

3.2.5.2 **Decision logic 3.2.2 for skin corrosion/irritation**

Classification of mixtures on the basis of information/data on similar tested mixtures and/or ingredients

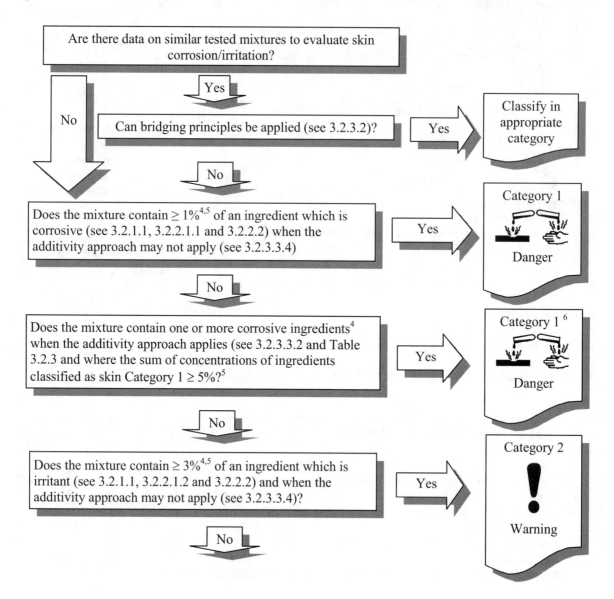

(Cont'd on next page)

---

⁴ *Where relevant < 1%, see 3.2.3.3.1.*

⁵ *For specific concentration limits, see 3.2.3.3.6. See also Chapter 1.3, para. 1.3.3.2 for "Use of cut-off values/concentration limits".*

⁶ *See note to Table 3.2.3 for details on use of Category 1 sub-categories.*

No

Does the mixture contain one or more corrosive or irritant ingredients[4] when the additivity approach applies (see 3.2.3.3.2 and Table 3.2.3) and where the sum of concentrations of ingredients classified as[5]:

(a) skin Category 1 ≥ 1% but < 5%, or

(b) skin Category 2 ≥ 10%, or

(c) $(10 \times$ skin Category 1) + skin Category 2 ≥ 10%?

Yes

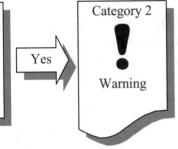

Category 2

Warning

No

Does the mixture contain one or more corrosive or irritant ingredients[4] when the additivity approach applies (see 3.2.3.3.2 and Table 3.2.3), and where the sum of concentrations of ingredients classified as[5]:

(a) skin Category 2 ≥ 1% but < 10%, or

(b) skin Category 3 ≥ 10%, or

(c) $(10 \times$ skin Category 1) + skin Category 2 ≥ 1% but < 10%, or

(d) $(10 \times$ skin Category 1) + skin Category 2 + skin Category 3 ≥ 10%?

Yes

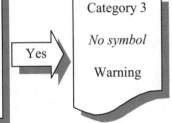

Category 3

No symbol

Warning

No

Not classified

---

[4]   *Where relevant < 1%, see 3.2.3.3.1.*

[5]   *For specific concentration limits, see 3.2.3.3.6. See also Chapter 1.3, para. 1.3.3.2 for "Use of cut-off values/concentration limits".*

3.2.5.3 *Background guidance*

3.2.5.3.1   Classification criteria for the skin and eye hazard classes are detailed in the GHS in terms of a 3-animal test. It has been identified that some older test methods may have used up to 6 animals. However, the GHS criteria do not specify how to classify based on existing data from tests with more than 3 animals. Guidance on how to classify based on existing data from studies with 4 or more animals is given in the following paragraphs.

3.2.5.3.2   Classification criteria based on a 3-animal test are detailed in 3.2.2.1. Evaluation of a 4, 5 or 6-animal study should follow the criteria in the following paragraphs, depending on the number of animals tested. Scoring for erythema/eschar and oedema should be performed at 24, 48 and 72 hours after exposure or, if reactions are delayed, from grades on 3 consecutive days after the onset of skin reactions.

3.2.5.3.3   In the case of a study with 6 animals the following principles apply:

(a)   The substance or mixture is classified as skin corrosion Category 1 if destruction of skin tissue (that is, visible necrosis through the epidermis and into the dermis) occurs in at least one animal after exposure up to 4 hours in duration;

(b)   The substance or mixture is classified as skin irritation Category 2 if at least 4 out of 6 animals show a mean score per animal of ≥ 2.3 and ≤ 4.0 for erythema/eschar or for oedema;

(c)   The substance or mixture is classified as skin irritation Category 3 if at least 4 out of 6 animals show a mean score per animal of ≥ 1.5 and < 2.3 for erythema/eschar or for oedema.

3.2.5.3.4   In the case of a study with 5 animals the following principles apply:

(a)   The substance or mixture is classified as skin corrosion Category 1 if destruction of skin tissue (that is, visible necrosis through the epidermis and into the dermis) occurs in at least one animal after exposure up to 4 hours in duration;

(b)   The substance or mixture is classified as skin irritation Category 2 if at least 3 out of 5 animals show a mean score per animal of ≥ 2.3 and ≤ 4.0 for erythema/eschar or for oedema;

(c)   The substance or mixture is classified as skin irritation Category 3 if at least 3 out of 5 animals show a mean score per animal of ≥ 1.5 and < 2.3 for erythema/eschar or for oedema.

3.2.5.3.5   In the case of a study with 4 animals the following principles apply:

(a)   The substance or mixture is classified as skin corrosion Category 1 if destruction of skin tissue (that is, visible necrosis through the epidermis and into the dermis) occurs in at least one animal after exposure up to 4 hours in duration;

(b)   The substance or mixture is classified as skin irritation Category 2 if at least 3 out of 4 animals show a mean score per animal of ≥ 2.3 and ≤ 4.0 for erythema/eschar or for oedema;

(c)   The substance or mixture is classified as skin irritation Category 3 if at least 3 out of 4 animals show a mean score per animal of ≥ 1.5 and < 2.3 for erythema/eschar or for oedema.

CHAPTER 3.3

SERIOUS EYE DAMAGE /EYE IRRITATION

3.3.1 Definitions and general considerations

3.3.1.1 *Serious eye damage* is the production of tissue damage in the eye, or serious physical decay of vision, following application of a test substance to the anterior surface of the eye, which is not fully reversible within 21 days of application[1].

Eye irritation is the production of changes in the eye following the application of test substance to the anterior surface of the eye, which are fully reversible within 21 days of application[1].

3.3.1.2 In a tiered approach, emphasis should be placed upon existing human data, followed by existing animal data, followed by *in vitro* data and then other sources of information. Classification results directly when the data satisfy the criteria. In other cases, classification of a substance or a mixture is made on the basis of the weight of evidence within a tier. In a total weight of evidence approach all available information bearing on the determination of serious eye damage/eye irritation is considered together, including the results of appropriate validated *in vitro* tests, relevant animal data, and human data such as epidemiological and clinical studies and well-documented case reports and observations (see Chapter 1.3, para. 1.3.2.4.9).

3.3.2 Classification criteria for substances

Substances are allocated to one of the categories within this hazard class, Category 1 (serious eye damage) or Category 2 (eye irritation), as follows:

(a) Category 1 (serious eye damage/irreversible effects on the eye):

substances that have the potential to seriously damage the eyes (see Table 3.3.1).

(b) Category 2 (eye irritation/reversible effects on the eye):

substances that have the potential to induce reversible eye irritation (see Table 3.3.2).

Those authorities desiring one category for classification of "eye irritation" may use the overall Category 2; others may want to distinguish between Category 2A and Category 2B (see Table 3.3.2).

3.3.2.1 *Classification based on standard animal test data*

3.3.2.1.1 *Serious eye damage (Category 1)/irreversible effects on the eye*

A single hazard category (Category 1) is adopted for substances that have the potential to seriously damage the eyes. This hazard category includes as criteria the observations listed in Table 3.3.1. These observations include animals with grade 4 cornea lesions and other severe reactions (e.g. destruction of cornea) observed at any time during the test, as well as persistent corneal opacity, discoloration of the cornea by a dye substance, adhesion, pannus, and interference with the function of the iris or other effects that impair sight. In this context, persistent lesions are considered those which are not fully reversible within an observation period of normally 21 days. Hazard classification as Category 1 also contains substances fulfilling the criteria of corneal opacity ≥ 3 or iritis > 1.5 observed in at least 2 of 3 tested animals, because severe lesions like these usually do not reverse within a 21 days observation period.

---

[1] *This is a working definition for the purpose of this document.*

Table 3.3.1: Serious eye damage/Irreversible effects on the eye category[a, b, c]

	Criteria
Category 1: **Serious eye damage/Irreversible effects on the eye**	A substance that produces: (a) in at least one animal effects on the cornea, iris or conjunctiva that are not expected to reverse or have not fully reversed within an observation period of normally 21 days; and/or (b) in at least 2 of 3 tested animals, a positive response of: (i) corneal opacity ≥ 3; and/or (ii) iritis > 1.5; calculated as the mean scores following grading at 24, 48 and 72 hours after instillation of the test material.

[a]   *The use of human data is addressed in 3.3.2.2 and in chapters 1.1 (para. 1.1.2.5 (c)) and 1.3 (para. 1.3.2.4.7).*

[b]   *Grading criteria are understood as described in OECD Test Guideline 405.*

[c]   *Evaluation of a 4, 5 or 6-animal study should follow the criteria given in 3.3.5.3.*

3.3.2.1.2   *Eye irritation (Category 2)/Reversible effects on the eye*

3.3.2.1.2.1   Substances that have the potential to induce reversible eye irritation should be classified in Category 2 where further categorization into Category 2A and Category 2B is not required by a competent authority or where data are not sufficient for further categorization. When a chemical is classified as Category 2, without further categorization, the classification criteria are the same as those for Category 2A.

3.3.2.1.2.2   For those authorities wanting more than one designation for reversible eye irritation, categories 2A and 2B are provided:

(a)   When data are sufficient and where required by a competent authority substances may be classified in Category 2A or 2B in accordance with the criteria in Table 3.3.2;

(b)   For substances inducing eye irritant effects reversing within an observation time of normally 21 days, Category 2A applies. For substances inducing eye irritant effects reversing within an observation time of 7 days, Category 2B applies.

3.3.2.1.2.3   For those substances where there is pronounced variability among animal responses, this information may be taken into account in determining the classification.

Table 3.3.2: Reversible effects on the eye categories [a, b, c]

	Criteria
	Substances that have the potential to induce reversible eye irritation
Category 2/2A	Substances that produce in at least 2 of 3 tested animals a positive response of: (a) corneal opacity ≥ 1; and/or (b) iritis ≥ 1; and/or (c) conjunctival redness ≥ 2; and/or (d) conjunctival oedema (chemosis) ≥ 2 calculated as the mean scores following grading at 24, 48 and 72 hours after instillation of the test material, and which fully reverses within an observation period of normally 21 days.
Category 2B	Within Category 2A an eye irritant is considered mildly irritating to eyes (Category 2B) when the effects listed above are fully reversible within 7 days of observation.

[a]   *The use of human data is addressed in 3.3.2.2 and in chapters 1.1 (para. 1.1.2.5(c)), and 1.3 (para. 1.3.2.4.7).*

[b]   *Grading criteria are understood as described in OECD Test Guideline 405.*

[c]   *Evaluation of a 4, 5 or 6-animal study should follow the criteria given in 3.3.5.3.*

3.3.2.2   *Classification in a tiered approach*

3.3.2.2.1   A tiered approach to the evaluation of initial information should be considered where applicable (Figure 3.3.1), recognizing that not all elements may be relevant.

3.3.2.2.2   Existing human and animal data should be the first line of evaluation as they give information directly relevant to effects on the eye. Possible skin corrosion has to be evaluated prior to consideration of any testing for serious eye damage/eye irritation in order to avoid testing for local effects on eyes with skin corrosive substances.

3.3.2.2.3   *In vitro* alternatives that have been validated and accepted should be used to make classification decisions.

3.3.2.2.4   Likewise, pH extremes like ≤ 2 and ≥ 11.5, may indicate serious eye damage, especially when associated with significant acid/alkaline reserve (buffering capacity). Generally such substances are expected to produce significant effects on the eyes. In the absence of any other information, a substance is considered to cause serious eye damage (Category 1) if it has a pH ≤ 2 or ≥ 11.5. However, if consideration of acid/alkaline reserve suggests the substance may not cause serious eye damage despite the low or high pH value, this needs to be confirmed by other data, preferably by data from an appropriate validated *in vitro* test.

3.3.2.2.5   In some cases sufficient information may be available from structurally related substances to make classification decisions.

3.3.2.2.6   The tiered approach provides guidance on how to organize existing information and to make a weight-of-evidence decision about hazard assessment and hazard classification (ideally without conducting new animal tests). Animal testing with corrosive substances should be avoided whenever possible. Although information might be gained from the evaluation of single parameters within a tier (see 3.3.2.1.1) consideration should be given to the totality of existing information and making an overall weight of evidence determination. This is especially true when there is conflict in information available on some parameters.

Step	Parameter	Finding	Conclusion
1a:	Existing human or animal serious eye damage/eye irritation data [a] → ↓ Negative data/Insufficient data/No data ↓	Serious eye damage ↘ Eye irritant →	Classify as causing **serious eye damage** → Classify as **eye irritant** [b]
1b:	Existing human or animal data, skin corrosion ↓ Negative data/Insufficient data/No data ↓	Skin corrosion →	Deemed to cause **serious eye damage**
1c:	Existing human or animal serious eye damage/eye irritation data [a] ↓ No/Insufficient data ↓	Existing data showing that substance does not cause serious eye damage or eye irritation →	**Not classified**
2:	Other, existing skin/eye data in animals [c] ↓ No/Insufficient data ↓	Yes; other existing data showing that substance may cause serious eye damage or eye irritation →	May be deemed to cause **serious eye damage** or to be an **eye irritant** [b]
3:	Existing *ex vivo/in vitro eye* data [d] ↓ No/Insufficient data/Negative response ↓	Positive: serious eye damage → ↘ Positive: eye irritant →	Classify as causing **serious eye damage** → Classify as **eye irritant** [b]
4:	pH-based assessment (with consideration of acid/alkaline reserve of the chemical) [e] ↓ Not pH extreme, no pH data or extreme pH with data showing low/no acid/alkaline reserve ↓	pH ≤ 2 or ≥ 11.5 with high acid/alkaline reserve or no data for acid/alkaline reserve →	Classify as causing **serious eye damage**
5:	Validated Structure Activity Relationship (SAR) methods ↓ No/Insufficient data ↓	↗ Severe damage to eyes → → Eye irritant → ↘ Skin corrosive →	Deemed to cause **serious eye damage** → Deemed to be **eye irritant** [b] → Deemed to cause **serious eye damage**
6:	Consideration of the total weight of evidence [f] ↓	Serious eye damage → ↘ Eye irritant →	Deemed to cause **serious eye damage** → Deemed to be **eye irritant** [b]
7:	**Not classified**		

(a)   *Existing human or animal data could be derived from single or repeated exposure(s), for example in occupational, consumer, transport, or emergency response scenarios; or from purposely-generated data from animal studies conducted according to validated and internationally accepted test methods. Although human data from accident or poison centre databases can provide evidence for classification, absence of incidents is not itself evidence for no classification as exposures are generally unknown or uncertain;*

(b)   *Classify in the appropriate category as applicable;*

(c)   Existing animal data should be carefully reviewed to determine if sufficient serious eye damage/eye irritation evidence is available through other, similar information. It is recognized that not all skin irritants are eye irritants. Expert judgment should be exercised prior to making such a determination;

(d)   Evidence from studies using validated protocols with isolated human/animal tissues or other non-tissue-based, validated protocols should be assessed. Examples of internationally accepted, validated test methods for identifying eye corrosives and severe irritants (i.e., Serious Eye Damage) include OECD Test Guidelines 437 (Bovine Corneal Opacity and Permeability (BCOP)) and 438 (Isolated Chicken Eye (ICE)). Presently there are no validated and internationally accepted in vitro test methods for identifying eye irritation. A positive test result from a validated in vitro test on skin corrosion would lead to the conclusion to classify as causing serious eye damage;

(e)   Measurement of pH alone may be adequate, but assessment of acid/alkaline reserve (buffering capacity) would be preferable. Presently, there is no validated and internationally accepted method for assessing this parameter;

(f)   All information that is available on a substance should be considered and an overall determination made on the total weight of evidence. This is especially true when there is conflict in information available on some parameters. The weight of evidence including information on skin irritation may lead to classification for eye irritation. Negative results from applicable validated in vitro tests are considered in the total weight of evidence evaluation.

3.3.3   Classification criteria for mixtures

3.3.3.1   *Classification of mixtures when data are available for the complete mixture*

3.3.3.1.1   The mixture should be classified using the criteria for substances, and taking into account the tiered approach to evaluate data for this hazard class (as illustrated in Figure 3.3.1).

3.3.3.1.2   When considering testing of the mixture, classifiers are encouraged to use a tiered weight of evidence approach as included in the criteria for classification of substances for skin corrosion and serious eye damage and eye irritation to help ensure an accurate classification, as well as to avoid unnecessary animal testing. In the absence of any other information, a mixture is considered to cause serious eye damage (Eye Category 1) if it has a pH ≤ 2 or ≥ 11.5. However, if consideration of alkali/acid reserve suggests the mixture may not cause serious eye damage despite the low or high pH value this needs to be confirmed by other data, preferably data from an appropriate validated *in vitro* test.

3.3.3.2   *Classification of mixtures when data are not available for the complete mixture: bridging principles*

3.3.3.2.1   Where the mixture itself has not been tested to determine its skin corrosivity or potential to cause serious eye damage or eye irritation, but there are sufficient data on both the individual ingredients and similar tested mixtures to adequately characterize the hazards of the mixture, these data will be used in accordance with the following agreed bridging principles. This ensures that the classification process uses the available data to the greatest extent possible in characterizing the hazards of the mixture without the necessity for additional testing in animals.

3.3.3.2.2   *Dilution*

If a tested mixture is diluted with a diluent which has an equivalent or lower classification for serious eye damage/eye irritation than the least seriously eye damaging/eye irritant original ingredient and which is not expected to affect the serious eye damage /eye irritancy of other ingredients, then the new diluted mixture may be classified as equivalent to the original tested mixture. Alternatively, the method explained in 3.3.3.3 could be applied.

3.3.3.2.3   *Batching*

The serious eye damage/eye irritation potential of a tested production batch of a mixture can be assumed to be substantially equivalent to that of another untested production batch of the same commercial product when produced by or under the control of the same manufacturer, unless there is reason to believe there is significant variation such that the serious eye damage/eye irritation potential of the untested batch has changed. If the latter occurs, a new classification is necessary.

3.3.3.2.4   *Concentration of mixtures of the highest serious eye damage/eye irritation category*

If a tested mixture classified for serious eye damage (Category 1) is concentrated, the more concentrated untested mixture should be classified for serious eye damage (Category 1) without additional testing. If a tested mixture classified for eye irritation (Category 2 or 2A) is concentrated and does not contain serious eye damage ingredients, the more concentrated untested mixture should be classified in the same category (Category 2 or 2A) without additional testing.

3.3.3.2.5   *Interpolation within one hazard category*

For three mixtures (A, B and C) with identical ingredients, where mixtures A and B have been tested and are in the same serious eye damage/eye irritation hazard category, and where untested mixture C has the same toxicologically active ingredients as mixtures A and B but has concentrations of toxicologically active ingredients intermediate to the concentrations in mixtures A and B, then mixture C is assumed to be in the same serious eye damage/eye irritation category as A and B.

3.3.3.2.6   *Substantially similar mixtures*

Given the following:

(a)   Two mixtures: (i)   A +B
                         (ii) C + B;

(b)   The concentration of ingredient B is essentially the same in both mixtures;

(c)   The concentration of ingredient A in mixture (i) equals that of ingredient C in mixture (ii);

(d)   Data on serious eye damage/eye irritation for A and C are available and substantially equivalent, i.e. they are in the same hazard category and are not expected to affect the serious eye damage/eye irritation potential of B.

If mixture (i) or (ii) is already classified by testing, the other mixture can be assigned in the same hazard category.

3.3.3.2.7   *Aerosols*

An aerosol form of a mixture may be classified in the same hazard category as the tested non-aerosolized form of mixture provided that the added propellant does not affect the serious eye damage/eye irritation properties of the mixture upon spraying[2].

---

[2]   *Bridging principles apply for the intrinsic hazard classification of aerosols, however, the need to evaluate the potential for "mechanical" eye damage from the physical force of the spray is recognized.*

3.3.3.3 *Classification of mixtures when data are available for all ingredients or only for some ingredients of the mixture*

3.3.3.3.1   In order to make use of all available data for purposes of classifying the serious eye damage/eye irritation properties of the mixtures, the following assumption has been made and is applied where appropriate in the tiered approach:

The "relevant ingredients" of a mixture are those which are present in concentrations ≥ 1% (w/w for solids, liquids, dusts, mists and vapours and v/v for gases), unless there is a presumption (e.g. in the case of corrosive ingredients) that an ingredient present at a concentration < 1% can still be relevant for classifying the mixture for serious eye damage/eye irritation.

3.3.3.3.2   In general, the approach to classification of mixtures as seriously damaging to the eye or eye irritant when data are available on the ingredients, but not on the mixture as a whole, is based on the theory of additivity, such that each corrosive or serious eye damaging/eye irritant ingredient contributes to the overall serious eye damage/eye irritation properties of the mixture in proportion to its potency and concentration. A weighting factor of 10 is used for corrosive and serious eye damaging ingredients when they are present at a concentration below the concentration limit for classification with Category 1, but are at a concentration that will contribute to the classification of the mixture as serious eye damaging/eye irritant. The mixture is classified as seriously damaging to the eye or eye irritant when the sum of the concentrations of such ingredients exceeds a threshold cut-off value/concentration limit.

3.3.3.3.3   Table 3.3.3 provides the cut-off value/concentration limits to be used to determine if the mixture should be classified as seriously damaging to the eye or an eye irritant.

3.3.3.3.4   Particular care must be taken when classifying certain types of chemicals such as acids and bases, inorganic salts, aldehydes, phenols, and surfactants. The approach explained in 3.3.3.3.1 and 3.3.3.3.2 might not work given that many such substances are seriously damaging to the eye/eye irritating at concentrations < 1%. For mixtures containing strong acids or bases the pH should be used as classification criterion (see 3.3.3.1.2) since pH will be a better indicator of serious eye damage (subject to consideration of acid/alkali reserve) than the concentration limits in Table 3.3.3. A mixture containing corrosive or serious eye damaging/eye irritating ingredients that cannot be classified based on the additivity approach applied in Table 3.3.3 due to chemical characteristics that make this approach unworkable, should be classified as Eye Category 1 if it contains ≥ 1% of a corrosive or serious eye damaging ingredient and as Eye Category 2 when it contains ≥ 3% of an eye irritant ingredient. Classification of mixtures with ingredients for which the approach in Table 3.3.3 does not apply is summarized in Table 3.3.4.

3.3.3.3.5   On occasion, reliable data may show that the irreversible/reversible eye effects of an ingredient will not be evident when present at a level above the generic cut-off values/concentration limits mentioned in Tables 3.3.3 and 3.3.4. In these cases the mixture could be classified according to those data (see also 1.3.3.2 *"Use of cut-off values/Concentration limits"*). On occasion, when it is expected that the skin corrosion/irritation or the irreversible/reversible eye effects of an ingredient will not be evident when present at a level above the generic concentration/cut-off levels mentioned in Tables 3.3.3 and 3.3.4, testing of the mixture may be considered. In those cases, the tiered weight of evidence approach should be applied as referred to in section 3.3.3, Figure 3.3.1 and explained in detail in this chapter.

3.3.3.3.6   If there are data showing that (an) ingredient(s) may be corrosive to the skin or seriously damaging to the eye/eye irritating at a concentration of < 1% (corrosive to the skin or seriously damaging to the eye) or < 3% (eye irritant), the mixture should be classified accordingly (see also 1.3.3.2 *"Use of cut-off values/concentration limits"*).

Table 3.3.3: Concentration of ingredients of a mixture classified as skin Category 1 and/or eye Category 1 or 2 that would trigger classification of the mixture as hazardous to the eye (Category 1 or 2)

Sum of ingredients classified as	Concentration triggering classification of a mixture as	
	Serious eye damage	Eye irritation
	Category 1	Category 2/2A
Skin Category 1 + Eye Category 1 [a]	≥ 3%	≥ 1% but < 3%
Eye Category 2		≥ 10% [b]
10 × (skin Category 1 + eye Category 1) [a] + eye Category 2		≥ 10%

[a]   *If an ingredient is classified as both skin Category 1 and eye Category 1 its concentration is considered only once in the calculation;*

[b]   *A mixture may be classified as eye Category 2B when all relevant ingredients are classified as eye Category 2B.*

Table 3.3.4: Concentration of ingredients of a mixture when the additivity approach does not apply, that would trigger classification of the mixture as hazardous to the eye

Ingredient	Concentration	Mixture classified as: Eye
Acid with pH ≤ 2	≥ 1%	Category 1
Base with pH ≥ 11.5	≥ 1%	Category 1
Other corrosive (eye Category 1) ingredient	≥ 1%	Category 1
Other eye irritant (eye Category 2) ingredient	≥ 3%	Category 2

3.3.4   Hazard communication

General and specific considerations concerning labelling requirements are provided in *Hazard communication: Labelling* (Chapter 1.4). Annex 1 contains summary tables about classification and labelling. Annex 3 contains examples of precautionary statements and pictograms which can be used where allowed by the competent authority.

Table 3.3.5: Label elements for serious eye damage/eye irritation [a]

	Category 1	Category 2A	Category 2B
Symbol	Corrosion	Exclamation mark	*No symbol*
Signal word	Danger	Warning	Warning
Hazard statement	Causes serious eye damage	Causes serious eye irritation	Causes eye irritation

[a]   *Where a chemical is classified as skin Category 1, labelling for serious eye damage/eye irritation may be omitted as this information is already included in the hazard statement for skin Category 1 (Causes severe skin burns and eye damage) (see Chapter 1.4, para. 1.4.10.5.3.3).*

3.3.5 Decision logics and guidance

The decision logics which follow are not part of the harmonized classification system but are provided here as additional guidance. It is strongly recommended that the person responsible for classification study the criteria before and during use of the decision logics.

3.3.5.1 *Decision logic 3.3.1 for serious eye damage/eye irritation*

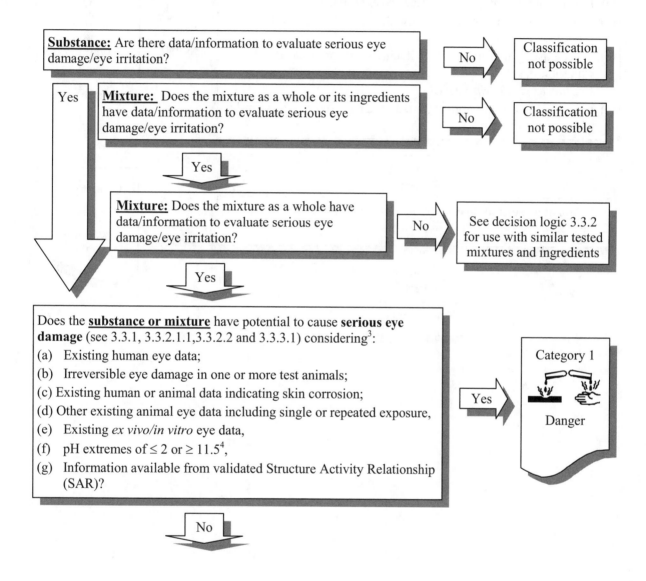

---

[3] *Taking into account consideration of the total weight of evidence as needed*

[4] *Not applicable if consideration of pH and acid/alkaline reserve indicates the substance or mixture many not cause serious eye damage and confirmed by other data, preferably by data from an appropriate validated in vitro test.*

- 143 -

No

Is the **substance or mixture** an **eye irritant** (see 3.3.1, 3.3.2.1.2, 3.3.2.2 and 3.3.3.1) considering[3]:

(a) Existing human data, single or repeated exposure;

(b) Eye irritation data from an animal study (see 3.3.2.1.2, Table 3.3.2 for criteria for Category 2/2A)

(c) Other existing animal eye data including single or repeated exposure,

(d) Existing *ex vivo/in vitro* data,

(e) Information available from validated Structure/Activity Relationship (SAR) methods?

Yes →

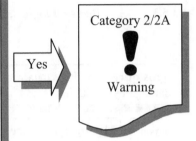

Category 2/2A

Warning

No

Is the **substance or mixture** an irritant Category 2B (see 3.3.2.1.2, Table 3.3.2?

Yes →

Category 2B

No symbol

Warning

No

Not classified

---

[3]   *Taking into account consideration of the total weight of evidence as needed.*

3.3.5.2   Decision logic 3.3.2 for serious eye damage/eye irritation

Classification of mixtures on the basis of information/data on similar tested mixtures and ingredients

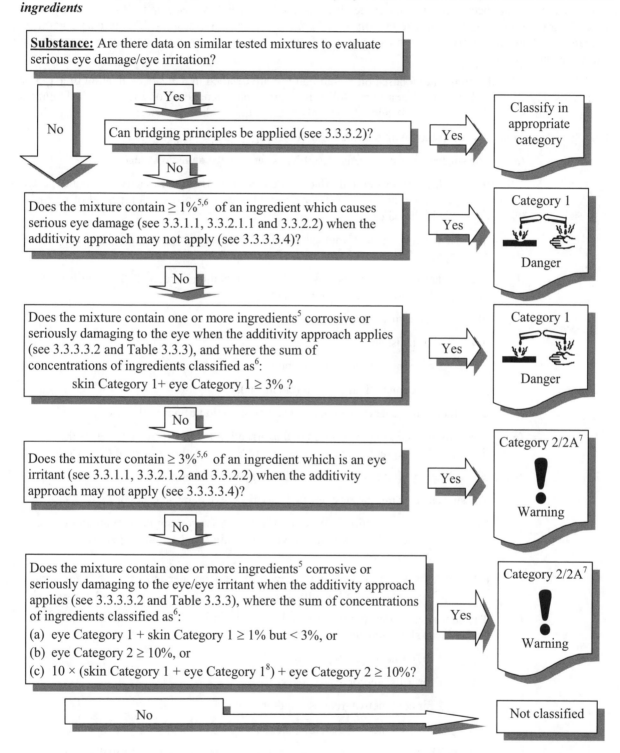

Substance: Are there data on similar tested mixtures to evaluate serious eye damage/eye irritation?

Yes → Can bridging principles be applied (see 3.3.3.2)? → Yes → Classify in appropriate category

No

No

Does the mixture contain $\geq 1\%^{5,6}$ of an ingredient which causes serious eye damage (see 3.3.1.1, 3.3.2.1.1 and 3.3.2.2) when the additivity approach may not apply (see 3.3.3.3.4)? → Yes → Category 1 — Danger

No

Does the mixture contain one or more ingredients[5] corrosive or seriously damaging to the eye when the additivity approach applies (see 3.3.3.3.2 and Table 3.3.3), and where the sum of concentrations of ingredients classified as[6]:

skin Category 1+ eye Category 1 $\geq 3\%$? → Yes → Category 1 — Danger

No

Does the mixture contain $\geq 3\%^{5,6}$ of an ingredient which is an eye irritant (see 3.3.1.1, 3.3.2.1.2 and 3.3.2.2) when the additivity approach may not apply (see 3.3.3.3.4)? → Yes → Category 2/2A[7] — Warning

No

Does the mixture contain one or more ingredients[5] corrosive or seriously damaging to the eye/eye irritant when the additivity approach applies (see 3.3.3.3.2 and Table 3.3.3), where the sum of concentrations of ingredients classified as[6]:

(a) eye Category 1 + skin Category 1 $\geq 1\%$ but $< 3\%$, or

(b) eye Category 2 $\geq 10\%$, or

(c) $10 \times$ (skin Category 1 + eye Category 1[8]) + eye Category 2 $\geq 10\%$? → Yes → Category 2/2A[7] — Warning

No → Not classified

---

[5]   *Where relevant < 1%, see 3.3.3.3.1.*

[6]   *For specific concentration limits, see 3.3.3.3.5 and 3.3.3.3.6. See also Chapter 1.3, para. 1.3.3.2 "Use of cut-off values/concentration limits".*

[7]   *A mixture may be classified as eye Category 2B in case all relevant ingredients are classified as eye Category 2B.*

[8]   *If an ingredient is classified as both skin Category 1 and eye Category 1 its concentration is considered only once in the calculation.*

3.3.5.3   *Background guidance*

3.3.5.3.1   Classification criteria for the skin and eye hazard classes are detailed in the GHS in terms of a 3-animal test. It has been identified that some older test methods may have used up to 6 animals. However, the GHS criteria do not specify how to classify based on existing data from tests with more than 3 animals. Guidance on how to classify based on existing data from studies with 4 or more animals is given in the following paragraphs.

3.3.5.3.2   Classification criteria based on a 3-animal test are detailed in 3.3.2.1. Evaluation of a 4, 5 or 6 animal study should follow the criteria in the following paragraphs, depending on the number of animals tested. Scoring should be done at 24, 48 and 72 hours after instillation of the test material.

3.3.5.3.3   In the case of a study with 6 animals the following principles apply:

   (a)   The substance or mixture is classified as serious eye damage Category 1 if:

   (i)   at least in one animal effects on the cornea, iris or conjunctiva are not expected to reverse or have not fully reversed within an observation period of normally 21 days; and/or

   (ii)   at least 4 out of 6 animals show a mean score per animal of ≥ 3 for corneal opacity and/or > 1.5 for iritis.

   (b)   The substance or mixture is classified as eye irritation Category 2/2A if at least 4 out of 6 animals show a mean score per animal of:

   (i) ≥ 1 for corneal opacity; and/or

   (ii) ≥ 1 for iritis; and/or

   (iii) ≥ 2 for conjunctival redness; and/or

   (iv) ≥ 2 for conjunctival oedema (chemosis),

   and which fully reverses within an observation period of normally 21 days.

   (c)   The substance or mixture is classified as irritating to eyes (Category 2B) if the effects listed in sub-paragraph (b) above are fully reversible within 7 days of observation.

3.3.5.3.4   In the case of a study with 5 animals the following principles apply:

   (a)   The substance or mixture is classified as serious eye damage Category 1 if:

   (i)   at least in one animal effects on the cornea, iris or conjunctiva are not expected to reverse or have not fully reversed within an observation period of normally 21 days; and/or

   (ii)   at least 3 out of 5 animals show a mean score per animal of ≥ 3 for corneal opacity and/or > 1.5 for iritis.

   (b)   The substance or mixture is classified as eye irritation Category 2/2A if at least 3 out of 5 animals show a mean score per animal of:

   (i) ≥ 1 for corneal opacity; and/or

   (ii) ≥ 1 for iritis; and/or

   (iii) ≥ 2 for conjunctival redness; and/or

   (iv) ≥ 2 for conjunctival oedema (chemosis),

   and which fully reverses within an observation period of normally 21 days.

   (c)   The substance or mixture is classified as irritating to eyes (Category 2B) if the effects listed in sub-paragraph (b) above are fully reversible within 7 days of observation.

3.3.5.3.5   In the case of a study with 4 animals the following principles apply:

(a)   The substance or mixture is classified as serious eye damage Category 1 if:

(i)   at least in one animal effects on the cornea, iris or conjunctiva are not expected to reverse or have not fully reversed within an observation period of normally 21 days; and/or

(ii)   at least 3 out of 4 animals show a mean score per animal of ≥ 3 for corneal opacity and/or > 1.5 for iritis.

(b)   Classification as eye irritation Category 2/2A if at least 3 out of 4 animals show a mean score per animal of:

(i) ≥ 1 for corneal opacity; and/or

(ii) ≥ 1 for iritis; and/or

(iii) ≥ 2 for conjunctival redness; and/or

(iv) ≥ 2 for conjunctival oedema (chemosis),

and which fully reverses within an observation period of normally 21 days.

(c)   The substance or mixture is classified as irritating to eyes (Category 2B) if the effects listed in sub-paragraph (b) above are fully reversible within 7 days of observation.

CHAPTER 3.4

RESPIRATORY OR SKIN SENSITIZATION

3.4.1 Definitions and general considerations

3.4.1.1 A *respiratory sensitizer* is a substance that will lead to hypersensitivity of the airways following inhalation of the substance[1].

A *skin sensitizer* is a substance that will lead to an allergic response following skin contact[1].

3.4.1.2 For the purpose of this chapter, sensitization includes two phases: the first phase is induction of specialized immunological memory in an individual by exposure to an allergen. The second phase is elicitation, i.e. production of a cell-mediated or antibody-mediated allergic response by exposure of a sensitized individual to an allergen.

3.4.1.3 For respiratory sensitization, the pattern of induction followed by elicitation phases is shared in common with skin sensitization. For skin sensitization, an induction phase is required in which the immune system learns to react; clinical symptoms can then arise when subsequent exposure is sufficient to elicit a visible skin reaction (elicitation phase). As a consequence, predictive tests usually follow this pattern in which there is an induction phase, the response to which is measured by a standardized elicitation phase, typically involving a patch test. The local lymph node assay is the exception, directly measuring the induction response. Evidence of skin sensitization in humans normally is assessed by a diagnostic patch test.

3.4.1.4 Usually, for both skin and respiratory sensitization, lower levels are necessary for elicitation than are required for induction. Provisions for alerting sensitized individuals to the presence of a particular sensitizer in a mixture can be found in 3.4.4.2.

3.4.1.5 The hazard class "respiratory or skin sensitization" is differentiated into:

    (a) Respiratory sensitization; and

    (b) Skin sensitization

3.4.2 Classification criteria for substances

3.4.2.1 *Respiratory sensitizers*

3.4.2.1.1 *Hazard categories*

3.4.2.1.1.1 Respiratory sensitizers shall be classified in Category 1 where sub-categorization is not required by a competent authority or where data are not sufficient for sub-categorization.

3.4.2.1.1.2 Where data are sufficient and where required by a competent authority, a refined evaluation according to 3.4.2.1.1.3 allows the allocation of respiratory sensitizers into sub-category 1A, strong sensitizers, or sub-category 1B for other respiratory sensitizers.

3.4.2.1.1.3 Effects seen in either humans or animals will normally justify classification in a weight of evidence approach for respiratory sensitizers. Substances may be allocated to one of the two sub-categories 1A or 1B using a weight of evidence approach in accordance with the criteria given in Table 3.4.1 and on the basis of reliable and good quality evidence from human cases or epidemiological studies and/or observations from appropriate studies in experimental animals.

---

[1] *This is a working definition for the purpose of this document.*

Table 3.4.1: Hazard category and sub-categories for respiratory sensitizers

CATEGORY 1:	Respiratory sensitizer
	A substance is classified as a respiratory sensitizer: (a) if there is evidence in humans that the substance can lead to specific respiratory hypersensitivity and/or (b) if there are positive results from an appropriate animal test[2].
Sub-category 1A:	Substances showing a high frequency of occurrence in humans; or a probability of occurrence of a high sensitization rate in humans based on animal or other tests [2]. Severity of reaction may also be considered.
Sub-category 1B:	Substances showing a low to moderate frequency of occurrence in humans; or a probability of occurrence of a low to moderate sensitization rate in humans based on animal or other tests[2]. Severity of reaction may also be considered.

3.4.2.1.2 *Human evidence*

3.4.2.1.2.1   Evidence that a substance can lead to specific respiratory hypersensitivity will normally be based on human experience. In this context, hypersensitivity is normally seen as asthma, but other hypersensitivity reactions such as rhinitis/conjunctivitis and alveolitis are also considered. The condition will have the clinical character of an allergic reaction. However, immunological mechanisms do not have to be demonstrated.

3.4.2.1.2.2   When considering the human evidence, it is necessary for a decision on classification to take into account, in addition to the evidence from the cases:

      (a)   the size of the population exposed;

      (b)   the extent of exposure.

3.4.2.1.2.3   The evidence referred to above could be:

      (a)   clinical history and data from appropriate lung function tests related to exposure to the substance, confirmed by other supportive evidence which may include:

            (i)   *in vivo* immunological test (e.g. skin prick test);

            (ii)   *in vitro* immunological test (e.g. serological analysis);

            (iii)   studies that may indicate other specific hypersensitivity reactions where immunological mechanisms of action have not been proven, e.g. repeated low-level irritation, pharmacologically mediated effects;

            (iv)   a chemical structure related to substances known to cause respiratory hypersensitivity;

      (b)   data from positive bronchial challenge tests with the substance conducted according to accepted guidelines for the determination of a specific hypersensitivity reaction.

3.4.2.1.2.4   Clinical history should include both medical and occupational history to determine a relationship between exposure to a specific substance and development of respiratory hypersensitivity. Relevant information includes aggravating factors both in the home and workplace, the onset and progress of the disease, family history and medical history of the patient in question. The medical history should also include a note of other allergic or airway disorders from childhood, and smoking history.

---

[2]   *At present, recognized and validated animal models for the testing of respiratory hypersensitivity are not available. Under certain circumstances, data from animal studies may provide valuable information in a weight of evidence assessment.*

3.4.2.1.2.5   The results of positive bronchial challenge tests are considered to provide sufficient evidence for classification on their own. It is however recognized that in practice many of the examinations listed above will already have been carried out.

3.4.2.1.3   *Animal studies*

Data from appropriate animal studies[2] which may be indicative of the potential of a substance to cause sensitization by inhalation in humans[3] may include:

(a)   measurements of Immunoglobulin E (IgE) and other specific immunological parameters, for example in mice;

(b)   specific pulmonary responses in guinea pigs.

3.4.2.2   *Skin sensitizers*

3.4.2.2.1   *Hazard categories*

3.4.2.2.1.1   Skin sensitizers shall be classified in Category 1 where sub-categorization is not required by a competent authority or where data are not sufficient for sub-categorization.

3.4.2.2.1.2   Where data are sufficient and where required by a competent authority, a refined evaluation according to 3.4.2.2.1.3 allows the allocation of skin sensitizers into sub-category 1A, strong sensitizers, or sub-category 1B for other skin sensitizers.

3.4.2.2.1.3   Effects seen in either humans or animals will normally justify classification in a weight of evidence approach for skin sensitizers as described in 3.4.2.2.2. Substances may be allocated to one of the two sub-categories 1A or 1B using a weight of evidence approach in accordance with the criteria given in Table 3.4.2 and on the basis of reliable and good quality evidence from human cases or epidemiological studies and/or observations from appropriate studies in experimental animals according to the guidance values provided in 3.4.2.2.2.1 and 3.4.2.2.3.2 for sub-category 1A and in 3.4.2.2.2.2 and 3.4.2.2.3.3 for sub-category 1B.

Table 3.4.2: Hazard category and sub-categories for skin sensitizers

CATEGORY 1:	Skin sensitizer
	A substance is classified as a skin sensitizer: (a) if there is evidence in humans that the substance can lead to sensitization by skin contact in a substantial number of persons, or (b) if there are positive results from an appropriate animal test.
Sub-category 1A:	Substances showing a high frequency of occurrence in humans and/or a high potency in animals can be presumed to have the potential to produce significant sensitization in humans. Severity of reaction may also be considered.
Sub-category 1B:	Substances showing a low to moderate frequency of occurrence in humans and/or a low to moderate potency in animals can be presumed to have the potential to produce sensitization in humans. Severity of reaction may also be considered.

---

[2]   *At present, recognized and validated animal models for the testing of respiratory hypersensitivity are not available. Under certain circumstances, data from animal studies may provide valuable information in a weight of evidence assessment.*

[3]   *The mechanisms by which substances induce symptoms of asthma are not yet fully known. For preventative measures, these substances are considered respiratory sensitizers. However, if on the basis of the evidence, it can be demonstrated that these substances induce symptoms of asthma by irritation only in people with bronchial hyperreactivity, they should not be considered as respiratory sensitizers.*

3.4.2.2.2   Human evidence

3.4.2.2.2.1   Human evidence for sub-category 1A can include:

(a)   positive responses at ≤ 500 $\mu g/cm^2$ (HRIPT, HMT – induction threshold);

(b)   diagnostic patch test data where there is a relatively high and substantial incidence of reactions in a defined population in relation to relatively low exposure;

(c)   other epidemiological evidence where there is a relatively high and substantial incidence of allergic contact dermatitis in relation to relatively low exposure.

3.4.2.2.2.2   Human evidence for sub-category 1B can include:

(a)   positive responses at > 500 $\mu g/cm^2$ (HRIPT, HMT – induction threshold);

(b)   diagnostic patch test data where there is a relatively low but substantial incidence of reactions in a defined population in relation to relatively high exposure;

(c)   other epidemiological evidence where there is a relatively low but substantial incidence of allergic contact dermatitis in relation to relatively high exposure.

3.4.2.2.3   *Animal studies*

3.4.2.2.3.1   For Category 1, when an adjuvant type test method for skin sensitization is used, a response of at least 30% of the animals is considered as positive. For a non-adjuvant Guinea pig test method a response of at least 15% of the animals is considered positive. For Category 1, a stimulation index of three or more is considered a positive response in the local lymph node assay. Test methods for skin sensitization are described in the OECD Guideline 406 (the Guinea Pig Maximisation test and the Buehler guinea pig test) and Guideline 429 (Local Lymph Node Assay). Other methods may be used provided that they are well-validated and scientific justification is given. The Mouse Ear Swelling Test (MEST), appears to be a reliable screening test to detect moderate to strong sensitizers, and can be used as a first stage in the assessment of skin sensitization potential.

3.4.2.2.3.2   Animal test results for sub-category 1A can include data with values indicated in Table 3.4.3 below:

Table 3.4.3: Animal test results for sub-category 1A

Assay	Criteria
Local lymph node assay	EC3 value $\leq 2\%$
Guinea pig maximisation test	$\geq 30\%$ responding at $\leq 0.1\%$ intradermal induction dose <u>or</u> $\geq 60\%$ responding at $> 0.1\%$ to $\leq 1\%$ intradermal induction dose
Buehler assay	$\geq 15\%$ responding at $\leq 0.2\%$ topical induction dose <u>or</u> $\geq 60\%$ responding at $> 0.2\%$ to $\leq 20\%$ topical induction dose

3.4.2.2.3.3   Animal test results for sub-category 1B can include data with values indicated in Table 3.4.4 below:

Table 3.4.4: Animal test results for sub-category 1B

Assay	Criteria
Local lymph node assay	EC3 value $> 2\%$
Guinea pig maximisation test	$\geq 30\%$ to $< 60\%$ responding at $> 0.1\%$ to $\leq 1\%$ intradermal induction dose or $\geq 30\%$ responding at $> 1\%$ intradermal induction dose
Buehler assay	$\geq 15\%$ to $< 60\%$ responding at $> 0.2\%$ to $\leq 20\%$ topical induction dose or $\geq 15\%$ responding at $> 20\%$ topical induction dose

3.4.2.2.4   *Specific considerations*

3.4.2.2.4.1   For classification of a substance, evidence should include any or all of the following using a weight of evidence approach:

(a)   Positive data from patch testing, normally obtained in more than one dermatology clinic;

(b)   Epidemiological studies showing allergic contact dermatitis caused by the substance; Situations in which a high proportion of those exposed exhibit characteristic symptoms are to be looked at with special concern, even if the number of cases is small;

(c)   Positive data from appropriate animal studies;

(d)   Positive data from experimental studies in man (see Chapter 1.3, para. 1.3.2.4.7);

(e)   Well documented episodes of allergic contact dermatitis, normally obtained in more than one dermatology clinic;

(f)   Severity of reaction may also be considered.

3.4.2.2.4.2   Evidence from animal studies is usually much more reliable than evidence from human exposure. However, in cases where evidence is available from both sources, and there is conflict between the results, the quality and reliability of the evidence from both sources must be assessed in order to resolve the question of classification on a case-by-case basis. Normally, human data are not generated in controlled experiments with volunteers for the purpose of hazard classification but rather as part of risk assessment to confirm lack of effects seen in animal tests. Consequently, positive human data on skin sensitization are usually derived from case-control or other, less defined studies. Evaluation of human data must therefore be carried out with caution as the frequency of cases reflect, in addition to the inherent properties of the substances, factors such as the exposure situation, bioavailability, individual predisposition and preventive measures taken. Negative human data should not normally be used to negate positive results from animal studies. For both animal and human data, consideration should be given to the impact of vehicle.

3.4.2.2.4.3   If none of the above mentioned conditions are met, the substance need not be classified as a skin sensitizer. However, a combination of two or more indicators of skin sensitization as listed below may alter the decision. This shall be considered on a case-by-case basis.

(a)   Isolated episodes of allergic contact dermatitis;

(b)   Epidemiological studies of limited power, e.g. where chance, bias or confounders have not been ruled out fully with reasonable confidence;

(c)   Data from animal tests, performed according to existing guidelines, which do not meet the criteria for a positive result described in 3.4.2.2.3, but which are sufficiently close to the limit to be considered significant;

(d)   Positive data from non-standard methods;

(e)   Positive results from close structural analogues.

3.4.2.2.4.4   *Immunological contact urticaria*

Substances meeting the criteria for classification as respiratory sensitizers may in addition cause immunological contact urticaria. Consideration should be given to classifying these substances also as skin sensitizers. Substances which cause immunological contact urticaria without meeting the criteria for respiratory sensitizers should also be considered for classification as skin sensitizers.

There is no recognized animal model available to identify substances which cause immunological contact urticaria. Therefore, classification will normally be based on human evidence which will be similar to that for skin sensitization.

3.4.3 Classification criteria for mixtures

3.4.3.1 *Classification of mixtures when data are available for the complete mixture*

When reliable and good quality evidence from human experience or appropriate studies in experimental animals, as described in the criteria for substances, is available for the mixture, then the mixture can be classified by weight of evidence evaluation of these data. Care should be exercised in evaluating data on mixtures that the dose used does not render the results inconclusive. (For special labelling required by some competent authorities, see the note to Table 3.4.5 of this chapter and 3.4.4.2.)

3.4.3.2 *Classification of mixtures when data are not available for the complete mixture: bridging principles*

3.4.3.2.1   Where the mixture itself has not been tested to determine its sensitizing properties, but there are sufficient data on both the individual ingredients and similar tested mixtures to adequately characterize the hazards of the mixture, these data will be used in accordance with the following agreed bridging principles. This ensures that the classification process uses the available data to the greatest extent possible in characterizing the hazards of the mixture without the necessity for additional testing in animals.

3.4.3.2.2   *Dilution*

If a tested mixture is diluted with a diluent which is not a sensitizer and which is not expected to affect the sensitization of other ingredients, then the new diluted mixture may be classified as equivalent to the original tested mixture.

3.4.3.2.3   *Batching*

The sensitizing properties of a tested production batch of a mixture can be assumed to be substantially equivalent to that of another untested production batch of the same commercial product when produced by or under the control of the same manufacturer, unless there is reason to believe there is significant variation such that the sensitization potential of the untested batch has changed. If the latter occurs, a new classification is necessary.

3.4.3.2.4   Concentration of mixtures of the highest sensitizing category/sub-category

If a tested mixture is classified in Category 1 or sub-category 1A, and the concentration of the ingredients of the tested mixture that are in Category 1 and sub-category 1A is increased, the resulting untested mixture should be classified in Category 1 or sub-category 1A without additional testing.

3.4.3.2.5   Interpolation within one category/sub-category

For three mixtures (A, B and C) with identical ingredients, where mixtures A and B have been tested and are in the same category/sub-category, and where untested mixture C has the same toxicologically active ingredients as mixtures A and B but has concentrations of toxicologically active ingredients intermediate to the concentrations in mixtures A and B, then mixture C is assumed to be in the same category/sub-category as A and B.

3.4.3.2.6   *Substantially similar mixtures*

Given the following:

(a)   Two mixtures: (i)   A + B;
                                    (ii) C + B;

(b)   The concentration of ingredient B is essentially the same in both mixtures;

(c)   The concentration of ingredient A in mixture (i) equals that of ingredient C in mixture (ii);

(d)   Ingredient B is a sensitizer and ingredients A and C are not sensitizers;

(e)   A and C are not expected to affect the sensitizing properties of B.

If mixture (i) or (ii) is already classified by testing, then the other mixture can be assigned the same hazard category.

3.4.3.2.7   *Aerosols*

An aerosol form of the mixture may be classified in the same hazard category as the tested non-aerosolized form of the mixture provided that the added propellant does not affect the sensitizing properties of the mixture upon spraying.

3.4.3.3   *Classification of mixtures when data are available for all ingredients or only for some ingredients of the mixture*

The mixture should be classified as a respiratory or skin sensitizer when at least one ingredient has been classified as a respiratory or skin sensitizer and is present at or above the appropriate cut-off value/concentration limit for the specific endpoint as shown in Table 3.4.5 for solid/liquid and gas respectively.

Table 3.4.5: Cut-off values/concentration limits of ingredients of a mixture classified as either respiratory sensitizers or skin sensitizers that would trigger classification of the mixture

Ingredient classified as:	Cut-off values/concentration limits triggering classification of a mixture as:		
	Respiratory sensitizer Category 1		Skin sensitizer Category 1
	Solid/Liquid	Gas	All physical states
Respiratory sensitizer Category 1	≥ 0.1% (see note)	≥ 0.1% (see note)	--
	≥ 1.0%	≥ 0.2%	
Respiratory sensitizer Sub-category 1A	≥ 0.1%	≥ 0.1%	
Respiratory sensitizer Sub-category 1B	≥ 1.0%	≥ 0.2%	
Skin sensitizer Category 1	--	--	≥ 0.1% (see note)
	--	--	≥ 1.0%
Skin sensitizer Sub-category 1A	--	--	≥ 0.1%
Skin sensitizer Sub-category 1B	--	--	≥ 1.0%

NOTE: Some competent authorities may require SDS and/or supplemental labelling only, as described in 3.4.4.2 for mixtures containing a sensitizing ingredient at concentrations between 0.1 and 1.0% (or between 0.1 and 0.2% for a gaseous respiratory sensitizer). While the current cut-off values reflect existing systems, all recognize that special cases may require information to be conveyed below that level.

3.4.4 Hazard communication

3.4.4.1 General and specific considerations concerning labelling requirements are provided in *Hazard communication: Labelling* (Chapter 1.4). Annex 1 contains summary tables about classification and labelling. Annex 3 contains examples of precautionary statements and pictograms which can be used where allowed by the competent authority. Table 3.4.6 below presents specific label elements for substances and mixtures that are classified as respiratory and skin sensitizers based on the criteria in this chapter.

Table 3.4.6: Label elements for respiratory or skin sensitization

	Respiratory sensitization Category 1 and sub-categories 1A and 1B	Skin sensitization Category 1 and sub-categories 1A and 1B
Symbol	Health hazard	Exclamation mark
Signal word	Danger	Warning
Hazard statement	May cause allergy or asthma symptoms or breathing difficulties if inhaled	May cause an allergic skin reaction

3.4.4.2 Some chemicals that are classified as sensitizers may elicit a response, when present in a mixture in quantities below the cut-offs established in Table 3.4.5, in individuals who are already sensitized to the chemicals. To protect these individuals, certain authorities may choose to require the name of the ingredients as a supplemental label element whether or not the mixture as a whole is classified as sensitizer.

3.4.5 **Decision logic**

The decision logics which follow are not part of the harmonized classification system but are provided here as additional guidance. It is strongly recommended that the person responsible for classification study the criteria before and during use of the decision logics.

3.4.5.1 *Decision logic 3.4.1 for respiratory sensitization*

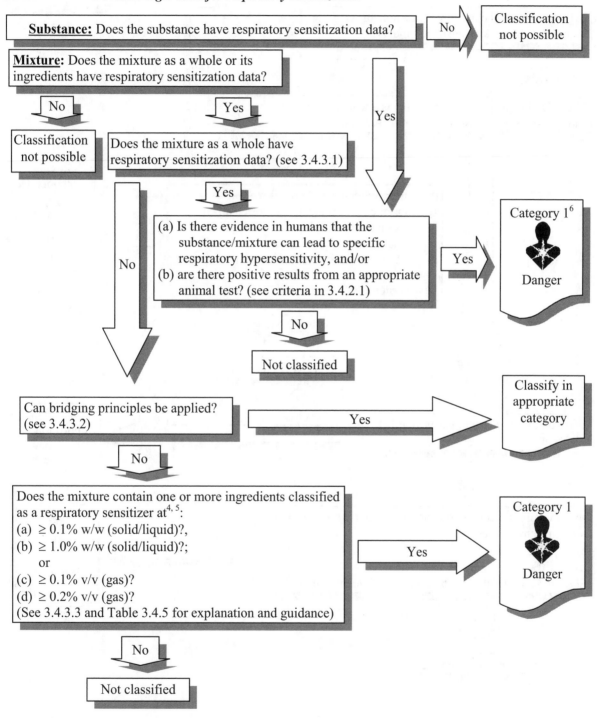

---
[4]   *For specific concentration limits, see "The use of cut-off values/concentration limits" in Chapter 1.3, para. 1.3.3.2.*

[5]   *See 3.4.4.2.*

[6]   *See 3.4.2.1.1 for details on use of Category 1 sub-categories.*

3.4.5.2   *Decision logic 3.4.2 for skin sensitization*

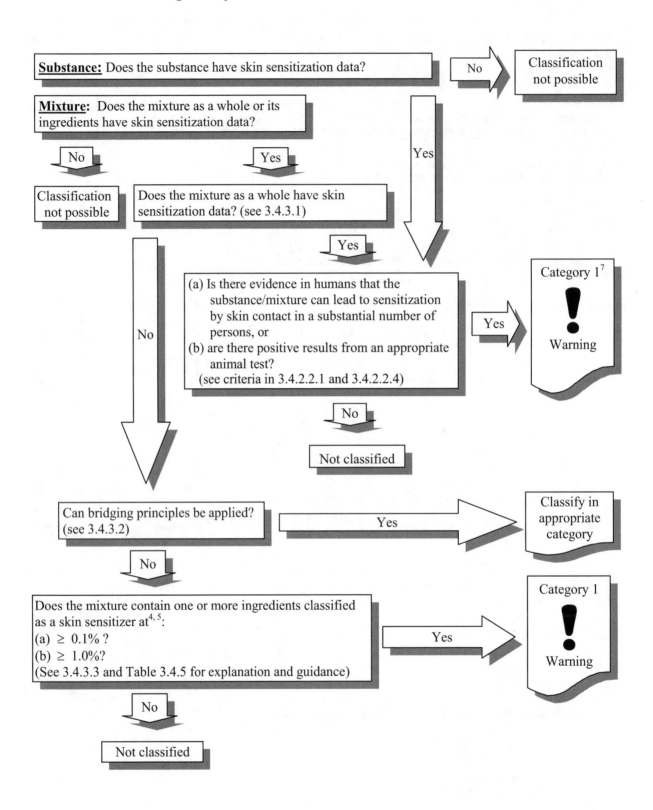

---

4   *For specific concentration limits, see "The use of cut-off values/concentration limits" in Chapter 1.3, para. 1.3.3.2.*

5   *See 3.4.4.2.*

7   *See 3.4.2.2.1 for details on use of Category 1 sub-categories.*

CHAPTER 3.5

GERM CELL MUTAGENICITY

3.5.1 Definitions and general considerations

3.5.1.1   This hazard class is primarily concerned with chemicals that may cause mutations in the germ cells of humans that can be transmitted to the progeny. However, mutagenicity/genotoxicity tests *in vitro* and in mammalian somatic cells *in vivo* are also considered in classifying substances and mixtures within this hazard class.

3.5.1.2   In the present context, commonly found definitions of the terms "mutagenic", "mutagen", "mutations" and "genotoxic" are used. A *mutation* is defined as a permanent change in the amount or structure of the genetic material in a cell.

3.5.1.3   The term *mutation* applies both to heritable genetic changes that may be manifested at the phenotypic level and to the underlying DNA modifications when known (including, for example, specific base pair changes and chromosomal translocations). The term *mutagenic* and *mutagen* will be used for agents giving rise to an increased occurrence of mutations in populations of cells and/or organisms.

3.5.1.4   The more general terms *genotoxic* and *genotoxicity* apply to agents or processes which alter the structure, information content, or segregation of DNA, including those which cause DNA damage by interfering with normal replication processes, or which in a non-physiological manner (temporarily) alter its replication. Genotoxicity test results are usually taken as indicators for mutagenic effects.

3.5.2 Classification criteria for substances

3.5.2.1   The classification system provides for two different categories of germ cell mutagens to accommodate the weight of evidence available. The two-category system is described in the following.

3.5.2.2   To arrive at a classification, test results are considered from experiments determining mutagenic and/or genotoxic effects in germ and/or somatic cells of exposed animals. Mutagenic and/or genotoxic effects determined in *in vitro* tests may also be considered.

3.5.2.3   The system is hazard based, classifying substances on the basis of their intrinsic ability to induce mutations in germ cells. The scheme is, therefore, not meant for the (quantitative) risk assessment of substances.

3.5.2.4   Classification for heritable effects in human germ cells is made on the basis of well conducted, sufficiently validated tests, preferably as described in OECD Test Guidelines. Evaluation of the test results should be done using expert judgement and all the available evidence should be weighed for classification.

3.5.2.5   Examples of *in vivo* heritable germ cell mutagenicity tests are:

> Rodent dominant lethal mutation test (OECD 478)
> Mouse heritable translocation assay (OECD 485)
> Mouse specific locus test

3.5.2.6   Examples of *in vivo* somatic cell mutagenicity tests are:

> Mammalian bone marrow chromosome aberration test (OECD 475)
> Mouse spot test (OECD 484)[1] Mammalian erythrocyte micronucleus test (OECD 474)

---

[1]   *This Test Guideline has been cancelled but may continue to be used until 2 April 2014.*

CATEGORY 1:	**Substances known to induce heritable mutations or to be regarded as if they induce heritable mutations in the germ cells of humans**
Category 1A:	**Substances known to induce heritable mutations in germ cells of humans**
	Positive evidence from human epidemiological studies.
Category 1B:	**Substances which should be regarded as if they induce heritable mutations in the germ cells of humans**

(a) Positive result(s) from *in vivo* heritable germ cell mutagenicity tests in mammals; or

(b) Positive result(s) from *in vivo* somatic cell mutagenicity tests in mammals, in combination with some evidence that the substance has potential to cause mutations to germ cells. This supporting evidence may, for example, be derived from mutagenicity/genotoxic tests in germ cells *in vivo*, or by demonstrating the ability of the substance or its metabolite(s) to interact with the genetic material of germ cells; or

(c) Positive results from tests showing mutagenic effects in the germ cells of humans, without demonstration of transmission to progeny; for example, an increase in the frequency of aneuploidy in sperm cells of exposed people.

CATEGORY 2: **Substances which cause concern for humans owing to the possibility that they may induce heritable mutations in the germ cells of humans**

Positive evidence obtained from experiments in mammals and/or in some cases from *in vitro* experiments, obtained from:

(a) Somatic cell mutagenicity tests *in vivo*, in mammals; or

(b) Other *in vivo* somatic cell genotoxicity tests which are supported by positive results from *in vitro* mutagenicity assays.

NOTE: *Substances which are positive in in vitro mammalian mutagenicity assays, and which also show structure activity relationship to known germ cell mutagens, should be considered for classification as Category 2 mutagens.*

3.5.2.7   Examples of mutagenicity/genotoxicity tests in germ cells are:

(a)   Mutagenicity tests:

Mammalian spermatogonial chromosome aberration test (OECD 483)
Spermatid micronucleus assay

(b)   Genotoxicity tests:

Sister chromatid exchange analysis in spermatogonia
Unscheduled DNA synthesis test (UDS) in testicular cells

3.5.2.8   Examples of genotoxicity tests in somatic cells are:

Liver Unscheduled DNA Synthesis (UDS) *in vivo* (OECD 486)
Mammalian bone marrow Sister Chromatid Exchanges (SCE)

3.5.2.9   Examples of *in vitro* mutagenicity tests are:

In vitro mammalian chromosome aberration test (OECD 473)
In vitro mammalian cell gene mutation test (OECD 476)
Bacterial reverse mutation tests (OECD 471)

3.5.2.10   The classification of individual substances should be based on the total weight of evidence available, using expert judgement. In those instances where a single well-conducted test is used for classification, it should provide clear and unambiguously positive results. If new, well validated, tests arise these may also be used in the total weight of evidence to be considered. The relevance of the route of exposure used in the study of the substance compared to the route of human exposure should also be taken into account.

3.5.3   Classification criteria for mixtures

3.5.3.1   *Classification of mixtures when data are available for the mixture itself*

Classification of mixtures will be based on the available test data for the individual ingredients of the mixture using cut-off values/concentration limits for the ingredients classified as germ cell mutagens. The classification may be modified on a case-by-case basis based on the available test data for the mixture as a whole. In such cases, the test results for the mixture as a whole must be shown to be conclusive taking into account dose and other factors such as duration, observations and analysis (e.g. statistical analysis, test sensitivity) of germ cell mutagenicity test systems. Adequate documentation supporting the classification should be retained and made available for review upon request.

3.5.3.2   *Classification of mixtures when data are not available for the complete mixture: bridging principles*

3.5.3.2.1   Where the mixture itself has not been tested to determine its germ cell mutagenicity hazard, but there are sufficient data on both the individual ingredients and similar tested mixtures to adequately characterize the hazards of the mixture, these data will be used in accordance with the following agreed bridging principles. This ensures that the classification process uses the available data to the greatest extent possible in characterizing the hazards of the mixture without the necessity for additional testing in animals.

3.5.3.2.2   *Dilution*

If a tested mixture is diluted with a diluent which is not expected to affect the germ cell mutagenicity of other ingredients, then the new diluted mixture may be classified as equivalent to the original tested mixture.

3.5.3.2.3   *Batching*

The germ cell mutagenic potential of a tested production batch of a mixture can be assumed to be substantially equivalent to that of another untested production batch of the same commercial product, when produced by or under the control of the same manufacturer unless there is reason to believe there is significant variation in composition such that the germ cell mutagenic potential of the untested batch has changed. If the latter occurs, a new classification is necessary.

3.5.3.2.4   *Substantially similar mixtures*

Given the following:

(a)   Two mixtures: (i)   A + B;
                         (ii)   C + B;

(b)   The concentration of mutagen ingredient B is the same in both mixtures;

(c)   The concentration of ingredient A in mixture (i) equals that of ingredient C in mixture (ii);

(d)   Data on toxicity for A and C are available and substantially equivalent, i.e. they are in the same hazard category and are not expected to affect the germ cell mutagenicity of B.

If mixture (i) or (ii) is already classified by testing, then the other mixture can be classified in the same hazard category.

3.5.3.3 *Classification of mixtures when data are available for all ingredients or only for some ingredients of the mixture*

The mixture will be classified as a mutagen when at least one ingredient has been classified as a Category 1 or Category 2 mutagen and is present at or above the appropriate cut-off value/concentration limit as shown in Table 3.5.1 below for Category 1 and 2 respectively.

Table 3.5.1: Cut-off values/concentration limits of ingredients of a mixture classified as germ cell mutagens that would trigger classification of the mixture

Ingredient classified as:	Cut-off/concentration limits triggering classification of a mixture as:		
	Category 1 mutagen		Category 2 mutagen
	Category 1A	Category 1B	
Category 1A mutagen	$\geq 0.1\%$	--	--
Category 1B mutagen	--	$\geq 0.1\%$	
Category 2 mutagen	--	--	$\geq 1.0\%$

Note: *The cut-off values/concentration limits in the table above apply to solids and liquids (w/w units) as well as gases (v/v units).*

3.5.4   Hazard communication

General and specific considerations concerning labelling requirements are provided in *Hazard communication: Labelling* (Chapter 1.4). Annex 1 contains summary tables about classification and labelling. Annex 3 contains examples of precautionary statements and pictograms which can be used where allowed by the competent authority. The table below presents specific label elements for substances and mixtures classified as germ cell mutagens based on the criteria in this chapter.

Table 3.5.2: Label elements for germ cell mutagenicity

	Category 1 (Category 1A, 1B)	Category 2
Symbol	Health hazard	Health hazard
Signal word	Danger	Warning
Hazard statement	May cause genetic defects (state route of exposure if it is conclusively proven that no other routes of exposure cause the hazard)	Suspected of causing genetic defects (state route of exposure if it is conclusively proven that no other routes of exposure cause the hazard)

3.5.5   **Decision logic and guidance**

3.5.5.1   *Decision logic for germ cell mutagenicity*

       The decision logic which follows is not part of the harmonized classification system but is provided here as additional guidance. It is strongly recommended that the person responsible for classification study the criteria before and during use of the decision logic.

3.5.5.1.1   *Decision logic 3.5.1 for substances*

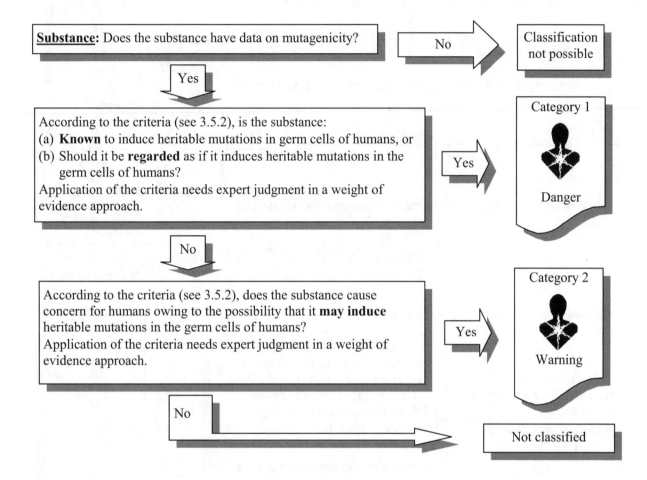

3.5.5.1.2   *Decision logic 3.5.2 for mixtures*

Mixture:
Classification of mixtures will be based on the available test data for the **individual ingredients** of the mixture, using cut-off values/concentration limits for those ingredients. The classification may **be modified on a case-by-case basis** based on the available test data for the mixture itself or based on bridging principles. See modified classification on a case-by-case basis below. For further details see criteria in 3.5.3.

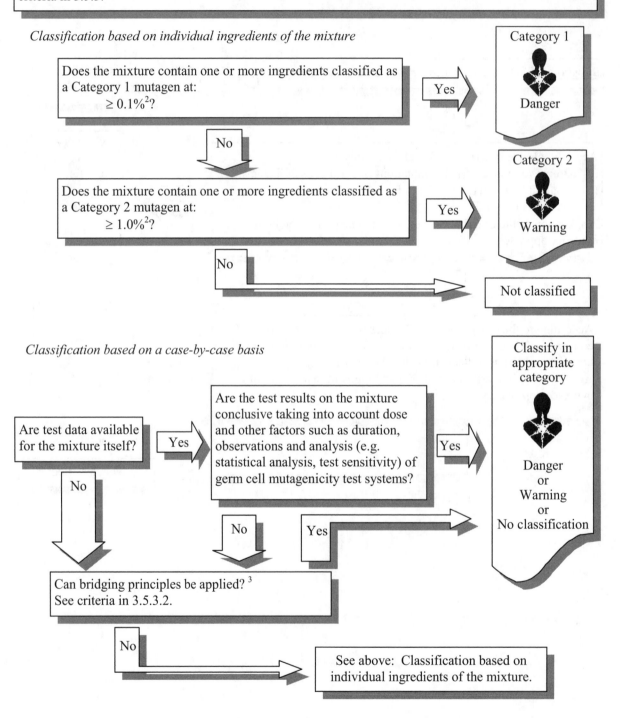

Classification based on individual ingredients of the mixture

Does the mixture contain one or more ingredients classified as a Category 1 mutagen at: $\geq 0.1\%^2$?

Yes → Category 1 ☠ Danger

No ↓

Does the mixture contain one or more ingredients classified as a Category 2 mutagen at: $\geq 1.0\%^2$?

Yes → Category 2 ☠ Warning

No → Not classified

Classification based on a case-by-case basis

Are test data available for the mixture itself?

Yes → Are the test results on the mixture conclusive taking into account dose and other factors such as duration, observations and analysis (e.g. statistical analysis, test sensitivity) of germ cell mutagenicity test systems?

Yes → Classify in appropriate category ☠ Danger or Warning or No classification

No ↓

No ↓   Yes →

Can bridging principles be applied? [3] See criteria in 3.5.3.2.

No → See above: Classification based on individual ingredients of the mixture.

---

2   *For specific concentration limits, see "The use of cut-off values/concentration limits" in Chapter 1.3, para. 1.3.3.2 and Table 3.5.1 of this Chapter.*

3   *If data on another mixture are used in the application of bridging principles, the data on that mixture must be conclusive in accordance with 3.5.3.2.*

3.5.5.2 *Guidance*

It is increasingly accepted that the process of chemical-induced tumorigenesis in man and animals involves genetic changes in proto-oncogenes and/or tumour suppresser genes of somatic cells. Therefore, the demonstration of mutagenic properties of chemicals in somatic and/or germ cells of mammals *in vivo* may have implications for the potential classification of these chemicals as carcinogens (see also Carcinogenicity, Chapter 3.6, para. 3.6.2.5.3).

CHAPTER 3.6

CARCINOGENICITY

3.6.1 Definitions

The term *carcinogen* denotes a substance or a mixture which induces cancer or increases its incidence. Substances and mixtures which have induced benign and malignant tumours in well performed experimental studies on animals are considered also to be presumed or suspected human carcinogens unless there is strong evidence that the mechanism of tumour formation is not relevant for humans.

Classification of a substance or mixture as posing a carcinogenic hazard is based on its inherent properties and does not provide information on the level of the human cancer risk which the use of the substance or mixture may represent.

3.6.2 Classification criteria for substances

3.6.2.1   For the purpose of classification for carcinogenicity, substances are allocated to one of two categories based on strength of evidence and additional considerations (weight of evidence). In certain instances, route specific classification may be warranted.

Figure 3.6.1: Hazard categories for carcinogens

CATEGORY 1:	**Known or presumed human carcinogens**
	The placing of a substance in Category 1 is done on the basis of epidemiological and/or animal data. An individual substance may be further distinguished:
Category 1A:	**Known to have carcinogenic potential for humans; the placing of a substance is largely based on human evidence.**
Category 1B:	**Presumed to have carcinogenic potential for humans; the placing of a substance is largely based on animal evidence.**
	Based on strength of evidence together with additional considerations, such evidence may be derived from human studies that establish a causal relationship between human exposure to a substance and the development of cancer (known human carcinogen). Alternatively, evidence may be derived from animal experiments for which there is sufficient evidence to demonstrate animal carcinogenicity (presumed human carcinogen). In addition, on a case by case basis, scientific judgement may warrant a decision of presumed human carcinogenicity derived from studies showing limited evidence of carcinogenicity in humans together with limited evidence of carcinogenicity in experimental animals.
	Classification: Category 1 (A and B) Carcinogen
CATEGORY 2:	**Suspected human carcinogens**
	The placing of a substance in Category 2 is done on the basis of evidence obtained from human and/or animal studies, but which is not sufficiently convincing to place the substance in Category 1. Based on strength of evidence together with additional considerations, such evidence may be from either limited evidence of carcinogenicity in human studies or from limited evidence of carcinogenicity in animal studies.
	Classification: Category 2 Carcinogen

3.6.2.2   Classification as a carcinogen is made on the basis of evidence from reliable and acceptable methods, and is intended to be used for substances which have an intrinsic property to produce such toxic effects. The evaluations should be based on all existing data, peer-reviewed published studies and additional data accepted by regulatory agencies.

3.6.2.3   *Carcinogen classification* is a one-step, criterion-based process that involves two interrelated determinations: evaluations of strength of evidence and consideration of all other relevant information to place substances with human cancer potential into hazard categories.

3.6.2.4   *Strength of evidence* involves the enumeration of tumours in human and animal studies and determination of their level of statistical significance. Sufficient human evidence demonstrates causality between human exposure and the development of cancer, whereas sufficient evidence in animals shows a causal relationship between the agent and an increased incidence of tumours. Limited evidence in humans is demonstrated by a positive association between exposure and cancer, but a causal relationship cannot be stated. Limited evidence in animals is provided when data suggest a carcinogenic effect, but are less than sufficient. The terms "sufficient" and "limited" are used here as they have been defined by the International Agency for Research on Cancer (IARC) and are outlined in 3.6.5.3.1.

3.6.2.5   *Additional considerations (weight of evidence)*: Beyond the determination of the strength of evidence for carcinogenicity, a number of other factors should be considered that influence the overall likelihood that an agent may pose a carcinogenic hazard in humans. The full list of factors that influence this determination is very lengthy, but some of the important ones are considered here.

3.6.2.5.1   The factors can be viewed as either increasing or decreasing the level of concern for human carcinogenicity. The relative emphasis accorded to each factor depends upon the amount and coherence of evidence bearing on each. Generally there is a requirement for more complete information to decrease than to increase the level of concern. Additional considerations should be used in evaluating the tumour findings and the other factors in a case-by-case manner.

3.6.2.5.2   Some important factors which may be taken into consideration, when assessing the overall level of concern are:

(a)   Tumour type and background incidence;

(b)   Multisite responses;

(c)   Progression of lesions to malignancy;

(d)   Reduced tumour latency;

Additional factors which may increase or decrease the level of concern include:

(e)   Whether responses are in single or both sexes;

(f)   Whether responses are in a single species or several species;

(g)   Structural similarity or not to a substance(s) for which there is good evidence of carcinogenicity;

(h)   Routes of exposure;

(i)   Comparison of absorption, distribution, metabolism and excretion between test animals and humans;

(j)   The possibility of a confounding effect of excessive toxicity at test doses;

(k)   Mode of action and its relevance for humans, such as mutagenicity, cytotoxicity with growth stimulation, mitogenesis, immunosuppression.

Guidance on how to consider important factors in classification of carcinogenicity is included in 3.6.5.3.

3.6.2.5.3   *Mutagenicity:* It is recognized that genetic events are central in the overall process of cancer development. Therefore evidence of mutagenic activity *in vivo* may indicate that a substance has a potential for carcinogenic effects.

3.6.2.5.4   The following additional considerations apply to classification of substances into either Category 1 or Category 2. A substance that has not been tested for carcinogenicity may in certain instances be classified in Category 1 or Category 2 based on tumour data from a structural analogue together with substantial support from consideration of other important factors such as formation of common significant metabolites, e.g. for benzidine congener dyes.

3.6.2.5.5   The classification should also take into consideration whether or not the substance is absorbed by a given route(s); or whether there are only local tumours at the site of administration for the tested route(s), and adequate testing by other major route(s) show lack of carcinogenicity.

3.6.2.5.6   It is important that whatever is known of the physico-chemical, toxicokinetic and toxicodynamic properties of the substances, as well as any available relevant information on chemical analogues, i.e. structure activity relationship, is taken into consideration when undertaking classification.

3.6.2.6   It is realized that some regulatory authorities may need flexibility beyond that developed in the hazard classification scheme. For inclusion into Safety Data Sheets, positive results in any carcinogenicity study performed according to good scientific principles with statistically significant results may be considered.

3.6.2.7   The relative hazard potential of a chemical is a function of its intrinsic potency. There is great variability in potency among chemicals, and it may be important to account for these potency differences. The work that remains to be done is to examine methods for potency estimation Carcinogenic potency as used here does not preclude risk assessment. The proceedings of a WHO/IPCS workshop on the *Harmonization of Risk Assessment for Carcinogenicity and Mutagenicity (Germ cells)-A Scoping Meeting (1995, Carshalton, UK)*, points to a number of scientific questions arising for classification of chemicals, e.g. mouse liver tumours, peroxisome proliferation, receptor-mediated reactions, chemicals which are carcinogenic only at toxic doses and which do not demonstrate mutagenicity. Accordingly, there is a need to articulate the principles necessary to resolve these scientific issues which have led to diverging classifications in the past. Once these issues are resolved, there would be a firm foundation for classification of a number of chemical carcinogens.

3.6.3   Classification criteria for mixtures

3.6.3.1   *Classification of mixtures when data are available for the complete mixture*

Classification of mixtures will be based on the available test data of the individual ingredients of the mixture using cut-off values/concentration limits for those ingredients. The classification may be modified on a case-by-case basis based on the available test data for the mixture as a whole. In such cases, the test results for the mixture as a whole must be shown to be conclusive taking into account dose and other factors such as duration, observations and analysis (e.g. statistical analysis, test sensitivity) of carcinogenicity test systems. Adequate documentation supporting the classification should be retained and made available for review upon request.

3.6.3.2   *Classification of mixtures when data are not available for the complete mixture: bridging principles*

3.6.3.2.1   Where the mixture itself has not been tested to determine its carcinogenic hazard, but there are sufficient data on both the individual ingredients and similar tested mixtures to adequately characterize the hazards of the mixture, these data will be used in accordance with the following agreed bridging principles. This ensures that the classification process uses the available data to the greatest extent possible in characterizing the hazards of the mixture without the necessity for additional testing in animals.

3.6.3.2.2   *Dilution*

If a tested mixture is diluted with a diluent that is not expected to affect the carcinogenicity of other ingredients, then the new diluted mixture may be classified as equivalent to the original tested mixture.

3.6.3.2.3   *Batching*

The carcinogenic potential of a tested production batch of a mixture can be assumed to be substantially equivalent to that of another untested production batch of the same commercial product, when produced by or under the control of the same manufacturer unless there is reason to believe there is significant variation in composition such that the carcinogenic potential of the untested batch has changed. If the latter occurs, a new classification is necessary.

3.6.3.2.4   *Substantially similar mixtures*

Given the following:

(a)   Two mixtures: (i)   A + B;
                        (ii)   C + B;

(b)   The concentration of carcinogen ingredient B is the same in both mixtures;

(c)   The concentration of ingredient A in mixture (i) equals that of ingredient C in mixture (ii);

(d)   Data on toxicity for A and C are available and substantially equivalent, i.e. they are in the same hazard category and are not expected to affect the carcinogenicity of B.

If mixture (i) or (ii) is already classified by testing, then the other mixture can be assigned the same hazard category.

3.6.3.3   *Classification of mixtures when data are available for all ingredients or only for some ingredients of the mixture*

The mixture will be classified as a carcinogen when at least one ingredient has been classified as a Category 1 or Category 2 carcinogen and is present at or above the appropriate cut-off value/concentration limit as shown in Table 3.6.1 for Category 1 and 2 respectively.

Table 3.6.1: Cut-off values/concentration limits of ingredients of a mixture classified as carcinogen that would trigger classification of the mixture [a]

Ingredient classified as:	Cut-off/concentration limits triggering classification of a mixture as:		
	Category 1 carcinogen		Category 2 carcinogen
	Category 1A	Category 1B	
Category 1A carcinogen	≥ 0.1 %	--	--
Category 1B carcinogen	--	≥ 0.1 %	
Category 2 carcinogen	--	--	≥ 0.1% (note 1)
			≥ 1.0% (note 2)

[a]   *This compromise classification scheme involves consideration of differences in hazard communication practices in existing systems. It is expected that the number of affected mixtures will be small; the differences will be limited to label warnings; and the situation will evolve over time to a more harmonized approach.*

***NOTE 1**:   If a Category 2 carcinogen ingredient is present in the mixture at a concentration between 0.1% and 1%, every regulatory authority would require information on the SDS for a product. However, a* *label warning would be optional. Some authorities will choose to label when the ingredient is present in the mixture between 0.1% and 1%, whereas others would normally not require a label in this case.*

NOTE 2: *If a Category 2 carcinogen ingredient is present in the mixture at a concentration of $\geq 1\%$, both an SDS and a label would generally be expected.*

3.6.4 Hazard communication

General and specific considerations concerning labelling requirements are provided in *Hazard communication: Labelling* (Chapter 1.4). Annex 1 contains summary tables about classification and labelling. Annex 3 contains examples of precautionary statements and pictograms which can be used where allowed by the competent authority. Table 3.6.2 below presents specific label elements for substances and mixtures that are classified as carcinogenic based on the criteria set forth in this chapter.

Table 3.6.2: Label elements for carcinogenicity

	Category 1 (Category 1A, 1B)	Category 2
Symbol	Health hazard	Health hazard
Signal word	Danger	Warning
Hazard statement	May cause cancer (state route of exposure if it is conclusively proven that no other routes of exposure cause the hazard)	Suspected of causing cancer (state route of exposure if it is conclusively proven that no other routes of exposure cause the hazard)

3.6.5 **Decision logic and guidance**

The decision logics which follow is not part of the harmonized classification system but is provided here as additional guidance. It is strongly recommended that the person responsible for classification study the criteria before and during use of the decision logic.

3.6.5.1 *Decision logic 3.6.1 for substances*

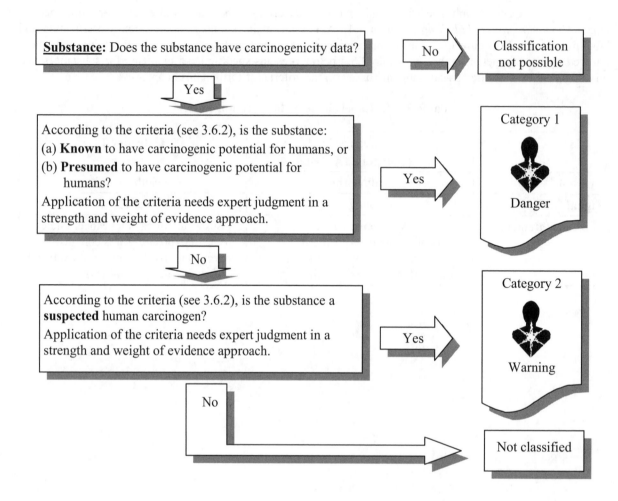

3.6.5.2   *Decision logic 3.6.2 for mixtures*

Mixture:
Classification of mixtures will be based on the available test data for the **individual ingredients** of the mixture, using cut-off values/concentration limits for those ingredients. The classification may be **modified on a case-by-case basis** based on the available test data for the mixture as a whole or based on bridging principles. See modified classification on a case-by-case basis below. For further details see criteria in 3.6.2.7 and 3.6.3.1 to 3.6.3.2.

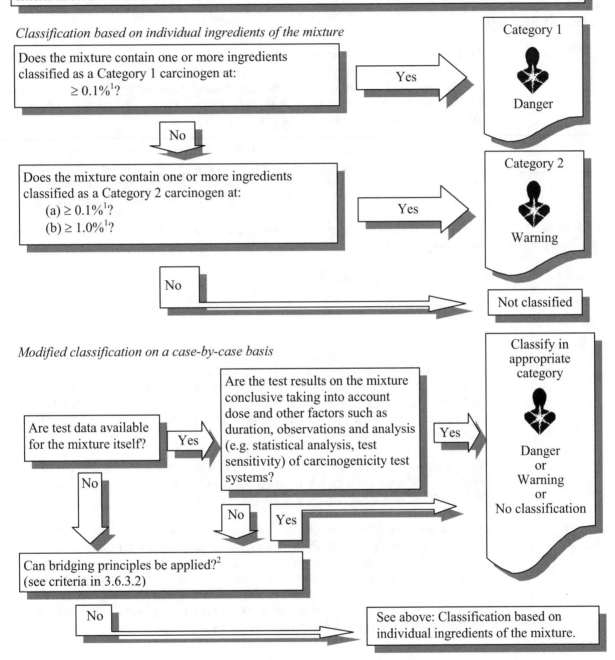

Classification based on individual ingredients of the mixture

Does the mixture contain one or more ingredients classified as a Category 1 carcinogen at:
$\geq 0.1\%^{1}$?

→ Yes → **Category 1** / Danger

No ↓

Does the mixture contain one or more ingredients classified as a Category 2 carcinogen at:
(a) $\geq 0.1\%^{1}$?
(b) $\geq 1.0\%^{1}$?

→ Yes → **Category 2** / Warning

No → Not classified

Modified classification on a case-by-case basis

Are test data available for the mixture itself? → Yes → Are the test results on the mixture conclusive taking into account dose and other factors such as duration, observations and analysis (e.g. statistical analysis, test sensitivity) of carcinogenicity test systems? → Yes → **Classify in appropriate category** / Danger or Warning or No classification

No ↓   No ↓   Yes →

Can bridging principles be applied?[2] (see criteria in 3.6.3.2)

No → See above: Classification based on individual ingredients of the mixture.

---

[1]   *For specific concentration limits, see "The use of cut-off values/concentration limits" in Chapter 1.3, para. 1.3.3.2 and in Table 3.6.1 of this Chapter.*

[2]   *If data of another mixture are used in the application of bridging principles, the data on that mixture must be conclusive in accordance with 3.6.3.2.*

3.6.5.3   *Background guidance*

3.6.5.3.1   Excerpts[3] from monographs of the International Agency for Research on Cancer (IARC) *Monographs programme on the evaluation of the strength of evidence of carcinogenic risks to humans* follow as in 3.6.5.3.1.1 and 3.6.5.3.1.2[4].

3.6.5.3.1.1   *Carcinogenicity in humans*

3.6.5.3.1.1.1   The evidence relevant to carcinogenicity from studies in humans is classified into one of the following categories:

> (a)   Sufficient evidence of carcinogenicity: the working group considers that a causal relationship has been established between exposure to the agent, mixture or exposure circumstance and human cancer. That is, a positive relationship has been observed between the exposure and cancer in studies in which chance, bias and confounding could be ruled out with reasonable confidence;

> (b)   Limited evidence of carcinogenicity: A positive association has been observed between exposure to the agent, mixture or exposure circumstance and cancer for which a causal interpretation is considered by the working group to be credible, but chance, bias or confounding could not be ruled out with reasonable confidence.

3.6.5.3.1.1.2   In some instances the above categories may be used to classify the degree of evidence related to carcinogenicity in specific organs or tissues.

3.6.5.3.1.2   *Carcinogenicity in experimental animals*

The evidence relevant to carcinogenicity in experimental animals is classified into one of the following categories:

> a)   Sufficient evidence of carcinogenicity: The working group considers that a causal relationship has been established between the agent or mixture and an increased incidence of malignant neoplasms or of an appropriate combination of benign and malignant neoplasms in (i) two or more species of animals or (ii) in two or more independent studies in one species carried out at different times or in different laboratories or under different protocols;

> (b)   Exceptionally, a single study in one species might be considered to provide sufficient evidence of carcinogenicity when malignant neoplasms occur to an unusual degree with regard to incidence, site, type of tumour or age at onset;

> (c)   Limited evidence of carcinogenicity: the data suggest a carcinogenic effect but are limited for making a definitive evaluation because, e.g. (i) the evidence of carcinogenicity is restricted to a single experiment; or (ii) there are unresolved questions regarding the adequacy of the design, conduct or interpretation of the study; or (iii) the agent or mixture increases the incidence only of benign neoplasms or lesions of uncertain neoplastic potential, or of certain neoplasms which may occur spontaneously in high incidences in certain strains.

---

[3]   *The excerpts from IARC Monographs, which follow, are taken from the OECD Integrated Document on Harmonization of Classification and Labelling. They are not part of the agreed text on the harmonized classification system developed by the OECD Task Force-HCL, but are provided here as additional guidance.*

[4]   *See 3.6.2.4.*

3.6.5.3.2   *Guidance on how to consider important factors in classification of carcinogenicity**

The guidance provides an approach to analysis rather than hard and fast rules. This section provides some considerations. The weight of evidence analysis called for in GHS is an integrative approach which considers important factors in determining carcinogenic potential along with the strength of evidence analysis. The IPCS "*Conceptual Framework for Evaluating a Mode of Action for Chemical carcinogenesis*" (2001), the International Life Sciences Institute (ILSI) "*Framework for Human Relevance Analysis of Information on Carcinogenic Modes of Action*" (Meek et al., 2003; Cohen et al., 2003, 2004) and the IARC (Preamble section 12(b)) provide a basis for systematic assessments which may be performed in a consistent fashion internationally; the IPCS also convened a panel in 2004 to further develop and clarify the human relevance framework. However, the internationally available documents are not intended to dictate answers, nor provide lists of criteria to be checked off.

3.6.5.3.2.1   Mode of action

The various international documents on carcinogen assessment all note that mode of action in and of itself, or consideration of comparative metabolism, should be evaluated on a case-by-case basis and are part of an analytic evaluative approach. One must look closely at any mode of action in animal experiments taking into consideration comparative toxicokinetics/toxicodynamics between the animal test species and humans to determine the relevance of the results to humans. This may lead to the possibility of discounting very specific effects of certain types of chemicals. Life stage-dependent effects on cellular differentiation may also lead to qualitative differences between animals and humans. Only if a mode of action of tumour development is conclusively determined not to be operative in humans may the carcinogenic evidence for that tumour be discounted. However, a weight of evidence evaluation for a substance calls for any other tumorigenic activity to be evaluated as well.

3.6.5.3.2.2   Responses in multiple animal experiments

Positive responses in several species add to the weight of evidence, that a chemical is a carcinogen. Taking into account all of the factors listed in 3.6.2.5.2 and more, such chemicals with positive outcomes in two or more species would be provisionally considered to be classified in GHS Category 1B until human relevance of animal results are assessed in their entirety. It should be noted, however, that positive results for one species in at least two independent studies, or a single positive study showing unusually strong evidence of malignancy may also lead to Category 1B.

3.6.5.3.2.3   Responses are in one sex or both sexes

Any case of gender-specific tumours should be evaluated in light of the total tumorigenic response to the substance observed at other sites (multi-site responses or incidence above background) in determining the carcinogenic potential of the substance.

If tumours are seen only in one sex of an animal species, the mode of action should be carefully evaluated to see if the response is consistent with the postulated mode of action. Effects seen only in one sex in a test species may be less convincing than effects seen in both sexes, unless there is a clear patho-physiological difference consistent with the mode of action to explain the single sex response.

3.6.5.3.2.4   Confounding effects of excessive toxicity or localized effects

Tumours occurring only at excessive doses associated with severe toxicity generally have doubtful potential for carcinogenicity in humans. In addition, tumours occurring only at sites of contact and/or only at excessive doses need to be carefully evaluated for human relevance for carcinogenic hazard. For example, forestomach tumours, following administration by gavage of an irritating or corrosive, non-mutagenic chemical, may be of questionable relevance. However, such determinations must be evaluated carefully in justifying the carcinogenic potential for humans; any occurrence of other tumours at distant sites must also be considered.

3.6.5.3.2.5   Tumour type, reduced tumour latency

Unusual tumour types or tumours occurring with reduced latency may add to the weight of evidence for the carcinogenic potential of a substance, even if the tumours are not statistically significant.

Toxicokinetic behaviour is normally assumed to be similar in animals and humans, at least from a qualitative perspective. On the other hand, certain tumour types in animals may be associated with toxicokinetics or toxicodynamics that are unique to the animal species tested and may not be predictive of carcinogenicity in humans. Very few such examples have been agreed internationally. However, one example is the lack of human relevance of kidney tumours in male rats associated with compounds causing α2u-globulin nephropathy (IARC, Scientific Publication N° 147). Even when a particular tumour type may be discounted, expert judgment must be used in assessing the total tumour profile in any animal experiment.

---

*   *References:*

Cohen, S.M., J. Klaunig, M.E. Meek, R.N. Hill, T. Pastoor, L. Lehman-McKeeman, J. Bucher, D.G. Longfellow, J. Seed, V. Dellarco, P. Fenner-Crisp, and D. Patton. 2004. Evaluating the human relevance of chemically induced animal tumors. Toxicol. Sci., 78(2): 181-186.

Cohen, S.M., M.E. Mkke, J.E. Klaunig, D.E. Patton, P.A. Fenner-Crisp. 2003. The human relevance of information on carcinogenic modes of action: overview. Crit. Rev. Toxicol. 33(6), 581-9.

Meek, M.E., J.R. Bucher, S.M. Cohen, V. Dellarco, R.N. Hill, L. Lehman-McKeeman, D.G. Longfellow, T. Pastoor, J. Seed, D.E. Patton. 2003. A framework for human relevance analysis of information on carcinogenic modes of action. Crit. Rev.Toxicol., 33(6), 591-653.

Sonich-Mullin, C., R. Fielder, J. Wiltse, K. Baetcke, J. Dempsey, P. Fenner-Crisp, D. Grant, M. Hartley, A. Knapp, D. Kroese, I. Mangelsdorf, E. Meek, J.M. Rice, and M. Younes. 2001. The Conceptual Framework for Evaluating a Mode of Action for Chemical Carcinogenesis. Reg. Tox. Pharm. 34, 146-152.

International Programme on Chemical Safety Harmonization Group. 2004 Report of the First Meeting of the Cancer Working Group. World Health Organization. Report IPCS/HSC-CWG-1/04. Geneva

International Agency for Research on Cancer. IARC Monographs on the Evaluation of Carcinogenic Risks to Human. Preambles to volumes. World Health Organization. Lyon, France.

S.M. Cohen, P.A.Fenner-Crisp, and D.E. Patton. 2003. Special Issue: Cancer Modes of Action and Human Relevance. Critical Reviews in Toxicology, R.O. McClellan, ed., Volume 33/Issue 6. CRC Press.

C.C. Capen, E. Dybing and J.D. Wilbourn. 1999. Species differences in Thyroid, Kidney and Urinary Bladder Carcinogenesis. International Agency for Research on Cancer, Scientific Publication N° 147.

CHAPTER 3.7

REPRODUCTIVE TOXICITY

3.7.1 Definitions and general considerations

3.7.1.1 *Reproductive toxicity*

Reproductive toxicity includes adverse effects on sexual function and fertility in adult males and females, as well as developmental toxicity in the offspring. The definitions presented below are adapted from those agreed as working definitions in IPCS/EHC Document N°225 Principles for evaluating health risks to reproduction associated with exposure to chemicals. For classification purposes, the known induction of genetically based inheritable effects in the offspring is addressed in *Germ cell mutagenicity* (Chapter 3.5), since in the present classification system it is considered more appropriate to address such effects under the separate hazard class of germ cell mutagenicity.

In this classification system, reproductive toxicity is subdivided under two main headings:

(a)   Adverse effects on sexual function and fertility;

(b)   Adverse effects on development of the offspring.

Some reproductive toxic effects cannot be clearly assigned to either impairment of sexual function and fertility or to developmental toxicity. Nonetheless, chemicals with these effects would be classified as reproductive toxicants with a general hazard statement.

3.7.1.2 *Adverse effects on sexual function and fertility*

Any effect of chemicals that would interfere with sexual function and fertility. This may include, but not be limited to, alterations to the female and male reproductive system, adverse effects on onset of puberty, gamete production and transport, reproductive cycle normality, sexual behaviour, fertility, parturition, pregnancy outcomes, premature reproductive senescence, or modifications in other functions that are dependent on the integrity of the reproductive systems.

Adverse effects on or via lactation are also included in reproductive toxicity, but for classification purposes, such effects are treated separately (see 3.7.2.1). This is because it is desirable to be able to classify chemicals specifically for an adverse effect on lactation so that a specific hazard warning about this effect can be provided for lactating mothers.

3.7.1.3 *Adverse effects on development of the offspring*

Taken in its widest sense, developmental toxicity includes any effect which interferes with normal development of the conceptus, either before or after birth, and resulting from exposure of either parent prior to conception, or exposure of the developing offspring during prenatal development, or postnatally, to the time of sexual maturation. However, it is considered that classification under the heading of developmental toxicity is primarily intended to provide a hazard warning for pregnant women and men and women of reproductive capacity. Therefore, for pragmatic purposes of classification, developmental toxicity essentially means adverse effects induced during pregnancy, or as a result of parental exposure. These effects can be manifested at any point in the life span of the organism. The major manifestations of developmental toxicity include death of the developing organism, structural abnormality, altered growth and functional deficiency.

3.7.2   *Classification criteria for substances*

3.7.2.1   *Hazard categories*

For the purpose of classification for reproductive toxicity, substances are allocated to one of two categories. Effects on sexual function and fertility, and on development, are considered. In addition, effects on lactation are allocated to a separate hazard category.

Figure 3.7.1 (a): Hazard categories for reproductive toxicants

<u>**CATEGORY 1:**</u>	**Known or presumed human reproductive toxicant** This category includes substances which are known to have produced an adverse effect on sexual function and fertility or on development in humans or for which there is evidence from animal studies, possibly supplemented with other information, to provide a strong presumption that the substance has the capacity to interfere with reproduction in humans. For regulatory purposes, a substance can be further distinguished on the basis of whether the evidence for classification is primarily from human data (<u>Category 1A</u>) or from animal data (<u>Category 1B</u>).
<u>**CATEGORY 1A:**</u>	**Known human reproductive toxicant** The placing of the substance in this category is largely based on evidence from humans.
<u>**CATEGORY 1B:**</u>	**Presumed human reproductive toxicant** The placing of the substance in this category is largely based on evidence from experimental animals. Data from animal studies should provide clear evidence of an adverse effect on sexual function and fertility or on development in the absence of other toxic effects, or if occurring together with other toxic effects the adverse effect on reproduction is considered not to be a secondary non-specific consequence of other toxic effects. However, when there is mechanistic information that raises doubt about the relevance of the effect for humans, classification in Category 2 may be more appropriate.
<u>**CATEGORY 2:**</u>	**Suspected human reproductive toxicant** This category includes substances for which there is some evidence from humans or experimental animals, possibly supplemented with other information, of an adverse effect on sexual function and fertility, or on development, in the absence of other toxic effects, or if occurring together with other toxic effects the adverse effect on reproduction is considered not to be a secondary non-specific consequence of the other toxic effects, and where the evidence is not sufficiently convincing to place the substance in Category 1. For instance, deficiencies in the study may make the quality of evidence less convincing, and in view of this Category 2 could be the more appropriate classification.

Figure 3.7.1 (b): Hazard category for effects on or via lactation

---

EFFECTS ON OR VIA LACTATION

Effects on or via lactation are allocated to a separate single category. It is appreciated that for many substances there is no information on the potential to cause adverse effects on the offspring via lactation. However, substances which are absorbed by women and have been shown to interfere with lactation, or which may be present (including metabolites) in breast milk in amounts sufficient to cause concern for the health of a breastfed child, should be classified to indicate this property hazardous to breastfed babies. This classification can be assigned on the basis of:

(a) absorption, metabolism, distribution and excretion studies that would indicate the likelihood the substance would be present in potentially toxic levels in breast milk; and/or

(b) results of one or two generation studies in animals which provide clear evidence of adverse effect in the offspring due to transfer in the milk or adverse effect on the quality of the milk; and/or

(c) human evidence indicating a hazard to babies during the lactation period.

3.7.2.2   Basis of classification

3.7.2.2.1   Classification is made on the basis of the appropriate criteria, outlined above, and an assessment of the total weight of evidence. Classification as a reproductive toxicant is intended to be used for chemicals which have an intrinsic, specific property to produce an adverse effect on reproduction and chemicals should not be so classified if such an effect is produced solely as a non-specific secondary consequence of other toxic effects.

3.7.2.2.2   In the evaluation of toxic effects on the developing offspring, it is important to consider the possible influence of maternal toxicity.

3.7.2.2.3   For human evidence to provide the primary basis for a Category 1A classification there must be reliable evidence of an adverse effect on reproduction in humans. Evidence used for classification should ideally be from well conducted epidemiological studies which include the use of appropriate controls, balanced assessment, and due consideration of bias or confounding factors. Less rigorous data from studies in humans should be supplemented with adequate data from studies in experimental animals and classification in Category 1B should be considered.

3.7.2.3   *Weight of evidence*

3.7.2.3.1   Classification as a reproductive toxicant is made on the basis of an assessment of the total weight of evidence. This means that all available information that bears on the determination of reproductive toxicity is considered together. Included is information such as epidemiological studies and case reports in humans and specific reproduction studies along with sub-chronic, chronic and special study results in animals that provide relevant information regarding toxicity to reproductive and related endocrine organs. Evaluation of substances chemically related to the material under study may also be included, particularly when information on the material is scarce. The weight given to the available evidence will be influenced by factors such as the quality of the studies, consistency of results, nature and severity of effects, level of statistical significance for intergroup differences, number of endpoints affected, relevance of route of administration to humans and freedom from bias. Both positive and negative results are assembled together into a weight of evidence determination. However, a single, positive study performed according to good scientific principles and with statistically or biologically significant positive results may justify classification (see also 3.7.2.2.3).

3.7.2.3.2   Toxicokinetic studies in animals and humans, site of action and mechanism or mode of action study results may provide relevant information, which could reduce or increase concerns about the hazard to human health. If it can be conclusively demonstrated that the clearly identified mechanism or mode of action has no relevance for humans or when the toxicokinetic differences are so marked that it is certain that the hazardous property will not be expressed in humans then a substance which produces an adverse effect on reproduction in experimental animals should not be classified.

3.7.2.3.3 In some reproductive toxicity studies in experimental animals the only effects recorded may be considered of low or minimal toxicological significance and classification may not necessarily be the outcome. These include for example small changes in semen parameters or in the incidence of spontaneous defects in the foetus, small changes in the proportions of common foetal variants such as are observed in skeletal examinations, or in foetal weights, or small differences in postnatal developmental assessments.

3.7.2.3.4 Data from animal studies ideally should provide clear evidence of specific reproductive toxicity in the absence of other, systemic, toxic effects. However, if developmental toxicity occurs together with other toxic effects in the dam, the potential influence of the generalized adverse effects should be assessed to the extent possible. The preferred approach is to consider adverse effects in the embryo/foetus first, and then evaluate maternal toxicity, along with any other factors, which are likely to have influenced these effects, as part of the weight of evidence. In general, developmental effects that are observed at maternally toxic doses should not be automatically discounted. Discounting developmental effects that are observed at maternally toxic doses can only be done on a case-by-case basis when a causal relationship is established or refuted.

3.7.2.3.5 If appropriate information is available it is important to try to determine whether developmental toxicity is due to a specific maternally mediated mechanism or to a non-specific secondary mechanism, like maternal stress and the disruption of homeostasis. Generally, the presence of maternal toxicity should not be used to negate findings of embryo/foetal effects, unless it can be clearly demonstrated that the effects are secondary non-specific effects. This is especially the case when the effects in the offspring are significant, e.g. irreversible effects such as structural malformations. In some situations it is reasonable to assume that reproductive toxicity is due to a secondary consequence of maternal toxicity and discount the effects, for example if the chemical is so toxic that dams fail to thrive and there is severe inanition; they are incapable of nursing pups; or they are prostrate or dying.

3.7.2.4 *Maternal toxicity*

3.7.2.4.1 Development of the offspring throughout gestation and during the early postnatal stages can be influenced by toxic effects in the mother either through non-specific mechanisms related to stress and the disruption of maternal homeostasis, or by specific maternally-mediated mechanisms. So, in the interpretation of the developmental outcome to decide classification for developmental effects it is important to consider the possible influence of maternal toxicity. This is a complex issue because of uncertainties surrounding the relationship between maternal toxicity and developmental outcome. Expert judgement and a weight of evidence approach, using all available studies, should be used to determine the degree of influence that should be attributed to maternal toxicity when interpreting the criteria for classification for developmental effects. The adverse effects in the embryo/foetus should be first considered, and then maternal toxicity, along with any other factors which are likely to have influenced these effects, as weight of evidence, to help reach a conclusion about classification.

3.7.2.4.2 Based on pragmatic observation, it is believed that maternal toxicity may, depending on severity, influence development via non-specific secondary mechanisms, producing effects such as depressed foetal weight, retarded ossification, and possibly resorptions and certain malformations in some strains of certain species. However, the limited numbers of studies which have investigated the relationship between developmental effects and general maternal toxicity have failed to demonstrate a consistent, reproducible relationship across species. Developmental effects, which occur even in the presence of maternal toxicity are considered to be evidence of developmental toxicity, unless it can be unequivocally demonstrated on a case by case basis that the developmental effects are secondary to maternal toxicity. Moreover, classification should be considered where there is significant toxic effect in the offspring, e.g. irreversible effects such as structural malformations, embryo/foetal lethality, significant post-natal functional deficiencies.

3.7.2.4.3 Classification should not automatically be discounted for chemicals that produce developmental toxicity only in association with maternal toxicity, even if a specific maternally-mediated mechanism has been demonstrated. In such a case, classification in Category 2 may be considered more appropriate than Category 1. However, when a chemical is so toxic that maternal death or severe inanition results, or the dams are prostrate and incapable of nursing the pups, it may be reasonable to assume that developmental toxicity is produced solely as a secondary consequence of maternal toxicity and discount the developmental effects. Classification may not necessarily be the outcome in the case of minor developmental changes e.g. small reduction in foetal/pup body weight, retardation of ossification when seen in association with maternal toxicity.

3.7.2.4.4   Some of the end-points used to assess maternal toxicity are provided below. Data on these end points, if available, need to be evaluated in light of their statistical or biological significance and dose response relationship.

(a)   Maternal mortality: an increased incidence of mortality among the treated dams over the controls should be considered evidence of maternal toxicity if the increase occurs in a dose-related manner and can be attributed to the systemic toxicity of the test material. Maternal mortality greater than 10% is considered excessive and the data for that dose level should not normally be considered for further evaluation.

(b)   Mating index (N° animals with seminal plugs or sperm/N° mated × 100)[1]

(c)   Fertility index (N° animals with implants/N° of matings × 100)[1]

(d)   Gestation length (if allowed to deliver)

(e)   Body weight and body weight change: consideration of the maternal body weight change and/or adjusted (corrected) maternal body weight should be included in the evaluation of maternal toxicity whenever such data are available. The calculation of an adjusted (corrected) mean maternal body weight change, which is the difference between the initial and terminal body weight minus the gravid uterine weight (or alternatively, the sum of the weights of the foetuses), may indicate whether the effect is maternal or intrauterine. In rabbits, the body weight gain may not be useful indicators of maternal toxicity because of normal fluctuations in body weight during pregnancy.

(f)   Food and water consumption (if relevant): the observation of a significant decrease in the average food or water consumption in treated dams compared to the control group may be useful in evaluating maternal toxicity, particularly when the test material is administered in the diet or drinking water. Changes in food or water consumption should be evaluated in conjunction with maternal body weights when determining if the effects noted are reflective of maternal toxicity or more simply, unpalatability of the test material in feed or water.

(g)   Clinical evaluations (including clinical signs, markers, haematology and clinical chemistry studies): The observation of increased incidence of significant clinical signs of toxicity in treated dams relative to the control group may be useful in evaluating maternal toxicity. If this is to be used as the basis for the assessment of maternal toxicity, the types, incidence, degree and duration of clinical signs should be reported in the study. Examples of frank clinical signs of maternal intoxication include: coma, prostration, hyperactivity, loss of righting reflex, ataxia, or laboured breathing.

(h)   Post-mortem data: increased incidence and/or severity of post-mortem findings may be indicative of maternal toxicity. This can include gross or microscopic pathological findings or organ weight data, e.g. absolute organ weight, organ-to-body weight ratio, or organ-to-brain weight ratio. When supported by findings of adverse histopathological effects in the affected organ(s), the observation of a significant change in the average weight of suspected target organ(s) of treated dams, compared to those in the control group, may be considered evidence of maternal toxicity.

---

[1]   *It is recognized that this index can also be affected by the male.*

3.7.2.5   *Animal and experimental data*

3.7.2.5.1   A number of internationally accepted test methods are available; these include methods for developmental toxicity testing (e.g. OECD Test Guideline 414, ICH Guideline S5A, 1993), methods for peri- and post-natal toxicity testing (e.g. ICH S5B, 1995) and methods for one or two-generation toxicity testing (e.g. OECD Test Guidelines 415, 416).

3.7.2.5.2   Results obtained from Screening Tests (e.g. OECD Guidelines 421 - Reproduction/ Developmental Toxicity Screening Test, and 422 - Combined Repeated Dose Toxicity Study with Reproduction/Development Toxicity Screening Test) can also be used to justify classification, although it is recognized that the quality of this evidence is less reliable than that obtained through full studies.

3.7.2.5.3   Adverse effects or changes, seen in short- or long-term repeated dose toxicity studies, which are judged likely to impair reproductive function and which occur in the absence of significant generalized toxicity, may be used as a basis for classification, e.g. histopathological changes in the gonads.

3.7.2.5.4   Evidence from *in vitro* assays, or non-mammalian tests, and from analogous substances using structure-activity relationship (SAR), can contribute to the procedure for classification. In all cases of this nature, expert judgement must be used to assess the adequacy of the data. Inadequate data should not be used as a primary support for classification.

3.7.2.5.5   It is preferable that animal studies are conducted using appropriate routes of administration which relate to the potential route of human exposure. However, in practice, reproductive toxicity studies are commonly conducted using the oral route, and such studies will normally be suitable for evaluating the hazardous properties of the substance with respect to reproductive toxicity. However, if it can be conclusively demonstrated that the clearly identified mechanism or mode of action has no relevance for humans or when the toxicokinetic differences are so marked that it is certain that the hazardous property will not be expressed in humans then a substance which produces an adverse effect on reproduction in experimental animals should not be classified.

3.7.2.5.6   Studies involving routes of administration such as intravenous or intraperitoneal injection, which may result in exposure of the reproductive organs to unrealistically high levels of the test substance, or elicit local damage to the reproductive organs, e.g. by irritation, must be interpreted with extreme caution and on their own would not normally be the basis for classification.

3.7.2.5.7   There is general agreement about the concept of a limit dose, above which the production of an adverse effect may be considered to be outside the criteria which lead to classification. However, there was no agreement within the OECD Task Force regarding the inclusion within the criteria of a specified dose as a limit dose. Some Test Guidelines specify a limit dose, other Test Guidelines qualify the limit dose with a statement that higher doses may be necessary if anticipated human exposure is sufficiently high that an adequate margin of exposure would not be achieved. Also, due to species differences in toxicokinetics, establishing a specific limit dose may not be adequate for situations where humans are more sensitive than the animal model.

3.7.2.5.8   In principle, adverse effects on reproduction seen only at very high dose levels in animal studies (for example doses that induce prostration, severe inappetence, excessive mortality) would not normally lead to classification, unless other information is available, e.g. toxicokinetics information indicating that humans may be more susceptible than animals, to suggest that classification is appropriate. Please also refer to the section on Maternal Toxicity for further guidance in this area.

3.7.2.5.9   However, specification of the actual "limit dose" will depend upon the test method that has been employed to provide the test results, e.g. in the OECD Test Guideline for repeated dose toxicity studies by the oral route, an upper dose of 1000 mg/kg unless expected human response indicates the need for a higher dose level, has been recommended as a limit dose.

3.7.2.5.10   Further discussions are needed on the inclusion within the criteria of a specified dose as a limit dose.

3.7.3   **Classification criteria for mixtures**

3.7.3.1   *Classification of mixtures when data are available for the complete mixture*

Classification of mixtures will be based on the available test data of the individual constituents of the mixture using cut-off values/concentration limits for the ingredients of the mixture. The classification may be modified on a case-by-case basis based on the available test data for the mixture as a whole. In such cases, the test results for the mixture as a whole must be shown to be conclusive taking into account dose and other factors such as duration, observations and analysis (e.g. statistical analysis, test sensitivity) of reproduction test systems. Adequate documentation supporting the classification should be retained and made available for review upon request.

3.7.3.2   *Classification of mixtures when data are not available for the complete mixture: bridging principles*

3.7.3.2.1   Where the mixture itself has not been tested to determine its reproductive toxicity, but there are sufficient data on both the individual ingredients and similar tested mixtures to adequately characterize the hazards of the mixture, these data will be used in accordance with the following agreed bridging rules. This ensures that the classification process uses the available data to the greatest extent possible in characterizing the hazards of the mixture without the necessity for additional testing in animals.

3.7.3.2.2   *Dilution*

If a tested mixture is diluted with a diluent which is not expected to affect the reproductive toxicity of other ingredients, then the new diluted mixture may be classified as equivalent to the original tested mixture.

3.7.3.2.3   *Batching*

The reproductive toxicity potential of a tested production batch of a mixture can be assumed to be substantially equivalent to that of another untested production batch of the same commercial product, when produced by or under the control of the same manufacturer unless there is reason to believe there is significant variation in composition such that the reproductive toxicity potential of the untested batch has changed. If the latter occurs, a new classification is necessary.

3.7.3.2.4   *Substantially similar mixtures*

Given the following:

(a)   Two mixtures: (i)   A + B;
                              (ii)   C + B;

(b)   The concentration of ingredient B, toxic to reproduction, is the same in both mixtures;

(c)   The concentration of ingredient A in mixture (i) equals that of ingredient C in mixture (ii);

(d)   Data on toxicity for A and C are available and substantially equivalent, i.e. they are in the same hazard category and are not expected to affect the reproductive toxicity of B.

If mixture (i) or (ii) is already classified by testing, then the other mixture can be assigned the same hazard category.

3.7.3.3 *Classification of mixtures when data are available for all ingredients or only for some ingredients of the mixture*

3.7.3.3.1 The mixture will be classified as a reproductive toxicant when at least one ingredient has been classified as a Category 1 or Category 2 reproductive toxicant and is present at or above the appropriate cut-off value/concentration limit as shown in Table 3.7.1 below for Category 1 and 2 respectively.

3.7.3.3.2 The mixture will be classified for effects on or via lactation when at least one ingredient has been classified for effects on or via lactation and is present at or above the appropriate cut-off value/concentration limit as shown in Table 3.7.1 for the additional category for effects on or via lactation.

Table 3.7.1: Cut-off values/concentration limits of ingredients of a mixture classified as reproductive toxicants or for effects on or via lactation that would trigger classification of the mixtures[a]

Ingredients classified as:	Cut-off/concentration limits triggering classification of a mixture as:			
	Category 1 reproductive toxicant		Category 2 reproductive toxicant	Additional category for effects on or via lactation
	Category 1A	Category 1B		
Category 1A reproductive toxicant	$\geq 0.1\%$ (note 1)	--	--	--
	$\geq 0.3\%$ (note 2)			
Category 1B reproductive toxicant	--	$\geq 0.1\%$ (note 1)	--	--
		$\geq 0.3\%$ (note 2)		
Category 2 reproductive toxicant	--	--	$\geq 0.1\%$ (note 3)	--
			$\geq 3.0\%$ (note 4)	
Additional category for effects on or via lactation	--	--	--	$\geq 0.1\%$ (note 1)
				$\geq 0.3\%$ (note 2)

[a] *This compromise classification scheme involves consideration of differences in hazard communication practices in existing systems. It is expected that the number of affected mixtures will be small; the differences will be limited to label warnings; and the situation will evolve over time to a more harmonized approach.*

NOTE 1: *If a Category 1 reproductive toxicant or substance classified in the additional category for effects on or via lactation is present in the mixture as an ingredient at a concentration between 0.1% and 0.3%, every regulatory authority would require information on the SDS for a product. However, a label warning would be optional. Some authorities will choose to label when the ingredient is present in the mixture between 0.1% and 0.3%, whereas others would normally not require a label in this case.*

NOTE 2: *If a Category 1 reproductive toxicant or substance classified in the additional category for effects on or via lactation is present in the mixture as an ingredient at a concentration of $\geq 0.3\%$, both an SDS and a label would generally be expected.*

NOTE 3: *If a Category 2 reproductive toxicant is present in the mixture as an ingredient at a concentration between 0.1% and 3.0%, every regulatory authority would require information on the SDS for a product. However, a label warning would be optional. Some authorities will choose to label when the ingredient is present in the mixture between 0.1% and 3.0%, whereas others would normally not require a label in this case.*

NOTE 4: *If a Category 2 reproductive toxicant is present in the mixture as an ingredient at a concentration of $\geq 3.0\%$, both an SDS and a label would generally be expected.*

3.7.4   **Hazard communication**

General and specific considerations concerning labelling requirements are provided in *Hazard communication: Labelling* (Chapter 1.4). Annex 1 contains summary tables about classification and labelling. Annex 3 contains examples of precautionary statements and pictograms which can be used where allowed by the competent authority.

Table 3.7.2: Label elements for reproductive toxicity

	Category 1 (Category 1A, 1B)	Category 2	Additional category for effects on or via lactation
Symbol	Health hazard	Health hazard	*No symbol*
Signal word	Danger	Warning	*No signal word*
Hazard statement	May damage fertility or the unborn child (state specific effect if known)(state route of exposure if it is conclusively proven that no other routes of exposure cause the hazard)	Suspected of damaging fertility or the unborn child (state specific effect if known) (state route of exposure if it is conclusively proven that no other routes of exposure cause the hazard)	May cause harm to breast-fed children.

3.7.5   **Decision logics for classification**

3.7.5.1   *Decision logic for reproductive toxicity*

     The decision logic which follows is not part of the harmonized classification system but is provided here as additional guidance. It is strongly recommended that the person responsible for classification study the criteria before and during use of the decision logic.

3.7.5.1.1   *Decision logic 3.7.1 for substances*

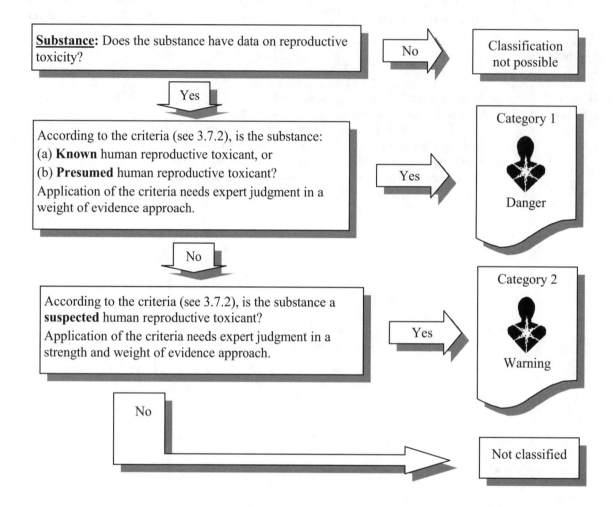

Mixture: Classification of mixtures will be based on the available test data for the **individual ingredients** of the mixture, using cut-off values/concentration limits for those ingredients. The classification may be **modified on a case-by-case basis** based on the available test data for the mixture as a whole or based on bridging principles. See modified classification on a case-by-case basis below. For further details see criteria in 3.7.3.1, 3.7.3.2 and 3.7.3.3.

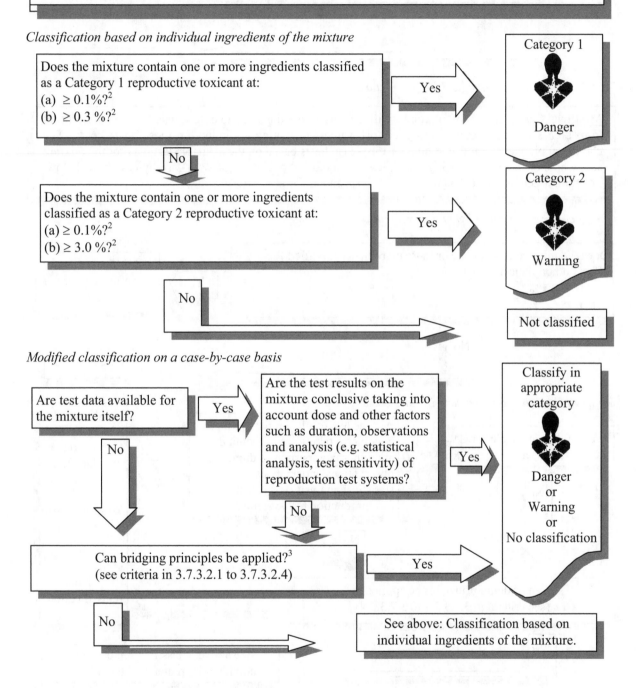

Classification based on individual ingredients of the mixture

Does the mixture contain one or more ingredients classified as a Category 1 reproductive toxicant at:
(a) $\geq 0.1\%?^2$
(b) $\geq 0.3\%?^2$

Yes → Category 1 — Danger

No

Does the mixture contain one or more ingredients classified as a Category 2 reproductive toxicant at:
(a) $\geq 0.1\%?^2$
(b) $\geq 3.0\%?^2$

Yes → Category 2 — Warning

No → Not classified

Modified classification on a case-by-case basis

Are test data available for the mixture itself?

Yes → Are the test results on the mixture conclusive taking into account dose and other factors such as duration, observations and analysis (e.g. statistical analysis, test sensitivity) of reproduction test systems?

Yes → Classify in appropriate category — Danger or Warning or No classification

No

No

Can bridging principles be applied?³ (see criteria in 3.7.3.2.1 to 3.7.3.2.4)

Yes →

No → See above: Classification based on individual ingredients of the mixture.

---

²   *For specific concentration limits, see "The use of cut-off values/concentration limits" in Chapter 1.3, para. 1.3.3.2, and in Table 3.7.1 of this Chapter.*

³   *If data on another mixture are used in the application of bridging principles, the data on that mixture must be conclusive in accordance with 3.7.3.2.*

3.7.5.2 *Decision logic for effects on or via lactation*

3.7.5.2.1 *Decision logic 3.7.3 for substances*

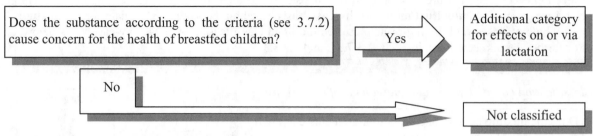

3.7.5.2.2 *Decision logic 3.7.4 for mixtures*

Mixture: Classification of mixtures will be based on the available test data for the **individual ingredients** of the mixture, using cut-off values/concentration limits for those ingredients. The classification may be **modified on a case-by-case basis** based on the available test data for the mixture as a whole or based on bridging principles. See modified classification on a case-by-case basis below. For further details see criteria in 3.7.3.1, 3.7.3.2 and 3.7.3.3.

Classification based on individual ingredients of the mixture

Modified classification on a case-by-case basis

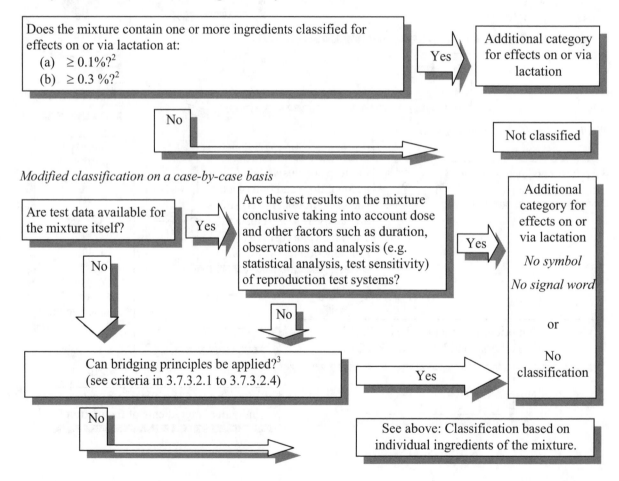

---

[2] *For specific concentration limits, see "The use of cut-off values/concentration limits" in Chapter 1.3, para. 1.3.3.2, and in Table 3.7.1 of this Chapter.*

[3] *If data on another mixture are used in the application of bridging principles, the data on that mixture must be conclusive in accordance with 3.7.3.2.*

CHAPTER 3.8

SPECIFIC TARGET ORGAN TOXICITY
SINGLE EXPOSURE

3.8.1 Definitions and general considerations

3.8.1.1 The purpose of this chapter is to provide a means of classifying substances and mixtures that produce specific, non lethal target organ toxicity arising from a single exposure. All significant health effects that can impair function, both reversible and irreversible, immediate and/or delayed and not specifically addressed in chapters 3.1 to 3.7 and 3.10 are included (see also para. 3.8.1.6).

3.8.1.2 Classification identifies the substance or mixture as being a specific target organ toxicant and, as such, it may present a potential for adverse health effects in people who are exposed to it.

3.8.1.3 Classification depends upon the availability of reliable evidence that a single exposure to the substance or mixture has produced a consistent and identifiable toxic effect in humans, or, in experimental animals, toxicologically significant changes which have affected the function or morphology of a tissue/organ, or has produced serious changes to the biochemistry or haematology of the organism and these changes are relevant for human health. It is recognized that human data will be the primary source of evidence for this hazard class.

3.8.1.4 Assessment should take into consideration not only significant changes in a single organ or biological system but also generalized changes of a less severe nature involving several organs.

3.8.1.5 Specific target organ toxicity can occur by any route that is relevant for humans, i.e. principally oral, dermal or inhalation.

3.8.1.6 Specific target organ toxicity following a repeated exposure is classified in the GHS as described in *Specific target organ toxicity – Repeated exposure* (Chapter 3.9) and is therefore excluded from the present chapter. Other specific toxic effects, listed below are assessed separately in the GHS and consequently are not included here:

    (a)   acute toxicity (Chapter 3.1);

    (b)   skin corrosion/irritation (Chapter 3.2);

    (c)   serious eye damage/eye irritation (Chapter 3.3);

    (d)   respiratory or skin sensitization (Chapter 3.4);

    (e)   germ cell mutagenicity (Chapter 3.5);

    (f)   carcinogenicity (Chapter 3.6);

    (g)   reproductive toxicity (Chapter 3.7); and

    (h)   aspiration toxicity (Chapter 3.10).

3.8.1.7 The classification criteria in this chapter are organized as criteria for substances Categories 1 and 2 (see 3.8.2.1), criteria for substances Category 3 (see 3.8.2.2) and criteria for mixtures (see 3.8.3). See also Figure 3.8.1.

3.8.2   **Classification criteria for substances**

3.8.2.1   *Substances of Category 1 and Category 2*

3.8.2.1.1   Substances are classified for immediate or delayed effects separately, by the use of expert judgement on the basis of the weight of all evidence available, including the use of recommended guidance values (see 3.8.2.1.9). Then substances are placed in Category 1 or 2, depending upon the nature and severity of the effect(s) observed (Figure 3.8.1).

Figure 3.8.1: Hazard categories for specific target organ toxicity following single exposure

<table>
<tr>
<td><u>CATEGORY 1:</u></td>
<td>Substances that have produced significant toxicity in humans, or that, on the basis of evidence from studies in experimental animals can be presumed to have the potential to produce significant toxicity in humans following single exposure

Placing a substance in Category 1 is done on the basis of:

(a) reliable and good quality evidence from human cases or epidemiological studies; or

(b) observations from appropriate studies in experimental animals in which significant and/or severe toxic effects of relevance to human health were produced at generally low exposure concentrations. Guidance dose/concentration values are provided below (see 3.8.2.1.9) to be used as part of weight-of-evidence evaluation.</td>
</tr>
<tr>
<td><u>CATEGORY 2:</u></td>
<td>Substances that, on the basis of evidence from studies in experimental animals can be presumed to have the potential to be harmful to human health following single exposure

Placing a substance in Category 2 is done on the basis of observations from appropriate studies in experimental animals in which significant toxic effects, of relevance to human health, were produced at generally moderate exposure concentrations. Guidance dose/concentration values are provided below (see 3.8.2.1.9) in order to help in classification.

In exceptional cases, human evidence can also be used to place a substance in Category 2 (see 3.8.2.1.9).</td>
</tr>
<tr>
<td><u>CATEGORY 3:</u></td>
<td>Transient target organ effects

There are target organ effects for which a substance/mixture may not meet the criteria to be classified in Categories 1 or 2 indicated above. These are effects which adversely alter human function for a short duration after exposure and from which humans may recover in a reasonable period without leaving significant alteration of structure or function. This category only includes narcotic effects and respiratory tract irritation. Substances/mixtures may be classified specifically for these effects as discussed in 3.8.2.2.</td>
</tr>
<tr>
<td colspan="2">NOTE: For these categories the specific target organ/system that has been primarily affected by the classified substance may be identified, or the substance may be identified as a general toxicant. Attempts should be made to determine the primary target organ/system of toxicity and classify for that purpose, e.g. hepatotoxicants, neurotoxicants. One should carefully evaluate the data and, where possible, not include secondary effects, e.g. a hepatotoxicant can produce secondary effects in the nervous or gastro-intestinal systems.</td>
</tr>
</table>

3.8.2.1.2   The relevant route of exposure by which the classified substance produces damage should be identified.

3.8.2.1.3   Classification is determined by expert judgement, on the basis of the weight of all evidence available including the guidance presented below.

3.8.2.1.4   Weight of evidence of all data, including human incidents, epidemiology, and studies conducted in experimental animals, is used to substantiate specific target organ toxic effects that merit classification.

3.8.2.1.5   The information required to evaluate specific target organ toxicity comes either from single exposure in humans, e.g. exposure at home, in the workplace or environmentally, or from studies conducted in experimental animals. The standard animal studies in rats or mice that provide this information are acute toxicity studies which can include clinical observations and detailed macroscopic and microscopic examination to enable the toxic effects on target tissues/organs to be identified. Results of acute toxicity studies conducted in other species may also provide relevant information.

3.8.2.1.6   In exceptional cases, based on expert judgement, it may be appropriate to place certain substances with human evidence of target organ toxicity in Category 2: (a) when the weight of human evidence is not sufficiently convincing to warrant Category 1 classification, and/or (b) based on the nature and severity of effects. Dose/concentration levels in humans should not be considered in the classification and any available evidence from animal studies should be consistent with the Category 2 classification. In other words, if there are also animal data available on the chemical that warrant Category 1 classification, the substance should be classified as Category 1.

3.8.2.1.7   *Effects considered to support classification for Category 1 and 2*

3.8.2.1.7.1   Evidence associating single exposure to the substance with a consistent and identifiable toxic effect demonstrates support for classification.

3.8.2.1.7.2   It is recognized that evidence from human experience/incidents is usually restricted to reports of adverse health consequences, often with uncertainty about exposure conditions, and may not provide the scientific detail that can be obtained from well-conducted studies in experimental animals.

3.8.2.1.7.3   Evidence from appropriate studies in experimental animals can furnish much more detail, in the form of clinical observations, and macroscopic and microscopic pathological examination and this can often reveal hazards that may not be life-threatening but could indicate functional impairment. Consequently all available evidence, and relevance to human health, must be taken into consideration in the classification process.

Examples of relevant toxic effects in humans and/or animals are provided below:

(a)   Morbidity resulting from single exposure;

(b)   Significant functional changes, more than transient in nature, in the respiratory system, central or peripheral nervous systems, other organs or other organ systems, including signs of central nervous system depression and effects on special senses (e.g. sight, hearing and sense of smell);

(c)   Any consistent and significant adverse change in clinical biochemistry, haematology, or urinalysis parameters;

(d)   Significant organ damage that may be noted at necropsy and/or subsequently seen or confirmed at microscopic examination;

(e)   Multifocal or diffuse necrosis, fibrosis or granuloma formation in vital organs with regenerative capacity;

(f)   Morphological changes that are potentially reversible but provide clear evidence of marked organ dysfunction;

(g)   Evidence of appreciable cell death (including cell degeneration and reduced cell number) in vital organs incapable of regeneration.

3.8.2.1.8   *Effects considered not to support classification for Category 1 and 2*

It is recognized that effects may be seen that would not justify classification.

Examples of such effects in humans and/or animals are provided below:

(a)   Clinical observations or small changes in bodyweight gain, food consumption or water intake that may have some toxicological importance but that do not, by themselves, indicate "significant" toxicity;

(b)   Small changes in clinical biochemistry, haematology or urinalysis parameters and/or transient effects, when such changes or effects are of doubtful or minimal toxicological importance;

(c)   Changes in organ weights with no evidence of organ dysfunction;

(d)   Adaptive responses that are not considered toxicologically relevant;

(e)   Substance-induced species-specific mechanisms of toxicity, i.e. demonstrated with reasonable certainty to be not relevant for human health, should not justify classification.

3.8.2.1.9   *Guidance values to assist with classification based on the results obtained from studies conducted in experimental animals for Category 1 and 2*

3.8.2.1.9.1   In order to help reach a decision about whether a substance should be classified or not, and to what degree it would be classified (Category 1 vs. Category 2), dose/concentration "guidance values" are provided for consideration of the dose/concentration which has been shown to produce significant health effects. The principal argument for proposing such guidance values is that all chemicals are potentially toxic and there has to be a reasonable dose/concentration above which a degree of toxic effect is acknowledged.

3.8.2.1.9.2   Thus, in animal studies, when significant toxic effects are observed, that would indicate classification, consideration of the dose/concentration at which these effects were seen, in relation to the suggested guidance values, can provide useful information to help assess the need to classify (since the toxic effects are a consequence of the hazardous property(ies) and also the dose/concentration).

3.8.2.1.9.3   The guidance value ranges proposed for single-dose exposure which has produced a significant non-lethal toxic effect are those applicable to acute toxicity testing, as indicated in Table 3.8.1.

Table 3.8.1: Guidance value ranges for single-dose exposures[a]

Route of exposure	Units	Guidance value ranges for:		
		Category 1	Category 2	Category 3
Oral (rat)	mg/kg body weight	$C \le 300$	$2000 \ge C > 300$	Guidance values do not apply[b]
Dermal (rat or rabbit)	mg/kg body weight	$C \le 1000$	$2000 \ge C > 1000$	
Inhalation (rat) gas	ppmV/4h	$C \le 2500$	$20000 \ge C > 2500$	
Inhalation (rat) vapour	mg/l/4h	$C \le 10$	$20 \ge C > 10$	
Inhalation (rat) dust/mist/fume	mg/l/4h	$C \le 1.0$	$5.0 \ge C > 1.0$	

[a]   *The guidance values and ranges mentioned in Table 3.8.1. above are intended only for guidance purposes, i.e. to be used as part of the weight of evidence approach, and to assist with decision about classification. They are not intended as strict demarcation values.*

[b]   *Guidance values are not provided since this classification is primarily based on human data. Animal data may be included in the weight of evidence evaluation.*

3.8.2.1.9.4   Thus it is feasible that a specific profile of toxicity is seen to occur at a dose/concentration below the guidance value, e.g. < 2000 mg/kg body weight by the oral route, however the nature of the effect may result in the decision not to classify. Conversely, a specific profile of toxicity may be seen in animal studies occurring at above a guidance value, e.g. ≥ 2000 mg/kg body weight by the oral route, and in addition there is supplementary information from other sources, e.g. other single dose studies, or human case experience, which supports a conclusion that, in view of the weight of evidence, classification would be the prudent action to take.

3.8.2.1.10   *Other considerations*

3.8.2.1.10.1   When a substance is characterized only by use of animal data (typical of new substances, but also true for many existing substances), the classification process would include reference to dose/concentration guidance values as one of the elements that contribute to the weight of evidence approach.

3.8.2.1.10.2   When well-substantiated human data are available showing a specific target organ toxic effect that can be reliably attributed to single exposure to a substance, the substance may be classified. Positive human data, regardless of probable dose, predominates over animal data. Thus, if a substance is unclassified because specific target organ toxicity observed was considered not relevant or significant to humans, if subsequent human incident data become available showing a specific target organ toxic effect, the substance should be classified.

3.8.2.1.10.3   A substance that has not been tested for specific target organ toxicity may in certain instances, where appropriate, be classified on the basis of data from a validated structure activity relationship and expert judgement-based extrapolation from a structural analogue that has previously been classified together with substantial support from consideration of other important factors such as formation of common significant metabolites.

3.8.2.1.10.4   It is recognized that saturated vapour concentration may be used as an additional element by some regulatory systems to provide for specific health and safety protection.

3.8.2.2   *Substances of Category 3*

3.8.2.2.1   *Criteria for respiratory tract irritation*

The criteria for respiratory tract irritation as Category 3 are:

(a)   Respiratory irritant effects (characterized by localized redness, edema, pruritis and/or pain) that impair function with symptoms such as cough, pain, choking, and breathing difficulties are included. It is recognized that this evaluation is based primarily on human data;

(b)   Subjective human observations could be supported by objective measurements of clear respiratory tract irritation (RTI) (e.g. electrophysiological responses, biomarkers of inflammation in nasal or bronchoalveolar lavage fluids);

(c)   The symptoms observed in humans should also be typical of those that would be produced in the exposed population rather than being an isolated idiosyncratic reaction or response triggered only in individuals with hypersensitive airways. Ambiguous reports simply of "irritation" should be excluded as this term is commonly used to describe a wide range of sensations including those such as smell, unpleasant taste, a tickling sensation, and dryness, which are outside the scope of this classification endpoint;

(d)   There are currently no validated animal tests that deal specifically with RTI, however, useful information may be obtained from the single and repeated inhalation toxicity tests. For example, animal studies may provide useful information in terms of clinical signs of toxicity (dyspnoea, rhinitis etc) and histopathology (e.g. hyperemia, edema, minimal inflammation, thickened mucous layer) which are reversible and may be reflective of the characteristic clinical symptoms described above. Such animal studies can be used as part of weight of evidence evaluation;

(e) This special classification would occur only when more severe organ effects including in the respiratory system are not observed.

3.8.2.2.2   *Criteria for narcotic effects*

The criteria for narcotic effects as Category 3 are:

(a) Central nervous system depression including narcotic effects in humans such as drowsiness, narcosis, reduced alertness, loss of reflexes, lack of coordination, and vertigo are included. These effects can also be manifested as severe headache or nausea, and can lead to reduced judgment, dizziness, irritability, fatigue, impaired memory function, deficits in perception and coordination, reaction time, or sleepiness;

(b) Narcotic effects observed in animal studies may include lethargy, lack of coordination righting reflex, narcosis, and ataxia. If these effects are not transient in nature, then they should be considered for classification as Category 1 or 2.

3.8.3   Classification criteria for mixtures

3.8.3.1   Mixtures are classified using the same criteria as for substances, or alternatively as described below. As with substances, mixtures may be classified for specific target organ toxicity following single exposure, repeated exposure, or both.

3.8.3.2   *Classification of mixtures when data are available for the complete mixture*

When reliable and good quality evidence from human experience or appropriate studies in experimental animals, as described in the criteria for substances, is available for the mixture, then the mixture can be classified by weight of evidence evaluation of this data. Care should be exercised in evaluating data on mixtures, that the dose, duration, observation or analysis, do not render the results inconclusive.

3.8.3.3   *Classification of mixtures when data are not available for the complete mixture: bridging principles*

3.8.3.3.1   Where the mixture itself has not been tested to determine its specific target organ toxicity, but there are sufficient data on both the individual ingredients and similar tested mixtures to adequately characterize the hazards of the mixture, these data can be used in accordance with the following bridging principles. This ensures that the classification process uses the available data to the greatest extent possible in characterizing the hazards of the mixture without the necessity of additional testing in animals.

3.8.3.3.2   *Dilution*

If a tested mixture is diluted with a diluent which has the same or a lower toxicity classification as the least toxic original ingredient and which is not expected to affect the toxicity of other ingredients, then the new diluted mixture may be classified as equivalent to the original tested mixture.

3.8.3.3.3   *Batching*

The toxicity of a tested production batch of a mixture can be assumed to be substantially equivalent to that of another untested production batch of the same commercial product when produced by or under the control of the same manufacturer, unless there is reason to believe there is significant variation such that the toxicity of the untested batch has changed. If the latter occurs, a new classification is necessary.

3.8.3.3.4   *Concentration of highly toxic mixtures*

If in a tested mixture of Category 1, the concentration of a toxic ingredient is increased, the resulting concentrated mixture should be classified in Category 1 without additional testing.

3.8.3.3.5   *Interpolation within one hazard category*

For three mixtures (A, B and C) with identical ingredients, where mixtures A and B have been tested and are in the same hazard category, and where untested mixture C has the same toxicologically active ingredients as mixtures A and B but has concentrations of toxicologically active ingredients intermediate to the concentrations in mixtures A and B, then mixture C is assumed to be in the same hazard category as A and B.

3.8.3.3.6   *Substantially similar mixtures*

Given the following:

(a)   Two mixtures: (i)   A + B;
                        (ii)   C + B;

(b)   The concentration of ingredient B is essentially the same in both mixtures;

(c)   The concentration of ingredient A in mixture (i) equals that of ingredient C in mixture (ii);

(d)   Data on toxicity for A and C are available and substantially equivalent, i.e. they are in the same hazard category and are not expected to affect the toxicity of B.

If mixture (i) or (ii) is already classified by testing, then the other mixture can be assigned the same hazard category.

3.8.3.3.7   *Aerosols*

An aerosol form of a mixture may be classified in the same hazard category as the tested, non-aerosolized form of the mixture for oral and dermal toxicity provided the added propellant does not affect the toxicity of the mixture on spraying. Classification of aerosolized mixtures for inhalation toxicity should be considered separately.

3.8.3.4   Classification of mixtures when data are available for all ingredients or only for some ingredients of the mixture

3.8.3.4.1   Where there is no reliable evidence or test data for the specific mixture itself, and the bridging principles cannot be used to enable classification, then classification of the mixture is based on the classification of the ingredient substances. In this case, the mixture will be classified as a specific target organ toxicant (specific organ specified), following single exposure, repeated exposure, or both when at least one ingredient has been classified as a Category 1 or Category 2 specific target organ toxicant and is present at or above the appropriate cut-off value/concentration limit as mentioned in Table 3.8.2 below for Category 1 and 2 respectively.

Table 3.8.2: Cut-off values/concentration limits of ingredients of a mixture classified as a specific target organ toxicant that would trigger classification of the mixture as Category 1 or 2[a]

Ingredient classified as:	Cut-off/concentration limits triggering classification of a mixture as:	
	Category 1	**Category 2**
Category 1 Target organ toxicant	≥ 1.0% (note 1)	1.0 ≤ ingredient < 10% (note 3)
	≥ 10% (note 2)	
Category 2 Target organ toxicant	--	≥ 1.0% (note 4)
		≥ 10% (note 5)

[a]   *This compromise classification scheme involves consideration of differences in hazard communication practices in existing systems. It is expected that the number of affected mixtures will be small; the differences will be limited to label warnings; and the situation will evolve over time to a more harmonized approach.*

NOTE 1:   *If a Category 1 specific target organ toxicant is present in the mixture as an ingredient at a concentration between 1.0% and 10%, every regulatory authority would require information on the SDS for a product. However, a label warning would be optional. Some authorities will choose to label when the ingredient is present in the mixture between 1.0% and 10%, whereas others would normally not require a label in this case.*

NOTE 2:   *If a Category 1 specific target organ toxicant is present in the mixture as an ingredient at a concentration of ≥ 10%, both an SDS and a label would generally be expected.*

NOTE 3:   *If a Category 1 specific target organ toxicant is present in the mixture as an ingredient at a concentration between 1.0% and 10%, some authorities classify this mixture as a Category 2 specific target organ toxicant, whereas others would not.*

NOTE 4:   *If a Category 2 specific target organ toxicant is present in the mixture as an ingredient at a concentration between 1.0% and 10%, every regulatory authority would require information on the SDS for a product. However, a label warning would be optional. Some authorities will choose to label when the ingredient is present in the mixture between 1.0% and 10%, whereas others would normally not require a label in this case.*

NOTE 5:   *If a Category 2 specific target organ toxicant is present in the mixture as an ingredient at a concentration of ≥ 10%, both an SDS and a label would generally be expected.*

3.8.3.4.2   These cut-off values and consequent classifications should be applied equally and appropriately to both single- and repeated-dose target organ toxicants.

3.8.3.4.3   Mixtures should be classified for either or both single and repeated dose toxicity independently.

3.8.3.4.4   Care should be exercised when toxicants affecting more than one organ system are combined that the potentiation or synergistic interactions are considered, because certain substances can cause target organ toxicity at < 1% concentration when other ingredients in the mixture are known to potentiate its toxic effect.

3.8.3.4.5   Care should be exercised when extrapolating the toxicity of a mixture that contains Category 3 ingredient(s). A cut-off value/concentration limit of 20% has been suggested; however, it should be recognized that this cut-off value concentration limit may be higher or less depending on the Category 3 ingredient(s) and that some effects such as respiratory tract irritation may not occur below a certain concentration while other effects such as narcotic effects may occur below this 20% value. Expert judgment should be exercised. Respiratory tract irritation and narcotic effects are to be evaluated separately in accordance with the criteria given in 3.8.2.2. When conducting classifications for these hazards, the contribution of each ingredient should be considered additive, unless there is evidence that the effects are not additive.

3.8.4 Hazard communication

3.8.4.1   General and specific considerations concerning labelling requirements are provided in *Hazard communication: Labelling* (Chapter 1.4). Annex 1 contains summary tables about classification and labelling. Annex 3 contains examples of precautionary statements and pictograms which can be used where allowed by the competent authority.

Table 3.8.3: Label elements for specific target organ toxicity after single exposure

	Category 1	**Category 2**	**Category 3**
Symbol	Health hazard	Health hazard	Exclamation mark
Signal word	Danger	Warning	Warning
Hazard statement	Causes damage to organs (or state all organs affected, if known) (state route of exposure if it is conclusively proven that no other routes of exposure cause the hazard)	May cause damage to organs (or state all organs affected, if known) (state route of exposure if it is conclusively proven that no other routes of exposure cause the hazard)	May cause respiratory irritation; or May cause drowsiness or dizziness

3.8.5 Decision logic for specific target organ toxicity following single exposure

The decision logic which follows is not part of the harmonized classification system but is provided here as additional guidance. It is strongly recommended that the person responsible for classification study the criteria before and during use of the decision logic.

3.8.5.1   *Decision logic 3.8.1*

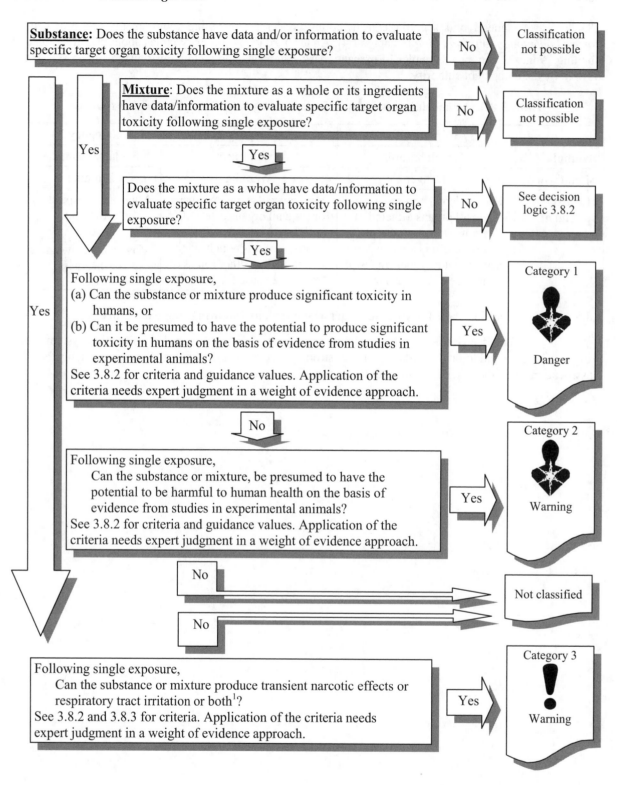

---
[1]   *Classification in Category 3 would only occur when classification into Category 1 or Category 2 (based on more severe respiratory effects or narcotic effects that are not transient) is not warranted. See 3.8.2.2.1 (e) (respiratory effects) and 3.8.2.2.2 (b) (narcotic effects).*

3.8.5.2   *Decision logic 3.8.2*

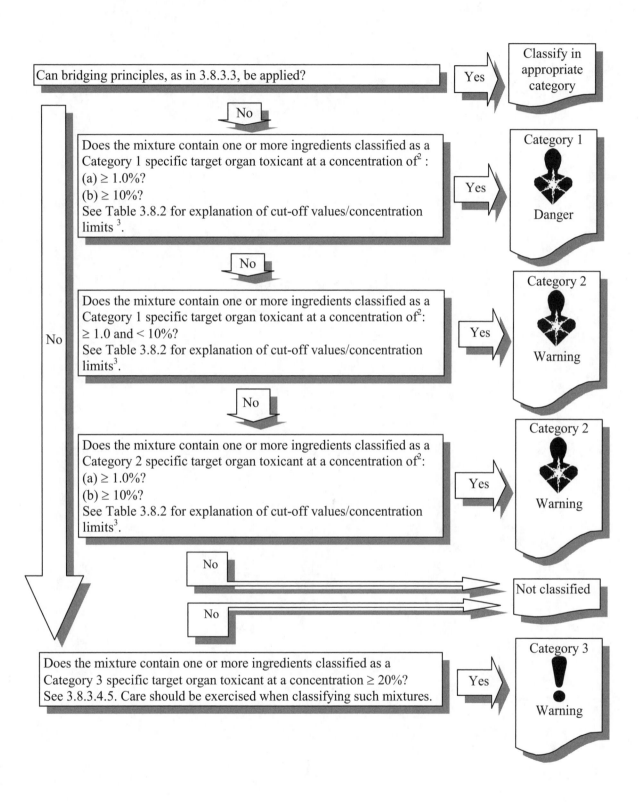

Can bridging principles, as in 3.8.3.3, be applied?	**Yes** → Classify in appropriate category

No ↓

Does the mixture contain one or more ingredients classified as a Category 1 specific target organ toxicant at a concentration of[2] : (a) ≥ 1.0%? (b) ≥ 10%? See Table 3.8.2 for explanation of cut-off values/concentration limits [3].	**Yes** → Category 1 Danger

No ↓

Does the mixture contain one or more ingredients classified as a Category 1 specific target organ toxicant at a concentration of[2]: ≥ 1.0 and < 10%? See Table 3.8.2 for explanation of cut-off values/concentration limits[3].	**Yes** → Category 2 Warning

No ↓

Does the mixture contain one or more ingredients classified as a Category 2 specific target organ toxicant at a concentration of[2]: (a) ≥ 1.0%? (b) ≥ 10%? See Table 3.8.2 for explanation of cut-off values/concentration limits[3].	**Yes** → Category 2 Warning

No → Not classified

No → Not classified

Does the mixture contain one or more ingredients classified as a Category 3 specific target organ toxicant at a concentration ≥ 20%? See 3.8.3.4.5. Care should be exercised when classifying such mixtures.	**Yes** → Category 3 Warning

---

[2]   *See 3.8.2 of this chapter and "The use of cut-off values/concentration limits" in Chapter 1.3, para. 1.3.3.2.*

[3]   *See 3.8.3.4 and Table 3.8.2 for explanation and guidance.*

CHAPTER 3.9

SPECIFIC TARGET ORGAN TOXICITY
REPEATED EXPOSURE

3.9.1 Definitions and general considerations

3.9.1.1 The purpose of this chapter is to provide a means of classifying substances and mixtures that produce specific target organ toxicity arising from a repeated exposure. All significant health effects that can impair function, both reversible and irreversible, immediate and/or delayed are included.

3.9.1.2 Classification identifies the substance or mixture as being a specific target organ toxicant and, as such, it may present a potential for adverse health effects in people who are exposed to it.

3.9.1.3 Classification depends upon the availability of reliable evidence that a repeated exposure to the substance or mixture has produced a consistent and identifiable toxic effect in humans, or, in experimental animals, toxicologically significant changes which have affected the function or morphology of a tissue/organ, or has produced serious changes to the biochemistry or haematology of the organism and these changes are relevant for human health. It is recognized that human data will be the primary source of evidence for this hazard class.

3.9.1.4 Assessment should take into consideration not only significant changes in a single organ or biological system but also generalized changes of a less severe nature involving several organs.

3.9.1.5 Specific target organ toxicity can occur by any route that is relevant for humans, i.e. principally oral, dermal or inhalation.

3.9.1.6 Non-lethal toxic effects observed after a single-event exposure are classified in the GHS as described in *Specific target organ toxicity – Single exposure* (Chapter 3.8) and are therefore excluded from the present chapter. Other specific toxic effects, such as acute toxicity, serious eye damage/eye irritation, skin corrosion/irritation, respiratory or skin sensitization, carcinogenicity, germ cell mutagenicity, reproductive toxicity and aspiration toxicity are assessed separately in the GHS and consequently are not included here.

3.9.2 Classification criteria for substances

3.9.2.1 Substances are classified as specific target organ toxicant by expert judgement on the basis of the weight of all evidence available, including the use of recommended guidance values which take into account the duration of exposure and the dose/concentration which produced the effect(s), (see 3.9.2.9), and are placed in one of two categories, depending upon the nature and severity of the effect(s) observed.

Figure 3.9.1: Hazard categories for specific target organ toxicity following repeated exposure

CATEGORY 1:	**Substances that have produced significant toxicity in humans, or that, on the basis of evidence from studies in experimental animals can be presumed to have the potential <u>to produce significant toxicity in humans</u> following repeated exposure**
	Placing a substance in Category 1 is done on the basis of:
	(a) reliable and good quality evidence from human cases or epidemiological studies; or,
	(b) observations from appropriate studies in experimental animals in which significant and/or severe toxic effects, of relevance to human health, were produced at generally low exposure concentrations. Guidance dose/concentration values are provided below (see 3.9.2.9) to be used as part of weight-of-evidence evaluation.
CATEGORY 2:	**Substances that, on the basis of evidence from studies in experimental animals can be presumed to have the potential <u>to be harmful to human health</u> following repeated exposure**
	Placing a substance in Category 2 is done on the basis of observations from appropriate studies in experimental animals in which significant toxic effects, of relevance to human health, were produced at generally moderate exposure concentrations. Guidance dose/concentration values are provided below (see 3.9.2.9) in order to help in classification.
	In exceptional cases human evidence can also be used to place a substance in Category 2 (see 3.9.2.6).
NOTE:	*For both categories the specific target organ/system that has been primarily affected by the classified substance may be identified, or the substance may be identified as a general toxicant. Attempts should be made to determine the primary target organ/system of toxicity and classify for that purpose, e.g. hepatotoxicants, neurotoxicants. One should carefully evaluate the data and, where possible, not include secondary effects, e.g. a hepatotoxicant can produce secondary effects in the nervous or gastro-intestinal systems.*

3.9.2.2   The relevant route of exposure by which the classified substance produces damage should be identified.

3.9.2.3   Classification is determined by expert judgement, on the basis of the weight of all evidence available including the guidance presented below.

3.9.2.4   Weight of evidence of all data, including human incidents, epidemiology, and studies conducted in experimental animals, is used to substantiate specific target organ toxic effects that merit classification. This taps the considerable body of industrial toxicology data collected over the years. Evaluation should be based on all existing data, including peer-reviewed published studies and additional data acceptable to regulatory agencies.

3.9.2.5   The information required to evaluate specific target organ toxicity comes either from repeated exposure in humans, e.g. exposure at home, in the workplace or environmentally, or from studies conducted in experimental animals. The standard animal studies in rats or mice that provide this information are 28 day, 90 day or lifetime studies (up to 2 years) that include haematological, clinico-chemical and detailed macroscopic and microscopic examination to enable the toxic effects on target tissues/organs to be identified. Data from repeat dose studies performed in other species may also be used. Other long-term exposure studies, e.g. for carcinogenicity, neurotoxicity or reproductive toxicity, may also provide evidence of specific target organ toxicity that could be used in the assessment of classification.

3.9.2.6   In exceptional cases, based on expert judgement, it may be appropriate to place certain substances with human evidence of specific target organ toxicity in Category 2: (a) when the weight of human evidence is not sufficiently convincing to warrant Category 1 classification, and/or (b) based on the nature and severity of effects. Dose/concentration levels in humans should not be considered in the classification and any available evidence from animal studies should be consistent with the Category 2 classification. In other words, if there are also animal data available on the substance that warrant Category 1 classification, the substance should be classified as Category 1.

3.9.2.7   *Effects considered to support classification*

3.9.2.7.1   Reliable evidence associating repeated exposure to the substance with a consistent and identifiable toxic effect demonstrates support for classification.

3.9.2.7.2   It is recognized that evidence from human experience/incidents is usually restricted to reports of adverse health consequences, often with uncertainty about exposure conditions, and may not provide the scientific detail that can be obtained from well-conducted studies in experimental animals.

3.9.2.7.3   Evidence from appropriate studies in experimental animals can furnish much more detail, in the form of clinical observations, haematology, clinical chemistry, macroscopic and microscopic pathological examination and this can often reveal hazards that may not be life-threatening but could indicate functional impairment. Consequently all available evidence, and relevance to human health, must be taken into consideration in the classification process. Examples of relevant toxic effects in humans and/or animals are provided below:

(a)   Morbidity or death resulting from repeated or long-term exposure. Morbidity or death may result from repeated exposure, even to relatively low doses/concentrations, due to bioaccumulation of the substance or its metabolites, or due to the overwhelming of the de-toxification process by repeated exposure;

(b)   Significant functional changes in the central or peripheral nervous systems or other organ systems, including signs of central nervous system depression and effects on special senses (e.g. sight, hearing and sense of smell);

(c)   Any consistent and significant adverse change in clinical biochemistry, haematology, or urinalysis parameters;

(d)   Significant organ damage that may be noted at necropsy and/or subsequently seen or confirmed at microscopic examination;

(e)   Multifocal or diffuse necrosis, fibrosis or granuloma formation in vital organs with regenerative capacity;

(f)   Morphological changes that are potentially reversible but provide clear evidence of marked organ dysfunction (e.g. severe fatty change in the liver);

(g)   Evidence of appreciable cell death (including cell degeneration and reduced cell number) in vital organs incapable of regeneration.

3.9.2.8   *Effects considered not to support classification*

It is recognized that effects may be seen that would not justify classification. Examples of such effects in humans and/or animals are provided below:

(a)   Clinical observations or small changes in bodyweight gain, food consumption or water intake that may have some toxicological importance but that do not, by themselves, indicate "significant" toxicity;

(b)   Small changes in clinical biochemistry, haematology or urinalysis parameters and/or transient effects, when such changes or effects are of doubtful or minimal toxicological importance;

(c)   Changes in organ weights with no evidence of organ dysfunction;

(d)   Adaptive responses that are not considered toxicologically relevant;

(e)   Substance-induced species-specific mechanisms of toxicity, i.e. demonstrated with reasonable certainty to be not relevant for human health, should not justify classification.

3.9.2.9   *Guidance values to assist with classification based on the results obtained from studies conducted in experimental animals*

3.9.2.9.1   In studies conducted in experimental animals, reliance on observation of effects alone, without reference to the duration of experimental exposure and dose/concentration, omits a fundamental concept of toxicology, i.e. all substances are potentially toxic, and what determines the toxicity is a function of the dose/concentration and the duration of exposure. In most studies conducted in experimental animals the test guidelines use an upper limit dose value.

3.9.2.9.2   In order to help reach a decision about whether a substance should be classified or not, and to what degree it would be classified (Category 1 vs. Category 2), dose/concentration "guidance values" are provided in Table 3.9.1 for consideration of the dose/concentration which has been shown to produce significant health effects. The principal argument for proposing such guidance values is that all chemicals are potentially toxic and there has to be a reasonable dose/concentration above which a degree of toxic effect is acknowledged. Also, repeated-dose studies conducted in experimental animals are designed to produce toxicity at the highest dose used in order to optimize the test objective and so most studies will reveal some toxic effect at least at this highest dose. What is therefore to be decided is not only what effects have been produced, but also at what dose/concentration they were produced and how relevant is that for humans.

3.9.2.9.3   Thus, in animal studies, when significant toxic effects are observed, that would indicate classification, consideration of the duration of experimental exposure and the dose/concentration at which these effects were seen, in relation to the suggested guidance values, can provide useful information to help assess the need to classify (since the toxic effects are a consequence of the hazardous property(ies) and also the duration of exposure and the dose/concentration).

3.9.2.9.4   The decision to classify at all can be influenced by reference to the dose/concentration guidance values at or below which a significant toxic effect has been observed.

3.9.2.9.5   The guidance values proposed refer basically to effects seen in a standard 90-day toxicity study conducted in rats. They can be used as a basis to extrapolate equivalent guidance values for toxicity studies of greater or lesser duration, using dose/exposure time extrapolation similar to Haber's rule for inhalation, which states essentially that the effective dose is directly proportional to the exposure concentration and the duration of exposure. The assessment should be done on a case-by-case basis; e.g. for a 28-day study the guidance values below would be increased by a factor of three.

3.9.2.9.6   Thus for Category 1 classification, significant toxic effects observed in a 90-day repeated-dose study conducted in experimental animals and seen to occur at or below the (suggested) guidance values as indicated in Table 3.9.1 would justify classification:

Table 3.9.1: Guidance values to assist in Category 1 classification

Route of exposure	Units	Guidance values (dose/concentration)
Oral (rat)	mg/kg bw/d	≤ 10
Dermal (rat or rabbit)	mg/kg bw/d	≤ 20
Inhalation (rat) gas	ppmV/6h/d	≤ 50
Inhalation (rat) vapour	mg/litre/6h/d	≤ 0.2
Inhalation (rat) dust/mist/fume	mg/litre/6h/d	≤ 0.02

Note: "bw" is for "body weight", "h" for" hour" and "d" for "day".

3.9.2.9.7   For Category 2 classification, significant toxic effects observed in a 90-day repeated-dose study conducted in experimental animals and seen to occur within the (suggested) guidance value ranges as indicated in Table 3.9.2 would justify classification:

Table 3.9.2: Guidance values to assist in Category 2 classification

Route of exposure	Units	Guidance value range (dose/concentration)
Oral (rat)	mg/kg bw/d	$10 < C \leq 100$
Dermal (rat or rabbit)	mg/kg bw/d	$20 < C \leq 200$
Inhalation (rat) gas	ppmV/6h/d	$50 < C \leq 250$
Inhalation (rat) vapour	mg/litre/6h/d	$0.2 < C \leq 1.0$
Inhalation (rat) dust/mist/fume	mg/litre/6h/d	$0.02 < C \leq 0.2$

Note: "bw" is for body weight,"h" for" hour" and "d" for "day".

3.9.2.9.8   The guidance values and ranges mentioned in 3.9.2.9.6 and 3.9.2.9.7 are intended only for guidance purposes, i.e. to be used as part of the weight of evidence approach, and to assist with decisions about classification. They are not intended as strict demarcation values.

3.9.2.9.9   Thus it is feasible that a specific profile of toxicity is seen to occur in repeat-dose animal studies at a dose/concentration below the guidance value, eg. < 100 mg/kg bw/day by the oral route, however the nature of the effect, e.g. nephrotoxicity seen only in male rats of a particular strain known to be susceptible to this effect, may result in the decision not to classify. Conversely, a specific profile of toxicity may be seen in animal studies occurring at above a guidance value, eg. $\geq$ 100 mg/kg bw/day by the oral route, and in addition there is supplementary information from other sources, e.g. other long-term administration studies, or human case experience, which supports a conclusion that, in view of the weight of evidence, classification would be the prudent action to take.

3.9.2.10   *Other considerations*

3.9.2.10.1   When a substance is characterized only by use of animal data (typical of new substances, but also true for many existing substances), the classification process would include reference to dose/concentration guidance values as one of the elements that contribute to the weight of evidence approach.

3.9.2.10.2   When well-substantiated human data are available showing a specific target organ toxic effect that can be reliably attributed to repeated or prolonged exposure to a substance, the substance may be classified. Positive human data, regardless of probable dose, predominates over animal data. Thus, if a substance is unclassified because no specific target organ toxicity was seen at or below the proposed dose/concentration guidance value for animal testing, if subsequent human incident data become available showing a specific target organ toxic effect, the substance should be classified.

3.9.2.10.3   A substance that has not been tested for specific target organ toxicity may in certain instances, where appropriate, be classified on the basis of data from a validated structure activity relationship and expert judgement-based extrapolation from a structural analogue that has previously been classified together with substantial support from consideration of other important factors such as formation of common significant metabolites.

3.9.2.10.4   It is recognized that saturated vapour concentration may be used as an additional element by some regulatory systems to provide for specific health and safety protection.

3.9.3   Classification criteria for mixtures

3.9.3.1   Mixtures are classified using the same criteria as for substances, or alternatively as described below. As with substances, mixtures may be classified for specific target organ toxicity following single exposure, repeated exposure, or both.

3.9.3.2   *Classification of mixtures when data are available for the complete mixture*

When reliable and good quality evidence from human experience or appropriate studies in experimental animals, as described in the criteria for substances, is available for the mixture, then the mixture can be classified by weight of evidence evaluation of this data. Care should be exercised in evaluating data on mixtures, that the dose, duration, observation or analysis, do not render the results inconclusive.

3.9.3.3   *Classification of mixtures when data are not available for the complete mixture: bridging principles*

3.9.3.3.1   Where the mixture itself has not been tested to determine its specific target organ toxicity, but there are sufficient data on both the individual ingredients and similar tested mixtures to adequately characterize the hazards of the mixture, these data can be used in accordance with the following bridging principles. This ensures that the classification process uses the available data to the greatest extent possible in characterizing the hazards of the mixture without the necessity of additional testing in animals.

3.9.3.3.2   *Dilution*

If a tested mixture is diluted with a diluent which has the same or a lower toxicity classification as the least toxic original ingredient and which is not expected to affect the toxicity of other ingredients, then the new diluted mixture may be classified as equivalent to the original tested mixture.

3.9.3.3.3   *Batching*

The toxicity of a tested production batch of a mixture can be assumed to be substantially equivalent to that of another untested production batch of the same commercial product when produced by or under the control of the same manufacturer, unless there is reason to believe there is significant variation such that the toxicity of the untested batch has changed. If the latter occurs, a new classification is necessary.

3.9.3.3.4   *Concentration of highly toxic mixtures*

If in a tested mixture of Category 1, the concentration of a toxic ingredient is increased, the resulting concentrated mixture should be classified in Category 1 without additional testing.

3.9.3.3.5   *Interpolation within one hazard category*

For three mixtures (A, B and C) with identical ingredients, where mixtures A and B have been tested and are in the same hazard category, and where untested mixture C has the same toxicologically active ingredients as mixtures A and B but has concentrations of toxicologically active ingredients intermediate to the concentrations in mixtures A and B, then mixture C is assumed to be in the same hazard category as A and B.

3.9.3.3.6   *Substantially similar mixtures*

Given the following:

(a)   Two mixtures: (i)   A + B;
                                    (ii)   C + B;

(b)   The concentration of ingredient B is essentially the same in both mixtures;

(c)   The concentration of ingredient A in mixture (i) equals that of ingredient C in mixture (ii);

(d)   Data on toxicity for A and C are available and substantially equivalent, i.e. they are in the same hazard category and are not expected to affect the toxicity of B.

If mixture (i) or (ii) is already classified by testing, then the other mixture can be assigned the same hazard category.

3.9.3.3.7   *Aerosols*

An aerosol form of a mixture may be classified in the same hazard category as the tested, non-aerosolized form of the mixture for oral and dermal toxicity provided the added propellant does not affect the toxicity of the mixture on spraying. Classification of aerosolized mixtures for inhalation toxicity should be considered separately.

3.9.3.4   *Classification of mixtures when data are available for all ingredients or only for some ingredients of the mixture*

3.9.3.4.1   Where there is no reliable evidence or test data for the specific mixture itself, and the bridging principles cannot be used to enable classification, then classification of the mixture is based on the classification of the ingredient substances. In this case, the mixture will be classified as a specific target organ toxicant (specific organ specified), following single exposure, repeated exposure, or both when at least one ingredient has been classified as a Category 1 or Category 2 specific target organ toxicant and is present at or above the appropriate cut-off value/concentration limit as mentioned in Table 3.9.3 for Category 1 and 2 respectively.

Table 3.9.3: Cut-off values/concentration limits of ingredients of a mixture classified as a specific target organ toxicant that would trigger classification of the mixture[a]

Ingredient classified as:	Cut-off/concentration limits triggering classification of a mixture as:	
	Category 1	**Category 2**
Category 1 Target organ toxicant	≥ 1.0% (note 1)	1.0 ≤ ingredient < 10% (note 3)
	≥ 10% (note 2)	1.0 ≤ ingredient < 10% (note 3)
Category 2 Target organ toxicant		≥ 1.0% (note 4)
		≥ 10% (note 5)

[a]   *This compromise classification scheme involves consideration of differences in hazard communication practices in existing systems. It is expected that the number of affected mixtures will be small; the differences will be limited to label warnings; and the situation will evolve over time to a more harmonized approach.*

NOTE 1*:   If a Category 1 specific target organ toxicant is present in the mixture as an ingredient at a concentration between 1.0% and 10%, every regulatory authority would require information on the SDS for a product. However, a label warning would be optional. Some authorities will choose to label when the ingredient is present in the mixture between 1.0% and 10%, whereas others would normally not require a label in this case.*

NOTE 2*:   If a Category 1 specific target organ toxicant is present in the mixture as an ingredient at a concentration of ≥ 10%, both an SDS and a label would generally be expected.*

NOTE 3:   *If a Category 1 specific target organ toxicant is present in the mixture as an ingredient at a concentration between 1.0% and 10%, some authorities classify this mixture as a Category 2 target organ toxicant, whereas others would not.*

NOTE 4:   *If a Category 2 specific target organ toxicant is present in the mixture as an ingredient at a concentration between 1.0% and 10%, every regulatory authority would require information on the SDS for a product. However, a label warning would be optional. Some authorities will choose to label when the ingredient is present in the mixture between 1.0% and 10%, whereas others would normally not require a label in this case.*

NOTE 5:   *If a Category 2 specific target organ toxicant is present in the mixture as an ingredient at a concentration of ≥ 10%, both an SDS and a label would generally be expected.*

3.9.3.4.2   These cut-off values and consequent classifications should be applied equally and appropriately to both single- and repeated-dose target organ toxicants.

3.9.3.4.3   Mixtures should be classified for either or both single- and repeated-dose toxicity independently.

3.9.3.4.4   Care should be exercised when toxicants affecting more than one organ system are combined that the potentiation or synergistic interactions are considered, because certain substances can cause specific target organ toxicity at < 1% concentration when other ingredients in the mixture are known to potentiate its toxic effect.

3.9.4   Hazard communication

General and specific considerations concerning labelling requirements are provided in *Hazard communication: Labelling* (Chapter 1.4). Annex 1 contains summary tables about classification and labelling. Annex 3 contains examples of precautionary statements and pictograms which can be used where allowed by the competent authority.

Table 3.9.4: Label elements for specific target organ toxicity following repeated exposure

	Category 1	**Category 2**
Symbol	Health hazard	Health hazard
Signal word	Danger	Warning
Hazard statement	Causes damage to organs (state all organs affected, if known) through prolonged or repeated exposure (state route of exposure if it is conclusively proven that no other routes of exposure cause the hazard)	May cause damage to organs (state all organs affected, if known) through prolonged or repeated exposure (state route of exposure if it is conclusively proven that no other routes of exposure cause the hazard)

3.9.5   Decision logic for specific target organ toxicity following repeated exposure

The decision logic which follows is not part of the harmonized classification system but is provided here as additional guidance. It is strongly recommended that the person responsible for classification studies the criteria before and during use of the decision logic.

3.9.5.1   *Decision logic 3.9.1*

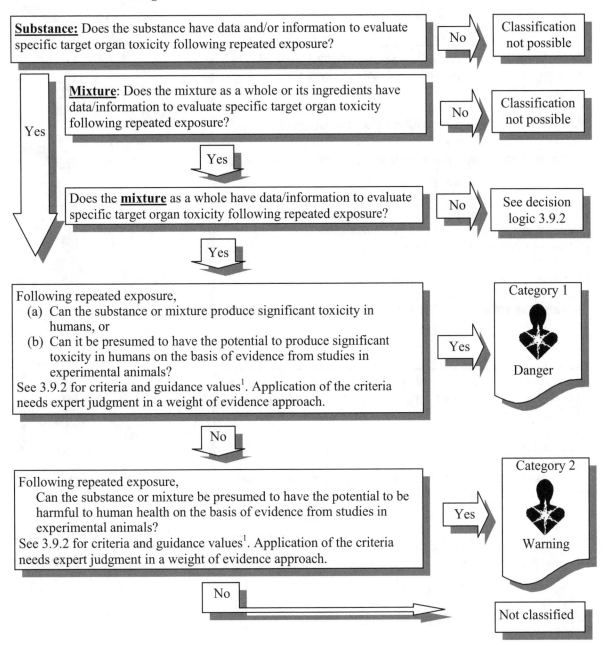

---

¹   *See 3.9.2, Tables 3.9.1 and 3.9.2, and in Chapter 1.3, para. 1.3.3.2 "The use of cut-off values/concentration limits".*

3.9.5.2   Decision logic 3.9.2

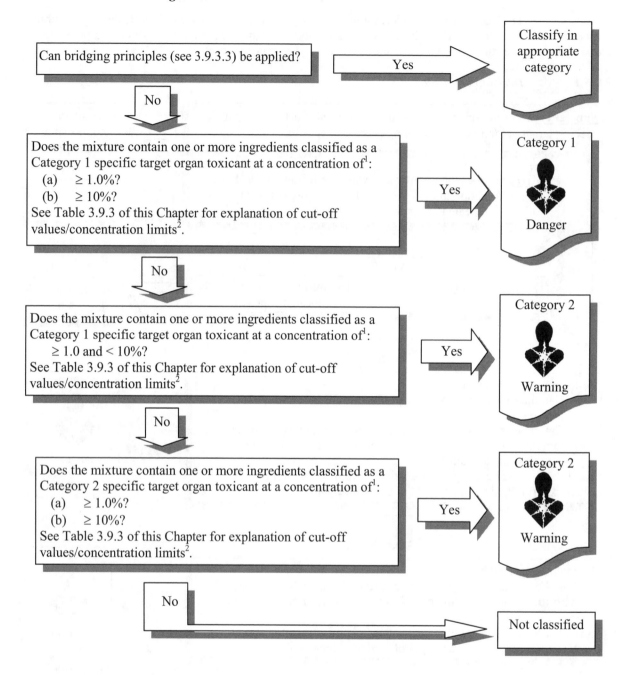

Can bridging principles (see 3.9.3.3) be applied? — Yes → Classify in appropriate category

No ↓

Does the mixture contain one or more ingredients classified as a Category 1 specific target organ toxicant at a concentration of[1]:
(a)   ≥ 1.0%?
(b)   ≥ 10%?
See Table 3.9.3 of this Chapter for explanation of cut-off values/concentration limits[2]. — Yes → Category 1 / Danger

No ↓

Does the mixture contain one or more ingredients classified as a Category 1 specific target organ toxicant at a concentration of[1]:
   ≥ 1.0 and < 10%?
See Table 3.9.3 of this Chapter for explanation of cut-off values/concentration limits[2]. — Yes → Category 2 / Warning

No ↓

Does the mixture contain one or more ingredients classified as a Category 2 specific target organ toxicant at a concentration of[1]:
(a)   ≥ 1.0%?
(b)   ≥ 10%?
See Table 3.9.3 of this Chapter for explanation of cut-off values/concentration limits[2]. — Yes → Category 2 / Warning

No → Not classified

---

[1]   See 3.9.2, Tables 3.9.1 and 3.9.2, and in Chapter 1.3, para. 1.3.3.2 "The use of cut-off values/concentration limits".

[2]   See 3.9.3.4 and 3.9.4 and Table 3.9.3 for explanation and guidance.

CHAPTER 3.10

ASPIRATION HAZARD

3.10.1 Definitions and general and specific considerations

3.10.1.1 The purpose of this chapter is to provide a means of classifying substances or mixtures that may pose an aspiration toxicity hazard to humans.

3.10.1.2 *Aspiration* means the entry of a liquid or solid chemical directly through the oral or nasal cavity, or indirectly from vomiting, into the trachea and lower respiratory system.

3.10.1.3 Aspiration toxicity includes severe acute effects such as chemical pneumonia, varying degrees of pulmonary injury or death following aspiration.

3.10.1.4 Aspiration is initiated at the moment of inspiration, in the time required to take one breath, as the causative material lodges at the crossroad of the upper respiratory and digestive tracts in the laryngopharyngeal region.

3.10.1.5 Aspiration of a substance or mixture can occur as it is vomited following ingestion. This may have consequences for labelling, particularly where, due to acute toxicity, a recommendation may be considered to induce vomiting after ingestion. However, if the substance/mixture also presents an aspiration toxicity hazard, the recommendation to induce vomiting may need to be modified.

3.10.1.6 *Specific considerations*

3.10.1.6.1 A review of the medical literature on chemical aspiration revealed that some hydrocarbons (petroleum distillates) and certain chlorinated hydrocarbons have been shown to pose an aspiration hazard in humans. Primary alcohols, and ketones have been shown to pose an aspiration hazard only in animal studies.

3.10.1.6.2 While a methodology for determination of aspiration hazard in animals has been utilized, it has not been standardized. Positive experimental evidence with animals can only serve as a guide to possible aspiration toxicity in humans. Particular care must be taken in evaluating animal data for aspiration hazards.

3.10.1.6.3 The classification criteria refer to kinematic viscosity. The following provides the conversion between dynamic and kinematic viscosity:

$$\frac{\text{Dynamic viscosity (mPa·s)}}{\text{Density (g/cm}^3)} = \text{Kinematic viscosity (mm}^2/\text{s)}$$

3.10.1.6.4 Although the definition of aspiration in 3.10.1.2 includes the entry of solids into the respiratory system, classification according to (b) in table 3.10.1 for Category 1 or for Category 2 is intended to apply to liquid substances and mixtures only.

3.10.1.6.5 *Classification of aerosol/mist products*

Aerosol and mist products are usually dispensed in containers such as self-pressurized containers, trigger and pump sprayers. The key to classifying these products is whether a pool of product is formed in the mouth, which then may be aspirated. If the mist or aerosol from a pressurized container is fine, a pool may not be formed. On the other hand, if a pressurized container dispenses product in a stream, a pool may be formed that may then be aspirated. Usually, the mist produced by trigger and pump sprayers is coarse and therefore, a pool may be formed that then may be aspirated. When the pump mechanism may be removed and contents are available to be swallowed then the classification of the products should be considered.

3.10.2   Classification criteria for substances

Table 3.10.1: Hazard categories for aspiration toxicity

Categories	Criteria
Category 1: Chemicals known to cause human aspiration toxicity hazards or to be regarded as if they cause human aspiration toxicity hazard	A substance is classified in Category 1: (a) Based on reliable and good quality human evidence (see note 1); or (b) If it is a hydrocarbon and has a kinematic viscosity ≤ 20.5 mm^2/s, measured at 40° C.
Category 2: Chemicals which cause concern owing to the presumption that they cause human aspiration toxicity hazard	On the basis of existing animal studies and expert judgment that takes into account surface tension, water solubility, boiling point, and volatility, substances, other than those classified in Category 1, which have a kinematic viscosity ≤ 14 mm^2/s, measured at 40° C (see note 2).

NOTE 1:   *Examples of substances included in Category 1 are certain hydrocarbons, turpentine and pine oil.*

NOTE 2:   *Taking this into account, some authorities would consider the following to be included in this Category: n-primary alcohols with a composition of at least 3 carbon atoms but not more than 13; isobutyl alcohol, and ketones with a composition of no more than 13 carbon atoms.*

3.10.3   Classification criteria for mixtures

3.10.3.1   *Classification when data are available for the complete mixture*

A mixture is classified in Category 1 based on reliable and good quality human evidence.

3.10.3.2   *Classification of mixtures when data are not available for the complete mixture: bridging principles*

3.10.3.2.1   Where the mixture itself has not been tested to determine its aspiration toxicity, but there are sufficient data on both the individual ingredients and similar tested mixtures to adequately characterize the hazard of the mixture, these data will be used in accordance with the following bridging principles. This ensures that the classification process uses the available data to the greatest extent possible in characterizing the hazards of the mixture without the necessity of additional testing in animals.

3.10.3.2.2   *Dilution*

If a tested mixture is diluted with a diluent that does not pose an aspiration toxicity hazard, and which is not expected to affect the aspiration toxicity of other ingredients or the mixture, then the new diluted mixture may be classified as equivalent to the original tested mixture. However, the concentration of aspiration toxicant(s) should not drop below 10%.

3.10.3.2.3   *Batching*

The aspiration toxicity of a tested production batch of a mixture can be assumed to be substantially equivalent to that of another untested production batch of the same commercial product, when produced by or under the control of the same manufacturer, unless there is reason to believe there is significant variation such that the aspiration toxicity, reflected by viscosity or concentration, of the untested batch has changed. If the latter occurs, a new classification is necessary.

3.10.3.2.4   *Concentration of Category 1 mixtures*

If a tested mixture is classified in Category 1, and the concentration of the ingredients of the tested mixture that are in Category 1 is increased, the resulting untested mixture should be classified in Category 1 without additional testing.

3.10.3.2.5   *Interpolation within one hazard category*

For three mixtures (A, B and C) with identical ingredients, where mixtures A and B have been tested and are in the same hazard category, and where untested mixture C has the same toxicologically active ingredients as mixtures A and B but has concentrations of toxicologically active ingredients intermediate to the concentrations in mixtures A and B, then mixture C is assumed to be in the same hazard category as A and B.

3.10.3.2.6   *Substantially similar mixtures*

Given the following:

(a)   Two mixtures: (i)   A + B;
                        (ii)   C + B;

(b)   The concentration of ingredient B is essentially the same in both mixtures;

(c)   The concentration of ingredient A in mixture (i) equals that of ingredient C in mixture (ii);

(d)   Aspiration toxicity for A and C is substantially equivalent, i.e. they are in the same hazard category and are not expected to affect the aspiration toxicity of B.

If mixture (i) or (ii) is already classified based on the criteria in table 3.10.1, then the other mixture can be assigned the same hazard category.

3.10.3.3   *Classification of mixtures when data are available for all ingredients or only for some ingredients of the mixture*

3.10.3.3.1   *Category 1*

3.10.3.3.1.1   A mixture which contains $\geq 10\%$ of an ingredient or ingredients classified in Category 1, and has a kinematic viscosity ≤ 20.5 mm^2/s, measured at 40 °C, will be classified in Category 1.

3.10.3.3.1.2   In the case of a mixture which separates into two or more distinct layers, one of which contains $\geq 10\%$ of an ingredient or ingredients classified in Category 1 and has a kinematic viscosity ≤ 20.5 mm^2/s, measured at 40 °C, then the entire mixture is classified in Category 1.

3.10.3.3.2   *Category 2*

3.10.3.3.2.1   A mixture which contains $\geq 10\%$ of an ingredient or ingredients classified in Category 2, and has a kinematic viscosity ≤ 14 mm^2/s, measured at 40 °C, will be classified in Category 2.

3.10.3.3.2.2   In classifying mixtures in this category, the use of expert judgment that considers surface tension, water solubility, boiling point, volatility is critical and especially when Category 2 substances are mixed with water.

3.10.3.3.2.3   In the case of classifying a mixture which separates into two or more distinct layers, one of which contains $\geq 10\%$ of an ingredient or ingredients classified in Category 2 and has a kinematic viscosity ≤ 14 mm^2/s, measured at 40 °C, then the entire mixture is classified in Category 2.

3.10.4 Hazard communication

3.10.4.1 General and specific considerations concerning labelling requirements are provided in *Hazard communication: Labelling* (Chapter 1.4). Annex 1 contains summary tables about classification and labelling. Annex 3 contains examples of precautionary statements and pictograms, which can be used where allowed by the competent authority. The table below presents specific label elements for substances and mixtures which are classified as posing an aspiration toxicity hazard, Categories 1 and 2, based on the criteria set forth in this chapter.

Table 3.10.2: Label elements for aspiration toxicity

	Category 1	**Category 2**
Symbol	Health hazard	Health hazard
Signal word	Danger	Warning
Hazard statement	May be fatal if swallowed and enters airways	May be harmful if swallowed and enters airways

3.10.5 Decision logic for aspiration toxicity

The decision logic which follows is not part of the harmonized classification system but is provided here as additional guidance. It is strongly recommended that the person responsible for classification study the criteria before and during use of the decision logic.

3.10.5.1 *Decision logic 3.10.1*

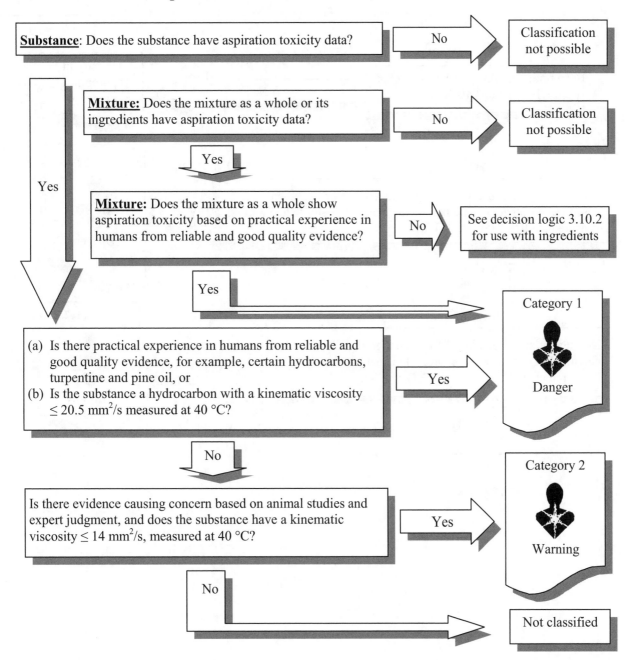

Substance: Does the substance have aspiration toxicity data? → No → Classification not possible

Mixture: Does the mixture as a whole or its ingredients have aspiration toxicity data? → No → Classification not possible

↓ Yes

Mixture: Does the mixture as a whole show aspiration toxicity based on practical experience in humans from reliable and good quality evidence? → No → See decision logic 3.10.2 for use with ingredients

Yes → Category 1 Danger

(a) Is there practical experience in humans from reliable and good quality evidence, for example, certain hydrocarbons, turpentine and pine oil, or
(b) Is the substance a hydrocarbon with a kinematic viscosity ≤ 20.5 mm^2/s measured at 40 °C? → Yes → Category 1 Danger

↓ No

Is there evidence causing concern based on animal studies and expert judgment, and does the substance have a kinematic viscosity ≤ 14 mm^2/s, measured at 40 °C? → Yes → Category 2 Warning

No → Not classified

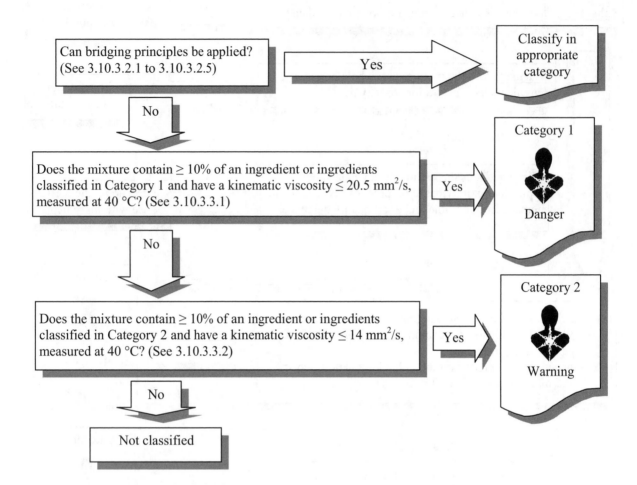

PART 4

ENVIRONMENTAL HAZARDS

CHAPTER 4.1

HAZARDOUS TO THE AQUATIC ENVIRONMENT

4.1.1 Definitions and general considerations

4.1.1.1 Definitions

Acute aquatic toxicity means the intrinsic property of a substance to be injurious to an organism in a short-term aquatic exposure to that substance.

Availability of a substance means the extent to which this substance becomes a soluble or disaggregate species. For metal availability, the extent to which the metal ion portion of a metal (M°) compound can disaggregate from the rest of the compound (molecule).

Bioavailability (or biological availability) means the extent to which a substance is taken up by an organism, and distributed to an area within the organism. It is dependent upon physico-chemical properties of the substance, anatomy and physiology of the organism, pharmacokinetics, and route of exposure. Availability is not a prerequisite for bioavailability.

Bioaccumulation means net result of uptake, transformation and elimination of a substance in an organism due to all routes of exposure (i.e. air, water, sediment/soil and food).

Bioconcentration means net result of uptake, transformation and elimination of a substance in an organism due to waterborne exposure.

Chronic aquatic toxicity means the intrinsic property of a substance to cause adverse effects to aquatic organisms during aquatic exposures which are determined in relation to the life-cycle of the organism.

Complex mixtures or multi-component substances or complex substances means mixtures comprising a complex mix of individual substances with different solubilities and physico-chemical properties. In most cases, they can be characterized as a homologous series of substances with a certain range of carbon chain length/number of degree of substitution.

Degradation means the decomposition of organic molecules to smaller molecules and eventually to carbon dioxide, water and salts.

ECx means the concentration associated with x% response.

Long-term (chronic) hazard, for classification purposes, means the hazard of a chemical caused by its chronic toxicity following long-term exposure in the aquatic environment.

NOEC (No Observed Effect Concentration) means the test concentration immediately below the lowest tested concentration with statistically significant adverse effect. The NOEC has no statistically significant adverse effect compared to the control.

Short-term (acute) hazard, for classification purposes, means the hazard of a chemical caused by its acute toxicity to an organism during short-term aquatic exposure to that chemical.

4.1.1.2   *Basic elements*

4.1.1.2.1   The basic elements for use within the harmonized system are:

     (a)   acute aquatic toxicity;

     (b)   chronic aquatic toxicity;

     (c)   potential for or actual bioaccumulation; and

     (d)   degradation (biotic or abiotic) for organic chemicals.

4.1.1.2.2   While data from internationally harmonized test methods are preferred, in practice, data from national methods may also be used where they are considered as equivalent. In general, it has been agreed that freshwater and marine species toxicity data can be considered as equivalent data and are preferably to be derived using OECD Test Guidelines or equivalent according to the principles of Good Laboratory Practices (GLP). Where such data are not available classification should be based on the best available data.

4.1.1.3   *Acute aquatic toxicity*

Acute aquatic toxicity would normally be determined using a fish 96 hour LC_{50} (OECD Test Guideline 203 or equivalent), a crustacea species 48 hour EC_{50} (OECD Test Guideline 202 or equivalent) and/or an algal species 72 or 96 hour EC_{50} (OECD Test Guideline 201 or equivalent). These species are considered as surrogate for all aquatic organisms and data on other species such as Lemna may also be considered if the test methodology is suitable.

4.1.1.4   *Chronic aquatic toxicity*

Chronic toxicity data are less available than acute data and the range of testing procedures less standardized. Data generated according to the OECD Test Guidelines 210 (Fish Early Life Stage), or 211 (Daphnia Reproduction) and 201 (Algal Growth Inhibition) can be accepted (see also Annex 9, para. A9.3.3.2). Other validated and internationally accepted tests could also be used. The NOECs or other equivalent ECx should be used.

4.1.1.5   *Bioaccumulation potential*

The potential for bioaccumulation would normally be determined by using the octanol/water partition coefficient, usually reported as a log K_{ow} determined by OECD Test Guideline 107 or 117. While this represents a potential to bioaccumulate, an experimentally determined Bioconcentration Factor (BCF) provides a better measure and should be used in preference when available. A BCF should be determined according to OECD Test Guideline 305.

4.1.1.6   *Rapid degradability*

4.1.1.6.1   Environmental degradation may be biotic or abiotic (e.g. hydrolysis) and the criteria used reflect this fact (see 4.1.2.11.3). Ready biodegradation can most easily be defined using the biodegradability tests (A-F) of OECD Test Guideline 301. A pass level in these tests can be considered as indicative of rapid degradation in most environments. These are freshwater tests and thus the use of the results from OECD Test Guideline 306 which is more suitable for marine environments has also been included. Where such data are not available, a BOD(5 days)/COD ratio ≥ 0.5 is considered as indicative of rapid degradation.

4.1.1.6.2   Abiotic degradation such as hydrolysis, primary degradation, both abiotic and biotic, degradation in non-aquatic media and proven rapid degradation in the environment may all be considered in defining rapid degradability. Special guidance on data interpretation is provided in the Guidance Document (Annex 9).

4.1.1.7   *Other considerations*

4.1.1.7.1   The harmonized system for classifying substances for the hazards they present to the aquatic environment is based on a consideration of existing systems listed in 4.1.1.7.3. The aquatic environment may be considered in terms of the aquatic organisms that live in the water, and the aquatic ecosystem of which they are part. To that extent, the proposal does not address aquatic pollutants for which there may be a need to consider effects beyond the aquatic environment such as the impacts on human health etc. The basis, therefore, of the identification of hazard is the aquatic toxicity of the substance, although this may be modified by further information on the degradation and bioaccumulation behaviour.

4.1.1.7.2   While the scheme is intended to apply to all substances and mixtures, it is recognized that for some substances, e.g. metals, poorly soluble substances, etc., special guidance will be necessary. Two guidance documents (see annexes 9 and 10) have been prepared to cover issues such as data interpretation and the application of the criteria defined below to such groups of substances. Considering the complexity of this endpoint and the breadth of the application of the system, the Guidance Documents are considered an important element in the operation of the harmonized scheme.

4.1.1.7.3   Consideration has been given to existing classification systems as currently in use, including the European Union supply and use scheme, the revised GESAMP hazard evaluation procedure, IMO scheme for marine pollutants, the European road and rail transport scheme (ADR/RID), the Canadian and United States of America pesticide systems and the United States of America land transport scheme. The harmonized scheme is considered suitable for use for packaged goods in both supply and use and multimodal transport schemes, and elements of it may be used for bulk land transport and bulk marine transport under MARPOL 73/78 Annex II insofar as this uses aquatic toxicity.

4.1.2   **Classification criteria for substances**

4.1.2.1   Whilst the harmonized classification system consists of three short-term (acute) classification categories and four long-term (chronic) classification categories, the core part of the harmonized classification system for substances consists of three short-term (acute) classification categories and three long-term (chronic) classification categories (see Table 4.1.1 (a) and (b)). The short-term (acute) and the long-term (chronic) classification categories are applied independently. The criteria for classification of a substance in Acute 1 to 3 are defined on the basis of the acute toxicity data only (EC_{50} or LC_{50}). The criteria for classification of a substance into Chronic 1 to 3 follow a tiered approach where the first step is to see if available information on chronic toxicity merits long-term hazard classification. In absence of adequate chronic toxicity data, the subsequent step is to combine two types of information, i.e. acute toxicity data and environmental fate data (degradability and bioaccumulation data) (see Figure 4.1.1).

4.1.2.2   The system also introduces a "safety net" classification (Chronic 4) for use when the data available do not allow classification under the formal criteria but there are nevertheless some grounds for concern. The precise criteria are not defined with one exception: for poorly water soluble substances for which no toxicity has been demonstrated, classification can occur if the substance is both not rapidly degraded and has a potential to bioaccumulate. It is considered that for such poorly soluble substances, the toxicity may not have been adequately assessed in the short-term test due to the low exposure levels and potentially slow uptake into the organism. The need for this classification can be negated by demonstrating that the substance does not require classification for aquatic long-term (chronic) hazards.

4.1.2.3   Substances with acute toxicities well below 1 mg/l or chronic toxicities well below 0.1 mg/l (if non-rapidly degradable) and 0.01 mg/l (if rapidly degradable) contribute as ingredients of a mixture to the toxicity of the mixture even at a low concentration and should be given increased weight in applying the summation method (see Note 2 to Table 4.1.1 and paragraph 4.1.3.5.5.5).

4.1.2.4   Substances classified under the following criteria (Table 4.1.1) will be categorized as "hazardous to the aquatic environment". These criteria describe in detail the classification categories. They are diagrammatically summarized in Table 4.1.2.

Table 4.1.1: Categories for substances hazardous to the aquatic environment *(Note 1)*

(a)   **Short-term (acute) aquatic hazard**

<table>
<tr><td colspan="2"><u>Category Acute 1:</u> (Note 2)</td></tr>
<tr><td>96 hr LC_{50} (for fish)</td><td>$\leq$ 1 mg/l and/or</td></tr>
<tr><td>48 hr EC_{50} (for crustacea)</td><td>$\leq$ 1 mg/l and/or</td></tr>
<tr><td>72 or 96hr ErC_{50} (for algae or other aquatic plants)</td><td>$\leq$ 1 mg/l (Note 3)</td></tr>
<tr><td colspan="2">Category Acute 1 may be subdivided for some regulatory systems to include a lower band at $L(E)C_{50} \leq 0.1$ mg/l</td></tr>
<tr><td colspan="2"><u>Category Acute 2:</u></td></tr>
<tr><td>96 hr LC_{50} (for fish)</td><td>>1 but $\leq$ 10 mg/l and/or</td></tr>
<tr><td>48 hr EC_{50} (for crustacea)</td><td>>1 but $\leq$ 10 mg/l and/or</td></tr>
<tr><td>72 or 96hr ErC_{50} (for algae or other aquatic plants)</td><td>>1 but $\leq$ 10 mg/l (Note 3)</td></tr>
<tr><td colspan="2"><u>Category Acute 3:</u></td></tr>
<tr><td>96 hr LC_{50} (for fish)</td><td>>10 but $\leq$ 100 mg/l and/or</td></tr>
<tr><td>48 hr EC_{50} (for crustacea)</td><td>>10 but $\leq$ 100 mg/l and/or</td></tr>
<tr><td>72 or 96hr ErC_{50} (for algae or other aquatic plants)</td><td>>10 but $\leq$ 100 mg/l (Note 3)</td></tr>
<tr><td colspan="2">Some regulatory systems may extend this range beyond an $L(E)C_{50}$ of 100 mg/l through the introduction of another category.</td></tr>
</table>

(b)   **Long-term (chronic) aquatic hazard** *(see also figure 4.1.1)*

(i)   **Non-rapidly degradable substances (Note 4) for which there are adequate chronic toxicity data available**

<table>
<tr><td colspan="2"><u>Category Chronic 1:</u> (Note 2)</td></tr>
<tr><td>Chronic NOEC or EC_x (for fish)</td><td>$\leq$ 0.1 mg/l and/or</td></tr>
<tr><td>Chronic NOEC or EC_x (for crustacea)</td><td>$\leq$ 0.1 mg/l and/or</td></tr>
<tr><td>Chronic NOEC or EC_x (for algae or other aquatic plants)</td><td>$\leq$ 0.1 mg/l</td></tr>
<tr><td colspan="2"><u>Category Chronic 2:</u></td></tr>
<tr><td>Chronic NOEC or EC_x (for fish)</td><td>$\leq$ 1 mg/l and/or</td></tr>
<tr><td>Chronic NOEC or EC_x (for crustacea)</td><td>$\leq$ 1 mg/l and/or</td></tr>
<tr><td>Chronic NOEC or EC_x (for algae or other aquatic plants)</td><td>$\leq$ 1 mg/l</td></tr>
</table>

(ii)   **Rapidly degradable substances for which there are adequate chronic toxicity data available**

<table>
<tr><td colspan="2"><u>Category Chronic 1:</u> (Note 2)</td></tr>
<tr><td>Chronic NOEC or EC_x (for fish)</td><td>$\leq$ 0.01 mg/l and/or</td></tr>
<tr><td>Chronic NOEC or EC_x (for crustacea)</td><td>$\leq$ 0.01 mg/l and/or</td></tr>
<tr><td>Chronic NOEC or EC_x (for algae or other aquatic plants)</td><td>$\leq$ 0.01 mg/l</td></tr>
<tr><td colspan="2"><u>Category Chronic 2:</u></td></tr>
<tr><td>Chronic NOEC or EC_x (for fish)</td><td>$\leq$ 0.1 mg/l and/or</td></tr>
<tr><td>Chronic NOEC or EC_x (for crustacea)</td><td>$\leq$ 0.1 mg/l and/or</td></tr>
<tr><td>Chronic NOEC or EC_x (for algae or other aquatic plants)</td><td>$\leq$ 0.1 mg/l</td></tr>
<tr><td colspan="2"><u>Category Chronic 3:</u></td></tr>
<tr><td>Chronic NOEC or EC_x (for fish)</td><td>$\leq$ 1 mg/l and/or</td></tr>
<tr><td>Chronic NOEC or EC_x (for crustacea)</td><td>$\leq$ 1 mg/l and/or</td></tr>
<tr><td>Chronic NOEC or EC_x (for algae or other aquatic plants)</td><td>$\leq$ 1 mg/l</td></tr>
</table>

(Cont'd on next page)

Table 4.1.1: Categories for substances hazardous to the aquatic environment *(Note 1) (cont'd)*

(iii)   Substances for which adequate chronic toxicity data are not available

Category Chronic 1: *(Note 2)*

96 hr LC_{50} (for fish)	≤ 1 mg/l and/or
48 hr EC_{50} (for crustacea)	≤ 1 mg/l and/or
72 or 96hr ErC_{50} (for algae or other aquatic plants)	≤ 1 mg/l *(Note 3)*

and the substance is not rapidly degradable and/or the experimentally determined BCF is ≥ 500 (or, if absent, the log K_{ow} ≥ 4). *(Notes 4 and 5)*

Category Chronic 2:

96 hr LC_{50} (for fish)	> 1 but ≤ 10 mg/l and/or
48 hr EC_{50} (for crustacea)	> 1 but ≤ 10 mg/l and/or
72 or 96hr ErC_{50} (for algae or other aquatic plants)	> 1 but ≤ 10 mg/l *(Note 3)*

and the substance is not rapidly degradable and/or the experimentally determined BCF is ≥ 500 (or, if absent, the log K_{ow} ≥ 4). *(Notes 4 and 5)*

Category Chronic 3:

96 hr LC_{50} (for fish)	> 10 but ≤ 100 mg/l and/or
48 hr EC_{50} (for crustacea)	> 10 but ≤ 100 mg/l and/or
72 or 96hr ErC_{50} (for algae or other aquatic plants)	> 10 but ≤ 100 mg/l *(Note 3)*

and the substance is not rapidly degradable and/or the experimentally determined BCF is ≥ 500 (or, if absent, the log K_{ow} ≥ 4). *(Notes 4 and 5)*.

(c)   "Safety net" classification

Category Chronic 4:

Poorly soluble substances for which no acute toxicity is recorded at levels up to the water solubility, and which are not rapidly degradable and have a log K_{ow} ≥ 4, indicating a potential to bioaccumulate, will be classified in this category unless other scientific evidence exists showing classification to be unnecessary. Such evidence would include an experimentally determined BCF < 500, or a chronic toxicity NOECs > 1 mg/l, or evidence of rapid degradation in the environment.

NOTE 1:   *The organisms fish, crustacea and algae are tested as surrogate species covering a range of trophic levels and taxa, and the test methods are highly standardized. Data on other organisms may also be considered, however, provided they represent equivalent species and test endpoints.*

NOTE 2:   *When classifying substances as Acute 1 and/or Chronic 1 it is necessary at the same time to indicate an appropriate M factor (see 4.1.3.5.5.5) to apply the summation method.*

NOTE 3:   *Where the algal toxicity ErC_{50} [= EC_{50} (growth rate)] falls more than 100 times below the next most sensitive species and results in a classification based solely on this effect, consideration should be given to whether this toxicity is representative of the toxicity to aquatic plants. Where it can be shown that this is not the case, professional judgment should be used in deciding if classification should be applied. Classification should be based on the ErC_{50}. In circumstances where the basis of the EC_{50} is not specified and no ErC_{50} is recorded, classification should be based on the lowest EC_{50} available.*

NOTE 4:   *Lack of rapid degradability is based on either a lack of ready biodegradability or other evidence of lack of rapid degradation. When no useful data on degradability are available, either experimentally determined or estimated data, the substance should be regarded as not rapidly degradable.*

NOTE 5:   *Potential to bioaccumulate, based on an experimentally derived BCF ≥ 500 or, if absent, a log K_{ow} ≥ 4, provided log K_{ow} is an appropriate descriptor for the bioaccumulation potential of the substance. Measured log K_{ow} values take precedence over estimated values and measured BCF values take precedence over log K_{ow} values.*

Figure 4.1.1: Categories for substances long-term (chronic) hazardous to the aquatic environment

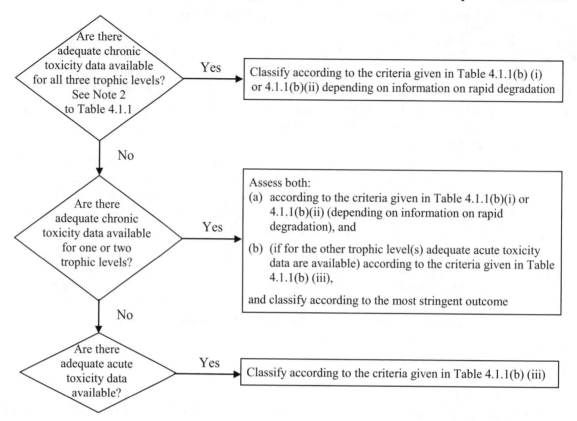

4.1.2.5   The system for classification recognizes that the core intrinsic hazard to aquatic organisms is represented by both the acute and chronic toxicity of a substance, the relative importance of which is determined by the specific regulatory system in operation. Distinction can be made between the short-term (acute) hazard and the long-term (chronic) hazard and therefore separate hazard categories are defined for both properties representing a gradation in the level of hazard identified. The lowest of the available toxicity values between and within the different trophic levels (fish, crustacean, algae) will normally be used to define the appropriate hazard category(ies). There may be circumstances, however, when a weight of evidence approach may be used. Acute toxicity data are the most readily available and the tests used are the most standardized.

4.1.2.6   Acute toxicity represents a key property in defining the hazard where transport of large quantities of a substance may give rise to short-term dangers arising from accidents or major spillages. Hazards categories up to $L(E)C_{50}$ values of 100 mg/l are thus defined although categories up to 1000 mg/l may be used in certain regulatory frameworks. The category Acute 1 may be further sub-divided to include an additional category for acute toxicity $L(E)C_{50} \leq 0.1$ mg/l in certain regulatory systems such as that defined by MARPOL 73/78 Annex II. It is anticipated that their use would be restricted to regulatory systems concerning bulk transport.

4.1.2.7   For packaged substances it is considered that the principal hazard is defined by chronic toxicity, although acute toxicity at $L(E)C_{50}$ levels ≤ 1 mg/l are also considered hazardous. Levels of substances up to 1 mg/l are considered as possible in the aquatic environment following normal use and disposal. At toxicity levels above this, it is considered that the acute toxicity itself does not describe the principal hazard, which arises from low concentrations causing effects over a longer time scale. Thus, a number of hazard categories are defined which are based on levels of chronic aquatic toxicity. Chronic toxicity data are not available for many substances, however, and in those cases it is necessary to use the available data on acute toxicity to estimate this property. The intrinsic properties of a lack of rapid degradability and/or a potential to bioconcentrate in combination with acute toxicity may be used to assign a substance to a long-term (chronic) hazard category. Where chronic toxicity is available showing NOECs greater than water solubility or greater than 1 mg/l, this would indicate that no classification in any of the long-term (chronic) hazard categories Chronic 1 to 3 would be necessary. Equally, for substances with an

L(E)C$_{50}$ > 100 mg/l, the toxicity is considered as insufficient to warrant classification in most regulatory systems.

4.1.2.8 Recognition is given to the classification goals of MARPOL 73/78 Annex II, which covers the transport of bulk quantities in ships tanks, which are aimed at regulating operational discharges from ships and assigning of suitable ship types. They go beyond that of protecting aquatic ecosystems, although that clearly is included. Additional hazard categories may thus be used which take account of factors such as physico-chemical properties and mammalian toxicity.

4.1.2.9 *Aquatic toxicity*

4.1.2.9.1 The organisms fish, crustacea and algae are tested as surrogate species covering a range of trophic levels and taxa, and the test methods are highly standardized. Data on other organisms may also be considered, however, provided they represent equivalent species and test endpoints. The algal growth inhibition test is a chronic test but the EC$_{50}$ is treated as an acute value for classification purposes. This EC$_{50}$ should normally be based on growth rate inhibition. If only the EC$_{50}$ based on reduction in biomass is available, or it is not indicated which EC$_{50}$ is reported, this value may be used in the same way.

4.1.2.9.2 Aquatic toxicity testing, by its nature, involves the dissolution of the substance under test in the water media used and the maintenance of a stable bioavailable exposure concentration over the course of the test. Some substances are difficult to test under standard procedures and thus special guidance will be developed on data interpretation for these substances and how the data should be used when applying the classification criteria.

4.1.2.10 *Bioaccumulation*

It is the bioaccumulation of substances within the aquatic organisms that can give rise to toxic effects over longer time scales even when actual water concentrations are low. The potential to bioaccumulate is determined by the partitioning between n-octanol and water. The relationship between the partition coefficient of an organic substance and its bioconcentration as measured by the BCF in fish has considerable scientific literature support. Using a cut-off value of log $K_{ow} \geq 4$ is intended to identify only those substances with a real potential to bioconcentrate. In recognition that the log K_{ow} is only an imperfect surrogate for a measured BCF, such a measured value would always take precedence. A BCF in fish of < 500 is considered as indicative of a low level of bioconcentration. Some relationships can be observed between chronic toxicity and bioaccumulation potential, as toxicity is related to the body burden.

4.1.2.11 *Rapid degradability*

4.1.2.11.1 Substances that rapidly degrade can be quickly removed from the environment. While effects can occur, particularly in the event of a spillage or accident, they will be localized and of short duration. The absence of rapid degradation in the environment can mean that a substance in the water has the potential to exert toxicity over a wide temporal and spatial scale. One way of demonstrating rapid degradation utilizes the biodegradation screening tests designed to determine whether a substance is "readily biodegradable". Thus a substance which passes this screening test is one that is likely to biodegrade "rapidly" in the aquatic environment, and is thus unlikely to be persistent. However, a fail in the screening test does not necessarily mean that the substance will not degrade rapidly in the environment. Thus a further criterion was added which would allow the use of data to show that the substance did actually degrade biotically or abiotically in the aquatic environment by > 70% in 28 days. Thus, if degradation could be demonstrated under environmentally realistic conditions, then the definition of "rapid degradability" would have been met. Many degradation data are available in the form of degradation half-lives and these can also be used in defining rapid degradation. Details regarding the interpretation of these data are further elaborated in the guidance document of Annex 9. Some tests measure the ultimate biodegradation of the substance, i.e. full mineralization is achieved. Primary biodegradation would not normally qualify in the assessment of rapid degradability unless it can be demonstrated that the degradation products do not fulfill the criteria for classification as hazardous to the aquatic environment.

4.1.2.11.2   It must be recognized that environmental degradation may be biotic or abiotic (e.g. hydrolysis) and the criteria used reflect this fact. Equally, it must be recognized that failing the ready biodegradability criteria in the OECD tests does not mean that the substance will not be degraded rapidly in the real environment. Thus where such rapid degradation can be shown, the substance should be considered as rapidly degradable. Hydrolysis can be considered if the hydrolysis products do not fulfil the criteria for classification as hazardous to the aquatic environment. A specific definition of rapid degradability is shown below. Other evidence of rapid degradation in the environment may also be considered and may be of particular importance where the substances are inhibitory to microbial activity at the concentration levels used in standard testing. The range of available data and guidance on its interpretation are provided in the guidance document of Annex 9.

4.1.2.11.3   Substances are considered rapidly degradable in the environment if the following criteria hold true:

(a)   if in 28-day ready biodegradation studies, the following levels of degradation are achieved:

(i)   tests based on dissolved organic carbon: 70%;

(ii)   tests based on oxygen depletion or carbon dioxide generation: 60% of theoretical maxima;

These levels of biodegradation must be achieved within 10 days of the start of degradation which point is taken as the time when 10% of the substance has been degraded, unless the substance is identified as a complex, multi-component substance with structurally similar constituents. In this case, and where there is sufficient justification, the 10-day window condition may be waived and the pass level applied at 28 days as explained in Annex 9 (A9.4.2.2.3).

(b)   if, in those cases where only BOD and COD data are available, when the ratio of BOD_5/COD is ≥ 0.5; or

(c)   if other convincing scientific evidence is available to demonstrate that the substance can be degraded (biotically and/or abiotically) in the aquatic environment to a level >70% within a 28-day period.

4.1.2.12   *Inorganic compounds and metals*

4.1.2.12.1   For inorganic compounds and metals, the concept of degradability as applied to organic compounds has limited or no meaning. Rather the substance may be transformed by normal environmental processes to either increase or decrease the bioavailability of the toxic species. Equally the use of bioaccumulation data should be treated with care. Specific guidance will be provided on how these data for such materials may be used in meeting the requirements of the classification criteria.

4.1.2.12.2   Poorly soluble inorganic compounds and metals may be acutely or chronically toxic in the aquatic environment depending on the intrinsic toxicity of the bioavailable inorganic species and the rate and amount of this species which may enter solution. A protocol for testing these poorly soluble materials is included in Annex 10. All evidence must be weighed in a classification decision. This would be especially true for metals showing borderline results in the Transformation/Dissolution Protocol.

4.1.2.13   *Use of QSARs*

While experimentally derived test data are preferred, where no experimental data are available, validated Quantitative Structure Activity Relationships (QSARs) for aquatic toxicity and log K_{ow} may be used in the classification process. Such validated QSARs may be used without modification to the agreed criteria, if restricted to chemicals for which their mode of action and applicability are well characterized. Reliable calculated toxicity and log K_{ow} values should be valuable in the safety net context. QSARs for predicting ready biodegradation are not yet sufficiently accurate to predict rapid degradation.

The classification criteria for substances diagrammatically summarized

Table 4.1.2: Classification scheme for substances hazardous to the aquatic environment

Classification categories			
Short-term (acute) hazard *(Note 1)*	**Long-term (chronic) hazard** *(Note 2)*		
	Adequate chronic toxicity data available		**Adequate chronic toxicity data not available** *(Note 1)*
	Non-rapidly degradable substances *(Note 3)*	**Rapidly degradable substances** *(Note 3)*	
Category: Acute 1 $L(E)C_{50} \leq 1.00$	**Category: Chronic 1** NOEC or $EC_x \leq 0.1$	**Category: Chronic 1** NOEC or $EC_x \leq 0.01$	**Category: Chronic 1** $L(E)C_{50} \leq 1.00$ and lack of rapid degradability and/or $BCF \geq 500$ or, if absent log $K_{ow} \geq 4$
Category: Acute 2 $1.00 < L(E)C_{50} \leq 10.0$	**Category: Chronic 2** $0.1 <$ NOEC or $EC_x \leq 1$	**Category: Chronic 2** $0.01 <$ NOEC or $EC_x \leq 0.1$	**Category: Chronic 2** $1.00 < L(E)C_{50} \leq 10.0$ and lack of rapid degradability and/or $BCF \geq 500$ or, if absent log $K_{ow} \geq 4$
Category: Acute 3 $10.0 < L(E)C_{50} \leq 100$		**Category: Chronic 3** $0.1 <$ NOEC or $EC_x \leq 1$	**Category: Chronic 3** $10.0 < L(E)C_{50} \leq 100$ and lack of rapid degradability and/or $BCF \geq 500$ or, if absent log $K_{ow} \geq 4$
	Category: Chronic 4 *(Note 4)* Example: *(Note 5)* No acute toxicity and lack of rapid degradability and $BCF \geq 500$ or, if absent log Kow ≥ 4, unless NOECs > 1 mg/l		

NOTE 1:   *Acute toxicity band based on $L(E)C_{50}$ values in mg/l for fish, crustacea and/or algae or other aquatic plants (or QSAR estimation if no experimental data).*

NOTE 2:   *Substances are classified in the various chronic categories unless there are adequate chronic toxicity data available for all three trophic levels above the water solubility or above 1 mg/l. ("Adequate" means that the data sufficiently cover the endpoint of concern. Generally this would mean measured test data, but in order to avoid unnecessary testing it can, on a case-by-case basis, also be estimated data, e.g. (Q)SAR, or for obvious cases expert judgment).*

NOTE 3:   *Chronic toxicity band based on NOEC or equivalent EC_x values in mg/l for fish or crustacea or other recognized measures for chronic toxicity.*

NOTE 4:   *The system also introduces a "safety net" classification (referred to as category Chronic 4) for use when the data available do not allow classification under the formal criteria but there are nevertheless some grounds for concern.*

NOTE 5:   *For poorly soluble substances for which no acute toxicity has been demonstrated at the solubility limit, and are both not rapidly degraded and have a potential to bioaccumulate, this category should apply unless it can be demonstrated that the substance does not require classification for aquatic long-term (chronic) hazards.*

4.1.3 Classification criteria for mixtures

4.1.3.1 The classification system for mixtures covers all classification categories which are used for substances, meaning categories Acute 1 to 3 and Chronic 1 to 4. In order to make use of all available data for purposes of classifying the aquatic environmental hazards of the mixture, the following assumption has been made and is applied where appropriate:

The "relevant ingredients" of a mixture are those which are present in a concentration equal to or greater than 0.1% (w/w) for ingredients classified as Acute and/or Chronic 1 and equal to or greater than 1% (w/w) for other ingredients, unless there is a presumption (e.g. in the case of highly toxic ingredients) that an ingredient present at a concentration less than 0.1% can still be relevant for classifying the mixture for aquatic environmental hazards.

4.1.3.2 The approach for classification of aquatic environmental hazards is tiered, and is dependent upon the type of information available for the mixture itself and for its ingredients. Elements of the tiered approach include classification based on tested mixtures, classification based on bridging principles, the use of "summation of classified ingredients" and/or an "additivity formula". Figure 4.1.2 outlines the process to be followed.

Figure 4.1.2: Tiered approach to classification of mixtures for short-term (acute) and long-term (chronic) aquatic environmental hazards

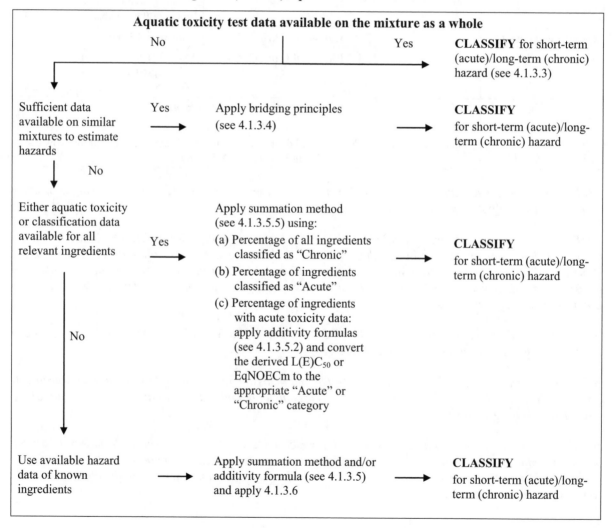

4.1.3.3   *Classification of mixtures when toxicity data are available for the complete mixture*

4.1.3.3.1   When the mixture as a whole has been tested to determine its aquatic toxicity, this information can be used for classifying the mixture according to the criteria that have been agreed for substances. The classification should normally be based on the data for fish, crustacea and algae/plants (see 4.1.1.3 and 4.1.1.4). When adequate acute or chronic data for the mixture as a whole are lacking, "bridging principles" or "summation method" should be applied (see paragraphs 4.1.3.4 and 4.1.3.5 and decision logic 4.1.5.2.2).

4.1.3.3.2   The long-term (chronic) hazard classification of mixtures requires additional information on degradability and in certain cases bioaccumulation. There are no degradability and bioaccumulation data for mixtures as a whole. Degradability and bioaccumulation tests for mixtures are not used as they are usually difficult to interpret, and such tests may be meaningful only for single substances.

4.1.3.3.3   *Classification for categories Acute 1, 2 and 3*

(a)   When there are adequate acute toxicity test data (LC_{50} or EC_{50}) available for the mixture as a whole showing $L(E)C_{50} \leq 100$ mg/l:

Classify the mixture as Acute 1, 2 or 3 in accordance with Table 4.1.1(a).

(b)   When there are acute toxicity test data ($LC_{50}(s)$ or $EC_{50}(s)$) available for the mixture as a whole showing $L(E)C_{50}(s) > 100$ mg/l, or above the water solubility:

No need to classify for short-term (acute) hazard

4.1.3.3.4   *Classification for categories Chronic 1, 2 and 3*

(a)   When there are adequate chronic toxicity data (EC_x or NOEC) available for the mixture as a whole showing EC_x or NOEC of the tested mixture ≤ 1 mg/l:

(i)   Classify the mixture as Chronic 1, 2 or 3 in accordance with Table 4.1.1 (b)(ii) (rapidly degradable) if the available information allows the conclusion that all relevant ingredients of the mixture are rapidly degradable;

(ii)   Classify the mixture as Chronic 1, 2 or 3 in all other cases in accordance with Table 4.1.1 (b)(i) (non-rapidly degradable);

(b)   When there are adequate chronic toxicity data (EC_x or NOEC) available for the mixture as a whole showing $EC_x(s)$ or NOEC(s) of the tested mixture > 1 mg/l or above the water solubility:

No need to classify for long-term (chronic) hazard, unless there are nevertheless reasons for concern.

4.1.3.3.5   *Classification for category Chronic 4*

If there are nevertheless reasons for concern:

Classify the mixture as Chronic 4 (safety net classification) in accordance with Table 4.1.1(c).

4.1.3.4 *Classification of mixtures when toxicity data are not available for the complete mixture: bridging principles*

4.1.3.4.1 Where the mixture itself has not been tested to determine its aquatic environmental hazard, but there are sufficient data on the individual ingredients and similar tested mixtures to adequately characterize the hazards of the mixture, this data will be used in accordance with the following agreed bridging principles. This ensures that the classification process uses the available data to the greatest extent possible in characterizing the hazards of the mixture without the necessity for additional testing in animals.

4.1.3.4.2 *Dilution*

Where a new mixture is formed by diluting a tested mixture or a substance with a diluent which has an equivalent or lower aquatic hazard classification than the least toxic original ingredient and which is not expected to affect the aquatic hazards of other ingredients, then the resulting mixture may be classified as equivalent to the original tested mixture or substance. Alternatively, the method explained in 4.1.3.5 could be applied.

4.1.3.4.3 *Batching*

The aquatic hazard classification of a tested production batch of a mixture can be assumed to be substantially equivalent to that of another untested production batch of the same commercial product when produced by or under the control of the same manufacturer, unless there is reason to believe there is significant variation such that the aquatic hazard classification of the untested batch has changed. If the latter occurs, new classification is necessary.

4.1.3.4.4 *Concentration of mixtures which are classified with the most severe classification categories (Chronic 1 and Acute 1)*

If a tested mixture is classified as Chronic 1 and/or Acute 1, and the ingredients of the mixture which are classified as Chronic 1 and/or Acute 1 are further concentrated, the more concentrated untested mixture should be classified with the same classification category as the original tested mixture without additional testing.

4.1.3.4.5 *Interpolation within one hazard category*

For three mixtures (A, B and C) with identical ingredients, where mixtures A and B have been tested and are in the same hazard category and where untested mixture C has the same toxicologically active ingredients as mixtures A and B but has concentrations of toxicologically active ingredients intermediate to the concentrations in mixtures A and B, then mixture C is assumed to be in the same hazard category as A and B.

4.1.3.4.6 *Substantially similar mixtures*

Given the following:

(a)   Two mixtures: (i)   A + B;
                       (ii)   C + B;

(b)   The concentration of ingredient B is essentially the same in both mixtures;

(c)   The concentration of ingredient A in mixture (i) equals that of ingredient C in mixture (ii);

(d)   Data on aquatic hazards for A and C are available and are substantially equivalent, i.e. they are in the same hazard category and are not expected to affect the aquatic toxicity of B.

If mixture (i) or (ii) is already classified based on test data, then the other mixture can be assigned the same hazard category.

4.1.3.5 Classification of mixtures when toxicity data are available for all ingredients or only for some ingredients of the mixture

4.1.3.5.1 The classification of a mixture is based on summation of the concentrations of its classified ingredients. The percentage of ingredients classified as "Acute" or "Chronic" will feed straight into the summation method. Details of the summation method are described in 4.1.3.5.5.

4.1.3.5.2 Mixtures can be made of a combination of both ingredients that are classified (as Acute 1, 2, 3 and/or Chronic 1, 2, 3, 4) and those for which adequate toxicity test data is available. When adequate toxicity data are available for more than one ingredient in the mixture, the combined toxicity of those ingredients may be calculated using the following additivity formulas (a) or (b), depending on the nature of the toxicity data:

(a) Based on acute aquatic toxicity:

$$\frac{\sum C_i}{L(E)C_{50_m}} = \sum_n \frac{C_i}{L(E)C_{50_i}}$$

where:

C_i = concentration of ingredient i (weight percentage);

$L(E)C_{50_i}$ = LC_{50} or EC_{50} for ingredient i, in (mg/l);

n = number of ingredients, and i is running from 1 to n;

$L(E)C_{50_m}$ = $L(E) C_{50}$ of the part of the mixture with test data;

The calculated toxicity may be used to assign that portion of the mixture a short-term (acute) hazard category which is then subsequently used in applying the summation method;

(b) Based on chronic aquatic toxicity:

$$\frac{\sum C_i + \sum C_j}{EqNOEC_m} = \sum_n \frac{C_i}{NOEC_i} + \sum_n \frac{C_j}{0.1 \times NOEC_j}$$

where:

C_i = concentration of ingredient i (weight percentage) covering the rapidly degradable ingredients;

C_j = concentration of ingredient j (weight percentage) covering the non- rapidly degradable ingredients;

$NOEC_i$ = NOEC (or other recognized measures for chronic toxicity) for ingredient i covering the rapidly degradable ingredients, in mg/l;

$NOEC_j$ = NOEC (or other recognized measures for chronic toxicity) for ingredient j covering the non-rapidly degradable ingredients, in mg/l;

n = number of ingredients, and i and j are running from 1 to n;

$EqNOEC_m$ = Equivalent NOEC of the part of the mixture with test data;

The equivalent toxicity thus reflects the fact that non-rapidly degrading substances are classified one hazard category level more "severe" than rapidly degrading substances.

The calculated equivalent toxicity may be used to assign that portion of the mixture a long-term (chronic) hazard category, in accordance with the criteria for rapidly degradable substances (Table 4.1.1(b)(ii)), which is then subsequently used in applying the summation method.

4.1.3.5.3   When applying the additivity formula for part of the mixture, it is preferable to calculate the toxicity of this part of the mixture using for each ingredient toxicity values that relate to the same taxonomic group (i.e. fish, crustacean or algae) and then to use the highest toxicity (lowest value) obtained (i.e. use the most sensitive of the three groups). However, when toxicity data for each ingredient are not available in the same taxonomic group, the toxicity value of each ingredient should be selected in the same manner that toxicity values are selected for the classification of substances, i.e. the higher toxicity (from the most sensitive test organism) is used. The calculated acute and chronic toxicity may then be used to classify this part of the mixture as Acute 1, 2 or 3 and/or Chronic 1, 2 or 3 using the same criteria described for substances.

4.1.3.5.4   If a mixture is classified in more than one way, the method yielding the more conservative result should be used.

4.1.3.5.5   *Summation method*

4.1.3.5.5.1   Rationale

4.1.3.5.5.1.1   In case of the ingredient classification categories Acute 1/Chronic 1 to Acute 3/Chronic 3, the underlying toxicity criteria differ by a factor of 10 in moving from one category to another. Ingredients with a classification in a high toxicity band may therefore contribute to the classification of a mixture in a lower band. The calculation of these classification categories therefore needs to consider the contribution of all ingredients classified Acute 1/Chronic 1 to Acute 3/Chronic 3 together.

4.1.3.5.5.1.2   When a mixture contains ingredients classified as Acute 1 or Chronic 1, attention should be paid to the fact that such ingredients, when their acute toxicity is well below 1 mg/l and/or chronic toxicity is well below 0.1 mg/l (if non rapidly degradable) and 0.01 mg/l (if rapidly degradable) contribute to the toxicity of the mixture even at a low concentration (see also *Classification of hazardous substances and mixtures* in Chapter 1.3, paragraph 1.3.3.2.1). Active ingredients in pesticides often possess such high aquatic toxicity but also some other substances like organometallic compounds. Under these circumstances the application of the normal cut-off values/concentration limits may lead to an "under-classification" of the mixture. Therefore, multiplying factors should be applied to account for highly toxic ingredients, as described in 4.1.3.5.5.5.

4.1.3.5.5.2   Classification procedure

In general a more severe classification for mixtures overrides a less severe classification, e.g. a classification with Chronic 1 overrides a classification with Chronic 2. As a consequence the classification procedure is already completed if the result of the classification is Chronic 1. A more severe classification than Chronic 1 is not possible, therefore it is not necessary to undergo the further classification procedure.

4.1.3.5.5.3   Classification for categories Acute 1, 2 and 3

4.1.3.5.5.3.1   First, all ingredients classified as Acute 1 are considered. If the sum of the concentrations (in %) of these ingredients is ≥ 25% the whole mixture is classified as Acute 1. If the result of the calculation is a classification of the mixture as Acute 1, the classification process is completed.

4.1.3.5.5.3.2   In cases where the mixture is not classified as Acute 1, classification of the mixture as Acute 2 is considered. A mixture is classified as Acute 2 if 10 times the sum of the concentrations (in %) of all ingredients classified as Acute 1 plus the sum of the concentrations (in %) of all ingredients classified as Acute 2 is ≥ 25%. If the result of the calculation is classification of the mixture as Acute 2, the classification process is completed.

4.1.3.5.5.3.3   In cases where the mixture is not classified either as Acute 1 or Acute 2, classification of the mixture as Acute 3 is considered. A mixture is classified as Acute 3 if 100 times the sum of the concentrations (in %) of all ingredients classified as Acute 1 plus 10 times the sum of the concentrations (in %) of all ingredients classified as Acute 2 plus the sum of the concentrations (in %) of all ingredients classified as Acute 3 is ≥ 25%.

4.1.3.5.5.3.4   The classification of mixtures for short-term (acute) hazards based on this summation of the concentrations of classified ingredients is summarized in Table 4.1.3.

Table 4.1.3: Classification of a mixture for short-term (acute) hazards based on summation of the concentrations of classified ingredients

Sum of the concentrations (in %) of ingredients classified as:		Mixture is classified as:
Acute 1 × M[a]	≥ 25%	Acute 1
(M × 10 × Acute 1) + Acute 2	≥ 25%	Acute 2
(M × 100 × Acute 1) + (10 × Acute 2) + Acute 3	≥ 25%	Acute 3

[a]   *For explanation of the M factor, see 4.1.3.5.5.5.*

4.1.3.5.5.4   Classification for categories Chronic 1, 2, 3 and 4

4.1.3.5.5.4.1   First, all ingredients classified as Chronic 1 are considered. If the sum of the concentrations (in %) of these ingredients is ≥ 25% the mixture is classified as Chronic 1. If the result of the calculation is a classification of the mixture as Chronic 1 the classification procedure is completed.

4.1.3.5.5.4.2   In cases where the mixture is not classified as Chronic 1, classification of the mixture as Chronic 2 is considered. A mixture is classified as Chronic 2 if 10 times the sum of the concentrations (in %) of all ingredients classified as Chronic 1 plus the sum of the concentrations (in %) of all ingredients classified as Chronic 2 is ≥ 25%. If the result of the calculation is classification of the mixture as Chronic 2, the classification process is completed.

4.1.3.5.5.4.3   In cases where the mixture is not classified either as Chronic 1 or Chronic 2, classification of the mixture as Chronic 3 is considered. A mixture is classified as Chronic 3 if 100 times the sum of the concentrations (in %) of all ingredients classified as Chronic 1 plus 10 times the sum of the concentrations (in %) of all ingredients classified as Chronic 2 plus the sum of the concentrations (in %) of all ingredients classified as Chronic 3 is ≥ 25%.

4.1.3.5.5.4.4   If the mixture is still not classified in either category Chronic 1, 2 or 3, classification of the mixture as Chronic 4 should be considered. A mixture is classified as Chronic 4 if the sum of the concentrations (in %) of ingredients classified as Chronic 1, 2, 3 and 4 is ≥ 25%.

4.1.3.5.5.4.5   The classification of mixtures for long-term (chronic) hazards based on this summation of the concentrations of classified ingredients is summarized in Table 4.1.4.

Table 4.1.4: Classification of a mixture for long-term (chronic) hazards based on summation of the concentrations of classified ingredients

Sum of the concentrations (in %) of ingredients classified as:		Mixture is classified as:
Chronic 1 × M[a]	≥ 25%	Chronic 1
(M × 10 × Chronic 1) + Chronic 2	≥ 25%	Chronic 2
(M × 100 × Chronic 1) + (10 × Chronic 2)+ Chronic 3	≥ 25%	Chronic 3
Chronic 1 + Chronic 2 + Chronic 3 + Chronic 4	≥ 25%	Chronic 4

[a]   *For explanation of the M factor, see 4.1.3.5.5.5.*

4.1.3.5.5.5   Mixtures with highly toxic ingredients

Acute 1 or Chronic 1 ingredients with acute toxicities well below 1 mg/l and/or chronic toxicities well below 0.1 mg/l (if non-rapidly degradable) and 0.01 mg/l (if rapidly degradable) may influence the toxicity of the mixture and should be given increased weight in applying the summation method. When a mixture contains ingredients classified as Acute or Chronic 1, the tiered approach described in 4.1.3.5.5.3 and 4.1.3.5.5.4 should be applied using a weighted sum by multiplying the concentrations of Acute 1 and Chronic 1 ingredients by a factor, instead of merely adding up the percentages. This means that the concentration of "Acute 1" in the left column of Table 4.1.3 and the concentration of "Chronic 1" in the left column of Table 4.1.4 are multiplied by the appropriate multiplying factor. The multiplying factors to be applied to these ingredients are defined using the toxicity value, as summarized in Table 4.1.5 below. Therefore, in order to classify a mixture containing Acute/Chronic 1 ingredients, the classifier needs to be informed of the value of the M factor in order to apply the summation method. Alternatively, the additivity formula (see 4.1.3.5.2) may be used when toxicity data are available for all highly toxic ingredients in the mixture and there is convincing evidence that all other ingredients, including those for which specific acute and/or chronic toxicity data are not available, are of low or no toxicity and do not significantly contribute to the environmental hazard of the mixture.

Table 4.1.5: Multiplying factors for highly toxic ingredients of mixtures

Acute toxicity	M factor	Chronic toxicity	M factor	
$L(E)C_{50}$ value		NOEC value	NRD^a ingredients	RD^b ingredients
$0.1 < L(E)C_{50} \leq 1$	1	$0.01 < NOEC \leq 0.1$	1	-
$0.01 < L(E)C_{50} \leq 0.1$	10	$0.001 < NOEC \leq 0.01$	10	1
$0.001 < L(E)C_{50} \leq 0.01$	100	$0.0001 < NOEC \leq 0.001$	100	10
$0.0001 < L(E)C_{50} \leq 0.001$	1000	$0.00001 < NOEC \leq 0.0001$	1000	100
$0.00001 < L(E)C_{50} \leq 0.0001$	10000	$0.000001 < NOEC \leq 0.00001$	10000	1000
(continue in factor 10 intervals)		(continue in factor 10 intervals)		

[a]   *Non-rapidly degradable*
[b]   *Rapidly degratdable*

4.1.3.6   *Classification of mixtures with ingredients without any useable information*

In the event that no useable information on acute and/or chronic aquatic toxicity is available for one or more relevant ingredients, it is concluded that the mixture cannot be attributed (a) definitive hazard category(ies). In this situation the mixture should be classified based on the known ingredients only, with the additional statement that: "× % of the mixture consists of ingredient(s) of unknown hazards to the aquatic environment". The competent authority can decide to specify that the additional statement is communicated on the label or on the SDS or both, or to leave the choice of where to place the statement to the manufacturer/supplier.

4.1.4   Hazard communication

General and specific considerations concerning labelling requirements are provided in *Hazard communication: Labelling* (Chapter 1.4). Annex 1 contains summary tables about classification and labelling. Annex 3 contains examples of precautionary statements and pictograms which can be used where allowed by the competent authority.

Table 4.1.6: Label elements for hazardous to the aquatic environment

SHORT-TERM (ACUTE) AQUATIC HAZARD

	Category 1	Category 2	Category 3
Symbol	Environment	*No symbol*	*No symbol*
Signal word	Warning	*No signal word*	*No signal word*
Hazard statement	Very toxic to aquatic life	Toxic to aquatic life	Harmful to aquatic life

LONG-TERM (CHRONIC) AQUATIC HAZARD

	Category 1	Category 2	Category 3	Category 4
Symbol	Environment	Environment	*No symbol*	*No symbol*
Signal word	Warning	*No signal word*	*No signal word*	*No signal word*
Hazard statement	Very toxic to aquatic life with long lasting effects	Toxic to aquatic life with long lasting effects	Harmful to aquatic life with long lasting effects	May cause long lasting harmful effects to aquatic life

4.1.5   Decision logic for substances and mixtures hazardous to the aquatic environment

The decision logics which follow are not part of the harmonized classification system but are provided here as additional guidance. It is strongly recommended that the person responsible for classification study the criteria before and during use of the decision logic.

4.1.5.1 *Short-term (acute) aquatic hazard classification*

4.1.5.1.1 *Decision logic 4.1.1 for substances and mixtures hazardous to the aquatic environment*

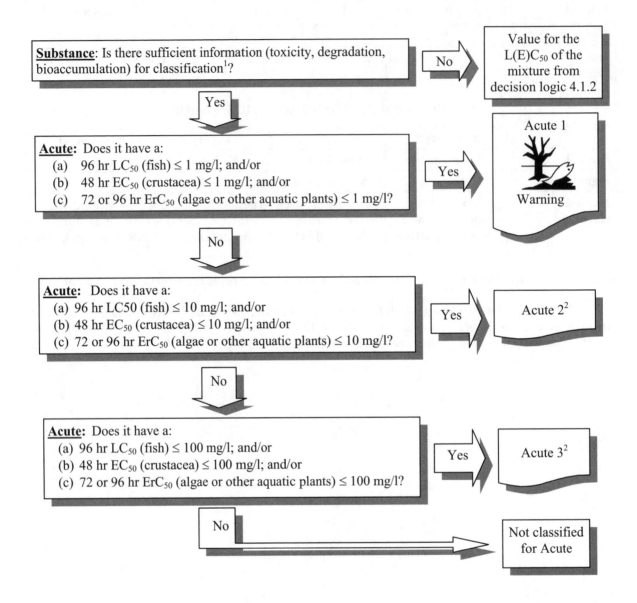

---

[1]   *Classification can be based on either measured data and/or calculated data (see 4.1.2.13 and Annex 9) and/or analogy decisions (see A9.6.4.5 in Annex 9).*

[2]   *Labelling requirements differ from one regulatory system to another, and certain classification categories may only be used in one or a few regulations.*

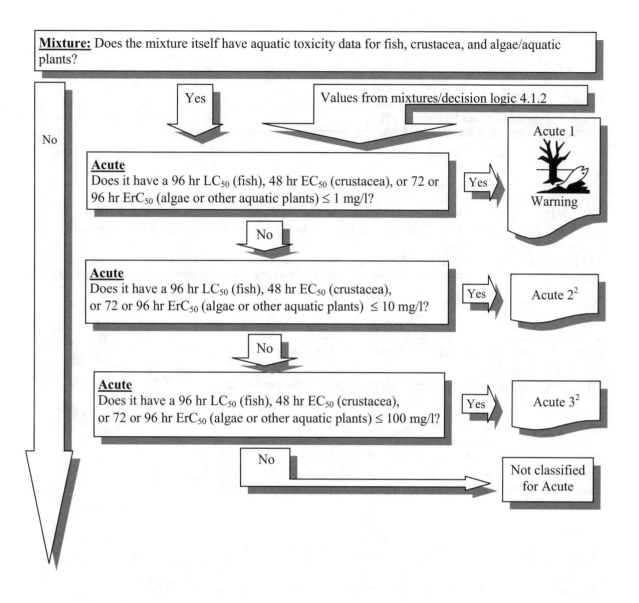

Mixture: Does the mixture itself have aquatic toxicity data for fish, crustacea, and algae/aquatic plants?

No

Yes

Values from mixtures/decision logic 4.1.2

Acute
Does it have a 96 hr LC_{50} (fish), 48 hr EC_{50} (crustacea), or 72 or 96 hr ErC_{50} (algae or other aquatic plants) $\leq$ 1 mg/l?

Yes

Acute 1

Warning

No

Acute
Does it have a 96 hr LC_{50} (fish), 48 hr EC_{50} (crustacea), or 72 or 96 hr ErC_{50} (algae or other aquatic plants) $\leq$ 10 mg/l?

Yes

Acute 2[2]

No

Acute
Does it have a 96 hr LC_{50} (fish), 48 hr EC_{50} (crustacea), or 72 or 96 hr ErC_{50} (algae or other aquatic plants) $\leq$ 100 mg/l?

Yes

Acute 3[2]

No

Not classified for Acute

---

[2]   *Labelling requirements differ from one regulatory system to another, and certain classification categories may only be used in one or a few regulations.*

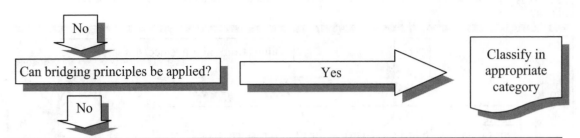

No

Can bridging principles be applied? ——— Yes ———▶ Classify in appropriate category

No

Use all available ingredient information in the summation method as follows [3]:
(a) For ingredients with available toxicity value(s) apply the additivity formula (decision logic 4.1.2), determine the hazard category for that part of the mixture and use this information in the summation method below;
(b) Classified ingredients will feed directly into the summation method below.

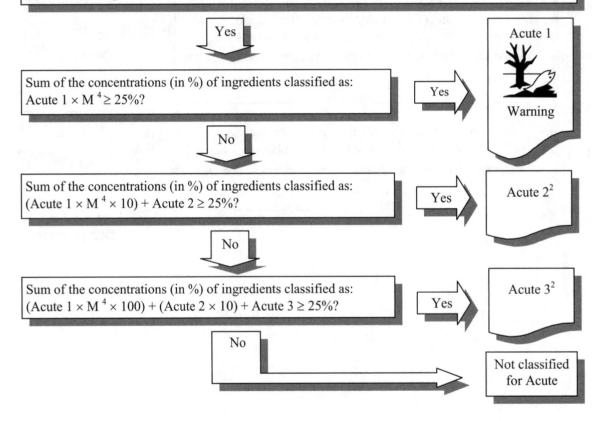

Yes

Sum of the concentrations (in %) of ingredients classified as:
Acute $1 \times M^4 \geq 25\%$? ——— Yes ———▶ Acute 1 [picture] Warning

No

Sum of the concentrations (in %) of ingredients classified as:
$(Acute 1 \times M^4 \times 10) + Acute 2 \geq 25\%$? ——— Yes ———▶ Acute 2[2]

No

Sum of the concentrations (in %) of ingredients classified as:
$(Acute 1 \times M^4 \times 100) + (Acute 2 \times 10) + Acute 3 \geq 25\%$? ——— Yes ———▶ Acute 3[2]

No ——————————————————————————▶ Not classified for Acute

---

[2]   *Labelling requirements differ from one regulatory system to another, and certain classification categories may only be used in one or a few regulations.*

[3]   *If not all ingredients have information, include the statement "x % of the mixture consists of ingredients(s) of unknown hazards to the aquatic environment" on the label. The competent authority can decide to specify that the additional statement be communicated on the label or on the SDS or both, or to leave the choice of where to place the statement to the manufacturer/supplier. Alternatively, in the case of a mixture with highly toxic ingredients, if toxicity values are available for these highly toxic ingredients and all other ingredients do not significantly contribute to the hazard of the mixture, then the additivity formula may be applied (see 4.1.3.5.5.5). In this case and other cases where toxicity values are available for all ingredients, the short-term (acute) classification may be made solely on the basis of the additivity formula.*

[4]   *For explanation of M factor see 4.1.3.5.5.5.*

Apply the additivity formula:

$$\frac{\sum C_i}{L(E)C_{50_m}} = \sum_n \frac{C_i}{L(E)C_{50_i}}$$

where:

C_i = concentration of ingredient i (weight percentage)

$L(E)C_{50_i}$ = (mg/l) LC_{50} or EC_{50} for ingredient i

n = number of ingredients, and i is running from 1 to n

$L(E)C_{50_m}$ = $L(E)C_{50}$ of the part of the mixture with test data

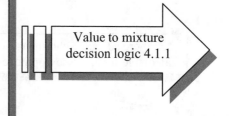

Value to mixture decision logic 4.1.1

4.1.5.2 *Long-term (chronic) aquatic hazard classification*

4.1.5.2.1 *Decision logic 4.1.3 (a) for substances*

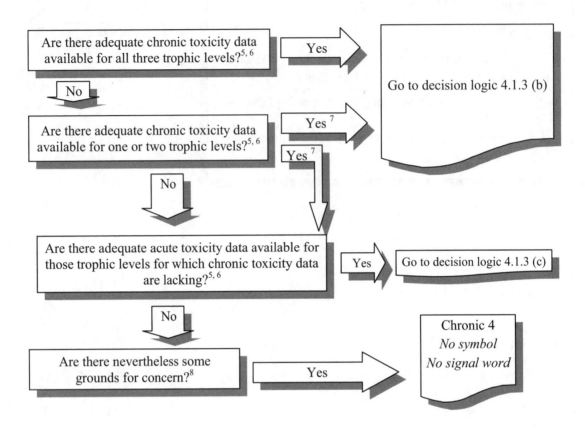

---

[5]   *Data are preferably to be derived using internationally harmonized test methods (e.g. OECD Test Guidelines or equivalent) according to the principles of good laboratory practices (GLP), but data from other test methods such as national methods may also be used where they are considered as equivalent (see 4.1.1.2.2 and A9.3.2 of Annex 9).*

[6]   *See Figure 4.1.1.*

[7]   *Follow the flowchart in both ways and choose the most stringent classification outcome.*

[8]   *Note that the system also introduces a "safety net" classification (referred to as Category: Chronic 4) for use when the data available do not allow classification under the formal criteria but there are nevertheless some grounds for concern.*

4.1.5.2.2 *Decision logic 4.1.3 (b) for substances (when adequate chronic toxicity data are available for all three trophic levels)*[5]

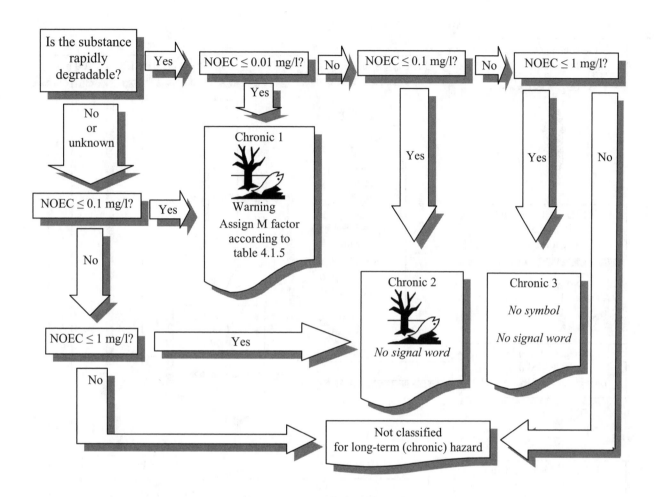

---

[5] *Data are preferably to be derived using internationally harmonized test methods (e.g. OECD Test Guidelines or equivalent) according to the principles of good laboratory practices (GLP), but data from other test methods such as national methods may also be used where they are considered as equivalent (see 4.1.1.2.2 and A9.3.2 of Annex 9).*

4.1.5.2.3 *Decision logic 4.1.3 (c) for substances (when adequate chronic toxicity data not are available for all three trophic levels)*[5]

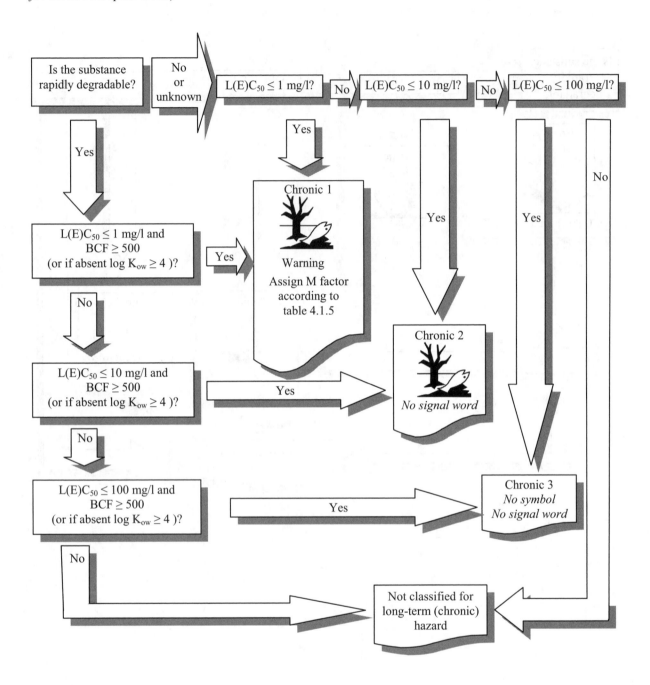

---

[5]   *Data are preferably to be derived using internationally harmonized test methods (e.g. OECD Test Guidelines or equivalent) according to the principles of good laboratory practices (GLP), but data from other test methods such as national methods may also be used where they are considered as equivalent (see 4.1.1.2.2 and A9.3.2 of Annex 9).*

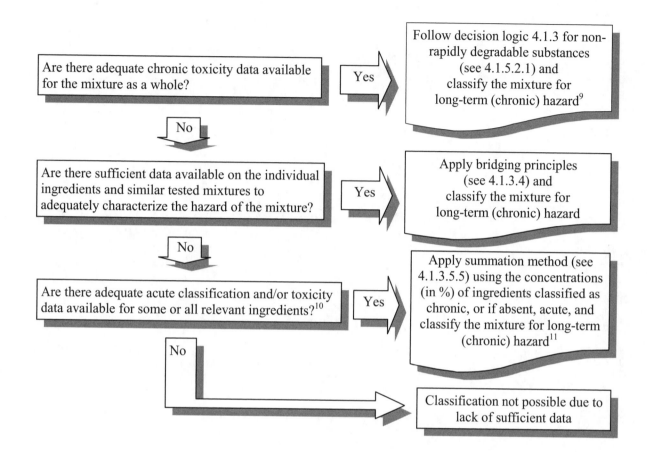

---

[9]   *Degradability and bioaccumulation tests for mixtures are not used as they are usually difficult to interpret, and such tests may be meaningful only for single substances. The mixture is therefore by default regarded as non-rapidly degradable. However, if the available information allows the conclusion that all relevant ingredients of the mixture are rapidly degradable the mixture can, for classification purposes, be regarded as rapidly degradable.*

[10]   *In the event that no useable information on acute and/or chronic aquatic toxicity is available for one or more relevant ingredients, it is concluded that the mixture cannot be attributed (a) definitive hazard category(ies). In this situation the mixture should be classified based on the known ingredients only, with the additional statement that: "× % of the mixture consists of ingredient(s) of unknown hazards to the aquatic environment". The competent authority can decide to specify that the additional statement be communicated on the label or on the SDS or both, or to leave the choice of where to place the statement to the manufacturer/supplier.*

[11]   *When adequate toxicity data are available for more than one ingredient in the mixture, the combined toxicity of those ingredients may be calculated using the additivity formulas (a) or (b) in 4.1.3.5.2, depending on the nature of the toxicity data. The calculated toxicity may be used to assign that portion of the mixture a short-term (acute) or long-term (chronic) hazard category which is then subsequently used in applying the summation method. (It is preferable to calculate the toxicity of this part of the mixture using for each ingredient a toxicity value that relate to the same taxonomic group (e.g. fish, crustacea or algae) and then to use the highest toxicity (lowest value) obtained (i.e. use the most sensitive of the three groups) (see 4.1.3.5.3)).*

CHAPTER 4.2

HAZARDOUS TO THE OZONE LAYER

4.2.1 Definitions

Ozone Depleting Potential (ODP) is an integrative quantity, distinct for each halocarbon source species, that represents the extent of ozone depletion in the stratosphere expected from the halocarbon on a mass-for-mass basis relative to CFC-11. The formal definition of ODP is the ratio of integrated perturbations to total ozone, for a differential mass emission of a particular compound relative to an equal emission of CFC-11.

Montreal Protocol is the Montreal Protocol on Substances that Deplete the Ozone Layer as either adjusted and/or amended by the Parties to the Protocol.

4.2.2 Classification criteria[1]

A substance or mixture shall be classified as Category 1 according to the following table:

Table 4.2.1: Criteria for substances and mixtures hazardous to the ozone layer

Category	Criteria
1	Any of the controlled substances listed in Annexes to the Montreal Protocol; or Any mixture containing at least one ingredient listed in the Annexes to the Montreal Protocol, at a concentration $\geq 0.1\%$

4.2.3 Hazard communication

General and specific considerations concerning labelling requirements are provided in *Hazard Communication: Labelling* (Chapter 1.4). Annex 1 contains summary tables about classification and labelling. Annex 3 contains examples of precautionary statements and pictograms which can be used where allowed by the competent authority.

Table 4.2.2: Label elements for substances and mixtures hazardous to the ozone layer

	Category 1
Symbol	Exclamation mark
Signal word	Warning
Hazard statement	Harms public health and the environment by destroying ozone in the upper atmosphere

---

[1] *The criteria in this chapter are intended to be applied to substances and mixtures. Equipment, articles or appliances (such as refrigeration or air conditioning equipment) containing substances hazardous to the ozone layer are beyond the scope of these criteria. Consistent with 1.1.2.5 (a)(iii) regarding pharmaceutical products, GHS classification and labelling criteria do not apply to medical inhalers at the point of intentional intake.*

4.2.4   **Decision logic for substances and mixtures hazardous to the ozone layer**

The decision logic which follows is not part of the harmonized classification system but is provided here as additional guidance. It is strongly recommended that the person responsible for classification study the criteria before and during use of the decision logic.

Decision logic 4.2.1

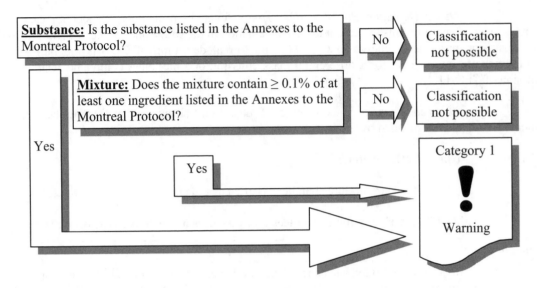

ANNEXES

ANNEX 1

CLASSIFICATION AND LABELLING
SUMMARY TABLES

Annex 1

CLASSIFICATION AND LABELLING SUMMARY TABLES

NOTE: *The codification of hazard statements is further explained in Annex 3 (Section 1). The hazard statement codes are intended to be used for reference purposes only. They are not part of the hazard statement text and should not be used to replace it.*

A1.1   Explosives (see Chapter 2.1 for classification criteria)

Classification		Labelling				Hazard statement codes
Hazard class	Hazard category	Pictogram		Signal word	Hazard statement	
		GHS	UN Model Regulations[a]			
Explosives	Unstable explosive		*(Transport not allowed)*	Danger	Unstable explosive	H200
	Division 1.1				Explosive; mass explosion hazard	H201
	Division 1.2				Explosive; severe projection hazard	H202
	Division 1.3				Explosive; fire, blast or projection hazard	H203
	Division 1.4			Warning	Fire or projection hazard	H204
	Division 1.5	*No pictogram*		Danger	May mass explode in fire	H205
	Division 1.6	*No pictogram*		*No signal word*	*No hazard statement*	*None*

[a]   *(*) Place for compatibility group.*

The pictogram for Divisions 1.1, 1.2 and 1.3 is also assigned to substances which have an explosive subsidiary risk, but without the indication of the division number and the compatibility group (see also "Self-reactive substances and mixtures" and "Organic peroxides").

A1.2 Flammable gases (including chemically unstable gases) (see Chapter 2.2 for classification criteria)

Classification		Labelling				Hazard statement codes
Hazard class	Hazard category	Pictogram		Signal word	Hazard statement	
		GHS	UN Model Regulations[a]			
Flammable gases (including chemically unstable gases)	1			**Danger**	Extremely flammable gas	H220
	2	*No pictogram*	*Not required*	**Warning**	Flammable gas	H221
	A (chemically unstable gases)	*No additional pictogram*	*Not required*	*No additional signal word*	*Additional hazard statement:* May react explosively even in the absence of air	H230
	B (chemically unstable gases)	*No additional pictogram*	*Not required*	*No additional signal word*	*Additional hazard statement:* May react explosively even in the absence of air at elevated pressure and/or temperature	H231

[a] *Under the UN Recommendations on the Transport of Dangerous Goods, Model Regulations, the symbol, number and border line may be shown in black instead of white. The background colour stays red in both cases.*

A1.3 Aerosols (see Chapter 2.3 for classification criteria)

Classification		Labelling				Hazard statement codes
Hazard class	Hazard category	Pictogram		Signal word	Hazard statement	
		GHS	UN Model Regulations[a]			
Aerosols	1			**Danger**	Extremely flammable aerosol	H222
					Pressurized container: may burst if heated	H229
	2			**Warning**	Flammable aerosol	H223
					Pressurized container: may burst if heated	H229
	3	*No pictogram*		**Warning**	Pressurized container: may burst if heated	H229

[a] *Under the UN Recommendations on the Transport of Dangerous Goods, Model Regulations, the symbol, number and border line may be shown in black or white. The background colour stays red in the first two cases and green in the third case.*

A1.4   **Oxidizing gases** (see Chapter 2.4 for classification criteria)

Classification		Labelling				Hazard statement code
Hazard class	Hazard category	Pictogram		Signal word	Hazard statement	
		GHS	UN Model Regulations			
Oxidizing gases	1			**Danger**	May cause or intensify fire; oxidizer	H270

A1.5   **Gases under pressure** (see Chapter 2.5 for classification criteria)

Classification		Labelling				Hazard statement codes
Hazard class	Hazard category	Pictogram		Signal word	Hazard statement	
		GHS	UN Model Regulations[a]			
Gases under pressure	Compressed gas			**Warning**	Contains gas under pressure; may explode if heated	H280
	Liquefied gas			**Warning**	Contains gas under pressure; may explode if heated	H280
	Refrigerated liquefied gas			**Warning**	Contains refrigerated gas; may cause cryogenic burns or injury	H281
	Dissolved gas			**Warning**	Contains gas under pressure; may explode if heated	H280

[a] *Under the UN Recommendations on the Transport of Dangerous Goods, Model Regulations, the symbol, number and border line may be shown in white instead of black. The background colour stays green in both cases. This pictogram is not required for toxic or flammable gases (see also note "a" to tables A1.17 and A1.2).*

A1.6   **Flammable liquids** (see Chapter 2.6 for classification criteria)

Classification		Labelling				Hazard statement codes
Hazard class	**Hazard category**	**Pictogram**		**Signal word**	**Hazard statement**	
		GHS	**UN Model Regulations**[a]			
Flammable liquids	1			**Danger**	Extremely flammable liquid and vapour	H224
	2			**Danger**	Highly flammable liquid and vapour	H225
	3			**Warning**	Flammable liquid and vapour	H226
	4	*No pictogram*	*Not required*	**Warning**	Combustible liquid	H227

[a]   *Under the UN Recommendations on the Transport of Dangerous Goods, Model Regulations, the symbol, number and border line may be shown in black instead of white. The background colour stays red in both cases.*

A1.7   **Flammable solids** (see Chapter 2.7 for classification criteria)

Classification		Labelling				Hazard statement codes
Hazard class	**Hazard category**	**Pictogram**		**Signal word**	**Hazard statement**	
		GHS	**UN Model Regulations**			
Flammable solids	1			**Danger**	Flammable solid	H228
	2			**Warning**	Flammable solid	H228

A1.8   Self-reactive substances and mixtures (see Chapter 2.8 for classification criteria)

Classification		Labelling				Hazard statement codes
Hazard class	Hazard category	Pictogram		Signal word	Hazard statement	
		GHS	UN Model Regulations[a]			
Self-reactive substances and mixtures	Type A		*(Transport may not be allowed)[b]*	**Danger**	Heating may cause an explosion	H240
	Type B			**Danger**	Heating may cause a fire or explosion	H241
	Types C and D			**Danger**	Heating may cause a fire	H242
	Types E and F			**Warning**	Heating may cause a fire	H242
	Type G	*No pictogram*	*Not required*	*No signal word*	*No hazard statement*	*None*

[a]   *For Type B, under the UN Recommendations on the Transport of Dangerous Goods, Model Regulations, special provision 181 may apply (Exemption of explosive label with competent authority approval. See Chapter 3.3 of the UN Model Regulations for more details).*

[b]   *May not be acceptable for transport in the packaging in which it is tested (See Chapter 2.5, par. 2.5.3.2.2 of the UN Model Regulations).*

A1.9   Pyrophoric liquids (see Chapter 2.9 for classification criteria)

Classification		Labelling				Hazard statement code
Hazard class	Hazard category	Pictogram		Signal word	Hazard statement	
		GHS	UN Model Regulations			
Pyrophoric liquids	1			**Danger**	Catches fire spontaneously if exposed to air	H250

A1.10   Pyrophoric solids (see Chapter 2.10 for classification criteria)

Classification		Labelling				Hazard statement code
Hazard class	Hazard category	Pictogram		Signal word	Hazard statement	
		GHS	UN Model Regulations			
Pyrophoric solids	1			Danger	Catches fire spontaneously if exposed to air	H250

A1.11   Self-heating substances and mixtures (see Chapter 2.11 for classification criteria)

Classification		Labelling				Hazard statement codes
Hazard class	Hazard category	Pictogram		Signal word	Hazard statement	
		GHS	UN Model Regulations			
Self-heating substances and mixtures	1			Danger	Self-heating; may catch fire	H251
	2			Warning	Self-heating in large quantities; may catch fire	H252

A1.12   Substances and mixtures, which in contact with water, emit flammable gases (see Chapter 2.12 for classification criteria)

Classification		Labelling				Hazard statement codes
Hazard class	Hazard category	Pictogram		Signal word	Hazard statement	
		GHS	UN Model Regulations[a]			
Substances and mixtures, which in contact with water, emit flammable gases	1			Danger	In contact with water releases flammable gases which may ignite spontaneously	H260
	2			Danger	In contact with water releases flammable gases	H261
	3			Warning	In contact with water releases flammable gases	H261

[a]   *Under the UN Recommendations on the Transport of Dangerous Goods, Model Regulations, the symbol, number and border line may be shown in black instead of white. The background colour stays blue in both cases.*

A1.13 **Oxidizing liquids** (see Chapter 2.13 for classification criteria)

Classification		Labelling				Hazard statement codes
Hazard class	Hazard category	Pictogram		Signal word	Hazard statement	
		GHS	UN Model Regulations			
Oxidizing liquids	1			Danger	May cause fire or explosion; strong oxidizer	H271
	2			Danger	May intensify fire; oxidizer	H272
	3			Warning	May intensify fire; oxidizer	H272

A1.14 **Oxidizing solids** (see Chapter 2.14 for classification criteria)

Classification		Labelling				Hazard statement codes
Hazard class	Hazard category	Pictogram		Signal word	Hazard statement	
		GHS	UN Model Regulations			
Oxidizing solids	1			Danger	May cause fire or explosion; strong oxidizer	H271
	2			Danger	May intensify fire; oxidizer	H272
	3			Warning	May intensify fire; oxidizer	H272

A1.15 **Organic peroxides** (see Chapter 2.15 for classification criteria)

Classification		Labelling				Hazard statement codes
Hazard class	Hazard category	Pictogram		Signal word	Hazard statement	
		GHS	UN Model Regulations[a]			
Organic peroxides	Type A		*(Transport may not be allowed)[b]*	**Danger**	Heating may cause an explosion	H240
	Type B			**Danger**	Heating may cause a fire or explosion	H241
	Types C and D			**Danger**	Heating may cause a fire	H242
	Types E and F			**Warning**	Heating may cause a fire	H242
	Type G	*No pictogram*	*Not required*	*No signal word*	*No hazard statement*	*None*

[a]   *For Type B, under the UN Recommendations on the Transport of Dangerous Goods, Model Regulations, special provision 181 may apply (Exemption of explosive label with competent authority approval. See Chapter 3.3 of UN Model Regulations for more details).*

[b]   *May not be acceptable for transport in the packaging in which it is tested (See Chapter 2.5, par. 2.5.3.2.2 of the UN Model Regulations).*

A1.16 **Corrosive to metals** (see Chapter 2.16 for classification criteria)

Classification		Labelling				Hazard statement code
Hazard class	Hazard category	Pictogram		Signal word	Hazard statement	
		GHS	UN Model Regulations			
Corrosive to metals	1			**Warning**	May be corrosive to metals	H290

A1.17   Acute toxicity (see Chapter 3.1 for classification criteria)

Classification			Labelling				Hazard statement codes
Hazard class	Hazard category		Pictogram		Signal word	Hazard statement	
			GHS	UN Model Regulations[a]			
Acute toxicity	1	Oral	☠	☠ 6	Danger	Fatal if swallowed	H300
		Dermal				Fatal in contact with skin	H310
		Inhalation				Fatal if inhaled	H330
	2	Oral	☠	☠ 6	Danger	Fatal if swallowed	H300
		Dermal				Fatal in contact with skin	H310
		Inhalation				Fatal if inhaled	H330
	3	Oral	☠	☠ 6	Danger	Toxic if swallowed	H301
		Dermal				Toxic in contact with skin	H311
		Inhalation				Toxic if inhaled	H331
	4	Oral	❗	Not required	Warning	Harmful if swallowed	H302
		Dermal				Harmful in contact with skin	H312
		Inhalation				Harmful if inhaled	H332
	5	Oral	No pictogram	Not required	Warning	May be harmful if swallowed	H303
		Dermal				May be harmful in contact with skin	H313
		Inhalation				May be harmful if inhaled	H333

[a]   For gases, under the UN Recommendations on the Transport of Dangerous Goods, Model Regulations, replace the number "6" in the bottom corner of the pictogram by "2".

A1.18   Skin corrosion/irritation (see Chapter 3.2 for classification criteria)

Classification			Labelling			Hazard statement codes
Hazard class	Hazard category	Pictogram		Signal word	Hazard statement	
		GHS	UN Model Regulations			
Skin corrosion/irritation	1	🧪	🧪 8	Danger	Causes severe skin burns and eye damage	H314
	2	❗	Not required	Warning	Causes skin irritation	H315
	3[a]	No pictogram	Not required	Warning	Causes mild skin irritation	H316

[a]   Applies to some authorities.

A1.19   Serious eye damage/eye irritation (see Chapter 3.3 for classification criteria)

Classification		Labelling				Hazard statement codes
Hazard class	Hazard category	Pictogram		Signal word	Hazard statement	
		GHS	UN Model Regulations			
Serious eye damage/eye irritation	1		*Not required*	**Danger**	Causes serious eye damage	H318
	2/2A		*Not required*	**Warning**	Causes serious eye irritation	H319
	2B	*No pictogram*	*Not required*	**Warning**	Causes eye irritation	H320

A1.20   Respiratory sensitizer (see Chapter 3.4 for classification criteria)

Classification		Labelling				Hazard statement codes
Hazard class	Hazard category	Pictogram		Signal word	Hazard statement	
		GHS	UN Model Regulations			
Respiratory sensitization	1		*Not required*	**Danger**	May cause allergy or asthma symptoms or breathing difficulties if inhaled	H334
	1A[a]		*Not required*	**Danger**	May cause allergy or asthma symptoms or breathing difficulties if inhaled	H334
	1B[a]		*Not required*	**Danger**	May cause allergy or asthma symptoms or breathing difficulties if inhaled	H334

[a]   *Sub-categories may be applied where data are sufficient and where required by a competent authority.*

A1.21   Skin sensitizer (see Chapter 3.4 for classification criteria)

Classification		Labelling				Hazard statement codes
Hazard class	**Hazard category**	**Pictogram**		**Signal word**	**Hazard statement**	
		GHS	**UN Model Regulations**			
Skin sensitization	1		*Not required*	**Warning**	May cause an allergic skin reaction	H317
	1A[a]		*Not required*	**Warning**	May cause an allergic skin reaction	H317
	1B[a]		*Not required*	**Warning**	May cause an allergic skin reaction	H317

[a]   *Sub-categories may be applied where data are sufficient and where required by a competent authority.*

A1.22   Germ cell mutagenicity (see Chapter 3.5 for classification criteria)

Classification		Labelling				Hazard statement codes
Hazard class	**Hazard category**	**Pictogram**		**Signal word**	**Hazard statement**	
		GHS	**UN Model Regulations**			
Germ cell mutagenicity	1 (both 1A and 1B)		*Not required*	**Danger**	May cause genetic defects *(state route of exposure if it is conclusively proven that no other routes of exposure cause the hazard)*	H340
	2		*Not required*	**Warning**	Suspected of causing genetic defects *(state route of exposure if it is conclusively proven that no other routes of exposure cause the hazard)*	H341

A1.23   Carcinogenicity (see Chapter 3.6 for classification criteria)

Classification		Labelling				Hazard statement codes
Hazard class	**Hazard category**	**Pictogram**		**Signal word**	**Hazard statement**	
		GHS	**UN Model Regulations**			
Carcinogenicity	1 (both 1A and 1B)		*Not required*	**Danger**	May cause cancer *(state route of exposure if it is conclusively proven that no other routes of exposure cause the hazard)*	H350
	2		*Not required*	**Warning**	Suspected of causing cancer *(state route of exposure if it is conclusively proven that no other routes of exposure cause the hazard)*	H351

A1.24   Toxic to reproduction (see Chapter 3.7 for classification criteria)

Classification		Labelling					Hazard statement codes
Hazard class	Hazard category	Pictogram		Signal word	Hazard statement		
		GHS	UN Model Regulations				
Reproductive toxicity	1 (both 1A and 1B)		*Not required*	**Danger**	May damage fertility or the unborn child *(state specific effect if known) (state route of exposure if it is conclusively proven that no other routes of exposure cause the hazard)*		H360
	2		*Not required*	**Warning**	Suspected of damaging fertility or the unborn child *(state specific effect if known) (state route of exposure if it is conclusively proven that no other routes of exposure cause the hazard)*		H361
	Additional category for effects on or via lactation	*No pictogram*	*Not required*	*No signal word*	May cause harm to breast-fed children		H362

A1.25   Specific target organ toxicity following single exposure (see Chapter 3.8 for classification criteria)

Classification		Labelling					Hazard statement codes
Hazard class	Hazard category	Pictogram		Signal word	Hazard statement		
		GHS	UN Model Regulations				
Specific target organ toxicity – single exposure	1		*Not required*	**Danger**	Causes damage to organs *(or state all organs affected, if known) (state route of exposure if it is conclusively proven that no other routes of exposure cause the hazard)*		H370
	2		*Not required*	**Warning**	May cause damage to organs *(or state all organs affected, if known) (state route of exposure if it is conclusively proven that no other routes of exposure cause the hazard)*		H371
	3		*Not required*	**Warning**	May cause respiratory irritation		H335
					or		
					May cause drowsiness or dizziness		H336

A1.26   Specific target organ toxicity following repeated exposure (see Chapter 3.9 for classification criteria)

Classification		Labelling				Hazard statement codes
Hazard class	Hazard category	Pictogram		Signal word	Hazard statement	
		GHS	UN Model Regulations			
Specific target organ toxicity – repeated exposure	1		*Not required*	**Danger**	Causes damage to organs *(state all organs affected, if known)* through prolonged or repeated exposure *(state route of exposure if it is conclusively proven that no other routes of exposure cause the hazard)*	H372
	2		*Not required*	**Warning**	May cause damage to organs *(state all organs affected, if known)* through prolonged or repeated exposure *(state route of exposure if it is conclusively proven that no other routes of exposure cause the hazard)*	H373

A1.27   Aspiration hazard (See chapter 3.10 for classification criteria)

Classification		Labelling				Hazard statement codes
Hazard class	Hazard category	Pictogram		Signal word	Hazard statement	
		GHS	UN Model Regulations			
Aspiration hazard	1		*Not required*	**Danger**	May be fatal if swallowed and enters airways	H304
	2		*Not required*	**Warning**	May be harmful if swallowed and enters airways	H305

A1.28 (a)   Hazardous to the aquatic environment, short-term (acute) (see Chapter 4.1 for classification criteria)

Classification		Labelling				Hazard statement codes
Hazard class	Hazard category	Pictogram		Signal word	Hazard statement	
		GHS	UN Model Regulations[a]			
Hazardous to the aquatic environment, short-term (Acute)	Acute 1			**Warning**	Very toxic to aquatic life	H400
	Acute 2	*No pictogram*	*Not required*	*No signal word*	Toxic to aquatic life	H401
	Acute 3	*No pictogram*	*Not required*	*No signal word*	Harmful to aquatic life	H402

[a]   *For Category 1, under the UN Recommendations on the Transport of Dangerous Goods, Model Regulations, the pictogram is not required if the substance presents any other hazards covered by UN Model Regulations. If no other hazard is presented, this pictogram is required as a mark in addition to the UN Model Regulations Class 9 label.*

A1.28 (b) **Hazardous to the aquatic environment, long-term (chronic)** (see Chapter 4.1 for classification criteria)

Classification		Labelling				Hazard statement codes
Hazard class	**Hazard category**	**Pictogram**		**Signal word**	**Hazard statement**	
		GHS	**UN Model Regulations**[a]			
Hazardous to the aquatic environment, long-term (Chronic)	**Chronic 1**			**Warning**	Very toxic to aquatic life with long lasting effects	H410
	Chronic 2			*No signal word*	Toxic to aquatic life with long lasting effects	H411
	Chronic 3	*No pictogram*	*Not required*	*No signal word*	Harmful to aquatic life with long lasting effects	H412
	Chronic 4	*No pictogram*	*Not required*	*No signal word*	May cause long lasting harmful effects to aquatic life	H413

[a] *For categories 1 and 2, under the UN Recommendations on the Transport of Dangerous Goods, Model Regulations, the pictogram is not required if the substance presents any other hazards covered by UN Model Regulations. If no other hazard is presented, this pictogram is required as a mark in addition to the UN Model Regulations Class 9 label.*

A1.29   **Hazard to the ozone layer** (see Chapter 4.2 for classification criteria)

Classification		Labelling				Hazard statement code
Hazard class	**Hazard category**	**Pictogram**		**Signal word**	**Hazard statement**	
		GHS	**UN Model Regulations**			
Hazardous to the ozone layer	1		*Not required*	**Warning**	Harms public health and the environment by destroying ozone in the upper atmosphere	H420

ANNEX 2

(Reserved)

ANNEX 3

CODIFICATION OF HAZARD STATEMENTS, CODIFICATION AND USE OF PRECAUTIONARY STATEMENTS, CODIFICATION OF HAZARD PICTOGRAMS AND EXAMPLES OF PRECAUTIONARY PICTOGRAMS

Annex 3

Section 1

CODIFICATION OF HAZARD STATEMENTS

A3.1.1 Introduction

A3.1.1.1   *Hazard statement* means a statement assigned to a hazard class and category that describes the nature of the hazards of a hazardous product, including, where appropriate, the degree of hazard.

A3.1.1.2   This section contains the recommended codes assigned to each of the hazard statements applicable to the hazard categories under the GHS.

A3.1.1.3   The hazard statement codes are intended to be used for reference purposes. They are not part of the hazard statement text and should not be used to replace it.

A3.1.2 Codification of hazard statements

A3.1.2.1   Hazard statements are assigned a unique alphanumerical code which consists of one letter and three numbers, as follows:

  (a)   the letter "H" (for "hazard statement");

  (b)   a number designating the type of hazard to which the hazard statement is assigned according to the numbering of the different parts of the GHS, as follows:

     –   "2" for physical hazards;
     –   "3" for health hazards;
     –   "4" for environmental hazards;

  (c)   two numbers corresponding to the sequential numbering of hazards arising from the intrinsic properties of the substance or mixture, such as explosivity (codes from 200 to 210), flammability (codes from 220 to 230), etc.

A3.1.2.2   The codes to be used for designating hazard statements are listed, in numerical order, in Table A3.1.1 for physical hazards, Table A3.1.2 for health hazards and Table A3.1.3 for environmental hazards. Each table is divided into 4 columns containing the following information:

  Column (1)   The hazard statement code;

  Column (2)   The hazard statement text;

  The text in bold should appear on the label, except as otherwise specified. The information in italics should also appear as part of the hazard statement when the information is known.

  For example: "**causes damages to organs** *(or state all organs affected, if known)* **through prolonged or repeated exposure** *(state route of exposure if it is conclusively proven that no other routes of exposure cause the hazard)*".

  Column (3)   Hazard class, with a reference to the chapter of the GHS where information about the hazard class may be found.

  Column (4)   The hazard category or categories within a hazard class for which the use of a hazard statement is applicable.

A3.1.2.3   In addition to individual hazard statements, a number of combined hazard statements are given in Table A3.1.2.   The alphanumerical codes for the combined statements are constructed from the codes for the individual statements that are combined, conjoined with the plus ("+") sign.   For example, H300 + H310 indicates that the text to appear on the label is "Fatal if swallowed or in contact with skin".

A3.1.2.4   All assigned hazard statements should appear on the label unless otherwise specified in 1.4.10.5.3.3. The competent authority may specify the order in which they appear. Also, where a combined hazard statement is indicated for two or more hazard statements, the competent authority may specify whether the combined hazard statement or the corresponding individual statements should appear on the label, or may leave the choice to the manufacturer/supplier.

Table A3.1.1: Hazard statement codes for physical hazards

Code (1)	Physical hazard statements (2)	Hazard class (GHS chapter) (3)	Hazard category (4)
H200	**Unstable explosive**	Explosives (chapter 2.1)	Unstable explosive
H201	**Explosive; mass explosion hazard**	Explosives (chapter 2.1)	Division 1.1
H202	**Explosive; severe projection hazard**	Explosives (chapter 2.1)	Division 1.2
H203	**Explosive; fire, blast or projection hazard**	Explosives (chapter 2.1)	Division 1.3
H204	**Fire or projection hazard**	Explosives (chapter 2.1)	Division 1.4
H205	**May mass explode in fire**	Explosives (chapter 2.1)	Division 1.5
H220	**Extremely flammable gas**	Flammable gases (chapter 2.2)	1
H221	**Flammable gas**	Flammable gases (chapter 2.2)	2
H222	**Extremely flammable aerosol**	Aerosols (chapter 2.3)	1
H223	**Flammable aerosol**	Aerosols (chapter 2.3)	2
H224	**Extremely flammable liquid and vapour**	Flammable liquids (chapter 2.6)	1
H225	**Highly flammable liquid and vapour**	Flammable liquids (chapter 2.6)	2
H226	**Flammable liquid and vapour**	Flammable liquids (chapter 2.6)	3
H227	**Combustible liquid**	Flammable liquids (chapter 2.6)	4
H228	**Flammable solid**	Flammable solids (chapter 2.7)	1, 2
H229	**Pressurized container: may burst if heated**	Aerosols (chapter 2.3)	1, 2, 3
H230	**May react explosively even in the absence of air**	Flammable gases (including chemically unstable gases) (chapter 2.2)	A (Chemically unstable gases)
H231	**May react explosively even in the absence of air at elevated pressure and/or temperature**	Flammable gases (including chemically unstable gases) (chapter 2.2)	B (Chemically unstable gases)
H240	**Heating may cause an explosion**	Self-reactive substances and mixtures (chapter 2.8); and Organic peroxides (chapter 2.15)	Type A
H241	**Heating may cause a fire or explosion**	Self-reactive substances and mixtures (chapter 2.8); and Organic peroxides (chapter 2.15)	Type B
H242	**Heating may cause a fire**	Self-reactive substances and mixtures (chapter 2.8); and Organic peroxides (chapter 2.15)	Types C, D, E, F

Code (1)	Physical hazard statements (2)	Hazard class (GHS chapter) (3)	Hazard category (4)
H250	**Catches fire spontaneously if exposed to air**	Pyrophoric liquids (chapter 2.9); Pyrophoric solids (chapter 2.10)	1
H251	**Self-heating; may catch fire**	Self-heating substances and mixtures (chapter 2.11)	1
H252	**Self-heating in large quantities; may catch fire**	Self-heating substances and mixtures (chapter 2.11)	2
H260	**In contact with water releases flammable gases which may ignite spontaneously**	Substances and mixtures which, in contact with water, emit flammable gases (chapter 2.12)	1
H261	**In contact with water releases flammable gas**	Substances and mixtures which, in contact with water, emit flammable gases (chapter 2.12)	2, 3
H270	**May cause or intensify fire; oxidizer**	Oxidizing gases (chapter 2.4)	1
H271	**May cause fire or explosion; strong oxidizer**	Oxidizing liquids (chapter 2.13); Oxidizing solids (chapter 2.14)	1
H272	**May intensify fire; oxidizer**	Oxidizing liquids (chapter 2.13); Oxidizing solids (chapter 2.14)	2, 3
H280	**Contains gas under pressure; may explode if heated**	Gases under pressure (chapter 2.5)	Compressed gas Liquefied gas Dissolved gas
H281	**Contains refrigerated gas; may cause cryogenic burns or injury**	Gases under pressure (chapter 2.5)	Refrigerated liquefied gas
H290	**May be corrosive to metals**	Corrosive to metals (chapter 2.16)	1

Table A3.1.2: Hazard statement codes for health hazards

Code (1)	Health hazard statements (2)	Hazard class (GHS chapter) (3)	Hazard category (4)
H300	**Fatal if swallowed**	Acute toxicity, oral (chapter 3.1)	1, 2
H301	**Toxic if swallowed**	Acute toxicity, oral (chapter 3.1)	3
H302	**Harmful if swallowed**	Acute toxicity, oral (chapter 3.1)	4
H303	**May be harmful if swallowed**	Acute toxicity, oral (chapter 3.1)	5
H304	**May be fatal if swallowed and enters airways**	Aspiration hazard (chapter 3.10)	1
H305	**May be harmful if swallowed and enters airways**	Aspiration hazard (chapter 3.10)	2
H310	**Fatal in contact with skin**	Acute toxicity, dermal (chapter 3.1)	1, 2
H311	**Toxic in contact with skin**	Acute toxicity, dermal (chapter 3.1)	3
H312	**Harmful in contact with skin**	Acute toxicity, dermal (chapter 3.1)	4
H313	**May be harmful in contact with skin**	Acute toxicity, dermal (chapter 3.1)	5
H314	**Causes severe skin burns and eye damage**	Skin corrosion/irritation (chapter 3.2)	1A, 1B, 1C
H315	**Causes skin irritation**	Skin corrosion/irritation (chapter 3.2)	2
H316	**Causes mild skin irritation**	Skin corrosion/irritation (chapter 3.2)	3
H317	**May cause an allergic skin reaction**	Sensitisation, skin (chapter 3.4)	1, 1A, 1B
H318	**Causes serious eye damage**	Serious eye damage/eye irritation (chapter 3.3)	1
H319	**Causes serious eye irritation**	Serious eye damage/eye irritation (chapter 3.3)	2A
H320	**Causes eye irritation**	Serious eye damage/eye irritation (chapter 3.3)	2B
H330	**Fatal if inhaled**	Acute toxicity, inhalation (chapter 3.1)	1, 2
H331	**Toxic if inhaled**	Acute toxicity, inhalation (chapter 3.1)	3
H332	**Harmful if inhaled**	Acute toxicity, inhalation (chapter 3.1)	4
H333	**May be harmful if inhaled**	Acute toxicity, inhalation (chapter 3.1)	5
H334	**May cause allergy or asthma symptoms or breathing difficulties if inhaled**	Sensitisation, respiratory (chapter 3.4)	1, 1A, 1B
H335	**May cause respiratory irritation**	Specific target organ toxicity, single exposure; Respiratory tract irritation (chapter 3.8);	3
H336	**May cause drowsiness or dizziness**	Specific target organ toxicity, single exposure; Narcotic effects (chapter 3.8)	3
H340	**May cause genetic defects** *(state route of exposure if it is conclusively proven that no other routes of exposure cause the hazard)*	Germ cell mutagenicity (chapter 3.5)	1A, 1B
H341	**Suspected of causing genetic defects** *(state route of exposure if it is conclusively proven that no other routes of exposure cause the hazard)*	Germ cell mutagenicity (chapter 3.5)	2
H350	**May cause cancer** *(state route of exposure if it is conclusively proven that no other routes of exposure cause the hazard)*	Carcinogenicity (chapter 3.6)	1A, 1B

Code	Health hazard statements	Hazard class (GHS chapter)	Hazard category
(1)	(2)	(3)	(4)
H351	**Suspected of causing cancer** *(state route of exposure if it is conclusively proven that no other routes of exposure cause the hazard)*	Carcinogenicity (chapter 3.6)	2
H360	**May damage fertility or the unborn child** *(state specific effect if known)(state route of exposure if it is conclusively proven that no other routes of exposure cause the hazard)*	Reproductive toxicity (chapter 3.7)	1A, 1B
H361	**Suspected of damaging fertility or the unborn child** *(state specific effect if known)(state route of exposure if it is conclusively proven that no other routes of exposure cause the hazard)*	Reproductive toxicity (chapter 3.7)	2
H362	**May cause harm to breast-fed children**	Reproductive toxicity, effects on or via lactation (chapter 3.7)	Additional category
H370	**Causes damage to organs** *(or state all organs affected, if known) (state route of exposure if it is conclusively proven that no other routes of exposure cause the hazard)*	Specific target organ toxicity, single exposure (chapter 3.8)	1
H371	**May cause damage to organs** *(or state all organs affected, if known)(state route of exposure if it is conclusively proven that no other routes of exposure cause the hazard)*	Specific target organ toxicity, single exposure (chapter 3.8)	2
H372	**Causes damage to organs** *(state all organs affected, if known)* **through prolonged or repeated exposure** *(state route of exposure if it is conclusively proven that no other routes of exposure cause the hazard)*	Specific target organ toxicity, repeated exposure (chapter 3.9)	1
H373	**May cause damage to organs** *(state all organs affected, if known)* **through prolonged or repeated exposure** *(state route of exposure if it is conclusively proven that no other routes of exposure cause the hazard)*	Specific target organ toxicity, repeated exposure (chapter 3.9)	2
H300 + H310	**Fatal if swallowed or in contact with skin**	Acute toxicity, oral (chapter 3.1) and acute toxicity dermal (chapter 3.1)	1, 2
H300 + H330	**Fatal if swallowed or if inhaled**	Acute toxicity, oral (chapter 3.1) and acute toxicity, inhalation (chapter 3.1)	1, 2
H310 + H330	**Fatal in contact with skin or if inhaled**	Acute toxicity, dermal (chapter 3.1) and acute toxicity, inhalation (chapter 3.1)	1, 2
H300 + H310 + H330	**Fatal if swallowed, in contact with skin or if inhaled**	Acute toxicity, oral (chapter 3.1), acute toxicity, dermal (chapter 3.1) and acute toxicity, inhalation (chapter 3.1)	1, 2
H301 + H311	**Toxic if swallowed or in contact with skin**	Acute toxicity, oral (chapter 3.1) and acute toxicity dermal (chapter 3.1)	3

Code (1)	Health hazard statements (2)	Hazard class (GHS chapter) (3)	Hazard category (4)
H301 + H331	**Toxic if swallowed or if inhaled**	Acute toxicity, oral (chapter 3.1) and acute toxicity, inhalation (chapter 3.1)	3
H311 + H331	**Toxic in contact with skin or if inhaled**	Acute toxicity, dermal (chapter 3.1) and acute toxicity, inhalation (chapter 3.1)	3
H301 + H311 + H331	**Toxic if swallowed, in contact with skin or if inhaled**	Acute toxicity, oral (chapter 3.1), acute toxicity, dermal (chapter 3.1) and acute toxicity, inhalation (chapter 3.1)	3
H302 + H312	**Harmful if swallowed or in contact with skin**	Acute toxicity, oral (chapter 3.1) and acute toxicity dermal (chapter 3.1)	4
H302 + H332	**Harmful if swallowed or if inhaled**	Acute toxicity, oral (chapter 3.1) and acute toxicity, inhalation (chapter 3.1)	4
H312 + H332	**Harmful in contact with skin or if inhaled**	Acute toxicity, dermal (chapter 3.1) and acute toxicity, inhalation (chapter 3.1)	4
H302 + H312 + H332	**Harmful if swallowed, in contact with skin or if inhaled**	Acute toxicity, oral (chapter 3.1), acute toxicity, dermal (chapter 3.1) and acute toxicity, inhalation (chapter 3.1)	4
H303 + H313	**May be harmful if swallowed or in contact with skin**	Acute toxicity, oral (chapter 3.1) and acute toxicity dermal (chapter 3.1)	5
H303 + H333	**May be harmful if swallowed or if inhaled**	Acute toxicity, oral (chapter 3.1) and acute toxicity, inhalation (chapter 3.1)	5
H313 + H333	**May be harmful in contact with skin or if inhaled**	Acute toxicity, dermal (chapter 3.1) and acute toxicity, inhalation (chapter 3.1)	5
H303 + H313 + H333	**May be harmful if swallowed, in contact with skin or if inhaled**	Acute toxicity, oral (chapter 3.1), acute toxicity, dermal (chapter 3.1) and acute toxicity, inhalation (chapter 3.1)	5
H315 + H320	**Causes skin and eye irritation**	Skin corrosion/irritation (chapter 3.2) and serious eye damage/eye irritation (chapter 3.3)	2 (skin)/2B (eye)

Table A3.1.3: Hazard statement codes for environmental hazards

Code (1)	Environmental hazard statements (2)	Hazard class (GHS chapter) (3)	Hazard category (4)
H400	**Very toxic to aquatic life**	Hazardous to the aquatic environment, acute hazard (chapter 4.1)	1
H401	**Toxic to aquatic life**	Hazardous to the aquatic environment, acute hazard (chapter 4.1)	2
H402	**Harmful to aquatic life**	Hazardous to the aquatic environment, acute hazard (chapter 4.1)	3
H410	**Very toxic to aquatic life with long lasting effects**	Hazardous to the aquatic environment, long-term hazard (chapter 4.1)	1
H411	**Toxic to aquatic life with long lasting effects**	Hazardous to the aquatic environment, long-term hazard (chapter 4.1)	2
H412	**Harmful to aquatic life with long lasting effects**	Hazardous to the aquatic environment, long-term hazard (chapter 4.1)	3
H413	**May cause long lasting harmful effects to aquatic life**	Hazardous to the aquatic environment, long-term hazard (chapter 4.1)	4
H420	**Harms public health and the environment by destroying ozone in the upper atmosphere**	Hazardous to the ozone layer (chapter 4.2)	1

Annex 3

Section 2

CODIFICATION OF PRECAUTIONARY STATEMENTS

A3.2.1   Introduction

A3.2.1.1   A *precautionary statement* is a phrase (and/or pictogram) which describes recommended measures that should be taken to minimize or prevent adverse effects resulting from exposures to a hazardous product, or improper storage or handling of a hazardous product (see 1.4.10.5.2 (c)).

A3.2.1.2   For the purposes of the GHS, there are five types of precautionary statements: **general, prevention, response** (in case of accidental spillage or exposure, emergency response and first-aid)**, storage** and **disposal**. For guidance on the use of GHS precautionary statements, including advice on the selection of the appropriate statements for each GHS hazard class and category, see section 3 to this annex.

A3.2.1.3   This section contains the recommended codes for each of the precautionary statement included in this annex.

A3.2.2   Codification of precautionary statements

A3.2.2.1   Precautionary statements are assigned a unique alphanumerical code which consists of one letter and three numbers as follows:

(a)   a letter "P" (for "precautionary statement")

(b)   one number designating the type of precautionary statement as follows:

– "1" for general precautionary statements;
– "2" for prevention precautionary statements;
– "3" for response precautionary statements;
– "4" for storage precautionary statements;
– "5" for disposal precautionary statements;

(c)   two numbers (corresponding to the sequential numbering of precautionary statements)

A3.2.2.2   The precautionary statement codes are intended to be used for reference purposes. They are not part of the precautionary statement text and should not be used to replace it.

A3.2.2.3   The codes to be used for designating precautionary statements are listed, in numerical order, in Table A3.2.1 for general precautionary statements, Table A3.2.2 for prevention precautionary statements, Table A3.2.3 for response precautionary statements, Table A3.2.4 for storage precautionary statements and Table A3.2.5 for disposal precautionary statements.

A3.2.3   Structure of the precautionary statement codification tables

A3.2.3.1   Each table is divided into 5 columns containing the following information:

Column (1)   The precautionary statement code;

Column (2)   The precautionary statement text;

Column (3)   The hazard class and the route of exposure, where relevant, for which the use of a precautionary statement is recommended together with a reference to the chapter of the GHS where information about the hazard class may be found.

Column (4)   The hazard category or categories within a hazard class for which the use of a precautionary statement is applicable.

Column (5)   Where applicable, conditions relating to the use of a precautionary statement;

A3.2.3.2   The tables show the **core part of the precautionary statements in bold print** in column (2). This is the text, except as otherwise specified, that should appear on the label. Derogations from the recommended labelling statements are at the discretion of competent authorities.

A3.2.3.3   When a forward slash or diagonal mark [/] appears in a precautionary statement text in column (2), it indicates that a choice has to be made between the phrases they separate. In such cases, the manufacturer or supplier can choose, or the competent authorities may prescribe one or more appropriate phrase(s). For example in P280 "**Wear protective gloves/protective clothing/eye protection/face protection**" could read "**wear eye protection**" or "**wear eye and face protection**".

A3.2.3.4   When three full stops [...] appears in a precautionary statement text in column (2), they indicate that all applicable conditions are not listed. For example in P241 "**Use explosion-proof [electrical/ventilating/lighting/...] equipment**", the use of "..." indicates that other equipment may need to be specified. Further details of the information to be provided may be found in column (5). In such cases the manufacturer or supplier can choose, or the competent authorities may prescribe the other conditions to be specified.

A3.2.3.5   In cases where additional information is required or information has to be specified, this is indicated by a relevant entry in column (5) in plain text.

A3.2.3.6   When *text in italics* is used in column (5), this indicates specific conditions applying to the use or allocation of the precautionary statement. This may relate to conditions attaching to either the general use of a precautionary statement or its use for a particular hazard class and/or hazard category. For example, for P241 "**Use explosion-proof [electrical/ventilating/lighting/...]equipment**", only applies for flammable solids "*if dust clouds can occur*".

A3.2.3.7   Where square brackets [...] appear around some text in a precautionary statement, this indicates that the text in square brackets is not appropriate in every case and should be used only in certain circumstances. In these cases, conditions for use explaining when the text should be used are given in column (5). For example, P284 states: "**[In case of inadequate ventilation] wear respiratory protection.**" This statement is given with the condition for use "*– text in square brackets may be used if additional information is provided with the chemical at the point of use that explains what type of ventilation would be adequate for safe use*". The application of the condition for use should be interpreted as follows: If additional information is provided with the chemical explaining what type of ventilation would be adequate for safe use, the text in square brackets <u>may</u> be used. In this case, the statement would read: "**In case of inadequate ventilation wear respiratory protection.**" However, if the chemical is supplied without such information, the text in square brackets should <u>not</u> be used, and the precautionary statement should read: "**Wear respiratory protection.**"

A3.2.3.8   To facilitate translation into the languages of users, precautionary statements have been broken down into individual sentences or parts of sentences in the tables in this section. In a number of instances the text that appears on a GHS label requires that these be added back together. This is indicated in this annex by codes conjoined with a plus sign "+". For example P305 + P351 + P338 indicates that the text to appear on the label is "**IF IN EYES: Rinse cautiously with water for several minutes. Remove contact lenses, if present and easy to do. Continue rinsing**". These additive precautionary statements can also be found at the end of each of the precautionary statement tables in this section. Translation of only the single precautionary statements is required, as this will enable the compilation of the additive precautionary statements.

Table A3.2.1: Codification of general precautionary statements

Code	General precautionary statements	Hazard class	Hazard category	Conditions for use
(1)	(2)	(3)	(4)	(5)
P101	**If medical advice is needed, have product container or label at hand.**	as appropriate		Consumer products
P102	**Keep out of reach of children.**	as appropriate		Consumer products
P103	**Read label before use.**	as appropriate		Consumer products

Table A3.2.2: Codification of prevention precautionary statements

Code	Prevention precautionary statements	Hazard class	Hazard category	Conditions for use
(1)	(2)	(3)	(4)	(5)
P201	**Obtain special instructions before use.**	Explosives (chapter 2.1)	Unstable explosive	
		Germ cell mutagenicity (chapter 3.5)	1A, 1B, 2	
		Carcinogenicity (chapter 3.6)	1A, 1B, 2	
		Reproductive toxicity (chapter 3.7)	1A, 1B, 2	
		Reproductive toxicity, effects on or via lactation (chapter 3.7)	Additional category	
P202	**Do not handle until all safety precautions have been read and understood.**	Flammable gases (including chemically unstable gases) (chapter 2.2)	A, B (chemically unstable gases)	
		Germ cell mutagenicity (chapter 3.5)	1A, 1B, 2	
		Carcinogenicity (chapter 3.6)	1A, 1B, 2	
		Reproductive toxicity (chapter 3.7)	1A, 1B, 2	

Code	Prevention precautionary statements	Hazard class	Hazard category	Conditions for use
(1)	(2)	(3)	(4)	(5)
P210	Keep away from heat, hot surfaces, sparks, open flames and other ignition sources. No smoking.	Explosives (chapter 2.1)	Divisions 1.1, 1.2, 1.3, 1.4, 1.5	
		Flammable gases (chapter 2.2)	1, 2	
		Aerosols (chapter 2.3)	1, 2, 3	
		Flammable liquids (chapter 2.6)	1, 2, 3, 4	
		Flammable solids (chapter 2.7)	1, 2	
		Self-reactive substances and mixtures (chapter 2.8)	Types A, B, C, D, E, F	
		Pyrophoric liquids (chapter 2.9)	1	
		Pyrophoric solids (chapter 2.10)	1	
		Oxidizing liquids (chapter 2.13)	1, 2, 3	
		Oxidizing solids (chapter 2.14)	Types A, B, C, D, E, F	
		Organic peroxides (chapter 2.15)	1, 2, 3	
P211	Do not spray on an open flame or other ignition source.	Aerosols (chapter 2.3)	1, 2	
P220	Keep away from clothing and other combustible materials.	Oxidizing gases (chapter 2.4)	1	
		Oxidizing liquids (chapter 2.13)	1, 2, 3	
		Oxidizing solids (chapter 2.14)	1, 2, 3	
P222	Do not allow contact with air.	Pyrophoric liquids (chapter 2.9)	1	− *if emphasis of the hazard statement is deemed necessary.*
		Pyrophoric solids (chapter 2.10)	1	
P223	Do not allow contact with water.	Substances and mixtures which, in contact with water, emit flammable gases (chapter 2.12)	1, 2	− *if emphasis of the hazard statement is deemed necessary.*
P230	Keep wetted with ...	Explosives (chapter 2.1)	Divisions 1.1, 1.2, 1.3, 1.5	− *for substances and mixtures which are wetted, diluted, dissolved or suspended with a phlegmatizer in order to reduce or suppress their explosive properties (desensitized explosives).* ...Manufacturer/supplier or the competent authority to specify appropriate material.

Code	Prevention precautionary statements	Hazard class	Hazard category	Conditions for use
(1)	(2)	(3)	(4)	(5)
P231	Handle and store contents under inert gas/...	Pyrophoric liquids (chapter 2.9)	1	...Manufacturer/supplier or the competent authority to specify appropriate liquid or gas if "inert gas" is not appropriate.
		Pyrophoric solids (chapter 2.10)	1	
		Substances and mixtures which, in contact with water, emit flammable gases (chapter 2.12)	1, 2, 3	– if the substance or mixture reacts readily with moisture in air. ...Manufacturer/supplier or the competent authority to specify appropriate liquid or gas if "inert gas" is not appropriate.
P232	Protect from moisture.	Substances and mixtures which, in contact with water, emit flammable gases (chapter 2.12)	1, 2, 3	
P233	Keep container tightly closed.	Flammable liquids (chapter 2.6)	1, 2, 3	– if the liquid is volatile and may generate an explosive atmosphere.
		Pyrophoric liquids (chapter 2.9)	1	
		Pyrophoric solids (chapter 2.10)	1	
		Acute toxicity, inhalation (chapter 3.1)	1, 2, 3	– if the chemical is volatile and may generate a hazardous atmosphere.
		Specific target organ toxicity, single exposure; respiratory tract irritation (chapter 3.8)	3	
		Specific target organ toxicity, single exposure; narcotic effects (chapter 3.8)	3	
P234	Keep only in original packaging.	Explosives (chapter 2.1)	Divisions 1.1, 1.2, 1.3, 1.4, 1.5	
		Self-reactive substances and mixtures (chapter 2.8)	Types A, B, C, D, E, F	
		Organic peroxides (chapter 2.15)	Types A, B, C, D, E, F	
		Corrosive to metals (chapter 2.16)	1	
P235	Keep cool.	Flammable liquids (chapter 2.6)	1, 2, 3	– for flammable liquids Category 1 and other flammable liquids that are volatile and may generate an explosive atmosphere.
		Self-reactive substances and mixtures (chapter 2.8)	Types A, B, C, D, E, F	– may be omitted if P411 is given on the label.
		Self-heating substances and mixtures (chapter 2.11)	1, 2	– may be omitted if P413 is given on the label.
		Organic peroxides (chapter 2.15)	Types A, B, C, D, E, F	– may be omitted if P411 is given on the label.

Code	Prevention precautionary statements	Hazard class	Hazard category	Conditions for use
(1)	(2)	(3)	(4)	(5)
P240	Ground and bond container and receiving equipment.	Explosives (chapter 2.1)	Divisions 1.1, 1.2, 1.3, 1.4, 1.5	– if the explosive is electrostatically sensitive.
		Flammable liquids (chapter 2.6)	1, 2, 3	– if the liquid is volatile and may generate an explosive atmosphere.
		Flammable solids (chapter 2.7)	1, 2	– if the solid is electrostatically sensitive.
		Self-reactive substances and mixtures (chapter 2.8)	Types A, B, C, D, E, F	– if electrostatically sensitive and able to generate an explosive atmosphere.
		Organic peroxides (chapter 2.15)	Types A, B, C, D, E, F	– if electrostatically sensitive and able to generate an explosive atmosphere.
P241	Use explosion-proof [electrical/ventilating/lighting/…] equipment.	Flammable liquids (chapter 2.6)	1, 2, 3	– if the liquid is volatile and may generate an explosive atmosphere. – text in square brackets may be used to specify specific electrical, ventilating, lighting or other equipment if necessary and as appropriate. – precautionary statement may be omitted where local or national legislation introduces more specific provisions.
		Flammable solids (chapter 2.7)	1, 2	– if dust clouds can occur. – text in square brackets may be used to specify specific electrical, ventilating, lighting or other equipment if necessary and as appropriate. – precautionary statement may be omitted where local or national legislation introduces more specific provisions.
P242	Use non-sparking tools.	Flammable liquids (chapter 2.6)	1, 2, 3	– if the liquid is volatile and may generate an explosive atmosphere and if the minimum ignition energy is very low. (This applies to substances and mixtures where the minimum ignition energy is <0.1mJ, e.g. carbon disulphide).
P243	Take action to prevent static discharges.	Flammable liquids (chapter 2.6)	1, 2, 3	– if the liquid is volatile and may generate an explosive atmosphere. – may be omitted where local or national legislation introduces more specific provisions.
P244	Keep valves and fittings free from oil and grease.	Oxidizing gases (chapter 2.4)	1	

Code (1)	Prevention precautionary statements (2)	Hazard class (3)	Hazard category (4)	Conditions for use (5)
P250	Do not subject to grinding/shock/friction/....	Explosives (chapter 2.1)	Unstable explosives and divisions 1.1, 1.2, 1.3, 1.4, 1.5	– if the explosive is mechanically sensitive ...Manufacturer/supplier or the competent authority to specify applicable rough handling.
P251	Do not pierce or burn, even after use.	Aerosols (chapter 2.3)	1, 2, 3	
P260	Do not breathe dust/fume/gas/mist/vapours/spray.	Acute toxicity – inhalation (chapter 3.1)	1, 2	Manufacturer/supplier or the competent authority to specify applicable conditions.
		Specific target organ toxicity, single exposure (chapter 3.8)	1, 2	
		Specific target organ toxicity, repeated exposure (chapter 3.9)	1, 2	
		Skin corrosion (chapter 3.2)	1A, 1B, 1C	– specify do not breathe dusts or mists
		Reproductive toxicity – effects on or via lactation (chapter 3.7)	Additional category	– if inhalable particles of dusts or mists may occur during use.
P261	Avoid breathing dust/fume/gas/mist/vapours/spray.	Acute toxicity – inhalation (chapter 3.1)	3, 4	– may be omitted if P260 is given on the label.
		Respiratory sensitization (chapter 3.4)	1, 1A, 1B	Manufacturer/supplier or the competent authority to specify applicable conditions.
		Skin sensitization (chapter 3.4)	1, 1A, 1B	
		Specific target organ toxicity, single exposure; respiratory tract irritation (chapter 3.8)	3	
		Specific target organ toxicity, single exposure; narcotic effects (chapter 3.8)	3	
P262	Do not get in eyes, on skin, or on clothing.	Acute toxicity – dermal (chapter 3.1)	1, 2	
P263	Avoid contact during pregnancy and while nursing.	Reproductive toxicity – effects on or via lactation (chapter 3.7)	Additional category	
P264	Wash ... thoroughly after handling.	Acute toxicity – oral (chapter 3.1)	1, 2, 3, 4	...Manufacturer/supplier or the competent authority to specify parts of the body to be washed after handling.
		Acute toxicity – dermal (chapter 3.1)	1, 2	
		Skin corrosion (chapter 3.2)	1A, 1B, 1C	
		Skin irritation (chapter 3.2)	2	
		Eye irritation (chapter 3.3)	2A, 2B	
		Reproductive toxicity – effects on or via lactation (chapter 3.7)	Additional category	
		Specific target organ toxicity, single exposure (chapter 3.8)	1, 2	...Manufacturer/supplier or the competent authority to specify parts of the body to be washed after handling.
		Specific target organ toxicity, repeated exposure (chapter 3.9)	1	

Code (1)	Prevention precautionary statements (2)	Hazard class (3)	Hazard category (4)	Conditions for use (5)
P270	**Do not eat, drink or smoke when using this product.**	Acute toxicity – oral (chapter 3.1)	1, 2, 3, 4	
		Acute toxicity – dermal (chapter 3.1)	1, 2	
		Reproductive toxicity – effects on or via lactation (chapter 3.7)	Additional category	
		Specific target organ toxicity, single exposure (chapter 3.8)	1, 2	
		Specific target organ toxicity, repeated exposure (chapter 3.9)	1	
P271	**Use only outdoors or in a well-ventilated area.**	Acute toxicity – inhalation (chapter 3.1)	1, 2, 3, 4	
		Specific target organ toxicity, single exposure; respiratory tract irritation (chapter 3.8)	3	
		Specific target organ toxicity, single exposure; narcotic effects (chapter 3.8)	3	
P272	**Contaminated work clothing should not be allowed out of the workplace.**	Skin sensitization (chapter 3.4)	1, 1A, 1B	
P273	**Avoid release to the environment.**	Hazardous to the aquatic environment, acute hazard (chapter 4.1)	1, 2, 3	*– if this is not the intended use.*
		Hazardous to the aquatic environment, long-term hazard (chapter 4.1)	1, 2, 3, 4	
P280	**Wear protective gloves/protective clothing/eye protection/face protection.**	Explosives (chapter 2.1)	Unstable explosives and divisions 1.1, 1.2, 1.3, 1.4, 1.5	Manufacturer/supplier or the competent authority to specify the appropriate type of equipment.
		Flammable liquids (chapter 2.6)	1, 2, 3, 4	
		Flammable solids (chapter 2.7)	1, 2	
		Self-reactive substances and mixtures (chapter 2.8)	Types A, B, C, D, E, F	
		Pyrophoric liquids (chapter 2.9)	1	
		Pyrophoric solids (chapter 2.10)	1	
		Self-heating substances and mixtures (chapter 2.11)	1, 2	Manufacturer/supplier or the competent authority to specify the appropriate type of equipment.
		Substances and mixtures which, in contact with water, emit flammable gases (chapter 2.12)	1, 2, 3	

Code	Prevention precautionary statements	Hazard class	Hazard category	Conditions for use
(1)	(2)	(3)	(4)	(5)
P280 *(cont'd)*	**Wear protective gloves/protective clothing/eye protection/face protection.**	Oxidizing liquids (chapter 2.13)	1, 2, 3	Manufacturer/supplier or the competent authority to specify the appropriate type of equipment.
		Oxidizing solids (chapter 2.14)	1, 2, 3	
		Organic peroxides (chapter 2.15)	Types A, B, C, D, E, F	
		Acute toxicity – dermal (chapter 3.1)	1, 2, 3, 4	– *Specify protective gloves/clothing.* Manufacturer/supplier or the competent authority may further specify type of equipment where appropriate.
		Skin corrosion (chapter 3.2)	1A, 1B, 1C	– *Specify protective gloves/clothing and eye/face protection.* Manufacturer/supplier or the competent authority may further specify type of equipment where appropriate.
		Skin irritation (chapter 3.2)	2	– *Specify protective gloves.*
		Skin sensitization (chapter 3.4)	1, 1A, 1B	Manufacturer/supplier or the competent authority may further specify type of equipment where appropriate.
		Severe eye damage (chapter 3.3)	1	– *Specify eye/face protection.*
		Eye irritation (chapter 3.3)	2A	Manufacturer/supplier or the competent authority may further specify type of equipment where appropriate.
		Germ cell mutagenicity (chapter 3.5)	1A, 1B, 2	Manufacturer/supplier or the competent authority to specify the appropriate type of equipment.
		Carcinogenicity (chapter 3.6)	1A, 1B, 2	
		Reproductive toxicity (chapter 3.7)	1A, 1B, 2	
P282	**Wear cold insulating gloves and either face shield or eye protection.**	Gases under pressure (chapter 2.5)	Refrigerated liquefied gas	
P283	**Wear fire resistant or flame retardant clothing.**	Oxidizing liquids (chapter 2.13)	1	
		Oxidizing solids (chapter 2.14)	1	
P284	**[In case of inadequate ventilation] wear respiratory protection.**	Acute toxicity, inhalation (chapter 3.1)	1, 2	– *text in square brackets may be used if additional information is provided with the chemical at the point of use that explains what type of ventilation would be adequate for safe use.* Manufacturer/supplier or the competent authority to specify equipment.
		Respiratory sensitization (chapter 3.4)	1, 1A, 1B	

Code (1)	Prevention precautionary statements (2)	Hazard class (3)	Hazard category (4)	Conditions for use (5)
P231 + P232	**Handle and store contents under inert gas/.... Protect from moisture.**	Pyrophoric liquids (chapter 2.9)	1	...Manufacturer/supplier or the competent authority to specify appropriate liquid or gas if "inert gas" is not appropriate.
		Pyrophoric solids (chapter 2.10)	1	
		Substances and mixtures which, in contact with water, emit flammable gases (chapter 2.12)	1, 2, 3	– *if the substance or mixture reacts readily with moisture in air.* ...Manufacturer/supplier or the competent authority to specify appropriate liquid or gas if "inert gas" is not appropriate.

Table A3.2.3: Codification of response precautionary statements

Code (1)	Response precautionary statements (2)	Hazard class (3)	Hazard category (4)	Conditions for use (5)
P301	**IF SWALLOWED:**	Acute toxicity, oral (chapter 3.1)	1, 2, 3, 4	
		Skin corrosion (chapter 3.2)	1A, 1B, 1C	
		Aspiration hazard (chapter 3.10)	1, 2	
P302	**IF ON SKIN:**	Pyrophoric liquids (chapter 2.9)	1	
		Pyrophoric solids (chapter 2.10)	1	
		Substances and mixtures which, in contact with water, emit flammable gases (chapter 2.12)	1, 2	
		Acute toxicity, dermal (chapter 3.1)	1, 2, 3, 4	
		Skin irritation (chapter 3.2)	2	
		Skin sensitization (chapter 3.4)	1, 1A, 1B	
P303	**IF ON SKIN (or hair):**	Flammable liquids (chapter 2.6)	1, 2, 3	
		Skin corrosion (chapter 3.2)	1A, 1B, 1C	
P304	**IF INHALED:**	Acute toxicity, inhalation (chapter 3.1)	1, 2, 3, 4, 5	
		Skin corrosion (chapter 3.2)	1A, 1B, 1C	
		Respiratory sensitization (chapter 3.4)	1, 1A, 1B	
		Specific target organ toxicity, single exposure; respiratory tract irritation (chapter 3.8)	3	
		Specific target organ toxicity, single exposure; narcotic effects (chapter 3.8)	3	

Code (1)	Response precautionary statements (2)	Hazard class (3)	Hazard category (4)	Conditions for use (5)
P305	**IF IN EYES:**	Skin corrosion (chapter 3.2)	1A, 1B, 1C	
		Severe eye damage (chapter 3.3)	1	
		Eye irritation (chapter 3.3)	2A, 2B	
P306	**IF ON CLOTHING:**	Oxidizing liquids (chapter 2.13)	1	
		Oxidizing solids (chapter 2.14)	1	
P308	**IF exposed or concerned:**	Germ cell mutagenicity (chapter 3.5)	1A, 1B, 2	
		Carcinogenicity (chapter 3.6)	1A, 1B, 2	
		Reproductive toxicity (chapter 3.7)	1A, 1B, 2	
		Reproductive toxicity, effects on or via lactation (chapter 3.7)	Additional category	
		Specific target organ toxicity, single exposure (chapter 3.8)	1, 2	
P310	**Immediately call a POISON CENTER/doctor/…**	Acute toxicity, oral (chapter 3.1)	1, 2, 3	…Manufacturer/supplier or the competent authority to specify the appropriate source of emergency medical advice.
		Acute toxicity, dermal (chapter 3.1)	1, 2	
		Acute toxicity, inhalation (chapter 3.1)	1, 2	
		Skin corrosion (chapter 3.2)	1A, 1B, 1C	
		Severe eye damage (chapter 3.3)	1	
		Aspiration hazard (chapter 3.10)	1, 2	
P311	**Call a POISON CENTER/doctor/…**	Acute toxicity, inhalation (chapter 3.1)	3	…Manufacturer/supplier or the competent authority to specify the appropriate source of emergency medical advice.
		Respiratory sensitization (chapter 3.4)	1, 1A, 1B	
		Specific target organ toxicity, single exposure (chapter 3.8)	1, 2	
P312	**Call a POISON CENTER/doctor/…if you feel unwell.**	Acute toxicity, oral (chapter 3.1)	4	…Manufacturer/supplier or the competent authority to specify the appropriate source of emergency medical advice.
		Acute toxicity, oral (chapter 3.1)	5	
		Acute toxicity, dermal (chapter 3.1)	3, 4, 5	
		Acute toxicity, inhalation (chapter 3.1)	4	
		Acute toxicity, inhalation (chapter 3.1)	5	
		Specific target organ toxicity, single exposure; respiratory tract irritation (chapter 3.8)	3	
		Specific target organ toxicity, single exposure; narcotic effects (chapter 3.8)	3	

Code (1)	Response precautionary statements (2)	Hazard class (3)	Hazard category (4)	Conditions for use (5)
P313	**Get medical advice/attention.**	Skin irritation (chapter 3.2)	2, 3	Manufacturer/supplier or the competent authority to select medical advice or attention as appropriate.
		Eye irritation (chapter 3.3)	2A, 2B	
		Skin sensitization (chapter 3.4)	1, 1A, 1B	
		Germ cell mutagenicity (chapter 3.5)	1A, 1B, 2	
		Carcinogenicity (chapter 3.6)	1A, 1B, 2	
		Reproductive toxicity (chapter 3.7)	1A, 1B, 2	
		Reproductive toxicity, effects on or via lactation (chapter 3.7)	Additional category	
P314	**Get medical advice/attention if you feel unwell.**	Specific target organ toxicity, repeated exposure (chapter 3.9)	1, 2	Manufacturer/supplier or the competent authority to select medical advice or attention as appropriate.
P315	**Get immediate medical advice/attention.**	Gases under pressure (chapter 2.5)	Refrigerated liquefied gas	Manufacturer/supplier or the competent authority to select medical advice or attention as appropriate.
P320	**Specific treatment is urgent (see ... on this label).**	Acute toxicity, inhalation (chapter 3.1)	1, 2	– *if immediate administration of antidote is required.* ...Reference to supplemental first aid instruction.
P321	**Specific treatment (see ... on this label).**	Acute toxicity, oral (chapter 3.1)	1, 2, 3	– *if immediate administration of antidote is required.* ...Reference to supplemental first aid instruction.
		Acute toxicity, dermal (chapter 3.1)	1, 2, 3, 4	– *if immediate measures such as specific cleansing agent is advised.* ...Reference to supplemental first aid instruction.
		Acute toxicity, inhalation (chapter 3.1)	3	– *if immediate specific measures are required.* ...Reference to supplemental first aid instruction.
		Skin corrosion (chapter 3.2)	1A, 1B, 1C	...Reference to supplemental first aid instruction.
		Skin irritation (chapter 3.2)	2	anufacturer/supplier or the competent authority may specify a cleansing agent if appropriate.
		Skin sensitization (chapter 3.4)	1, 1A, 1B	
		Specific target organ toxicity, single exposure (chapter 3.8)	1	– *if immediate measures are required.* ...Reference to supplemental first aid instruction.
P330	**Rinse mouth.**	Acute toxicity, oral (chapter 3.1)	1, 2, 3, 4	
		Skin corrosion (chapter 3.2)	1A, 1B, 1C	
P331	**Do NOT induce vomiting.**	Skin corrosion (chapter 3.2)	1A, 1B, 1C	
		Aspiration hazard (chapter 3.10)	1, 2	

Code (1)	Response precautionary statements (2)	Hazard class (3)	Hazard category (4)	Conditions for use (5)
P332	If skin irritation occurs:	Skin irritation (chapter 3.2)	2, 3	
P333	If skin irritation or rash occurs:	Skin sensitization (chapter 3.4)	1, 1A, 1B	
P334	Immerse in cool water [or wrap in wet bandages].	Pyrophoric liquids (chapter 2.9)	1	– text in square brackets to be used for pyrophoric liquids and solids.
		Pyrophoric solids (chapter 2.10)	1	– use only "Immerse in cool water." Text in square brackets should not be used.
		Substances and mixtures which, in contact with water, emit flammable gases (chapter 2.12)	1, 2	
P335	Brush off loose particles from skin.	Pyrophoric solids (chapter 2.10)	1	
		Substances and mixtures which, in contact with water, emit flammable gases (chapter 2.12)	1, 2	
P336	Thaw frosted parts with lukewarm water. Do not rub affected area.	Gases under pressure (chapter 2.5)	Refrigerated liquefied gas	
P337	If eye irritation persists:	Eye irritation (chapter 3.3)	2A, 2B	
P338	Remove contact lenses, if present and easy to do. Continue rinsing.	Skin corrosion (chapter 3.2)	1A, 1B, 1C	
		Severe eye damage (chapter 3.3)	1	
		Eye irritation (chapter 3.3)	2A, 2B	
P340	Remove person to fresh air and keep comfortable for breathing.	Acute toxicity, inhalation (chapter 3.1)	1, 2, 3, 4	
		Skin corrosion (chapter 3.2)	1A, 1B, 1C	
		Respiratory sensitization (chapter 3.4)	1, 1A, 1B	
		Specific target organ toxicity, single exposure; respiratory tract irritation (chapter 3.8)	3	
		Specific target organ toxicity, single exposure; narcotic effects (chapter 3.8)	3	
P342	If experiencing respiratory symptoms:	Respiratory sensitization (chapter 3.4)	1, 1A, 1B	
P351	Rinse cautiously with water for several minutes.	Skin corrosion (chapter 3.2)	1A, 1B, 1C	
		Severe eye damage (chapter 3.3)	1	
		Eye irritation (chapter 3.3)	2A, 2B	
P352	Wash with plenty of water/...	Acute toxicity, dermal (chapter 3.1)	1, 2, 3, 4	...Manufacturer/supplier or the competent authority may specify a cleansing agent if appropriate, or may recommend an alternative agent in exceptional cases if water is clearly inappropriate.
		Skin irritation (chapter 3.2)	2	
		Skin sensitization (chapter 3.4)	1, 1A, 1B	

Code (1)	Response precautionary statements (2)	Hazard class (3)	Hazard category (4)	Conditions for use (5)
P353	**Rinse skin with water [or shower].**	Flammable liquids (chapter 2.6)	1, 2, 3	*– text in square brackets to be included where the manufacturer/supplier or the competent authority considers it appropriate for the specific chemical.*
		Skin corrosion (chapter 3.2)	1A, 1B, 1C	
P360	**Rinse immediately contaminated clothing and skin with plenty of water before removing clothes.**	Oxidizing liquids (chapter 2.13)	1	
		Oxidizing solids (chapter 2.14)	1	
P361	**Take off immediately all contaminated clothing.**	Flammable liquids (chapter 2.6)	1, 2, 3	
		Acute toxicity, dermal (chapter 3.1)	1, 2, 3	
		Skin corrosion (chapter 3.2)	1A, 1B, 1C	
P362	**Take off contaminated clothing.**	Acute toxicity, dermal (chapter 3.1)	4	
		Skin irritation (chapter 3.2)	2	
		Skin sensitization (chapter 3.4)	1, 1A, 1B	
P363	**Wash contaminated clothing before reuse.**	Skin corrosion (chapter 3.2)	1A, 1B, 1C	
P364	**And wash it before reuse.**	Acute toxicity, dermal (chapter 3.1)	1, 2, 3, 4	
		Skin irritation (chapter 3.2)	2	
		Skin sensitization (chapter 3.4)	1, 1A, 1B	
P370	**In case of fire:**	Explosives (chapter 2.1)	Unstable explosives and divisions 1.1, 1.2, 1.3, 1.4, 1.5	
		Oxidizing gases (chapter 2.4)	1	
		Flammable liquids (chapter 2.6)	1, 2, 3, 4	
		Flammable solids (chapter 2.7)	1, 2	
		Self-reactive substances and mixtures (chapter 2.8)	Types A, B, C, D, E, F	
		Pyrophoric liquids (chapter 2.9)	1	
		Pyrophoric solids (chapter 2.10)	1	
		Substances and mixtures which, in contact with water, emit flammable gases (chapter 2.12)	1, 2, 3	
		Oxidizing liquids (chapter 2.13)	1, 2, 3	
		Oxidizing solids (chapter 2.14)	1, 2, 3	
		Organic peroxides (chapter 2.15)	Types A, B, C. D, E, F	

- 290 -

Code (1)	Response precautionary statements (2)	Hazard class (3)	Hazard category (4)	Conditions for use (5)
P371	**In case of major fire and large quantities:**	Oxidizing liquids (chapter 2.13)	1	
		Oxidizing solids (chapter 2.14)	1	
P372	**Explosion risk.**	Explosives (chapter 2.1)	Unstable explosives and Divisions 1.1, 1.2, 1.3, and 1.5	
			Division 1.4	*– except for explosives of division 1.4 (compatibility group S) in transport packaging.*
		Self-reactive substances and mixtures (chapter 2.8)	Type A	
		Organic peroxides (chapter 2.15)	Type A	
P373	**DO NOT fight fire when fire reaches explosives.**	Explosives (chapter 2.1)	Unstable explosives and Divisions 1.1, 1.2, 1.3, and 1.5	
			Division 1.4	*– except for explosives of division 1.4 (compatibility group S) in transport packaging.*
		Self-reactive substances and mixtures (chapter 2.8)	Type A	
		Organic peroxides (chapter 2.15)	Type A	
P375	**Fight fire remotely due to the risk of explosion.**	Explosives (chapter 2.1)	Division 1.4	*– for explosives of division 1.4 (compatibility group S) in transport packaging.*
		Self-reactive substances and mixtures (chapter 2.8)	Type B	
		Oxidizing liquids (chapter 2.13)	1	
		Oxidizing solids (chapter 2.14)	1	
		Organic peroxides (chapter 2.15)	Type B	
P376	**Stop leak if safe to do so.**	Oxidizing gases (chapter 2.4)	1	
P377	**Leaking gas fire: Do not extinguish, unless leak can be stopped safely.**	Flammable gases (chapter 2.2)	1, 2	
P378	**Use ... to extinguish.**	Flammable liquids (chapter 2.6)	1, 2, 3, 4	*– if water increases risk.*
		Flammable solids (chapter 2.7)	1, 2	... Manufacturer/supplier or the competent authority to specify appropriate media.
		Self-reactive substances and mixtures (chapter 2.8)	Types B, C, D, E, F	
		Pyrophoric liquids (chapter 2.9)	1	
		Pyrophoric solids (chapter 2.10)	1	
		Substances and mixtures which, in contact with water, emit flammable gases (chapter 2.12)	1, 2, 3	
		Oxidizing liquids (chapter 2.13)	1, 2, 3	
		Oxidizing solids (chapter 2.14)	1, 2, 3	
		Organic peroxides (chapter 2.15)	Types B, C, D, E, F	

Code (1)	Response precautionary statements (2)	Hazard class (3)	Hazard category (4)	Conditions for use (5)
P380	Evacuate area.	Explosives (chapter 2.1)	Unstable explosives	
		Explosives (chapter 2.1)	Divisions 1.1, 1.2, 1.3, 1.4, 1.5	
		Self-reactive substances and mixtures (chapter 2.8)	Types A, B	
		Oxidizing liquids (chapter 2.13)	1	
		Oxidizing solids (chapter 2.14)	1	
		Organic peroxides (chapter 2.15)	Types A, B	
P381	In case of leakage, eliminate all ignition sources.	Flammable gases (chapter 2.2)	1, 2	
P390	Absorb spillage to prevent material-damage.	Corrosive to metals (chapter 2.16)	1	
P391	Collect spillage.	Hazardous to the aquatic environment, acute hazard (chapter 4.1)	1	
		Hazardous to the aquatic environment, long-term hazard (chapter 4.1)	1, 2	
P301 + P310	IF SWALLOWED: Immediately call a POISON CENTER/doctor/...	Acute toxicity, oral (chapter 3.1)	1, 2, 3	...Manufacturer/supplier or the competent authority to specify the appropriate source of emergency medical advice.
		Aspiration hazard (chapter 3.10)	1, 2	
P301 + P312	IF SWALLOWED: Call a POISON CENTER/doctor/...if you feel unwell.	Acute toxicity, oral (chapter 3.1)	4	...Manufacturer/supplier or the competent authority to specify the appropriate source of emergency medical advice.
P302 + P334	IF ON SKIN: Immerse in cool water [or wrap in wet bandages].	Pyrophoric liquids (chapter 2.9)	1	– text in square brackets to be used for pyrophoric liquids.
P302 + P352	IF ON SKIN: Wash with plenty of water/...	Acute toxicity, dermal (chapter 3.1)	1, 2, 3, 4	...Manufacturer/supplier or the competent authority may specify a cleansing agent if appropriate, or may recommend an alternative agent in exceptional cases if water is clearly inappropriate.
		Skin irritation (chapter 3.2)	2	
		Skin sensitization (chapter 3.4)	1, 1A, 1B	
P304 + P312	IF INHALED: Call a POISON CENTER/doctor/...if you feel unwell.	Acute toxicity, inhalation (chapter 3.1)	5	...Manufacturer/supplier or the competent authority to specify the appropriate source of emergency medical advice.

Code (1)	Response precautionary statements (2)	Hazard class (3)	Hazard category (4)	Conditions for use (5)
P304 + P340	**IF INHALED: Remove person to fresh air and keep comfortable for breathing.**	Acute toxicity, inhalation (chapter 3.1)	1, 2, 3, 4	
		Skin corrosion (chapter 3.2)	1A, 1B, 1C	
		Respiratory sensitization (chapter 3.4)	1, 1A, 1B	
		Specific target organ toxicity, single exposure; respiratory tract irritation (chapter 3.8)	3	
		Specific target organ toxicity, single exposure; narcotic effects (chapter 3.8)	3	
P306 + P360	**IF ON CLOTHING: Rinse immediately contaminated clothing and skin with plenty of water before removing clothes.**	Oxidizing liquids (chapter 2.13)	1	
		Oxidizing solids (chapter 2.14)	1	
P308 + P311	**IF exposed or concerned: Call a POISON CENTER/doctor/...**	Specific target organ toxicity, single exposure (chapter 3.8)	1, 2	...Manufacturer/supplier or the competent authority to specify the appropriate source of emergency medical advice.
P308 + P313	**IF exposed or concerned: Get medical advice/ attention.**	Germ cell mutagenicity (chapter 3.5)	1A, 1B, 2	Manufacturer/supplier or the competent authority to select medical advice or attention as appropriate.
		Carcinogenicity (chapter 3.6)	1A, 1B, 2	Manufacturer/supplier or the competent authority to select medical advice or attention as appropriate.
		Reproductive toxicity (chapter 3.7)	1A, 1B, 2	Manufacturer/supplier or the competent authority to select medical advice or attention as appropriate.
		Reproductive toxicity, effects on or via lactation (chapter 3.7)	Additional category	
P332 + P313	**If skin irritation occurs: Get medical advice/attention.**	Skin irritation (chapter 3.2)	2, 3	*– may be omitted when P333+P313 is given on the label.* Manufacturer/supplier or the competent authority to select medical advice or attention as appropriate.
P333 + P313	**If skin irritation or rash occurs: Get medical advice/attention.**	Skin sensitization (chapter 3.4)	1, 1A, 1B	Manufacturer/supplier or the competent authority to select medical advice or attention as appropriate.
P336 + P315	**Thaw frosted parts with lukewarm water. Do not rub affected area. Get immediate medical advice/attention**	Gases under pressure (chapter 2.5)	Refrigerated liquefied gas	
P337 + P313	**If eye irritation persists: Get medical advice/attention.**	Eye irritation (chapter 3.3)	2A, 2B	Manufacturer/supplier or the competent authority to select medical advice or attention as appropriate.
P342 + P311	**If experiencing respiratory symptoms: Call a POISON CENTER/doctor/...**	Respiratory sensitization (chapter 3.4)	1, 1A, 1B	...Manufacturer/supplier or the competent authority to specify the appropriate source of emergency medical advice.
P361 + P364	**Take off immediately all contaminated clothing and wash it before reuse.**	Acute toxicity, dermal (chapter 3.1)	1, 2, 3	

Code (1)	Response precautionary statements (2)	Hazard class (3)	Hazard category (4)	Conditions for use (5)
P362 + P364	Take off contaminated clothing and wash it before reuse.	Acute toxicity, dermal (chapter 3.1)	4	
		Skin irritation (chapter 3.2)	2	
		Skin sensitization (chapter 3.4)	1, 1A, 1B	
P370 + P376	In case of fire: Stop leak if safe to do so.	Oxidizing gases (chapter 2.4)	1	
P370 + P378	In case of fire: Use ... to extinguish.	Flammable liquids (chapter 2.6)	1, 2, 3, 4	*– if water increases risk.*
		Flammable solids (chapter 2.7)	1, 2	*... Manufacturer/supplier or the competent authority to specify appropriate media.*
		Self-reactive substances and mixtures (chapter 2.8)	Types C, D, E, F	
		Pyrophoric liquids (chapter 2.9)	1	
		Pyrophoric solids (chapter 2.10)	1	
		Substances and mixtures which, in contact with water, emit flammable gases (chapter 2.12)	1, 2, 3	
		Oxidizing liquids (chapter 2.13)	1, 2, 3	
		Oxidizing solids (chapter 2.14)	1, 2, 3	
		Organic peroxides (chapter 2.15)	Types C, D, E, F	
P301 + P330 + P331	IF SWALLOWED: Rinse mouth. Do NOT induce vomiting.	Skin corrosion (chapter 3.2)	1A, 1B, 1C	
P302 + P335 + P334	IF ON SKIN: Brush off loose particles from skin. Immerse in cool water [or wrap in wet bandages].	Pyrophoric solids (chapter 2.10)	1	*– text in square brackets to be used for pyrophoric solids*
		Substances and mixtures which, in contact with water, emit flammable gases (chapter 2.12)	1, 2	*– use only "Immerse in cool water." Text in square brackets should not be used.*
P303 + P361 + P353	IF ON SKIN (or hair): Take off immediately all contaminated clothing. Rinse skin with water [or shower].	Flammable liquids (chapter 2.6)	1, 2, 3	*– text in square brackets to be included where the manufacturer/supplier or the competent authority considers it appropriate for the specific chemical.*
		Skin corrosion (chapter 3.2)	1A, 1B, 1C	

Code (1)	Response precautionary statements (2)	Hazard class (3)	Hazard category (4)	Conditions for use (5)
P305 + P351 + P338	IF IN EYES: Rinse cautiously with water for several minutes. Remove contact lenses, if present and easy to do. Continue rinsing.	Skin corrosion (chapter 3.2)	1A, 1B, 1C	
		Severe eye damage (chapter 3.3)	1	
		Eye irritation (chapter 3.3)	2A, 2B	
P370 + P380 + P375	In case of fire: Evacuate area. Fight fire remotely due to the risk of explosion.	Explosives (chapter 2.1)	Division 1.4	– for explosives of division 1.4 (compatibility group S) in transport packaging
		Organic peroxides (chapter 2.15)	Type B	
P371 + P380 + P375	In case of major fire and large quantities: Evacuate area. Fight fire remotely due to the risk of explosion.	Oxidizing liquids (chapter 2.13)	1	
		Oxidizing solids (chapter 2.14)	1	
P370 + P372 + P380 + P373	In case of fire: Explosion risk. Evacuate area. DO NOT fight fire when fire reaches explosives.	Explosives (chapter 2.1)	Unstable explosives and divisions 1.1, 1.2, 1.3, 1.5	
			Division 1.4	– except for explosives of division 1.4 (compatibility group S) in transport packaging.
		Self-reactive substances and mixtures (chapter 2.8)	Type A	
		Organic peroxides (chapter 2.15)	Type A	
P370 + P380 + P375 [+ P378]	In case of fire: Evacuate area. Fight fire remotely due to the risk of explosion. [Use…to extinguish].	Self-reactive substances and mixtures (chapter 2.8)	Type B	– text in square brackets to be used if water increases risk. … Manufacturer/supplier or the competent authority to specify appropriate media.
		Organic peroxides (chapter 2.15)	Type B	

Table A3.2.4: Codification of storage precautionary statements

Code (1)	Storage precautionary statements (2)	Hazard class (3)	Hazard category (4)	Conditions for use (5)
P401	**Store in accordance with…**	Explosives (chapter 2.1)	Unstable explosives and Divisions 1.1, 1.2, 1.3, 1.4, 1.5	… Manufacturer/supplier or the competent authority to specify local/regional/ national/international regulations as applicable.
P402	**Store in a dry place.**	Substances and mixtures which, in contact with water, emit flammable gases (chapter 2.12)	1, 2, 3	
P403	**Store in a well-ventilated place.**	Flammable gases (chapter 2.2)	1, 2	
		Oxidizing gases (chapter 2.4)	1	
		Gases under pressure (chapter 2.5)	Compressed gas Liquefied gas Refrigerated liquefied gas Dissolved gas	
		Flammable liquids (chapter 2.6)	1, 2, 3, 4	*– for flammable liquids Category 1 and other flammable liquids that are volatile and may generate an explosive atmosphere.*
		Self-reactive substances and mixtures (chapter 2.8)	Types A, B, C, D, E, F	*– except for temperature controlled self-reactive substances and mixtures or organic peroxides because condensation and consequent freezing may take place.*
		Organic peroxides (chapter 2.15)	Types A, B, C, D, E, F	
		Acute toxicity, inhalation (chapter 3.1)	1, 2, 3	*– if the chemical is volatile and may generate a hazardous atmosphere.*
		Specific target organ toxicity, single exposure; respiratory tract irritation (chapter 3.8)	3	
		Specific target organ toxicity, single exposure; narcotic effects (chapter 3.8)	3	
P404	**Store in a closed container.**	Substances and mixtures which, in contact with water, emit flammable gases (chapter 2.12)	1, 2, 3	

Code (1)	Storage precautionary statements (2)	Hazard class (3)	Hazard category (4)	Conditions for use (5)
P405	Store locked up.	Acute toxicity, oral (chapter 3.1)	1, 2, 3	
		Acute toxicity, dermal (chapter 3.1)	1, 2, 3	
		Acute toxicity, inhalation (chapter 3.1)	1, 2, 3	
		Skin corrosion (chapter 3.2)	1A, 1B, 1C	
		Germ cell mutagenicity (chapter 3.5)	1A, 1B, 2	
		Carcinogenicity (chapter 3.6)	1A, 1B, 2	
		Reproductive toxicity (chapter 3.7)	1A, 1B, 2	
		Specific target organ toxicity, single exposure (chapter 3.8)	1, 2	
		Specific target organ toxicity, single exposure; respiratory tract irritation (chapter 3.8)	3	
		Specific target organ toxicity, single exposure; narcotic effects (chapter 3.8)	3	
		Aspiration hazard (chapter 3.10)	1, 2	
P406	Store in a corrosion resistant/...container with a resistant inner liner.	Corrosive to metals (chapter 2.16)	1	– *may be omitted if P234 is given on the label* ... Manufacturer/supplier or the competent authority to specify other compatible materials.
P407	Maintain air gap between stacks or pallets.	Self-heating substances and mixtures (chapter 2.11)	1, 2	
P410	Protect from sunlight.	Aerosols (chapter 2.3)	1, 2, 3	
		Gases under pressure (chapter 2.5)	Compressed gas Liquefied gas Dissolved gas	– *may be omitted for gases filled in transportable gas cylinders in accordance with packing instruction P200 of the UN Recommendations on the Transport of Dangerous Goods, Model Regulations, unless those gases are subject to (slow) decomposition or polymerisation, or the competent authority provides otherwise.*
		Self-heating substances and mixtures (chapter 2.11)	1, 2	
		Organic peroxides (chapter 2.15)	Types A, B, C, D, E, F	

Code (1)	Storage precautionary statements (2)	Hazard class (3)	Hazard category (4)	Conditions for use (5)
P411	Store at temperatures not exceeding …°C/…°F.	Self-reactive substances and mixtures (chapter 2.8)	Types A, B, C, D, E, F	– if temperature control is required (according to section 2.8.2.3 or 2.15.2.3 of the GHS) or if otherwise deemed necessary. …Manufacturer/supplier or the competent authority to specify temperature using applicable temperature scale.
		Organic peroxides (chapter 2.15)	Types A, B, C, D, E, F	
P412	Do not expose to temperatures exceeding 50 °C/122 °F.	Aerosols (chapter 2.3)	1, 2, 3	Manufacturer/supplier or the competent authority to use applicable temperature scale.
P413	Store bulk masses greater than … kg/…lbs at temperatures not exceeding …°C/…°F.	Self-heating substances and mixtures (chapter 2.11)	1, 2	…Manufacturer/supplier or the competent authority to specify mass and temperature using applicable scale.
P420	Store separately.	Self-reactive substances and mixtures (chapter 2.8)	Types A, B, C, D, E, F	
		Self-heating substances and mixtures (chapter 2.11)	1, 2	
		Oxidizing liquids (chapter 2.13)	1	
		Oxidizing solids (chapter 2.14)	1	
		Organic peroxides (chapter 2.15)	Types A, B, C, D, E, F	
P402 + P404	Store in a dry place. Store in a closed container.	Substances and mixtures which, in contact with water, emit flammable gases (chapter 2.12)	1, 2, 3	
P403 + P233	Store in a well-ventilated place. Keep container tightly closed.	Acute toxicity, inhalation (chapter 3.1)	1, 2, 3	– if the chemical is volatile and may generate a hazardous atmosphere.
		Specific target organ toxicity, single exposure; respiratory tract irritation (chapter 3.8)	3	
P403 + P235	Store in a well-ventilated place. Keep cool.	Specific target organ toxicity, single exposure; narcotic effects (chapter 3.8)	3	
		Flammable liquids (chapter 2.6)	1, 2, 3	– for flammable liquids Category 1 and other flammable liquids that are volatile and may generate an explosive atmosphere.

Code (1)	Storage precautionary statements (2)	Hazard class (3)	Hazard category (4)	Conditions for use (5)
P410 + P403	**Protect from sunlight. Store in a well-ventilated place.**	Gases under pressure (chapter 2.5)	Compressed gas Liquefied gas Dissolved gas	*– P410 may be omitted for gases filled in transportable gas cylinders in accordance with packing instruction P200 of the UN Recommendations on the Transport of Dangerous Goods, Model Regulations, unless those gases are subject to (slow) decomposition or polymerisation, or the competent authority provides otherwise.*
P410 + P412	**Protect from sunlight. Do not expose to temperatures exceeding 50 °C/122 °F.**	Aerosols (chapter 2.3)	1, 2, 3	Manufacturer/supplier or the competent authority to use applicable temperature scale.

Table A3.2.5: Codification of disposal precautionary statements

Code (1)	Disposal precautionary statements (2)	Hazard class (3)	Hazard category (4)	Conditions for use (5)
P501	**Dispose of contents/container to ...**	Explosives (chapter 2.1)	Unstable explosives and Divisions 1.1, 1.2, 1.3, 1.4, 1.5	... in accordance with local/regional/national/international regulation (to be specified).
		Flammable liquids (chapter 2.6)	1, 2, 3, 4	Manufacturer/supplier or the competent authority to specify whether disposal requirements apply to contents, container or both.
		Self-reactive substances and mixtures (chapter 2.8)	Types A, B, C, D, E, F	
		Substances and mixtures which, in contact with water, emit flammable gases (chapter 2.12)	1, 2, 3	
		Oxidizing liquids (chapter 2.13)	1, 2, 3	
		Oxidizing solids (chapter 2.14)	1, 2, 3	
		Organic peroxides (chapter 2.15)	Types A, B, C, D, E, F	
		Acute toxicity, oral (chapter 3.1)	1, 2, 3, 4	
		Acute toxicity, dermal (chapter 3.1)	1, 2, 3, 4	
		Acute toxicity, inhalation (chapter 3.1)	1, 2	

Code (1)	Disposal precautionary statements (2)	Hazard class (3)	Hazard category (4)	Conditions for use (5)
P501 (cont'd)	**Dispose of contents/container to ...**	Skin corrosion (chapter 3.2)	1A, 1B, 1C	... in accordance with local/regional/ national/international regulation (to be specified).
		Respiratory sensitization (chapter 3.4)	1, 1A, 1B	Manufacturer/supplier or the competent authority to specify whether disposal requirements apply to contents, container or both.
		Skin sensitization (chapter 3.4)	1, 1A, 1B	
		Germ cell mutagenicity (chapter 3.5)	1A, 1B, 2	
		Carcinogenicity (chapter 3.6)	1A, 1B, 2	
		Reproductive toxicity (chapter 3.7)	1A, 1B, 2	
		Specific target organ toxicity, single exposure (chapter 3.8)	1, 2	
		Specific target organ toxicity , single exposure; respiratory tract irritation (chapter 3.8)	3	
		Specific target organ toxicity, single exposure; narcotic effects (chapter 3.8)	3	
		Specific target organ toxicity, repeated exposure (chapter 3.9)	1, 2	
		Aspiration hazard (chapter 3.10)	1, 2	
		Hazardous to the aquatic environment, acute hazard (chapter 4.1)	1, 2, 3	
		Hazardous to the aquatic environment, long-term hazard (chapter 4.1)	1, 2, 3, 4	
P502	**Refer to manufacturer or supplier for information on recovery or recycling**	Hazardous to the ozone layer (chapter 4.2)	1	

Annex 3

Section 3

USE OF PRECAUTIONARY STATEMENTS

A3.3.1 Introduction

A3.3.1.1   This section provides guidance on the use of precautionary statements consistent with the GHS, including advice on the selection of appropriate statements for each GHS hazard class and category.

A3.3.1.2   The starting point for assigning precautionary statements is the hazard classification of the chemical product. The system of classifying hazards in the GHS is based on the intrinsic properties of the chemicals involved (see 1.3.2.2.1). In some systems, however, labelling may not be required for chronic hazards on consumer product labels, if information shows that the respective risks can be excluded under conditions of normal handling, normal use or foreseeable misuse (see Annex 5). If certain hazard statements are not required then the corresponding precautionary statements are also not necessary (see A5.1.1).

A3.3.1.3   The guidance for assigning the phrases in this section has been developed to provide the essential minimum phrases linking precautionary statements with relevant GHS hazard classification criteria and type of hazard.

A3.3.1.4   Existing precautionary statements have been used to the maximum extent as the basis for the development of this section. These existing systems have included the IPCS International Chemical Safety Card (ICSC) Compilers Guide, the American National Standards (ANSI Z129.1), the EU classification and labelling directives, the Emergency Response Guidebook (ERG 2004), and the Pesticide Label Review Manual of the Environmental Protection Agency (EPA) of the United States of America.

A3.3.1.5   The goal of this section is to promote a more consistent use of precautionary statements. Their use will reinforce safe handling procedures and will enable the key concepts and approaches to be emphasized in training and education activities.

A3.3.1.6   This section should be seen as a living document and therefore subject to further refinement and development over time. The basic concepts of the matrix and the philosophy given below will remain.

A3.3.2 Allocation of precautionary statements

A3.3.2.1   This section sets out a matrix which guides the selection of appropriate precautionary statements. It includes elements for all categories of precautionary action. All specific elements relating to particular hazard classes should be used. General elements not linked in particular to a certain hazard class or category should also be used where relevant.

A3.3.2.2   To provide flexibility in the application of precautionary phrases, a combination of statements is encouraged to save label space and improve their readability. Combination of phrases can also be useful for different types of hazard where the precautionary behaviour is similar, e.g. "**Keep away from heat, sparks and open flame and store in a cool well ventilated place**".

A3.3.2.3   Precautionary statements should appear on GHS labels along with the GHS hazard communication elements (pictograms, signal words and hazard statements). Additional supplemental information, such as directions for use, may also be provided at the discretion of the manufacturer/supplier and/or competent authority (see Chapter 1.2 and Chapter 1.4, para. 1.4.6.3). For some specific chemicals, supplementary first aid, treatment measures or specific antidotes or cleansing materials may be required. Poisons Centres and/or medical practitioners or specialist advice should be sought in such situations and included on labels.

A3.3.3 **General precautionary measures**

A3.3.3.1 General precautionary measures should be adopted for all substances and mixtures which are classified as hazardous to human health or the environment. To this end, the needs of and the information sources available to three groups of users or applicators should be taken into account: the general public, the commercial user and the industrial worker.

A3.3.3.2 The presumed observation of precautionary label information, specific safety guidelines, and the safety data sheet for each product before use are part of the labelling requirements and occupational health and safety procedures.

A3.3.3.3 In order to correctly implement precautionary measures concerning prevention, response, storage and disposal, it is also necessary to have information on the composition of products at hand, so that information shown on the container, label and safety data sheet can be taken into account when asking for further specialist advice.

A3.3.3.4 The following general precautionary statements on the GHS label are appropriate under the given conditions:

General public	GHS label, supplemental label information	P101	**If medical advice is needed: Have product container or label at hand.**
		P102	**Keep out of reach of children.**
		P103	**Read label before use.**
Industrial worker	GHS label, supplemental label information, Safety Data Sheet, workplace instructions		*none of the above*

A3.3.4 **Structure of the precautionary statements matrix**

A3.3.4.1 The tables making up the matrix show the core part of the precautionary statements in bold print. This is the text, except as otherwise specified, that should appear on the label. However, it is not necessary to insist on identical sets of words in all situations. Derogations from the recommended labelling statements are at the discretion of competent authorities. In all cases, clear plain language is essential to convey information on precautionary behaviour.

A3.3.4.2 Text in italics that starts with "– *if*" or "– *specify*" is intended to be an explanatory conditional note for the application of the precautionary statements and is not intended to appear on the label.

A3.3.4.3 When a forward slash or diagonal mark [/] appears in a precautionary statement text, it indicates that a choice needs to be made between the phrases they separate. In such cases, the manufacturer or supplier can choose or competent authorities may prescribe one or more appropriate phrase(s). For example, "**Wear protective gloves/protective clothing/eye protection/face protection**" could read "**Wear eye protection**" or "**Wear eye and face protection**".

A3.3.4.4 When three full stops [...] appear in a precautionary statement text, they indicate that all applicable conditions are not listed. In such cases the manufacturer or supplier can choose, or the competent authorities may prescribe the other conditions to be specified. For example, in the statement "**Use explosion-proof [electrical/ventilating/lighting/...]equipment**", the use of "..." indicates that other equipment may need to be specified.

A3.3.4.5 In the majority of cases, the recommended precautionary statements are independent, e.g. the phrases for explosive hazard do not modify those related to certain health hazards and products that are classified for both hazard classes should bear appropriate precautionary statements for both.

A3.3.4.6   Where a substance or mixture is classified for a number of health hazards, generally the most stringent set of precautionary statements should be selected. This applies mainly for the preventive measures. With respect to phrases concerning "Response", rapid action may be crucial. For example, if a chemical is carcinogenic and acutely toxic then the first aid measures for acute toxicity will take precedence over those for longer term effects. In addition, medical attention to delayed health effects may be required in cases of incidental exposure, even if not associated with immediate symptoms of intoxication.

A3.3.4.7   To protect people with different reading abilities, it might be useful to include both precautionary pictograms and precautionary statements in order to convey information in more than one way (see 1.4.4.1 (a)). It should be noted, however, that the protective effect of pictograms is limited and the examples in this annex do not cover all precautionary aspects to be addressed. While pictograms can be useful, they can be misinterpreted and are not a substitute for training.

A3.3.5   Matrix of precautionary statements by hazard class/category

A3.3.5.1   This matrix lists the recommended precautionary statements for each hazard class and hazard category of the GHS by type of precautionary statement (see A3.2.2.1) except for general precautionary statements. In each case the precautionary statement has the applicable code on the line immediately above.

**EXPLOSIVES
(CHAPTER 2.1)**

Hazard category	**Signal word**	**Hazard statement**	**Symbol**

Unstable explosive

Danger

H200   Unstable explosive

Exploding bomb

Precautionary statements

Prevention	Response	Storage	Disposal
P201 **Obtain special instructions before use.** P250 **Do not subject to grinding/shock/friction/...** – *if the explosive is mechanically sensitive.* ...Manufacturer/supplier or the competent authority to specify applicable rough handling. P280 **Wear protective gloves/protective clothing/eye protection/face protection.** Manufacturer/supplier or the competent authority to specify the appropriate type of equipment.	P370 + P372 + P380 + P373 **In case of fire: Explosion risk. Evacuate area. DO NOT fight fire when fire reaches explosives.**	P401 **Store in accordance with...** ... Manufacturer/supplier or the competent authority to specify local/regional/ national/international regulations as applicable.	P501 **Dispose of contents/container to ...** ...in accordance with local/regional/ national/international regulations (to be specified). Manufacturer/supplier or the competent authority to specify whether disposal requirements apply to contents, container or both.

**EXPLOSIVES
(CHAPTER 2.1)**

Hazard category	Signal word		Hazard statement	
Division 1.1	Danger		H201	Explosive; mass explosion hazard
Division 1.2	Danger		H202	Explosive; severe projection hazard
Division 1.3	Danger		H203	Explosive; fire, blast or projection hazard

Precautionary statements

Prevention	Response	Storage	Disposal
P210 **Keep away from heat, hot surfaces, sparks, open flames and other ignition sources. No smoking.** P230 **Keep wetted with…** *– for substances and mixtures which are wetted, diluted, dissolved or suspended with a phlegmatizer in order to reduce or suppress their explosive properties (desensitized explosives).* …Manufacturer/supplier or the competent authority to specify appropriate material. P234 **Keep only in original packaging.** P240 **Ground and bond container and receiving equipment.** *– if the explosive is electrostatically sensitive.* P250 **Do not subject to grinding/shock/friction/…** *– if the explosive is mechanically sensitive.* …Manufacturer/supplier or the competent authority to specify applicable rough handling. P280 **Wear protective gloves/protective clothing/eye protection/face protection.** Manufacturer/supplier or the competent authority to specify the appropriate type of equipment.	P370 + P372 + P380 + P373 **In case of fire: Explosion risk. Evacuate area. DO NOT fight fire when fire reaches explosives.**	P401 **Store in accordance with…** …Manufacturer/supplier or the competent authority to specify local/regional/national/international regulations as applicable.	P501 **Dispose of contents/container to …** … in accordance with local/ regional/national/international regulations (to be specified). Manufacturer/supplier or the competent authority to specify whether disposal requirements apply to contents, container or both.

**EXPLOSIVES
(CHAPTER 2.1)**

Hazard category	Signal word	Hazard statement	Symbol
Division 1.4	Warning	H204 Fire or projection hazard	Exploding bomb

Precautionary statements

Prevention	Response	Storage	Disposal
P210 **Keep away from heat, hot surfaces, sparks, open flames and other ignition sources. No smoking.** P234 **Keep only in original packaging.** P240 **Ground and bond container and receiving equipment.** *– if the explosive is electrostatically sensitive.* P250 **Do not subject to grinding/shock/friction/…** *– if the explosive is mechanically sensitive.* *…Manufacturer/supplier or the competent authority to specify applicable rough handling.* P280 **Wear protective gloves/protective clothing/eye protection/face protection.** *Manufacturer/supplier or the competent authority to specify the appropriate type of equipment.*	P370 + P372 + P380 + P373 **In case of fire: Explosion risk. Evacuate area. DO NOT fight fire when fire reaches explosives.** *– except for explosives of division 1.4 (compatibility group S) in transport packaging.* P370 + P380 + P375 **In case of fire: Evacuate area. Fight fire remotely due to the risk of explosion.** *– for explosives of division 1.4 (compatibility group S) in transport packaging.*	P401 **Store in accordance with…** *… Manufacturer/supplier or the competent authority to specify local/regional/ national/international regulations as applicable.*	P501 **Dispose of contents/container to…** *… in accordance with local/regional/national/international regulations (to be specified).* *Manufacturer/supplier or the competent authority to specify whether disposal requirements apply to contents, container or both.*

Hazard category	**Signal word**	**Hazard statement**	**Symbol**
Division 1.5	Danger	H205 May mass explode in fire	*No symbol*

Precautionary statements

Prevention	Response	Storage	Disposal
P210 **Keep away from heat, hot surfaces, sparks, open flames and other ignition sources. No smoking.** P230 **Keep wetted with...** *– for substances and mixtures which are wetted, diluted, dissolved or suspended with a phlegmatizer in order to reduce or suppress their explosive properties (desensitized explosives).* ... Manufacturer/supplier or the competent authority to specify appropriate material. P234 **Keep only in original packaging.** P240 **Ground and bond container and receiving equipment.** *– if the explosive is electrostatically sensitive.* P250 **Do not subject to grinding/shock/friction...** *– if the explosive is mechanically sensitive.* ...Manufacturer/supplier or the competent authority to specify applicable rough handling. P280 **Wear protective gloves/protective clothing/eye protection/face protection.** Manufacturer/supplier or competent authority to specify the appropriate type of equipment.	P370 + P372 + P380 + P373 **In case of fire: Explosion risk. Evacuate area. DO NOT fight fire when fire reaches explosives.**	P401 **Store in accordance with...** ... Manufacturer/supplier or the competent authority to specify local/regional/ national/international regulations as applicable.	P501 **Dispose of contents/container to ...** ... in accordance with local/regional/ national/international regulations (to be specified). Manufacturer/supplier or the competent authority to specify whether disposal requirements apply to contents, container or both.

FLAMMABLE GASES (INCLUDING CHEMICALLY UNSTABLE GASES)

(CHAPTER 2.2)
(Flammable gases)

Symbol	Flame

Hazard category

1

Signal word

Danger

Hazard statement

H220   Extremely flammable gas

Precautionary statements

Prevention	Response	Storage	Disposal
P210 **Keep away from heat, hot surfaces, sparks, open flames and other ignition sources. No smoking.**	P377 **Leaking gas fire:** **Do not extinguish, unless leak can be stopped safely.** P381 **In case of leakage, eliminate all ignition sources.**	P403 **Store in a well-ventilated place.**	

FLAMMABLE GASES (INCLUDING CHEMICALLY UNSTABLE GASES)
(CHAPTER 2.2)
(Flammable gases)

Hazard category	**Signal word**	**Hazard statement**	**Symbol**
2	Warning	H221 Flammable gas	*No symbol*

Precautionary statements

Prevention	Response	Storage	Disposal
P210 **Keep away from heat, hot surfaces, sparks, open flames and other ignition sources. No smoking.**	P377 **Leaking gas fire: Do not extinguish, unless leak can be stopped safely.** P381 **In case of leakage, eliminate all ignition sources.**	P403 **Store in a well-ventilated place.**	

FLAMMABLE GASES (INCLUDING CHEMICALLY UNSTABLE GASES)
(CHAPTER 2.2)
(Chemically unstable gases)

Symbol

No additional symbol

Hazard category

	Signal word	**Hazard statement**	
A	*No additional signal word*	H230	May react explosively even in the absence of air
B	*No additional signal word*	H231	May react explosively even in the absence of air at elevated pressure and/or temperature

Precautionary statements

Prevention	**Response**	**Storage**	**Disposal**
P202 **Do not handle until all safety precautions have been read and understood.**			

Note: *This table lists only the precautionary statement that is assigned due to the chemical instability of the gas. For the other precautionary statements that are assigned based on the flammability see the respective tables for flammable gases.*

AEROSOLS
(CHAPTER 2.3)

	Symbol
	Flame

Hazard category

1

2

Signal word

Danger

Warning

Hazard statement

H222	Extremely flammable aerosol
H229	Pressurized container: may burst if heated
H223	Flammable aerosol
H229	Pressurized container: may burst if heated

Precautionary statements

Prevention	Response	Storage	Disposal
P210 **Keep away from heat, hot surfaces, sparks, open flames and other ignition sources. No smoking.** P211 **Do not spray on an open flame or other ignition source.** P251 **Do not pierce or burn, even after use.**		P410 + P412 **Protect from sunlight. Do not expose to temperatures exceeding 50 °C/122 °F.** Manufacturer/supplier or the competent authority to use applicable temperature scale.	

AEROSOLS
(CHAPTER 2.3)

Symbol	*No symbol*

Hazard category

3

Signal word

Warning

Hazard statement

H229   Pressurized container: may burst if heated

Precautionary statements

Prevention	Response	Storage	Disposal
P210 **Keep away from heat, hot surfaces, sparks, open flames and other ignition sources. No smoking.** P251 **Do not pierce or burn, even after use.**		P410 + P412 **Protect from sunlight. Do not expose to temperatures exceeding 50 °C/122 °F.** Manufacturer/supplier or the competent authority to use applicable temperature scale.	

OXIDIZING GASES
(CHAPTER 2.4)

	Symbol
	Flame over circle

Hazard category

1

Signal word

Danger

Hazard statement

H270   May cause or intensify fire; oxidizer

Precautionary statements			
Prevention	**Response**	**Storage**	**Disposal**
P220 **Keep away from clothing and other combustible materials.** P244 **Keep valves and fittings free from oil and grease.**	P370 + P376 **In case of fire: Stop leak if safe to do so.**	P403 **Store in a well-ventilated place.**	

GASES UNDER PRESSURE
(CHAPTER 2.5)

	Symbol
	Gas cylinder

Hazard category

Compressed gas

Liquefied gas

Dissolved gas

Signal word

Warning

Warning

Warning

Hazard statement

H280 Contains gas under pressure; may explode if heated

H280 Contains gas under pressure; may explode if heated

H280 Contains gas under pressure; may explode if heated

Precautionary statements

Prevention	Response	Storage	Disposal
		P410 + P403 **Protect from sunlight. Store in a well-ventilated place.** *– P410 may be omitted for gases filled in transportable gas cylinders in accordance with packing instruction P200 of the UN Recommendations on the Transport of Dangerous Goods, Model Regulations, unless those gases are subject to (slow) decomposition or polymerisation, or the competent authority provides otherwise.*	

GASES UNDER PRESSURE
(CHAPTER 2.5)

		Symbol
		Gas cylinder

Hazard category	**Signal word**	**Hazard statement**
Refrigerated liquefied gas	Warning	H281 Contains refrigerated gas; may cause cryogenic burns or injury

Precautionary statements

Prevention	Response	Storage	Disposal
P282 **Wear cold insulating gloves and either face shield or eye protection.**	P336 + P315 **Thaw frosted parts with lukewarm water. Do not rub affected area. Get immediate medical advice/attention.** Manufacturer/supplier or the competent authority to select medical advice or attention as appropriate.	P403 **Store in a well-ventilated place.**	

FLAMMABLE LIQUIDS
(CHAPTER 2.6)

Hazard category	**Signal word**
1	Danger
2	Danger
3	Warning

Symbol
Flame

Hazard statement

H224	Extremely flammable liquid and vapour
H225	Highly flammable liquid and vapour
H226	Flammable liquid and vapour

Precautionary statements

Prevention	Response	Storage	Disposal
P210 **Keep away from heat, hot surfaces, sparks, open flames and other ignition sources. No smoking.** P233 **Keep container tightly closed.** *– if the liquid is volatile and may generate an explosive atmosphere.* P240 **Ground and bond container and receiving equipment.** *– if the liquid is volatile and may generate an explosive atmosphere.* P241 **Use explosion-proof [electrical/ventilating/lighting/...] equipment.** *– if the liquid is volatile and may generate an explosive atmosphere.* *– text in square brackets may be used to specify specific electrical, ventilating, lighting or other equipment if necessary and as appropriate.* *– precautionary statement may be omitted where local or national legislation introduces more specific provisions..* P242 **Use non-sparking tools.** *– if the liquid is volatile and may generate an explosive atmosphere and if the minimum ignition energy is very low. (This applies to substances and mixtures where the minimum ignition energy is <0.1mJ, e.g. carbon disulphide).* P243 **Take action to prevent static discharges.** *– if the liquid is volatile and may generate an explosive atmosphere.* *– may be omitted where local or national legislation introduces more specific provisions.* P280 **Wear protective gloves/protective clothing/eye protection/face protection** Manufacturer/supplier or the competent authority to specify the appropriate type of equipment.	P303 + P361 + P353 **IF ON SKIN (or hair): Take off immediately all contaminated clothing. Rinse skin with water [or shower].** *– text in square brackets to be included where the manufacturer/supplier or the competent authority considers it appropriate for the specific chemical.* P370 + P378 **In case of fire: Use ... to extinguish.** *– if water increases risk.* *... Manufacturer/supplier or the competent authority to specify appropriate media.*	P403 + P235 **Store in a well-ventilated place. Keep cool.** *– for flammable liquids Category 1 and other flammable liquids that are volatile and may generate an explosive atmosphere.*	P501 **Dispose of contents/container to...** *... in accordance with local/regional/national/international regulations (to be specified).* Manufacturer/supplier or the competent authority to specify whether disposal requirements apply to contents, container or both.

FLAMMABLE LIQUIDS
(CHAPTER 2.6)

Hazard category	Signal word	Hazard statement		Symbol
4	Warning	H227	Combustible liquid	*No symbol*

Precautionary statements

Prevention	Response	Storage	Disposal
P210 **Keep away from heat, hot surfaces, sparks, open flames and other ignition sources. No smoking.** P280 **Wear protective gloves/protective clothing/eye protection/face protection** Manufacturer/supplier or the competent authority to specify the appropriate type of equipment.	P370 + P378 **In case of fire: Use ... to extinguish.** *– if water increases risk.* ... Manufacturer/supplier or the competent authority to specify appropriate media.	P403 **Store in a well-ventilated place.** *– for flammable liquids Category 1 and other flammable liquids that are volatile and may generate an explosive atmosphere.*	P501 **Dispose of contents/container to...** *...in accordance with local/regional/ national/international regulations (to be specified).* Manufacturer/supplier or the competent authority to specify whether disposal requirements apply to contents, container or both.

FLAMMABLE SOLIDS
(CHAPTER 2.7)

Hazard category	Signal word
1	Danger
2	Warning

Hazard statement

H228	Flammable solid
H228	Flammable solid

Precautionary statements

Prevention	Response	Storage	Disposal
P210 **Keep away from heat, hot surfaces, sparks, open flames and other ignition sources. No smoking.** P240 **Ground and bond container and receiving equipment.** *– if the solid is electrostatically sensitive.* P241 **Use explosion-proof [electrical/ventilating/ lighting/...]equipment.** *– if dust clouds can occur.* *– text in square brackets may be used to specify specific electrical, ventilating, lighting or other equipment if necessary and as appropriate.* *– precautionary statement may be omitted where local or national legislation introduces more specific provisions.* P280 **Wear protective gloves/ protective clothing/eye protection/face protection** Manufacturer/supplier or the competent authority to specify the appropriate type of equipment.	P370 + P378 **In case of fire: Use ... to extinguish** *– if water increases risk.* ... Manufacturer/supplier or the competent authority to specify appropriate media.		

SELF-REACTIVE SUBSTANCES AND MIXTURES
(CHAPTER 2.8)

Hazard category	**Signal word**	**Hazard statement**		**Symbol**
Type A	Danger	H240	Heating may cause an explosion	Exploding bomb

Precautionary statements

Prevention	Response	Storage	Disposal
P210 **Keep away from heat, hot surfaces, sparks, open flames and other ignition sources. No smoking.** P234 **Keep only in original packaging.** P235 **Keep cool.** *– may be omitted if P411 is given on the label.* P240 **Ground and bond container and receiving equipment.** *– if electrostatically sensitive and able to generate an explosive atmosphere.* P280 **Wear protective gloves/protective clothing/eye protection/face protection.** Manufacturer/supplier or the competent authority to specify the appropriate type of equipment.	P370 + P372 + P380 + P373 **In case of fire: Explosion risk. Evacuate area. DO NOT fight fire when fire reaches explosives.**	P403 **Store in a well-ventilated place.** *– except for temperature controlled self-reactive substances and mixtures or organic peroxides because condensation and consequent freezing may take place.* P411 **Store at temperatures not exceeding ...°C/...°F.** *– if temperature control is required (according to section 2.8.2.3 or 2.15.2.3 of the GHS) or if otherwise deemed necessary.* ... Manufacturer/supplier or the competent authority to specify temperature using applicable temperature scale. P420 **Store separately.**	P501 **Dispose of contents/container to...** ... in accordance with local/regional/national/international regulations (to be specified). Manufacturer/supplier or the competent authority to specify whether disposal requirements apply to contents, container or both.

SELF-REACTIVE SUBSTANCES AND MIXTURES
(CHAPTER 2.8)

Hazard category
Type B

Signal word
Danger

Hazard statement
H241   Heating may cause a fire or explosion

Symbol
Exploding bomb and flame

Precautionary statements

Prevention	Response	Storage	Disposal
P210 **Keep away from heat, hot surfaces, sparks, open flames and other ignition sources. No smoking.** **P234** **Keep only in original packaging.** **P235** **Keep cool** *– may be omitted if P411 is given on the label.* **P240** **Ground and bond container and receiving equipment.** *– if electrostatically sensitive and able to generate an explosive atmosphere.* **P280** **Wear protective gloves/protective clothing/eye protection/face protection.** Manufacturer/supplier or the competent authority to specify the appropriate type of equipment.	**P370 + P380 + P375 [+ P378]** **In case of fire: Evacuate area. Fight fire remotely due to the risk of explosion. [Use…to extinguish]** *– text in square brackets to be included if water increases risk.* … Manufacturer/supplier or the competent authority to specify appropriate media.	**P403** **Store in a well-ventilated place.** *– except for temperature controlled self-reactive substances and mixtures or organic peroxides because condensation and consequent freezing may take place.* **P411** **Store at temperatures not exceeding …°C/…°F.** *– if temperature control is required (according to section 2.8.2.3 or 2.15.2.3 of the GHS) or if otherwise deemed necessary.* … Manufacturer/supplier or the competent authority to specify temperature using applicable temperature scale. **P420** **Store separately.**	**P501** **Dispose of contents/container to…** …in accordance with local/regional/national/international regulations (to be specified). Manufacturer/supplier or the competent authority to specify whether disposal requirements apply to contents, container or both.

SELF-REACTIVE SUBSTANCES AND MIXTURES
(CHAPTER 2.8)

Hazard category	Signal word	Hazard statement	
Type C	Danger	H242	Heating may cause a fire
Type D	Danger	H242	Heating may cause a fire
Type E	Warning	H242	Heating may cause a fire
Type F	Warning	H242	Heating may cause a fire

Symbol
Flame

Precautionary statements

Prevention	Response	Storage	Disposal
P210 **Keep away from heat, hot surfaces, sparks, open flames and other ignition sources. No smoking.** P234 **Keep only in original packaging.** P235 **Keep cool** *– may be omitted if P411 is given on the label.* P240 **Ground and bond container and receiving equipment.** *– if electrostatically sensitive and able to generate an explosive atmosphere.* P280 **Wear protective gloves/protective clothing/eye protection/face protection.** Manufacturer/supplier or the competent authority to specify the appropriate type of equipment.	P370 + P378 **In case of fire: Use ... to extinguish** *– if water increases risk.* ... Manufacturer/supplier or the competent authority to specify appropriate media.	P403 **Store in a well-ventilated place.** *– except for temperature controlled self-reactive substances and mixtures or organic peroxides because condensation and consequent freezing may take place.* P411 **Store at temperatures not exceeding ...°C/...°F.** *– if temperature control is required (according to section 2.8.2.3 or 2.15.2.3 of the GHS) or if otherwise deemed necessary.* ... Manufacturer/supplier or the competent authority to specify temperature using applicable temperature scale. P420 **Store separately.**	P501 **Dispose of contents/container to...** ...in accordance with local/regional/national/international regulations (to be specified). Manufacturer/supplier or the competent authority to specify whether disposal requirements apply to contents, container or both.

PYROPHORIC LIQUIDS
(CHAPTER 2.9)

Hazard category	Signal word	Hazard statement	Symbol
1	Danger	**H250** Catches fire spontaneously if exposed to air	Flame

Precautionary statements

Prevention	Response	Storage	Disposal
P210 **Keep away from heat, hot surfaces, sparks, open flames and other ignition sources. No smoking.** P222 **Do not allow contact with air.** *– if emphasis of the hazard statement is deemed necessary.* P231 + P232 **Handle and store contents under inert gas/….** **Protect from moisture.** …Manufacturer/supplier or the competent authority to specify appropriate liquid or gas if "inert gas" is not appropriate. P233 **Keep container tightly closed.** P280 **Wear protective gloves/protective clothing/eye protection/face protection.** Manufacturer/supplier or the competent authority to specify the appropriate type of equipment.	P302 + P334 **IF ON SKIN: Immerse in cool water or wrap in wet bandages.** P370 + P378 **In case of fire: Use … to extinguish** *– if water increases risk.* …Manufacturer/supplier or the competent authority to specify appropriate media.		

PYROPHORIC SOLIDS
(CHAPTER 2.10)

Hazard category

1

Signal word

Danger

Hazard statement

H250   Catches fire spontaneously if exposed to air

Symbol
Flame

Precautionary statements

Prevention	Response	Storage	Disposal
P210 **Keep away from heat, hot surfaces, sparks, open flames and other ignition sources. No smoking.** P222 **Do not allow contact with air.** – *if emphasis of the hazard statement is deemed necessary.* P231 + P232 **Handle and store contents under inert gas/…** **Protect from moisture.** …Manufacturer/supplier or the competent authority to specify appropriate liquid or gas if "inert gas" is not appropriate. P233 **Keep container tightly closed.** P280 **Wear protective gloves/protective clothing/eye protection/face protection** Manufacturer/supplier or the competent authority to specify the appropriate type of equipment.	P302 + P335 + P334 **IF ON SKIN: Brush off loose particles from skin. Immerse in cool water or wrap in wet bandages.** P370 + P378 **In case of fire: Use … to extinguish** – *if water increases risk.* …Manufacturer/supplier or the competent authority to specify appropriate media.		

- 323 -

SELF-HEATING SUBSTANCES AND MIXTURES
(CHAPTER 2.11)

Hazard category	Signal word	Hazard statement		
1	Danger	H251	Self-heating; may catch fire	
2	Warning	H252	Self-heating in large quantities; may catch fire	

	Symbol
	Flame

Precautionary statements

Prevention	Response	Storage	Disposal
P235 **Keep cool.** *– may be omitted if P413 is given on the label.* P280 **Wear protective gloves/protective clothing/eye protection/face protection.** Manufacturer/supplier or the competent authority to specify the appropriate type of equipment.		P407 **Maintain air gap between stacks or pallets.** P413 **Store bulk masses greater than ... kg/...lbs at temperatures not exceeding ...°C/...°F.** ... Manufacturer/supplier or the competent authority to specify mass and temperature using applicable scale. P420 **Store separately.**	

SUBSTANCES AND MIXTURES WHICH, IN CONTACT WITH WATER, EMIT FLAMMABLE GASES
(CHAPTER 2.12)

Symbol	
Flame	

Hazard category	Signal word	Hazard statement	
1	Danger	H260	In contact with water releases flammable gases, which may ignite spontaneously
2	Danger	H261	In contact with water releases flammable gas

Precautionary statements

Prevention	Response	Storage	Disposal
P223 **Do not allow contact with water.** – *if emphasis of the hazard statement is deemed necessary.* P231 + P232 **Handle and store contents under inert gas/…** **Protect from moisture.** – *if the substance or mixture reacts readily with moisture in air.* …Manufacturer/supplier or the competent authority to specify appropriate liquid or gas if "inert gas" is not appropriate. P280 **Wear protective gloves/protective clothing/eye protection/face protection.** Manufacturer/supplier or the competent authority to specify the appropriate type of equipment.	P302 + P335 + P334 **IF ON SKIN: Brush off loose particles from skin and immerse in cool water.** P370 + P378 **In case of fire: Use … to extinguish** – *if water increases risk.* … Manufacturer/supplier or the competent authority to specify appropriate media.	P402 + P404 **Store in a dry place. Store in a closed container.**	P501 **Dispose of contents/container to…** …in accordance with local/regional/national/ international regulations (to be specified). Manufacturer/supplier or the competent authority to specify whether disposal requirements apply to contents, container or both.

SUBSTANCES AND MIXTURES WHICH, IN CONTACT WITH WATER, EMIT FLAMMABLE GASES
(CHAPTER 2.12)

Hazard category	**Signal word**	**Hazard statement**	**Symbol**
3	Warning	H261 In contact with water releases flammable gas	Flame

Precautionary statements

Prevention	Response	Storage	Disposal
P231 + P232 **Handle and store contents under inert gas/...** **Protect from moisture.** *– if the substance or mixture reacts readily with moisture in air.* ...Manufacturer/supplier or the competent authority to specify appropriate liquid or gas if "inert gas" is not appropriate. P280 **Wear protective gloves/protective clothing/eye protection/face protection.** Manufacturer/supplier or the competent authority to specify the appropriate type of equipment.	P370 + P378 **In case of fire: Use ... to extinguish.** *– if water increases risk.* ...Manufacturer/supplier or the competent authority to specify appropriate media.	P402 + P404 **Store in a dry place. Store in a closed container.**	P501 **Dispose of contents/container to...** ... in accordance with local/regional/national/international regulations (to be specified). Manufacturer/supplier or the competent authority to specify whether disposal requirements apply to contents, container or both.

OXIDIZING LIQUIDS
(CHAPTER 2.13)

Hazard category	Signal word	Hazard statement	Symbol
1	Danger	H271 May cause fire or explosion; strong oxidizer	Flame over circle

Precautionary statements

Prevention	Response	Storage	Disposal
P210 **Keep away from heat, hot surfaces, sparks, open flames and other ignition sources. No smoking.** **P220** **Keep away from clothing and other combustible materials.** **P280** **Wear protective gloves/protective clothing/eye protection/face protection.** Manufacturer/supplier or the competent authority to specify the appropriate type of equipment. **P283** **Wear fire resistant or flame retardant clothing.**	**P306 + P360** **IF ON CLOTHING: Rinse immediately contaminated clothing and skin with plenty of water before removing clothes.** **P371 + P380 + P375** **In case of major fire and large quantities: Evacuate area. Fight fire remotely due to the risk of explosion.** **P370 + P378** **In case of fire: Use ... to extinguish.** – *if water increases risk...* Manufacturer/supplier or the competent authority to specify appropriate media.	**P420** **Store separately.**	**P501** **Dispose of contents/container to...** ...in accordance with local/regional/national/international regulations (to be specified). Manufacturer/supplier or the competent authority to specify whether disposal requirements apply to contents, container or both.

OXIDIZING LIQUIDS
(CHAPTER 2.13)

Symbol
Flame over circle

Hazard category	Signal word
2	Danger
3	Warning

Hazard statement

H272	May intensify fire; oxidizer
H272	May intensify fire; oxidizer

Precautionary statements

Prevention	Response	Storage	Disposal
P210 **Keep away from heat, hot surfaces, sparks, open flames and other ignition sources. No smoking.** P220 **Keep away from clothing and other combustible materials.** P280 **Wear protective gloves/protective clothing/eye protection/face protection.** Manufacturer/supplier or the competent authority to specify the appropriate type of equipment.	P370 + P378 **In case of fire: Use ... to extinguish.** – *if water increases risk.* ... Manufacturer/supplier or the competent authority to specify appropriate media.		P501 **Dispose of contents/container to...** ...in accordance with local/regional/national/international regulations (to be specified). Manufacturer/supplier or the competent authority to specify whether disposal requirements apply to contents, container or both.

OXIDIZING SOLIDS
(CHAPTER 2.14)

		Symbol
		Flame over circle

Hazard category

1

Signal word

Danger

Hazard statement

H271   May cause fire or explosion; strong oxidizer

Precautionary statements

Prevention	Response	Storage	Disposal
P210 **Keep away from heat, hot surfaces, sparks, open flames and other ignition sources. No smoking.** P220 **Keep away from clothing and other combustible materials.** P280 **Wear protective gloves/protective clothing/eye protection/face protection.** Manufacturer/supplier or the competent authority to specify the appropriate type of equipment. P283 **Wear fire resistant or flame retardant clothing.**	P306 + P360 **IF ON CLOTHING: Rinse immediately contaminated clothing and skin with plenty of water before removing clothes.** P371 + P380 + P375 **In case of major fire and large quantities: Evacuate area. Fight fire remotely due to the risk of explosion.** P370 + P378 **In case of fire: Use ... to extinguish.** – *if water increases risk.* ... Manufacturer/supplier or the competent authority to specify appropriate media.	P420 **Store separately.**	P501 **Dispose of contents/container to...** ...in accordance with local/regional/national/international regulations (to be specified). Manufacturer/supplier or the competent authority to specify whether disposal requirements apply to contents, container or both.

OXIDIZING SOLIDS
(CHAPTER 2.14)

	Symbol
	Flame over circle

Hazard category

2

3

Signal word

Danger

Warning

Hazard statement

H272   May intensify fire; oxidizer

H272   May intensify fire; oxidizer

Precautionary statements

Prevention	Response	Storage	Disposal
P210 **Keep away from heat, hot surfaces, sparks, open flames and other ignition sources. No smoking.** P220 **Keep away from clothing and other combustible materials.** P280 **Wear protective gloves/protective clothing/eye protection/face protection.** Manufacturer/supplier or the competent authority to specify the appropriate type of equipment.	P370 + P378 **In case of fire: Use ... to extinguish.** – *if water increases risk.* ... Manufacturer/supplier or the competent authority to specify appropriate media.		P501 **Dispose of contents/container to...** ... in accordance with local/regional/national/international regulations (to be specified). Manufacturer/supplier or the competent authority to specify whether disposal requirements apply to contents, container or both.

**ORGANIC PEROXIDES
(CHAPTER 2.15)**

Hazard category	Signal word		Symbol
Type A	Danger		Exploding bomb

Hazard statement

H240   Heating may cause an explosion

Precautionary statements

Prevention	Response	Storage	Disposal
P210 **Keep away from heat, hot surfaces, sparks, open flames and other ignition sources. No smoking.** P234 **Keep only in original container.** P235 **Keep cool.** *– may be omitted if P411 is given on the label.* P240 **Ground and bond container and receiving equipment.** *– if electrostatically sensitive and able to generate an explosive atmosphere.* P280 **Wear protective gloves/ protective clothing/eye protection/face protection.** Manufacturer/supplier or the competent authority to specify the appropriate type of equipment.	P370 + P372 + P380 + P373 **In case of fire: Explosion risk. Evacuate area. DO NOT fight fire when fire reaches explosives.**	P403 **Store in a well-ventilated place.** *– except for temperature controlled self-reactive substances and mixtures or organic peroxides because condensation and consequent freezing may take place.* P410 **Protect from sunlight.** P411 **Store at temperatures not exceeding …°C/…°F.** *– if temperature control is required (according to section 2.8.2.3 or 2.15.2.3 of the GHS) or if otherwise deemed necessary.* … Manufacturer/supplier or the competent authority to specify temperature using applicable temperature scale P420 **Store separately.**	P501 **Dispose of contents/container to…** … in accordance with local/regional/national/international regulations (to be specified). Manufacturer/supplier or the competent authority to specify whether disposal requirements apply to contents, container or both.

ORGANIC PEROXIDES
(CHAPTER 2.15)

		Symbol
		Exploding bomb and flame

Hazard category

Type B

Signal word

Danger

Hazard statement

H241   Heating may cause a fire or explosion

Precautionary statements

Prevention	Response	Storage	Disposal
P210 **Keep away from heat, hot surfaces, sparks, open flames and other ignition sources. No smoking.** P234 **Keep only in original packaging.** P235 **Keep cool.** *– may be omitted if P411 is given on the label.* P240 **Ground and bond container and receiving equipment.** *– if electrostatically sensitive and able to generate an explosive atmosphere.* P280 **Wear protective gloves/ protective clothing/eye protection/face protection.** Manufacturer/supplier or the competent authority to specify the appropriate type of equipment.	P370 + P380 + P375 [+ P378] **In case of fire: Evacuate area. Fight fire remotely due to the risk of explosion.** **[Use...to extinguish]** *– text in square brackets to be used if water increases risk.* ...Manufacturer/supplier or the competent authority to specify appropriate media.	P403 **Store in a well-ventilated place.** *– except for temperature controlled self-reactive substances and mixtures or organic peroxides because condensation and consequent freezing may take place.* P410 **Protect from sunlight.** P411 **Store at temperatures not exceeding ...°C/...°F.** *– if temperature control is required (according to section 2.8.2.3 or 2.15.2.3 of the GHS) or if otherwise deemed necessary.* ...Manufacturer/supplier or the competent authority to specify temperature using applicable temperature scale. P420 **Store separately.**	P501 **Dispose of contents/container to...** ... in accordance with local/regional/national/international regulations (to be specified). Manufacturer/supplier or the competent authority to specify whether disposal requirements apply to contents, container or both.

ORGANIC PEROXIDES
(CHAPTER 2.15)

		Symbol
		Flame

Hazard category	Signal word		Hazard statement	
Type C	Danger		H242	Heating may cause a fire
Type D	Danger		H242	Heating may cause a fire
Type E	Warning		H242	Heating may cause a fire
Type F	Warning		H242	Heating may cause a fire

Precautionary statements

Prevention	Response	Storage	Disposal
P210 **Keep away from heat, hot surfaces, sparks, open flames and other ignition sources. No smoking.** P234 **Keep only in original packaging.** P235 **Keep cool.** – *may be omitted if P411 is given on the label.* P240 **Ground and bond container and receiving equipment.** – *if electrostatically sensitive and able to generate an explosive atmosphere.* P280 **Wear protective gloves/ protective clothing/eye protection/face protection.** Manufacturer/supplier or the competent authority to specify the appropriate type of equipment.	P370 + P378 **In case of fire: Use ... to extinguish.** – *if water increases risk.* ... Manufacturer/supplier or the competent authority to specify appropriate media.	P403 **Store in a well-ventilated place.** – *except for temperature controlled self-reactive substances and mixtures or organic peroxides because condensation and consequent freezing may take place.* P410 **Protect from sunlight.** P411 **Store at temperatures not exceeding ... °C/... °F.** – *if temperature control is required (according to section 2.8.2.3 or 2.15.2.3 of the GHS) or if otherwise deemed necessary...* Manufacturer/supplier or the competent authority to specify temperature using applicable temperature scale. P420 **Store separately.**	P501 **Dispose of contents/container to...** ... in accordance with local/regional/national/international regulations (to be specified). Manufacturer/supplier or the competent authority to specify whether disposal requirements apply to contents, container or both.

**CORROSIVE TO METALS
(CHAPTER 2.16)**

Hazard category	**Signal word**
1	Warning

Hazard statement

H290   May be corrosive to metals

Symbol	
Corrosion	

Precautionary statements

Prevention	Response	Storage	Disposal
P234 **Keep only in original packaging.**	P390 **Absorb spillage to prevent material-damage.**	P406 **Store in a corrosion resistant/... container with a resistant inner liner.** *– may be omitted if P234 is given on the label* ... Manufacturer/supplier or the competent authority to specify other compatible materials.	

ACUTE TOXICITY – ORAL
(CHAPTER 3.1)

Hazard category	Signal word	Hazard statement		Symbol
1	Danger	H300	Fatal if swallowed	Skull and crossbones
2	Danger	H300	Fatal if swallowed	

Precautionary statements

Prevention	Response	Storage	Disposal
P264 **Wash …thoroughly after handling.** … Manufacturer/supplier or the competent authority to specify parts of the body to be washed after handling. P270 **Do not eat, drink or smoke when using this product.**	P301 + P310 **IF SWALLOWED: Immediately call a POISON CENTER/doctor/…** …Manufacturer/supplier or the competent authority to specify the appropriate source of emergency medical advice. P321 **Specific treatment (see .. on this label)** – *if immediate administration of antidote is required.* … Reference to supplemental first aid instruction. P330 **Rinse mouth.**	P405 **Store locked up.**	P501 **Dispose of contents/container to…** .. in accordance with local/regional/national/international regulations (to be specified). Manufacturer/supplier or the competent authority to specify whether disposal requirements apply to contents, container or both.

ACUTE TOXICITY – ORAL
(CHAPTER 3.1)

Hazard category	Signal word	Hazard statement	Symbol
3	Danger	H301 Toxic if swallowed	Skull and crossbones

Precautionary statements

Prevention	Response	Storage	Disposal
P264 **Wash ... thoroughly after handling.** ...Manufacturer/supplier or the competent authority to specify parts of the body to be washed after handling. P270 **Do not eat, drink or smoke when using this product.**	P301 + P310 **IF SWALLOWED: Immediately call a POISON CENTER/doctor/...** ...Manufacturer/supplier or the competent authority to specify the appropriate source of emergency medical advice. P321 **Specific treatment (see ... on this label)** – *if immediate administration of antidote is required.* ... Reference to supplemental first aid instruction. P330 **Rinse mouth.**	P405 **Store locked up.**	P501 **Dispose of contents/container to...** ...in accordance with local/regional/national/international regulations (to be specified). Manufacturer/supplier or the competent authority to specify whether disposal requirements apply to contents, container or both.

ACUTE TOXICITY – ORAL
(CHAPTER 3.1)

		Symbol
		Exclamation mark

Hazard category | **Signal word** | **Hazard statement**

4 | Warning | H302   Harmful if swallowed

Precautionary statements

Prevention	Response	Storage	Disposal
P264 **Wash ... thoroughly after handling.** ... Manufacturer/supplier or the competent authority to specify parts of the body to be washed after handling. P270 **Do not eat, drink or smoke when using this product.**	P301 + P312 **IF SWALLOWED: Call a POISON CENTER/ doctor/...if you feel unwell.** ...Manufacturer/supplier or the competent authority to specify the appropriate source of emergency medical advice. P330 **Rinse mouth.**		P501 **Dispose of contents/container to...** ... in accordance with local/regional/national/international regulations (to be specified). Manufacturer/supplier or the competent authority to specify whether disposal requirements apply to contents, container or both.

ACUTE TOXICITY – ORAL
(CHAPTER 3.1)

Symbol	
No symbol	

Hazard category

5

Signal word

Warning

Hazard statement

H303   May be harmful if swallowed

Precautionary statements

Prevention	Response	Storage	Disposal
	P312 **Call a POISON CENTER/doctor/…if you feel unwell.** …Manufacturer/supplier or the competent authority to specify the appropriate source of emergency medical advice.		

ACUTE TOXICITY – DERMAL
(CHAPTER 3.1)

	Symbol
	Skull and crossbones

Hazard category	Signal word	Hazard statement	
1	Danger	H310	Fatal in contact with skin
2	Danger	H310	Fatal in contact with skin

Precautionary statements

Prevention	Response	Storage	Disposal
P262 **Do not get in eyes, on skin, or on clothing.** P264 **Wash ... thoroughly after handling.** ...Manufacturer/supplier or the competent authority to specify parts of the body to be washed after handling. P270 **Do not eat, drink or smoke when using this product.** P280 **Wear protective gloves/protective clothing.** Manufacturer/supplier or the competent authority may further specify type of equipment where appropriate.	P302 + P352 **IF ON SKIN: Wash with plenty of water/...** ...Manufacturer/supplier or the competent authority may specify a cleansing agent if appropriate, or may recommend an alternative agent in exceptional cases if water is clearly inappropriate. P310 **Immediately call a POISON CENTER/doctor/...** ...Manufacturer/supplier or the competent authority to specify the appropriate source of emergency medical advice. P321 **Specific treatment (see ... on this label)** *– if immediate measures such as specific cleansing agent is advised.* ... Reference to supplemental first aid instruction. P361+ P364 **Take off immediately all contaminated clothing and wash it before reuse.**	P405 **Store locked up.**	P501 **Dispose of contents/container to...** ... in accordance with local/regional/national/international regulations (to be specified). Manufacturer/supplier or the competent authority to specify whether disposal requirements apply to contents, container or both.

ACUTE TOXICITY – DERMAL
(CHAPTER 3.1)

			Symbol
			Skull and crossbones

Hazard category	**Signal word**	**Hazard statement**
3	Danger	H311 Toxic in contact with skin

Precautionary statements

Prevention	Response	Storage	Disposal
P280 **Wear protective gloves/protective clothing.** Manufacturer/supplier or the competent authority may further specify type of equipment where appropriate.	P302 + P352 **IF ON SKIN: Wash with plenty of water/...** ...Manufacturer/supplier or the competent authority may specify a cleansing agent if appropriate, or may recommend an alternative agent in exceptional cases if water is clearly inappropriate. P312 **Call a POISON CENTER/doctor/...if you feel unwell.** ...Manufacturer/supplier or the competent authority to specify the appropriate source of emergency medical advice. P321 **Specific treatment (see ... on this label)** *– if immediate measures such as specific cleansing agent is advised.* ... Reference to supplemental first aid instruction. P361 + P364 **Take off immediately all contaminated clothing and wash it before reuse.**	P405 **Store locked up.**	P501 **Dispose of contents/container to...** ... in accordance with local/regional/national/international regulations (to be specified). Manufacturer/supplier or the competent authority to specify whether disposal requirements apply to contents, container or both.

ACUTE TOXICITY – DERMAL
(CHAPTER 3.1)

Symbol	Exclamation mark

Hazard category	Signal word	Hazard statement
4	Warning	H312 Harmful in contact with skin

Precautionary statements

Prevention	Response	Storage	Disposal
P280 **Wear protective gloves/protective clothing** Manufacturer/supplier or the competent authority may further specify type of equipment where appropriate.	P302 + P352 **IF ON SKIN: Wash with plenty of water/...** ...Manufacturer/supplier or the competent authority may specify a cleansing agent if appropriate, or may recommend an alternative agent in exceptional cases if water is clearly inappropriate. P312 **Call a POISON CENTER/doctor/...if you feel unwell.** ...Manufacturer/supplier or the competent authority to specify the appropriate source of emergency medical advice. P321 **Specific treatment (see ... on this label)** – *if immediate measures such as specific cleansing agent is advised.* ... Reference to supplemental first aid instruction. P362 + P364 **Take off contaminated clothing and wash it before reuse.**		P501 **Dispose of contents/container to...** ... in accordance with local/regional/national/international regulations (to be specified). Manufacturer/supplier or the competent authority to specify whether disposal requirements apply to contents, container or both.

ACUTE TOXICITY – DERMAL
(CHAPTER 3.1)

Hazard category	Signal word	Hazard statement		Symbol
5	Warning	H313 May be harmful in contact with skin		*No symbol*

Precautionary statements

Prevention	Response	Storage	Disposal
	P312 **Call a POISON CENTER/doctor/…if you feel unwell.** …Manufacturer/supplier or the competent authority to specify the appropriate source of emergency medical advice.		

**ACUTE TOXICITY – INHALATION
(CHAPTER 3.1)**

Hazard category	Signal word	Hazard statement		Symbol
				Skull and crossbones
1	Danger	H330	Fatal if inhaled	
2	Danger	H330	Fatal if inhaled	

Precautionary statements

Prevention	Response	Storage	Disposal
P260 **Do not breathe dust/fume/gas/mist/ vapours/spray.** Manufacturer/supplier or the competent authority to specify applicable conditions.	P304 + P340 **IF INHALED: Remove person to fresh air and keep comfortable for breathing.**	P403 + P233 **Store in a well-ventilated place. Keep container tightly closed.** *– if the chemical is volatile and may generate a hazardous atmosphere.*	P501 **Dispose of contents/container to...** *... in accordance with local/regional/national/international regulations (to be specified).* Manufacturer/supplier or the competent
P271 **Use only outdoors or in a well-ventilated area.**	P310 **Immediately call a POISON CENTER/doctor/...** *...Manufacturer/supplier or the competent authority to specify the appropriate source of emergency medical advice.*	P405 **Store locked up.**	authority to specify whether disposal requirements apply to contents, container or both.
P284 **[In case of inadequate ventilation] wear respiratory protection.** *– text in square brackets may be used if additional information is provided with the chemical at the point of use that explains what type of ventilation would be adequate for safe use.* Manufacturer/supplier or the competent authority to specify equipment.	P320 **Specific treatment is urgent (see ... on this label)** *– if immediate administration of antidote is required.* *... Reference to supplemental first aid instruction.*		

ACUTE TOXICITY – INHALATION

(CHAPTER 3.1)

Hazard category	Signal word	Hazard statement	Symbol
3	Danger	H331 Toxic if inhaled	Skull and crossbones

Precautionary statements

Prevention	Response	Storage	Disposal
P261 **Avoid breathing dust/fume/gas/mist/ vapours/spray.** – *may be omitted if P260 is given on the label* Manufacturer/supplier or the competent authority to specify applicable conditions. P271 **Use only outdoors or in a well-ventilated area.**	P304 + P340 **IF INHALED: Remove person to fresh air and keep comfortable for breathing.** P311 **Call a POISON CENTER/doctor...** ...Manufacturer/supplier or the competent authority to specify the appropriate source of emergency medical advice. P321 **Specific treatment (see ... on this label)** – *if immediate specific measures are required.* ... Reference to supplemental first aid instruction.	P403 + P233 **Store in a well-ventilated place. Keep container tightly closed.** – *if the chemical is volatile and may generate a hazardous atmosphere.* P405 **Store locked up.**	P501 **Dispose of content/container to...** ... in accordance with local/regional/national/international regulations (to be specified). Manufacturer/supplier or the competent authority to specify whether disposal requirements apply to contents, container or both.

ACUTE TOXICITY – INHALATION
(CHAPTER 3.1)

Hazard category	Signal word	Hazard statement		Symbol
4	Warning	H332 Harmful if inhaled		Exclamation mark

Precautionary statements

Prevention	Response	Storage	Disposal
P261 **Avoid breathing dust/fume/gas/mist/vapours/spray.** *– may be omitted if P260 is given on the label* Manufacturer/supplier or the competent authority to specify applicable conditions. P271 **Use only outdoors or in a well-ventilated area.**	P304 + P340 **IF INHALED: Remove person to fresh air and keep comfortable for breathing.** P312 **Call a POISON CENTER/doctor/…if you feel unwell.** …Manufacturer/supplier or the competent authority to specify the appropriate source of emergency medical advice.		

ACUTE TOXICITY – INHALATION

(CHAPTER 3.1)

Hazard category	Signal word	Hazard statement	Symbol
5	Warning	H333 May be harmful if inhaled	*No symbol*

Precautionary statements			
Prevention	**Response**	**Storage**	**Disposal**
	P304 + P312 **IF INHALED:** **Call a POISON CENTER/doctor/…if you feel unwell.** …Manufacturer/supplier or the competent authority to specify the appropriate source of emergency medical advice.		

SKIN CORROSION/IRRITATION
(CHAPTER 3.2)

Hazard category	**Signal word**	**Hazard statement**	**Symbol**
1A to 1C	Danger	H314 Causes severe skin burns and eye damage	Corrosion 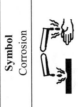

Precautionary statements

Prevention	Response	Storage	Disposal
P260 **Do not breathe dusts or mists.** *– if inhalable particles of dusts or mists may occur during use.* P264 **Wash …thoroughly after handling.** …Manufacturer/supplier or the competent authority to specify parts of the body to be washed after handling. P280 **Wear protective gloves/protective clothing/eye protection/face protection.** Manufacturer/supplier or the competent authority may further specify type of equipment where appropriate.	P301 + P330 + P331 **IF SWALLOWED: Rinse mouth. Do NOT induce vomiting.** P303 + P361 + P353 **IF ON SKIN (or hair): Take off immediately all contaminated clothing. Rinse skin with water [or shower].** *– text in square brackets to be included where the manufacturer/supplier or the competent authority considers it appropriate for the specific chemical.* P363 **Wash contaminated clothing before reuse.** P304 + P340 **IF INHALED: Remove person to fresh air and keep comfortable for breathing.** P310 **Immediately call a POISON CENTER/doctor/…** …Manufacturer/supplier or the competent authority to specify the appropriate source of emergency medical advice. P321 **Specific treatment (see … on this label)** … Reference to supplemental first aid instruction. Manufacturer/supplier or the competent authority may specify a cleansing agent if appropriate. P305 + P351 + P338 **IF IN EYES: Rinse cautiously with water for several minutes. Remove contact lenses, if present and easy to do. Continue rinsing.**	P405 **Store locked up.**	P501 **Dispose of contents/container to…** … in accordance with local/regional/national/international regulations (to be specified). Manufacturer/supplier or the competent authority to specify whether disposal requirements apply to contents, container or both.

SKIN CORROSION/IRRITATION
(CHAPTER 3.2)

Hazard category	Signal word	Hazard statement	Symbol
2	Warning	H315 Causes skin irritation	Exclamation mark

Precautionary statements

Prevention	Response	Storage	Disposal
P264 **Wash ... thoroughly after handling.** ... Manufacturer/supplier or the competent authority to specify parts of the body to be washed after handling. **P280** **Wear protective gloves.** Manufacturer/supplier or the competent authority may further specify type of equipment where appropriate.	**P302 + P352** **IF ON SKIN: Wash with plenty water/...** ...Manufacturer/supplier or the competent authority may specify a cleansing agent if appropriate, or may recommend an alternative agent in exceptional cases if water is clearly inappropriate. **P321** **Specific treatment (see ... on this label)** ... Reference to supplemental first aid instruction. Manufacturer/supplier or the competent authority may specify a cleansing agent if appropriate. **P332 + P313** **If skin irritation occurs: Get medical advice/attention.** *– may be omitted when P333+P313 appears on the label* Manufacturer/supplier or the competent authority to select medical advice or attention as appropriate. **P362 + P364** **Take off contaminated clothing and wash it before reuse.**		

SKIN CORROSION/IRRITATION
(CHAPTER 3.2)

Symbol	
No symbol	

Hazard category

3

Signal word

Warning

Hazard statement

H316   Causes mild skin irritation

Precautionary statements

Prevention	Response	Storage	Disposal
	P332 + P313 **If skin irritation occurs: Get medical advice/attention.** *– may be omitted when P333+P313 appears on the label.* Manufacturer/supplier or the competent authority to select medical advice or attention as appropriate.		

EYE DAMAGE/IRRITATION
(CHAPTER 3.3)

Hazard category	Signal word	Hazard statement		Symbol
				Corrosion
1	Danger	H318 Causes serious eye damage		

Precautionary statements

Prevention	Response	Storage	Disposal
P280 **Wear eye protection/face protection.** Manufacturer/supplier or the competent authority may further specify type of equipment where appropriate.	P305 + P351 + P338 **IF IN EYES: Rinse cautiously with water for several minutes. Remove contact lenses, if present and easy to do. Continue rinsing.** P310 **Immediately call a POISON CENTER/doctor/…** …Manufacturer/supplier or the competent authority to specify the appropriate source of emergency medical advice.		

EYE DAMAGE/IRRITATION
(CHAPTER 3.3)

		Symbol
		Exclamation mark

Hazard category   **Signal word**   **Hazard statement**

2A   Warning   H319   Causes serious eye irritation

Precautionary statements

Prevention	Response	Storage	Disposal
P264 **Wash ... thoroughly after handling.** ...Manufacturer/supplier or the competent authority to specify parts of the body to be washed after handling.	P305 + P351 + P338 **IF IN EYES: Rinse cautiously with water for several minutes. Remove contact lenses, if present and easy to do. Continue rinsing.**		
P280 **Wear eye protection/face protection.** Manufacturer/supplier or the competent authority may further specify type of equipment where appropriate.	P337 + P313 **If eye irritation persists: Get medical advice/attention.** Manufacturer/supplier or the competent authority to select medical advice or attention as appropriate.		

EYE DAMAGE/IRRITATION
(CHAPTER 3.3)

Hazard category	**Signal word**	**Hazard statement**		**Symbol**
2B	Warning	H320 Causes eye irritation		*No symbol*

Precautionary statements

Prevention	Response	Storage	Disposal
P264 **Wash … thoroughly after handling.** …Manufacturer/supplier or the competent authority to specify parts of the body to be washed after handling.	P305 + P351 + P338 **IF IN EYES: Rinse cautiously with water for several minutes. Remove contact lenses, if present and easy to do. Continue rinsing.** P337 + P313 **If eye irritation persists: Get medical advice/attention.** Manufacturer/supplier or the competent authority to select medical advice or attention as appropriate.		

SENSITIZATION – RESPIRATORY
(CHAPTER 3.4)

Symbol
Symbol Health hazard

Hazard category

1, 1A, 1B

Signal word

Danger

Hazard statement

H334   May cause allergy or asthma symptoms or breathing difficulties if inhaled

Precautionary statements

Prevention	Response	Storage	Disposal
P261 **Avoid breathing dust/fume/gas/mist/vapours/spray.** – *may be omitted if P260 is given on the label* Manufacturer/supplier or the competent authority to specify applicable conditions. P284 **[In case of inadequate ventilation] wear respiratory protection.** – *text in square brackets may be used if additional information is provided with the chemical at the point of use that explains what type of ventilation would be adequate for safe use.* Manufacturer/supplier or the competent authority to specify equipment.	P304 + P340 **IF INHALED: remove person to fresh air and keep comfortable for breathing.** P342 + P311 **If experiencing respiratory symptoms: Call a POISON CENTER/doctor/...** ...Manufacturer/supplier or the competent authority to specify the appropriate source of emergency medical advice.		P501 **Dispose of contents/container to...** ... in accordance with local/regional/national/international regulations (to be specified). Manufacturer/supplier or the competent authority to specify whether disposal requirements apply to contents, container or both.

SENSITIZATION – SKIN
(CHAPTER 3.4)

Hazard category	**Signal word**	**Hazard statement**	**Symbol**

Hazard category

1, 1A, 1B

Signal word

Warning

Hazard statement

H317   May cause an allergic skin reaction

Symbol

Exclamation mark

Precautionary statements

Prevention	Response	Storage	Disposal
P261 **Avoid breathing dust/fume/gas/mist/ vapours/spray.** *– may be omitted if P260 is given on the label* Manufacturer/supplier or the competent authority to specify applicable conditions. P272 **Contaminated work clothing should not be allowed out of the workplace.** P280 **Wear protective gloves.** Manufacturer/supplier or the competent authority may further specify type of equipment where appropriate.	P302 + P352 **IF ON SKIN: Wash with plenty of water/...** ...Manufacturer/supplier or the competent authority may specify a cleansing agent if appropriate, or may recommend an alternative agent in exceptional cases if water is clearly inappropriate. P333 + P313 **If skin irritation or rash occurs: Get medical advice/attention.** Manufacturer/supplier or the competent authority to select medical advice or attention as appropriate. P321 **Specific treatment (see ... on this label)** ... Reference to supplemental first aid instruction. Manufacturer/supplier or the competent authority may specify a cleansing agent if appropriate. P362 + P364 **Take off contaminated clothing and wash it before reuse.**		P501 **Dispose of contents/container to...** ... in accordance with local/regional/national/international regulations (to be specified). Manufacturer/supplier or the competent authority to specify whether disposal requirements apply to contents, container or both.

GERM CELL MUTAGENICITY
(CHAPTER 3.5)

		Symbol
		Health hazard

Hazard category	**Signal word**	**Hazard statement**
1	Danger	H340 May cause genetic defects <...>
2	Warning	H341 Suspected of causing genetic defects <...>
		<...> *(state route of exposure if it is conclusively proven that no other routes of exposure cause the hazard)*

Precautionary statements

Prevention	Response	Storage	Disposal
P201 **Obtain special instructions before use.** P202 **Do not handle until all safety precautions have been read and understood.** P280 **Wear protective gloves/protective clothing/eye protection/face protection.** Manufacturer/supplier or the competent authority to specify the appropriate type of equipment.	P308 + P313 **IF exposed or concerned: Get medical advice/attention.** Manufacturer/supplier or the competent authority to select medical advice or attention as appropriate.	P405 **Store locked up.**	P501 **Dispose of contents/container to...** ... in accordance with local/regional/national/international regulations (to be specified). Manufacturer/supplier or the competent authority to specify whether disposal requirements apply to contents, container or both.

CARCINOGENICITY
(CHAPTER 3.6)

Hazard category	**Signal word**	**Hazard statement**
1	Danger	H350 May cause cancer <...>
2	Warning	H351 Suspected of causing cancer <...>
		<...> *(state route of exposure if it is conclusively proven that no other routes of exposure cause the hazard).*

Precautionary statements

Prevention	Response	Storage	Disposal
P201 **Obtain special instructions before use.** P202 **Do not handle until all safety precautions have been read and understood.** P280 **Wear protective gloves/protective clothing/eye protection/face protection.** Manufacturer/supplier or the competent authority to specify the appropriate type of equipment.	P308 + P313 **IF exposed or concerned: Get medical advice/attention.** Manufacturer/supplier or the competent authority to select medical advice or attention as appropriate.	P405 **Store locked up.**	P501 **Dispose of contents/container to...** ... in accordance with local/regional/national/international regulations (to be specified). Manufacturer/supplier or the competent authority to specify whether disposal requirements apply to contents, container or both.

REPRODUCTIVE TOXICITY
(CHAPTER 3.7)

			Symbol
			Health hazard

Hazard category | **Signal word** | **Hazard statement**
1 | Danger | H360 | May damage fertility or the unborn child <...> <<...>>
2 | Warning | H361 | Suspected of damaging fertility or the unborn child <...> <<...>>
| | <...> | (state specific effect if known)
| | <<...>> | (state route of exposure if it is conclusively proven that no other routes of exposure cause the hazard)

Precautionary statements

Prevention	Response	Storage	Disposal
P201 **Obtain special instructions before use.** P202 **Do not handle until all safety precautions have been read and understood.** P280 **Wear protective gloves/protective clothing/eye protection/face protection.** Manufacturer/supplier or the competent authority to specify the appropriate type of equipment.	P308 + P313 **IF exposed or concerned: Get medical advice/attention.** Manufacturer/supplier or the competent authority to select medical advice or attention as appropriate.	P405 **Store locked up.**	P501 **Dispose of contents/container to...** ... in accordance with local/regional/national/international regulations (to be specified). Manufacturer/supplier or the competent authority to specify whether disposal requirements apply to contents, container or both.

REPRODUCTIVE TOXICITY
(CHAPTER 3.7)
(effects on or via lactation)

Hazard category	**Signal word**	**Hazard statement**	**Symbol**
(additional)	*No signal word*	H362 May cause harm to breast-fed children	*No symbol*

Precautionary statements

Prevention	Response	Storage	Disposal
P201 **Obtain special instructions before use.** P260 **Do not breathe dusts or mists.** *– if inhalable particles of dusts or mists may occur during use.* P263 **Avoid contact during pregnancy and while nursing.** P264 **Wash … thoroughly after handling.** *…Manufacturer/supplier or the competent authority to specify parts of the body to be washed after handling.* P270 **Do not eat, drink or smoke when using this product.**	P308 + P313 **IF exposed or concerned: Get medical advice/attention.** Manufacturer/supplier or the competent authority to select medical advice or attention as appropriate.		

- 358 -

SPECIFIC TARGET ORGAN TOXICITY (SINGLE EXPOSURE)
(CHAPTER 3.8)

		Symbol
		Health hazard

Hazard category	**Signal word**	**Hazard statement**
1	Danger	H370 Causes damage to organs <...> <<...>>
		<...> *(or state all organs affected if known)*
		<<...>> *(state route of exposure if it is conclusively proven that no other routes of exposure cause the hazard)*

Precautionary statements

Prevention	**Response**	**Storage**	**Disposal**
P260 **Do not breathe dust/fume/gas/mist/ vapours/spray.** Manufacturer/supplier or the competent authority to specify applicable conditions. P264 **Wash ...thoroughly after handling.** ... Manufacturer/supplier or the competent authority to specify parts of the body to be washed after handling. P270 **Do not eat, drink or smoke when using this product.**	P308 + P311 **IF exposed or concerned: Call a POISON CENTER/doctor/...** ...Manufacturer/supplier or the competent authority to specify the appropriate source of emergency medical advice. P321 **Specific treatment (see ... on this label)** *– if immediate measures are required.* ... Reference to supplemental first aid instruction.	P405 **Store locked up.**	P501 **Dispose of contents/container to...** ... in accordance with local/regional/national/international regulations (to be specified). Manufacturer/supplier or the competent authority to specify whether disposal requirements apply to contents, container or both.

SPECIFIC TARGET ORGAN TOXICITY (SINGLE EXPOSURE)
(CHAPTER 3.8)

		Symbol
		Health hazard

Hazard category
2

Signal word
Warning

Hazard statement

H371　May cause damage to organs <...> <<...>>

<...>　*(or state all organs affected, if known)*

<<...>>　*(state route of exposure if it is conclusively proven that no other routes of exposure cause the hazard)*

Precautionary statements

Prevention	Response	Storage	Disposal
P260 **Do not breathe dust/fume/gas/mist/ vapours/spray.** Manufacturer/supplier or the competent authority to specify applicable conditions.	P308 + P311 **IF exposed or concerned: Call a POISON CENTER/doctor/...** ...Manufacturer/supplier or the competent authority to specify the appropriate source of emergency medical advice.	P405 **Store locked up.**	P501 **Dispose of contents/container to...** ...in accordance with local/regional/national/international regulations (to be specified). Manufacturer/supplier or the competent authority to specify whether disposal requirements apply to contents, container or both.
P264 **Wash ... thoroughly after handling.** ...Manufacturer/supplier or the competent authority to specify parts of the body to be washed after handling.			
P270 **Do not eat, drink or smoke when using this product.**			

SPECIFIC TARGET ORGAN TOXICITY (SINGLE EXPOSURE)
(CHAPTER 3.8)

Hazard category	Signal word	Hazard statement		Symbol
3	Warning	H335	May cause respiratory irritation; or	Exclamation mark
		H336	May cause drowsiness or dizziness	

Precautionary statements

Prevention	Response	Storage	Disposal
P261 **Avoid breathing dust/fume/gas/mist/ vapours/spray.** *– may be omitted if P260 is given on the label.* Manufacturer/supplier or the competent authority to specify applicable conditions. P271 **Use only outdoors or in a well-ventilated area.**	P304 + P340 **IF INHALED: Remove person to fresh air and keep comfortable for breathing.** P312 **Call a POISON CENTER/doctor/…if you feel unwell.** …Manufacturer/supplier or the competent authority to specify the appropriate source of emergency medical advice.	P403 + P233 **Store in a well-ventilated place. Keep container tightly closed.** *– if the chemical is volatile and may generate a hazardous atmosphere.* P405 **Store locked up.**	P501 **Dispose of contents/container to…** … in accordance with local/regional/national/international regulations (to be specified). Manufacturer/supplier or the competent authority to specify whether disposal requirements apply to contents, container or both.

SPECIFIC TARGET ORGAN TOXICITY (REPEATED EXPOSURE)
(CHAPTER 3.9)

Hazard category	**Signal word**	**Hazard statement**
1	Danger	**H372** Causes damage to organs <...> through prolonged or repeated exposure <<...>>

<...> *(state all organs affected, if known)*

<<...>> *(state route of exposure if it is conclusively proven that no other routes of exposure cause the hazard)*

Precautionary statements

Prevention	Response	Storage	Disposal
P260 **Do not breathe dust/fume/gas/mist/ vapours/spray.** Manufacturer/supplier or the competent authority to specify applicable conditions. P264 **Wash ... thoroughly after handling.** ...Manufacturer/supplier or the competent authority to specify parts of the body to be washed after handling. P270 **Do not eat, drink or smoke when using this product.**	P314 **Get medical advice/attention if you feel unwell.** Manufacturer/supplier or the competent authority to select medical advice or attention as appropriate.		P501 **Dispose of contents/container to...** ... in accordance with local/regional/national/international regulations (to be specified). Manufacturer/supplier or the competent authority to specify whether disposal requirements apply to contents, container or both.

SPECIFIC TARGET ORGAN TOXICITY (REPEATED EXPOSURE)
(CHAPTER 3.9)

		Symbol
		Health hazard

Hazard category	Signal word	Hazard statement
2	Warning	H373 May cause damage to organs <...> through prolonged or repeated exposure <<...>>
		<...> *(state all organs affected, if known)*
		<<...>> *(state route of exposure if it is conclusively proven that no other routes of exposure cause the hazard)*

Precautionary statements

Prevention	Response	Storage	Disposal
P260 **Do not breathe dust/fume/gas/mist/vapours/spray.** Manufacturer/supplier or the competent authority to specify applicable conditions.	P314 **Get medical advice/attention if you feel unwell.** Manufacturer/supplier or the competent authority to select medical advice or attention as appropriate.		P501 **Dispose of contents/container to...** ... in accordance with local/regional/national/international regulations (to be specified). Manufacturer/supplier or the competent authority to specify whether disposal requirements apply to contents, container or both.

ASPIRATION HAZARD
(CHAPTER 3.10)

	Symbol
	Health hazard

Hazard category

1

2

Signal word

Danger

Warning

Hazard statement

H304   May be fatal if swallowed and enters airways

H305   May be harmful if swallowed and enters airways

Precautionary statements

Prevention	Response	Storage	Disposal
	P301 + P310 **IF SWALLOWED: Immediately call a POISON CENTER/ doctor/...** ...Manufacturer/supplier or the competent authority to specify the appropriate source of emergency medical advice.	P405 **Store locked up.**	P501 **Dispose of contents/container to...** ... in accordance with local/regional/national/international regulations (to be specified). Manufacturer/supplier or the competent authority to specify whether disposal requirements apply to contents, container or both.
	P331 **Do NOT induce vomiting.**		

HAZARDOUS TO THE AQUATIC ENVIRONMENT – SHORT-TERM (ACUTE) HAZARD
(CHAPTER 4.1)

Hazard category

1

Signal word

Warning

Hazard statement

H400   Very toxic to aquatic life

Symbol
Environment

Precautionary statements

Prevention	Response	Storage	Disposal
P273 **Avoid release to the environment.** *– if this is not the intended use.*	P391 **Collect spillage.**		P501 **Dispose of contents/container to...** ... in accordance with local/regional/national/international regulations (to be specified). Manufacturer/supplier or the competent authority to specify whether disposal requirements apply to contents, container or both.

HAZARDOUS TO THE AQUATIC ENVIRONMENT – SHORT-TERM (ACUTE) HAZARD
(CHAPTER 4.1)

		Symbol
		No symbol

Hazard category

2

3

Signal word

No signal word

No signal word

Hazard statement

H401   Toxic to aquatic life

H402   Harmful to aquatic life

Precautionary statements

Prevention	Response	Storage	Disposal
P273 **Avoid release to the environment.** *– if this is not the intended use.*			P501 **Dispose of contents/container to...** ... in accordance with local/regional/national/international regulations (to be specified). Manufacturer/supplier or the competent authority to specify whether disposal requirements apply to contents, container or both.

HAZARDOUS TO THE AQUATIC ENVIRONMENT – LONG-TERM (CHRONIC) HAZARD

(CHAPTER 4.1)

		Symbol
		Environment

Hazard category   **Signal word**   **Hazard statement**

1   Warning   H410   Very toxic to aquatic life with long lasting effects

2   *No signal word*   H411   Toxic to aquatic life with long lasting effects

Precautionary statements

Prevention	**Response**	**Storage**	**Disposal**
P273 **Avoid release to the environment.** *– if this is not the intended use.*	P391 **Collect spillage.**		P501 **Dispose of contents/container to...** ... in accordance with local/regional/national/international regulations (to be specified). Manufacturer/supplier or the competent authority to specify whether disposal requirements apply to contents, container or both.

- 367 -

HAZARDOUS TO THE AQUATIC ENVIRONMENT – LONG-TERM (CHRONIC) HAZARD
(CHAPTER 4.1)

Symbol

No symbol

Hazard category

3

4

Signal word

No signal word

No signal word

Hazard statement

H412   Harmful to aquatic life with long lasting effects

H413   May cause long lasting harmful effects to aquatic life

Precautionary statements

Prevention	Response	Storage	Disposal
P273 **Avoid release to the environment.** *– if this is not the intended use.*			P501 **Dispose of contents/container to...** ... in accordance with local/regional/national/international regulations (to be specified). Manufacturer/supplier or the competent authority to specify whether disposal requirements apply to contents, container or both.

HAZARDOUS TO THE OZONE LAYER

(CHAPTER 4.2)

Hazard category	Signal word	Symbol
1	Warning	Exclamation mark

Hazard statement

H420   Harms public health and the environment by destroying ozone in the upper atmosphere

Precautionary statements

Prevention	Response	Storage	Disposal
			P502 **Refer to manufacturer or supplier for information on recovery or recycling**

Annex 3

Section 4

CODIFICATION OF PICTOGRAMS

A3.4.1 Introduction

A3.4.1.1 *Pictogram* means a graphical composition that may include a symbol plus other graphic elements, such as a border, background pattern or colour that is intended to convey specific information.

A3.4.1.2 This section contains the recommended code assigned to each of the pictograms prescribed by the GHS for sectors other than transport.

A3.4.1.3 The pictogram code is intended to be used for references purposes. It is not part of the pictogram and should not appear on labels or in section 2 of the safety data sheet.

A3.4.2 Codification of pictograms

A3.4.2.1 GHS pictograms for sectors other than transport are assigned a unique alphanumerical code as follows:

(a) the letters "GHS"; and

(b) a sequential number "01", "02", "03" etc. assigned in accordance with Table A3.4.1 below.

Table A3.4.1

Code	Hazard pictogram	Symbol
GHS01		Exploding bomb
GHS02		Flame
GHS03		Flame over circle
GHS04		Gas cylinder
GHS05		Corrosion
GHS06		Skull and crossbones
GHS07		Exclamation mark
GHS08		Health hazard
GHS09		Environment

Annex 3

Section 5

EXAMPLES OF PRECAUTIONARY PICTOGRAMS

A3.5.1   **Precautionary pictograms**

From European Union (Council Directive 92/58/EEC of 24 June 1992)

From South African Bureau of Standards (SABS 0265:1999)

ANNEX 4

GUIDANCE ON THE PREPARATION OF SAFETY DATA SHEETS (SDS)

Annex 4

GUIDANCE ON THE PREPARATION OF
SAFETY DATA SHEETS (SDS)

A4.1 Introduction

A4.1.1 This annex provides guidance on the preparation of an SDS under the requirements of the Globally Harmonized System of Classification and Labelling of Chemicals (GHS). SDS's are an important element of hazard communication in the GHS, as explained in Chapter 1.5. Use of this guidance document should support compliance with competent authority (CA) requirements and should allow the SDS to be prepared in accordance with the GHS.

A4.1.2 The use of this guidance document is dependent on importing countries requirements for SDS. It is hoped that the application of the GHS worldwide will eventually lead to a fully harmonized situation.

A4.1.3 Unless otherwise stated, all chapters, sections and tables referred to in this annex can be found in the main text of the GHS.

A4.2 General guidance for compiling an SDS

A4.2.1 *Scope and application*

Safety Data Sheets (SDS) should be produced for all substances and mixtures which meet the harmonized criteria for physical, health or environmental hazards under the GHS and for all mixtures which contain ingredients that meet the criteria for carcinogenic, toxic to reproduction or target organ toxicity in concentrations exceeding the cut-off limits for SDS specified by the criteria for mixtures (see Table 1.5.1 in Chapter 1.5). The competent authority (CA) may also require SDS for mixtures not meeting the criteria for classification as hazardous but which contain hazardous ingredients in certain concentrations (see Chapter 3.2). The CA may also require SDS for substances or mixtures that meet the criteria for classification as hazardous for non-GHS classes/end-points. An SDS is a well-accepted and effective method for the provision of information, and may be used to convey information for substances or mixtures that do not meet or are not included in the GHS classification criteria.

A4.2.2 General guidance

A4.2.2.1 The writer of the SDS needs to keep in mind that an SDS must inform its audience of the hazards of a substance or a mixture and provide information on the safe storage, handling and disposal of the substance or a mixture. An SDS contains information on the potential health effects of exposure and how to work safely with the substance or mixture. It also contains hazard information derived from physicochemical properties or environmental effects, on the use, storage, handling and emergency response measures related to that substance or mixture. The purpose of this guidance is to ensure consistency and accuracy in the content of each of the mandatory headings required under GHS, so that the resulting safety data sheets will enable users to take the necessary measures relating to protection of health and safety at the workplace, and the protection of the environment. The information in the SDS shall be written in a clear and concise manner. The SDS shall be prepared by a competent person who shall take into account the specific needs of the user audience, as far as it is known. Persons placing substances and mixtures on the market shall ensure that refresher courses and training on the preparation of SDS be regularly attended by the competent persons.

A4.2.2.2 When writing the SDS, information should be presented in a consistent and complete form, with the workplace audience firmly in mind. However, it should be considered that all or part of the SDS can be used to inform workers, employers, health and safety professionals, emergency personnel, relevant government agencies, as well as members of the community.

A4.2.2.3   Language used in the SDS should be simple, clear and precise, avoiding jargon, acronyms and abbreviations. Vague and misleading expressions should not be used. Phrases such as "may be dangerous", "no health effects", "safe under most conditions of use", or "harmless" are also not recommended. It may be that information on certain properties is of no significance or that it is technically impossible to provide; if so, the reasons for this must be clearly stated under each heading. If it is stated that a particular hazard does not exist, the safety data sheet should clearly differentiate between cases where no information is available to the classifier, and cases where negative test results are available.

A4.2.2.4   The date of issue of the SDS should be stated and be very apparent. The date of issue is the date the SDS version was made public. This generally occurs shortly after the SDS authoring and publishing process is completed. Revised SDS's should clearly state the date of issue as well as a version number, revision number, supersedes date or some other indication of what version is replaced.

A4.2.3   *SDS format*

A4.2.3.1   The information in the SDS should be presented using the following 16 headings in the order given below (see also 1.5.3.2.1):

1.   Identification;

2.   Hazard identification;

3.   Composition/information on ingredients;

4.   First-aid measures;

5.   Fire-fighting measures;

6.   Accidental release measures;

7.   Handling and storage;

8.   Exposure controls/personal protection;

9.   Physical and chemical properties;

10.   Stability and reactivity;

11.   Toxicological information;

12.   Ecological information;

13.   Disposal considerations;

14.   Transport information;

15.   Regulatory information;

16.   Other information

A4.2.3.2   An SDS is not a fixed length document. The length of the SDS should be commensurate with the hazard of the material and the information available.

A4.2.3.3   All pages of an SDS should be numbered and some indication of the end of the SDS should be given (for example: "page 1 of 3"). Alternatively, number each page and indicate whether there is a page following (e.g. "Continued on next page" or "End of SDS").

A4.2.4   SDS content

A4.2.4.1   General information on SDS content can be found in 1.5.3.3. More practical information is given below.

A4.2.4.2   The minimum information outlined in section A4.3 of this annex should be included on the SDS, where applicable and available[1], under the relevant headings. When information is not available or lacking this should be clearly stated. The SDS should not contain any blanks.

A4.2.4.3   In addition, the SDS should contain a brief summary/conclusion of the data given, making it easy even for non-experts in the field to identify all the hazards for the hazardous substance/mixture.

A4.2.4.4   Use of abbreviations is not recommended because they may lead to confusion or decreased understanding.

A4.2.5   Other information requirements

A4.2.5.1   There are information requirements for the preparation of an SDS. The minimum information requirements are outlined in A4.3.

A4.2.5.2   In addition to the minimum information requirements (see A4.2.4.2), the SDS may also contain "additional information". Where a material has additional relevant and available information about its nature and/or use, that information should be included in the SDS (see A4.3.16 for further advice on additional information requirements).

A4.2.6   Units

Numbers and quantities should be expressed in units appropriate to the region into which the product is being supplied. In general, the International System of Units (SI) should be used.

A4.3   Information requirements for the preparation of the SDS

This section describes the GHS information requirements for SDS's. Additional information may be required by competent authorities.

A4.3.1   SECTION 1: Identification

Identify the substance or mixture and provide the name of the supplier, recommended uses and the contact detail information of the supplier including an emergency contact in this section.

A4.3.1.1   *GHS Product identifier*

The identity of the substance or mixture (GHS product identifier) should be exactly as found on the label. If one generic SDS is used to cover several minor variants of a substance or mixture, all names and variants should be listed on the SDS or the SDS should clearly delineate the range of substances included.

A4.3.1.2   *Other means of identification*

In addition, or as an alternative, to the GHS product identifier, the substance or mixture may be identified by alternative names, numbers, company product codes, or other unique identifiers. Provide other names or synonyms by which the substance or mixture is labelled or commonly known, if applicable.

---

[1]   *Where "applicable" means where the information is applicable to the specific product covered by the SDS. Where "available" means where the information is available to the supplier or other entity that is preparing the SDS.*

A4.3.1.3   *Recommended use of the chemical and restrictions on use*

Provide the recommended or intended use of the substance or mixture, including a brief description of what it actually does, e.g. flame retardant, anti-oxidant, etc. Restrictions on use should, as far as possible, be stated including non-statutory recommendations by the supplier.

A4.3.1.4   *Supplier's details*

The name, full address and phone number(s) of the supplier should be included on the SDS.

A4.3.1.5   *Emergency phone number*

References to emergency information services should be included in all SDS. If any restrictions apply, such as hours of operation (e.g. Monday - Friday, 8:00 a.m. - 6:00 p.m., or 24 hours) or limits on specific types of information (e.g., medical emergencies, or transportation emergencies), this should be clearly stated.

A4.3.2   **SECTION 2: Hazard identification**

This section describes the hazards of the substance or mixture and the appropriate warning information (signal word, hazard statement(s) and precautionary statement(s)) associated with those hazards. The section should include a brief summary/conclusion of the data given as described in A4.2.4.3.

A4.3.2.1   *Classification of the substance or mixture*

A4.3.2.1.1   This sub-section indicates the hazard classification of the substance or mixture.

A4.3.2.1.2   If the substance or mixture is classified in accordance with Parts 2, 3 and/or 4 of the GHS, generally the classification is communicated by providing the appropriate hazard class and category/subcategory to indicate the hazard (for example, flammable liquid Category 1 and skin corrosive, Category 1A). However, when classification is differentiated within a hazard class and results in unique hazard statements, then the classification should also reflect that differentiation. For example, the route of exposure differentiates the acute toxicity classification as follows: acute oral toxicity Category 1, acute dermal toxicity Category 1 and acute inhalation toxicity Category 1. If a substance or mixture is classified into more than one category in a hazard class that is differentiated, then all classifications should be communicated.

A4.3.2.2   *GHS label elements, including precautionary statements*

A4.3.2.2.1   Based on the classification, provide the appropriate label elements: signal word(s), hazard statement(s) and precautionary statement(s).

A4.3.2.2.2   Pictograms (or hazard symbols) may be provided as a graphical reproduction of the symbols in black and white or the name of the symbol, e.g. "flame", "skull and crossbones".

A4.3.2.3   *Other hazards which do not result in classification*

Provide information on other hazards which do not result in classification but may contribute to the overall hazards of the material, for example, formation of air contaminants during hardening or processing, dust explosion hazards, suffocation, freezing or environmental effects such as hazards to soil-dwelling organisms. The statement "May form explosible dust-air mixture if dispersed" is appropriate in the case of a dust explosion hazard.

A4.3.3 **SECTION 3: Composition/information on ingredients**

Identify the ingredient(s) of the product in this section. This includes identifying impurities and stabilizing additives which are themselves classified and which contribute to the classification of the substance. This section may also be used to provide information on complex substances.

NOTE: *For information on ingredients, the competent authority rules for Confidential Business Information (CBI) take priority over the rules for product identification. When applicable, indicate that confidential information about the composition was omitted.*

A4.3.3.1 *Substances*

A4.3.3.1.1 *Chemical identity of the substance*

The identity of a substance is provided by its common chemical name. The chemical name can be identical to the GHS product identifier.

NOTE: *The "common chemical name" may, for example, be the CAS name or IUPAC name, as applicable.*

A4.3.3.1.2 *Common name(s), synonym(s) of the substance*

Common names and synonyms should be provided where appropriate.

A4.3.3.1.3 *CAS number and other unique identifiers for the substance*

The Chemical Abstract Service (CAS) registry number provides a unique chemical identification and should be provided when available. Other unique identifiers specific to a country or region, such as the European Community (EC) number could be added.

A4.3.3.1.4 *Impurities and stabilizing additives which are themselves classified and which contribute to the classification of the substance*

Identify any impurities and/or stabilizing additives, which are themselves classified and which contribute to the classification of the substance.

A4.3.3.2 *Mixtures*

A4.3.3.2.1 For a mixture, provide the chemical identity, identification number (within the meaning of A4.3.3.1.3) and concentration or concentration ranges of all hazardous ingredients, which are hazardous to health or the environment within the meaning of the GHS, and are present above their cut-off levels. Manufacturers or suppliers may choose to list all ingredients, including non-hazardous ingredients.

A4.3.3.2.2 The concentrations of the ingredients of a mixture should be described as:

(a) exact percentages in descending order by mass or volume; or

(b) ranges of percentages in descending order by mass or volume if such ranges are acceptable to the appropriate competent national authority.

A4.3.3.2.3 When using a proportion range, the health and environmental hazard effects should describe the effects of the highest concentration of each ingredient, provided that the effects of the mixture as a whole are not available.

NOTE: *The "proportion range" refers to the concentration or percentage range of the ingredient in the mixture.*

A4.3.4   **SECTION 4: First-aid measures**

This section describes the initial care that can be given by an untrained responder without the use of sophisticated equipment and without a wide selection of medications available. If medical attention is required, the instructions should state this, including its urgency. It may be useful to provide information on the immediate effects, by route of exposure, and indicate the immediate treatment, followed by possible delayed effects with specific medical surveillance required.

A4.3.4.1   *Description of necessary first-aid measures*

A4.3.4.1.1   Provide first-aid instructions by relevant routes of exposure. Use sub-headings to indicate the procedure for each route (e.g. inhalation, skin, eye and ingestion). Describe expected immediate and delayed symptoms.

A4.3.4.1.2   Provide advice whether:

(a)   immediate medical attention is required and if delayed effects can be expected after exposure;

(b)   movement of the exposed individual from the area to fresh air is recommended;

(c)   removal and handling of clothing and shoes from the individual is recommended; and

(d)   personal protective equipment (PPE) for first-aid responders is recommended.

A4.3.4.2   *Most important symptoms/effects, acute and delayed*

Provide information on the most important symptoms/effects, acute and delayed, from exposure.

A4.3.4.3   *Indication of immediate medical attention and special treatment needed, if necessary*

Where appropriate, provide information on clinical testing and medical monitoring for delayed effects, specific details on antidotes (where they are known) and contraindications.

A4.3.5   **SECTION 5: Fire-fighting measures**

This section covers the requirements for fighting a fire caused by the substance or mixture, or arising in its vicinity.

A4.3.5.1   *Suitable extinguishing media*

Provide information on the appropriate extinguishing media. In addition, indicate whether any extinguishing media are inappropriate for a particular situation involving the substance or mixture (e.g. avoid high pressure media which could cause the formation of a potentially explosive dust-air mixture).

A4.3.5.2   *Specific hazards arising from the chemical*

Provide advice on specific hazards that may arise from the chemical, such as hazardous combustion products that form when the substance or mixture burns. For example:

(a)   "may produce toxic fumes of carbon monoxide if burning"; or

(b)   "produces oxides of sulphur and nitrogen on combustion".

A4.3.5.3   *Special protective actions for fire-fighters*

A4.3.5.3.1   Provide advice on any protective actions to be taken during fire fighting. For example, "keep containers cool with water spray".

| A4.3.6 | **SECTION 6: Accidental release measures** |

This section recommends the appropriate response to spills, leaks, or releases in order to prevent or minimize the adverse effects on persons, property and the environment in this section. Distinguish between responses for large and small spills where the spill volume has a significant impact on the hazard. The procedures for containment and recovery may indicate that different practices are required.

| A4.3.6.1 | *Personal precautions, protective equipment and emergency procedures* |

| A4.3.6.1.1 | *For non-emergency personnel* |

Provide advice related to accidental spills and release of the substance or mixture such as:

(a) the wearing of suitable protective equipment (including personal protective equipment, see Section 8 of the SDS) to prevent any contamination of skin, eyes and personal clothing;

(b) removal of ignition sources and provision of sufficient ventilation; and

(c) emergency procedures such as the necessity to evacuate the danger area or to consult an expert.

| A4.3.6.1.2 | *For emergency responders* |

Provide advice related to suitable fabric for personal protective clothing (e.g.: "appropriate: Butylene; not appropriate: PVC).

| A4.3.6.2 | *Environmental precautions* |

Provide advice on any environmental precautions related to accidental spills and release of the substance or mixture, such as keeping away from drains, surface and ground water.

| A4.3.6.3 | *Methods and materials for containment and cleaning up* |

A4.3.6.3.1 Provide appropriate advice on how to contain and clean up a spill. Appropriate containment techniques may include:

(a) bunding[2], covering of drains; and

(b) capping procedures[3].

A4.3.6.3.2 Appropriate clean up procedures may include:

(a) neutralization techniques;

(b) decontamination techniques;

(c) adsorbent materials;

(d) cleaning techniques;

(e) vacuuming techniques; and

---

[2] A ***bund*** *is a provision of liquid collection facilities which, in the event of any leak or spillage from tanks or pipe work, will capture well in excess of the volume of liquids held, e.g. an embankment. Bunded areas should drain to a capture tank which should have facilities for water/oil separation.*

[3] *i.e. providing a cover or protection (e.g. to prevent damage or spillage).*

(f) equipment required for containment/clean up (include the use of non-sparking tools and equipment where applicable).

A4.3.6.3.3   Provide any other issues relating to spills and releases. For example, including advice on inappropriate containment or clean up techniques.

A4.3.7   **SECTION 7: Handling and storage**

This section provides guidance on safe handling practices that minimize the potential hazards to people, property and the environment from the substance or mixture. Emphasize precautions that are appropriate to the intended use and to the unique properties of the substance or mixture.

A4.3.7.1   *Precautions for safe handling*

A4.3.7.1.1   Provide advice that:

(a) allows safe handling of the substance or mixture;

(b) prevents handling of incompatible substances or mixtures;

(c) draws attention to operations and conditions which create new risks by altering the properties of the substance or mixture, and to appropriate countermeasures; and

(d) minimizes the release of the substance or mixture to the environment.

A4.3.7.1.2   It is good practice to provide advice on general hygiene. For example:

(a) "eating, drinking and smoking in work areas is prohibited";

(b) "wash hands after use"; and

(c) "remove contaminated clothing and protective equipment before entering eating areas".

A4.3.7.2   *Conditions for safe storage, including any incompatibilities*

Ensure that the advice provided is consistent with the physical and chemical properties in Section 9 (Physical and chemical properties) of the SDS. If relevant, provide advice on specific storage requirements including:

(a) How to avoid:

(i) explosive atmospheres;

(ii) corrosive conditions;

(iii) flammability hazards;

(iv) incompatible substances or mixtures;

(v) evaporative conditions; and

(vi) potential ignition sources (including electrical equipment).

(b) How to control the effects of:

(i) weather conditions;

(ii) ambient pressure;

　　　　　　　　(iii)　temperature;

　　　　　　　　(iv)　sunlight;

　　　　　　　　(v)　humidity; and

　　　　　　　　(vi)　vibration.

　　　　(c)　How to maintain the integrity of the substance or mixture by the use of:

　　　　　　　　(i)　stabilizers; and

　　　　　　　　(ii)　anti-oxidants.

　　　　(d)　Other advice including:

　　　　　　　　(i)　ventilation requirements;

　　　　　　　　(ii)　specific designs for storage rooms/vessels;

　　　　　　　　(iii)　quantity limits under storage conditions (if relevant); and

　　　　　　　　(iv)　packaging compatibilities.

A4.3.8　　　SECTION 8:　Exposure controls/personal protection

　　　　Within this guidance the term "occupational exposure limit(s)" refers to limits in the air of the workplace or biological limit values. In addition, for the purposes of this document "exposure control" means the full range of specific protection and prevention measures to be taken during use in order to minimize worker and environmental exposure. Engineering control measures that are needed to minimize exposure to, and risks associated with the hazards of, the substance or mixture should be included in this section.

A4.3.8.1　　　*Control parameters*

A4.3.8.1.1　　　Where available, list the occupational exposure limits (limits in the air of the workplace or biological limit values), including notations, for a substance and for each of the ingredients of a mixture. If air contaminants are formed when using the substance or mixture as intended available occupational exposure limits for these should also be listed. If an occupational exposure limit exists for the country or region in which the SDS is being supplied, this should be listed. The source of the occupational exposure limit should be stated on the SDS. When listing occupational exposure limits, use the chemical identity as specified in section 3 (Composition/Information on ingredients) of the SDS.

A4.3.8.1.2　　　Where available, list the biological limit values, including notations, for a substance and for each of the ingredients of a mixture. Where possible, the biological limit value should be relevant to the countries or regions in which the SDS is being supplied. The source of the biological limit value should be stated on the SDS. When listing biological limit values, use the chemical identity as specified in section 3 of the SDS.

A4.3.8.1.3　　　Where a control banding approach is recommended for providing protection in relation to specific uses then sufficient detail should be given to enable effective management of the risk. The context and limitations of the specific control banding recommendation should be made clear.

A4.3.8.2　　　*Appropriate engineering controls*

　　　　The description of appropriate exposure control measures should relate to the intended modes of use of the substance or mixture. Sufficient information should be provided to enable a proper risk assessment to be carried out. Indicate when special engineering controls are necessary, and specify which type. Examples include:

(a) "maintain air concentrations below occupational exposure standards", using engineering controls if necessary;

(b) "use local exhaust ventilation when…";

(c) "use only in an enclosed system";

(d) "use only in spray paint booth or enclosure";

(e) "use mechanical handling to reduce human contact with materials"; or

(f) "use explosive dust handling controls".

The information provided here should complement that provided under section 7 (Handling and storage) of the SDS.

A4.3.8.3 *Individual protection measures, such as personal protective equipment (PPE)*

A4.3.8.3.1   Consistent with good occupational hygiene practices, personal protective equipment (PPE) should be used in conjunction with other control measures, including engineering controls, ventilation and isolation. See also section 5 (Fire- fighting measures) of the SDS for specific fire/chemical PPE advice.

A4.3.8.3.2   Identify the PPE needed to minimize the potential for illness or injury due to exposure from the substance or mixture, including:

(a) Eye/face protection: specify the type of eye protection and/or face shield required, based on the hazard of the substance or mixture and potential for contact;

(b) Skin protection: specify the protective equipment to be worn (e.g. type of gloves, boots, bodysuit) based on the hazards associated with the substance or mixture and the potential for contact;

(c) Respiratory protection: specify appropriate types of respiratory protection based on the hazard and potential for exposure, including air-purifying respirators and the proper purifying element (cartridge or canister) or breathing apparatus; and

(d) Thermal hazards: when specifying protective equipment to be worn for materials that represent a thermal hazard, special consideration should be given to the construction of the PPE.

A4.3.8.3.3   Special requirements may exist for gloves or other protective clothing to prevent skin, eye or lung exposure. Where relevant, this type of PPE should be clearly stated. For example, "PVC gloves" or "nitrile rubber gloves", and thickness and breakthrough time of the glove material. Special requirements may exist for respirators.

A4.3.9 SECTION 9: Physical and chemical properties

A4.3.9.1   Describe the empirical data of the substance or mixture (if possible) in this section.

A4.3.9.2   In the case of a mixture, the entries should clearly indicate to which ingredient the data apply, unless it is valid for the whole mixture. The data included in this sub-section should apply to the substance or mixture.

A4.3.9.3   Clearly identify the following properties and specify appropriate units of measure and/or reference conditions where appropriate. If relevant for the interpretation of the numeric value, the method of determination should also be provided (e.g. for flash point, open-cup/closed-cup):

(a) Appearance (physical state, colour etc);

(b)   Odour;

(c)   Odour threshold;

(d)   pH;

(e)   Melting point/freezing point;

(f)   Initial boiling point and boiling range;

(g)   Flash point;

(h)   Evaporation rate;

(i)   Flammability (solid, gas);

(j)   Upper/lower flammability or explosive limits;

(k)   Vapour pressure;

(l)   Vapour density;

(m)   Relative density;

(n)   Solubility(ies);

(o)   Partition coefficient: n-octanol/water;

(p)   Auto-ignition temperature;

(q)   Decomposition temperature;

(r)   Viscosity.

If specific characteristics do not apply or are not available, they should still be listed on the SDS with a statement that they do not apply or not available.

Other physical or chemical parameters in addition to those listed above may also be included in this section of the SDS.

A4.3.10   SECTION 10: Stability and reactivity

A4.3.10.1   *Reactivity*

A4.3.10.1.1   Describe the reactivity hazards of the substance or mixture in this section. Provide specific test data for the substance or mixture as a whole, where available. However, the information may also be based on general data for the class or family of chemical if such data adequately represent the anticipated hazard of the substance or mixture.

A4.3.10.1.2   If data for mixtures are not available, ingredient data should be provided. In determining incompatibility, consider the substances, containers and contaminants that the substance or mixture might be exposed to during transportation, storage and use.

A4.3.10.2   *Chemical stability*

Indicate if the substance or mixture is stable or unstable under normal ambient and anticipated storage and handling conditions of temperature and pressure. Describe any stabilizers which are, or may need to be, used to maintain the product. Indicate the safety significance of any change in the physical appearance of the product.

A4.3.10.3 *Possibility of hazardous reactions*

If relevant, state if the substance or mixture will react or polymerize, releasing excess pressure or heat, or creating other hazardous conditions. Describe under what conditions the hazardous reactions may occur.

A4.3.10.4 *Conditions to avoid*

List conditions such as heat, pressure, shock, static discharge, vibrations or other physical stresses that might result in a hazardous situation.

A4.3.10.5 *Incompatible materials*

List classes of chemicals or specific substances with which the substance or mixture could react to produce a hazardous situation (e.g. explosion, release of toxic or flammable materials, liberation of excessive heat).

A4.3.10.6 *Hazardous decomposition products*

List known and reasonably anticipated hazardous decomposition products produced as a result of use, storage and heating. Hazardous combustion products should be included in section 5 (Fire-fighting measures) of the SDS.

A4.3.11   SECTION 11: Toxicological information

A4.3.11.1   This section is used primarily by medical professionals, occupational health and safety professionals and toxicologists. A concise but complete and comprehensible description of the various toxicological (health) effects, and the available data used to identify those effects, should be provided. Under GHS classification, the relevant hazards, for which data should be provided, are:

    (a)   acute toxicity;

    (b)   skin corrosion/irritation;

    (c)   serious eye damage/irritation;

    (d)   respiratory or skin sensitization;

    (e)   germ cell mutagenicity;

    (f)   carcinogenicity;

    (g)   reproductive toxicity;

    (h)   STOT-single exposure;

    (i)   STOT-repeated exposure; and

    (j)   aspiration hazard.

These hazards should always be listed on the SDS.

A4.3.11.2   The health effects included in the SDS should be consistent with those described in the studies used for the classification of the substance or mixture.

A4.3.11.3   Where there is a substantial amount of test data on the substance or mixture, it may be desirable to summarize results e.g. by route of exposure (see A4.3.11.1).

A4.3.11.4   The data included in this sub-section should apply to the substance or mixture as used. The toxicological data should describe the mixture. If that information is not available, the classification under GHS and the toxicological properties of the hazardous ingredients should be provided.

A4.3.11.5   General statements such as "Toxic" with no supporting data or "Safe if properly used" are not acceptable as they may be misleading and do not provide a description of health effects. Phrases such as "not applicable", "not relevant", or leaving blank spaces in the health effects section can lead to confusion and misunderstanding and should not be used. For health effects where information is not available, this should be clearly stated. Health effects should be described accurately and relevant distinctions made. For example, allergic contact dermatitis and irritant contact dermatitis should be distinguished from each other.

A4.3.11.6   If data for any of these hazards are not available, they should still be listed on the SDS with a statement that data are not available. Also provide information on the relevant negative data (see A4.2.2.3). If data are available showing that the substance or mixture does not meet the criteria for classification, it should be stated on the SDS that the substance or mixture has been evaluated and based on available data, does not meet the classification criteria. Additionally, if a substance or mixture is found to be not classified for other reasons, for example, due to technical impossibility to obtain data, or inconclusive data, this should be clearly stated on the SDS.

A4.3.11.7   *Information on the likely routes of exposure*

Provide information on the likely routes of exposure and the effects of the substance or mixture via each possible route of exposure, that is, through ingestion (swallowing), inhalation or skin/eye exposure. A statement should be made if health effects are not known.

A4.3.11.8   *Symptoms related to the physical, chemical and toxicological characteristics*

Describe the potential adverse health effects and symptoms associated with exposure to the substance or mixture and its ingredients or known by-products. Provide information on the symptoms related to the physical, chemical and toxicological characteristics of the substance or mixture following exposure related to the intended uses. Describe the first symptoms at the lowest exposures through to the consequences of severe exposure; for example, "headaches and dizziness may occur, proceeding to fainting or unconsciousness; large doses may result in coma and death".

A4.3.11.9   *Delayed and immediate effects and also chronic effects from short and long term exposure*

Provide information on whether delayed or immediate effects can be expected after short or long term exposure. Also provide information on acute and chronic health effects relating to human exposure to the substance or mixture. Where human data are not available, animal data should be summarised and the species clearly identified. It should be indicated in the SDS whether toxicological data is based on human or animal data.

A4.3.11.10   *Numerical measures of toxicity (such as acute toxicity estimates)*

Provide information on the dose, concentration or conditions of exposure that may cause adverse health effects. Where appropriate, doses should be linked to symptoms and effects, including the period of exposure likely to cause harm.

A4.3.11.11   *Interactive effects*

Information on interactions should be included if relevant and readily available.

A4.3.11.12   *Where specific chemical data are not available*

It may not always be possible to obtain information on the hazards of a substance or mixture. In cases where data on the specific substance or mixture are not available, data on the chemical class, if appropriate, may be used. Where generic data are used or where data are not available, this should be stated clearly in the SDS.

A4.3.11.13 *Mixtures*

If a mixture has not been tested for its health effects as a whole then information on each ingredient listed under A4.3.3.2.1 should be provided and the mixture should be classified using the processes that are described in the GHS (Section 1.3.2.3 and subsequent chapters).

A4.3.11.14 *Mixture versus ingredient information*

A4.3.11.14.1   Ingredients may interact with each other in the body resulting in different rates of absorption, metabolism and excretion. As a result, the toxic actions may be altered and the overall toxicity of the mixture may be different from its ingredients.

A4.3.11.14.2   It is necessary to consider whether the concentration of each ingredient is sufficient to contribute to the overall health effects of the mixture. The information on toxic effects should be presented for each ingredient, except:

(a)   if the information is duplicated, it is not necessary to list this more than once. For example, if two ingredients both cause vomiting and diarrhoea, it is not necessary to list this twice. Overall, the mixture is described as causing vomiting and diarrhoea;

(b)   if it is unlikely that these effects will occur at the concentrations present. For example, when a mild irritant is diluted in a non-irritating solution, there comes a point where the overall mixture would be unlikely to cause irritation;

(c)   Predicting the interactions between ingredients is extremely difficult, and where information on interactions is not available, assumptions should not be made and instead the health effects of each ingredient should be listed separately.

A4.3.11.15 *Other information*

Other relevant information on adverse health effects should be included even when not required by the GHS classification criteria.

A4.3.12   **SECTION 12: Ecological information**

A4.3.12.1   The information that shall be provided in this section is to enable evaluation of the environmental impact of the substance or mixture if it were released to the environment. This information can assist in handling spills, and evaluating waste treatment practices, control of release, accidental release measures, and transport.

A4.3.12.2   A concise but complete and comprehensible description of the various ecotoxicological (environment) properties, and the available data used to identify those properties, should be provided. The basic properties, for which data should be provided, are:

(a)   Toxicity;

(b)   Persistence and degradability;

(c)   Bioaccumulative potential;

(d)   Mobility in soil;

(e)   Other adverse effects.

These properties should always be listed on the SDS. Species, media, units, test duration and test conditions should be clearly indicated. (If data for any of these properties are not available, they should still be listed on the SDS with a statement that data are not available).

A4.3.12.3   Some ecotoxicological properties are substance specific, i.e. bioaccumulation, persistence and degradability. The information should therefore be given, where available and appropriate, for each relevant ingredient of the mixture (i.e. those which are required to be listed in Section 3 of the SDS).

A4.3.12.4   Provide also a short summary of the data given under A4.3.12.5 to A4.3.12.9 in relation to the hazard classification criteria. Where data are not available for classification, this should be clearly stated on the SDS for each basic property concerned. Additionally, if data are available showing that the substance or mixture does not meet the criteria for classification, it should be stated on the SDS that the substance or mixture has been evaluated and, based on available data, does not meet the classification criteria. Additionally, if a substance or mixture is found to be not classified for other reasons, for example, due to technical impossibility to obtain the data, or inconclusive data, this should be clearly stated on the SDS.

A4.3.12.5   *Toxicity*

Information on toxicity can be provided using data from tests performed on aquatic and/or terrestrial organisms. This should include relevant available data on both acute and chronic aquatic toxicity for fish, crustaceans, algae and other aquatic plants. In addition, toxicity data on other organisms (including soil micro-and macro-organisms) such as birds, bees and plants, should be included when available. Where the substance or mixture has inhibitory effects on the activity of micro-organisms, the possible impact on sewage treatment plants should be mentioned.

A4.3.12.6   *Persistence and degradability*

Persistence and degradability is the potential for the substance or the appropriate constituents of a mixture to degrade in the environment, either through biodegradation or other processes, such as oxidation or hydrolysis. Test results relevant to assess persistence and degradability should be given where available. If degradation half-lives are quoted it must be indicated whether these half-lives refer to mineralization or to primary degradation. The potential of the substance or certain constituents (see also A4.3.12.8) of a mixture to degrade in sewage treatment plants should also be mentioned.

A4.3.12.7   *Bioaccumulative potential*

Bioaccumulation is the potential for the substance or certain constituents of a mixture to accumulate in biota and, possibly, pass through the food chain. Test results relevant to assess the bioaccumulative potential should be given. This should include reference to the octanol-water partition coefficient (K_{ow}) and bioconcentration factor (BCF), if available.

A4.3.12.8   *Mobility in soil*

Mobility in soil is the potential of a substance or the constituents of a mixture, if released to the environment, to move under natural forces to the groundwater or to a distance from the site of release. The potential for mobility in soil should be given where available. Information on mobility can be determined from relevant mobility data such as adsorption studies or leaching studies. For example, K_{oc} values can be predicted from octanol/water partition coefficients (K_{ow}). Leaching and mobility can be predicted from models.

NOTE: *Where real data on the substance or mixture is available this data will take precedence over models and predictions.*

A4.3.12.9   *Other adverse effects*

Information on any other adverse effects to the environment should be included where available, such as environmental fate (exposure), ozone depletion potential, photochemical ozone creation potential, endocrine disrupting potential and/or global warming potential.

A4.3.13   **SECTION 13: Disposal considerations**

A4.3.13.1   *Disposal methods*

A4.3.13.1.1   Provide information for proper disposal, recycling or reclamation of the substance or mixture and/or its container to assist in the determination of safe and environmentally preferred waste management options, consistent with the requirements of the national competent authority. For the safety of persons conducting disposal, recycling or reclamation activities, please refer to the information in section 8 (exposure controls and personal protection) of the SDS.

A4.3.13.1.2   Specify disposal containers and methods.

A4.3.13.1.3   Discuss physical/chemical properties that may affect disposal options.

A4.3.13.1.4   Discourage sewage disposal.

A4.3.13.1.5   Where appropriate, identify any special precautions for incineration or landfill.

A4.3.14   **SECTION 14: Transport information**

This section provides basic classification information for the transporting/shipment of a hazardous substance or mixture by road, rail, sea or air. Where information is not available or relevant this should be stated.

A4.3.14.1   *UN Number*

Provide the UN Number (i.e. four-figure identification number of the substance or article) from the *UN Model Regulations*[4].

A4.3.14.2   *UN Proper Shipping Name*

Provide the UN proper shipping name from the UN Model Regulations[4]. For substances or mixtures the UN proper shipping name should be provided in this sub-section if it has not appeared as the GHS product identifier or national or regional identifiers.

A4.3.14.3   *Transport hazard class(es)*

Provide the transport class (and subsidiary risks) assigned to the substances or mixtures according to the most predominant hazard that they present in accordance with the UN Model Regulations[4].

A4.3.14.4   *Packing group, if applicable*

Provide the packing group number from the UN Model Regulations[4], if applicable. The packing group number is assigned to certain substances in accordance with their degree of hazard.

A4.3.14.5   *Environmental hazards*

Indicate whether the substance or mixture is a known marine pollutant according to the IMDG Code[5], and if so, whether it is a "marine pollutant" or a "severe marine pollutant". Also indicate whether the substance or mixture is environmentally hazardous according to the UN Model Regulations[4], ADR[6], RID[7] and ADN[8].

---

[4]   *UN Model Regulations means the Model Regulations annexed to the most recently revised edition of the Recommendations on the Transport of Dangerous Goods published by the United Nations.*

[5]   *IMDG Code means the International Maritime Dangerous Goods code, as amended.*

[6]   *ADR means the European Agreement concerning the International Carriage of Dangerous Goods by Road, as amended.*

A4.3.14.6　Special precautions for user

Provide information on any special precautions, which a user needs to be aware of, or needs to comply with in connection with transport.

A4.3.14.7　Transport in bulk according to Annex II of MARPOL 73/78[9] and the IBC Code[10]

This sub-section only applies when cargoes are intended to be carried in bulk according to the following IMO instruments: Annex II of MARPOL 73/78 and the IBC Code.

Provide the product name (if name is different to that given in A4.3.1.1) as required by the shipment document and in accordance with the name used in the lists of product names given in Chapters 17 or 18 of the IBC Code or the latest edition of the IMO's MEPC.2/Circular. Indicate ship type required and pollution category.

A4.3.15　SECTION 15: Regulatory information

Describe any other regulatory information on the substance or mixture that is not provided elsewhere in the SDS (e.g. whether the substance or mixture is subject to the Montreal Protocol[11], the Stockholm Convention[12] or the Rotterdam Convention[13]).

A4.3.15.1　*Safety, health and environmental regulations specific for the product in question*

Provide relevant national and/or regional information on the regulatory status of the substance or mixture (including its ingredients) under relevant safety, health and environmental regulations. This should include whether the substance is subject to any prohibitions or restrictions in the country or region into which it is being supplied.

A4.3.16　SECTION 16: Other information

Provide information relevant to the preparation of the SDS in this section. This should incorporate other information that does not belong in sections 1 to 15 of the SDS, including information on preparation and revision of the SDS such as:

(a)　the date of preparation of the latest revision of the SDS. When revisions are made to an SDS, unless it has been indicated elsewhere, clearly indicate where the changes have been made to the previous version of the SDS. Suppliers should maintain an explanation of the changes and be willing to provide it upon request;

(b)　a key/legend to abbreviations and acronyms used in the SDS; and

(c)　key literature references and sources for data used to compile the SDS.

NOTE:　*While references are not necessary in SDS's, references may be included in this section if desired.*

---

[7]　***RID*** *means the Regulations concerning the International Carriage of Dangerous Goods by Rail, as amended.*

[8]　***ADN*** *means the European Agreement concerning the International Transport of Dangerous Goods by Inland Waterways, as amended.*

[9]　***MARPOL 73/78*** *means the International Convention for the Prevention of Pollution from Ships, 1973, as modified by the Protocol of 1978 relating thereto, as amended*

[10]　***IBC Code*** *means the International Code for the Construction and Equipment of Ships carrying Dangerous Chemicals in Bulk (International Bulk Chemical Code).*

[11]　***Montreal Protocol*** *means the Montreal Protocol on Substances that Deplete the Ozone Layer, as either adjusted and/or amended.*

[12]　***Stockholm Convention*** *means the Stockholm Convention on Persistent Organic Pollutants.*

[13]　***Rotterdam Convention*** *means the Rotterdam Convention on the Prior Informed Consent Procedure for Certain Hazardous Chemicals and Pesticides in International Trade.*

ANNEX 5

CONSUMER PRODUCT LABELLING
BASED ON THE LIKELIHOOD OF INJURY

Annex 5

CONSUMER PRODUCT LABELLING BASED
ON THE LIKELIHOOD OF INJURY

A5.1   Introduction

A5.1.1   The Globally Harmonized System of Classification and Labelling of Chemicals is based on an assessment of the intrinsic hazardous properties of the chemicals involved. However, it has been recognized that some systems provide information about chronic health hazards in consumer products only after considering additional data regarding potential exposures to consumers under normal conditions of use or foreseeable misuse. These systems thus provide information based on an assessment of risk, or the likelihood of injury occurring from exposure to these products. Where this exposure assessment and determination of likelihood of injury reveal that the potential for harm to occur as a result of the expected exposures is insignificant, chronic health hazards may not be included on the product label for consumer use. This type of system was recognized in a paper clarifying the scope of the GHS work in 1998[1]:

"The application of the components of the system may vary by type of product or stage of the life cycle. Once a chemical is classified, the likelihood of adverse effects may be considered in deciding what informational or other steps should be taken for a given product or use setting".

A5.1.2   The work on the GHS has not addressed harmonization of this type of approach. Therefore, specific procedures to apply this approach would have to be developed and applied by the competent authority. However, in recognition that it is an approach that has been used, and will continue to be used in the future, this annex is being provided to give additional guidance on how such an approach may work in practice.

A5.1.3   Exposure assessments for some consumer products are used to determine what information is included on a label in this type of approach. Regulators and manufacturers obtain exposure data or generate hypothetical exposure data based on customary use or foreseeable misuse. These assumptions are then used to determine whether a chronic health hazard is included on a consumer product label, and what precautions are to be followed, under a risk-based approach. These decisions are thus made on the basis of considerations regarding the likelihood of harm occurring in the consumer exposure situations that have been identified.

A5.1.4   Consumer product labels in some systems are based on a combination of hazard and risk. However, acute and physical hazards may be indicated on the label, while chronic health effects labelling based on risk is not indicated. This may be due in part to the expectation that exposures to some consumer products are of short duration, and thus may not be sufficient to lead to the development of chronic health effects as a result of those exposures. These expectations may not be accurate where consumer products are used in a workplace, e.g. paints or adhesives used by construction workers on a regular basis

A5.1.5   While intrinsic hazards of a chemical can be determined for all sectors, information about exposure, and thus risk, varies significantly among the sectors covered by the GHS. The vehicle by which this information is then transmitted to the user also varies. In some cases, particularly in the consumer setting, the label is the sole source of information, while in others, especially the workplace, it is one piece of a comprehensive system, supplemented by SDS's and worker training. In transport, a label transmits the primary information, but additional information is provided by the transport documentation.

---

[1]   *IOMC Description and Further Clarification of the Anticipated Application of the Globally Harmonized System (GHS), IFCS/ISG3/98.32B.*

A5.2   **General principles**

A5.2.1   While the specific risk assessment approach has not been addressed or harmonized in the GHS, certain general principles are as follows:

       (a)   All chemicals should be classified based on GHS classification criteria

               The first step in the process of classifying hazards and communicating information should always be classification of intrinsic hazards based on the GHS criteria for substances and mixtures;

       (b)   Risk-based labelling can only be applied by the competent authorities to the chronic health hazards of chemicals in the consumer product setting. All acute health, environmental and physical hazards should be labelled based on intrinsic hazards

               The hazard classification should lead directly to labelling of acute health effects, environmental and physical hazards. The labelling approach that involves a risk assessment should only be applied to chronic health hazards, e.g. carcinogenicity, reproductive toxicity, or target organ toxicity based on repeated exposure. The only chemicals it may be applied to are those in the consumer product setting where consumer exposures are generally limited in quantity and duration;

       (c)   Estimates of possible exposures and risks to consumers should be based on conservative, protective assumptions to minimise the possibility of underestimating exposure or risk

               Exposure assessments or estimates should be based on data and/or conservative assumptions.

               Assessment of the risk and the approach to extrapolating animal data to humans should also involve a conservative margin of safety through establishment of uncertainty factors.

A5.2.2   **An example of risk-based labelling used in the United States Consumer Product Safety Commission**

A5.2.2.1   In general, consumers rely on product labels for information about the effects of a chemical. Whereas other sectors have additional sources of information (e.g. safety data sheets, transport documents) to expand upon or refine product information and relate risk to the hazard information provided, the consumer sector generally does not.

A5.2.2.2   As noted above, the general rule for the GHS is that the label information will be based on intrinsic properties (hazards) of the chemical in all sectors. The rationale for hazard based labelling in the GHS has been described earlier in this document, and may be applied to consumer products as well as products in other sectors.

A5.2.2.3   In particular, the principle of the user's "right-to-know" about the intrinsic hazards of the chemical is important and widely supported by many stakeholders. Hazard information is an incentive to choose less hazardous chemicals for use. It may not be possible to accurately predict the exposures when the products are used, and consumer protective measures are less certain than those in other more structured sectors.

A5.2.2.4   On the other hand some research has indicated [2-7] that a consumer's attention can be diverted by too much information on a label regarding all potential hazards. It appears there is some evidence that warnings focused on specific hazards that are likely to cause injury enhance consumer protection.

A5.2.2.5   To ensure that consumers have the information needed to take appropriate protective measures, a risk-based labelling approach examines likely or possible exposures and communicates information related to the actual risks of exposure. Consumer exposures from use, foreseeable use and accidents can be estimated since products are designed for specific use(s).

A5.2.2.6   The following process has not been harmonized in the GHS. It is consistent with US Consumer Product Safety Commission Guidelines[8] and with other national and international guidelines on conducting risk assessments[9-11]. A substance or product under evaluation for chronic hazard labelling for consumer use in the US must satisfy a two-part test. First, it must present one of the chronic hazards covered, i.e. be classified as a chronic hazard based on specific criteria. Second, a risk assessment must be carried out to establish whether it has the potential to cause substantial illness or injury during or as a result of "reasonably foreseeable handling or use or from ingestion by children". If the result of the risk assessment indicates the risk is very low, the substance or product need not be labelled for chronic hazard. In other words, whether a given substance is labelled for a chronic effect depends not only on whether it is hazardous, but also on exposure and risk.

A5.2.2.7   The extent of the exposure assessment would depend on the hazard. For example, for non-cancer chronic endpoints, an "acceptable daily intake" (ADI) would be calculated from the "no observed adverse effect level" (NOAEL). For a conservative estimate of exposure, one can assume that the consumer will use the entire consumer product in a day and/or assume that all of the hazardous substance/mixture that the consumer is exposed to will be absorbed. If the resulting exposure is lower than the "acceptable daily intake" no hazard communication would be required. If the exposure level is higher than the ADI, then a more refined quantitative assessment could be performed before making a final labelling decision. If refined data are not available, or a refined analysis is not done, the hazard would be communicated on the label.

A5.2.2.8   For carcinogens, a unit risk from exposure to the carcinogen would be calculated based on linear extrapolation with the multistage model as a default model. Life time exposures can be calculated either by assuming worst case scenarios (such as all of the substance in a product is reaching the target tissue at each use, exposure is daily/weekly/monthly), or by determining actual exposures during use, or some combination of these approaches.

A5.2.2.9   The competent authority will need to establish what level of risk is acceptable to implement such an approach to consumer product labelling for chronic effects. For example, CPSC recommends labelling for a cancer hazard if the lifetime excess risk exceeds one-in-a-million from exposure during "reasonably foreseeable handling and use."

References

1.   ILO. 1999. *Current Sector Uses of Risk Communication*, IOMC/ILO/HC3/99.7.

2.   A. Venema, M. Trommelen, and S. Akerboom. 1997. *Effectiveness of labelling of household chemicals*, Consumer Safety Institute, Amsterdam.

3.   Leen Petre. 1994. *Safety information on dangerous products: consumer assessment*, COFACE, Brussels, Belgium.

4.   European Commission. 1999. *DGIII Study on Comprehensibility of labels based on Directive 88/379/EEC on Dangerous Preparations.*

5.   Magat, W.A., W.K. Viscusi, and J. Huber, 1988. *Consumer processing of hazard warning information*, Journal of Risk and Uncertainty, 1, 201-232.

6.   Abt Associates, Inc. 1999. *Consumer Labelling Initiative: Phase II Report*, Cambridge, Massachusetts, Prepared for US EPA.

7.   Viscusi, W.K. 1991. *Toward a proper role for hazard warnings in products liability cases*, Journal of Products Liability, 13, 139-163.

8.   US Consumer Product Safety Commission. 2001. *Code of Federal Regulations, Subchapter C – Federal Hazardous Substances Act Regulations*, 16, Part 1500.

9.   Saouter, E., G. Van Hoof, C. Pittinger, and T. Feijtel. 2000. *A retrospective analysis of the environmental profile of laundry detergents*, submitted to: International Journal of life cycle analysis, October 2000.

10.   IPCS. 2001. *Principles for evaluating health risks to reproduction associated with exposure to chemicals*, Environmental Health Criteria No. 225.

11.   IPCS. 2000. *Human exposure assessment*, Environmental Health Criteria No. 214.

12.   IPCS. 1999. *Principles for assessment of risks to human health from exposure to chemicals*, Environmental Health Criteria No. 210.

ANNEX 6

COMPREHENSIBILITY TESTING METHODOLOGY

Annex 6

COMPREHENSIBILITY TESTING METHODOLOGY[1]

A6.1   This instrument aims to provide a methodology for the assessment of the comprehensibility of labels and Safety Data Sheets (SDS's) for chemical hazards. The tool has been developed with a particular focus on addressing the needs of workers and consumers in developing countries. The emphasis of instrument development has been to provide a tool that is, as far as possible, globally applicable taking into account varied levels of literacy and differences in cultural experience.

A6.2   Overview of the instrument

A6.2.1   The instrument is organized into a number of modules, directions for each of which is covered in this annex. Broadly speaking, the instrument consists of four parts:

(a)   Module 1: This is a focus group, whose main purpose is to ensure that the instruments used in Modules 2 to 11 are sensible across diverse cultures and settings. Its use is recommended in all categories of target populations (see Table A6.2 below) but it should be mandatory to commence with this module in groups of workers and community members from cultures different to the settings in which labels and SDS's have been produced;

(b)   Modules 2 to 8: These include a general questionnaire (Module 2) and a set of label and Safety Data Sheet questions and exercises (Modules 3 to 8). Depending on whether the subject is a worker and makes use of a Safety Data Sheet, some elements of these modules may not apply;

(c)   Module 9: This is a simulation exercise. One version is intended for workers and is applicable to most people involved in production, while the other version (Module 9a) is adapted for a consumer setting;

(d)   Module 10: Module 10 contains a final post-test questionnaire. It is applicable to all participants in the questionnaires (Modules 2 to 8) and the simulations (Module 9). It is also administered to participants in the group exercise (Module 11). The questionnaire is focused on training, and past experience, and offers an opportunity for open-ended feedback and comment on the testing process;

(e)   Module 11: This is a group exercise for workers that draws on all elements contained in previous modules and is intended to test comprehensibility in the context of group learning. It is designed to complement Modules 2 to 10 but is carried out on different subjects to those in Modules 1, 2 to 8, and 9.

A6.2.3   It is further proposed that follow-up testing be conducted at one and twelve months after comprehensibility testing. This testing should be repeated on the same subjects who underwent initial testing. Depending on resources and logistics, it may be possible to avoid re-testing on all the modules completed at baseline. Repeat testing would be important to gain insight into retention and real benefits of exposure to hazard messages.

A6.2.4   Table A6.1 summarizes the modules in the instrument, the main activities in the modules, and the objectives and outcomes to be derived from each module.

---

[1]   *Developed by a multidisciplinary team at the University of Cape Town, for the International Labour Office (ILO) Working Group on Hazard Communication as part of international efforts to promote a Global Harmonised System (GHS) for hazard communication.*

A6.2.5   Although the testing instrument has been designed as a self-contained package, it may be possible to make use of selective modules from the battery where there are local priorities and needs. Moreover, it is recognized that as global harmonization of hazard communication evolves, new needs for testing may arise. The instrument may be adapted to take account of new testing priorities over time by using adapted testing materials (labels and SDS's) in the same testing formats. For example, if new icons for hazard symbols are under consideration, module 4 can be amended to include new symbols.

A6.3   Use of Annex 6 and of the testing instrument

A6.3.1   Each module is the actual test questionnaire for a specific set of comprehensibility testing objectives. The layout of the modules is such that instructions are clearly marked in the questionnaires for those administering the comprehensibility tests. Accompanying each module, but presented separately, is a set of detailed guidance notes comprising the manual for the particular module. The manuals also outline the different labels and/or SDS's to be used in each module and the outputs and time requirements of each module.

A6.3.2   To avoid rendering the modules to lengthy, instructions on the modules have been kept to a minimum in the text of the modules, reserving the elaboration on instructions for the manual sections. Where key instructions are present in Modules 3 to 11, they are listed in bold text within shaded boxes to improve ease of administration. Italic font is used throughout the modules for all text to be read out to the subject.

A6.3.3   Some modules (Modules 3, 4, 6, 7, 8 and 9) require random selection of labels and/or SDS's. A box of cards is provided to the interviewer to expedite the selection of a random label/SDS or set of labels/SDS's. The interviewer will have a specific box of such cards marked for every relevant module.

A6.3.4   Labels and Safety Data Sheets are provided but should be to conform to the normative styles and presentations existing in the countries in which the tool is to be applied. The GHS will bring a certain degree of standardization in the content and layout of hazard communication methods but a great deal of variation will still arise in relation to local traditions, styles, size and preferences. Labels and SDS's used in testing must as far as possible reflect the typical local usage patterns. Therefore, although sample labels and SDS's are provided with this manual, users are encouraged to adapt the test materials within the limits of the experimental design requirements so that the materials appear as authentic as possible to local subjects.

A6.3.5   Notwithstanding attempts to simplify the relatively complex testing procedures required to measure hazard communication comprehensibility, the test instrument require careful administration and quality control. Training of interviewers is therefore critical. This is dealt with in more detail in the manuals for Modules 1 and 2.

Table A6.1: Comprehensibility testing: Objectives and outcomes by module

Module	Contents	Objectives	Outcome
Module 1	**Focus groups**	To shape research tool to the context, language, and cultural interpretations of the specific target group. To identify cultural specific definitions of words. To test whether ranking, the use of colour for attributing hazard, and the quantitative estimation of ambiguous variables are culturally transferable. Testing strategies used in subsequent modules are piloted for face validity and identify alternatives. To identify potential biases in the testing situation arising from cultural use of items.	Culturally consistent explanations for difficult words. Appropriate use of colour in local context. Account of cultural factors that would bias comprehensibility tests. Validation of colour blindness test methods. Interpretability of psychometric scales for non-Western populations. Contextual testing. Instruments to capture workers' experience. "Dummy" symbols.
Module 2	**General interview**	To ascertain demographic and other data as a basis for analysis of comprehensibility. To clarify competence in colour and visual acuity necessary for some of the subsequent tests. To collect data on work experience, critical to interpretation of comprehensibility assessments.	Relevant demographic and other data for linking to study results and analysis. Colour and visual acuity assessed. Role work experience plays in comprehensibility.
Module 3	**Recall, reading, and comprehensibility of labels and SDS's**	To evaluate subjects' familiarity with a label and an SDS. To test subjects' recall of label elements. To evaluate the sequence used to look at label elements. To test the comprehensibility of signal words, colours, symbols and hazard statements. To assess the impact of the label on the subjects': - Ranking of hazard, both to self and to spouse or child, - Intention to use, store and dispose of the chemical. Whether ranking and reporting change after questions on comprehensibility. Can subjects correctly identify the appropriate SDS? Can subjects correctly identify information on chemical name, health hazard, physical hazard and use of protective clothing?	Identify a priori familiarity with labels and SDS's. An assessment of the impact of different label fonts. Identification of poorly understood elements terms. Identify statements with highest comprehensibility. Hazard ranking, and intention to behave as a result of the label. The effect of detailed questions on comprehensibility on subjects' perceptions of hazard as a proxy for training. The impact of the Hawthorne effect will be gauged. Comparison of ranking of hazard to self differs from ranking of hazard to a close relative. Identifying whether subjects can link data from a label to an appropriate SDS in a meaningful way.

Table A6.1: Comprehensibility testing: Objectives and outcomes by module

Module	Contents	Objectives	Outcome
Module 4	**Rating and understanding of hazards:** **Signal words, colours and symbols**	To test subjects' relative ranking for severity of hazard for: - signal words, colours and symbols; - combinations of symbols and multiple symbols; - selected combinations of symbols, colour and signal words. To test understanding of signal words, colours, and symbols. To test opinion on the ability of signal words, colours, and symbols to attract attention. To test whether subjects' perception of the label will influence their reported intention to use, store or dispose of the chemical. To explore subjects' views as to why hazard elements are present on a label.	Signal words, Colours and Symbols will be rated for ability to denote level of hazard, and for comprehension both separately, and for selected combinations of elements. Quality control assessment of face validity of ranking. Ability of label elements to attract attention. Label rated highest for attracting attention will be explored for its ability to: Prompt the subject to identify further information, particularly health hazard information. Influence reported intention to behave in safe ways.
Module 5	**Comprehension of hazard symbols with and without text**	To test subjects' understanding of symbols representing hazard classes. To test subjects' understanding of concepts of hazard classes. To identify whether adding text words improves understanding of selected symbols representing hazard classes: reproductive, carcinogenic, and mutagenic. To identify whether adding signal words improve understanding of symbols representing classes.	Ability to identify the correct symbol for a hazard class. Identification of hazard classes for which symbols perform poorly; and of symbols which perform poorly as indicators of a hazard class. Identify symbols with ambiguous interpretations. The effectiveness of adding text to symbols for reproductive, carcinogenic and mutagenic hazards. The effectiveness of adding signal words to symbols denoting hazard class.
Module 6	**Size, placement background colour and border of symbols/pictograms**	To test the impact of varying symbol size, border and placement. To test the impact of varying background colour and varying icon size in a pictogram relative to border.	Impact of the symbol size, border and placement: - ability to identify chemical name; - perception of risk; - recall of symbol as proxy for attention to symbol; - recall of hazard statement as proxy for attention to hazard statement; - reported intention to behave; - sequence of reading; Comparison of whether ranking of hazard to self differs from ranking of hazard to a close relative.

Table A6.1: Comprehensibility testing: Objectives and outcomes by module

Module	Contents	Objectives	Outcome
Module 7	**Pictogram comprehension – additional testing (Pesticides)**	To test subjects' ability to identify information: - chemical name; - health hazards; To assess subjects' rating of hazard. To test subjects' understanding of pictograms. To assess subjects' sequence of reading.	Comprehensibility of pictograms: understanding, ranking of hazard, attention, access to key information. Comparison of whether ranking of hazard to self differs from ranking of hazard to a close relative.
Module 8	**Comprehensibility of safety data sheets (SDS's) by organization of data**	To test subjects' ability to identify safety information from an SDS. To test the understanding of hazard information on an SDS. To evaluate what the subject reads on an SDS and the sequence in which subjects report reading the elements of the SDS. To assess what information is useful, appropriate and understandable. To assess whether SDS information is related to intention to behave in safe ways. To evaluate the impact of different organisation of SDS information on the above.	Comprehension of SDS hazard information assessed from different aspects: (a) Interpretation of health hazard information; (b) Self-assessment of understandability to others; (c) Scoring of how the subject explains a hazard statement to a third party; (d) Reported intention to behave Agreement between these four measures of understanding will be estimated. The impact of different ways to organise SDS information will be estimated. Subjective assessment of the usefulness and appropriateness of sub-elements to identify areas for further review of SDS development.
Module 9	**Simulation exercise: impact of the use of labels and SDS's, and of symbols and signal words on labels on safe chemical practices**	To assess safety practices in relation to a simulated exercise in which a chemical is handled. To evaluate whether safety practices are improved by the presence of the signal word "Danger" and/or by the size of the hazard symbol "Skull and Crossbones". To identify whether past experience in relation to chemicals plays a significant role in both safety practices, and in the impact of signal words and symbols on safety practices.	Measures of actual behaviour observed and related to use of labels, SDS's prior to, and during the task. Safety behaviours include use of PPE and other preventive hygiene practices. The impact of varying label elements (with or without "Danger"; with different size hazard symbol) and SDS layout (explicit heath hazard heading versus health hazard data under regulatory information). Relationship between understanding, practice and experimental conditions to be explored.

Table A6.1: Comprehensibility testing: Objectives and outcomes by module

Module	Contents	Objectives	Outcome
Module 10	**Post interview/post simulation interview**	To ascertain past history of contact with chemicals and training. To test the effect of a brief explanation of symbols, signal words, colours and hazard statements on ranking for severity of hazard, and comprehension. To identify chemical information needs from subjects.	Variables derived from training and past experience for stratified analysis of responses to modules 3 to 9. Results will help to indicate whether training should be the subject of more detailed evaluation in the long term. Responses to questions on needs for chemical information can be useful to GHS efforts on chemical safety.
Module 11	**Group exercise - comprehension**	To test whether learning about hazard communication happens differently in a group context than with individuals. To test whether subjects working as a group come up with significantly different answers than when individual subjects are asked a questionnaire.	A quality control assessment on the affect of group versus individual learning. Groups coming up with significantly different responses from individuals indicate that the testing model needs to be revised. Implications for how training should be addressed in future as an element of hazard communication.

A6.3.6   *Consent*: Before conducting any of the modules in this instrument, participants should first give informed consent. To do so, the purpose of the exercises should be explained to them as well as the procedures that will be asked of them. Participants should not be coerced into participating and should know that they have the right to withdraw their participation at any time. The nature of the information provided in the consent procedure is sufficiently generic so as not to give away the explicit hypotheses being tested.

A6.3.7   *Consent procedures* are outlined in the opening sections of Modules 1 (focus group), 2 (commencement of interviews) and 10 (simulation exercises). Irrespective of whether the same subjects complete all modules or not, all three consent procedure should be applied when required. The consent procedure for the simulation is by necessity more of an explanation to obviate the obvious bias to be introduced by alerting the subject to the purpose of the exercise.

A6.3.8   *Policy on rewards or compensation to participants:* Each participating respondent in this study is to be given some form of compensation or incentive for participating in the study. Participating respondents should be told in consenting to the testing that at the end of the study some form of compensation will be presented to them. Compensation may vary from country to country depending on what is culturally appropriate and locally available. Some suggestions (based on other studies) are food (lunch), hats/caps, mugs, food (sugar, rice, mealie, meal), certificates, etc. It is up to the countries applying the tool to develop an appropriate policy on compensation for participants.

A6.4   Sampling

A6.4.1   *Target populations*

A6.4.1.1   Target populations are outlined in Table A6.2 below. These are largely adult working populations, typical of groups who use, distribute or manage chemicals, either directly or indirectly. Children are another important potential audience. However, although the ability to provide understandable safety messages to children is recognised as critically important, it has not been possible to address this area in this manual because of the specialised methods required for evaluation. Further development at some future point may be able to extend the comprehensibility testing to methods suitable for children.

A6.4.1.2   Proposed methods for attaining representative samples are outlined in the Manual sections for Modules 1 and 2. University students should not be used as they have been extensively used in previous hazard communication studies and are not considered representative of the target populations identified in this study.

A6.4.2   *Focus groups*

A6.4.2.1   Given the aim of the focus groups to ensure that the instruments used in Modules 2 to 11 are sensible across diverse cultures and settings, participants for focus groups should be as far as possible typical of the target groups to be evaluated. Emphasis should be placed on targeting groups of workers and community members from cultures different to the settings in which labels and SDS's have been produced. This will mainly apply to farm workers, non-agricultural workers and community/residents/consumer groups, both literate and non-literate, groups whose cultural and linguistic backgrounds may make hazard communication complex. Categories for focus groups are recommended in the Table A6.2 below.

A6.4.2.2   At least 2 focus groups are recommended per category. However, where results from a focus group in one category (e.g. non-literate farm workers) appear highly similar to an analogous group (e.g. non-literate non-agricultural workers), it may be possible to dispense with further groups. This should only be done if the testers are confident that no different results would be anticipated from additional testing. In general, once findings from different focus groups are consistent, it is recommended to proceed directly to the main evaluation (Modules 2 onward). Where findings appear vastly discrepant, or where inadequate information to inform the rest of the instrument has been obtained, it is recommended to continue assembling focus groups until such information is obtained. Under such circumstances, testing until results are consistent or clarity is achieved may require more groups than the 2 per category recommended.

A6.4.2.3   Focus group participants should preferably not be the same workers included in the testing under Modules 2 to 11 as some learning will take place through the focus group itself. Groups should aim, wherever possible, to be homogenous for language, inasmuch as all participants should be able to communicate in at least one common language.

A6.5   Questionnaire and experimental design

A6.5.1   Different sub-populations of working and non-working people will have different experiences that influence their comprehension of hazard communication messages. Modules 2 to 8, and Module 10 will test comprehension under different experimental conditions. Sample size calculations combined with considerations of logistical ease suggest that the minimum numbers of subjects to be tested are those contained in the Table A6.2 below. Modules 6 (effect of label font and layout on comprehensibility) and 9 (simulation test) include comparisons of different label types (8 and 11 strata respectively). Thus, larger numbers are needed for these modules to generate sufficient cases within each stratum. The other interview Modules (3, 4, 5, 7 and 8) have fewer strata (vary from one to four maximum) and thus can be managed with fewer subjects. Users of this instrument may choose to apply all the modules to all participants, in which case the minimum number of participants recommended is as for Modules 6 and 9 in Table A6.2. Modules 2 and 10 must be completed by all participants as indicated.

A6.5.2   In view of the length of the full battery of tests (see Table A6.3), it may be necessary for logistic reasons to break up the instrument by having different subjects complete only some of the modules. In this way, more participants are recruiting to the study but they complete only some parts of the evaluation. If this is the case, remember that all subjects must complete Modules 2 and 10, irrespective of how many of the other modules they complete. For example, the battery of modules could be sub-divided into sets consisting of:

(a)   Modules, 2, 3, 8 and 10;

(b)   Modules 2, 4 and 10;

(c)   Modules 2, 5, 6, 7 and 10;

(d)   Modules 2 and 11;

(e)   Modules 9, 2 and 10.

However, it is preferable that, if possible, participants are given the full battery of tests contained in the instrument, and are adequately compensated for their effort.

Table A6.2: Sample size - recommended numbers

Category	Sub-category		Focus group: Module 1	Interviews: Modules 2, 6 and 10; Simulation: Module 9	Interview: Modules 3, 4, 5, 7 and 8.
Target Group 1: Workplace a) Management	**Population 1**: Production Managers, engineering, technical		Optional	30-50[a]	25
	Population 2: Supervisory Managers in industry, agriculture		Optional	30-50[a]	25
b) Workers	Population: Farm workers	**3**. Literate	At least one group	100	50
		4. Non-literate	At least one group	100[a]	50
	Population: Workers other than in agriculture	**5**. Literate	At least one group	100	50
		6. Non-literate	At least one group	100[a]	50
Target Group 2: Transport	**Population 7**. Transport workers		Optional	30-50	25
Target Group 3: Community Residents/ Consumers/general public	**Population 8**: Literate		At least one group	100	50
	Population 9: Non-literate		At least one group	100[a]	50
	Population 10: Retailers and distributors		Optional	30-50[a]	25
Target Group 4: Emergency Responders	**Population 11**: Health Professionals, Technical Extension staff and Emergency Responders		Optional	30-50[a]	25
Target Group 5: Other	**Population 12**: Enforcement / Regulatory		Optional	30-50[a]	25

[a] *Recognizing the practical difficulties in organizing a simulation test, it is suggested that in these groups simulation testing only be carried out where resources are available and where practically feasible.*

A6.5.3   As far as possible, the selection of sub-groups should be done an as representative a sample as possible, using random selection of the population for participation. This is critical for generalizability of the results. Even where different participants are chosen from the same sub-group to complete different parts of the instrument, for reasons of length of the battery, selection of participants should emphasize representativeness. However, it is recognized that random selection may be very difficult to achieve in practice. Nonetheless, it should be borne in mind that whatever, selection is used, it should seek to generate a sample as representative as possible.

A6.5.4   Note that within the modules, randomization of subjects within the groups is essential and cannot be compromised on. Randomization is necessary for internal validity of the comparisons and is not the same as random selection of the sample, which is needed for generalizability of the study results.

A6.5.5   *Simulation studies:* Because simulations studies are relatively resource intensive exercises, it is proposed that the simulations only be conducted with limited target populations - workers, both agricultural and non-agricultural, transporters, and consumers. However, where resources permit, these simulations can easily be applied to other strata as desired.

A6.5.6   *Contamination and co-intervention*

A6.5.6.1   The testing design requires control circumstances. For this reason, the situation should be avoided where a participant is able to see or be told of the experimental materials of another participant. This will invalidate the comparisons being made where manipulation of the independent variable is key to the evaluation. Such events occurring in an experimental set up are called contamination.

A6.5.6.2   To avoid contamination, participants should avoid contact with each other whilst testing is being conducted. This may require considerable effort on the part of the testing team to ensure that chance meetings of subjects does not occur. Although difficult, every effort should be made to minimise the probability of contamination.

A6.5.6.3   A distinct but related problem is co-intervention, where both experimental groups are subjected to an intervention occurring independent of the experimental situation. This would occur when, for example, every worker in factory received detailed hazard safety training in the week before the testing was done. It may result in a masking of the effect of the different hazard communication elements and may lead to an under-estimation of the effect of different formulations of the label and SDS. Where this is not preventable, note should be taken of the possibility that co-intervention took place.

A6.5.7   *Group learning*

Module 11 is included to test comprehensibility in the context of group learning. It is applied only to workers (populations 3 to 6 in Table A6.2 above) and will need a sample separate from workers completing Modules 2 to 8. Ten groups should be tested in total including 5 groups of factory workers and 5 groups of farm workers. Groups should aim to be homogenous for literacy level and approximately equal numbers literate and non-literate groups. Each group should not be larger than 10 and not smaller than 6.

A6.5.8   *Context*

A6.5.8.1   The context under which comprehensibility testing is carried out is crucial to the accurate evaluation of meaning and understanding. This is particularly so amongst workers with little formal education who use contextual cues to improve their understanding of hazard messages. For this reason, the bulk of testing in this instrument makes use of complete labels rather than elements of a label or SDS. While well-educated subjects may find it conceptually easier to respond to the isolated elements, the interpretation of such elements may have little bearing to real world learning situations. For this reason, all testing is to be conducted using realistic labels and SDS's.

A6.5.8.2   To maximize realism, an in-site label attached to a container will be used. To attach a different label to each container may pose an unnecessary burden on the tester, so it is proposed that the label be attached to a standard container, and removed after testing. This procedure may require an assistant to the interviewer if overly burdensome for the interviewer. It is important that every visual cue be offered to subjects to maximise their possibilities of comprehension, particularly for workers with low levels of formal education who rely on contextual information to a greater degree. Therefore, the labels should be presented attached to container at all times. A Velcro strip attached to the container may make the procedure relatively simple.

A6.5.8.3   To standardize opportunities for comprehension, the actual chemicals identified in the labels will be spurious chemicals, although made to look as if they could be genuine agents. This aims to retain context, while not disadvantaging those unfamiliar with a particular chemical.

A6.5.8.4   As indicated above, users are encouraged to adapt the test materials within the limits of the experimental design requirements so that the materials appear as authentic as possible to local subjects so as to maximise context.

A6.5.9   *Sample sizes for sub-studies*

Sample sizes for the sub-studies have been calculated based on a two-sided alpha error of 0.1 and a power of 0.8, but have also been tempered by considerations of logistical feasibility. Preliminary piloting of the instrument confirms these estimates. In particular, the simulation exercise has been considered relatively selectively for a smaller number of subjects and target groups, largely because of anticipated logistical constraints.

A6.5.10   *Translations*

A6.5.10.1   Language is key to much hazard communication. Although the instrument seeks to take account as far as possible of language differences, poor and unstandardized translation may introduce considerable error into the testing. For this reason, careful attention needs to be paid to accurate translation. The following procedure should be followed:

(a)   Two persons fluent in English (the language of the current instrument) independently translate the questionnaire into the index language (the language of the target group);

(b)   Both translations are then translated back into English by a further pair of translators independent of each other and of the original translators.

A6.5.10.2   Back-translations should aim to achieve less than 5% errors on first round. Clarification of the errors in the translation should be conducted to correct ambiguities. Where possible, a combined translation should try to include all elements correctly translated and back translated from either questionnaire.

A6.5.10.3   If the latter is not possible, the translation with the lower rate of errors should be taken as the translation of preference. A second round of back translation will be necessary if errors exceed 5%.

A6.5.11   *Timing of interviews and focus groups*

A6.5.11.1   Interviews and focus groups must be set up at a convenient time for both the interviewee and their employer (when this applies). Farm workers should not be requested to attend an interview during a crucial and busy period for farmers (e.g. planting, ploughing, spraying, or harvest). Workers should be interviewed during working time and should not suffer financial loss for their participation. It is not recommended that workers participate in their own time (lunch or after hours) without adequate compensation. If workers agree to participate during lunch break, the time must be adequate and suitable recompense provided (time back, lunch provided, etc).

A6.5.11.2   Table A6.3 gives the estimated time needed for completion of individual modules based on preliminary piloting with two South African factories. Depending on the module and how skilled the administrators of the modules are, total testing time could vary from 20 minutes to 2 hours. Testing times will be prolonged with non-literate workforces.

Table A6.3: Approximate testing times for hazard communication comprehensibility testing

Module	Time (minutes)
1	60 – 120
2	30 – 45
3	45 – 75
4	75 – 105
5	20 – 30
6	20 – 30
7	20 – 30
8	45 – 75
9	30
10	30 - 45
11	120 – 180

A6.5.12   *Rating and coding of responses*

A6.5.12.1   Rating of responses to comprehensibility testing requires expert judgement as to the correctness of the response. Previous experience in Zimbabwe has shown that content analysis of open-ended responses may be feasible where observers are carefully standardized in their approach.

A6.5.12.2   This instrument requires the presence of a set of experts to conduct the rating required for comprehension. The panel of experts should be identified before commencing the study in a process outlined below:

(a)   Select a panel with a range of experience, including (one or more) employees, employers and practitioners, as well as researchers skilled in the field of coding and rating;

(b)   Convene a workshop with the panel to review the nature of potential responses to questions in each of the modules listed. Review the documentation of the GHS process and aim to arrive at consensus as to what responses would constitute the following categories:

(i)   Correct: Meaning is identical, or fully consistent with intention of the GHS construct. This includes responses which are not 100% the same as the GHS meaning but would suffice as the basis for a safety action or precaution;

(ii)   Partly correct: Some element of the meaning is correct but it would be insufficient to ensure adequate safety action or precaution;

(iii)   Incorrect: Meaning given is either completely wrong, or has very poor relation to the GHS intended meaning;

(iv)   Opposite meaning (critical confusions): Meaning given is not only incorrect but indicates an understanding opposite of the intention of the GHS system. Such a critical confusion may result in a dangerous behaviour or action;

(v)   Cannot answer/does not know;

(c)   Pilot the questionnaire amongst 5 or 10 subjects. Review the results in relation to the criteria selected;

(d)   If the results show significant discrepancy, iterate the process above until agreement reached about criteria.

A6.5.12.3   Further coding of responses to questions in the different modules is discussed under each module, where appropriate.

A6.5.13   *Analyses*

Analyses proposed for these modules are simple computations of proportions and means in relation to different strata. More complex analyses may be undertaken and are indicated in the different modules. An overall estimate for comprehensibility may be attempted by combining results from subjects in the different strata, but should be adjusted for weightings by stratum and by other demographic factors known to affect comprehensibility.

A6.5.14   *Feedback and follow up*

All subjects should be offered the opportunity of seeing the results of the comprehensibility evaluations, and to give feedback on the interview and testing procedures.

A6.5.15 *Follow up evaluation*

Subjects participating in these evaluations should be re-interviewed after 1 month and 1 year to assess retention and the medium and long-term benefits of exposure to the GHS hazard messages. Depending on resources and logistics, it may be possible to avoid re-testing on all the modules completed at baseline.

ANNEX 7

EXAMPLES OF ARRANGEMENTS
OF THE GHS LABEL ELEMENTS

Annex 7

EXAMPLES OF ARRANGEMENTS OF THE GHS LABEL ELEMENTS

The following examples are provided for illustrative purposes and are subject to further discussion and consideration by the GHS Sub-Committee.

Example 1:   **Combination packaging for a Category 2 flammable liquid**

Outer Packaging: Box with a flammable liquid transport label*
Inner Packaging: Plastic bottle with GHS hazard warning label**

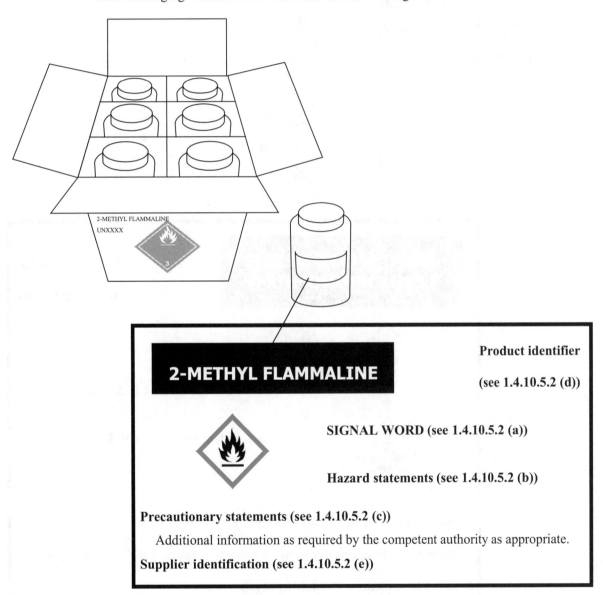

---

*   *Only the UN transport markings and labels are required for outer packagings.*

**   *A flammable liquid pictogram as specified in the "UN Recommendations on the Transport of Dangerous Goods, Model Regulations" may be used in place of the GHS pictogram shown on the inner packaging label.*

Example 2: **Combination packaging for a Category 1 specific target organ toxicant and Category 2 flammable liquid**

Outer Packaging: Box with a flammable liquid transport label*
Inner Packaging: Plastic bottle with GHS hazard warning label**

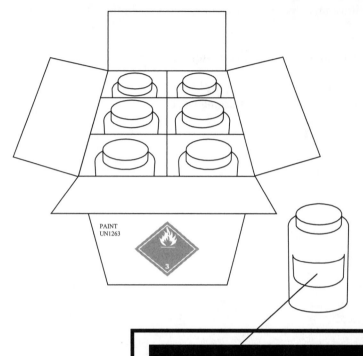

PAINT
UN1263

| **PAINT (FLAMMALINE, LEAD CHROMOMIUM)** | **Product identifier** (see 1.4.10.5.2 (d)) |

SIGNAL WORD (see 1.4.10.5.2 (a))

Hazard statements (see 1.4.10.5.2 (b))

Precautionary statements (see 1.4.10.5.2 (c))

Additional information as required by the competent authority as appropriate.

Supplier identification (see 1.4.10.5.2 (e))

---

* *Only the UN transport markings and labels are required for outer packagings.*

** *A flammable liquid pictogram as specified in the UN Recommendations on the Transport of Dangerous Goods, Model Regulations may be used in place of the GHS pictogram shown on the inner packaging label.*

Example 3: **Combination packaging for a Category 2 skin irritant and Category 2A eye irritant**

Outer Packaging: Box with no label required for transport*
Inner Packaging: Plastic bottle with GHS hazard warning label

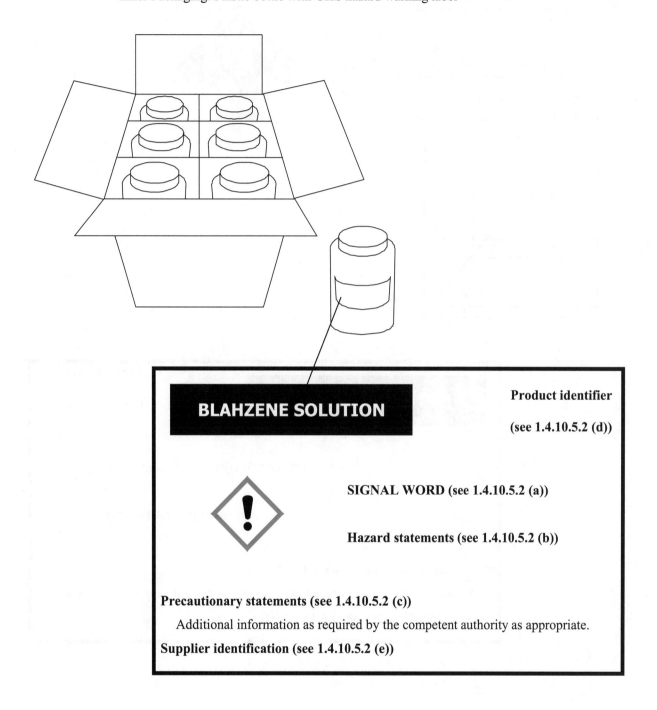

BLAHZENE SOLUTION

Product identifier

(see 1.4.10.5.2 (d))

SIGNAL WORD (see 1.4.10.5.2 (a))

Hazard statements (see 1.4.10.5.2 (b))

Precautionary statements (see 1.4.10.5.2 (c))

Additional information as required by the competent authority as appropriate.

Supplier identification (see 1.4.10.5.2 (e))

---

*   *Some competent authorities may require a GHS label on the outer packaging in the absence of a transport label.*

Example 4:   Single packaging (200 *l* drum) for a Category 2 flammable liquid

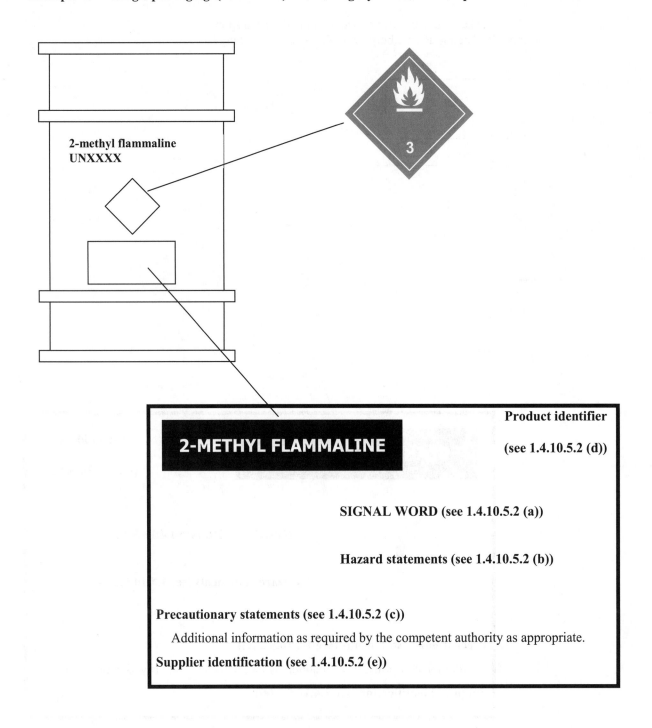

Note: *The GHS label and the flammable liquid pictogram and markings required by the "UN Recommendations on the Transport of Dangerous Goods, Model Regulations" may also be presented in a combined format.*

Example 5: **Single packaging for a Category 1 specific target organ toxicant and Category 2 flammable liquid**

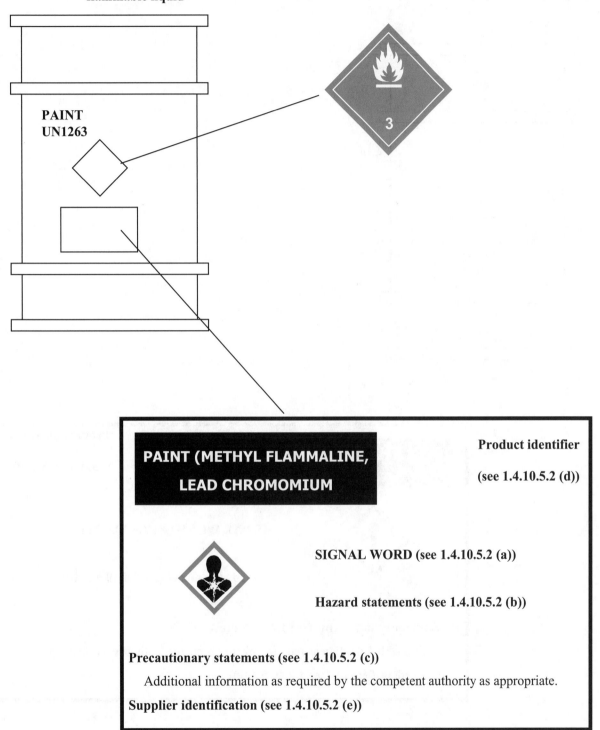

Note: *The GHS label and the flammable liquid pictogram and markings required by the "UN Recommendations on the Transport of Dangerous Goods, Model Regulations" may also be presented in a combined format.*

Example 6: **Single packaging for a Category 2 skin irritant and Category 2A eye irritant**

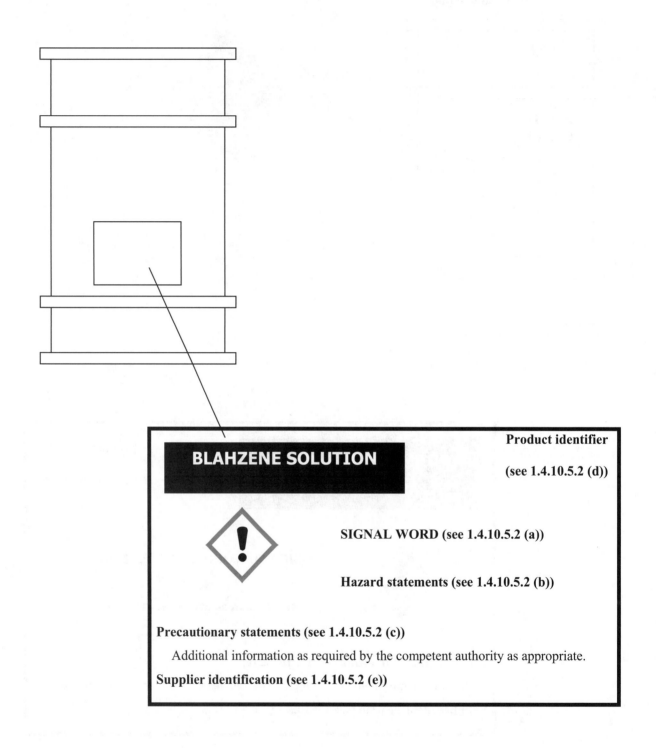

Example 7: **Additional guidance when transport and other GHS information appear on single packagings**

(a) Where transport and other GHS information appear on a single packaging (e.g. a 200 l drum), consideration must be given to ensure that the label elements are placed in a manner that addresses the needs of the different sectors;

(b) Transport pictograms must convey information immediately in an emergency situation. They must be able to be seen from a distance, as well as in conditions that are smoky or otherwise partially obscure the package;

(c) The transport-related pictograms are distinct in appearance from pictograms intended solely for non-transport purposes which helps to distinguish them;

(d) The transport pictograms may be placed on a separate panel of a GHS label to distinguish them from the other information or may be placed adjacent to the other GHS information on the packaging;

(e) The pictograms may be distinguished by adjusting their size. Generally speaking, the size of the non-transport pictograms should be proportional to the size of the text of the other label elements. This would generally be smaller than the transport-related pictograms, but such size adjustments should not affect the clarity or comprehensibility of the non-transport pictograms;

Following is an example of how such a label may appear:

Single packaging using 3 adjacent panels to convey multiple hazards.

Product classified as: (a) Category 2 Flammable liquid; (b) Category Acute 4 (by inhalation); and (c) Category 2 Specific target organ toxicant following repeated exposure.

CODE

PRODUCT NAME

COMPANY NAME

Street Address
City, State, Postal Code, Country
Phone Number
Emergency Phone Number

DIRECTIONS FOR USE:
XXXXXXXXXXXXXXXX
XXXXXXXXXXXXXXXXXX
XXXXXXXXXXXXXXXXXX

Fill weight:	XXXX	Lot Number:	XXXX
Gross weight:	XXXX	Fill Date:	XXXX
Expiration Date:	XXXX		

Danger
Keep out of the reach of children.
Read label before use.

Highly flammable liquid and vapour.
Harmful if inhaled.
May cause liver and kidney damage through prolonged or repeated exposure.

Keep container tightly closed.
Keep away from heat, hot surfaces, sparks, open flames and other ignition sources. No smoking.
Use only outdoors or in a well-ventilated area.
Do not breathe dust/fume/gas/mist/vapours/spray.
Wear protective gloves, protective clothing/eye protection/face protection [as specified....]
Ground and bond container and receiving equipment.

In case of fire: Use [as specified] to extinguish.

FIRST AID
IF INHALED: Remove person to fresh air and keep comfortable for breathing.
Call a POISON CENTER/doctor if you feel unwell.

Store in a well-ventilated place. Keep cool

UN Number
Proper shipping name

[Universal Product Code (UPC)]

ANNEX 8

AN EXAMPLE OF CLASSIFICATION IN THE GLOBALLY HARMONIZED SYSTEM

Annex 8

AN EXAMPLE OF CLASSIFICATION IN THE GLOBALLY HARMONIZED SYSTEM

A8.1   Classification proposal

The following classification proposal draws on the GHS criteria. The document includes both brief statements about the proposal for each health hazard class and details of all the available scientific evidence.

Classification is proposed for both the acute toxicity and the corrosivity of this substance based on standard and non-standard animal studies.

Proposed classification	GHS:	Acute oral toxicity Category 4
		Acute dermal (skin) toxicity Category 3
		Skin irritation/corrosion Category 1C
		Eye irritation/serious eye damage Category 1
		Flammable liquid Category 4

A8.2   Identification of the substance

1.1	EINECS Name If not in EINECS IUPAC Name	Globalene Hazexyl Systemol
		CAS No. 999-99-9 EINECS No. 222-222-2
1.2	Synonyms (state ISO name if available)	2-Hazanol Globalethylene
1.3	Molecular formula	$C_xH_yO_z$
1.4	Structural formula	
1.5	Purity (w/w)	
1.6	Significant impurities or additives	
1.7	Known uses	*Industrial:* Solvent for surface coatings and cleaning solutions. Chemical intermediate for Globalexyl UNoxy ILOate. *General public:* Toilet cleaner

A8.3   Physico-chemical characteristics

Classification as a Category 4 flammable liquid is proposed for the physico-chemical endpoints.

2.1	Physical form	Liquid
2.2	Molecular weight	146.2
2.3	Melting point/range (°C)	-45
2.4	Initial boiling point/ boiling range (°C)	208.3
2.5	Decomposition temperature	
2.6	Vapour pressure (Pa(°C))	7
2.7	Relative density (g/cm3)	0.887 - 0.890
2.8	Vapour density (air = 1)	5.04
2.9	Fat solubility (mg/kg, °C)	
2.10	Water solubility (mg/kg, °C)	Slightly soluble (0.99% w/w)
2.11	Partition coefficient (log Pow)	
2.12	Flammability flash point (°C) explosivity limits (%,v/v) auto-flammability temp. (°C)	closed cup: 81.7 open cup: 90.6 lower limit: 1.2 upper limit: 8.4
2.13	Explosivity	No data available
2.14	Oxidizing properties	
2.15	Other physico-chemical properties	

A8.4   Health and environmental characteristics

A8.4.1   *Acute toxicity*

A8.4.1.1   *Oral*

Classification under GHS Category 4 (300-2000 mg/kg) is justified.

Species	LD$_{50}$ (mg/kg)	Observations and remarks	Ref.
Rat	1480	No further details were available.	2
Rat	1500 (males) 740 (females)	The LD$_{50}$ values in mg/kg were calculated from ml/kg using the known density for EGHE of 0.89 g/cm^3.	8

A8.4.1.2   *Inhalation*

There were no deaths or signs of overt toxicity in animals exposed to the saturated vapour concentration of approximately 0.5 mg/l and therefore, the available data do not support classification.

Species	LC$_{50}$ (mg/l)	Exposure time (h)	Observations and remarks	Ref.
Rat	> 83 ppm. (approx = 0.5 mg/l).	4	No deaths, clinical signs or gross lesions occurred at 83 ppm (85 ppm is stated to be the saturated vapour concentration at room temperature).	3
Rat	Not stated	6	The animals were exposed to the saturated vapour concentration at room temperature (assumed to be 85 ppm). No deaths occurred and no signs of gross pathology were observed.	8
Rat	Not stated	8	No deaths occurred with exposure to the "saturated vapour concentration" at room temperature (assumed to be 85 ppm).	2

A8.4.1.3   *Skin*

Classification under GHS Category 3 (200-1000 mg/kg) is justified.

Species	LD$_{50}$ (mg/kg)	Observations and remarks	Ref.
Rat	790	No further details were available.	2
Rabbit (5/sex/ group)	720 (males) 830 (females)	Animals were exposed to up to 3560 mg/kg for 24 hours. All but 2 of the animals that died did so during the application period. Following the exposure period, local toxicity (erythema, oedema, necrosis and ecchymoses) was reported in an unstated number of animals, and persisted throughout the 14 day post-application observation period. Ulceration was also noted in an unstated number of animals at the end of the observation period.	8

A8.4.2   *Skin irritation/corrosion*

There are conflicting reports concerning the irritant nature of this substance. In a dedicated skin irritation study reported in the same paper as the acute dermal study, the author states that "necrosis" was observed in 3 of 6 treated rabbits which was still present on the last day of observation (day 7), along with mild to moderate erythema. Mild to marked oedema was also observed during the course of the study but had resolved within the 7-day observation period. Given that one animal showed no evidence of any skin response in this study and that only slight to moderate skin irritation was observed in the other animals the observation of "necrosis" in three of the animals is somewhat surprising. An acute dermal (skin) toxicity study in rabbits also reported signs of skin irritation including the description "necrosis" and ulceration but did not quantify the number of animals affected. In contrast to these findings, an old and briefly reported study indicated that there was little or no indication of skin irritation in rabbits.

Similarly mixed skin irritation findings have been observed with a closely related substance, for which both necrosis and no skin irritation has been reported. In addition a secondary source indicates that some other similar substances cause "moderate" skin irritation, and that prolonged exposure to these group of substances may cause burns. However, much shorter chain similar substances are not considered to be skin irritants.

It was considered that the reported necrosis in both the acute dermal and skin irritation studies cannot be dismissed and, taken together with the findings seen with structurally similar substances, this justifies classification. There are three Categories under the GHS for classification as corrosive. The data do not match the criteria readily, but Category 1C would be appropriate since the necrotic lesions observed occurred after an exposure period of 4 hours. There is no evidence to suggest that significantly shorter exposures would produce skin corrosion.

Species	No. of animals	Exposure time (h)	Conc. (w/w)	Dressing: (occlusive, semi-occlusive, open)	Observations and remarks (specify degree and nature of irritation and reversibility)	Ref.
Rabbit	6	4	0.5 ml of 100%	Occlusive	No signs of irritation were observed in one animal, and only slight erythema (grade 1) in another on day 1, which had resolved by day 7. Four animals showed a mild to moderate erythema (grade 1-2) and a mild to marked oedema (grade 1-3) after removal of the dressing. The oedema had resolved by day 7 post-exposure. "Necrosis" at the application site was reported in 3/6 rabbits from day 1 until the end of the observation period on day 7. Desquamation was observed in 4/6 rabbits on day 7.	8
Rabbit (albino)	5	24	100% (volume not stated)	Not stated	Little or no signs of skin irritation were found in this poorly reported study.	2

A8.4.3   *Serious damage to eyes/eye irritation*

The only available study involved exposure of rabbits to considerably lower amounts of the test substance than the standard protocols for this endpoint recommend. Relatively severe (e.g. conjunctival redness grade 3) but reversible effects were seen. It is predictable that under standard test conditions, the effects on the eye would be very severe and consequently GHS Category 1 (irreversible effects on the eye) would be justified.

Species	No. of animals	Conc. (w/w)	Observations and remarks (specify degree and nature if irritation, any serious lesions, reversibility)	Ref.
Rabbit	6	0.005 ml of 100%	One hour post-instillation conjunctival redness (grade 3) and discharge (grade 2.8) observed. The mean scores for the 24, 48 and 72 hour readings for corneal opacity, iris, conjunctival redness, chemosis and discharge were all approx 0.5. All lesions had resolved by day 7.	8
Rabbit	60	1 and 5%	A report in the secondary literature of severe eye injury observed in rabbits associated with instillation of an unstated amount of 5%, could not be substantiated as the information was not found in the reference stated.	1

A8.4.4   *Skin and respiratory sensitization*

No data are available. There are no additional grounds for concern (e.g. structure activity relationships) and no classification proposed.

A8.4.5   *Specific target organ toxicity following single or repeated exposure*

A8.4.5.1   *Toxicity following single exposure*

There is no reliable information available about the potential of this substance to produce specific, non-lethal target organ toxicity arising from a single exposure. Therefore, under GHS, no classification for specific target organ toxicity (STOT) single exposure is proposed.

A8.4.5.2   *Toxicity following repeated exposure*

A8.4.5.2.1   Oral

No oral repeat dose studies or human evidence are available and therefore no classification is proposed.

A8.4.5.2.2   Inhalation

There was no evidence of adverse toxicity in a 13-week rat inhalation study at 0.43 mg/l (approx. 72 ppm), an exposure level close to the saturated vapour concentration. No classification is justified according to GHS criteria.

Species	conc. mg/l	Exposure time (h)	Duration of treatment	Observations and remarks (specify group size, NOEL, effects of major toxicological significance)	Ref.
Rat (F344) 20/sex / group (plus 10/ sex/group - 4 week recovery groups)	0.12, 0.24 and 0.425	6	5 d/wk for 13 weeks	No deaths occurred. Decreased weight gain was observed in high dose animals of both sexes and medium dose females. There were no toxicologically significant changes in haematological or urinalysis parameters. High dose females showed an increase in alkaline phosphatase. High and medium dose males showed a statistically significant increase in absolute and relative kidney weight. A small increase in absolute liver weight (12%) was observed in high dose females. However, there were no gross or histopathological changes in any organs examined.	3

A8.4.5.2.3   Dermal

Unquantified haematological changes were reported in rabbits exposed to 444 mg/kg dermally for 11 days. However, due to the limited information provided, no conclusions can be drawn from this study and no classification is proposed.

Species	Dose mg/kg	Exposure time (h)	Duration of treatment	Observations and remarks (specify group size, NOEL, effects of major toxicological significance)	Ref.
Rabbit	0, 44, 222 and 444	6	9 doses applied over 11 days	This is an unpublished study reported in the secondary literature. Unquantified decreases in haematological parameters were noted in top dose animals. No description of local effects was provided.	1

A8.4.6   *Carcinogenicity (including chronic toxicity studies)*

No data available – no classification proposed.

A8.4.7   *Germ cell mutagenicity*

Negative results have been reported *in vitro* from Ames, cytogenetics, and gene mutation tests reported in the secondary literature. There are no *in vivo* data available. These data do not support classification.

In vitro studies

Test	Cell type	Conc. range	Observations and remarks	Ref.
Ames	Salmonella (strains unstated)	0.3-15 mg/plate	**Negative**, in the presence and absence of metabolic activation. This is an unpublished study described in a secondary source and no further information is available.	5
IVC	CHO	0.1-0.8 mg/ml (-S9), 0.08-0.4 mg/ml (+S9)	**Negative**, in the presence and absence of metabolic activation. This is an unpublished study described in a secondary source and no further information is available.	6
Gene mutation	CHO	Not stated	**Negative**. This is an unpublished study described in a secondary source and no further information is available.	7
SCE	CHO	Not stated	**Negative**. This is an unpublished study described in a secondary source and no further information is available.	7

A8.4.8   *Reproductive toxicity-Fertility*

No data available – no classification proposed.

A8.4.9   *Reproductive toxicity*

There was no evidence of reproductive toxicity in rats or rabbits following inhalation exposure to levels inducing slight maternal toxicity. It is noted that although shorter chain related substances are classified for reproductive toxicity, this toxicity decreases with increasing chain length such that there is no evidence of this hazard. No classification is proposed.

Species	Route	Dose	Exposure	Observations and remarks	Ref.
Rat	Inhalation	21, 41 and 80 ppm (0.12, 0.24 and 0.48 mg/l)	days 6-15 of gestation	The substance was tested up to approximately the saturated vapour concentration. Decreases in dam body weight gain, associated with decreases in food consumption, were observed in the medium and high dose groups during the exposure period. There was no evidence of reproductive toxicity.	4
Rabbit	Inhalation	21, 41 and 80 ppm (0.12, 0.24 and 0.48 mg/l)	days 6-18 of gestation	The substance was tested up to approximately the saturated vapour concentration. Decrease in absolute body weight during the exposure period was observed in the high dose animals. There was no evidence of reproductive toxicity.	4

A8.5   References

1.   Patty, F. (Ed.) (1994). Industrial Hygiene and Toxicology. 4th Ed. pxxxx-xx New York: Wiley-Interscience.

2.   Smyth, H.F., Carpenter, C.P., Weil, C.S. and Pozzani, U.S. (1954). Range finding toxicity data. *Arch. Ind. Hyg. Occup. Med.*

3.   Fasey, Headrick, Silk and Sundquist (1987). Acute, 9-day, and 13-week vapour inhalation studies on Globalene Hazexyl Systemol. *Fundamental and Applied Toxicology.*

4.   Wyeth, Gregor, Pratt and Obadia (1989). Evaluation of the developmental toxicity of Globalene Hazexyl Systemol in Fischer 344 rats and New Zealand White rabbits. *Fundamental and Applied Toxicology.*

5.   Etc.

ANNEX 9

GUIDANCE ON HAZARDS TO THE
AQUATIC ENVIRONMENT

Annex 9

GUIDANCE ON HAZARDS TO THE AQUATIC ENVIRONMENT

CONTENTS

Annex 9

GUIDANCE ON HAZARDS TO THE AQUATIC ENVIRONMENT[1]

A9.1   Introduction

A9.1.1   In developing the set of criteria for identifying substances hazardous to the aquatic environment, it was agreed that the detail needed to properly define the hazard to the environment resulted in a complex system for which some suitable guidance would be necessary. Therefore, the purpose of this document is twofold:

        (a)   to provide a description of and guidance to how the system will work;

        (b)   to provide a guidance to the interpretation of data for use in applying the classification criteria.

A9.1.2   The hazard classification scheme has been developed with the object of identifying those substances that present, through the intrinsic properties they possess, a danger to the aquatic environment. In this context, the aquatic environment is taken as the aquatic ecosystem in freshwater and marine, and the organisms that live in it. For most substances, the majority of data available addresses this environmental compartment. The definition is limited in scope in that it does not, as yet, include aquatic sediments, nor higher organisms at the top end of the aquatic food-chain, although these may to some extent be covered by the criteria selected.

A9.1.3   Although limited in scope, it is widely accepted that this compartment is both vulnerable, in that it is the final receiving environment for many harmful substances, and the organisms that live there are sensitive. It is also complex since any system that seeks to identify hazards to the environment must seek to define those effects in terms of wider effects on ecosystems rather than on individuals within a species or population. As will be described in detail in the subsequent sections, a limited set of specific properties of substances have been selected through which the hazard can be best described: acute aquatic toxicity; chronic aquatic toxicity; lack of degradability; and potential or actual bioaccumulation. The rationale for the selection of these data as the means to define the aquatic hazard will be described in more detail in Section A9.2.

A9.1.4   This annex is limited at this stage, to the application of the criteria to substances. The term substances covers a wide range of chemicals, many of which pose difficult challenges to a classification system based on rigid criteria. The following sections will thus provide some guidance as to how these challenges can be dealt with based both on experience in use and clear scientific rationale. While the harmonized criteria apply most easily to the classification of individual substances of defined structure (see definition in Chapter 1.2), some materials that fall under this category are frequently referred to as "complex mixtures". In most cases they can be characterized as a homologous series of substances with a certain range of carbon chain length/number or degree of substitution. Special methodologies have been developed for testing which provides data for evaluating the intrinsic hazard to aquatic organisms, bioaccumulation and degradation. More specific guidance is provided in the separate sections on these properties. For the purpose of this guidance document, these materials will be referred to as "complex substances" or "multi-component substances".

A9.1.5   Each of these properties (i.e. acute aquatic toxicity, chronic aquatic toxicity, degradability, bioaccumulation) can present a complex interpretational problem, even for experts. While internationally agreed testing guidelines exist and should be used for any and all new data produced, many data usable in classification will not have been generated according to such standard tests. Even where standard tests have been used, some substances, such as complex substances, hydrolytically unstable substances, polymers etc, present difficult interpretational problems when the results have to be used within the classification scheme.

---

[1]   *OECD Environment, Health and Safety Publications, Series on Testing and Assessment, No 27, Environment Directorate, Organization for economic Co-operation and Development, April 2001.*

Thus data are available for a wide variety of both standard and non-standard test organisms, both marine and freshwater, of varying duration and utilizing a variety of endpoints. Degradation data may be biotic or abiotic and can vary in environmental relevance. The potential to bioaccumulate can, for many organic chemicals, be indicated by the octanol-water partition coefficient. It can however be affected by many other factors and these will also need to be taken into account.

A9.1.6   It is clearly the objective of a globally harmonized system that, having agreed on a common set of criteria, a common data-set should also be used so that once classified, the classification is globally accepted. For this to occur, there must first be a common understanding of the type of data that can be used in applying the criteria, both in type and quality, and subsequently a common interpretation of the data when measured against the criteria. For that reason, it has been felt necessary to develop a transparent guidance document that would seek to expand and explain the criteria in such a way that a common understanding of their rationale and a common approach to data interpretation may be achieved. This is of particular importance since any harmonized system applied to the "universe of chemicals" will rely heavily on self-classification by manufacturers and suppliers, classifications that must be accepted across national boundaries without always receiving regulatory scrutiny. This guidance document, therefore, seeks to inform the reader, in a number of key areas, and as a result lead to classification in a consistent manner, thus ensuring a truly harmonized and self-operating system.

A9.1.7   Firstly, it will provide a detailed description of the criteria, a rationale for the criteria selected, and an overview of how the scheme will work in practice (Section A9.2). This section will address the common sources of data, the need to apply quality criteria, how to classify when the data-set is incomplete or when a large data-set leads to an ambiguous classification, and other commonly encountered classification problems.

A9.1.8   Secondly, the guidance will provide detailed expert advice on the interpretation of data derived from the available databases, including how to use non-standard data, and specific quality criteria that may apply for individual properties. The problems of data interpretation for "difficult substances", those substances for which standard testing methods either do not apply or give difficult interpretational problems, will be described and advice provided on suitable solutions. The emphasis will be on data interpretation rather than testing since the system will, as far as possible, rely on the best available existing data and data required for regulatory purposes. The four core properties, acute and chronic aquatic toxicity (Section A9.3), degradability (Section A9.4) and bioaccumulation (Section A9.5) are treated separately.

A9.1.9   The range of interpretational problems can be extensive and as a result such interpretation will always rely on the ability and expertise of the individuals responsible for classification. However, it is possible to identify some commonly occurring difficulties and provide guidance that distils accepted expert judgement that can act as an aid to achieving a reliable and consistent result. Such difficulties can fall into a number of overlapping issues:

a)   The difficulty in applying the current test procedures to a number of types of substance;

(b)   The difficulty in interpreting the data derived both from these "difficult to test" substances and from other substances;

(c)   The difficulty in interpretation of diverse data-sets derived from a wide variety of sources.

A9.1.10   For many organic substances, the testing and interpretation of data present no problems when applying both the relevant OECD Guideline and the classification criteria. There are a number of typical interpretational problems, however, that can be characterized by the type of substance being studied. These are commonly called "difficult substances":

(a)   poorly soluble substances: these substances are difficult to test because they present problems in solution preparation, and in concentration maintenance and verification during aquatic toxicity testing. In addition, many available data for such substances have been produced using "solutions" in excess of the water solubility resulting in major interpretational problems in defining the true $L(E)C_{50}$ or NOEC for the purposes of classification. Interpretation of the partitioning behaviour can also be problematic where the poor solubility in water and octanol may be compounded by insufficient sensitivity in the analytical method. Water solubility may be difficult to determine and is frequently recorded as simply being less than the detection limit, creating problems in interpreting both aquatic toxicity and bioaccumulation studies. In biodegradation studies, poor solubility may result in low bioavailability and thus lower than expected biodegradation rates. The specific test method or the choice of procedures used can thus be of key importance;

(b) unstable substances: such substances that degrade (or react) rapidly in the test system present both testing and interpretational problems. It will be necessary to determine whether the correct methodology has been used, whether it is the substance or the degradation/reaction product that has been tested, and whether the data produced is relevant to the classification of the parent substance;

(c) volatile substances: such substances that can clearly present testing problems when used in open systems should be evaluated to ensure adequate maintenance of exposure concentrations. Loss of test material during biodegradation testing is inevitable in certain methods and will lead to misinterpretation of the results;

(d) complex or multi-component substances: such substances, for example, hydrocarbon mixtures, frequently cannot be dissolved into a homogeneous solution, and the multiple components make monitoring impossible. Consideration therefore needs to be given to using the data derived from the testing of water accommodated fractions (WAFs) for aquatic toxicity, and the utilization of such data in the classification scheme. Biodegradation, bioaccumulation, partitioning behaviour and water solubility all present problems of interpretation, where each component of the mixture may behave differently;

(e) polymers: such substances frequently have a wide range of molecular masses, with only a fraction being water soluble. Special methods are available to determine the water soluble fraction and these data will need to be used in interpreting the test data against the classification criteria;

(f) inorganic compounds and metals: such substances, which can interact with the media, can produce a range of aquatic toxicities dependant on such factors as pH, water hardness etc. Difficult interpretational problems also arise from the testing of essential elements that are beneficial at certain levels. For metals and inorganic metal compounds, the concept of degradability as applied to organic compounds has limited or no meaning. Equally the use of bioaccumulation data should be treated with care;

(g) surface active substances: such substances can form emulsions in which the bioavailablity is difficult to ascertain, even with careful solution preparation. Micelle formation can result in an overestimation of the bioavailable fraction even when "solutions" are apparently formed. This presents significant problems of interpretation in each of the water solubility, partition coefficient, bioaccumulation and aquatic toxicity studies;

(h) ionizable substances: such substances can change the extent of ionization according to the level of counter ions in the media. Acids and bases, for example, will show radically different partitioning behaviour depending on the pH;

(i) coloured substances: such substance can cause problems in the algal/aquatic plant testing because of the blocking of incident light;

(j) impurities: some substances can contain impurities that can change in % and in chemical nature between production batches. Interpretational problems can arise where either or both the toxicity and water solubility of the impurities are greater than the parent substance, thus potentially influencing the toxicity data in a significant way.

A9.1.11   These represent some of the problems encountered in establishing the adequacy of data, interpreting the data and applying that data to the classification scheme. Detailed guidance on how to deal with these problems, as well as other issues related will be presented in the following sections. The interpretation of data on acute and on chronic aquatic toxicity will be covered in Section A9.3. This section will deal with the specific interpretational problems encountered for the above "difficult substances", including providing some advice on when and how such data can be used within the classification scheme. Also covered will be a general description of the test data used and the testing methodologies suitable for producing such data.

A9.1.12   A wide range of degradation data are available that must be interpreted according to the criteria for rapid degradability. Guidance is thus needed on how to use these data obtained by employing non-standard test methods, including the use of half-lives where these are available, of primary degradation, of soil degradation rates and their suitability for extrapolation to aquatic degradation and of environmental degradation rates. A short description of estimation techniques for evaluating degradability in relation to the classification criteria is also included. This guidance will be provided in Section A9.4.

A9.1.13   Methods by which the potential to bioaccumulate can be determined will be described in Section A9.5. This section will describe the relationship between the partition coefficient criteria and the bioconcentration factor (BCF), provide guidance on the interpretation of existing data, how to estimate the partition coefficient by the use of QSARs when no experimental data are available and in particular deal with the specific problems identified above for difficult substances. The problems encountered when dealing with substances of high molecular mass will also be covered.

A9.1.14   A section is also included which covers general issues concerning the use of QSARs within the system, when and how they may be used, for each of the three properties of concern. As a general approach, it is widely accepted that experimental data should be used rather than QSAR data when such data are available. The use of QSARs will thus be limited to such times when no reliable data are available. Not all substances are suitable for the application of QSAR estimations, however, and the guidance in Section A9.6 will address this issue.

A9.1.15   Finally, a section is devoted to the special problems associated with the classification of metals and their compounds. Clearly, for these compounds, a number of the specific criteria such as biodegradability and octanol-water partition coefficient cannot be applied although the principle of lack of destruction via degradation, and bioaccumulation remain important concepts. Thus it is necessary to adopt a different approach. Metals and metal compounds can undergo interactions with the media which affect the solubility of the metal ion, partitioning from the water column, and the species of metal ion that exists in the water column. In the water column, it is generally the dissolved metal ions which are of concern for toxicity. The interaction of the substance with the media may either increase or decrease the level of ions and hence toxicity. It is thus necessary to consider whether metal ions are likely to be formed from the substance and dissolve in the water, and if so whether they are formed rapidly enough to cause concern. A scheme for interpreting the results from this type of study is presented in Section A9.7.

A9.1.16   While the Guidance Document provides useful advice on how to apply the criteria to a wide variety of situations, it remains a guidance only. It cannot hope to cover all situations that arise in classification. It should therefore be seen as a living document that in part describes the fundamental principles of the system, e.g. hazard based rather than risk based, and the fixed criteria. It must also, in part, be a repository for the accumulated experience in using the scheme to include the interpretations which allow the apparently fixed criteria to be applied in a wide variety of non-standard situations.

A9.2   The harmonized classification scheme

A9.2.1   *Scope*

The criteria were developed taking into account existing systems for hazard classification, such as EU- Supply and Use System, the Canadian and US Pesticide systems, GESAMP hazard evaluation procedure, IMO Scheme for Marine Pollutant, the European Road and Rail Transport Scheme (RID/ADR), and the US Land Transport. These systems include supply and subsequent use of chemicals, the sea transport of chemicals as well as transport of chemicals by road and rail. The harmonized criteria are therefore intended to identify hazardous chemicals in a common way for use throughout all these systems. To address the needs for all different sectors (transport, supply and use) it was necessary to create two different sub-classes, one sub-class for short-term (acute) aquatic hazards, consisting of three categories and one sub-class for lont-term (chronic) aquatic hazards, consisting of 4 categories. The short-term (acute) classification sub-class makes provision for two short-term (acute) hazard categories (Acute 2 and 3) not normally used when considering packaged goods. For chemicals transported in bulk, there are a number of regulatory decisions that can uniquely arise because of the bulk quantities being considered. For these situations, for example where decisions are required on the ship type to be used, consideration of all short-term (acute) hazard categories as well as the long-term (chronic) hazard categories are considered important. The following paragraphs describe in detail the criteria to be used in defining each of these hazard categories.

A9.2.2 *Classification categories and criteria*

The hazard categories for acute and chronic aquatic toxicity and their related criteria are set out in Chapter 4.1, paragraph 4.1.2.4 and table 4.1.1.

A9.2.3 *Rationale*

A9.2.3.1 The harmonized system for classification recognizes that the intrinsic hazard to aquatic organisms is represented by both the acute and chronic or long-term toxicity of a substance, the relative importance of which is determined by the specific regulatory regimes in operation. Distinction can be made between the short-term (acute) hazard and the long-term (chronic) hazard and therefore hazard classes are defined for both properties representing a gradation in the level of hazard identified. Clearly the hazard identified by Chronic 1 is more severe than Chronic 2. Since the acute (short-term) hazard and long-term (chronic) hazard represent distinct types of hazard, they are not comparable in terms of their relative severity. Both hazard sub-classes should be applied independently for the classification of substances to establish a basis for all regulatory systems.

A9.2.3.2 The principal hazard classes defined by the criteria relate largely to the potential for long-term (chronic) hazard. This reflects the overriding concern with respect to chemicals in the environment, namely that the effects caused are usually sub-lethal, e.g. effects on reproduction, and caused by longer-term exposure. While recognizing that the long-term (chronic) hazard represents the principal concern, particularly for packaged goods where environmental release would be limited in scope, it must also be recognized that chronic toxicity data are expensive to generate and generally not readily available for most substances. On the other hand, acute toxicity data are frequently readily available, or can be generated to highly standardised protocols. It is this acute toxicity which has therefore been used as the core property in defining both the acute and the long-term (chronic) hazard if no adequate chronic test data are available. Nevertheless, it has been recognized that chronic toxicity data, if available should be preferred in defining the long-term (chronic) hazard category.

A9.2.3.3 The combination of chronic toxicity and intrinsic fate properties reflects the potential hazard of a substance. Substances that do not rapidly degrade have a higher potential for longer term exposures and therefore should be classified in a more severe category than substances which are rapidly degradable (see A9.3.3.2.2).

A9.2.3.4 While recognizing that acute toxicity itself is not a sufficiently accurate predictor of chronic toxicity to be used solely and directly for establishing hazard, it is considered that, in combination with either a potential to bioaccumulate (i.e. a log K_{ow} $\geq$4 unless BCF <500) or potential longer-term exposure (i.e. lack of rapid degradation) it can be used as a suitable surrogate for classification purposes. Substances rapidly biodegrading that show acute toxicity with a significant degree of bioaccumulation will normally show chronic toxicity at a significantly lower concentration. Equally substances that do not rapidly degrade have a higher potential for giving rise to longer term exposures which again may result in long-term toxicity being realized. Thus, for example, in absence of adequate chronic test data, category Chronic 1 should be assigned if either of the following criteria are met:

> (a) L(E)C$_{50}$ for any appropriate aquatic species $\leq$1 mg/l *and* a potential to bioaccumulate (log K_{ow} $\geq$4 unless BCF <500);

(b) $L(E)C_{50}$ for any appropriate aquatic species ≤1 mg/l <u>and</u> a lack of rapid degradation.

A9.2.3.5   The precise definitions of the core elements of this system are described in detail in sections A9.3, A9.4 and A9.5.

A9.2.3.6   For some poorly soluble substances, which are normally considered as those having a water solubility < 1 mg/l, no acute toxicity is expressed in toxicity tests performed at the solubility limit. If for such a substance, however, the BCF ≥ 500, or if absent, the log K_{ow} ≥ 4 (indicating a bioaccumulating potential) and the substance is also not rapidly degradable, a safety net classification is applied, Chronic 4. For these types of substance the exposure duration in short term tests may well be too short for a steady state concentration of the substance to be reached in the test organisms. Thus, even though no acute toxicity has been measured in a short term (acute) test, it remains a real possibility that such non-rapidly degradable and bioaccumulative substances may exert chronic effects, particularly since such low degradability may lead to an extended exposure period in the aquatic environment.

A9.2.3.7   In defining aquatic toxicity, it is not possible to test all species present in an aquatic ecosystem. Representative species are therefore chosen which cover a range of trophic levels and taxonomic groupings. The taxa chosen, fish, crustacea and aquatic plants that represent the "base-set" in most hazard profiles, represent a minimum data-set for a fully valid description of hazard. The lowest of the available toxicity values will normally be used to define the hazard category. Given the wide range of species in the environment, the three tested can only be a poor surrogate and the lowest value is therefore taken for cautious reasons to define the hazard category. In doing so, it is recognized that the distribution of species sensitivity can be several orders of magnitude wide and that there will thus be both more and less sensitive species in the environment. Thus, when data are limited, the use of the most sensitive species tested gives a cautious but acceptable definition of the hazard. There are some circumstances where it may not be appropriate to use the lowest toxicity value as the basis for classification. This will usually only arise where it is possible to define the sensitivity distribution with more accuracy than would normally be possible, such as when large data-sets are available. Such large data-sets should be evaluated with due caution.

A9.2.4   *Application*

A9.2.4.1   Generally speaking, in deciding whether a substance should be classified, a search of appropriate databases and other sources of data should be made for the following data elements:

(a)   water solubility;

(b)   acute aquatic toxicity ($L(E)C_{50}s$);

(c)   chronic aquatic toxicity (NOECs and/or equivalent ECx);

(d)   available degradation (and specifically evidence of ready biodegradability);

(e)   stability data, in water;

(f)   fish bioconcentration factor (BCF);

(g)   octanol/water partition coefficient (log K_{ow});

The water solubility and stability data, although not used directly in the criteria, are nevertheless important since they are a valuable help in the data interpretation of the other properties (see A9.1.10).

A9.2.4.2   To classify, a review should first be made of the available aquatic toxicity data. It will be necessary to consider all the available data and select those which meet the necessary quality criteria for classification. If there are no data available that meet the quality criteria required by the internationally standardized methods, it will be necessary to examine any available data to determine whether a classification can be made. If the data indicate that the acute aquatic toxicity $L(E)C_{50}$ is greater than 100 mg/l for soluble substances and the chronic aquatic toxicity is greater than 1 mg/l, then the substance is not classified as hazardous. There are a number of cases where no effects are observed in the test and the aquatic toxicity is thus recorded as a > water solubility value, i.e. there is no acute toxicity within the range of the water solubility in the test media. Where this is the case, and the water solubility in the test media is ≥ 1 mg/l, again, no classification need be applied.

A9.2.4.3   If chronic aquatic toxicity data are available, cut-off values will depend on whether the substance is rapidly degradable or not. Therefore, for non-rapidly degradable substances and those for which no information on degradation is available, the cut-off levels are higher than for those substances where rapid degradability can be confirmed (see Chapter 4.1, Tables 4.1.1 and 4.1.2).

A9.2.4.4   Where the lowest acute aquatic toxicity data are below 100 mg/l and no adequate chronic toxicity data are available, it is necessary to first decide which hazard category the toxicity falls in, and then to determine whether the chronic and/or the acute sub-class should be applied. This can simply be achieved by examining the available data on the partition coefficient, log K_{ow} and the available data on degradation. If either the log $K_{ow} \geq 4$ or the substance cannot be considered as rapidly degradable, then the appropriate long-term (chronic) hazard category and the corresponding acute (short-term) hazard category are applied independently. It should be noted that, although the log K_{ow} is the most readily available indication of a potential to bioaccumulate, an experimentally derived BCF is preferred. Where this is available, this should be used rather than the partition coefficient. In these circumstances, a BCF ≥ 500 would indicate bioaccumulation sufficient to classify in the appropriate long-term (chronic) hazard category. If the substance is both rapidly degradable and has a low potential to bioaccumulate (BCF < 500 or, if absent, log $K_{ow} < 4$) then it should not be assigned to a long-term (chronic) hazard category, unless the chronic toxicity data indicate otherwise (see A9.2.4.3).

A9.2.4.5   For poorly soluble substances, generally speaking, those with a water solubility in the test media of < 1 mg/l, for which no aquatic toxicity has been found, should be further examined to determine whether Chronic Category 4 needs to be applied. Thus, if the substance is both not rapidly degradable and has a potential to bioaccumulate (BCF ≥ 500 or, if absent log $K_{ow} \geq 4$), the Chronic 4 should be applied.

A9.2.5   *Data availability*

The data used to classify a substance can be drawn from data required for regulatory purposes as well as the relevant literature, although a number of internationally recognized data-bases exist which can act as a good starting point. Such databases vary widely in quality and comprehensiveness and it is unlikely that any one database will hold all he information necessary for classification to be made. Some databases specialize in aquatic toxicity and others in environmental fate. There is an obligation on the chemical supplier to make the necessary searches and checks to determine the extent and quality of the data available and to use it in assigning the appropriate hazard category.

A9.2.6   *Data quality*

A9.2.6.1   The precise use of the available data will be described in the relevant section but, as a general rule, data generated to standard international guidelines and to GLP is to be preferred over other types of data. Equally, however, it is important to appreciate that classification can be made based on the best available data. Thus if no data is available which conforms to the quality standard detailed above, classification can still be made provided the data used is not considered invalid. To assist this process, a quality scoring guide has been developed and used extensively in a number of fora and generally conforms to the following categories:

(a)   Data derived from official data sources that have been validated by regulatoryauthorities, such as EU Water Quality Monographs, US-EPA Water Quality Criteria. These data can be considered as valid for classification purposes. No assumption should be made that these are the only data available, however, and due regard should be given to the date of the relevant report. Newly available data may not have been considered;

(b)   Data derived from recognized international guidelines (e.g. OECD Guidelines) or national guidelines of equivalent quality. Subject to the data interpretation issues raised in the following sections, these data can be used for classification;

(c)   Data derived from testing which, while not strictly according to a guideline detailed above, follows accepted scientific principles and procedures and/or has been peer reviewed prior to publication. For such data, where all the experimental detail is not recorded, some judgement may be required to determine validity. Normally, such data may be used within the classification scheme;

(d) Data derived from testing procedures which deviate significantly from standard guidelines and are considered as unreliable, should not be used in classification;

(e) QSAR data. The circumstances of use and validity of QSAR data are discussed in the relevant sections;

(f) Data derived from secondary sources such as handbooks, reviews, citation, etc. where the data quality cannot be directly evaluated. Such data should be examined where data from quality 1, 2 and 3 are not available, to determine whether it can be used. Such data should have sufficient detail to allow quality to be assessed. In determining the acceptability of these data for the purposes of classification, due regard should be given to the difficulties in testing that may have affected data quality and the significance of the reported result in terms of the level of hazard identified (see A9.3.6.2.3).

A9.2.6.2   Classification may also be made on incomplete toxicity data-sets, e.g. where data are not available on all three trophic levels. In these cases, the classification may be considered as "provisional" and subject to further information becoming available. In general, all the data available will need to be considered prior to assigning a classification. Where good quality data are not available, lower quality data will need to be considered. In these circumstances, a judgement will need to be made regarding the true level of hazard. For example, where good quality data are available for a particular species or taxa, this should be used in preference to any lower quality data which might also be available for that species or taxa. However, good quality data may not always be available for all the basic data set trophic levels. It will be necessary to consider data of lower quality for those trophic levels for which good quality data are not available. Consideration of such data, however, will also need to consider the difficulties that may have affected the likelihood of achieving a valid result. For example, the test details and experimental design may be critical to the assessment of the usability of some data, such as that from hydrolytically unstable chemicals, while less so for other chemicals. Such difficulties are described further in Section A9.3.

A9.2.6.3   Normally, the identification of hazard, and hence the classification will be based on information directly obtained from testing of the substance being considered. There are occasions, however, where this can create difficulties in the testing or the outcomes do not conform to common sense. For example, some chemicals, although stable in the bottle, will react rapidly (or slowly) in water giving rise to degradation products that may have different properties. Where such degradation is rapid, the available test data will frequently define the hazard of the degradation products since it will be these that have been tested. These data may be used to classify the parent substance in the normal way. However, where degradation is slower, it may be possible to test the parent substance and thus generate hazard data in the normal manner. The subsequent degradation may then be considered in determining whether a short-term (acute) or long-term (chronic) hazard category should apply. There may be occasions, however, when a substance so tested may degrade to give rise to a more hazardous product. In these circumstances, the classification of the parent should take due account of the hazard of the degradation product, and the rate at which it can be formed under normal environmental conditions.

A9.3   Aquatic toxicity

A9.3.1   *Introduction*

The basis for the identification of hazard to the aquatic environment for a substance is the aquatic toxicity of that substance. Classification is predicated on having toxicity data for fish, crustacea, and algae/aquatic plant available. These taxa are generally accepted as representative of aquatic fauna and flora for hazard identification. Data on these particular taxa are more likely to be found because of this general acceptance by regulatory authorities and the chemical industry. Other information on the degradation and bioaccumulation behaviour is used to better delineate the aquatic hazard. This section describes the appropriate tests for ecotoxicity, provides some basic concepts in evaluating the data and using combinations of testing results for classification, summarizes approaches for dealing with difficulty substances, and includes a brief discussion on interpretation of data quality.

A9.3.2   *Description of tests*

A9.3.2.1   For classifying substances in the harmonized system, freshwater and marine species toxicity data can be considered as equivalent data. It should be noted that some types of substances, e.g. ionizable organic chemicals or organometallic substances may express different toxicities in freshwater and marine environments. Since the purpose of classification is to characterize hazard in the aquatic environment, the result showing the highest toxicity should be chosen.

A9.3.2.2   The GHS criteria for determining health and environmental hazards should be test method neutral, allowing different approaches as long as they are scientifically sound and validated according to international procedures and criteria already referred to in existing systems for the endpoints of concern and produce mutually acceptable data. According to the proposed system (OECD 1998):

> *"Acute toxicity would normally be determined using a fish 96 hour LC50 (OECD Test Guideline 203 or equivalent), a crustacea species 48 hour EC50 (OECD Test Guideline 202 or equivalent) and/or an algal species 72 or 96 hour EC50 (OECD Test Guideline 201 or equivalent). These species are considered as surrogate for all aquatic organisms and data on other species such as the duckweed Lemna may also be considered if the test methodology is suitable."*

Chronic testing generally involves an exposure that is lingering or continues for a longer time; the term can signify periods from days to a year, or more depending on the reproductive cycle of the aquatic organism. Chronic tests can be done to assess certain endpoints relating to growth, survival, reproduction and development.

> *"Chronic toxicity data are less available than acute data and the range of testing procedures less standardised. Data generated according to the OECD Test Guidelines 210 (Fish Early Life Stage), 202 Part 2 or 211 (Daphnia Reproduction) and 201 (Algal Growth Inhibition) can be accepted. Other validated and internationally accepted tests could also be used. The NOECs or other equivalent L(E)Cx should be used."*

An OECD document describes the main statistical methods for the analysis of data of standardized ecotoxicity tests (OECD 2006).

A9.3.2.3   It should be noted that several of the OECD guidelines cited as examples for classification are being revised or are being planned for updating. Such revisions may lead to minor modifications of test conditions. Therefore, the expert group that developed the harmonized criteria for classification intended some flexibility in test duration or even species used.

A9.3.2.4   Guidelines for conducting acceptable tests with fish, crustacea, and algae can be found in many sources (OECD, 1999; EPA, 1996; ASTM, 1999; ISO EU). The OECD monograph No.11, Detailed Review Paper on Aquatic Toxicity Testing for Industrial Chemicals and Pesticides, is a good compilation of pelagic test methods and sources of testing guidance. This document is also a source of appropriate test methodologies.

A9.3.2.5   *Fish Tests*

A9.3.2.5.1   Acute testing

Acute tests are generally performed with young juveniles 0.1 - 5 g in size for a period of 96 hours. The observational endpoint in these tests is mortality. Fish larger than this range and/or durations shorter than 96 hours are generally less sensitive. However, for classification, they could be used if no acceptable data with the smaller fish for 96 hours are available or the results of these tests with different size fish or test durations would influence classification in a more hazardous category. Tests consistent with OECD Test Guideline 203 (Fish 96 hour LC50) or equivalent should be used for classification.

A9.3.2.5.2   Chronic testing

Chronic or long term tests with fish can be initiated with fertilized eggs, embryos, juveniles, or reproductively active adults. Tests consistent with OECD Test Guideline 210 (Fish Early Life Stage), the fish life-cycle test (US EPA 850.1500), or equivalent can be used in the classification scheme. Durations can vary widely depending on the test purpose (anywhere from 7 days to over 200 days). Observational endpoints can include hatching success, growth (length and weight changes), spawning success, and survival. Technically, the OECD 210 Guideline (Fish Early Life Stage) is not a "chronic" test, but a sub-chronic test on sensitive life stages. It is widely accepted as a predictor of chronic toxicity and is used as such for purposes of classification in the harmonized system. Fish early life stage toxicity data are much more available than fish life cycle or reproduction studies.

A9.3.2.6   *Crustacea tests*

A9.3.2.6.1   Acute testing

Acute tests with crustacea generally begin with first instar juveniles. For daphnids, a test duration of 48 hours is used. For other crustacea, such as mysids or others, a duration of 96 hours is typical. The observational endpoint is mortality or immobilization as a surrogate to mortality. Immobilization is defined as unresponsive to gentle prodding. Tests consistent with OECD Test Guideline 202 Part 1 (Daphnia acute) or USA-EPA OPPTS 850.1035 (Mysid acute toxicity) or their equivalents should be used for classification.

A9.3.2.6.2   Chronic testing

Chronic tests with crustacea also generally begin with first instar juveniles and continue through maturation and reproduction. For daphnids, 21 days is sufficient for maturation and the production of 3 broods. For mysids, 28 days is necessary. Observational endpoints include time to first brood, number of offspring produced per female, growth, and survival. It is recommended that tests consistent with OECD Test Guideline 202 Part 2 (Daphnia reproduction) or US-EPA 850.1350 (Mysid chronic) or their equivalents be used in the classification scheme.

A9.3.2.7   *Algae/Plant tests*

A9.3.2.7.1   Tests in algae

Algae are cultured and exposed to the test substance in a nutrient-enriched medium. Tests consistent with OECD Test Guideline 201 (Algal growth inhibition) should be used. Standard test methods employ a cell density in the inoculum in order to ensure exponential growth through the test, usually 3 to 4 days duration.

The algal test is a short-term test that provides both acute and chronic endpoints. The preferred observational endpoint in this study is algal growth rate inhibition because it is not dependent on the test design, whereas biomass depends both on growth rate of the test species as well as test duration and other elements of test design. If the endpoint is reported only as reduction in biomass or is not specified, then this value may be interpreted as an equivalent endpoint.

A9.3.2.7.2   Tests in aquatic macrophytes

The most commonly used vascular plants for aquatic toxicity tests are duckweeds (*Lemna gibba* and *Lemna minor*). The Lemna test is a short-term test and, although it provides both acute and sub-chronic endpoints, only the acute EC_{50} is used for classification in the harmonized system. The tests last for up to 14 days and are performed in nutrient enriched media similar to that used for algae, but may be increased in strength. The observational endpoint is based on change in the number of fronds produced. Tests consistent with OECD Test Guideline on Lemna (in preparation) and US-EPA 850.4400 (aquatic plant toxicity, Lemna) should be used.

A9.3.3   *Aquatic toxicity concepts*

This section addresses the use of acute and chronic toxicity data in classification, and special considerations for exposure regimes, algal toxicity testing, and use of QSARs. For a more detailed discussion of aquatic toxicity concepts, one can refer to Rand (1996).

A9.3.3.1   *Acute toxicity*

A9.3.3.1.1   Acute toxicity for purposes of classification refers to the intrinsic property of a substance to be injurious to an organism in a short-term exposure to that substance. Acute toxicity is generally expressed in terms of a concentration which is lethal to 50% of the test organisms (LC_{50}), causes a measurable adverse effect to 50% of the test organisms (e.g. immobilization of daphnids), or leads to a 50% reduction in test (treated) organism responses from control (untreated) organism responses (e.g. growth rate in algae).

A9.3.3.1.2   Substances with an acute toxicity determined to be less than one part per million (1 mg/l) are generally recognized as being very toxic. The handling, use, or discharge into the environment of these substances poses a high degree of hazard and they are classified in Chronic 1 and/or Acute 1. Decimal bands are accepted for categorizing acute toxicity above this category. Substances with an acute toxicity measured from one to ten parts per million (1 - 10 mg/l) are classified in Acute 2, from ten to one hundred parts per million (10 - 100 mg/l) are classified in Acute 3, and those over one hundred parts per million (> 100 mg/l) are regarded as practically non-toxic.

A9.3.3.2   *Chronic toxicity*

A9.3.3.2.1   Chronic toxicity, for purposes of classification, refers to the intrinsic property of a substance to cause adverse effects to aquatic organisms during exposures which are determined in relation to the life-cycle of the organism. Such chronic effects usually include a range of sublethal endpoints and are generally expressed in terms of a No Observable Effect Concentration (NOEC), or an equivalent ECx. Observable endpoints typically include survival, growth and/or reproduction. Chronic toxicity exposure durations can vary widely depending on test endpoint measured and test species used.

A9.3.3.2.2   For the classification based on chronic toxicity a differentiation is made between rapidly degradable and non-rapidly degradable substances. Substances that do rapidly degrade are classified in category Chronic 1 when a chronic toxicity determined to be ≤ 0.01 mg/l. Decimal bands are accepted for categorizing chronic toxicity above this category. Substances with a chronic toxicity measured from 0.01 to 0.1 mg/l are classified in category Chronic 2 for chronic toxicity, from 0.1 to 1.0 mg/l are classified in category Chronic 3 for chronic toxicity, and those over 1.0 mg/l are regarded as practically non-toxic. For substances that do not rapidly degrade or where no information on rapid degradation is available two chronic categories are used: Chronic 1 when a chronic toxicity determined to be ≤ 0.1 mg/l and Chronic 2 when chronic toxicity is measured from 0.1 to 1.0 mg/l.

A9.3.3.2.3   Since chronic toxicity data are less common in certain sectors than acute data, for classification schemes, the potential for chronic toxicity is, in absence of adequate chronic toxicity data, identified by appropriate combinations of acute toxicity, lack of degradability and/or the potential or actual bioaccumulation. However, where adequate chronic toxicity data exist, this shall be used in preference over the classification based on the combination of acute toxicity with degradability and/or bioaccumulation. In this context, the following general approach should be used:

(a)   If adequate chronic toxicity data are available for all three trophic levels this can be used directly to determine an appropriate long-term (chronic) hazard category;

(b)   If adequate chronic toxicity data are available for one or two trophic levels, it should be examined if acute toxicity data are available for the other trophic level(s). A potential classification is made for the trophic level(s) with chronic data and compared with that made using the acute toxicity data for the other trophic level(s). The final classification shall be made according to the most stringent outcome;

(c)   In order to remove or lower a chronic classification, using chronic toxicity data, it must be demonstrated that the NOEC(s) (or equivalent ECx) used would be suitable to remove or lower the concern for all taxa which resulted in classification based on acute data in combination with degradability, and/or bioaccumulation. This can often be achieved by using a long-term NOEC for the most sensitive species identified by the acute toxicity. Thus, if a classification has been based on a fish acute LC_{50}, it would generally not be possible to remove or lower this classification using a long-term NOEC from an invertebrate toxicity test. In this case, the NOEC would normally need to be derived from a long-term fish test of the same species or one of equivalent or greater sensitivity. Equally, if classification has resulted from the acute toxicity to more than one taxa, it is likely that NOECs from each taxa will be needed. In case of classification of a substance as Chronic 4, sufficient evidence should be provided that the NOEC or equivalent ECx for each taxa is greater than 1 mg/l or greater than the water solubility of the substances under consideration.

A9.3.3.2.4   Testing with algae/Lemna cannot be used for removing or lowering a classification because:

(a)   the algae and Lemna tests are not long-term studies;

(b)   the acute to chronic ratio is generally narrow; and

(c)   the endpoints are more consistent with the acute endpoints for other organisms.

However where classification is applied solely due to the acute toxicity ($L(E)C_{50}$) observed in single algae/aquatic plant tests, but there is evidence from a range of other algae tests that the chronic toxicity (NOECs) for this taxonomic group is in the toxicity band corresponding to a less stringent classification category or above 1mg/l, this evidence could be used to consider removing or lowering a classification. At present this approach cannot be applied to aquatic plants since no standardized chronic toxicity tests have been developed.

A9.3.3.3   *Exposure regimes*

Four types of exposure conditions are employed in both acute and chronic tests and in both freshwater and saltwater media: static, static-renewal (semi-static), recirculation, and flow-through. The choice for which test type to use usually depends on test substance characteristics, test duration, test species, and regulatory requirements.

A9.3.3.4   *Test media for algae*

Algal tests are performed in nutrient-enriched media and the use of one common constituent, EDTA, or other chelators, should be considered carefully. When testing the toxicity of organic chemicals, trace amounts of a chelator like EDTA are needed to complex micronutrients in the culture medium; if omitted, algal growth can be significantly reduced and compromise test utility. However, chelators can reduce the observed toxicity of metal test substances. Therefore, for metal compounds, it is desirable that data from tests with high concentration of chelators and/or tests with stoichiometrical excess of chelator relative to iron should be critically evaluated. Free chelator may mask heavy metal toxicity considerably, in particular with strong chelators like EDTA. However, in the absence of available iron in the medium the growth of algae can become iron limited, and consequently data from tests with no or with reduced iron and EDTA should be treated with caution.

A9.3.3.5   *Use of QSARs*

For purpose of classification, and in the absence of experimental data, QSARs can be relied upon to provide predictions of acute toxicity for fish, daphnia, and algae for non-electrolyte, non-electrophilic, and otherwise non-reactive substances (See Section A9.6 on *Use of QSAR*). Problems remain for substances such as organophosphates which operate by means of special mechanisms such as functional groups which interact with biological receptors, or which can form sulfhydryl bonds with cellular proteins. Reliable QSARs have been derived for chemicals acting by a basic narcosis mechanism. These chemicals are nonelectrolytes of low reactivity such as hydrocarbons, alcohols, ketones and certain aliphatic chlorinated hydrocarbons which produce their biological effects as a function of their partition coefficients. Every organic chemical can produce narcosis. However, if the chemical is an electrolyte or contains specific functional groups leading to non-narcotic mechanisms as well, any calculations of toxicity based on partition coefficient alone would severely underestimate the toxicity. QSARs for acute aquatic toxicity of parent compounds cannot be used to predict the effects of toxic metabolites or degradates, when these arise after a longer time period than the duration of acute tests.

A9.3.4   *Weight of evidence*

A9.3.4.1   The best quality data should be used as the fundamental basis for classification. Classification should preferably be based on primary data sources. It is essential that test conditions are clearly and completely articulated.

A9.3.4.2   Where multiple studies for a taxonomic group are available, a decision on what is the most sensitive and highest quality must be made. A judgement has to be made on a case by case basis whether a non-GLP study with a more sensitive observation is used in lieu of a GLP study. It would appear that results that indicate high toxicity from tests performed according to non-standard or non-GLP guidelines should be able to be used for classification, whereas studies, which demonstrate negligible toxicity, would require more careful consideration. Substances, which are difficult to test, may yield apparent results that are more or less severe than the true toxicity. Expert judgement would also be needed for classification in these cases.

A9.3.4.3   Where more than one acceptable test is available for the same taxonomic group, the most sensitive (the one with the lowest L(E)C50 or NOEC) is generally used for classification. However, this must be dealt with on a case-by-case basis. When larger data sets (4 or more values) are available for the same species, the geometric mean of toxicity values may be used as the representative toxicity value for that species. In estimating a mean value, it is not advisable to combine tests of different species within a taxa group or in different life stages or tested under different conditions or duration.

A9.3.5   *Difficult to test substances*

A9.3.5.1   Valid aquatic toxicity tests require the dissolution of the test substance in the water media under the test conditions recommended by the guideline. In addition, a bioavailable exposure concentration should be maintained for the duration of the test. Some substances are difficult to test in aquatic systems and guidance has been developed to assist in testing these materials (DoE 1996; ECETOC 1996; and US EPA 1996). OECD is in the process of finalizing a Guidance Document on Aquatic Toxicity testing of Difficult Substances and Mixtures (OECD, 2000). This latter document is a good source of information on the types of substances that are difficult to test and the steps needed to ensure valid conclusions from tests with these materials.

A9.3.5.2   Nevertheless, much test data exist that may have used testing methodologies which, while not in conformity with what might be considered best practice today, can still yield information suitable for application of the classification criteria. Such data require special guidance on interpretation, although ultimately, expert judgement must be used in determining data validity. Such difficult to test substances may be poorly soluble, volatile, or subject to rapid degradation due to such processes as phototransformation, hydrolysis, oxidation, or biotic degradation. When testing algae, coloured materials may interfere with the test endpoint by attenuating the light needed for cell growth. In a similar manner, substances tested as cloudy dispersions above solubility may give rise to false toxicity measurements. Loading of the water column with test material can be an issue for particulates or solids such as metals. Petroleum distillate fractions can also pose loading problems, as well as difficult interpretational problems when deciding on the appropriate concentrations for determining $L(E)C_{50}$ values. The draft Guidance Document on Aquatic Toxicity Testing of Difficult Substances and Mixtures describes the more common properties of many types of substances which are likely to pose testing difficulties.

(a)   Stability: If test chemical concentrations are expected to fall below 80% of nominal, testing, in order to be valid, may require exposure regimes which provide for renewal of the test material. Semi-static or flow-through conditions are preferred. Special problems arise, therefore, with respect to testing on algae, where the standard guidelines generally include static tests to be conducted. While alternative exposure regimes are possible for crustacea and fish, these tests are frequently conducted on static conditions as included in the internationally agreed guidelines. In these tests, a certain level of degradation as well as other relevant factors have to be tolerated and appropriate account must be taken in calculations of toxic concentrations. Some approaches on how this can be dealt with are covered in A9.3.5.6. Where degradation occurs, it is also important to consider the influence of the toxicity of the degradation products on the recorded toxicity in the test. Expert judgement will need to be exercised when deciding if the data can be used for classification;

(b)   Degradation: When a compound breaks down or degrades under test condition, expert judgement should be used in calculating toxicity for classification, including consideration of known or likely breakdown products. Concentrations of the parent material and all significant toxic degradates are desirable. If degradates are expected to be relatively non-toxic, renewable exposure regimes are desirable in order to ensure that levels of the parent compounds are maintained;

(c)   Saturation: For single component substances, classification should be based only on toxic responses observed in the soluble range, and not on total chemical loading above solubility. Frequently, data are available which indicate toxicity at levels in excess of water solubility and, while these data will often be regarded as not valid, some interpretation may be possible. These problems generally apply when testing poorly soluble substances, and guidance on how to interpret such data is included in A9.3.5.7 (see also the Guidance document on aquatic toxicity testing of difficult substances and mixtures);

(d)   Perturbation of test media: Special provisions may be needed to ensure dissolution of difficult to test substances. Such measures should not lead to significant changes in the test media when such changes are likely to lead to an increase or decrease in the apparent toxicity and hence the classification level of the test substance;

(e)   Complex substances: Many substances covered by the classification scheme are in fact mixtures, for which measurement of exposure concentrations is difficult, and in some cases impossible. Substances such as petroleum distillate fractions, polymers, substances with significant levels of impurities, etc can pose special problems since the toxic concentration is difficult to define and impossible to verify. Typical testing procedures often rely on the formation of a Water Soluble Fraction (WSF) or Water Accommodated Fraction (WAF) and data are reported in terms of loading rates. These data may be used in applying the classification criteria.

A9.3.5.3   For classification of organic compounds, it is desirable to have stabilized and analytically measured test concentrations. Although measured concentrations are preferred, classification may be based on nominal concentration studies when these are the only valid data available under certain circumstances. If the material is likely to substantially degrade or otherwise be lost from the water column, care must be taken in data interpretation and classification should be done taking the loss of the toxicant during the test into account, if relevant and possible. Additionally, metals present their own set of difficulties and are discussed separately. Table A9.3.1 lists several properties of difficult to test substances and their relevance for classification.

A9.3.5.4   In most difficult to test conditions, the actual test concentration is likely to be less than the nominal or expected test concentration. Where acute toxicities ($L(E)C_{50}s$) are estimated to be < 1 mg/l for a difficult to test substance, one can be fairly confident the classification in the Acute 1 (and Chronic 1 if appropriate) is warranted. However, if the estimated acute toxicity is greater than 1 mg/l, the estimated toxicity is likely to under-represent the toxicity. In these circumstances, expert judgement is needed to determine the acceptability of a test with a difficult to test substance for use in classification. Where the nature of the testing difficulty is believed to have a significant influence on the actual test concentration when acute toxicity is estimated to be greater than 1 mg/l and the test concentration is not measured, then the test should be used with due caution in classification.

A9.3.5.5   The following paragraphs provide some detailed guidance on some of these interpretational problems. In doing so it should be remembered that this is guidance and hard and fast rules cannot be applied. The nature of many of the difficulties mean that expert judgement must always be applied both in determining whether there is sufficient information in a test for a judgement to be made on its validity, and also whether a toxicity level can be determined suitable for use in applying the classification criteria.

A9.3.5.6   *Unstable substances*

A9.3.5.6.1   While testing procedures should ideally have been adopted which minimized the impacts of instability in the test media, in practice, in certain tests, it can be almost impossible to maintain a concentration throughout the test. Common causes of such instability are oxidation, hydrolysis, photodegradation and biodegradation. While the latter forms of degradation can more readily be controlled, such controls are frequently absent in much existing testing. Nevertheless, for some testing, particularly acute and chronic fish toxicity testing, a choice of exposure regimes is available to help minimize losses due to instability, and this should be taken into account in deciding on the test data validity.

A9.3.5.6.2   Where instability is a factor in determining the level of exposure during the test, an essential prerequisite for data interpretation is the existence of measured exposure concentrations at suitable time points throughout the test. In the absence of analytically measured concentrations at least at the start and end of test, no valid interpretation can be made and the test should be considered as invalid for classification purposes. Where measured data are available, a number of practical rules can be considered by way of guidance in interpretation:

(a)   where measured data are available for the start and end of test (as is normal for the acute Daphnia and algal tests), the $L(E)C_{50,}$ for classification purposes, may be calculated based on the geometric mean of the start and end of test concentrations. Where the end of test concentrations are below the analytical detection limit, such concentrations shall be considered to be half that detection limit;

(b)   where measured data are available at the start and end of media renewal periods (as may be available for the semi-static tests), the geometric mean for each renewal period should be calculated, and the mean exposure over the whole exposure period calculated from these data;

(c)   where the toxicity can be attributed to a degradation breakdown product, and the concentrations of this are known, the $L(E)C_{50}$ for classification purposes, may be calculated based on the geometric mean of the degradation product concentration, back calculated to the parent substance;

(d)   similar principles may be applied to measured data in chronic toxicity testing.

A9.3.5.7   *Poorly soluble substances*

A9.3.5.7.1   These substances, usually taken to be those with a solubility in water <1 mg/l, are frequently difficult to dissolve in the test media, and the dissolved concentrations will often prove difficult to measure at the low concentrations anticipated. For many substances, the true solubility in the test media will be unknown, and will often be recorded as < detection limit in purified water. Nevertheless such substances can show toxicity, and where no toxicity is found, judgement must be applied to whether the result can be considered valid for classification. Judgement should err on the side of caution and should not underestimate the hazard.

A9.3.5.7.2   Ideally, tests using appropriate dissolution techniques and with accurately measured concentrations within the range of water solubility should be used. Where such test data are available, they should be used in preference to other data. It is normal, however, particularly when considering older data, to find such substances with toxicity levels recorded in excess of the water solubility, or where the dissolved levels are below the detection limit of the analytical method. Thus, in both circumstances, it is not possible to verify the actual exposure concentrations using measured data. Where these are the only data available on which to classify, some practical rules can be considered by way of general guidance:

(a)   where the acute toxicity is recorded at levels in excess of the water solubility, the $L(E)C_{50}$ for classification purposes, may be considered to be equal to or below the measured water solubility. In such circumstances it is likely that Chronic 1 and/or Acute 1 should be applied. In making this decision, due attention should be paid to the possibility that the excess undissolved substance may have given rise to physical effects on the test organisms. Where this is considered the likely cause of the effects observed, the test should be considered as invalid for classification purposes;

(b)   where no acute toxicity is recorded at levels in excess of the water solubility, the $L(E)C_{50}$ for classification purposes may be considered to be greater than the measured water solubility. In such circumstances, consideration should be given to whether the Chronic 4 should apply. In making a decision that the substance shows no acute toxicity, due account should be taken of the techniques used to achieve the maximum dissolved concentrations. Where these are not considered as adequate, the test should be considered as invalid for classification purposes;

(c)   where the water solubility is below the detection limit of the analytical method for a substance, and acute toxicity is recorded, the $L(E)C_{50}$ for classification purposes, may be considered to be less than the analytical detection limit. Where no toxicity is observed, the $L(E)C_{50}$ for classification purposes, may be considered to be greater than the water solubility. Due consideration should also be given to the quality criteria mentioned above;

(d)   where chronic toxicity data are available, the same general rules should apply. Again, where these data cannot be validated by consideration of measured concentrations, the techniques used to achieve the maximum dissolved concentrations must be considered as appropriate.

A9.3.5.8   *Other factors contributing to concentration loss*

A number of other factors can also contribute to losses of concentration and, while some can be avoided by correct study design, interpretation of data where these factors have contributed may, from time to time, be necessary.

(a)   sedimentation: this can occur during a test for a number of reasons. A common explanation is that the substance has not truly dissolved despite the apparent absence of particulates, and agglomeration occurs during the test leading to precipitation. In these circumstances, the $L(E)C_{50}$ or NOEC for classification purposes, may be considered to be based on the end of test concentrations. Equally, precipitation can occur through reaction with the media. This is considered under instability above;

(b)   adsorption: this can occur for substances of high adsorption characteristics such as high log Kow substances. Where this occurs, the loss of concentration is usually rapid and exposure may best be characterized by the end of test concentrations;

(c)   bioaccumulation: losses may occur through the bioaccumulation of a substance into the test organisms. This may be particularly important where the water solubility is low and log K_{ow} correspondingly high. The $L(E)C_{50}$ or NOEC for classification purposes, may be calculated based on the geometric mean of the start and end of test concentrations.

A9.3.5.9   *Perturbation of the test media*

A9.3.5.9.1   Strong acids and bases may appear toxic because they may alter pH. Generally however changes of the pH in aquatic systems are normally prevented by buffer systems in the test medium. If no data are available on a salt, the salt should generally be classified in the same way as the anion or cation, i.e. as the ion that receives the most stringent classification. If the effect concentration is related to only one of the ions, the classification of the salt should take the molecular weight difference into consideration by correcting the effect concentration by multiplying with the ratio: MW_{salt}/MW_{ion}.

A9.3.5.9.2   Polymers are typically not available in aquatic systems. Dispersible polymers and other high molecular mass materials can perturb the test system and interfere with uptake of oxygen, and give rise to mechanical or secondary effects. These factors need to be taken into account when considering data from these substances. Many polymers behave like complex substances, however, having a significant low molecular mass fraction which can leach from the bulk polymer. This is considered further below.

A9.3.5.10   *Complex substances*

A9.3.5.10.1   Complex substances are characterized by a range of chemical structures, frequently in a homologous series, but covering a wide range of water solubilities and other physico-chemical characteristics. On addition to water, an equilibrium will be reached between the dissolved and undissolved fractions which will be characteristic of the loading of the substance. For this reason, such complex substances are usually tested as a WSF or WAF, and the $L(E)C_{50}$ recorded based on the loading or nominal concentrations. Analytical support data are not normally available since the dissolved fraction will itself be a complex mixtures of components. The toxicity parameter is sometimes referred to as LL_{50}, related to the lethal loading level. This loading level from the WSF or WAF may be used directly in the classification criteria.

A9.3.5.10.2   Polymers represent a special kind of complex substance, requiring consideration of the polymer type and their dissolution/dispersal behaviour. Polymers may dissolve as such without change, (true solubility related to particle size), be dispersible, or portions consisting of low molecular weight fractions may go into solution. In the latter case, in effect, the testing of a polymer is a test of the ability of low molecular mass material to leach from the bulk polymer, and whether this leachate is toxic. It can thus be considered in the same way as a complex mixture in that a loading of polymer can best characterize the resultant leachate, and hence the toxicity can be related to this loading.

Table A9.3.1: Classification of difficult test substances

Property	Nature of difficulty	Relevance for classification
Poorly water soluble	Achieving/maintaining required exposure concentration. Analysing exposure.	When toxic responses are observed above apparent solubility, expert judgement is required to confirm whether effects are due to chemical toxicity or a physical effect; if no effects are observed, it should be demonstrated that full, saturated dissolution has been achieved.
Toxic at low concentrations	Achieving/maintaining required exposure concentration. Analysing exposure.	Classified based on toxicity < 1 mg/l
Volatile	Maintaining and measuring exposure concentration.	Classification should be based on reliable measurement of concentrations.
Photo-degradable	Maintaining exposure concentrations. Toxicity of breakdown products.	Classification requires expert judgement and should be based on measured concentrations. Toxicity of significant breakdown products should be characterized.
Hydrolytically unstable	Maintaining exposure concentrations. Toxicity of breakdown products. Comparison of degradation half-lives to the exposure regimen used in testing.	Classification requires expert judgement, should be based on measured concentrations, and needs to address the toxicity of significant breakdown products.
Oxidizable	Achieving, maintaining and measuring exposure concentration. Toxicity of modified chemical structures or breakdown products. Comparison of degradation half-lives to the exposure regimen used in testing.	Classification requires expert judgement, should be based on measured concentrations, and needs to address the toxicity of significant breakdown products.
Subject to corrosion/ transformation (this refers to metals /metal compounds)	Achieving, maintaining and measuring exposure concentration. Comparison of partitioning from the water column half-lives to the exposure regimen used in testing.	Classification requires expert judgement, should be based on measured concentrations, and needs to address the toxicity of significant breakdown products.
Biodegradable	Maintaining exposure concentrations. Toxicity of breakdown products. Comparison of degradation half-lives to the exposure regimen used in testing.	Classification requires expert judgement, should be based on measured concentrations, and needs to address the toxicity of significant breakdown products.
Adsorbing	Maintaining exposure concentrations. Analysing exposure. Toxicity mitigation due to reduced availability of test substance.	Classification should use measured concentration of available material.
Chelating	Distinguishing chelated and non-chelated fractions in media.	Classification should use measurement of concentration of bioavailable material.
Coloured	Light attenuation (an algal problem).	Classification must distinguish toxic effects from reduced growth due to light attenuation.
Hydrophobic	Maintaining constant exposure concentrations.	Classification should use measured concentration.
Ionized	Maintaining exposure concentrations. Toxicity of breakdown products. Comparison of degradation half-lives to the exposure regime used in testing.	Classification requires expert judgement, should be based on measured concentrations, and needs to address the toxicity of significant breakdown products.
Multi-component	Preparing representative test batches.	Considered same as complex mixture.

A9.3.6 *Interpreting data quality*

A9.3.6.1 *Standardization*

Many factors can influence the results of toxicity tests with aquatic organisms. These factors include characteristics of the test water, experimental design, chemical characteristics of the test material, and biological characteristics of the test organisms. Therefore, it is important in conducting aquatic toxicity tests to use standardized test procedures to reduce the influence of these sources of extraneous variability. The goal of test standardization and international harmonization of these standards is to reduce test variability and improve precision, reproducibility, and consistency of test results.

A9.3.6.2 *Data hierarchies*

A9.3.6.2.1   Classification should be based on primary data of good quality. Preference is given to data conforming to OECD Test Guidelines or equivalent and Good Laboratory Practices (GLP). While data from internationally harmonized test methods performed on standard test species are preferred, results of tests performed using widely recognized international or national methods or their equivalent may also be used, e.g. ISO or ASTM methods. Data from tests that appear to conform to accepted guidelines but which lacks provisions for GLP can be used in the absence of pertinent GLP data.

A9.3.6.2.2   Pedersen et al (1995) provides a data quality-scoring system, which is compatible with many others in current use, including that, used by the US-EPA for its AQUIRE database. See also Mensink et al (1995) for discussions of data quality. The data quality scoring system described in Pedersen *et al.* includes a reliability ranking scheme, which can be a model for use with in classifying under the harmonized scheme. The first three levels of data described by Pedersen are for preferred data.

A9.3.6.2.3   Data for classification under the harmonized scheme should come from primary sources. However, since many nations and regulatory authorities will perform classification using the globally harmonized scheme, classification should allow for use of reviews from national authorities and expert panels as long as the reviews are based on primary sources. Such reviews should include summaries of test conditions, which are sufficiently detailed for weight of evidence and classification decisions to be made. It may be possible to use the reviews, which were made by a well-recognized group such as GESAMP for which the primary data are accessible.

A9.3.6.2.4   In the absence of empirical test data, validated Quantitative Structure Activity Relationships (QSARs) for aquatic toxicity may be used. Test data always take precedence over QSAR predictions, providing the test data are valid.

A9.4 Degradation

A9.4.1 *Introduction*

A9.4.1.1   Degradability is one of the important intrinsic properties of substances that determine their potential environmental hazard. Non-degradable substances will persist in the environment and may consequently have a potential for causing long-term adverse effects on biota. In contrast, degradable substances may be removed in the sewers, in sewage treatment plants or in the environment.

Classification of substances is primarily based on their intrinsic properties. However, the degree of degradation depends not only on the intrinsic recalcitrance of the molecule, but also on the actual conditions in the receiving environmental compartment as e.g. redox potential, pH, presence of suitable micro-organisms, concentration of the substances and occurrence and concentration of other substrates. The interpretation of the degradation properties in an aquatic hazard classification context therefore requires detailed criteria that balance the intrinsic properties of the substance and the prevailing environmental conditions into a concluding statement on the potential for long-term adverse effects. The purpose of the present section is to present guidance for interpretation of data on degradability of organic substances. The guidance is based on an analysis of the above mentioned aspects regarding degradation in the aquatic environment. Based on the guidance a detailed decision scheme for use of existing degradation data for classification purposes is proposed. The types of degradation data included in this Guidance Document are ready biodegradability data, simulation data for transformation in water, aquatic sediment and soil, BOD$_5$/COD-data and techniques for estimation of rapid degradability in the aquatic environment. Also considered are anaerobic degradability, inherent biodegradability, sewage treatment plant simulation test data, abiotic transformation data such as hydrolysis and photolysis, removal process such as volatilization and finally, data obtained from field investigations and monitoring studies.

A9.4.1.2   The term degradation is defined in Chapter 4.1 as the decomposition of organic molecules to smaller molecules and eventually to carbon dioxide, water and salts. For inorganic compounds and metals, the concept of degradability as applied to organic compounds has limited or no meaning. Rather the substance may be transformed by normal environmental processes to either increase or decrease the bioavailability of the toxic species. Therefore, the present section deals only with organic substances and organo-metals. Environmental partitioning from the water column is discussed in Section A9.7.

A9.4.1.3   Data on degradation properties of a substance may be available from standardized tests or from other types of investigations, or they may be estimated from the structure of the molecules. The interpretation of such degradation data for classification purposes often requires detailed evaluation of the test data. Guidance is given in the present section and more details can be found in two paragraphs describing available methods (Appendix A9.I) and factors influencing degradation in aquatic environments (Appendix A9.II).

A9.4.2   *Interpretation of degradability data*

A9.4.2.1   *Rapid degradability*

Aquatic hazard classification of substances is normally based on existing data on their environmental properties. Only seldom will test data be produced with the main purpose of facilitating a classification. Often a diverse range of test data is available that does not necessarily fits directly with the classification criteria. Consequently, guidance is needed on interpretation of existing test data in the context of the aquatic hazard classification. Based on the harmonized criteria, guidance for interpretation of degradation data is prepared below for the three types of data comprised by the expression "rapid degradation" in the aquatic environment (see A9.1.8, A9.1.9, A9.1.2.3.1 to A9.2.3.4 and the definition in Chapter 4.1, para. 4.1.2.11.3).

A9.4.2.2   *Ready biodegradability*

A9.4.2.2.1   Ready biodegradability is defined in the OECD Test Guidelines No. 301 (OECD 1992). All organic substances that degrade to a level higher than the pass level in a standard OECD ready biodegradability test or in a similar test should be considered readily biodegradable and consequently also rapidly degradable. Many literature test data, however, do not specify all of the conditions that should be evaluated to demonstrate whether or not the test fulfils the requirements of a ready biodegradability test. Expert judgement is therefore needed as regards the validity of the data before use for classification purposes. Before concluding on the ready biodegradability of a test substance, however, at least the following parameters should be considered.

A9.4.2.2.2   Concentration of test substance

Relatively high concentrations of test substance are used in the OECD ready biodegradability tests (2-100 mg/l). Many substances may, however, be toxic to the inocula at such high concentrations causing a low degradation in the tests although the substances might be rapidly degradable at lower non-toxic concentrations. A toxicity test with micro-organisms (as e.g. the OECD Test Guideline 209 "Activated Sludge, Respiration Inhibition Test", the ISO 9509 nitrification inhibition test, or the ISO 11348 luminescent bacteria inhibition test) may demonstrate the toxicity of the test substance. When it is likely that inhibition is the reason for a substance being not readily degradable, results from a test employing lower non-toxic concentrations of the test substance should be used when available. Such test results could on a case by case basis be considered in relation to the classification criteria for rapid degradation, even though surface water degradation test data with environmentally realistic microbial biomass and non toxic realistic low concentration of the test substance in general are preferred, if available.

A9.4.2.2.3   Time window

The harmonized criteria (see 4.1.2.11.3) include a general requirement for all of the ready biodegradability tests on achievement of the pass level within 10 days. This is not in line with the OECD Test Guideline 301 in which the 10-days time window applies to the OECD ready biodegradability tests except to the MITI I test (OECD Test Guideline 301C). In the Closed Bottle test (OECD Test Guideline 301D), a 14-days window may be used instead when measurements have not been made after 10 days. Moreover, often only limited information is available in references of biodegradation tests. Thus, as a pragmatic approach the percentage of degradation reached after 28 days may be used directly for assessment of ready biodegradability when no information on the 10-days time window is available. This should, however, only be accepted for existing test data and data from tests where the 10-days window does not apply.

Where there is sufficient justification, the 10-day window condition may be waived for complex, multi-component substances and the pass level applied at 28 days. The constituents of such substances may have different chain-lengths, degree and/or site of branching or stereo-isomers, even in their most purified commercial forms. Testing of each individual component may be costly and impractical. If a test on the complex, multi-component substance is performed and it is anticipated that a sequential biodegradation of the individual structures is taking place, then the 10-day window should not be applied to interpret the results of the test. A case by case evaluation should however take place on whether a biodegradability test on such a substance would give valuable information regarding its biodegradability as such (i.e. regarding the degradability of all the constituents) or whether instead an investigation of the degradability of carefully selected individual components of the complex, multi-component substance is required.

A9.4.2.3   *BOD$_5$/COD*

Information on the 5-day biochemical oxygen demand (BOD$_5$) will be used for classification purposes only when no other measured degradability data are available. Thus, priority is given to data from ready biodegradability tests and from simulation studies regarding degradability in the aquatic environment. The BOD$_5$ test is a traditional biodegradation test that is now replaced by the ready biodegradability tests. Therefore, this test should not be performed today for assessment of the ready biodegradability of substances. Older test data may, however, be used when no other degradability data are available. For substances where the chemical structure is known, the theoretical oxygen demand (ThOD) can be calculated and this value should be used instead of the chemical oxygen demand (COD).

A9.4.2.4   *Other convincing scientific evidence*

A9.4.2.4.1   Rapid degradation in the aquatic environment may be demonstrated by other data than referred to in Chapter 4.1, paragraph 4.1.2.11.3 (a) and (b). These may be data on biotic and/or abiotic degradation. Data on primary degradation can only be used where it is demonstrated that the degradation products shall not be classified as hazardous to the aquatic environment, i.e. that they do not fulfil the classification criteria.

A9.4.2.4.2   The fulfilment of paragraph 4.1.2.11.3 (c) requires that the substance is degraded in the aquatic environment to a level of >70% within a 28-day period. If first-order kinetics are assumed, which is reasonable at the low substance concentrations prevailing in most aquatic environments, the degradation rate will be relatively constant for the 28-day period. Thus, the degradation requirement will be fulfilled with an average degradation rate constant, $k > -(\ln 0.3 - \ln 1)/28 = 0.043$ day^{-1}. This corresponds to a degradation half-life, $t_{1/2} < \ln 2/0.043 = 16$ days.

A9.4.2.4.3   Moreover, as degradation processes are temperature dependent, this parameter should also be taken into account when assessing degradation in the environment. Data from studies employing environmentally realistic temperatures should be used for the evaluation. When data from studies performed at different temperatures need to be compared, the traditional Q10 approach could be used, i.e. that the degradation rate is halved when the temperature decreases by 10 °C.

A9.4.2.4.4   The evaluation of data on fulfilment of this criterion should be conducted on a case-by-case basis by expert judgement. However, guidance on the interpretation of various types of data that may be used for demonstrating a rapid degradation in the aquatic environment is given below. In general, only data from aquatic biodegradation simulation tests are considered directly applicable. However simulation test data from other environmental compartments could be considered as well, but such data require in general more scientific judgement before use.

A9.4.2.4.5   Aquatic simulation tests

Aquatic simulation tests are tests conducted in laboratory, but simulating environmental conditions and employing natural samples as inoculum. Results of aquatic simulation tests may be used directly for classification purposes, when realistic environmental conditions in surface waters are simulated, i.e.:

(a)   substance concentration that is realistic for the general aquatic environment (often in the low µg/l range);

(b)   inoculum from a relevant aquatic environment;

(c)   realistic concentration of inoculum (10^3-10^6 cells/ml);

(d)   realistic temperature (e.g. 5 °C to 25 °C); and

(e)   ultimate degradation is determined (i.e. determination of the mineralization rate or the individual degradation rates of the total biodegradation pathway).

Substances that under these conditions are degraded at least 70% within 28 days, i.e. with a half-life < 16 days, are considered rapidly degradable.

A9.4.2.4.6   Field investigations

Parallels to laboratory simulation tests are field investigations or mesocosm experiments. In such studies, fate and/or effects of chemicals in environments or environmental enclosures may be investigated. Fate data from such experiments might be used for assessing the potential for a rapid degradation. This may, however, often be difficult, as it requires that an ultimate degradation can be demonstrated. This may be documented by preparing mass balances showing that no non-degradable intermediates are formed, and which take the fractions into account that are removed from the aqueous system due to other processes such as sorption to sediment or volatilization from the aquatic environment.

A9.4.2.4.7   Monitoring data

Monitoring data may demonstrate the removal of contaminants from the aquatic environment. Such data are, however, very difficult to use for classification purposes. The following aspects should be considered before use:

(a)   Is the removal a result of degradation, or is it a result of other processes such as dilution or distribution between compartments (sorption, volatilization)?

(b)   Is formation of non-degradable intermediates excluded?

Only when it can be demonstrated that removal as a result of ultimate degradation fulfils the criteria for rapid degradability, such data be considered for use for classification purposes. In general, monitoring data should only be used as supporting evidence for demonstration of either persistence in the aquatic environment or a rapid degradation.

A9.4.2.4.8   Inherent biodegradability tests

Substances that are degraded more than 70% in tests for inherent biodegradability (OECD Test Guidelines 302) have the potential for ultimate biodegradation. However, because of the optimum conditions in these tests, the rapid biodegradability of inherently biodegradable substances in the environment cannot be assumed. The optimum conditions in inherent biodegradability tests stimulate adaptation of the micro-organisms thus increasing the biodegradation potential, compared to natural environments. Therefore, positive results in general should not be interpreted as evidence for rapid degradation in the environment[2].

A9.4.2.4.9   Sewage treatment plant simulation tests

Results from tests simulating the conditions in a sewage treatment plant (STP) (e.g. the OECD Test Guideline 303) cannot be used for assessing the degradation in the aquatic environment. The main reasons for this are that the microbial biomass in a STP is significantly different from the biomass in the environment, that there is a considerably different composition of substrates, and that the presence of rapidly mineralized organic matter in waste water facilitates degradation of the test substance by co-metabolism.

A9.4.2.4.10   Soil and sediment degradation data

It has been argued that for many non-sorptive (non-lipophilic) substances more or less the same degradation rates are found in soil and in surface water. For lipophilic substances, a lower degradation rate may generally be expected in soil than in water due to partial immobilization caused by sorption. Thus, when a substance has been shown to be degraded rapidly in a soil simulation study, it is most likely also rapidly degradable in the aquatic environment. It is therefore proposed that an experimentally determined rapid degradation in soil is sufficient documentation for a rapid degradation in surface waters when:

(a)   no pre-exposure (pre-adaptation) of the soil micro-organisms has taken place; and

(b)   an environmentally realistic concentration of substance is tested; and

(c)   the substance is ultimately degraded within 28 days with a half-life < 16 days corresponding to a degradation rate > 0.043 day^{-1}.

The same argumentation is considered valid for data on degradation in sediment under aerobic conditions.

A9.4.2.4.11   Anaerobic degradation data

Data regarding anaerobic degradation cannot be used in relation to deciding whether a substance should be regarded as rapidly degradable, because the aquatic environment is generally regarded as the aerobic compartment where the aquatic organisms, such as those employed for aquatic hazard classification, live.

A9.4.2.4.12   Hydrolysis

Data on hydrolysis (e.g. OECD Test Guideline 111) might be considered for classification purposes only when the longest half-life $t_{1/2}$ determined within the pH range 4-9 is shorter than 16 days. However, hydrolysis is not an ultimate degradation and various intermediate degradation products may be formed, some of which may be only slowly degradable. Only when it can be satisfactorily demonstrated that the hydrolysis products formed do not fulfil the criteria for classification as hazardous for the aquatic environment, data from hydrolysis studies could be considered.

---

[2]   *In relation to interpretation of degradation data equivalent with the harmonised OECD criteria for Chronic 4, the standing EU working group for environmental hazard classification of substances is discussing whether certain types of data from inherent biodegradability tests may be used in a case by case evaluation as a basis for not classifying substances otherwise fulfilling this classification criterion.*

The inherent biodegradability tests concerned are the Zahn Wellens test (OECD TG 302 B) and the MITI II test (OECD TG 302 C). The conditions for use in this regard are:

    (a)   The methods must not employ pre-exposed (pre-adapted) micro-organisms;

    (b)   The time for adaptation within each test should be limited, the test endpoint should refer to the mineralization only and the pass level and time for reaching these should be, respectively:

        (i)   MITI II pass level > 60 % within 14 days

        (ii)   Zahn Wellens Test > 70 % within 7 days.

When a substance is quickly hydrolysed (e.g. with $t_{1/2}$ < a few days), this process is a part of the degradation determined in biodegradation tests. Hydrolysis may be the initial transformation process in biodegradation.

A9.4.2.4.13   Photochemical degradation

Information on photochemical degradation (e.g. OECD, 1997) is difficult to use for classification purposes. The actual degree of photochemical degradation in the aquatic environment depends on local conditions (e.g. water depth, suspended solids, turbidity) and the hazard of the degradation products is usually not known. Probably only seldom will enough information be available for a thorough evaluation based on photochemical degradation.

A9.4.2.4.14   Estimation of degradation

A9.4.2.4.14.1   Certain QSARs have been developed for prediction of an approximate hydrolysis half-life, which should only be considered when no experimental data are available. However, a hydrolysis half-life can only be used in relation to classification with great care, because hydrolysis does not concern ultimate degradability (see "Hydrolysis" of this Section). Furthermore the QSARs developed until now have a rather limited applicability and are only able to predict the potential for hydrolysis on a limited number of chemical classes. The QSAR program HYDROWIN (version 1.67, Syracuse Research Corporation) is for example only able to predict the potential for hydrolysis on less than 1/5th of the existing EU substances which have a defined (precise) molecular structure (Niemelä, 2000).

A9.4.2.4.14.2   In general, no quantitative estimation method (QSAR) for estimating the degree of biodegradability of organic substances is yet sufficiently accurate to predict rapid degradation. However, results from such methods may be used to predict that a substance is not rapidly degradable. For example, when in the Biodegradation Probability Program (e.g. BIOWIN version 3.67, Syracuse Research Corporation) the probability is < 0.5 estimated by the linear or non-linear methods, the substances should be regarded as not rapidly degradable (OECD, 1994; Pedersen *et al.*, 1995 & Langenberg *et al.*, 1996). Also other (Q)SAR methods may be used as well as expert judgement, for example, when degradation data for structurally analogue compounds are available, but such judgement should be conducted with great care. In general, a QSAR prediction that a substance is not rapidly degradable is considered a better documentation for a classification than application of a default classification, when no useful degradation data are available.

A9.4.2.4.15   Volatilization

Chemicals may be removed from some aquatic environments by volatilization. The intrinsic potential for volatilization is determined by the Henry's Law constant (H) of the substance. Volatilization from the aquatic environment is highly dependent on the environmental conditions of the specific water body in question, such as the water depth, the gas exchange coefficients (depending on wind speed and water flow) and stratification of the water body. Because volatilization only represents removal of a chemical from water phase, the Henry's Law constant cannot be used for assessment of degradation in relation to aquatic hazard classification of substances. Substances that are gases at ambient temperature may however for example be considered further in this regard (see also Pedersen *et al.*, 1995).

A9.4.2.5   *No degradation data available*

When no useful data on degradability are available - either experimentally determined or estimated data - the substance should be regarded as not rapidly degradable.

A9.4.3   **General interpretation problems**

A9.4.3.1   *Complex substances*

The harmonized criteria for classification of chemicals as hazardous for the aquatic environment focus on single substances. A certain type of intrinsically complex substance are multi-component substances. They are typically of natural origin and need occasionally to be considered. This may be the case for chemicals that are produced or extracted from mineral oil or plant material. Such complex chemicals are normally considered as single substances in a regulatory context. In most cases they are defined as a homologous series of substances within a certain range of carbon chain length and/or degree of substitution. When this is the case, no major difference in degradability is foreseen and the degree of degradability can be established from tests of the complex chemical. One exception would be when a borderline degradation is found because in this case some of the individual substances may be rapidly degradable and other may be not rapidly degradable. This requires a more detailed assessment of the degradability of the individual components in the complex substance. When not-rapidly-degradable components constitute a significant part of the complex substance (e.g. more than 20%, or for a hazardous component, an even lower content), the substance should be regarded as not rapidly degradable.

A9.4.3.2   *Availability of the substance*

A9.4.3.2.1   Degradation of organic substances in the environment takes place mostly in the aquatic compartments or in aquatic phases in soil or sediment. Hydrolysis, of course, requires the presence of water. The activity of micro-organisms depends on the presence of water. Moreover, biodegradation requires that the micro-organisms are directly in contact with the substance. Dissolution of the substance in the water phase that surrounds the micro-organisms is therefore the most direct way for contact between the bacteria and fungi and the substrate.

A9.4.3.2.2   The present standard methods for investigating degradability of substances are developed for readily soluble test compounds. However, many organic substances are only slightly soluble in water. As the standard tests require 2-100 mg/l of the test substance, sufficient availability may not be reached for substances with a low water solubility. Tests with continuous mixing and/or an increased exposure time, or tests with a special design where concentrations of the test substance lower than the water solubility have been employed, may be available on slightly soluble compounds.

A9.4.3.3   *Test duration less than 28 days*

A9.4.3.3.1   Sometimes degradation is reported for tests terminated before the 28 day period specified in the standards (e.g. the MITI, 1992). These data are of course directly applicable when a degradation greater than or equal to the pass level is obtained. When a lower degradation level is reached, the results need to be interpreted with caution. One possibility is that the duration of the test was too short and that the chemical structure would probably have been degraded in a 28-day biodegradability test. If substantial degradation occurs within a short time period, the situation may be compared with the criterion $BOD_5/COD \geq 0.5$ or with the requirements on degradation within the 10-days time window. In these cases, a substance may be considered readily degradable (and hence rapidly degradable), if:

    (a)   the ultimate biodegradability > 50% within 5 days; or

    (b)   the ultimate degradation rate constant in this period is > 0.1 day^{-1} corresponding to a half-life of 7 days.

A9.4.3.3.2   These criteria are proposed in order to ensure that rapid mineralization did occur, although the test was ended before 28 days and before the pass level was attained. Interpretation of test data that do not comply with the prescribed pass levels must be made with great caution. It is mandatory to consider whether a biodegradability below the pass level was due to a partial degradation of the substance and not a complete mineralization. If partial degradation is the probable explanation for the observed biodegradability, the substance should be considered not readily biodegradable.

A9.4.3.4   *Primary biodegradation*

In some tests, only the disappearance of the parent compound (i.e. primary degradation) is determined for example by following the degradation by specific or group specific chemical analyses of the test substance. Data on primary biodegradability may be used for demonstrating rapid degradability only when it can be satisfactorily demonstrated that the degradation products formed do not fulfil the criteria for classification as hazardous to the aquatic environment.

A9.4.3.5 *Conflicting results from screening tests*

A9.4.3.5.1   The situation where more degradation data are available for the same substance introduces the possibility of conflicting results. In general, conflicting results for a substance which has been tested several times with an appropriate biodegradability test could be interpreted by a "weight of evidence approach". This implies that if both positive (i.e. higher degradation than the pass level) and negative results have been obtained for a substance in ready biodegradability tests, then the data of the highest quality and the best documentation should be used for determining the ready biodegradability of the substance. However, positive results in ready biodegradability tests could be considered valid, irrespective of negative results, when the scientific quality is good and the test conditions are well documented, i.e. guideline criteria are fulfilled, including the use of non-pre-exposed (non-adapted) inoculum. None of the various screening tests are suitable for the testing of all types of substances, and results obtained by the use of a test procedure which is not suitable for the specific substance should be evaluated carefully before a decision on the use is taken.

A9.4.3.5.2   Thus, there are a number of factors that may explain conflicting biodegradability data from screening tests:

(a)   inoculum;

(b)   toxicity of test substance;

(c)   test conditions;

(d)   solubility of the test substance; and

(e)   volatilization of the test substance.

A9.4.3.5.3   The suitability of the inoculum for degrading the test substance depends on the presence and amount of competent degraders. When the inoculum is obtained from an environment that has previously been exposed to the test substance, the inoculum may be adapted as evidenced by a degradation capacity, which is greater than that of an inoculum from a non-exposed environment. As far as possible the inoculum must be sampled from an unexposed environment, but for substances that are used ubiquitously in high volumes and released widespread or more or less continuously, this may be difficult or impossible. When conflicting results are obtained, the origin of the inoculum should be checked in order to clarify whether or not differences in the adaptation of the microbial community may be the reason.

A9.4.3.5.4   As mentioned above, many substances may be toxic or inhibitory to the inoculum at the relatively high concentrations tested in ready biodegradability tests. Especially in the Modified MITI (I) test (OECD Test Guideline 301C) and the Manometric Respirometry test (OECD Test Guideline 301F) high concentrations (100 mg/l) are prescribed. The lowest test substance concentrations are prescribed in the Closed Bottle test (OECD Test Guideline 301D) where 2-10 mg/l is used. The possibility of toxic effects may be evaluated by including a toxicity control in the ready biodegradability test or by comparing the test concentration with toxicity test data on micro-organisms, e.g. the respiration inhibition tests (OECD Test Guideline 209), the nitrification inhibition test (ISO 9509) or, if other microbial toxicity tests are not available, the bioluminescence inhibition test (ISO 11348). When conflicting results are found, this may becaused by toxicity of the test substance. If the substance is not inhibitory at environmentally realistic concentrations, the greatest degradation measured in screening tests may be used as a basis for classification. If simulation test data are available in such cases, consideration of these data may be especially important, because a low non inhibitory concentration of the substance may have been employed, thus giving a more reliable indication of the biodegradation half-life of the substance under environmentally realistic conditions.

A9.4.3.5.5   When the solubility of the test substance is lower than the concentrations employed in a test, this parameter may be the limiting factor for the actual degradation measured. In these cases, results from tests employing the lowest concentrations of test substance should prevail, i.e. often the Closed Bottle test (OECD Test Guideline 301D). In general, the DOC Die-Away test (OECD Test Guideline 301A) and the Modified OECD Screening test (OECD Test Guideline 301E) are not suitable for testing the biodegradability of poorly soluble substances (e.g. OECD Test Guideline 301).

A9.4.3.5.6   Volatile substances should only be tested in closed systems as the Closed Bottle test (OECD Test Guideline 301D), the MITI I test (OECD Test Guideline 301C) and the Manometric Respirometry test (OECD Test Guideline 301F). Results from other tests should be evaluated carefully and only considered if it can be demonstrated, e.g. by mass balance estimates, that the removal of the test substance is not a result of volatilization.

A9.4.3.6   *Variation in simulation test data*

A number of simulation test data may be available for certain high priority chemicals. Often such data provide a range of half lives in environmental media such as soil, sediment and/or surface water. The observed differences in half-lives from simulation tests performed on the same substance may reflect differences in test conditions, all of which may be environmentally relevant. A suitable half life in the higher end of the observed range of half lives from such investigations should be selected for classification by employing a weight of evidence approach and taking the realism and relevance of the employed tests into account in relation to environmental conditions. In general, simulation test data of surface water are preferred relative to aquatic sediment or soil simulation test data in relation to the evaluation of rapid degradability in the aquatic environment.

A9.4.4   *Decision scheme*

The following decision scheme may be used as a general guidance to facilitate decisions in relation to rapid degradability in the aquatic environment and classification of chemicals hazardous to the aquatic environment.

A substance is considered to be not rapidly degradable unless at least one of the following is fulfilled:

(a)   the substance is demonstrated to be readily biodegradable in a 28-day test for ready biodegradability. The pass level of the test (70% DOC removal or 60% theoretical oxygen demand) must be achieved within 10 days from the onset of biodegradation, if it is possible to evaluate this according to the available test data. If this is not possible, then the pass level should be evaluated within a 14 days time window if possible, or after the end of the test; or

(b)   the substance is demonstrated to be ultimately degraded in a surface water simulation test[3] with a half-life of < 16 days (corresponding to a degradation of > 70% within 28 days); or

(c)   the substance is demonstrated to be primarily degraded (biotically or abiotically) in the aquatic environment with a half-life < 16 days (corresponding to a degradation of > 70% within 28 days) and it can be demonstrated that the degradation products do not fulfil the criteria for classification as hazardous to the aquatic environment.

When these data are not available rapid degradation may be demonstrated if either of the following criteria are justified:

(d)   the substance is demonstrated to be ultimately degraded in an aquatic sediment or soil simulation test[3] with a half-life of < 16 days (corresponding to a degradation of > 70% within 28 days); or

(e)   in those cases where only BOD_5 and COD data are available, the ratio of BOD_5/COD is ≥ 0.5. The same criterion applies to ready biodegradability tests of a shorter duration than 28 days, if the half-life furthermore is < 7 days.

---

[3]   *Simulations tests should reflect realistic environmental conditions such as low concentration of the chemical, realistic temperature and employment of ambient microbial biomass not pre-exposed to the chemical.*

If none of the above types of data are available then the substance is considered as not rapidly degradable. This decision may be supported by fulfilment of at least one of the following criteria:

(i)   the substance is not inherently degradable in an inherent biodegradability test; or

(ii)   the substances is predicted to be slowly biodegradable by scientifically valid QSARs, e.g. for the Biodegradation Probability Program, the score for rapid degradation (linear or non-linear model) < 0.5; or

(iii)   the substance is considered to be not rapidly degradable based on indirect evidence, as e.g. knowledge from structurally similar substances; or

(iv)   no other data regarding degradability are available.

A9.5   Bioaccumulation

A9.5.1   *Introduction*

A9.5.1.1   Bioaccumulation is one of the important intrinsic properties of substances that determine the potential environmental hazard. Bioaccumulation of a substance into an organism is not a hazard in itself, but bioconcentration and bioaccumulation will result in a body burden, which may or may not lead to toxic effects. In the harmonized integrated hazard classification system for human health and environmental effects of chemical substances (OECD, 1998), the wording "potential for bioaccumulation" is given. A distinction should, however, be drawn between bioconcentration and bioaccumulation. Here bioconcentration is defined as the net result of uptake, transformation, and elimination of a substance in an organism due to waterborne exposure, whereas bioaccumulation includes all routes of exposure (i.e. via air, water, sediment/soil, and food). Finally, biomagnification is defined as accumulation and transfer of substances via the food chain, resulting in an increase of internal concentrations in organisms on higher levels of the trophic chain (European Commission, 1996). For most organic chemicals uptake from water (bioconcentration) is believed to be the predominant route of uptake. Only for very hydrophobic substances does uptake from food becomes important. Also, the harmonized classification criteria use the bioconcentration factor (or the octanol/water partition coefficient) as the measure of the potential for bioaccumulation. For these reasons, the present guidance document only considers bioconcentration and does not discuss uptake via food or other routes.

A9.5.1.2   Classification of a substance is primarily based on its intrinsic properties. However, the degree of bioconcentration also depends on factors such as the degree of bioavailability, the physiology of test organism, maintenance of constant exposure concentration, exposure duration, metabolism inside the body of the target organism and excretion from the body. The interpretation of the bioconcentration potential in a chemical classification context therefore requires an evaluation of the intrinsic properties of the substance, as well as of the experimental conditions under which bioconcentration factor (BCF) has been determined. Based on the guide, a decision scheme for application of bioconcentration data or log K_{ow} data for classification purposes has been developed. The emphasis of the present section is organic substances and organo-metals. Bioaccumulation of metals is also discussed in Section A9.7.

A9.5.1.3   Data on bioconcentration properties of a substance may be available from standardized tests or may be estimated from the structure of the molecule. The interpretation of such bioconcentration data for classification purposes often requires detailed evaluation of test data. In order to facilitate this evaluation two additional appendixes are enclosed. These appendixes describe available methods (Appendix III of Annex 9) and factors influencing the bioconcentration potential (Appendix IV of Annex 9). Finally, a list of standardized experimental methods for determination of bioconcentration and K_{ow} are attached (Appendix V of Annex 9) together with a list of references (Appendix VI of Annex 9).

A9.5.2.1   Environmental hazard classification of a substance is normally based on existing data on its environmental properties. Test data will only seldom be produced with the main purpose of facilitating a classification. Often a diverse range of test data is available which does not necessarily match the classification criteria. Consequently, guidance is needed on interpretation of existing test data in the context of hazard classification.

A9.5.2.2   Bioconcentration of an organic substance can be experimentally determined in bioconcentration experiments, during which BCF is measured as the concentration in the organism relative to the concentration in water under steady-state conditions and/or estimated from the uptake rate constant (k_1) and the elimination rate constant (k_2) (OECD 305, 1996). In general, the potential of an organic substance to bioconcentrate is primarily related to the lipophilicity of the substance. A measure of lipophilicity is the n-octanol-water partition coefficient (K_{ow}) which, for lipophilic non-ionic organic substances, undergoing minimal metabolism or biotransformation within the organism, is correlated with the bioconcentration factor. Therefore, K_{ow} is often used for estimating the bioconcentration of organic substances, based on the empirical relationship between log BCF and log K_{ow}. For most organic substances, estimation methods are available for calculating the K_{ow}. Data on the bioconcentration properties of a substance may thus be (i) experimentally determined, (ii) estimated from experimentally determined K_{ow}, or (iii) estimated from K_{ow} values derived by use of Quantitative Structure Activity Relationships (QSARs). Guidance for interpretation of such data is given below together with guidance on assessment of chemical classes, which need special attention.

A9.5.2.3   *Bioconcentration factor (BCF)*

A9.5.2.3.1   The bioconcentration factor is defined as the ratio on a weight basis between the concentration of the chemical in biota and the concentration in the surrounding medium, here water, at steady state. BCF can thus be experimentally derived under steady-state conditions, on the basis of measured concentrations. However, BCF can also be calculated as the ratio between the first-order uptake and elimination rate constants; a method which does not require equilibrium conditions.

A9.5.2.3.2   Different test guidelines for the experimental determination of bioconcentration in fish have been documented and adopted, the most generally applied being the OECD test guideline (OECD 305, 1996).

A9.5.2.3.3   Experimentally derived BCF values of high quality are ultimately preferred for classification purposes as such data override surrogate data, e.g. K_{ow}.

A9.5.2.3.4   High quality data are defined as data where the validity criteria for the test method applied are fulfilled and described, e.g. maintenance of constant exposure concentration; oxygen and temperature variations, and documentation that steady-state conditions have been reached, etc. The experiment will be regarded as a high-quality study, if a proper description is provided (e.g. by Good Laboratory Practice (GLP)) allowing verification that validity criteria are fulfilled. In addition, an appropriate analytical method must be used to quantify the chemical and its toxic metabolites in the water and fish tissue (see section 1, Appendix III for further details).

A9.5.2.3.5   BCF values of low or uncertain quality may give a false and too low BCF value; e.g. application of measured concentrations of the test substance in fish and water, but measured after a too short exposure period in which steady-state conditions have not been reached (cf. OECD 306, 1996, regarding estimation of time to equilibrium). Therefore, such data should be carefully evaluated before use and consideration should be given to using K_{ow} instead.

A9.5.2.3.6   If there is no BCF value for fish species, high-quality data on the BCF value for other species may be used (e.g. BCF determined on blue mussel, oyster, scallop (ASTM E 1022-94)). Reported BCFs for microalgae should be used with caution.

A9.5.2.3.7   For highly lipophilic substances, e.g. with log K_{ow} above 6, experimentally derived BCF values tend to decrease with increasing log K_{ow}. Conceptual explanations of this non-linearity mainly refer to either reduced membrane permeation kinetics or reduced biotic lipid solubility for large molecules. A low bioavailability and uptake of these substances in the organism will thus occur. Other factors comprise experimental artefacts, such as equilibrium not being reached, reduced bioavailability due to sorption to organic matter in the aqueous phase, and analytical errors. Special care should thus be taken when evaluating experimental data on BCF for highly lipophilic substances as these data will have a much higher level of uncertainty than BCF values determined for less lipophilic substances.

A9.5.2.3.8   BCF in different test species

A9.5.2.3.8.1   BCF values used for classification are based on whole body measurements. As stated previously, the optimal data for classification are BCF values derived using the OECD 305 test method or internationally equivalent methods, which uses small fish. Due to the higher gill surface to weight ratio for smaller organisms than larger organisms, steady-state conditions will be reached sooner in smaller organisms than in larger ones. The size of the organisms (fish) used in bioconcentration studies is thus of considerable importance in relation to the time used in the uptake phase, when the reported BCF value is based solely on measured concentrations in fish and water at steady-state. Thus, if large fish, e.g. adult salmon, have been used in bioconcentration studies, it should be evaluated whether the uptake period was sufficiently long for steady state to be reached or to allow for a kinetic uptake rate constant to be determined precisely.

A9.5.2.3.8.2   Furthermore, when using existing data for classification, it is possible that the BCF values could be derived from several different fish or other aquatic species (e.g. clams) and for different organs in the fish. Thus, to compare these data to each other and to the criteria, some common basis or normalization will be required. It has been noted that there is a close relationship between the lipid content of a fish or an aquatic organism and the observed BCF value. Therefore, when comparing BCF values across different fish species or when converting BCF values for specific organs to whole body BCFs, the common approach is to express the BCF values on a common lipid content. If e.g. whole body BCF values or BCF values for specific organs are found in the literature, the first step is to calculate the BCF on a % lipid basis using the relative content of fat in the fish (cf. literature/test guideline for typical fat content of the test species) or the organ. In the second step the BCF for the whole body for a typical aquatic organism (i.e. small fish) is calculated assuming a common default lipid content. A default value of 5% is most commonly used (Pedersen et al., 1995) as this represents the average lipid content of the small fish used in OECD 305 (1996).

A9.5.2.3.8.3   Generally, the highest valid BCF value expressed on this common lipid basis is used to determine the wet weight based BCF-value in relation to the cut off value for BCF of 500 of the harmonized classification criteria (see Chapter 4.1, Table 4.1.1).

A9.5.2.3.9   Use of radiolabelled substances

A9.5.2.3.9.1   The use of radiolabelled test substances can facilitate the analysis of water and fish samples. However, unless combined with a specific analytical method, the total radioactivity measurements potentially reflect the presence of the parent substance as well as possible metabolite(s) and possible metabolized carbon, which have been incorporated in the fish tissue in organic molecules. BCF values determined by use of radiolabelled test substances are therefore normally overestimated.

A9.5.2.3.9.2   When using radiolabelled substances, the labelling is most often placed in the stable part of the molecule, for which reason the measured BCF value includes the BCF of the metabolites. For some substances it is the metabolite which is the most toxic and which has the highest bioconcentration potential. Measurements of the parent substance as well as the metabolites may thus be important for the interpretation of the aquatic hazard (including the bioconcentration potential) of such substances.

A9.5.2.3.9.3   In experiments where radiolabelled substances have been used, high radiolabel concentrations are often found in the gall bladder of fish. This is interpreted to be caused by biotransformation in the liver and subsequently by excretion of metabolites in the gall bladder (Comotto et al., 1979; Wakabayashi et al., 1987; Goodrich et al., 1991; Toshima et al., 1992). When fish do not eat, the content of the gall bladder is not emptied into the gut, and high concentrations of metabolites may build up in the gall bladder. The feeding regime may thus have a pronounced effect on the measured BCF. In the literature many studies are found where radiolabelled compounds are used, and where the fish are not fed. As a result high concentrations of radioactive material are found in the gall bladder. In these studies the bioconcentration may in most cases have been overestimated. Thus when evaluating experiments, in which radiolabelled compounds are used, it is essential to evaluate the feeding regime as well.

A9.5.2.3.9.4   If the BCF in terms of radiolabelled residues is documented to be ≥ 1000, identification and quantification of degradation products, representing $\geq 10\%$ of total residues in fish tissues at steady-state, are for e.g. pesticides strongly recommended in the OECD guideline No. 305 (1996). If no identification and quantification of metabolites are available, the assessment of bioconcentration should be based on the measured radiolabelled BCF value. If, for highly bioaccumulative substances (BCF ≥ 500), only BCFs based on the parent compound and on radiolabelled measurements are available, the latter should thus be used in relation to classification.

A9.5.2.4   *Octanol-water-partitioning coefficient (K_{ow})*

A9.5.2.4.1   For organic substances experimentally derived high-quality K_{ow} values, or values which are evaluated in reviews and assigned as the "recommended values", are preferred over other determinations of Kow. When no experimental data of high quality are available, validated Quantitative Structure Activity Relationships (QSARs) for log K_{ow} may be used in the classification process. Such validated QSARs may be used without modification to the agreed criteria if they are restricted to chemicals for which their applicability is well characterized. For substances like strong acids and bases, substances which react with the eluent, or surface-active substances, a QSAR estimated value of K_{ow} or an estimate based on individual *n*-octanol and water solubilities should be provided instead of an analytical determination of K_{ow} (EEC A.8., 1992; OECD 117, 1989). Measurements should be taken on ionizable substances in their non-ionized form (free acid or free base) only by using an appropriate buffer with pH below pK for free acid or above the pK for free base.

A9.5.2.4.2   Experimental determination of K_{ow}

For experimental determination of K_{ow} values, several different methods, Shake-flask, and HPLC, are described in standard guidelines, e.g. OECD Test Guideline 107 (1995); OECD Test Guideline 117 (1989); EEC A.8. (1992); EPA-OTS (1982); EPA-FIFRA (1982); ASTM (1993); the pH-metric method (OECD Test Guideline in preparation). The shake-flask method is recommended when the log K_{ow} value falls within the range from –2 to 4. The shake-flask method applies only to essential pure substances soluble in water and *n*-octanol. For highly lipophilic substances, which slowly dissolve in water, data obtained by employing a slow-stirring method are generally more reliable. Furthermore, the experimental difficulties, associated with the formation of microdroplets during the shake-flask experiment, can to some degree be overcome by a slow-stirring method where water, octanol, and test compound are equilibrated in a gently stirred reactor. With the slow-stirring method (OECD Test Guideline in preparation) a precise and accurate determination of K_{ow} of compounds with log K_{ow} of up to 8.2 is allowed (OECD draft Guideline, 1998). As for the shake-flask method, the slow-stirring method applies only to essentially pure substances soluble in water and *n*-octanol. The HPLC method, which is performed on analytical columns, is recommended when the log K_{ow} value falls within the range 0 to 6. The HPLC method is less sensitive to the presence of impurities in the test compound compared to the shake-flask method. Another technique for measuring log K_{ow} is the generator column method (USEPA 1985).

As an experimental determination of the K_{ow} is not always possible, e.g. for very water-soluble substances, very lipophilic substances, and surfactants, a QSAR-derived K_{ow} may be used.

A9.5.2.4.3   Use of QSARs for determination of log K_{ow}

When an estimated K_{ow} value is found, the estimation method has to be taken into account. Numerous QSARs have been and continue to be developed for the estimation of K_{ow}. Four commercially available PC programmes (CLOGP, LOGKOW (KOWWIN), AUTOLOGP, SPARC) are frequently used for risk assessment if no experimentally derived data are available. CLOGP, LOGKOW and AUTOLOGP are based upon the addition of group contributions, while SPARC is based upon a more fundamental chemical structure algorithm. Only SPARC can be employed in a general way for inorganic or organometallic compounds. Special methods are needed for estimating log K_{ow} for surface-active compounds, chelating compounds and mixtures. CLOGP is recommended in the US EPA/EC joint project on validation of QSAR estimation methods (US EPA/EC 1993). Pedersen *et al.* (1995) recommended the CLOGP and the LOGKOW programmes for classification purposes because of their reliability, commercial availability, and convenience of use. The following estimation methods are recommended for classification purposes (Table A9.5.1).

Table A9.5.1: Recommended QSARs for estimation of K_{ow}

Model	log K_{ow} range	Substance utility
CLOGP	$0 < \log K_{ow} < 9$ [a]	The program calculates log K_{ow} for organic compounds containing C, H, N, O, Hal, P, and/or S.
LOGKOW (KOWWIN)	$-4 < \log K_{ow} < 8$ [b]	The program calculates log K_{ow} for organic compounds containing C, H, N, O, Hal, Si, P, Se, Li, Na, K, and/or Hg. Some surfactants (e.g. alcohol ethoxylates, dyestuffs, and dissociated substances may be predicted by the program as well.
AUTOLOGP	log $K_{ow} > 5$	The programme calculates log K_{ow} for organic compounds containing C, H, N, O, Hal, P and S. Improvements are in progress in order to extend the applicability of AUTOLOGP.
SPARC	Provides improved results over KOWWIN and CLOGP for compounds with log $K_{ow} > 5$	SPARC is a mechanistic model based on chemical thermodynamic principles rather than a deterministic model rooted in knowledge obtained from observational data. Therefore, SPARC differs from models that use QSARs (i.e. KOWWIN, CLOGP, AUTOLOGP) in that no measured log K_{ow} data are needed for a training set of chemicals. Only SPARC can be employed in a general way for inorganic or organometallic compounds.

[a] *A validation study performed by Niemelä, who compared experimental determined log K_{ow} values with estimated values, showed that the program precisely predicts the log K_{ow} for a great number of organic chemicals in the log K_{ow} range from below 0 to above 9 (n = 501, r^2 = 0.967) (TemaNord 1995: 581).*

[b] *Based on a scatter plot of estimated vs. experimental log K_{ow} (Syracuse Research Corporation, 1999), where 13058 compound have been tested, the LOGKOW is evaluated being valid for compounds with a log K_{ow} in the interval -4 - 8.*

A9.5.3 *Chemical classes that need special attention with respect to BCF and K_{ow} values*

A9.5.3.1   There are certain physico-chemical properties, which can make the determination of BCF or its measurement difficult. These may be substances, which do not bioconcentrate in a manner consistent with their other physico-chemical properties, e.g. steric hindrance or substances which make the use of descriptors inappropriate, e.g. surface activity, which makes both the measurement and use of log K_{ow} inappropriate.

A9.5.3.2   *Difficult substances*

A9.5.3.2.1   Some substances are difficult to test in aquatic systems and guidance has been developed to assist in testing these materials (DoE, 1996; ECETOC 1996; and US EPA 1996). OECD is in the process of finalizing a guidance document for the aquatic testing of difficult substances (OECD, 2000). This latter document is a good source of information, also for bioconcentration studies, on the types of substances that are difficult to test and the steps needed to ensure valid conclusions from tests with these substances. Difficult to test substances may be poorly soluble, volatile, or subject to rapid degradation due to such processes as phototransformation, hydrolysis, oxidation, or biotic degradation.

A9.5.3.2.2   To bioconcentrate organic compounds, a substance needs to be soluble in lipids, present in the water, and available for transfer across the fish gills. Properties which alter this availability will thus change the actual bioconcentration of a substance, when compared with the prediction. For example, readily biodegradable substances may only be present in the aquatic compartment for short periods of time. Similarly, volatility, and hydrolysis will reduce the concentration and the time during which a substance is available for bioconcentration. A further important parameter, which may reduce the actual exposure concentration of a substance, is adsorption, either to particulate matter or to surfaces in general. There are a number of substances, which have shown to be rapidly transformed in the organism, thus leading to a lower BCF value than expected. Substances that form micelles or aggregates may bioconcentrate to a lower extent than would be predicted from simple physico-chemical properties. This is also the case for hydrophobic substances that are contained in micelles formed as a consequence of the use of dispersants. Therefore, the use of dispersants in bioaccumulation tests is discouraged.

A9.5.3.2.3   In general, for difficult to test substances, measured BCF and K_{ow} values – based on the parent substance – are a prerequisite for the determination of the bioconcentration potential. Furthermore, proper documentation of the test concentration is a prerequisite for the validation of the given BCF value.

A9.5.3.3   *Poorly soluble and complex substances*

Special attention should be paid to poorly soluble substances. Frequently the solubility of these substances is recorded as less than the detection limit, which creates problems in interpreting the bioconcentration potential. For such substances the bioconcentration potential should be based on experimental determination of log K_{ow} or QSAR estimations of log K_{ow}.

When a multi-component substance is not fully soluble in water, it is important to attempt to identify the components of the mixture as far as practically possible and to examine the possibility of determining its bioaccumulation potential using available information on its components. When bioaccumulating components constitute a significant part of the complex substance (e.g. more than 20% or for hazardous components an even lower content), the complex substance should be regarded as being bioaccumulating.

A9.5.3.4   *High molecular weight substances*

Above certain molecular dimensions, the potential of a substance to bioconcentrate decreases.. This is possibly due to steric hindrance of the passage of the substance through gill membranes. It has been proposed that a cut-off limit of 700 for the molecular weight could be applied (e.g. European Commission, 1996). However, this cut-off has been subject to criticism and an alternative cut-off of 1000 has been proposed in relation to exclusion of consideration of substances with possible indirect aquatic effects (CSTEE, 1999). In general, bioconcentration of possible metabolites or environmental degradation products of large molecules should be considered. Data on bioconcentration of molecules with a high molecular weight should therefore be carefully evaluated and only be used if such data are considered to be fully valid in respect to both the parent compound and its possible metabolites and environmental degradation products.

A9.5.3.5   *Surface-active agents*

A9.5.3.5.1   Surfactants consist of a lipophilic (most often an alkyl chain) and a hydrophilic part (the polar headgroup). According to the charge of the headgroup, surfactants are subdivided into classes of anionic, cationic, non-ionic, or amphoteric surfactants. Due to the variety of different headgroups, surfactants are a structurally diverse class of compounds, which is defined by surface activity rather than by chemical structure. The bioaccumulation potential of surfactants should thus be considered in relation to the different subclasses (anionic, cationic, non-ionic, or amphoteric) instead of to the group as a whole. Surface-active substances may form emulsions, in which the bioavailability is difficult to ascertain. Micelle formation can result in a change of the bioavailable fraction even when the solutions are apparently formed, thus giving problems in interpretation of the bioaccumulation potential.

A9.5.3.5.2   Experimentally derived bioconcentration factors

Measured BCF values on surfactants show that BCF may increase with increasing alkyl chain length and be dependant of the site of attachment of the head group, and other structural features.

A9.5.3.5.3   Octanol-water-partition coefficient (K_{ow})

The octanol-water partition coefficient for surfactants can not be determined using the shake-flask or slow stirring method because of the formation of emulsions. In addition, the surfactant molecules will exist in the water phase almost exclusively as ions, whereas they will have to pair with a counter-ion in order to be dissolved in octanol. Therefore, experimental determination of K_{ow} does not characterize the partition of ionic surfactants (Tolls, 1998). On the other hand, it has been shown that the bioconcentration of anionic and non-ionic surfactants increases with increasing lipophilicity (Tolls, 1998). Tolls (1998) showed that for some surfactants, an estimated log K_{ow} value using LOGKOW could represent the bioaccumulation potential; however, for other surfactants some 'correction' to the estimated log K_{ow} value using the method of Roberts (1989) was required. These results illustrate that the quality of the relationship between log K_{ow} estimates and bioconcentration depends on the class and specific type of surfactants involved. Therefore, the classification of the bioconcentration potential based on log K_{ow} values should be used with caution.

A9.5.4 *Conflicting data and lack of data*

A9.5.4.1 *Conflicting BCF data*

In situations where multiple BCF data are available for the same substance, the possibility of conflicting results might arise. In general, conflicting results for a substance, which has been tested several times with an appropriate bioconcentration test, should be interpreted by a "weight of evidence approach". This implies that if experimental determined BCF data, both $\geq$ and < 500, have been obtained for a substance the data of the highest quality and with the best documentation should be used for determining the bioconcentration potential of the substance. If differences still remain, if e.g. high-quality BCF values for different fish species are available, generally the highest valid value should be used as the basis for classification.

When larger data sets (4 or more values) are available for the same species and life stage, the geometric mean of the BCF values may be used as the representative BCF value for that species.

A9.5.4.2 *Conflicting log K_{ow} data*

The situations, where multiple log K_{ow} data are available for the same substance, the possibility of conflicting results might arise. If log K_{ow} data both $\geq$ and < 4 have been obtained for a substance, then the data of the highest quality and the best documentation should be used for determining the bioconcentration potential of the substance. If differences still exist, generally the highest valid value should take precedence. In such situation, QSAR estimated log K_{ow} could be used as a guidance.

A9.5.4.3 *Expert judgement*

If no experimental BCF or log K_{ow} data or no predicted log K_{ow} data are available, the potential for bioconcentration in the aquatic environment may be assessed by expert judgement. This may be based on a comparison of the structure of the molecule with the structure of other substances for which experimental bioconcentration or log K_{ow} data or predicted K_{ow} are available.

A9.5.5 *Decision scheme*

A9.5.5.1   Based on the above discussions and conclusions, a decision scheme has been elaborated which may facilitate decisions as to whether or not a substance has the potential for bioconcentration in aquatic species.

A9.5.5.2   Experimentally derived BCF values of high quality are ultimately preferred for classification purposes. BCF values of low or uncertain quality should not be used for classification purposes if data on log K_{ow} are available because they may give a false and too low BCF value, e.g. due to a too short exposure period in which steady-state conditions have not been reached. If no BCF is available for fish species, high quality data on the BCF for other species (e.g. mussels) may be used.

A9.5.5.3   For organic substances, experimentally derived high quality K_{ow} values, or values which are evaluated in reviews and assigned as the "recommended values", are preferred. If no experimentally data of high quality are available validated Quantitative Structure Activity Relationships (QSARs) for log K_{ow} may be used in the classification process. Such validated QSARs may be used without modification in relation to the classification criteria, if restricted to chemicals for which their applicability is well characterized. For substances like strong acids and bases, metal complexes, and surface-active substances a QSAR estimated value of K_{ow} or an estimate based on individual *n*-octanol and water solubilities should be provided instead of an analytical determination of K_{ow}.

A9.5.5.4   If data are available but not validated, expert judgement should be used.

A9.5.5.5   Whether or not a substance has a potential for bioconcentration in aquatic organisms could thus be decided in accordance with the following scheme:

(a)   Valid/high quality experimentally determined BCF value = YES:

(i)   BCF ≥ 500: *The substance has a potential for bioconcentration*
(ii)   BCF < 500: *The substance does not have a potential for bioconcentration.*

(b)   Valid/high quality experimentally determined BCF value = NO:

Valid/high quality experimentally determined log K_{ow} value =YES:

(i)   log K_{ow} ≥ 4: *The substance has a potential for bioconcentration*
(ii)   log K_{ow} < 4: *The substance does not have a potential for bioconcentration.*

(c)   Valid/high quality experimentally determined BCF value = NO:

Valid/high quality experimentally determined log K_{ow} value =NO:

Use of validated QSAR for estimating a log K_{ow} value = YES:

(i)   log K_{ow} ≥ 4: *The substance has a potential for bioconcentration*
(ii)   log K_{ow} < 4: *The substance does not have a potential for bioconcentration.*

A9.6   Use of QSAR

A9.6.1   *History*

A9.6.1.1   Quantitative Structure-Activity Relationships (QSAR) in aquatic toxicology can be traced to the work of Overton in Zürich (Lipnick, 1986) and Meyer in Marburg (Lipnick, 1989a). They demonstrated that the potency of substances producing narcosis in tadpoles and small fish is in direct proportion to their partition coefficients measured between olive oil and water. Overton postulated in his 1901 monograph "Studien über die Narkose," that this correlation reflects toxicity taking place at a standard molar concentration or molar volume within some molecular site within the organism (Lipnick, 1991a). In addition, he concluded that this corresponds to the same concentration or volume for a various organisms, regardless of whether uptake is from water or via gaseous inhalation. This correlation became known in anaesthesia as the Meyer-Overton theory.

A9.6.1.2   Corwin Hansch and co-workers at Pomona College proposed the use of n-octanol/water as a standard partitioning system, and found that these partition coefficients were an additive, constitutive property that can be directly estimated from chemical structure. In addition, they found that regression analysis could be used to derive QSAR models, providing a statistical analysis of the findings. Using this approach, in 1972 these workers reported 137 QSAR models in the form log $(1/C)$ = A log K_{ow} + B, where K_{ow} is the n-octanol/water partition coefficient, and C is the molar concentration of a chemical yielding a standard biological response for the effect of simple non-electrolyte non-reactive organic compounds on whole animals, organs, cells, or even pure enzymes. Five of these equations, which relate to the toxicity of five simple monohydric alcohols to five species of fish, have almost identical slopes and intercepts that are in fact virtually the same as those found by Könemann in 1981, who appears to have been unaware of Hansch's earlier work. Könemann and others have demonstrated that such simple non-reactive non-electrolytes all act by a narcosis mechanism in an acute fish toxicity test, giving rise to minimum or baseline toxicity (Lipnick, 1989b).

A9.6.2　　　*Experimental artifacts causing underestimation of hazard*

A9.6.2.1　　　Other non-electrolytes can be more toxic than predicted by such a QSAR, but not less toxic, except as a result of a testing artefact. Such testing artefacts include data obtained for compounds such as hydrocarbons which tend to volatilize during the experiment, as well as very hydrophobic compounds for which the acute testing duration may be inadequate to achieve steady state equilibrium partitioning between the concentration in the aquatic phase (aquarium test solution), and the internal hydrophobic site of narcosis action. A QSAR plot of log K_{ow} vs log C for such simple non-reactive non-electrolytes exhibits a linear relationship so long as such equilibrium is established within the test duration. Beyond this point, a bilinear relationship is observed, with the most toxic chemical being the one with the highest log K_{ow} value for which such equilibrium is established (Lipnick, 1995).

A9.6.2.2　　　Another testing problem is posed by water solubility cut-off. If the toxic concentration required to produce the effect is above the compound's water solubility, no effect will be observed even at water saturation. Compounds for which the predicted toxic concentration is close to water solubility will also show no effect if the test duration is insufficient to achieve equilibrium partitioning. A similar cut-off is observed for surfactants if toxicity is predicted at a concentration beyond the critical micelle concentration. Although such compounds may show no toxicity under these conditions when tested alone, their toxic contributions to mixtures are still present. For compounds with the same log K_{ow} value, differences in water solubility reflect differences in enthalpy of fusion related to melting point. Melting point is a reflection of the degree of stability of the crystal lattice and is controlled by intermolecular hydrogen bonding, lack of conformational flexibility, and symmetry. The more highly symmetric a compound, the higher the melting point (Lipnick, 1990).

A9.6.3　　　*QSAR modelling issues*

A9.6.3.1　　　Choosing an appropriate QSAR implies that the model will yield a reliable prediction for the toxicity or biological activity of an untested chemical. Generally speaking, reliability decreases with increasing complexity of chemical structure, unless a QSAR has been derived for a narrowly defined set of chemicals similar in structure to the candidate substance. QSAR models derived from narrowly defined classes of chemicals are commonly employed in the development of pharmaceuticals once a new lead compound is identified and there is a need to make minor structural modifications to optimize activity (and decrease toxicity). Overall, the objective is make estimates by interpolation rather than extrapolation.

A9.6.3.2　　　For example, if 96-h LC_{50} test data for fathead minnow are available for ethanol, n-butanol, n-hexanol, and n-nonanol, there is some confidence in making a prediction for this endpoint for n-propanol and n-pentanol. In contrast, there is would have less confidence in making such a prediction for methanol, which is an extrapolation, with fewer carbon atoms than any of the tested chemicals. In fact, the behaviour of the first member of such a homologous is typically the most anomalous, and should not be predicted using data from remaining members of the series. Even the toxicity of branched chain alcohols may be an unreasonable extrapolation, depending upon the endpoint in question. Such extrapolation becomes more unreliable to the extent that toxicity is related to production of metabolites for a particular endpoint, as opposed to the properties of the parent compound. Also, if toxicity is mediated by a specific receptor binding mechanism, dramatic effects may be observed with small changes in chemical structure.

A9.6.3.3　　　What ultimately governs the validity of such predictions is the degree to which the compounds used to derive the QSAR for a specific biological endpoint, are acting by a common molecular mechanism. In many and perhaps most cases, a QSAR does not represent such a mechanistic model, but merely a correlative one. A truly valid mechanistic model must be derived from a series of chemicals all acting by a common molecular mechanism, and fit to an equation using one or more parameters that relate directly to one or more steps of the mechanism in question. Such parameters or properties are more generally known as molecular descriptors. It is also important to keep in mind that many such molecular descriptors in common use may not have a direct physical interpretation. For a correlative model, the statistical fit of the data are likely to be poorer than a mechanistic one given these limitations. Mechanisms are not necessarily completely understood, but enough information may be known to provide confidence in this approach. For correlative models, the predictive reliability increases with the narrowness with which each is defined, e.g. categories of electrophiles, such as acrylates, in which the degree of reactivity may be similar and toxicity can be estimated for a "new" chemical using a model based solely on the log K_{ow} parameter.

A9.6.3.4   As an example, primary and secondary alcohols containing a double or triple bond that is conjugated with the hydroxyl function (i.e. allylic or propargylic) are more toxic than would be predicted for a QSAR for the corresponding saturated compounds. This behaviour has been ascribed to a proelectrophile mechanism involving metabolic activation by the ubiquitous enzyme alcohol dehydrogenase to the corresponding α,β-unsaturated aldehydes and ketones which can act as electrophiles via a Michael-type acceptor mechanism (Veith *et al.*, 1989). In the presence of an alcohol dehydrogenase inhibitor, these compounds behave like other alcohols and do not show excess toxicity, consistent with the mechanistic hypothesis.

A9.6.3.5   The situation quickly becomes more complex once one goes beyond such a homologous series of compounds. Consider, for example, simple benzene derivatives. A series of chlorobenzenes may be viewed as similar to a homologous series. Not much difference is likely in the toxicities of the three isomeric dichlorobenzenes, so that a QSAR for chlorobenzenes based upon test data for one of these isomers is likely to be adequate. What about the substitution of other functional groups on benzene ring? Unlike an aliphatic alcohol, addition of a hydroxyl functionality to a benzene ring produces a phenol which is no longer neutral, but an ionizable acidic compound, due to the resonance stabilization of the resulting negative charge. For this reason, phenol does not act as a true narcotic agent. With the addition of electron withdrawing substituents to phenol (e.g. chlorine atoms), there is a shift to these compounds acting as uncouplers of oxidative phosphorylation (e.g. the herbicide dinoseb). Substitution of an aldehyde group leads to increased toxicity via an electrophile mechanism for such compounds react with amino groups, such as the lysine ε-amino group to produce a Schiff Base adduct. Similarly, a benzylic chloride acts as an electrophile to form covalent abducts with sulfhydryl groups. In tackling a prediction for an untested compound, the chemical reactivity of these and many other functional groups and their interaction with one another should be carefully studied, and attempts made to document these from the chemical literature (Lipnick, 1991b).

A9.6.3.6   Given these limitations in using QSARs for making predictions, it is best employed as a means of establishing testing priorities, rather than as a means of substituting for testing, unless some mechanistic information is available on the untested compound itself. In fact, the inability to make a prediction along with known environmental release and exposure may in itself be adequate to trigger testing or the development of a new QSAR for a class of chemicals for which such decisions are needed. A QSAR model can be derived by statistical analysis, e.g. regression analysis, from such a data set. The most commonly employed molecular descriptor, log K_{ow}, may be tried as a first attempt.

A9.6.3.7   By contrast, derivation of a mechanism based QSAR model requires an understanding or working hypothesis of molecular mechanism and what parameter or parameters would appropriately model these actions. It is important to keep in mind that this is different from a hypothesis regarding mode of action, which relates to biological/physiological response, but not molecular mechanism.

A9.6.4   *Use of QSARs in aquatic classification*

A9.6.4.1   The following inherent properties of substances are relevant for classification purposes concerning the aquatic environment:

(a)   partition coefficient n-octanol-water log K_{ow};

(b)   bioconcentration factor BCF;

(c)   degradability - abiotic and biodegradation;

(d)   acute aquatic toxicity for fish, daphnia and algae;

(e)   prolonged toxicity for fish and daphnia.

A9.6.4.2   Test data always take precedence over QSAR predications, providing the test data are valid, with QSARs used for filling data gaps for purposes of classification. Since the available QSARs are of varying reliability and application range, different restrictions apply for the prediction of each of these endpoints. Nevertheless, if a tested compound belongs to a chemical class or structure type (see above) for which there is some confidence in the predictive utility of the QSAR model, it is worthwhile to compare this prediction with the experimental data, as it is not unusual to use this approach to detect some of the experimental artefacts (volatilization, insufficient test duration to achieve equilibrium, and water solubility cut-off) in the measured data, which would mostly result in classifying substances as lower than actual toxicity.

A9.6.4.3   When two or more QSARs are applicable or appear to be applicable, it is useful to compare the predictions of these various models in the same way that predicted data should be compared with measured (as discussed above). If there is no discrepancy between these models, the result provides encouragement of the validity of the predictions. Of course, it may also mean that the models were all developed using data on similar compounds and statistical methods. On the other hand, if the predictions are quite different, this result needs to be examined further. There is always the possibility that none of the models used provides a valid prediction. As a first step, the structures and properties of the chemicals used to derive each of the predictive models should be examined to determine if any models are based upon chemicals similar in both of these respects to the one for which a prediction is needed. If one data set contains such an appropriate analogue used to derive the model, the measured value in the database for that compound vs model prediction should be tested. If the results fit well with the overall model, it is likely the most reliable one to use. Likewise, if none of the models contain test data for such an analogue, testing of the chemical in question is recommended.

A9.6.4.4   The U.S. EPA has recently posted a draft document on its website "Development of Chemical Categories in the HPV Challenge Program," that proposes the use of chemical categories to "... voluntarily compile a Screening Information Data Set (SIDS) on all chemicals on the US HPV list ... [to provide] basic screening data needed for an initial assessment of the physicochemical properties, environmental fate, and human and environmental effects of chemicals" (US EPA, 1999). This list consists of "...about 2,800 HPV chemicals which were reported for the Toxic Substances Control Act's 1990 Inventory Update Rule (IUR)".

A9.6.4.5   One approach being proposed "...where this is scientifically justifiable ... is to consider closely related chemicals as a group, or category, rather than test them as individual chemicals. In the category approach, not every chemical needs to be tested for every SIDS endpoint". Such limited testing could be justified providing that the "...final data set must allow one to assess the untested endpoints, ideally by interpolation between and among the category members." The process for defining such categories and in the development of such data are described in the proposal.

A9.6.4.6   A second potentially less data intensive approach being considered (US EPA, 2000a) is "... applying SAR principles to a single chemical that is closely related to one or more better characterized chemicals ("analogs")." A third approach proposed consists of using "... a combination of the analogue and category approaches ... [for] individual chemicals ... [similar to that] used in ECOSAR (US EPA, 2000b), a SAR-based computer program that generates ecotoxicity values. ". The document also details the history of the use of SARs within the U.S. EPA new chemicals program, and how to go about collecting and analysing data for the sake of such SAR approaches.

A9.6.4.7   The Nordic Council of Ministers issued a report (Pederson et al., 1995) entitled "Environmental Hazard Classification," that includes information on data collection and interpretation, as well as a section (5.2.8) entitled "QSAR estimates of water solubility and acute aquatic toxicity". This section also discusses the estimation of physicochemical properties, including log K_{ow}. For the sake of classification purposes, estimation methods are recommended for prediction of "minimum acute aquatic toxicity," for "...neutral, organic, non-reactive and non-ionizable compounds such as alcohols, ketones, ethers, alkyl, and aryl halides, and can also be used for aromatic hydrocarbons, halogenated aromatic and aliphatic hydrocarbons as well as sulphides and disulphides," as cited in an earlier OECD Guidance Document (OECD, 1995). The Nordic document also includes diskettes for a computerized application of some of these methods.

A9.6.4.8   The European Centre for Ecotoxicology and Toxicology of Chemicals (ECETOC) has published a report entitled "QSARs in the Assessment of the Environmental Fate and Effects of Chemicals," which describes the use of QSARs to "...check the validity of data or to fill data gaps for priority setting, risk assessment and classification" (ECETOC, 1998). QSARs are described for predicting environmental fate and aquatic toxicity. The report notes that "a consistent dataset for [an endpoint] covered ... for a well defined scope of chemical structures ("domain") [is needed] ... from which a training set is developed. The document also discusses the advantage of mechanism based models, the use of statistical analysis in the development of QSARs, and how to assess "outliers".

A9.6.4.9   *Octanol-water-partition coefficient (K_{ow})*

A9.6.4.9.1   Computerized methods such as CLOGP (US EPA, 1999), LOGKOW (US EPA, 2000a) and SPARC (US EPA, 2000b) are available to calculate log K_{ow} directly from chemical structure. CLOGP and LOGKOW are based upon the addition of group contributions, while SPARC is based upon a more fundamental chemical structure algorithm. Caution should be used in using calculated values for compounds that can undergo hydrolysis in water or some other reaction, since these transformations need to be considered in the interpretation of aquatic toxicity test data for such reactive chemicals. Only SPARC can be employed in a general way for inorganic or organometallic compounds. Special methods are needed in making estimates of log K_{ow} or aquatic toxicity for surface-active compounds, chelating compounds, and mixtures.

A9.6.4.9.2   Values of log K_{ow} can be calculated for pentachlorophenol and similar compounds, both for the ionized and unionized (neutral) forms. These values can potentially be calculated for certain reactive molecules (e.g. benzotrichloride), but the reactivity and subsequent hydrolysis also need to be considered. Also, for such ionizable phenols, pKa is a second parameter. Specific models can be used to calculate log K_{ow} values for organometallic compounds, but they need to be applied with caution since some of these compounds really exist in the form of ion pairs in water.

A9.6.4.9.3   For compounds of extremely high lipophilicity, measurements up to about 6 to 6.5 can be made by shake flask, and can be extended up to about log K_{ow} of 8 using the slow stirring approach (Bruijn *et al.*, 1989). Calculations are considered useful even in extrapolating beyond what can be measured by either of these methods. Of course, it should be kept in mind that if the QSAR models for toxicity, etc. are based on chemicals with lower log K_{ow} values, the prediction itself will also be an extrapolation; in fact, it is known that in the case of bioconcentration, the relationship with log K_{ow} becomes non-linear at higher values. For compounds with low log K_{ow} values, the group contribution can also be applied, but this is not very useful for hazard purposes since for such substances, particularly with negative log K_{ow} values, little if any partitioning can take place into lipophilic sites and as Overton reported, these substances produce toxicity through osmotic effects (Lipnick, 1986).

A9.6.4.10   *Bioconcentration factor BCF*

A9.6.4.10.1   If experimentally determined BCF values are available, these values should be used for classification. Bioconcentration measurements must be performed using pure samples at test concentrations within water solubility, and for an adequate test duration to achieve steady state equilibrium between the aqueous concentration and that in the fish tissue. Moreover, with bioconcentration tests of extended duration, the correlation with log K_{ow} levels off and ultimately decreases. Under environmental conditions, bioconcentration of highly lipophilic chemicals takes place by a combination of uptake from food and water, with the switch to food taking place at log $K_{ow} \approx 6$. Otherwise log K_{ow} values can be used with a QSAR model as a predictor of the bioaccumulation potential of organic compounds. Deviations from these QSARs tend to reflect differences in the extent to which the chemicals undergo metabolism in the fish. Thus, some chemicals, such as phthalate, can bioconcentrate significantly less than predicted for this reason. Also, caution should be applied in comparing predicted BCF values with those using radiolabeled compounds, where the tissue concentration thus detected may represent a mix of parent compound and metabolites or even covalently bound parent or metabolite.

A9.6.4.10.2   Experimental log K_{ow} values are to be used preferentially. However, older shake flask values above 5.5 are not reliable and in many cases it is better to use some average of calculated values or to have these remeasured using the slow stirring method (Bruijn *et al.*, 1989). If there is reasonable doubt about the accuracy of the measured data, calculated log K_{ow} values shall be used.

A9.6.4.11   *Degradability - abiotic and biodegradation*

        QSARs for abiotic degradation in water phases are narrowly defined linear free energy relationships (LFERs) for specific classes of chemicals and mechanisms. For example, such LFERs are available for hydrolysis of benzylic chlorides with various substituents on the aromatic ring. Such narrowly defined LFER models tend to be very reliable if the needed parameters are available for the Substituent(s) in question. Photo degradation, i.e. reaction with UV produced reactive species, may be extrapolated from estimates for the air compartment. While these abiotic processes do not usually result in complete degradation of organic compounds, they are frequently significant starting points, and may be rate limiting. QSARs for calculating biodegradability are either compound specific (OECD, 1995) or group contribution models like the BIODEG program (Hansch and Leo, 1995; Meylan and Howard 1995; Hilal *et al.*, 1994; Howard *et al.*, 1992; Boethling *et al.*, 1994; Howard and Meylan 1992; Loonen *et al.*, 1999). While validated compound class specific models are very limited in their application range, the application range of group contribution models is potentially much broader, but limited to compounds containing the model substructures. Validation studies have suggested that the biodegradability predictions by currently available group contribution models may be used for prediction of "not ready biodegradability" (Pedersen *et al.*, 1995; Langenberg *et al.*, 1996; USEPA, 1993) – and thus in relation to aquatic hazard classification "not rapid degradability."

A9.6.4.12   *Acute aquatic toxicity for fish, daphnia and algae*

The acute aquatic toxicity of non-reactive, non-electrolyte organic chemicals (baseline toxicity) can be predicted from their log K_{ow} value with a quite high level of confidence, provided the presence of electrophile, proelectrophile, or special mechanism functional groups (see above) were not detected. Problems remain for such specific toxicants, for which the appropriate QSAR has to be selected in a prospective manner. Since straightforward criteria for the identification of the relevant modes of action are still lacking, empirical expert judgement needs to be applied for selecting a suitable model. Thus, if an inappropriate QSAR is employed, the predictions may be in error by several orders of magnitude, and in the case of baseline toxicity, will be predicted less toxic, rather than more.

A9.6.4.13   *Prolonged toxicity for fish and Daphnia*

Calculated values for chronic toxicity to fish and Daphnia should not be used to overrule classification based on experimental acute toxicity data. Only a few validated models are available for calculating prolonged toxicity for fish and Daphnia. These models are based solely on log K_{ow} correlations and are limited in their application to non-reactive, non-electrolyte organic compounds, and are not suitable for chemicals with specific modes of action under prolonged exposure conditions. The reliable estimation of chronic toxicity values depends on the correct discrimination between non-specific and specific chronic toxicity mechanisms; otherwise, the predicted toxicity can be wrong by orders of magnitude. It should be noted that although for many compounds, excess toxicity[4] in a chronic test correlates with excess toxicity in an acute test, this is not always the case.

A9.7   Classification of metals and metal compounds

A9.7.1   *Introduction*

A9.7.1.1   The harmonized system for classifying substances is a hazard-based system, and the basis of the identification of hazard is the aquatic toxicity of the substances, and information on the degradation and bioaccumulation behaviour (OECD 1998). Since this document deals only with the hazards associated with a given substance when the substance is dissolved in the water column, exposure from this source is limited by the solubility of the substance in water and bioavailability of the substance in species in the aquatic environment. Thus, the hazard classification schemes for metals and metal compounds are limited to the hazards posed by metals and metal compounds when they are available (i.e. exist as dissolved metal ions, for example, as M^+ when present as $M-NO_3$), and do not take into account exposures to metals and metal compounds that are not dissolved in the water column but may still be bioavailable, such as metals in foods. This section does not take into account the non-metallic ion (e.g. CN-) of metal compounds which may be toxic or which may be organic and may pose bioaccumulation or persistence hazards. For such metal compounds the hazards of the non-metallic ions must also be considered.

A9.7.1.2   The level of the metal ion which may be present in solution following the addition of the metal and/or its compounds, will largely be determined by two processes: the extent to which it can be

---

4   *Excess toxicity, T_e = (Predicted baseline toxicity)/Observed toxicity.*

dissolved, i.e. its water solubility, and the extent to which it can react with the media to transform to water soluble forms. The rate and extent at which this latter process, known as "transformation" for the purposes of this guidance, takes place can vary extensively between different compounds and the metal itself, and is an important factor in determining the appropriate hazard class. Where data on transformation are available, they should be taken into account in determining the classification. The Protocol for determining this rate is available in Annex 10.

A9.7.1.3   Generally speaking, the rate at which a substance dissolves is not considered relevant to the determination of its intrinsic toxicity. However, for metals and many poorly soluble inorganic metal compounds, the difficulties in achieving dissolution through normal solubilization techniques is so severe that the two processes of solubilization and transformation become indistinguishable. Thus, where the compound is sufficiently poorly soluble that the levels dissolved following normal attempts at solubilization do not exceed the available $L(E)C_{50}$, it is the rate and extent of transformation, which must be considered. The transformation will be affected by a number of factors, not least of which will be the properties of the media with respect to pH, water hardness, temperature etc. In addition to these properties, other factors such as the size and specific surface area of the particles which have been tested, the length of time over which exposure to the media takes place and, of course the mass or surface area loading of the substance in the media will all play a part in determining the level of dissolved metal ions in the water. Transformation data can generally, therefore, only be considered as reliable for the purposes of classification if conducted according to the standard Protocol in Annex 10.

A9.7.1.4   This Protocol aims at standardizing the principal variables such that the level of dissolved ion can be directly related to the loading of the substance added. It is this loading level which yields the level of metal ion equivalent to the available $L(E)C_{50}$ that can then be used to determine the hazard category appropriate for classification. The testing methodology is detailed in Annex 10. The strategy to be adopted in using the data from the testing protocol, and the data requirements needed to make that strategy work, will be described.

A9.7.1.5   In considering the classification of metals and metal compounds, both readily and poorly soluble, recognition has to be paid to a number of factors. As defined in Chapter 4.1, the term "degradation" refers to the decomposition of organic molecules. For inorganic compounds and metals, clearly the concept of degradability, as it has been considered and used for organic substances, has limited or no meaning. Rather, the substance may be transformed by normal environmental processes to either increase or decrease the bioavailability of the toxic species. Equally, the log K_{ow} cannot be considered as a measure of the potential to accumulate. Nevertheless, the concepts that a substance, or a toxic metabolite/reaction product may not be rapidly lost from the environment and/or may bioaccumulate are as applicable to metals and metal compounds as they are to organic substances.

A9.7.1.6   Speciation of the soluble form can be affected by pH, water hardness and other variables, and may yield particular forms of the metal ion which are more or less toxic. In addition, metal ions could be made non-available from the water column by a number of processes (e.g. mineralization and partitioning). Sometimes these processes can be sufficiently rapid to be analogous to degradation in assessing chronic classification. However, partitioning of the metal ion from the water column to other environmental media does not necessarily mean that it is no longer bioavailable, nor does it mean that the metal has been made permanently unavailable.

A9.7.1.7   Information pertaining to the extent of the partitioning of a metal ion from the water column, or the extent to which a metal has been or can be converted to a form that is less toxic or non-toxic is frequently not available over a sufficiently wide range of environmentally relevant conditions, and thus, a number of assumptions will need to be made as an aid in classification. These assumptions may be modified if available data show otherwise. In the first instance it should be assumed that the metal ions, once in the water, are not rapidly partitioned from the water column and thus these compounds do not meet the criteria. Underlying this is the assumption that, although speciation can occur, the species will remain available under environmentally relevant conditions. This may not always be the case, as described above, and any evidence available that would suggest changes to the bioavailability over the course of 28 days, should be carefully examined. The bioaccumulation of metals and inorganic metal compounds is a complex process and bioaccumulation data should be used with care. The application of bioaccumulation criteria will need to be considered on a case-by-case basis taking due account of all the available data.

A9.7.1.8   A further assumption that can be made, which represents a cautious approach, is that, in the absence of any solubility data for a particular metal compound, either measured or calculated, the substance will be sufficiently soluble to cause toxicity at the level of the L(E)C$_{50}$, and thus may be classified in the same way as other soluble salts. Again, this is clearly not always the case, and it may be wise to generate appropriate solubility data.

A9.7.1.9   This section deals with metals and metal compounds. Within the context of this Guidance Document, metals and metal compounds are characterized as follows, and therefore, organo-metals are outside the scope of this section:

(a)   metals, M^0, in their elemental state are not soluble in water but may transform to yield the available form. This means that a metal in the elemental state may react with water or a dilute aqueous electrolyte to form soluble cationic or anionic products, and in the process the metal will oxidize, or transform, from the neutral or zero oxidation state to a higher one;

(b)   in a simple metal compound, such as an oxide or sulphide, the metal already exists in the oxidized state, so that further metal oxidation is unlikely to occur when the compound is introduced into an aqueous medium.

However, while oxidization may not change, interaction with the media may yield more soluble forms. A sparingly soluble metal compound can be considered as one for which a solubility product can be calculated, and which will yield a small amount of the available form by dissolution. However, it should be recognized that the final solution concentration may be influenced by a number of factors, including the solubility product of some metal compounds precipitated during the transformation/dissolution test, e.g. aluminium hydroxide.

A9.7.2   *Application of aquatic toxicity data and solubility data for classification*

A9.7.2.1   *Interpretation of aquatic toxicity data*

A9.7.2.1.1   Aquatic toxicity studies carried out according to a recognized protocol should normally be acceptable as valid for the purposes of classification. Section A9.3 should also be consulted for generic issues that are common to assessing any aquatic toxicity data point for the purposes of classification.

A9.7.2.1.2   Metal complexation and speciation

A9.7.2.1.2.1   The toxicity of a particular metal in solution, appears to depend primarily on (but is not strictly limited to) the level of dissolved free metal ions. Abiotic factors including alkalinity, ionic strength and pH can influence the toxicity of metals in two ways: (i) by influencing the chemical speciation of the metal in water (and hence affecting the availability) and (ii) by influencing the uptake and binding of available metal by biological tissues.

A9.7.2.1.2.2   Where speciation is important, it may be possible to model the concentrations of the different forms of the metal, including those that are likely to cause toxicity. Analysis methods for quantifying exposure concentrations, which are capable of distinguishing between the complexed and uncomplexed fractions of a test substance, may not always be available or economic.

A9.7.2.1.2.3   Complexation of metals to organic and inorganic ligands in test media and natural environments can be estimated from metal speciation models. Speciation models for metals, including pH, hardness, DOC, and inorganic substances such as MINTEQ (Brown and Allison, 1987), WHAM (Tipping, 1994) and CHESS (Santore and Driscoll, 1995) can be used to calculate the uncomplexed and complexed fractions of the metal ions. Alternatively, the Biotic Ligand Model (BLM), allows for the calculation of the concentration of metal ion responsible for the toxic effect at the level of the organism. The BLM model has at present only been validated for a limited number of metals, organisms, and end-points (Santore and Di Toro, 1999). The models and formula used for the characterization of metal complexation in the media should always be clearly reported, allowing for their translation back to natural environments (OECD, 2000).

A9.7.2.2   *Interpretation of solubility data*

A9.7.2.2.1   When considering the available data on solubility, their validity and applicability to the identification of the hazard of metal compounds should be assessed. In particular, a knowledge of the pH at which the data were generated should be known.

A9.7.2.2.2   Assessment of existing data

Existing data will be in one of three forms. For some well-studied metals, there will be solubility products and/or solubility data for the various inorganic metal compounds. It is also possible that the pH relationship of the solubility will be known. However, for many metals or metal compounds, it is probable that the available information will be descriptive only, e.g. poorly soluble. Unfortunately there appears to be very little (consistent) guidance about the solubility ranges for such descriptive terms. Where these are the only information available it is probable that solubility data will need to be generated using the Transformation/Dissolution Protocol (Annex 10).

A9.7.2.2.3   Screening test for assessing solubility of metal compounds

In the absence of solubility data, a simple "Screening Test" for assessing solubility, based on the high rate of loading for 24 h, can be used for metal compounds as described in the Transformation/Dissolution Protocol (Annex 10). The function of the screening test is to identify those metal compounds which undergo either dissolution or rapid transformation such that they are indistinguishable from soluble forms and hence may be classified based on the dissolved ion concentration. Where data are available from the screening test detailed in the Transformation/Dissolution Protocol, the maximum solubility obtained over the tested pH range should be used. Where data are not available over the full pH range, a check should be made that this maximum solubility has been achieved by reference to suitable thermodynamic speciation models or other suitable methods (see A9.7.2.1.2.3). It should be noted that this test is only intended to be used for metal compounds.

A9.7.2.2.4   Full test for assessing solubility of metals and metal compounds

The first step in this part of the study is, as with the screening test, an assessment of the pH(s) at which the study should be conducted. Normally, the Full Test should have been carried out at the pH that maximizes the concentration of dissolved metal ions in solution. In such cases, the pH may be chosen following the same guidance as given for the screening test.

Based on the data from the Full Test, it is possible to generate a concentration of the metal ions in solution after 7 days for each of the three loadings (i.e. 1 mg/l as "low", 10 mg/l as "medium" and 100 mg/l as "high") used in the test. If the purpose of the test is to assess the long-term (chronic) hazard of the substance, then the test at the low loading may be extended to 28 days, at an appropriate pH.

A9.7.2.3   *Comparison of aquatic toxicity data and solubility data*

A decision whether or not the substance be classified will be made by comparing aquatic toxicity data and solubility data. If the $L(E)C_{50}$ is exceeded, irrespective of whether the toxicity and dissolution data are at the same pH and if this is the only data available then the substance should be classified. If other solubility data are available to show that the dissolution concentration would not exceed the $L(E)C_{50}$ across the entire pH range then the substance should not be classified on its soluble form. This may involve the use of additional data either from ecotoxicological testing or from applicable bioavailability-effect models.

A9.7.3   *Assessment of environmental transformation*

A9.7.3.1   Environmental transformation of one species of a metal to another species of the same does not constitute degradation as applied to organic compounds and may increase or decrease the availability and bioavailability of the toxic species. However as a result of naturally occurring geochemical processes metal ions can partition from the water column. Data on water column residence time, the processes involved at the water – sediment interface (i.e. deposition and re-mobilization) are fairly extensive, but have not been integrated into a meaningful database. Nevertheless, using the principles and assumptions discussed above in A9.7.1, it may be possible to incorporate this approach into classification.

A9.7.3.2   Such assessments are very difficult to give guidance for and will normally be addressed on a case by case approach. However, the following may be taken into account:

(a)   Changes in speciation if they are to non-available forms, however, the potential for the reverse change to occur must also be considered;

(b)   Changes to a metal compound which is considerably less soluble than that of the metal compound being considered.

Some caution is recommended, see A9.7.1.5 and A9.7.1.6.

A9.7.4   *Bioaccumulation*

A9.7.4.1   While log K_{ow} is a good predictor of BCF for certain types of organic compounds e.g. non-polar organic substances, it is of course irrelevant for inorganic substances such as inorganic metal compounds.

A9.7.4.2   The mechanisms for uptake and depuration rates of metals are very complex and variable and there is at present no general model to describe this. Instead the bioaccumulation of metals according to the classification criteria should be evaluated on a case-by-case basis using expert judgement.

A9.7.4.3   While BCFs are indicative of the potential for bioaccumulation there may be a number of complications in interpreting measured BCF values for metals and inorganic metal compounds. For some metals and inorganic metal compounds the relationship between water concentration and BCF in some aquatic organisms is inverse, and bioconcentration data should be used with care. This is particularly relevant for metals that are biologically essential. Metals that are biologically essential are actively regulated in organisms in which the metal is essential. Since nutritional requirement of the organisms can be higher than the environmental concentration, this active regulation can result in high BCFs and an inverse relationship between BCFs and the concentration of the metal in water. When environmental concentrations are low, high BCFs may be expected as a natural consequence of metal uptake to meet nutritional requirements and in these instances can be viewed as a normal phenomenon. Additionally, if internal concentration is regulated by the organism, then measured BCFs may decline as external concentration increases. When external concentrations are so high that they exceed a threshold level or overwhelm the regulatory mechanism, this can cause harm to the organism. Also, while a metal may be essential in a particular organism, it may not be essential in other organisms. Therefore, where the metal is not essential or when the bioconcentration of an essential metal is above nutritional levels special consideration should be given to the potential for bioconcentration and environmental concern.

A9.7.5   *Application of classification criteria to metals and metal compounds*

A9.7.5.1   *Introduction to the classification strategy for metals and metal compounds*

A9.7.5.1.1   The schemes for the classification of metals and metal compounds are described below and summarized diagrammatically in Figure A9.7.1. There are several stages in these schemes where data are used for decision purposes. It is not the intention of the classification schemes to generate new data. In the absence of valid data, it will be necessary to use all available data and expert judgement.

In the following sections, the reference to the $L(E)C_{50}$ refers to the data point(s) that will be used to select the class for the metal or metal compound.

A9.7.5.1.2   When considering $L(E)C_{50}$ data for metal compounds, it is important to ensure that the data point to be used as the justification for the classification is expressed in the weight of the molecule of the metal compound to be classified. This is known as correcting for molecular weight. Thus while most metal data is expressed in, for example, mg/l of the metal, this value will need to be adjusted to the corresponding weight of the metal compound. Thus:

$$L(E)C_{50} \text{ metal compounds} = L(E)C_{50} \text{ of metal} \times (\text{Molecular weight of metal compound} / \text{Atomic weight of metal})$$

NOEC data may also need to be adjusted to the corresponding weight of the metal compounds.

A9.7.5.2 *Classification strategy for metals*

A9.7.5.2.1 Where the $L(E)C_{50}$ for the metal ions of concern is greater than 100 mg/l, the metals need not be considered further in the classification scheme.

A9.7.5.2.2 Where the $L(E)C_{50}$ for the metal ions of concern is $\leq$100 mg/l, consideration must be given to the data available on the rate and extent to which these ions can be generated from the metal. Such data, to be valid and useable should have been generated using the Transformation/Dissolution Protocol (Annex 10).

A9.7.5.2.3 Where such data are unavailable, i.e. there is no clear data of sufficient validity to show that the transformation to metal ions will not occur, the safety net classification (Chronic 4) should be applied since the known classifiable toxicity of these soluble forms is considered to produce sufficient concern.

A9.7.5.2.4 Where data from dissolution protocol are available, then, the results should be used to aid classification according to the following rules:

A9.7.5.2.4.1 7 day Transformation test

If the dissolved metal ion concentration after a period of 7 days (or earlier) exceeds that of the $L(E)C_{50}$, then the default classification for the metals is replaced by the following classification:

(a) If the dissolved metal ion concentration at the low loading rate is $\geq L(E)C_{50}$, then classify as Acute 1. Classify also as Chronic 1, unless there is evidence of both rapid partitioning from the water column and no bioaccumulation;

(b) If the dissolved metal ion concentration at the medium loading rate is $\geq L(E)C_{50}$, then classify as Acute 2. Classify also as Chronic 2 unless there is evidence of both rapid partitioning from the water column and no bioaccumulation;

(c) If the dissolved metal ion concentration at the high loading rate is $\geq L(E)C_{50}$, then classify as Acute 3. Classify also as Chronic 3 unless there is evidence of both rapid partitioning from the water column and no bioaccumulation.

A9.7.5.2.4.2 28 day transformation test

If the process described in A9.7.5.2.4.1 results in classification as Chronic 1, no further assessment is required, as the metal will be classified irrespective of any further information.

In all other cases, further data may have been generated through the dissolution/transformation test in order to show that the classification may be amended. If for substances classified as Chronic 2, 3 or 4, the dissolved metal ion concentration at the low loading rate after a total period of 28 days is $\leq$ long-term NOECs, then the classification is removed.

A9.7.5.3 *Classification strategy for metal compounds*

A9.7.5.3.1 Where the $L(E)C_{50}$ for the metal ions of concern is > 100 mg/l, the metal compounds need not be considered further in the classification scheme.

A9.7.5.3.2 If solubility $\geq L(E)C_{50}$, classify on the basis of soluble ion.

A9.7.5.3.2.1 All metal compounds with a water solubility (either measured e.g. through 24-hour Dissolution Screening test or estimated e.g. from the solubility product) $\geq L(E)C_{50}$ of the dissolved metal ion concentration are considered as readily soluble metal compounds. Care should be exercised for compounds whose solubility is close to the acute toxicity value as the conditions under which solubility is measured could differ significantly from those of the acute toxicity test. In these cases the results of the Dissolution Screening Test are preferred.

A9.7.5.3.2.2   Readily soluble metal compounds are classified on the basis of the $L(E)C_{50}$ (corrected where necessary for molecular weight):

(a)   If the $L(E)C_{50}$ of the dissolved metal ion is ≤ 1 mg/l then classify as Acute 1. Classify also as Chronic 1 unless there is evidence of both rapid partitioning from the water column and no bioaccumulation;

(b)   If the $L(E)C_{50}$ of the dissolved metal ion is >1 mg/l but ≤ 10 mg/l then classify as Acute 2. Classify also as Chronic 2 unless there is evidence of both rapid partitioning from the water column and no bioaccumulation;

(c)   If the $L(E)C_{50}$ of the dissolved metal ion is > 10 mg/l and ≤ 100 mg/l then classify as Acute 3. Classify also as Chronic 3 unless there is evidence of both rapid partitioning from the water column and no bioaccumulation.

A9.7.5.3.3   *If solubility $< L(E)C_{50}$, classify default Chronic 4*

A9.7.5.3.3.1   In the context of the classification criteria, poorly soluble compounds of metals are defined as those with a known solubility (either measured e.g. through 24-hour Dissolution Screening test or estimated e.g. from the solubility product) less than the $L(E)C_{50}$ of the soluble metal ion. In those cases when the soluble forms of the metal of poorly soluble metal compounds have a $L(E)C_{50} \leq 100$ mg/l and the substance can be considered as poorly soluble the default safety net classification (Chronic 4) should be applied.

A9.7.5.3.3.2   7-day transformation test

For poorly soluble metal compounds classified with the default safety net classification further information that may be available from the 7-day transformation/dissolution test can also be used. Such data should include transformation levels at low, medium and high loading levels.

If the dissolved metal ion concentration after a period of 7 days (or earlier) exceeds that of the $L(E)C_{50}$, then the default classification for the metals is replaced by the following classification:

(a)   If the dissolved metal ion concentration at the low loading rate is $\geq L(E)C_{50}$, then classify as Acute 1. Classify also as Chronic 1, unless there is evidence of both rapid partitioning from the water column and no bioaccumulation;

(b)   If the dissolved metal ion concentration at the medium loading rate is $\geq L(E)C_{50}$, then classify as Acute 2. Classify also as Chronic 2 unless there is evidence of both rapid partitioning from the water column and no bioaccumulation;

(c)   If the dissolved metal ion concentration at the high loading rate is $\geq L(E)C_{50}$, then classify as Acute 3 . Classify also as Chronic 3 unless there is evidence of both rapid partitioning from the water column and no bioaccumulation.

A9.7.5.3.3.3   28-day transformation test

If the process described in A9.7.5.3.3.2 results in classification as Chronic 1, no further assessment is required as the metal compound will be classified irrespective of any further information.

In all other cases, further data may have been generated through the dissolution/transformation test for 28 days in order to show that the classification may be amended. If for poorly soluble metal compounds classified as Chronic 2, 3 or 4, the dissolved metal ion concentration at the low loading rate after a total period of 28 days is less than or equal to the long-term NOECs, then classification is removed.

A9.7.5.4 *Particle size and surface area*

A9.7.5.4.1 Particle size, or moreover surface area, is a crucial parameter in that any variation in the size or surface area tested may cause a significant change in the levels of metals ions released in a given time-window. Thus, this particle size or surface area is fixed for the purposes of the transformation test, allowing the comparative classifications to be based solely on the loading level. Normally, the classification data generated would have used the smallest particle size marketed to determine the extent of transformation. There may be cases where data generated for a particular metal powder is not considered as suitable for classification of the massive forms. For example, where it can be shown that the tested powder is structurally a different material (e.g. different crystallographic structure) and/or it has been produced by a special process and cannot be generated from the massive metal, classification of the massive can be based on testing of a more representative particle size or surface area, if such data are available. The powder may be classified separately based on the data generated on the powder. However, in normal circumstances it is not anticipated that more than two classification proposals would be made for the same metal.

A9.7.5.4.2 Metals with a particle size smaller than the default diameter value of 1 mm can be tested on a case-by-case basis. One example of this is where metal powders are produced by a different production technique or where the powders give rise to a higher dissolution (or reaction) rate than the massive form leading to a more stringent classification.

A9.7.5.4.3 The particle sizes tested depend on the substance being assessed and are shown in the table below:

Type	Particle size	Comments
Metal compounds	Smallest representative size sold	Never larger than 1 mm
Metals – powders	Smallest representative size sold	May need to consider different sources if yielding different crystallographic/morphologic properties
Metals – massive	1 mm	Default value may be altered if sufficient justification

A9.7.5.4.4 For some forms of metals, it may be possible, using the Transformation/Dissolution Protocol (OECD 2001), to obtain a correlation between the concentration of the metal ion after a specified time interval as a function of the surface area loadings of the forms tested. In such cases, it could then be possible to estimate the level of dissolved metal ion concentration of the metal with different particles, using the critical surface area approach as proposed by Skeaff *et. al.* (2000) (See reference in appendix VI, part 5, Metals and metal compounds). That is, from this correlation and a linkage to the appropriate toxicity data, it may be possible to determine a critical surface area of the substance that delivers the $L(E)C_{50}$ to the medium and then to convert the critical surface area to the low, medium and high mass loadings used in hazard identification. While this approach is not normally used for classification it may provide useful information for labelling and downstream decisions.

Figure A9.7.1: Classification strategy for metals and metal compounds

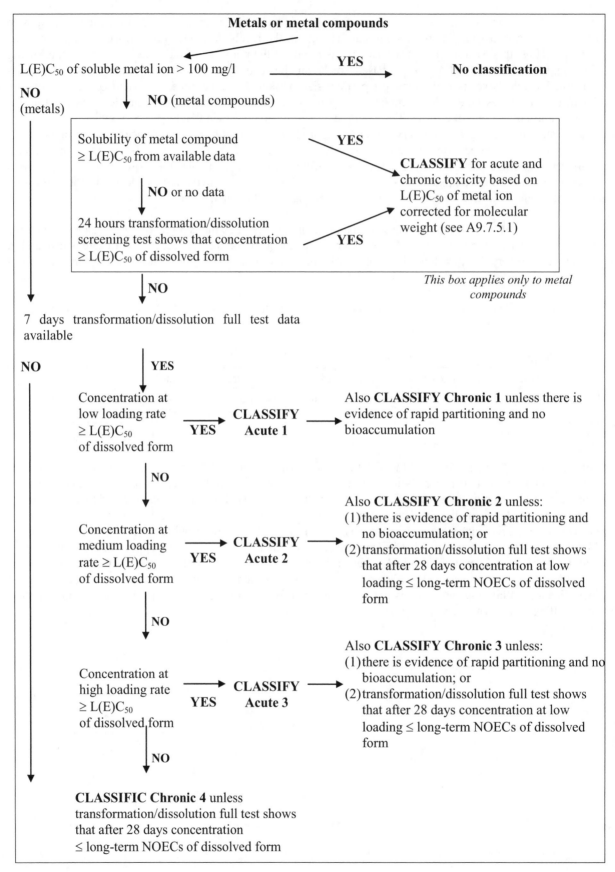

Annex 9

APPENDIX I

Determination of degradability of organic substances

1.   Organic substances may be degraded by abiotic or biotic processes or by a combination of these. A number of standard procedures or tests for determination of the degradability are available. The general principles of some of these are described below. It is by no way the intention to present a comprehensive review of degradability test methods, but only to place the methods in the context of aquatic hazard classification.

2.   Abiotic degradability

2.1   Abiotic degradation comprises chemical transformation and photochemical transformation. Usually abiotic transformations will yield other organic compounds but will not cause a full mineralization (Schwarzenbach *et al.*, 1993). Chemical transformation is defined as transformation that happens without light and without the mediation of organisms whereas photochemical transformations require light.

2.2   Examples of relevant chemical transformation processes in aqueous environment are hydrolysis, nucleophilic substitution, elimination, oxidation and reduction reactions (Schwarzenbach *et al.*, 1993). Of these, hydrolysis is often considered the most important and it is the only chemical transformation process for which international test guidelines are generally available. The tests for abiotic degradation of chemicals are generally in the form of determination of transformation rates under standardized conditions.

2.3   *Hydrolysis*

2.3.1   Hydrolysis is the reaction of the nucleophiles H_2O or OH^- with a chemical where a (leaving) group of the chemical is exchanged with an OH group. Many compounds, especially acid derivatives, are susceptible to hydrolysis. Hydrolysis can both be abiotic and biotic, but in regard to testing only abiotic hydrolysis is considered. Hydrolysis can take place by different mechanisms at different pHs, neutral, acid- or base-catalysed hydrolysis, and hydrolysis rates may be very dependent on pH.

2.3.2   Currently two guidelines for evaluating abiotic hydrolysis are generally available, the OECD Test Guideline 111 Hydrolysis as a function of pH (corresponding to OPPTS 835.2110) and OPPTS 835.2130 Hydrolysis as a function of pH and temperature. In OECD Test Guideline 111, the overall hydrolysis rate at different pHs in pure buffered water is determined. The test is divided in two, a preliminary test that is performed for chemicals with unknown hydrolysis rates and a more detailed test that is performed for chemicals that are known to be hydrolytically unstable and for chemicals for which the preliminary test shows fast hydrolysis. In the preliminary test the concentration of the chemical in buffered solutions at pHs in the range normally found in the environment (pHs of 4, 7 and 9) at 50°C is measured after 5 days. If the concentration of the chemical has decreased less than 10 % it is considered hydrolytically stable, otherwise the detailed test may be performed. In the detailed test, the overall hydrolysis rate is determined at three pHs (4, 7 and 9) by measuring the concentration of the chemical as a function of time. The hydrolysis rate is determined at different temperatures so that interpolations or extrapolations to environmentally relevant temperatures can be made. The OPPTS 835.2130 test is almost identical in design to the OECD Test Guideline 111, the difference mainly being in the treatment of data.

2.3.3   It should be noted that apart from hydrolysis the hydrolysis rate constants determined by the tests include all other abiotic transformations that may occur without light under the given test conditions. Good agreement has been found between hydrolysis rates in natural and in pure waters (OPPTS 835.2110).

2.4   *Photolysis*

2.4.1   At present, there is no OECD guideline on aqueous photodegradation, but a guidance document, concerning aquatic direct photolysis, is available (OECD, 1997). The Guidance Document is supposed to form the basis for a scheduled guideline. According to the definitions set out in this Guidance Document, phototransformation of compounds in water can be in the form of primary or secondary phototransformation, where the primary phototransformation (photolysis) can be divided further into direct and indirect photolysis. Direct phototransformation (photolysis) is the case where the chemical absorbs light and as a direct result hereof undergoes transformation. Indirect phototransformation is the case where other excited species transfer energy, electrons or H-atoms to the chemical and thereby induces a transformation (sensitized photolysis). Secondary phototransformation is the case where chemical reactions occur between the chemical and reactive short lived species like hydroxy radicals, peroxy radicals or singlet oxygen that are formed in the presence of light by reactions of excited species like excited humic or fulvic acids or nitrate.

2.4.2   The only currently available guidelines on phototransformation of chemicals in water are therefore OPPTS 835.2210 *Direct photolysis rate in water by sunlight* and OPPTS 835.5270 *Indirect photolysis screening test*. The OPPTS 835.2210 test uses a tiered approach. In Tier 1 the maximum direct photolysis rate constant (minimum half-life) is calculated from a measured molar absorptivity. In Tier 2 there are two phases. In Phase 1 the chemical is photolysed with sunlight and an approximate rate constant is obtained. In Phase 2, a more accurate rate constant is determined by using an actinometer that quantifies the intensity of the light that the chemical has actually been exposed to. From the parameters measured, the actual direct photodegradation rate at different temperatures and for different latitudes can be calculated. This degradation rate will only apply to the uppermost layer of a water body, e.g. the first 50 cm or less and only when the water is pure and air saturated which may clearly not be the case in environment. However, the results can be extended over other environmental conditions by the use of a computer programme incorporating attenuation in natural waters and other relevant factors.

2.4.3   The OPPTS 835.5270 screening test concerns indirect photolysis of chemicals in waters that contain humic substances. The principle of the test is that in natural waters exposed to natural sunlight a measured phototransformation rate will include both direct and indirect phototransformation, whereas only direct phototransformation will take place in pure water. Therefore, the difference between the direct photodegradation rate in pure water and the total photodegradation in natural water is the sum of indirect photolysis and secondary photodegradation according to the definitions set out in the Annex 9 Guidance Document. In the practical application of the test, commercial humic substances are used to make up a synthetic humic water, which mimics a natural water. It should be noted that the indirect phototransformation rate determined is only valid for the season and latitude for which it is determined and it is not possible to transfer the results to other latitudes and seasons.

3.   Biotic degradability

3.1   Only a brief overview of the test methods is given below. For more information, the comprehensive OECD Detailed Review Paper on Biodegradability Testing (OECD, 1995) should be consulted.

3.2   *Ready biodegradability*

3.2.1   Standard tests for determination of the ready biodegradability of organic substances are developed by a number of organisations including OECD (OECD Test Guidelines 301A-F), EU (C.4 tests), OPPTS (835.3110) and ISO (9408, 9439, 10707).

3.2.2   The ready biodegradability tests are stringent tests, which provide limited opportunity for biodegradation and acclimatization to occur. The basic test conditions ensuring these specifications are:

(a)   high concentration of test substance (2-100 mg/l);

(b)   the test substance is the sole carbon and energy source;

(c)   low to medium concentration of inoculum (10^4-10^8 cells/mL);

(d)   no pre-adaptation of inoculum is allowed;

(e)   28 days test period with a 10-days time window (except for the MITI I method (OECD Test Guideline 301C)) for degradation to take place;

(f)   test temperature < 25 °C; and

(g)   pass levels of 70% (DOC removal) or 60% (O_2 demand or CO_2 evolution) demonstrating complete mineralization (as the remaining carbon of the test substance is assumed to be built into the growing biomass).

3.2.3   It is assumed that a positive result in one of the ready biodegradability tests demonstrates that the substance will degrade rapidly in the environment (OECD Test Guidelines).

3.2.4   Also the traditional BOD_5 tests (e.g. the EU C.5 test) may demonstrate whether a substance is readily biodegradable. In this test, the relative biochemical oxygen demand in a period of 5 days is compared to the theoretical oxygen demand (ThOD) or, when this is not available, the chemical oxygen demand (COD). The test is completed within five days and consequently, the pass level defined in the proposed hazard classification criteria at 50% is lower than in the ready biodegradability tests.

3.2.5   The screening test for biodegradability in seawater (OECD Test Guideline 306) may be seen as seawater parallel to the ready biodegradability tests. Substances that reach the pass level in OECD Test Guideline 306 (i.e. >70% DOC removal or >60 theoretical oxygen demand) may be regarded as readily biodegradable, since the degradation potential is normally lower in seawater than in the freshwater degradation tests.

3.3   *Inherent biodegradability*

3.3.1   Tests for inherent biodegradability are designed to assess whether a substance has any potential for biodegradation. Examples of such tests are the OECD Test Guidelines 302A-C tests, the EU C.9 and C.12 tests, and the ASTM E 1625-94 test.

3.3.2   The basic test conditions favouring an assessment of the inherent biodegradation potential are:

(a)   a prolonged exposure of the test substance to the inoculum allowing adaptation within the test period;

(b)   a high concentration of micro-organisms;

(c)   a favourable substance/biomass ratio.

3.3.3   A positive result in an inherent test indicates that the test substance will not persist indefinitely in the environment, however a rapid and complete biodegradation can not be assumed. A result demonstrating more than 70% mineralization indicates a potential for ultimate biodegradation, a degradation of more than 20% indicates inherent, primary biodegradation, and a result of less than 20% indicates that the substance is persistent. Thus, a negative result means that non-biodegradability (persistence) should be assumed (OECD Test Guidelines).

3.3.4   In many inherent biodegradability tests only the disappearance of the test substance is measured. Such a result only demonstrates a primary biodegradability and not a total mineralization. Thus, more or less persistent degradation products may have been formed. Primary biodegradation of a substance is no indication of ultimate degradability in the environment.

3.3.5   The OECD inherent biodegradation tests are very different in their approach and especially, the MITI II test (OECD Test Guideline 302C) employs a concentration of inoculum that is only three times higher than in the corresponding MITI I ready biodegradability test (OECD Test Guideline 301C). Also the Zahn-Wellens test (OECD Test Guideline 302B) is a relatively "weak" inherent test. However, although the degradation potential in these tests is not very much stronger than in the ready biodegradability tests, the results can not be extrapolated to conditions in the ready biodegradability tests and in the aquatic environment.

3.4   *Aquatic simulation tests*

3.4.1   A simulation test attempts to simulate biodegradation in a specific aquatic environment. As examples of a standard test for simulation of degradation in the aquatic environment may be mentioned the ISO/DS14592 Shake flask batch test with surface water or surface water/sediment suspensions (Nyholm and Toräng, 1999), the ASTM E1279-89(95) test on biodegradation by a shake-flask die-away method and the similar OPPTS 835.3170 test. Such test methods are often referred to as river die-away tests.

3.4.2   The features of the tests that ensure simulation of the conditions in the aquatic environment are:

        (a)   use of a natural water (and sediment) sample as inoculum; and

        (b)   low concentration of test substance (1-100 µg/l) ensuring first-order degradation kinetics.

3.4.3   The use of a radiolabelled test compound is recommended as this facilitates the determination of the ultimate degradation. If only the removal of the test substance by chemical analysis is determined, only the primary degradability is determined. From observation of the degradation kinetics, the rate constant for the degradation can be derived. Due to the low concentration of the test substance, first-order degradation kinetics are assumed to prevail.

3.4.4   The test may also be conducted with natural sediment simulating the conditions in the sediment compartment. Moreover, by sterilizing the samples, the abiotic degradation under the test conditions can be determined.

3.5   *STP simulation tests*

Tests are also available for simulating the degradability in a sewage treatment plant (STP), e.g. the OECD Test Guideline 303A Coupled Unit test, ISO 11733 Activated sludge simulation test, and the EU C.10 test. Recently, a new simulation test employing low concentrations of organic pollutants has been proposed (Nyholm et. al., 1996).

3.6   *Anaerobic degradability*

3.6.1   Test methods for anaerobic biodegradability determine the intrinsic potential of the test substance to undergo biodegradation under anaerobic conditions. Examples of such tests are the ISO 11734:1995(E) test, the ASTM E 1196-92 test and the OPPTS 835.3400 test.

3.6.2   The potential for anaerobic degradation is determined during a period of up to eight weeks and with the test conditions indicated below:

        (a)   performance of the test in sealed vessels in the absence of O_2 (initially in a pure N_2 atmosphere);

        (b)   use of digested sludge;

        (c)   a test temperature of 35 °C; and

        (d)   determination of head-space gas pressure (CO_2 and CH_4 formation).

3.6.3   The ultimate degradation is determined by determining the gas production. However, also primary degradation may be determined by measuring the remaining parent substance.

3.7 *Degradation in soil and sediment*

3.7.1 Many substances end up in the soil or sediment compartments and an assessment of their degradability in these environments may therefore be of importance. Among standard methods may be mentioned the OECD Test Guideline 304A test on inherent biodegradability in soil, which corresponds to the OPPTS 835.3300 test.

3.7.2 The special test characteristics ensuring the determination of the inherent degradability in soil are:

(a) natural soil samples are used without additional inoculation;

(b) radiolabelled test substance is used; and

(c) evolution of radiolabelled CO_2 is determined.

3.7.3 A standard method for determining the biodegradation in sediment is the OPPTS 835.3180 Sediment/water microcosm biodegradation test. Microcosms containing sediment and water are collected from test sites and test compounds are introduced into the system. Disappearance of the parent compound (i.e. primary biodegradation) and, if feasible, appearance of metabolites or measurements of ultimate biodegradation may be made.

3.7.4 Currently, two new OECD guidelines are being drafted on aerobic and anaerobic transformation in soil (OECD Test Guideline, 1999a) and in aquatic sediment systems (OECD Test Guideline 1999b), respectively. The experiments are performed to determine the rate of transformation of the test substance and the nature and rates of formation and decline of transformation products under environmentally realistic conditions including a realistic concentration of the test substance. Either complete mineralization or primary degradability may be determined depending on the analytical method employed for determining the transformation of the test substance.

3.8 *Methods for estimating biodegradability*

3.8.1 In recent years, possibilities for estimating environmental properties of substances have been developed and, among these, also methods for predicting the biodegradability potential of organic substances (e.g. the Syracuse Research Corporation's Biodegradability Probability Program, BIOWIN). Reviews of methods have been performed by OECD (1993) and by Langenberg *et al.* (1996). They show that group contribution methods seem to be the most successful methods. Of these, the Biodegradation Probability Program (BIOWIN) seems to have the broadest application. It gives a qualitative estimate of the probability of slow or fast biodegradation in the presence of a mixed population of environmental micro-organisms. The applicability of this program has been evaluated by the US EPA/EC Joint Project on the Evaluation of (Q)SARs (OECD, 1994), and by Pedersen *et al.* (1995). The latter is briefly referred below.

3.8.2 A validation set of experimentally determined biodegradation data was selected among the data from MITI (1992), but excluding substances for which no precise degradation data were available and substances already used for development of the programme. The validation set then consisted of 304 substances. The biodegradability of these substances were estimated by use of the programme's non-linear estimation module (the most reliable) and the results compared with the measured data. 162 substances were predicted to degrade "fast", but only 41 (25%) were actually readily degradable in the MITI I test. 142 substances were predicted to degrade "slowly", which was confirmed by 138 (97%) substances being not readily degradable in the MITI I test. Thus, it was concluded that the programme may be used for classification purposes only when no experimental degradation data can be obtained, and when the programme predicts a substance to be degraded "slowly". In this case, the substance can be regarded as not rapidly degradable.

3.8.3   The same conclusion was reached in the US EPA/EC Joint Project on the Evaluation of (Q)SARs by use of experimental and QSAR data on new substances notified in the EU. The evaluation was based on an analysis of QSAR predictions on 115 new substances also tested experimentally in ready biodegradability tests. Only 9 of the substances included in this analysis were readily biodegradable. The employed QSAR methodology is not fully specified in the final report of the Joint US EPA/EC project (OECD, 1994), but it is likely that the majority of predictions were made by using methods which later have been integrated in the Biodegradation Probability Program.

3.8.4   Also in the EU TGD (EC, 1996) it is recommended that estimated biodegradability by use of the Biodegradation Probability Program is used only in a conservative way, i.e. when the programme predicts fast biodegradation, this result should not be taken into consideration, whereas predictions of slow biodegradation may be considered (EC, 1996).

3.8.5   Thus, the use of results of the Biodegradability Probability Program in a conservative way may fulfil the needs for evaluating biodegradability of some of the large number of substances for which no experimental degradation data are available.

Annex 9

APPENDIX II

Factors influencing degradability in the aquatic environment

1.   Introduction

1.1   The OECD classification criteria are considering the hazards to the aquatic environment only. However, the hazard classification is primarily based on data prepared by conduction of tests under laboratory conditions that only seldom are similar to the conditions in the environment. Thus, the interpretation of laboratory test data for prediction of the hazards in the aquatic environment should be considered.

1.2   Interpretation of test results on biodegradability of organic substances has been considered in the OECD Detailed Review Paper on Biodegradability Testing (OECD, 1995).

1.3   The conditions in the environment are typically very different from the conditions in the standardized test systems, which make the extrapolation of degradation data from laboratory tests to the environment difficult. Among the differences, the following have significant influence on the degradability:

  (a)   Organism related factors (presence of competent micro-organisms);

  (b)   Substrate related factors (concentration of the substance and presence of other substrates); and

  (c)   Environment related factors (physico-chemical conditions, presence of nutrients, bioavailability of the substance).

These aspects will be discussed further below.

2.   Presence of competent micro-organisms

2.1   Biodegradation in the aquatic environment is dependent on the presence of competent micro-organisms in sufficient numbers. The natural microbial communities consist of a very diverse biomass and when a 'new' substance is introduced in a sufficiently high concentration, the biomass may be adapted to degrade this substance. Frequently, the adaptation of the microbial population is caused by the growth of specific degraders that by nature are competent to degrade the substance. However, also other processes as enzyme induction, exchange of genetic material and development of tolerance to toxicity may be involved.

2.2   Adaptation takes place during a "lag" phase, which is the time period from the onset of the exposure until a significant degradation begins. It seems obvious that the length of the lag phase will depend on the initial presence of competent degraders. This will again depend on the history of the microbial community, i.e. whether the community formerly has been exposed to the substance. This means that when a xenobiotic substance has been used and emitted ubiquitously in a number of years, the likelihood of finding competent degraders will increase. This will especially be the case in environments receiving emissions as e.g. biological wastewater treatment plants. Often more consistent degradation results are found in tests where inocula from polluted waters are used compared to tests with inocula from unpolluted water (OECD, 1995; Nyholm and Ingerslev, 1997).

2.3   A number of factors determine whether the potential for adaptation in the aquatic environment is comparable with the potential in laboratory tests. Among other things adaptation depends on:

  (a)   initial number of competent degraders in the biomass (fraction and number);

  (b)   presence of surfaces for attachment;

  (c)   concentration and availability of substrate; and

  (d)   presence of other substrates.

2.4   The length of the lag phase depends on the initial number of competent degraders and, for toxic substances, the survival and recovery of these. In standard ready biodegradability tests, the inoculum is sampled in sewage treatment plants. As the load with pollutants is normally higher than in the environment, both the fraction and the number of competent degraders may be higher than in the less polluted aquatic environment. It is, however, difficult to estimate how much longer the lag phase will be in the aquatic environment than in a laboratory test due to the likely lower initial number of competent degraders.

2.5   Over long periods of time, the initial concentration of competent degraders is not important as they will grow up when a suitable substrate is present in sufficient concentrations. However, if the degradability in a short period of time is of concern, the initial concentration of competent degrading micro-organisms should be considered (Scow, 1982).

2.6   The presence of flocs, aggregates and attached micro-organisms may also enhance adaptation by e.g. development of microbial niches with consortia of micro-organisms. This is of importance when considering the capability of adaptation in the diverse environments in sewage treatment plants or in sediment or soil. However, the total number of micro-organisms in ready biodegradability tests and in the aquatic environment are of the same orders of magnitude (10^4-10^8 cells/ml in ready biodegradability tests and 10^3-10^6 cells/ml or more in surface water (Scow, 1982). Thus, this factor is probably of minor importance.

2.7   When discussing the extrapolation to environmental conditions it may be valuable to discriminate between oligotrophic and eutrophic environments. Micro-organisms thriving under oligotrophic conditions are able to mineralize organic substrates at low concentrations (fractions of mg C/L), and they normally have a greater affinity for the substrate but lower growth rates and higher generation times than eutrophic organisms (OECD, 1995). Moreover, oligotrophs are unable to degrade chemicals in concentrations higher than 1 mg/l and may even be inhibited at high concentrations. Opposite to that, eutrophs require higher substrate concentrations before mineralization begins and they thrive at higher concentrations than oligotrophs. Thus, the lower threshold limit for degradation in the aquatic environment will depend on whether the microbial population is an oligotroph or an eutroph population. It is, however, not clear whether oligotrophs and eutrophs are different species or whether there is only an oligotrophic and an eutrophic way of life (OECD, 1995). Most pollutants reach the aquatic environment directly through discharge of wastewater and consequently, these recipients are mostly eutrophic.

2.8   From the above discussion it may thus be concluded that the chance of presence of competent degraders is greatest in highly exposed environments, i.e. in environments continuously receiving substances (which more frequently occurs for high production volume chemicals than for low production volume chemicals). These environments are often eutrophic and therefore, the degradation may require relatively high concentrations of substances before onset. On the other hand, in pristine waters competent species may be lacking, especially species capable of degradation of chemicals only occasionally released as low production volume chemicals.

3.   Substrate related factors

3.1   *Concentration of test substance*

3.1.1   In most laboratory tests, the test substance is applied in very high concentrations (2-100 mg/l) compared to the concentrations in the lower µg/l range that may be expected in the aquatic environment. In general, growth of micro-organisms is not supported when a substrate is present in concentrations below a threshold level of around 10 µg/l and at lower concentrations, even the energy requirement for maintenance is not met (OECD, 1995). The reason for this lower threshold level is possibly a lack of sufficient stimulus to initiate an enzymatic response (Scow, 1982). This means in general that the concentrations of many substances in the aquatic environment are at a level where they can only hardly be the primary substrate for degrading micro-organisms.

3.1.2   Moreover, the degradation kinetics depends on substance concentration (S_0) compared with the saturation constant (K_s) as described in the Monod equation. The saturation constant is the concentration of the substrate resulting in a specific growth rate of 50% of the maximum specific growth rate. At substrate concentrations much lower than the saturation constant, which is the normal situation in most of the aquatic environment, the degradation can be described by first order or logistic kinetics (OECD, 1995). When a low density of micro-organisms (lower than 10^3-10^5 cells/ml) prevails (e.g. in oligotrophic waters), the population grows at ever decreasing rates which is typical of logistic kinetics. At a higher density of micro-organisms (e.g. in eutrophic waters), the substrate concentration is not high enough to support growth of the cells and first order kinetics apply, i.e. the degradation rate is proportional with the substance concentration. In practice, it may be impossible to distinguish between the two types of degradation kinetics due to uncertainty of the data (OECD, 1995).

3.1.3   In conclusion, substances in low concentrations (i.e. below 10 µg/l) are probably not degraded as primary substrates in the aquatic environment. At higher concentrations, readily degradable substances will probably be degraded as primary substrates in the environment at a degradation rate more or less proportional with the concentration of the substance. The degradation of substances as secondary substrates is discussed below.

3.2   *Presence of other substrates*

3.2.1   In the standard tests, the test substance is applied as the sole substrate for the micro-organisms while in the environment, a large number of other substrates are present. In natural waters, concentrations of dissolved organic carbon are often found in the range 1-10 mg C/l, i.e. up to a factor 1000 higher than a pollutant. However, much of this organic carbon is relatively persistent with an increasing fraction of persistent matter the longer the distance from the shore.

3.2.2   Bacteria in natural waters are primarily nourishing on exudates from algae. These exudates are mineralized very quickly (within minutes) demonstrating that there is a high degradation potential in the natural micro-organism communities. Thus, as micro-organisms compete for the variety of substrates in natural waters, there is a selection pressure among micro-organisms resulting in growth of opportunistic species capable of nourishing on quickly mineralized substrates, while growth of more specialized species is suppressed. Experiences from isolation of bacteria capable of degrading various xenobiotics have demonstrated that these organisms are often growing relatively slowly and survive on complex carbon sources in competition with more rapidly growing bacteria. When competent micro-organisms are present in the environment, their numbers may increase if the specific xenobiotic substrate is continuously released and reach a concentration in the environment sufficient to support growth. However, most of the organic pollutants in the aquatic environment are present in low concentrations and will only be degraded as secondary substrates not supporting growth.

3.2.3   On the other hand, the presence of quickly mineralized substrates in higher concentrations may facilitate an initial transformation of the xenobiotic molecule by co-metabolism. The co-metabolized substance may then be available for further degradation and mineralization. Thus, the presence of other substrates may increase the possibilities for a substance to be degraded.

3.2.4   It may then be concluded that the presence of a variety of substrates in natural waters and among them quickly mineralized substrates, may on the one hand cause a selection pressure suppressing growth of micro-organisms competent of degrading micro-pollutants. On the other hand it may facilitate an increased degradation by an initial co-metabolism followed by a further mineralization. The relative importance of these processes under natural conditions may vary depending on both the environmental conditions and the substance and no generalization can yet be established.

4.   Environment related factors

4.1   The environmental variables control the general microbial activity rather than specific degradation processes. However, the significance of the influence varies between different ecosystems and microbial species (Scow, 1982).

4.2   *Redox potential*

One of the most important environment related factors influencing the degradability is probably the presence of oxygen. The oxygen content and the related redox potential determines the presence of different types of micro-organisms in aquatic environments with aerobic organisms present in the water phase, in the upper layer of sediments and in parts of sewage treatment plants, and anaerobic organisms present in sediments and parts of sewage treatment plants. In most parts of the water phase, aerobic conditions are prevailing and the prediction of the biodegradability should be based on results from aerobic tests. However, in some aquatic environments the oxygen content may be very low in periods of the year due to eutrophication and the following decay of produced organic matter. In these periods, aerobic organisms will not be able to degrade the chemical, but anaerobic processes may take over if the chemical is degradable under anaerobic conditions.

4.3   *Temperature*

Another important parameter is the temperature. Most laboratory tests are performed at 20-25 °C (standard aerobic ready biodegradability tests), but anaerobic tests may be performed at 35 °C as this better mimics the conditions in a sludge reactor. Microbial activity is found in the environment at temperatures ranging from below 0 °C to 100 °C. However, optimum temperatures are probably in the range from 10 °C to 30 °C and roughly, the degradation rate doubles for every 10 °C increase of temperature in this range (de Henau, 1993). Outside this optimum range the activity of the degraders is reduced drastically although some specialized species (termo- and psycrophilic bacteria) may thrive. When extrapolating from laboratory conditions, it should be considered that some aquatic environments are covered by ice in substantial periods of the year and that only minor or even no degradation can be expected during the winter season.

4.4   *pH*

Active micro-organisms are found in the entire pH range found in the environment. However, for bacteria as a group, slightly alkaline conditions favour the activity and the optimum pH range is 6-8. At a pH lower than 5, the metabolic activity in bacteria is significantly decreased. For fungi as a group, slightly acidic conditions favour the activity with an optimum pH range of 5-6 (Scow, 1982). Thus, an optimum for the degrading activity of micro-organisms will probably be within the pH range of 5-8, which is the range most often prevailing in the aquatic environment.

4.5   *Presence of nutrients*

The presence of inorganic nutrients (nitrogen and phosphorus) is often required for microbial growth. However, these are only seldom the activity limiting factors in the aquatic environment where growth of micro-organisms is often substrate limited. However, the presence of nutrient influences the growth of primary producers and then again the availability of readily mineralized exudates.

Annex 9

APPENDIX III

Basic principles of the experimental and estimation methods for determination of BCF and K_{ow} of organic substances

1.   Bioconcentration factor (BCF)

1.1   *Definition*

The bioconcentration factor is defined as the ratio between the concentration of the chemical in biota and the concentration in the surrounding medium, here water, at steady state. BCF can be measured experimentally directly under steady-state conditions or calculated by the ratio of the first-order uptake and elimination rate constants, a method that does not require equilibrium conditions.

1.2   *Appropriate methods for experimental determination of BCF*

1.2.1   Different test guidelines for the experimental determination of bioconcentration in fish have been documented and adopted; the most generally applied being the OECD test guideline (OECD 305, 1996) and the ASTM standard guide (ASTM E 1022-94). OECD 305 (1996) was revised and replaced the previous version OECD 305A-E, (1981). Although flow-through test regimes are preferred (OECD 305, 1996), semi-static regimes are allowed (ASTM E 1022-94), provided that the validity criteria on mortality and maintenance of test conditions are fulfilled. For lipophilic substances (log K_{ow} > 3), flow-through methods are preferred.

1.2.2   The principles of the OECD 305 and the ASTM guidelines are similar, but the experimental conditions described are different, especially concerning:

(a)   method of test water supply (static, semi-static or flow through);

(b)   the requirement for carrying out a depuration study;

(c)   the mathematical method for calculating BCF;

(d)   sampling frequency: Number of measurements in water and number of samples of fish;

(e)   requirement for measuring the lipid content of the fish;

(f)   the minimum duration of the uptake phase;

1.2.3   In general, the test consists of two phases: The exposure (uptake) and post-exposure (depuration) phases. During the uptake phase, separate groups of fish of one species are exposed to at least two concentrations of the test substance. A 28-day exposure phase is obligatory unless a steady state has been reached within this period. The time needed for reaching steady-state conditions may be set on the basis of $K_{ow} - k_2$ correlations (e.g. log $k_2 = 1.47 - 0.41$ log K_{ow} (Spacie and Hamelink, 1982) or log $k_2 = 1.69 - 0.53$ log K_{ow} (Gobas *et al.*, 1989)). The expected time (d) for e.g. 95% steady state may thus be calculated by: $-\ln(1-0.95)/k_2$, provided that the bioconcentration follows first order kinetics. During the depuration phase the fish are transferred to a medium free of the test substance. The concentration of the test substance in the fish is followed through both phases of the test. The BCF is expressed as a function of the total wet weight of the fish. As for many organic substances, there is a significant relationship between the potential for bioconcentration and the lipophilicity, and furthermore, there is a corresponding relationship between the lipid content of the test fish and the observed bioconcentration of such substances. Therefore, to reduce this source of variability in the test results for the substances with high lipophilicity, bioconcentration should be expressed in relation to the lipid content in addition to whole body weight (OECD 305 (1996), ECETOC (1995)). The guidelines mentioned are based on the assumption that bioconcentration may be approximated by a first-order process (one-compartment model) and thus that BCF = k_1/k_2 (k_1: first-order uptake rate, k_2: first-order depuration rate, described by a log-linear approximation). If the depuration follows biphasic kinetics, i.e. two distinct depuration rates can be identified, the approximation k_1/k_2 may significantly underestimate BCF. If a second order kinetic has been indicated, BCF may be estimated from the relation: C_{Fish}/C_{Water}, provided that "steady-state" for the fish-water system has been reached.

1.2.4　　　　Together with details of sample preparation and storage, an appropriate analytical method of known accuracy, precision, and sensitivity must be available for the quantification of the substance in the test solution and in the biological material. If these are lacking it is impossible to determine a true BCF. The use of radiolabelled test substance can facilitate the analysis of water and fish samples. However, unless combined with a specific analytical method, the total radioactivity measurements potentially reflect the presence of parent substance, possible metabolite(s), and possible metabolized carbon, which have been incorporated in the fish tissue in organic molecules. For the determination of a true BCF it is essential to clearly discriminate the parent substance from possible metabolites. If radiolabelled materials are used in the test, it is possible to analyse for total radio label (i.e. parent and metabolites) or the samples may be purified so that the parent compound can be analysed separately.

1.2.5　　　　In the log K_{ow} range above 6, the measured BCF data tend to decrease with increasing log K_{ow}. Conceptual explanations of non-linearity mainly refer to either biotransformation, reduced membrane permeation kinetics or reduced biotic lipid solubility for large molecules. Other factors consider experimental artefacts, such as equilibrium not being reached, reduced bioavailability due to sorption to organic matter in the aqueous phase, and analytical errors. Moreover, care should be taken when evaluating experimental data on BCF for substances with log K_{ow} above 6, as these data will have a much higher level of uncertainty than BCF values determined for substances with log K_{ow} below 6.

2.　　　　log K_{ow}

2.1　　　　*Definition and general considerations*

2.1.1　　　　The log *n*-octanol-water partition coefficient (log K_{ow}) is a measure of the lipophilicity of a substance. As such, log K_{ow} is a key parameter in the assessment of environmental fate. Many distribution processes are driven by log K_{ow}, e.g. sorption to soil and sediment and bioconcentration in organisms.

2.1.2　　　　The basis for the relationship between bioconcentration and log K_{ow} is the analogy for the partition process between the lipid phase of fish and water and the partition process between n-octanol and water. The reason for using K_{ow} arises from the ability of octanol to act as a satisfactory surrogate for lipids in fish tissue. Highly significant relationships between log K_{ow} and the solubility of substances in cod liver oil and triolin exist (Niimi, 1991). Triolin is one of the most abundant triacylglycerols found in freshwater fish lipids (Henderson and Tocher, 1987).

2.1.3　　　　The determination of the *n*-octanol-water partition coefficient (K_{ow}) is a requirement of the base data set to be submitted for notified new and priority existing substances within the EU. As the experimental determination of the K_{ow} is not always possible, e.g. for very water-soluble and for very lipophilic substances, a QSAR derived K_{ow} may be used. However, extreme caution should be exercized when using QSARs for substances where the experimental determination is not possible (as for e.g. surfactants).

2.2　　　　*Appropriate methods for experimental determination of K_{ow} values*

2.2.1　　　　For experimental determination of K_{ow} values, two different methods, Shake-flask and HPLC, have been described in standard guidelines e.g. OECD 107 (1995); OECD 117 (1983); EEC A.8. (1992); EPA-OTS (1982); EPA-FIFRA (1982); ASTM (1993). Not only data obtained by the employment of the shake-flask or the HPLC method according to standard guidelines are recommended. For highly lipophilic substances, which are slowly soluble in water, data obtained by employing a slow-stirring method are generally more reliable (De Bruijn *et al.*, 1989; Tolls and Sijm, 1993; OECD draft Guideline, 1998). The slow stirring method is currently being ringtested for development of a final OECD guideline.

2.2.2 Shake-flask method

The basic principle of the method is to measure the dissolution of the substance in two different phases, water and n-octanol. In order to determine the partition coefficient, equilibrium between all interacting components of the system must be achieved after which the concentration of the substances dissolved in the two phases is determined. The shake-flask method is applicable when the log K_{ow} value falls within the range from -2 to 4 (OECD 107, 1995). The shake-flask method applies only to essential pure substances soluble in water and n-octanol and should be performed at a constant temperature ($\pm 1°C$) in the range 20-25 °C.

2.2.3 HPLC method

HPLC is performed on analytical columns packed with a commercially available solid phase containing long hydrocarbon chains (e.g. C_8, C_{18}) chemically bound onto silica. Chemicals injected onto such a column move along at different rates because of the different degrees of partitioning between the mobile aqueous phase and the stationary hydrocarbon phase. The HPLC method is not applicable to strong acids and bases, metals complexes, surface-active materials, or substances that react with the eluent. The HPLC method is applicable when the log K_{ow} value falls within the range 0 to 6 (OECD 117, 1989). The HPLC method is less sensitive to the presence of impurities in the test compound compared to the shake-flask method.

2.2.4 Slow stirring method

With the slow-stirring method a precise and accurate determination of K_{ow} of compounds with log K_{ow} up till 8.2 is allowed (De Bruijn et al., 1989). For highly lipophilic compounds the shake-flask method is prone to produce artefacts (formation of microdroplets), and with the HPLC method K_{ow} needs to be extrapolated beyond the calibration range to obtain estimates of K_{ow}.

In order to determine a partition coefficient, water, n-octanol, and test compound are equilibrated with each other after which the concentration of the test compound in the two phases is determined. The experimental difficulties associated with the formation of microdroplets during the shake-flask experiment can to some degree be overcome in the slow-stirring experiment as water, octanol, and the test compound are equilibrated in a gently stirred reactor. The stirring creates a more or less laminar flow between the octanol and the water, and exchange between the phases is enhanced without microdroplets being formed.

2.2.5 Generator column method

Another very versatile method for measuring log K_{ow} is the generator column method. In this method, a generator column method is used to partition the test substance between the octanol and water phases. The column is packed with a solid support and is saturated with a fixed concentration of the test substance in n-octanol. The test substance is eluted from the octanol -saturated generator column with water. The aqueous solution exiting the column represents the equilibrium concentration of the test substance that has partitioned from the octanol phase into the water phase. The primary advantage of the generator column method over the shake flask method is that the former completely avoids the formation of micro-emulsions. Therefore, this method is particularly useful for measuring K_{ow} for substances values over 4.5 (Doucette and Andren, 1987 and 1988; Shiu et al., 1988) as well as for substances having log K_{ow} values less than 4.5. A disadvantage of the generator column method is that it requires sophisticated equipment. A detailed description of the generator column method is presented in the "Toxic Substances Control Act Test Guidelines" (USEPA 1985).

2.3   *Use of QSARs for determination of log K_{ow} (see also in A9.6, « Use of QSARs »)*

2.3.1   Numerous QSARs have been and continue to be developed for the estimation of K_{ow}. Commonly used methods are based on fragment constants. The fragmental approaches are based on a simple addition of the lipophilicity of the individual molecular fragments of a given molecule. Three commercially available PC programs are recommended in the European Commission's Technical Guidance Document (European Commission, 1996) for risk assessment, part III, if no experimentally derived data are available.

2.3.2   CLOGP (Daylight Chemical Information Systems, 1995) was initially developed for use in drug design. The model is based on the Hansch and Leo calculation procedure (Hansch and Leo, 1979). The program calculates log K_{ow} for organic compounds containing C, H, N, O, Hal, P, and/or S. Log K_{ow} for salts and for compounds with formal charges cannot be calculated (except for nitro compounds and nitrogen oxides). The calculation results of log K_{ow} for ionizable substances, like phenols, amines, and carboxylic acids, represent the neutral or unionized form and will be pH dependent. In general, the program results in clear estimates in the range of log Kow between 0 and 5 (European Commission, 1996, part III). However a validation study performed by Niemelä (1993), who compared experimental determined log K_{ow} values with estimated values, showed that the program precisely predicts the log K_{ow} for a great number of organic chemicals in the log K_{ow} range from below 0 to above 9 (n = 501, r^2 = 0.967). In a similar validation study on more than 7000 substances the results with the CLOGP-program (PC version 3.32, EPA version 1.2) were r^2 = 0.89, s.d.= 0.58, n = 7221. These validations show that the CLOGP-program may be used for estimating reliable log K_{ow} values when no experimental data are available. For chelating compounds and surfactants the CLOGP program is stated to be of limited reliability (OECD, 1993). However, as regards anionic surfactants (LAS) a correction method for estimating adjusted CLOGP values has been proposed (Roberts, 1989).

2.3.3   LOGKOW or KOWWIN (Syracuse Research Corporation) uses structural fragments and correction factors. The program calculates log K_{ow} for organic compounds containing the following atoms: C, H, N, O, Hal, Si, P, Se, Li, Na, K, and/or Hg. Log K_{ow} for compounds with formal charges (like nitrogenoxides and nitro compounds) can also be calculated. The calculation of log K_{ow} for ionizable substances, like phenols, amines and carboxylic acids, represent the neutral or unionized form, and the values will thus be pH dependent. Some surfactants (e.g. alcohol ethoxylates (Tolls, 1998), dyestuffs, and dissociated substances may be predicted by the LOGKOW program (Pedersen *et al*, 1995). In general, the program gives clear estimates in the range of log K_{ow} between 0 and 9 (TemaNord 1995:581). Like the CLOGP-program, LOGKOW has been validated (Table 2) and is recommended for classification purposes because of its reliability, commercial availability, and convenience of use.

2.3.4   AUTOLOGP (Devillers *et al.*, 1995) has been derived from a heterogeneous data set, comprising 800 organic chemicals collected from literature. The program calculates log K_{ow} values for organic chemicals containing C, H, N, O, Hal, P, and S. The log K_{ow} values of salts cannot be calculated. Also the log K_{ow} of some compounds with formal charges cannot be calculated, with the exception of nitro compounds. The log K_{ow} values of ionizable chemicals like phenols, amines, and corboxylic acids can be calculated although pH-dependencies should be noted. Improvements are in progress in order to extend the applicability of AUTOLOGP. According to the presently available information, AUTOLOGP gives accurate values especially for highly lipophilic substances (log K_{ow} > 5) (European Commission, 1996).

2.3.5   SPARC. The SPARC model is still under development by EPA's Environmental Research Laboratory in Athens, Georgia, and is not yet public available. SPARC is a mechanistic model based on chemical thermodynamic principles rather than a deterministic model rooted in knowledge obtained from observational data. Therefore, SPARC differs from models that use QSARs (i.e. KOWWIN, LOGP) in that no measured log K_{ow} data are needed for a training set of chemicals. EPA does occasionally run the model for a list of CAS numbers, if requested. SPARC provides improved results over KOWWIN and CLOGP only for compounds with log K_{ow} values greater than 5. Only SPARC can be employed in a general way for inorganic or organometallic compounds.

In Table 1, this Appendix, an overview of log K_{ow} estimation methods based on fragmentation methodologies is presented. Also other methods for the estimation of log K_{ow} values exist, but they should only be used on a case-by-case basis and only with appropriate scientific justification.

Table 1: Overview of QSAR methods for estimation of log K_{ow} based on fragmentation methodologies (Howard and Meylan (1997))

Method	Methodology	Statistics
CLOGP Hansch and Leo (1979), CLOGP Daylight (1995)	Fragments + correction factors	Total n = 8942, r^2= 0,917, sd = 0,482 Validation: n = 501, r^2 = 0,967 Validation: n = 7221, r^2 = 0,89, sd = 0,58
LOGKOW (KOWWIN) Meylan and Howard (1995), SRC	140 fragments 260 correction factors	Calibration: n = 2430, r^2= 0,981, sd = 0,219, me = 0,161 Validation: n = 8855, r^2= 0,95, sd = 0,427, me = 0,327
AUTOLOGP Devillers et al. (1995)	66 atomic and group contributions from Rekker and Manhold (1992)	Calibration: n = 800, r^2= 0,96, sd = 0,387
SPARC Under development by EPA, Athens, Georgia.	Based upon fundamental chemical structure algorithm.	No measured log Kow data are needed for a training set of chemicals.
Rekker and De Kort (1979)	Fragments + correction factors	Calibration n = 1054, r^2 = 0,99 Validation: n = 20, r^2 = 0,917, sd = 0,53, me = 0,40
Niemi et al. (1992)	MCI	Calibration n = 2039, r^2 = 0,77 Validation: n = 2039, r^2 = 0,49
Klopman et al (1994)	98 fragments + correction factors	Calibration n = 1663, r^2 = 0,928, sd = 0,3817
Suzuki and Kudo (1990)	424 fragments	Total: n= 1686, me = 0,35 Validation: n = 221, me = 0,49
Ghose et al. (1988) ATOMLOGP	110 fragments	Calibration: n = 830, r^2= 0,93, sd = 0,47 Validation: n = 125, r^2= 0,87, sd = 0,52
Bodor and Huang (1992)	Molecule orbital	Calibration: n = 302, r^2= 0,96, sd = 0,31, me = 0,24 Validation: n = 128, sd = 0,38
Broto et al. (1984) ProLogP	110 fragments	Calibration: n = 1868, me= ca. 0,4

Annex 9

APPENDIX IV

Influence of external and internal factors on the bioconcentration potential of organic substances

1. Factors influencing the uptake

The uptake rate for lipophilic compounds is mainly a function of the size of the organism (Sijm and Linde, 1995). External factors such as the molecular size, factors influencing the bioavailability, and different environmental factors are of great importance to the uptake rate as well.

1.1 *Size of organism*

Since larger fish have a relatively lower gill surface to weight ratio, a lower uptake rate constant (k_1) is to be expected for large fish compared to small fish (Sijm and Linde, 1995; Opperhuizen and Sijm, 1990). The uptake of substances in fish is further controlled by the water flow through the gills; the diffusion through aqueous diffusion layers at the gill epithelium; the permeation through the gill epithelium; the rate of blood flow through the gills, and the binding capacity of blood constituents (ECETOC, 1995).

1.2 *Molecular size*

Ionized substances do not readily penetrate membranes; as aqueous pH can influence the substance uptake. Loss of membrane permeability is expected for substances with a considerable cross-sectional area (Opperhuizen *et al.*, 1985; Anliker *et al.*, 1988) or long chain length (> 4.3 nm) (Opperhuizen, 1986). Loss of membrane permeability due to the size of the molecules will thus result in total loss of uptake. The effect of molecular weight on bioconcentration is due to an influence on the diffusion coefficient of the substance, which reduces the uptake rate constants (Gobas *et al.*, 1986).

1.3 *Availability*

Before a substance is able to bioconcentrate in an organism it needs to be present in water and available for transfer across fish gills. Factors, which affect this availability under both natural and test conditions, will alter the actual bioconcentration in comparison to the estimated value for BCF. As fish are fed during bioconcentration studies, relatively high concentrations of dissolved and particulate organic matter may be expected, thus reducing the fraction of chemical that is actually available for direct uptake via the gills. McCarthy and Jimenez (1985) have shown that adsorption of lipophilic substances to dissolved humic materials reduces the availability of the substance, the more lipophilic the substance the larger reduction in availability (Schrap and Opperhuizen, 1990). Furthermore, adsorption to dissolved or particulate organic matter or surfaces in general may interfere during the measurement of BCF (and other physical-chemical properties) and thus make the determination of BCF or appropriate descriptors difficult. As bioconcentration in fish is directly correlated with the available fraction of the chemical in water, it is necessary for highly lipophilic substances to keep the available concentration of the test chemical within relatively narrow limits during the uptake period.

Substances, which are readily biodegradable, may only be present in the test water for a short period, and bioconcentration of these substances may thus be insignificant. Similarly, volatility and hydrolysis will reduce the concentration and time in which the substance is available for bioconcentration.

1.4 *Environmental factors*

Environmental parameters influencing the physiology of the organism may also affect the uptake of substances. For instance, when the oxygen content of the water is lowered, fish have to pass more water over their gills in order to meet respiratory demands (McKim and Goeden, 1982). However, there may be species dependency as indicated by Opperhuizen and Schrap (1987). It has, furthermore, been shown that the temperature may have an influence on the uptake rate constant for lipophilic substances (Sijm *et al.* 1993), whereas other authors have not found any consistent effect of temperature changes (Black *et al.* 1991).

2. Factors influencing the elimination rate

The elimination rate is mainly a function of the size of the organism, the lipid content, the biotransformation process of the organism, and the lipophilicity of the test compound.

2.1 *Size of organism*

As for the uptake rate the elimination rate is dependent on the size of the organism. Due to the higher gill surface to weight ratio for small organisms (e.g. fish larvae) than that of large organisms, steady-state and thus "toxic dose equilibrium" has shown to be reached sooner in early life stages than in juvenile/adult stages of fish (Petersen and Kristensen, 1998). As the time needed to reach steady-state conditions is dependent on k_2, the size of fish used in bioconcentration studies has thus an important bearing on the time required for obtaining steady-state conditions.

2.2 *Lipid content*

Due to partitioning relationships, organisms with a high fat content tend to accumulate higher concentrations of lipophilic substances than lean organisms under steady-state conditions. Body burdens are therefore often higher for "fatty" fish such as eel, compared to "lean" fish such as cod. In addition, lipid "pools" may act as storage of highly lipophilic substances. Starvation or other physiological changes may change the lipid balance and release such substances and result in delayed impacts.

2.3 *Metabolism*

2.3.1 In general, metabolism or biotransformation leads to the conversion of the parent compound into more water-soluble metabolites. As a result, the more hydrophilic metabolites may be more easily excreted from the body than the parent compound. When the chemical structure of a compound is altered, many properties of the compound are altered as well. Consequently the metabolites will behave differently within the organism with respect to tissue distribution, bioaccumulation, persistence, and route and rate of excretion. Biotransformation may also alter the toxicity of a compound. This change in toxicity may either be beneficial or harmful to the organism. Biotransformation may prevent the concentration in the organism from becoming so high that a toxic response is expressed (detoxification). However, a metabolite may be formed which is more toxic than the parent compound (bioactivation) as known for e.g. benzo(a)pyrene.

2.3.2 Terrestrial organisms have a developed biotransformation system, which is generally better than that of organisms living in the aquatic environment. The reason for this difference may be the fact that biotransformation of xenobiotics may be of minor importance in gill breathing organisms as they can relatively easily excrete the compound into the water (Van Den Berg *et al.* 1995). Concerning the biotransformation capacity in aquatic organisms the capacity for biotransformation of xenobiotics increases in general as follows: Molluscs < crustaceans < fish (Wofford *et al.*, 1981).

3. Lipophilicity of substance

A negative linear correlation between k_2 (depuration constant) and log K_{ow} (or BCF) has been shown in fish by several authors (e.g. Spacie and Hamelink, 1982; Gobas *et al.*, 1989; Petersen and Kristensen, 1998), whereas k_1 (uptake rate constant) is more or less independent of the lipophilicity of the substance (Connell, 1990). The resultant BCF will thus generally increase with increasing lipophilicity of the substances, i.e. log BCF and log K_{ow} correlate for substances which do not undergo extensive metabolism.

APPENDIX V

Test guidelines

1. **Most of the guidelines mentioned are found in compilations from the organisation issuing them. The main references to these are:**

(a) EC guidelines: Commission Regulation (EC) No 440/2008 of 30 May 2008 laying down test methods pursuant to Regulation (EC) No 1907/2006 of the European Parliament and of the Council on the Registration, Evaluation, Authorisation and Restriction of Chemicals (REACH);

(b) ISO guidelines: Available from the national standardisation organisations or ISO (Homepage: http://www.iso.org/iso/home.htm);

(c) OECD guidelines for the testing of chemicals. OECD, Paris, 1993 with regular updates (http://www.oecd.org/env/testguidelines);

(d) OPPTS guidelines: US-EPA homepage (http://www.epa.gov/opptsfrs/home/guidelin.htm);

(e) ASTM: ASTM's homepage (http://www.astm.org). Further search via "standards".

2. **Test guidelines for aquatic toxicity[1]**

OECD Test Guideline 201 (1984) Alga, Growth Inhibition Test
OECD Test Guideline 202 (1984) Daphnia sp. Acute Immobilisation Test and Reproduction Test
OECD Test Guideline 203 (1992) Fish, Acute Toxicity Test
OECD Test Guideline 204 (1984) Fish, Prolonged Toxicity Test: 14-Day Study[2]
OECD Test Guideline 210 (1992) Fish, Early-Life Stage Toxicity Test
OECD Test Guideline 211 (1998) Daphnia magna Reproduction Test
OECD Test Guideline 212 (1998) Fish, Short-term Toxicity Test on Embryo and Sac-Fry Stages
OECD Test Guideline 215 (2000) Fish, Juvenile Growth Test
OECD Test Guideline 221 (in preparation) Lemna sp. Growth inhibition test
EC C.1: Acute Toxicity for Fish (1992)
EC C.2: Acute Toxicity for Daphnia (1992)
EC C.3: Algal Inhibition Test (1992)
EC C.14: Fish Juvenile Growth Test (2001)
EC C.15: Fish, Short-term Toxicity Test on Embryo and Sac-Fry Stages (2001)
EC C.20: Daphnia Magna Reproduction Test (2001)

OPPTS Testing Guidelines for Environmental Effects (850 Series Public Drafts):

850.1000 Special consideration for conducting aquatic laboratory studies
850.1000 Special consideration for conducting aquatic laboratory studies
850.1010 Aquatic invertebrate acute toxicity, test, freshwater daphnids
850.1010 Aquatic invertebrate acute toxicity, test, freshwater daphnids
850.1020 Gammarid acute toxicity test
850.1020 Gammarid acute toxicity test
850.1035 Mysid acute toxicity test
850.1035 Mysid acute toxicity test

---

[1] The list below will need to be regularly updated as new guidelines are adopted or draft guidelines are elaborated.

[2] This Test Guideline has been cancelled but may continue to be used until 2 April 2014.

850.1045 Penaeid acute toxicity test
850.1045 Penaeid acute toxicity test
850.1075 Fish acute toxicity test, freshwater and marine
850.1075 Fish acute toxicity test, freshwater and marine
850.1300 Daphnid chronic toxicity test
850.1300 Daphnid chronic toxicity test
850.1350 Mysid chronic toxicity test
850.1350 Mysid chronic toxicity test
850.1400 Fish early-life stage toxicity test
850.1400 Fish early-life stage toxicity test
850.1500 Fish life cycle toxicity
850.1500 Fish life cycle toxicity
850.1730 Fish BCF
850.1730 Fish BCF
850.4400 Aquatic plant toxicity test using Lemna spp. Tiers I and II
850.4400 Aquatic plant toxicity test using Lemna spp. Tiers I and II
850.4450 Aquatic plants field study, Tier III
850.4450 Aquatic plants field study, Tier III
850.5400 Algal toxicity, Tiers I and II
850.5400 Algal toxicity, Tiers I and II

3.   Test guidelines for biotic and abiotic degradation [3]

ASTM E 1196-92

ASTM E 1279-89(95) Standard test method for biodegradation by a shake-flask die-away method

ASTM E 1625-94 Standard test method for determining biodegradability of organic chemicals in semi-continuous activated sludge (SCAS)

EC C.4. A to F: Determination of ready biodegradability. Directive 67/548/EEC, Annex V. (1992)

EC C.5. Degradation: biochemical oxygen demand. Directive 67/548/EEC, Annex V. (1992)

EC C.7. Degradation: abiotic degradation: hydrolysis as a function of pH. Directive 67/548/EEC, Annex V. (1992)

EC C.9. Biodegradation: Zahn-Wellens test. Directive 67/548/EEC, Annex V. (1988)

EC C.10. Biodegradation: Activated sludge simulation tests. Directive 67/548/EEC, Annex V. (1998)

EC C.11. Biodegradation: Activated sludge respiration inhibition test. Directive 67/548/EEC, AnnexV.(1988)

EC C.12. Biodegradation: Modified SCAS test. Directive 67/548/EEC, Annex V. (1998)

ISO 9408 (1991). Water quality - Evaluation in an aqueous medium of the "ultimate" biodegradability of organic compounds - Method by determining the oxygen demand in a closed respirometer

ISO 9439 (1990). Water quality - Evaluation in an aqueous medium of the "ultimate" biodegradability of organic compounds - Method by analysis of released carbon dioxide

ISO 9509 (1996). Water quality - Method for assessing the inhibition of nitrification of activated sludge micro-organisms by chemicals and wastewaters

ISO 9887 (1992). Water quality - Evaluation of the aerobic biodegradability of organic compounds in an aqueous medium - Semicontinuous activated sludge method (SCAS)

ISO 9888 (1991). Water quality - Evaluation of the aerobic biodegradability of organic compounds in an aqueous medium - Static test (Zahn-Wellens method)

---

[3]   *The list below will need to be regularly updated as new guidelines are adopted or draft guidelines are elaborated.*

ISO 10707 (1994). Water quality - Evaluation in an aqueous medium of the "ultimate" biodegradability of organic compounds - Method by analysis of biochemical oxygen demand (closed bottle test)

ISO 11348 (1997). Water quality - Determination of the inhibitory effect of water samples on the light emission of *Vibrio fischeri* (Luminescent bacteria test)

ISO 11733 (1994). Water quality - Evaluation of the elimination and biodegradability of organic compounds in an aqueous medium - Activated sludge simulation test

ISO 11734 (1995). Water quality - Evaluation of the "ultimate" anaerobic biodegradability of organic compounds in digested sludge - Method by measurement of the biogas production

ISO/DIS 14592 .(1999) Water quality - Evaluation of the aerobic biodegradability of organic compounds at low concentrations in water. Part 1: Shake flask batch test with surface water or surface water/sediment suspensions (22.11.1999)

OECD Test Guideline 111 (1981). Hydrolysis as a function of pH. OECD guidelines for testing of chemicals

OECD Test Guideline 209 (1984). Activated sludge, respiration inhibition test. OECD guidelines for testing of chemicals

OECD Test Guideline 301 (1992). Ready biodegradability. OECD guidelines for testing of chemicals

OECD Test Guideline 302A (1981). Inherent biodegradability: Modified SCAS test. OECD guidelines for testing of chemicals

OECD Test Guideline 302B (1992). Zahn-Wellens/EMPA test. OECD guidelines for testing of chemicals

OECD Test Guideline 302C (1981). Inherent biodegradability: Modified MITI test (II). OECD guidelines for testing of chemicals

OECD Test Guideline 303A (1981). Simulation test - aerobic sewage treatment: Coupled units test. OECD guidelines for testing of chemicals. Draft update available 1999

OECD Test Guideline 304A (1981). Inherent biodegradability in soil. OECD guidelines for testing of chemicals

OECD Test Guideline 306 (1992). Biodegradability in seawater. OECD guidelines for testing of chemicals

OECD (1998b). Aerobic and anaerobic transformation in aquatic sediment systems. Draft proposal for a new guideline, December 1999

OECD (1999). Aerobic and anaerobic transformation in soil. Final text of a draft proposal for a new guideline, October. 1999

OECD (2000). Simulation test - Aerobic Transformation in Surface Water. Draft proposal for a new guideline, May 2000

OPPTS 835.2110 Hydrolysis as a function of pH

OPPTS 835.2130 Hydrolysis as a function of pH and temperature

OPPTS 835.2210 Direct photolysis rate in water by sunlight

OPPTS 835.3110 Ready biodegradability

OPPTS 835.3170 Shake flask die-away test

OPPTS 835.3180 Sediment/water microcosm biodegradability test

OPPTS 835.3200 Zahn-Wellens/EMPA test

OPPTS 835.3210 Modified SCAS test

OPPTS 835.3300 Soil biodegradation

OPPTS 835.3400 Anaerobic biodegradability of organic chemicals

OPPTS 835.5270 Indirect photolysis screening test: Sunlight photolysis in waters containing dissolved humic substances

4. Test guidelines for bioaccumulation [4]

ASTM, 1993. ASTM Standards on Aquatic Toxicology and Hazard Evaluation. Sponsored by ASTM Committee E-47 on Biological Effects and Environmental Fate. American Society for Testing and Materials. 1916 Race Street, Philadelphia, PA 19103. ASTM PCN: 03-547093-16., ISBN 0-8032-1778-7

ASTM E 1022-94. 1997. Standard Guide for Conducting Bioconcentration Tests with Fishes and Saltwater Bivalve Molluscs. American Society for Testing and Materials

EC, 1992. EC A.8. Partition coefficient. Annex V (Directive 67/548/EEC). Methods for determination of physico-chemical properties, toxicity and ecotoxicity

EC, 1998. EC.C.13 Bioconcentration: Flow-through Fish Test

EPA-OTS, 1982. Guidelines and support documents for environmental effects testing. Chemical fate test guidelines and support documents. United States Environmental Protection Agency. Office of Pesticides and Toxic Substances, Washington, D.C. 20960. EPA 560/6-82-002. (August 1982 and updates), cf. also Code of Federal Regulations. Protection of the Environment Part 790 to End. Revised as of July 1, 1993. ONLINE information regarding the latest updates of these test guidelines: US National Technical Information System

EPA-FIFRA, 1982. The Federal Insecticide, Fungicide and Rodenticide Act. Pesticide Assessment Guidelines, subdivision N: chemistry: Environmental fate, and subdivision E, J & L: Hazard Evaluation. Office of Pesticide Programs. US Environmental Protection Agency, Washington D.C. (1982 and updates). ONLINE information regarding the latest updates of these test guidelines: US National Technical Information System

OECD Test Guideline 107, 1995. OECD Guidelines for testing of chemicals. Partition Coefficient (n-octanol/water): Shake Flask Method

OECD Test Guideline 117, 1989. OECD Guideline for testing of chemicals. Partition Coefficient (n-octanol/water), High Performance Liquid Chromatography (HPLC) Method

OECD Test Guideline 305, 1996. Bioconcentration: Flow-through Fish Test. OECD Guidelines for testing of Chemicals

OECD Test Guidelines 305 A-E, 1981. Bioaccumulation. OECD Guidelines for testing of chemicals

OECD draft Test Guideline, 1998. Partition Coefficient n-Octanol/Water Pow. Slow-stirring method for highly hydrophobic chemicals. Draft proposal for an OECD Guideline for Testing of Chemicals

---

[4] *The list below will need to be regularly updated as new guidelines are adopted or draft guidelines are elaborated.*

1. Aquatic toxicity

APHA 1992. Standard Methods for the Examination of Water and Wastewater, 18th edition. American Public Health Association, Washington, DC

ASTM 1999. Annual Book of ASTM standards, Vol. 11.04. American Society for Testing and Materials, Philadelphia, PA

DoE 1996. Guidance on the Aquatic Toxicity Testing of Difficult Substances. United Kingdom Department of the Environment, London

ECETOC 1996. Aquatic Toxicity Testing of Sparingly Soluble, Volatile and Unstable Substances. ECETOC Monograph No. 26, ECETOC, Brussels

Lewis, M. A. 1995. Algae and vascular plant tests. In: Rand, G. M. (ed.) 1995. Fundamentals of Aquatic Toxicology, Second Edition. Taylor & Francis, Washington, DC. pp. 135-169

Mensink, B. J. W. G., M. Montforts, L. Wijkhuizen-Maslankiewicz, H. Tibosch, and J.B.H.J. Linders 1995. Manual for Summarising and Evaluating the Environmental Aspects of Pesticides. Report No. 679101022 RIVM, Bilthoven, The Netherlands

OECD 1998. Harmonized Integrated Hazard Classification System for Human Health and Environmental Effects of Chemical Substances. OECD, Paris. (Document ENV/JM/MONO(2001)6)

OECD 1999. Guidelines for Testing of Chemicals. Organisation for Economic Co-operation and Development, Paris

OECD 2000. Revised Draft Guidance Document on Aquatic Toxicity Testing of Difficult Substances and Mixtures, OECD, Paris

OECD 2006. "Current approaches in the statistical analysis of ecotoxicity data: A guidance to application", OECD Environment Health and Safety Publications Series Testing and Assessment N.54

Pedersen, F., H. Tyle, J. R. Niemeldi, B. Guttmann, L. Lander, and A. Wedebrand 1995. Environmental Hazard Classification – data collection and interpretation guide. TemaNord 1995:581

US EPA 1996. Ecological Effects Test Guidelines – OPPTS 850.1000. Special Considerations for Conducting Aquatic Laboratory Studies. Public Draft, EPA 712-C-96-113. United States Environmental Protection Agency. http://www.epa.gov/opptsfrs/home/testmeth.htm

OECD Monograph 11, Detailed Review Paper on Aquatic Toxicity Testing for Industrial Chemicals and Pesticides

Rand, Gary M., Fundamentals of Aquatic toxicology: Effects, Environmental Fate, and Risk Assessment

2. Biotic and abiotic degradation

Boesten J.J.T.I. & A.M.A. van der Linden (1991). Modeling the influence of sorption and transformation on pesticide leaching and persistence. *J. Environ. Qual.* 20, 425-435

Boethling R.S., P.H. Howard, J.A. Beauman & M.E. Larosche (1995). Factors for intermedia extrapolation in biodegradability assessment. *Chemosphere* 30(4), 741-752

de Henau H. (1993). Biodegradation. In: P. Calow. Handbook of Ecotoxicology, vol. I. Blackwell Scientific Publications, London. Chapter 18, pp. 355-377

EC (1996). Technical guidance documents in support of the Commission Directive 93/67/EEC on risk assessment for new notified substances and the Commission Regulation (EC) No. 1488/94 on risk assessment for existing substances. European Commission, Ispra

ECETOC (1998): QSARs in the Assessment of the Environmental Fate and Effects of Chemicals, Technical report No. 74. Brussels, June 1998

Federle T.W., S.D. Gasior & B.A. Nuck (1997). Extrapolating mineralisation rates from the ready CO_2 screening test to activated sludge, river water, and soil. *Environmental Toxicology and Chemistry* 16, 127-134

Langenberg J.H., W.J.G.M. Peijnenburg & E. Rorije (1996). On the usefulness and reliability of existing QSBRs for risk assessment and priority setting. *SAR and QSAR in Environmental Research* 5, 1-16

Loonen H., F. Lindgren, B. Hansen & W. Karcher (1996). Prediction of biodegradability from chemical structure. In: Peijnenburg W.J.G.M. & J. Damborsky (eds.). Biodegradability Prediction. Kluwer Academic Publishers

MITI (1992). Biodegradation and bioaccumulation data on existing data based on the CSCL Japan. Japan chemical industry, Ecology-toxicology & information center. ISBN 4-89074-101-1

Niemelä J (2000). Personal communication to OECD Environment Directorate, 20 March 2000

Nyholm N., U.T. Berg & F. Ingerslev (1996). Activated sludge biodegradability simulation test. Danish EPA, Environmental Report No. 337

Nyholm N. & F. Ingerslev (1997). Kinetic biodegradation tests with low test substance concentrations: Shake flask test with surface water and short term rate measurement in activated sludge. In: Hales S.G. (ed.). Biodegradation Kinetics: Generation and use of data for regulatory decision making. From the SETAC-Europe Workshop. Port- Sunlight. September 1996. pp. 101-115. SETAC-Europe, Brussels

Nyholm N. & L. Toräng (1999). Report of 1998/1999 Ring-test: Shalke flask batch test with surface water or surface water / sediment suspensions. ISO/CD 14592-1 Water Quality- Evaluation of the aerobic biodegradability of organic compounds at low concentrations, ISO/TC 147/ SC5/WG4 Biodegradability

OECD (1993). Structure-Activity Relationships for Biodegradation. OECD Environment Monographs No. 68. Paris 1993

OECD (1994): "US EPA/EC Joint Project on the Evaluation of (Quantitative) Structure Activity Relationships." OECD Environment Monograph No. 88. Paris

OECD (1995). Detailed Review Paper on Biodegradability Testing. OECD Environmental Monograph No. 98. Paris

OECD (1997). Guidance document on direct phototransformation of chemical in water. OECD/GD(97)21. Paris

OECD (1998). Harmonized integrated hazard classification system for human health and environmental effects of chemical substances. Paris. (Document ENV/JM/MONO(2001)6)

Pedersen F., H. Tyle, J. R. Niemelä, B. Guttmann. L. Lander & A. Wedebrand (1995). Environmental Hazard Classification – data collection and interpretation guide for substances to be evaluated for classification as dangerous for the environment. Nordic Council of Ministers. 2nd edition. TemaNord 1995:581, 166 pp

Schwarzenbach R.P., P.M. Gschwend & D.M. Imboden (1993). Environmental organic chemistry 1st ed. John Wiley & Sons, Inc. New York

Scow K.M. (1982). Rate of biodegradation. In: Lyman W.J., W.F. Reehl & D.H. Rosenblatt (1982): Handbook of Chemical Property Estimation Methods Environmental Behaviour of Organic Compounds. American Chemical Society. Washington DC (ISBN 0-8412-1761-0). Chapter 9

Struijs J. & R. van den Berg (1995). Standardized biodegradability tests: Extrapolation to aerobic environments. *Wat. Res.* 29(1), 255-262

Syracuse Research Corporation. Biodegradation Probability Program (BIOWIN). Syracuse. N.Y. http://esc.syrres.com/~esc1/biodeg.htm

Westermann P., B.K. Ahring & R.A. Mah (1989). Temperature compensation in *Methanosarcina barkeri* by modulation of hydrogen and acetate affinity. *Applied and Environmental Microbiology* 55(5), 1262-1266

3. Bioaccumulation

Anliker, R., Moser, P., Poppinger, D. 1988. Bioaccumulation of dyestuffs and organic pigments in fish. Relationships to hydrophobicity and steric factors. Chem. 17(8):1631-1644

Bintein, S.; Devillers, J. and Karcher, W. 1993. Nonlinear dependence of fish bioconcentration on *n*-octanol/water partition coefficient. SAR and QSAR in Environmental Research. Vol.1.pp.29-39

Black, M.C., Millsap, D.S., McCarthy, J.F. 1991. Effects of acute temperature change on respiration and toxicant uptake by rainbow trout, *Salmo gairdneri* (Richardson). Physiol. Zool. 64:145-168

Bodor, N., Huang, M.J. 1992. J. Pharm. Sci. 81:272-281

Broto, P., Moreau, G., Vandycke, C. 1984. Eur. J. Med. Chem. 19:71-78

Chiou, T. 1985. Partition coefficients of organic compounds in lipid-water systems and correlations with fish bioconcentration factors. Environ. Sci. Technol 19:57-62

CLOGP. 1995. Daylight Chemical Information Systems, Inf. Sys. Inc. Irvine, Ca

CSTEE (1999): DG XXIV Scientific Committee for Toxicity and Ecotoxicity and the Environment Opinion on revised proposal for a list of Priority substances in the context of the water framework directive (COMMs Procedure) prepared by the Frauenhofer-Institute, Germany,. Final report opinion adopted at the 11th CSTEE plenary meeting on 28th of September 1999

Comotto, R.M., Kimerle, R.A., Swisher, R.D. 1979. Bioconcentration and metabolism of linear alkylbenzenesulfonate by Daphnids and Fathead minnows. L.L.Marking, R.A. Kimerle, Eds., Aquatic Toxicology (ASTM, 1979), vol. ASTM STP 667

Connell, D.W., Hawker, D.W. 1988. Use of polynomial expressions to describe the bioconcentration of hydrophobic chemicals by fish. Ecotoxicol. Environ. Saf. 16:242-257

Connell, D.W. 1990. Bioaccumulation of xenobiotic compounds, Florida: CRC Press, Inc. pp.1-213

De Bruijn, J., Busser, F., Seinen, W. & Hermens, J. 1989. Determination of octanol/water partition coefficients with the "slow stirring" method. Environ. Toxicol. Chem. 8:499-512

Devillers, J., Bintein, S., Domine, D. 1996. Comparison of BCF models based on log P. Chemosphere 33(6):1047-1065

DoE, 1996. Guidance on the aquatic toxicity testing of difficult substance. Unites Kingdom Department of the Environment, London

Doucette, W.J., Andren, A.W. 1987. Correlation of octanol/water partition coefficients and total molecular surface area for highly hydrophobic aromatic compounds. Environ. Sci. Technol., 21, pages 821-824

Doucette, W.J., Andren, A.W. 1988. Estimation of octanol/water partition coefficients: evaluation of six methods for highly hydrophobic aromatic compounds. Chemosphere, 17, pages 345-359

Driscoll, S.K., McElroy, A.E. 1996. Bioaccumulation and metabolism of benzo(a)pyrene in three species of polychaete worms. Environ. Toxicol. Chem. 15(8):1401-1410

ECETOC, 1995. The role of bioaccumulation in environmental risk assessment: The aquatic environment and related food webs, Brussels, Belgium

ECEOOC, 1996. Aquatic toxicity testing of sparingly soluble, volatile and unstable substances. ECETOC Monograph No. 26, ECETOC, Brussels

European Commission, 1996. Technical Guidance Document in support of Commission Directive 93/96/EEC on Risk Assessment for new notified substances and Commission Regulation (EC) No 1488/94 on Risk Assessment for Existing Substances. Brussels

Ghose, A.K., Prottchet, A., Crippen, G.M. 1988. J. Computational Chem. 9:80-90

Gobas, F.A.P.C., Opperhuizen, A., Hutzinger, O. 1986. Bioconcentration of hydrophobic chemicals in fish: Relationship with membrane permeation. Environ. Toxicol. Chem. 5:637-646

Gobas, F.A.P.C., Clark, K.E., Shiu, W.Y., Mackay, D. 1989. Bioconcentration of polybrominated benzenes and biphenyls and related superhydrophobic chemicals in fish: Role of bioavailability and elimination into feces. Environ. Toxicol. Chem. 8:231-245

Goodrich, M.S., Melancon, M.J., Davis, R.A., Lech J.J. 1991. The toxicity, bioaccumulation, metabolism, and elimination of dioctyl sodium sulfosuccinate DSS in rainbow trout (*Oncorhynchus mykiss*) Water Res. 25: 119-124

Hansch, C., Leo, A. 1979. Substituent constants for correlation analysis in chemistry and biology. Wiley, New York, NY, 1979

Henderson, R.J., Tocher, D.R. 1987. The lipid composition and biochemistry of freshwater fish. Prog. Lipid. Res. 26:281-347

Howard, P.H. and Meyland, W.M., 1997. Prediction of physical properties transport and degradation for environmental fate and exposure assessments, QSAR in environmental science VII. Eds. Chen, F. and Schüürmann, G. pp. 185-205

Kimerle, R.A., Swisher, R.D., Schroeder-Comotto, R.M. 1975. Surfactant structure and aquatic toxicity, Symposium on Structure-Activity correlations in Studies on Toxicity and Bioconcentration with Aquatic Organisms, Burlington, Ontario, Canada, pp. 22-35

Klopman, G., Li, J.Y., Wang, S., Dimayuga, M. 1994. Computer automated log P calculations based on an extended group contribution approach. J. Chem. Inf. Comput. Sci. 34:752-781

Knezovich, J.P., Lawton, M.P., Inoue, L.S. 1989. Bioaccumulation and tissue distribution of a quaternary ammonium surfactant in three aquatic species. Bull. Environ. Contam. Toxicol. 42:87-93

Knezovich, J.P., Inoue, L.S. 1993. The influence of sediment and colloidal material on the bioavailability of a quaternary ammonium surfactant. Ecotoxicol. Environ. Safety. 26:253-264

Kristensen, P. 1991. Bioconcentration in fish: Comparison of BCFs derived from OECD and ASTM testing methods; influence of particulate matter to the bioavailability of chemicals. Danish Water Quality Institute

Mackay, D. 1982. Correlation of bioconcentration factors. Environ. Sci. Technol. 16:274-278

McCarthy, J.F., Jimenez, B.D. 1985. Reduction in bioavailability to bluegills of polycyclic aromatic hydrocarbons bound to dissolved humic material. Environ. Toxicol. Chem. 4:511-521

McKim, J.M., Goeden, H.M. 1982. A direct measure of the uptake efficiency of a xenobiotic chemical across the gill of brook trout (*Salvelinus fontinalis*) under normoxic and hypoxic conditions. Comp. Biochem. Physiol. 72C:65-74

Meylan, W.M. and Howard, P.H., 1995. Atom/Fragment Contribution Methods for Estimating Octanol-Water Partition Coefficients. J.Pharm.Sci. 84, 83

Niemelä, J.R. 1993. QTOXIN-program (ver 2.0). Danish Environmental Protection Agency

Niemi, G.J., Basak, S.C., Veith, G.D., Grunwald, G. Environ. Toxicol. Chem. 11:893-900

Niimi, A.J. 1991. Solubility of organic chemicals in octanol, triolin and cod liver oil and relationships between solubility and partition coefficients. Wat. Res. 25:1515-1521

OECD, 1993. Application of structure activity relationships to the estimation of properties important in exposure assessment. OECD Environment Directorate. Environment Monograph No. 67

OECD, 1998. Harmonized integrated hazard classification system for human health and environmental effects of chemical substances. As endorsed by the 28th joint meeting of the chemicals committee and the working party on chemicals in November 1998

OECD, 2000. Guidance Document on Aquatic Toxicity Testing of Difficult Substances and Mixtures, OECD, Paris

Opperhuizen, A., Van der Velde, E.W., Gobas, F.A.P.C., Liem, A.K.D., Van der Steen, J.M.D., Hutzinger, O. 1985. Relationship between bioconcentration in fish and steric factors of hydrophobic chemicals. Chemosphere 14:1871-1896

Opperhuizen, A. 1986. Bioconcentration of hydrophobic chemicals in fish. In: Poston T.M., Purdy, R. (eds), Aquatic Toxicology and Environmental Fate: Ninth Volume, ASTM STP 921. American Society for Testing and Materials, Philadelphia, PA, 304-315

Opperhuizen, A., Schrap, S.M. 1987. Relationship between aqueous oxygen concentration and uptake and elimination rates during bioconcentration of hydrophobic chemicals in fish. Environ. Toxicol. Chemosphere 6:335-342

Opperhuizen, A., Sijm, D.T.H.M. 1990. Bioaccumulation and biotransformation of polychlorinated dibenzo-p-dioxins and dibenzofurans in fish. Environ. Toxicol. Chem. 9:175-186

Pedersen, F., Tyle, H., Niemelä, J.R., Guttmann, B., Lander,L. and Wedebrand, A., 1995. Environmental Hazard Classification – data collection and interpretation guide (2nd edition). TemaNord 1995:581

Petersen, G.I., Kristensen, P. 1998. Bioaccumulation of lipophilic substances in fish early life stages. Environ. Toxicol. Chem. 17(7):1385-1395

Rekker, R.F., de Kort, H.M. 1979. The hydrophobic fragmental constant: An extension to a 1000 data point set. Eur. J. Med. Chem. – Chim. Ther. 14:479-488

Roberts, D.W. 1989. Aquatic toxicity of linear alkyl benzene sulphonates (LAS) – a QSAR analysis. Communicaciones Presentadas a las Jornadas del Comite Espanol de la Detergencia, 20 (1989) 35-43. Also in J.E. Turner, M.W. England, T.W. Schultz and N.J. Kwaak (eds.) QSAR 88. Proc. Third International Workshop on Qualitative Structure-Activity Relationships in Environmental Toxicology, 22-26 May 1988, Knoxville, Tennessee, pp. 91-98. Available from the National Technical Information Service, US Dept. of Commerce, Springfield, VA

Schrap, S.M., Opperhuizen, A. 1990. Relationship between bioavailability and hydrophobicity: reduction of the uptake of organic chemicals by fish due to the sorption of particles. Environ. Toxicol. Chem. 9:715-724

Shiu, WY, Doucette, W., Gobas, FAPC., Andren, A., Mackay, D. 1988. Physical-chemical properties of chlorinated dibenzo-p-dioxins. Environ. Sci. Technol. 22: pages 651-658

Sijm, D.T.H.M., van der Linde, A. 1995. Size-dependent bioconcentration kinetics of hydrophobic organic chemicals in fish based on diffusive mass transfer and allometric relationships. Environ. Sci. Technol. 29:2769-2777

Sijm, D.T.H.M., Pärt, P., Opperhuizen, A. 1993. The influence of temperature on the uptake rate constants of hydrophobic compounds determined by the isolated perfused gill of rainbow trout (Oncorhynchus mykiss). Aquat. Toxicol. 25:1-14

Spacie, A., Hamelink, J.L. 1982. Alternative models for describing the bioconcentration of organics in fish. Environ. Toxicol. Chem. 1:309-320

Suzuki, T., Kudo, Y.J. 1990. J. Computer-Aided Molecular Design 4:155-198

Syracuse Research Corporation, 1999.

Tas, J.W., Seinen, W., Opperhuizen, A. 1991. Lethal body burden of triphenyltin chloride in fish: Preliminary results. Comp. Biochem. Physiol. 100C(1/2):59-60

Tolls J. & Sijm, D.T.H.M., 1993. Bioconcentration of surfactants, RITOX, the Netherlands (9. Nov. 1993). Procter and Gamble Report (ed.: M.Stalmans)

Tolls, J. 1998. Bioconcentration of surfactants. Ph.D. Thesis. Utrecht University, Utrecht, The Netherlands

Toshima, S., Moriya, T. Yoshimura, K. 1992. Effects of polyoxyethylene (20) sorbitan monooleate on the acute toxicity of linear alkylbenzenesulfonate (C_{12}-LAS) to fish. Ecotoxicol. Environ. Safety 24: 26-36

USEPA 1985. U.S. Environmental Protection Agency. Office of Toxic Substances. Toxic Substances Control Act Test Guidelines. 50 FR 39252

US EPA/EC, 1993. US EPA/EC Joint Project on the Evaluation of (Quantitative) Structure Activity Relationships

US EPA, 1996. Ecological effects test guidelines – OPPTS 850.1000. Special considerations for conducting aquatic laboratory studies. Public Draft, EPA712-C-96-113. United States Environmental Protection Agency. http://www.epa.gov/opptsfrs/home/testmeth.htm

Van Den Berg, M., Van De Meet, D., Peijnenburg, W.J.G.M., Sijm, D.T.H.M., Struijs, J., Tas, J.W. 1995. Transport, accumulation and transformation processes. In: Risk Assessment of Chemicals: An Introduction. van Leeuwen, C.J., Hermens, J.L.M. (eds). Dordrecht, NL. Kluwer Academic Publishers, 37-102

Wakabayashi, M., Kikuchi, M., Sato, A. Yoshida, T. 1987. Bioconcentration of alcohol ethoxylates in carp (*Cyprinus carpio*), Ecotoxicol. Environ. Safety 13, 148-163

Wofford, H.W., C.D. Wilsey, G.S. Neff, C.S. Giam & J.M. Neff (1981): Bioaccumulation and metabolism of phthalate esters by oysters, brown shrimp and sheepshead minnows. Ecotox.Environ.Safety 5:202-210, 1981

4. Reference for QSAR

Boethling, R.S., Howard, P.H., Meylan, W.M. Stiteler, W.M., Beauman, J.A., and Tirado, N. (1994). Group contribution method for predicting probability and rate of aerobic biodegradation. Envir. Sci. Technol., 28, 459-465

De Bruijn, J, Busser, F., Seinen, W., and Hermens, J. (1989), Determination of octanol/water partition coefficients for hydrophobic organic chemicals with the "slow-stirring method," Environ. Toxicol. Chem., 8, 499-512

ECETOC (1998), QSARs in the Assessment of the Environmental Fate and Effects of Chemicals, Technical report No 74

Hansch, C. and A. Leo (1995), *Exploring QSAR*, American Chemical Society

Hilal, S. H., L. A. Carreira and S. W. Karickhoff (1994), *Quantitative Treatments of Solute/solvent Interactions, Theoretical and Computational Chemistry, Vol. 1,* 291-353, Elsevier Science

Howard, P.H., Boethling, R.S, Stiteler, W.M., Meylan, W.M., Hueber, A.E., Beaumen, J.A. and Larosche, M.E. (1992). Predictive model for aerobic biodegradation developed from a file of evaluated biodegradation data. Envir. Toxicol. Chem. 11, 593-603

Howard, P. And Meylan, W.M. (1992). Biodegradation Probability Program, Version 3, Syracuse Research Corp., NY

Langenberg, J.H., Peijnenburg, W.J.G.M. and Rorije, E. (1996). On the usefulness and reliability of existing QSARs for risk assessment and priority setting. SAR QSAR Environ. Res., 5, 1-16

R.L. Lipnick (1986). Charles Ernest Overton: Narcosis studies and a contribution to general pharmacology. *Trends Pharmacol. Sci.*, 7, 161-164

R.L. Lipnick (1989a). Hans Horst Meyer and the lipoid theory of narcosis, *Trends Pharmacol. Sci.*, 10 (7) July, 265-269; Erratum: 11 (1) Jan (1990), p. 44

R.L. Lipnick (1989b). Narcosis, electrophile, and proelectrophile toxicity mechanisms. Application of SAR and QSAR. *Environ. Toxicol. Chem.*, 8, 1-12

R.L. Lipnick (1990). Narcosis: Fundamental and Baseline Toxicity Mechanism for Nonelectrolyte Organic Chemicals. In: W. Karcher and J. Devillers (eds.) *Practical Applications of Quantitative Structure-Activity Relationships (QSAR) in Environmental Chemistry and Toxicology*, Kluwer Academic Publishers, Dordrecht, The Netherlands, pp. 129-144

R.L. Lipnick (ed.) (1991a). *Charles Ernest Overton: Studies of Narcosis and a Contribution to General Pharmacology*, Chapman and Hall, London, and Wood Library-Museum of Anesthesiology

R.L. Lipnick (1991b). Outliers: their origin and use in the classification of molecular mechanisms of toxicity, *Sci. Tot. Environ.*, 109/110 131-153

R.L. Lipnick (1995). Structure-Activity Relationships. In: Fundamentals of Aquatic Toxicology, 2nd edition, (G.R. Rand, ed.), Taylor & Francis, London, 609-655

Loonen, H., Lindgren, F., Hansen, B., Karcher, W., Niemela, J., Hiromatsu, K., Takatsuki, M., Peijnenburg, W., Rorije, E., and Struijs, J. (1999). Prediction of biodegradability from chemical structure: modeling of ready biodegradation test data. Environ. Toxicol. Chem., 18, 1763-1768

Meylan, W. M. and P. H. Howard (1995), *J. Pharm. Sci.*, 84, 83-92

OECD (1993), Structure-Activity Relationships for Biodegradation. OECD Environment Monograph No. 68 OECD, Paris, France

OECD (1995). Environment Monographs No. 92. Guidance Document for Aquatic Effects Assessment. OECD, Paris

F. Pedersen, H. Tyle, J. R. Niemelä, B. Guttmann, L. Lander, and A. Wedebrand (1995), Environmental Hazard Classification: Data Collection and Interpretation Guide for Substances to be Evaluated for Classification as Dangerous for the Environment, 2nd Edition, TemaNord 1995:581, Nordic Council of Ministers, Copenhagen, January

US EPA (1999) Development of Chemical Categories in the HPV Challenge Program, http://www.epa.gov/HPV/pubs/general/categuid.htm

US EPA (2000a), The Use of Structure-Activity Relationships (SAR) in the High Production Volume Chemicals Challenge Program, http://www.epa.gov/hpv/pubs/general/sarfinl1.htm

US EPA (2000b), ECOSAR, http://www.epa.gov/oppt/newchems/tools/21ecosar.htm

US EPA/EC (1993): US EPA Joint Project on the Evaluation of (Quantitative) Structure Activity Relationships, Commission of European Communities, Final Report, July

G.D. Veith, R.L. Lipnick, and C.L. Russom (1989). The toxicity of acetylenic alcohols to the fathead minnow, Pimephales promelas. Narcosis and proelectrophile activation. *Xenobiotica*, 19(5), 555-565

5.   Metals and metal compounds

Brown, D.S. and Allison, J.D. (1987). MINTEQA1 Equilibrium Metal Speciation Model: A user's manual. Athens, Georgia, USEPA Environmental Research Laboratory, Office of Research and Development

OECD (1998). Harmonized Integrated Hazard Classification System for Human Health and Environmental Effects of Chemical Substances (Document ENV/JM/MONO(2001)6)

OECD (2000). Guidance Document on Aquatic Toxicity Testing of Difficult Substances and Mixtures

OECD (2001). Guidance Document on Transformation/Dissolution of Metals and Metals Compounds in Aqueous Media

Santore, R.C. and Driscoll, C.T. (1995). The CHESS Model for Calculating Chemical Equilibria in Soils and Solutions, Chemical Equilibrium and Reaction Models. The Soil Society of America, American Society of Agronomy

Santore, R.C. and Di Toro, D.M. et al (1999). A biotic ligand model of the acute toxicity of metals. II. Application to fish and daphnia exposure to copper. Environ. Tox. Chem. Submitted

Skeaff, J., Delbeke, K., Van Assche, F. and Conard, B. (2000) A critical surface are concept for acute hazard classification of relatively insoluble metal-containing powders in aquatic environments. Environ. Tox. Chem. 19:1681-1691

Tipping, E. (1994). WHAM – A computer equilibrium model and computer code for waters, sediments, and soils incorporating discrete site/electrostatic model of ion-binding by humic substances. Computers and Geoscience 20 (6): 073-1023

ANNEX 10

GUIDANCE ON TRANSFORMATION/DISSOLUTION OF METALS AND METAL COMPOUNDS IN AQUEOUS MEDIA

Annex 10

GUIDANCE ON TRANSFORMATION/DISSOLUTION OF METALS AND METAL COMPOUNDS IN AQUEOUS MEDIA[1]

A10.1 Introduction

A10.1.1   This Test Guidance is designed to determine the rate and extent to which metals and sparingly soluble metal compounds can produce soluble available ionic and other metal-bearing species in aqueous media under a set of standard laboratory conditions representative of those generally occurring in the environment. Once determined, this information can be used to evaluate the short term and long term aquatic toxicity of the metal or sparingly soluble metal compound from which the soluble species came. This Test Guidance is the outcome of an international effort under the OECD to develop an approach for the toxicity testing and data interpretation of metals and sparingly soluble inorganic metal compounds (SSIMs) (reference 1, this annex and section A9.7 of Annex 9). As a result of recent meetings and discussions held within the OECD and EU, the experimental work on several metals and metal compounds upon which this Test Guidance is based has been conducted and reported (references 5 to 11, this annex).

A10.1.2   The evaluation of the short term and long term aquatic toxicity of metals and sparingly soluble metal compounds is to be accomplished by comparison of (a) the concentration of the metal ion in solution, produced during transformation or dissolution in a standard aqueous medium with (b) appropriate standard ecotoxicity data as determined with the soluble metal salt (acute and chronic values). This document gives guidance for performing the transformation/dissolution tests. The strategy to derive an environmental hazard classification using the results of the dissolution/transformation protocol is not within the scope of this Guidance document and can be found in Annex 9, section A9.7.

A10.1.3   For this Test Guidance, the transformations of metals and sparingly soluble metal compounds are, within the context of the test, defined and characterized as follows:

(a)   metals, M^0, in their elemental state are not soluble in water but may transform to yield the available form. This means that a metal in the elemental state may react with the media to form soluble cationic or anionic products, and in the process the metal will oxidize, or transform, from the neutral or zero oxidation state to a higher one;

(b)   in a simple metal compound, such as an oxide or sulphide, the metal already exists in an oxidized state, so that further metal oxidation is unlikely to occur when the compound is introduced into an aqueous medium. However, while oxidization state may not change, interaction with the media may yield more soluble forms. A sparingly soluble metal compound can be considered as one for which a solubility product can be calculated, and which will yield small amount of the available form by dissolution. However, it should be recognized that the final solution concentration may be influenced by a number of factors, including the solubility product of some metal compounds precipitated during the transformation/dissolution test, e.g. aluminium hydroxide.

A10.2 Principles

A10.2.1   This Test Guidance is intended to be a standard laboratory transformation/ dissolution protocol based on a simple experimental procedure of agitating various quantities of the test substance in a pH buffered aqueous medium, and sampling and analysing the solutions at specific time intervals to determine the concentrations of dissolved metal ions in the water. Two different types of tests are described in the text below:

---

[1]   *OECD Environment, Health and Safety Publications, Series on Testing and Assessment, No. 29, Environment Directorate, Organisation for Economic Co-operation and Development, April 2001.*

A10.2.2 *Screening transformation/dissolution test – sparingly soluble metal compounds*

A10.2.2.1   For sparingly soluble metal compounds, the maximum concentration of total dissolved metal can be determined by the solubility limit of the metal compound or from a screening transformation/dissolution test. The intent of the screening test, performed at a single loading, is to identify those compounds which undergo either dissolution or rapid transformation such that their ecotoxicity potential is indistinguishable from soluble forms.

A10.2.2.2   Sparingly soluble metal compounds, having the smallest representative particle size on the market are introduced into the aqueous medium at a single loading of 100 mg/l. Such dissolution as will occur is achieved by agitation during a 24 hours period. After 24 hours agitation, the dissolved metal ion concentration is measured.

A10.2.3   *Full transformation/dissolution test - metals and sparingly soluble metal compounds*

A10.2.3.1   The full transformation/dissolution test is intended to determine level of the dissolution or transformation of metals and metal compounds after a certain time period at different loadings of the aqueous phase. Normally massive forms and/or powders are introduced into the aqueous medium at three different loadings: 1, 10 and 100 mg/l. A single loading of 100 mg/l may be used if a significant release of dissolved metal species is not anticipated. Transformation/dissolution is accomplished by standardized agitation, without causing abrasion of the particles. The short term transformation/dissolution endpoints are based on the dissolved metal ion concentrations obtained after a 7 days transformation/dissolution period. The long term transformation/dissolution endpoint is obtained during a 28 days transformation/dissolution test, using a single load of 1 mg/l.

A10.2.3.2   As pH has a significant influence on transformation/dissolution both the screening test and the full test should in principle be carried out at a pH that maximizes the concentration of the dissolved metal ions in solution. With reference to the conditions generally found in the environment a pH range of 6 to 8.5 must be used, except for the 28 day full test where the pH range of 5.5 to 8.5 should be used in order to take into consideration possible long term effects on acidic lakes.

A10.2.3.3   As in addition the surface area of the particles in the test sample has an important influence on the rate and extent of transformation/dissolution, powders are tested at the smallest representative particle size as placed on the market, while massives are tested at a particle size representative of normal handling and use. A default diameter value of 1 mm should be used in absence of this information. For massive metals, this default may only be exceeded when sufficiently justified. The specific surface area should be determined in order to characterize and compare similar samples.

A10.3   **Applicability of the test**

This test applies to all metals and sparingly soluble inorganic metal compounds. Exceptions, such as certain water reactive metals, should be justified.

A10.4   **Information on the test substance**

Substances as placed on the market should be used in the transformation/dissolution tests. In order to allow for correct interpretation of the test results, it is important to obtain the following information on the test substance(s):

(a)   substance name, formula and use on the market;

(b)   physical-chemical method of preparation;

(c)   identification of the batch used for testing;

(d)   chemical characterization: overall purity (%) and specific impurities (% or ppm);

(e)   density (g/cm^3) or specific gravity;

(f)   measured specific surface area (m^2/g)- measured by BET N_2 adsorption desorption or equivalent technique;

(g)   storage, expiration date;

(h)   known solubility data and solubility products;

(i)   hazard identification and safe handling precautions;

(j)   Safety Data Sheets (SDS) or equivalent.

A10.5   Description of the test method

A10.5.1   *Apparatus and reagents*

A10.5.1.1   The following apparatus and reagents are necessary for performing tests:

(a)   pre-cleaned and acid rinsed closed glass sample bottles (A10.5.1.2);

(b)   transformation /dissolution medium (ISO 6341) (A10.5.1.3);

(c)   test solution buffering facilities (A10.5.1.4);

(d)   agitation equipment: orbital shaker, radial impeller, laboratory shaker or equivalent (A10.5.1.5);

(e)   appropriate filters (e.g.0.2 μm Acrodisc) or centrifuge for solids-liquid separation (A10.5.1.7) acrodisc filter should be flushed at least three times with fresh medium to avoid elevetaed trace metals in sample at time 0;

(f)   means to control the temperature of the reaction vessels to ± 1.5 °C in the range 20-23 °C, such as a temperature controlled cabinet or a water bath;

(g)   syringes and/or automatic pipettes;

(h)   pH meter showing acceptable results within + 0.2 pH units;

(i)   dissolved oxygen meter, with temperature reading capability;

(j)   thermometer or thermocouple; and

(k)   analytical equipment for metal analysis (e.g. atomic adsorption spectrometry, inductively coupled axial plasma spectrometry) of acceptable accuracy, preferably with a limit of quantification (LOQ) five times lower than the lowest chronic ecotoxicity reference value;

A10.5.1.2   All glass test vessels must be carefully cleaned by standard laboratory practices, acid-cleaned (e.g. HCl) and subsequently rinsed with de-ionized water. The test vessel volume and configuration (one- or two-litre reaction kettles) should be sufficient to hold 1 or 2 *l* of aqueous medium without overflow during the agitation specified. If air buffering is used (tests carried out at pH 8), it is advised to increase the air buffering capacity of the medium by increasing the headspace/liquid ratio (e.g. 1 *l* medium in 2.8 *l* flasks).

A10.5.1.3   A reconstituted standard water based on ISO 6341 should be used[2], as the standard transformation/dissolution medium. The medium should be sterilized by filtration (0.2 μm) before use in the tests. The chemical composition of the standard transformation/dissolution medium (for tests carried out at pH 8) is as follows:

$$NaHCO_3 \quad : \quad 65.7 \text{ mg/l}$$
$$KCl \quad : \quad 5.75 \text{ mg/l}$$
$$CaCl_2.2H_2O \quad : \quad 294 \text{ mg/l}$$
$$MgSO_4.7H_2O \quad : \quad 123 \text{ mg/l}$$

For tests carried out at lower or higher pH values, adjusted chemical compositions are given in A10.5.1.7.

A10.5.1.4   The concentration of total organic carbon in the medium should not exceed 2.0 mg/l.

A10.5.1.5   In addition to the fresh water medium, the use of a standardized marine test medium may also be considered when the solubility or transformation of the metal compound is expected to be significantly affected by the high chloride content or other unique chemical characteristics of marine waters and when toxicity test data are available on marine species. When marine waters are considered, the chemical composition of the standard marine medium is as follows:

$$NaF \quad : \quad 3\text{mg/l}$$
$$SrCl_2.6H_2O \quad : \quad 20 \text{ mg/l}$$
$$H_3BO_3 \quad : \quad 30 \text{ mg/l}$$
$$KBr \quad : \quad 100 \text{ mg/l}$$
$$KCl \quad : \quad 700 \text{ mg/l}$$
$$CaCl_2.2H2O \quad : \quad 1.47\text{g/l}$$
$$Na_2SO_4 \quad : \quad 4.0 \text{ g/l}$$
$$MgCl_2.6H2O \quad : \quad 10.78 \text{ g/l}$$
$$NaCl \quad : \quad 23.5 \text{ g/l}$$
$$Na_2SiO_3.9H2O \quad : \quad 20 \text{ mg/l}$$
$$NaHCO_3 \quad : \quad 200 \text{ mg/l}$$

The salinity should be 34 ± 0.5 g/kg and the pH should be 8.0 ± 0.2. The reconstituted salt water should also be stripped of trace metals (from ASTM E 729-96).

A10.5.1.6   The transformation/dissolution tests are to be carried out at a pH that maximizes the concentration of the dissolved metal ions in solution within the prescribed pH range. A pH-range of 6 to 8.5 must be used for the screening test and the 7 day full test, and a range of 5.5 to 8.5 for the 28 day full test (A10.2.3.2).

A10.5.1.7   Buffering at pH 8 may be established by equilibrium with air, in which the concentration of CO_2 provides a natural buffering capacity sufficient to maintain the pH within an average of ± 0.2 pH units over a period of one week (reference 7, Annex 10). An increase in the headspace/liquid ratio can be used to improve the air buffering capacity of the medium.

For pH adjustment and buffering down to pH 7 and 6 and up to pH 8 and 8.5, Table A10.1 shows the recommended chemical compositions of the media, as well as the CO_2 concentrations in air to be passed through the headspace, and the calculated pH values under these conditions.

---

[2]   *For hazard classification purposes the results of the dissolution/transformation protocol are compared with existing ecotoxicity data for metals and metal compounds. However, for purposes such as data validation, there might be cases where it may be appropriate to use the aqueous medium from a completed transformation test directly in an OECD 202 and 203 daphnia and fish ecotoxicity test. If the $CaCl_2.2H_2O$ and $MgSO_4.7H_2O$ concentrations of the transformation medium are reduced to one-fifth of the ISO 6341 medium, the completed transformation medium can also be used (upon the addition of micronutrients) in an OECD 201 algae ecotoxicity test.*

Table A10.1: Recommended chemical composition of testing medium

Chemical composition of medium	NaHCO₃	6.5 mg/l	12.6 mg/l	64.75 mg/l	194.25 mg/l
	KCl	0.58 mg/l	2.32 mg/l	5.75 mg/l	5.74 mg/l
	CaCl₂.2H₂O	29.4 mg/l	117.6 mg/l	294 mg/l	29.4 mg/l
	MgSO₄.7H₂O	12.3 mg/l	49.2 mg/l	123.25 mg/l	123.25 mg/l
CO₂ concentration (balance is air) in test vessel		0.50%	0.10%	0.038% (air)	0.038%(air)
Calculated pH		6.09	7.07	7.98	8.5

NOTE 1: *The pH values were calculated using the FACT (Facility for the Analysis of Chemical Thermodynamics) System (http://www.crct.polymtl.ca/fact/fact.htm).*

NOTE 2: *While the protocol was only validated for the pH range 6.0-8.0, this table does not prevent attaining pH 5.5. Composition for pH 8.5 has not been verified experimentally in presence of metal.*

A10.5.1.8   Alternative equivalent buffering methods may be used if the influence of the applied buffer on the chemical speciation and transformation rate of the dissolved metal fraction would be minimal. pH should not be adjusted during the test using an acid or alkali.

A10.5.1.9   During the full transformation/dissolution tests, agitation should be used which is sufficient to maintain the flow of aqueous medium over the test substance while maintaining the integrity of the surface of the test substance and of any solid reaction product coatings formed during the test. For 1 *l* of aqueous medium, this may be accomplished by the use of:

(a)   a radial impeller set at 200 r.p.m., with blades deployed 5 cm from the bottom of a 1 *l* reaction kettle. The radial impellers consist of two fixed polypropylene blades of dimensions 40 mm width by 15 mm height on a PVC-coated steel rod 8 mm diameter and 350 mm long; or

(b)   a 1.0 to 3.0 *l* flask capped with a rubber stopper and placed on an orbital or laboratory shaker set at 100 r.p.m.

Other methods of gentle agitation may be used provided they meet the criteria of surface integrity and homogeneous solution.

A10.5.1.10   The choice of solids-liquid separation method depends on whether adsorption of soluble metal ions on filters occurs and whether or not a suspension is generated by the agitation prescribed in A10.5.1.9, which will in turn depend on particle size distributions and particle density. For solids of density greater than approximately 6 g/cm^3 and particle size ranges as low as 50% < 8 µm, experience has shown that the gentle agitation methods prescribed in A10.5.1.9 are unlikely to result in suspensions. Hence, filtration of a sample through e.g. a 25 mm diameter 0.2 µm hydrophilic polyethersulphone membrane syringe filter (as an option, overlain by a 0.8 µm prefilter) will result in a solution essentially free of solids.

However, in the event that suspensions occur, stopping the agitation to allow the suspension to settle for about 5 minutes prior to taking a solution sample may be useful.

A10.5.2   *Prerequisites*

A10.5.2.1   *Analytical method*

     A suitable validated analytical method for the total dissolved metal analysis is essential to the study. The analytical detection limit should be lower than the appropriate chronic or long term value from the exotoxicity tests.

     The following analytical validation aspects are at a minimum to be reported:

(a)   detection and quantification limit of the analytical method;

(b)   analytical linearity range within the applicable analytical range;

(c)   a blank run consisting of transformation medium (this can be done during the tests);

(d)   matrix effect of the transformation medium on the measurement of the dissolved metal ion;

(e)   mass balance (%) after completion of the transformation test;

(f)   reproducibility of the analysis;

(g)   adsorptive properties of the soluble metal ions on the filters (if filtration is used for the separation of the soluble from the solid metal ion).

A10.5.2.2   *Determination of the appropriate pH of the dissolution medium*

     If no relevant literature data exist, a preliminary screening test may need to be carried out in order to ensure that the test is performed at a pH maximizing transformation/dissolution within the pH range described in A10.2.3.2 and A10.5.1.6.

A10.5.2.3   *Reproducibility of transformation data*

A10.5.2.3.1   For a standard set-up of three replicate test vessels and two replicate samples per test vessel at each sampling time, it is reasonable to anticipate that for a constant loading of a substance, tested in a narrow particle size (e.g. 37 - 44 μm) and total surface area range, the within-vessel variation in transformation data should be < 10% and the between-vessel variation should be < 20 % (reference 5, this annex).

A10.5.2.3.2   To estimate the reproducibility of the transformation test, some Guidance is given in the following. The results can be used to eventually improve on reproducibility by adjusting the final test set-up through varying the number of replica test vessels and/or replica samples or further screening of the particles. The preliminary tests also allow for a first evaluation of the transformation rate of the tested substance and can be used to establish the sampling frequency.

A10.5.2.3.3   In preparing the transformation/dissolution medium, the pH of the medium should be adjusted to the desired pH (air buffering or CO_2 buffering) by agitation for about half an hour to bring the aqueous medium into equilibrium with the buffering atmosphere. At least three samples (e.g. 10 - 15 ml) are drawn from the test medium prior to addition of the substance, and the dissolved metal concentrations are measured as controls and background.

     At least five test vessels, containing the metal or metal compound (e.g.100 mg solid/l medium), are agitated as described in A10.5.1.9 at a temperature ± 1.5 °C in the range 20 - 23 °C, and triplicate samples are taken by syringe from each test vessel after 24 hours. The solid and solution are separated by membrane filter as described in A10.5.1.10, the solution is acidified with one or two drops of trace metal grade HNO_3 with the target pH 1 and analyzed for total dissolved metal concentration.

A10.5.2.3.4   The within-test vessel and between-test vessel means and coefficients of variation of the measured dissolved metal concentrations are calculated.

A10.5.2.3.5   To ensure reproducibility of transformation data, it is recommended that:

(a)   new laboratories use a training set;

(b)   one metal powder with specified surface conditions be used as standard control; and

(c)   one or two laboratories be responsible for reference chemicals.

It may be necessary to check specific surface areas of the powders.

A10.5.3   *Test performance*

A10.5.3.1   *Dissolution screening test – sparingly soluble metal compounds*

A10.5.3.1.1   After dissolution medium is prepared, add the medium into at least three test vessels (number of test vessels depend on the reproducibility obtained during the preliminary test). After a half-hour of agitation to bring the aqueous medium into equilibrium with the atmosphere or buffering system (paras. A10.5.1.6 to A10.5.1.8), the pH, temperature and dissolved O_2 concentrations of the medium are measured. Then at least two 10 - 15 ml samples are taken from the test medium (prior to addition of the solids) and the dissolved metal concentration measured as controls and background.

A10.5.3.1.2   The metal compound is added to the test vessels at a loading of 100 mg/l and the test vessels are covered and agitated rapidly and vigorously. After the 24 hours agitation, the pH, temperature and dissolved O_2 concentrations are measured in each test vessel, and two to three solution samples are drawn by syringe from each test vessel and the solution is passed through a membrane filter as described in A10.5.1.10 above, acidified (e.g. 1 % HNO_3) and analysed for total dissolved metal concentration.

A10.5.3.2   *Full test - metals and metal compounds*

A10.5.3.2.1   Repeat A10.5.3.1.1

A10.5.3.2.2   For 7 day test, substance loadings of 1, 10 and 100 mg/l, respectively, are added to the test vessels (number of which depends on the reproducibility as established in sub-section A10.5.2.3), containing the aqueous medium. The test vessels are closed and agitated as described in A10.5.1.9. If a 28-day test is to be conducted, the test with 1 mg/l loading may be extended to 28 days, provided that the same pH value is to be chosen for both 7 day and 28-day tests. However, since 7-day tests are only conducted at pH ranges of 6 and higher, separate 28-day tests are needed to cover the pH range between 5.5 and 6. It may also be useful to include a concurrent control test with no substance loaded (i.e. a blank test solution). At established time intervals (e.g. 2 hours, 6 hours, 1, 4 and 7 days), the temperature, pH and dissolved O_2 concentrations are measured in each test vessel, and at least two samples (e.g. 10 - 15 ml) are drawn by syringe from each test vessel. The solid and dissolved fractions are separated as per A10.5.1.10 above. The solutions are acidified (e.g. 1 % HNO_3) and analysed for dissolved metal concentration. After the first 24 hours, the solution volumes should be replenished with a volume of fresh dissolution medium equal to that already drawn. Repeat after subsequent samplings. The maximum total volume taken from the test solutions should not exceed 20% of the initial test solution volume. The test can be stopped when three subsequent total dissolved metal concentration data points vary no more than 15%. The maximum duration for the loadings of 10 and 100 mg/l is seven days (the short term test) and 28 days for the loading of 1 mg/l test medium (long term test).

A10.5.4   *Test conditions*

A10.5.4.1   The transformation/dissolution tests should be done at a controlled ambient temperature ± 1.5 °C in the range 20 – 23 °C.

A10.5.4.2   The transformation/dissolution tests are to be carried out within the pH range described in A10.2.3.2 and A10.5.1.6. The test solution pH should be recorded at each solution sampling interval. The pH can be expected to remain constant (± 0.2 units) during most tests, although some short-term pH variations have been encountered at 100 mg/l loadings of reactive fine powders (reference 7, this annex), due to the inherent properties of the substance in the finely divided state.

A10.5.4.3   Above the aqueous medium, the head space provided by the reaction vessel should be adequate in most instances to maintain the dissolved oxygen concentration above about 6.0 mg/l, which is 70% of the saturation level of 8.5 mg/l. However, in certain instances, reaction kinetics may be limited not by the availability of molecular oxygen in the head space above the solution but by the transfer of dissolved oxygen to, and removal of reaction product away from, the solid-solution interface. In this case, little can be done, other than await the restoration of equilibrium.

A10.5.4.4   To reduce chemical and biological contamination as well as evaporation, the transformation/dissolution kinetics must be performed in closed vessels and in the dark, whenever possible.

A10.6   **Treatment of the results**

A10.6.1   *Screening test*

The mean dissolved metal concentrations at 24 hours are calculated (with confidence intervals).

A10.6.2   *Full test: Determination of the extent of transformation/dissolution*

A10.6.2.1   *Short term test*

The dissolved metal concentrations, measured during the different short term (7 days) tests, are plotted versus time, and the transformation/dissolution kinetics may be determined, if possible. The following kinetic models could be used to describe the transformation/dissolution curves:

(a)   Linear model:

$$C_t \quad = \quad C_0 + kt, \text{ mg/l}$$

where:

C_0 = initial total dissolved metal concentration (mg/l) at time $t = 0$;
C_t = total dissolved metal concentration (mg/l) at time t;
k = linear rate constant, mg/l-days.

(b)   First order model:

$$C_t \quad = \quad A\,(1\text{-}e^{(-kt)}), \text{ mg/l}$$

where:

A = limiting dissolved metal concentration (mg/l) at apparent equilibrium = constant;
C_t = total dissolved metal concentration (mg/l) at time t;
k = first order rate constant, 1/days.
(c)   Second order model:
C_t = $A\,(1\text{-}e(\text{-}at)) + B\,(1\text{-}e(\text{-}bt))$, mg/l

where:

C_t = total dissolved metal concentration (mg/l), at time t;
a = first order rate constant, 1/days;
b = second order rate constant, 1/days;
C = A + B = limiting dissolved metal concentration (mg/l).

(d) Reaction kinetic equation:

$$C_t = a\,[1-e^{-bt} - (c/n)\{1 + (b\,e^{-nt} - n\,e^{-bt})/(n - b)\}],\ \text{mg/l}$$

where:

C_t = total dissolved metal concentration (mg/l) at time t;
a = regression coefficient (mg/l);
b,c,d = regression coefficients (1/days);
n = c+d.

Other reaction kinetic equations may also apply (reference 7 and 8, this annex).

For each replicate vessel in the transformation test, these model parameters are to be estimated by regression analyses. The approach avoids possible problems of correlation between successive measurements of the same replicate. The mean values of the coefficients can be compared using standard analysis of variance if at least three replicate test vessel were used. The coefficient of determination, r^2, is estimated as a measure of the "goodness of fit" of the model.

A10.6.2.1   *Long term test*

The dissolved metal concentrations, measured from the 1 mg/l loading during the 28 day test, are plotted versus time and the transformation/dissolution kinetics determined, if possible, as described in A10.6.1 and A10.6.2.

A10.7   Test report

The test report should include (but is not limited to) the following information (see also A10.4 and A10.5.2.1):

(a) Identification of the sponsor and testing facility;

(b) Description of the tested substance;

(c) Description of the reconstituted test medium and metal loadings;

(d) Test medium buffering system used and validation of the pH used (as per paras. A10.2.3.2 and A10.5.1.6 to A10.5.1.8) description of the analytical method;

(e) Detailed descriptions of the test apparatus and procedure;

(f) Preparation of the standard metal solution;

(g) Results of the method validation;

(h) Results from the analyses of metal concentrations, pH, temperature, oxygen;

(i) Dates of tests and analyses at the various time intervals;

(j) Mean dissolved metal concentration at different time intervals (with confidence intervals);

(k)   Transformation curves (total dissolved metal as a function of time);

(l)   Results from transformation/dissolution kinetics, if determined;

(m)   Estimated reaction kinetic quation, if determined;

(n)   Deviations from the study plan if any and reasons;

(o)   Any circumstances that may have affected the results; and

(p)   Reference to the records and raw data.

Annex 10

APPENDIX

References

1. "Draft Report of the OECD Workshop on Aquatic Toxicity Testing of Sparingly Soluble Metals, Inorganic Metal Compounds and Minerals", Sept. 5-8, 1995, Ottawa

2. OECD Metals Working Group Meeting, Paris, June 18-19, 1996

3. European Chemicals Bureau. Meeting on Testing Methods for Metals and Metal Compounds, Ispra, February 17-18, 1997

4. OECD Metals Working Group Meeting, Paris, October 14-15, 1997

5. LISEC [1] Staff, "Final report "transformation/dissolution of metals and sparingly soluble metal compounds in aqueous media - zinc", LISEC no. BO-015 (1997)

6. J.M. Skeaff [2] and D. Paktunc, "Development of a Protocol for Measuring the Rate and Extent of Transformations of Metals and Sparingly Soluble Metal Compounds in Aqueous Media. Phase I, Task 1: Study of Agitation Method." Final Report, January 1997. Mining and Mineral Sciences Laboratories Division Report 97-004(CR)/Contract No. 51545

7. Jim Skeaff and Pierrette King, "Development of a Protocol For Measuring the Rate and Extent of Transformations of Metals and Sparingly Soluble Metal Compounds in Aqueous Media. Phase I, Tasks 3 and 4: Study of pH and of Particle Size/Surface Area.", Final Report, December 1997. Mining and Mineral Sciences Laboratories Division Report 97-071(CR)/Contract No. 51590

8. Jim Skeaff and Pierrette King, Development of Data on the Reaction Kinetics of Nickel Metal and Nickel Oxide in Aqueous Media for Hazard Identification, Final Report, January 1998. Mining and Mineral Sciences Laboratories Division Report 97-089(CR)/Contract No. 51605

9. LISEC Staff, "Final report "transformation/dissolution of metals and sparingly soluble metal compounds in aqueous media - zinc oxide", LISEC no. BO-016 (January, 1997)

10. LISEC Staff, "Final report "transformation/dissolution of metals and sparingly soluble metal compounds in aqueous media - cadmium", LISEC no. WE-14-002 (January, 1998)

11. LISEC Staff, "Final report "transformation/dissolution of metals and sparingly soluble metal compounds in aqueous media - cadmium oxide", LISEC no. WE-14-002 (January, 1998)

Bibliography

1. OECD Guideline for testing of chemicals, Paris (1984). Guideline 201 Alga, Growth Inhibition test

2. OECD Guideline for testing of chemicals, Paris (1984). Guideline 202:Daphnia sp. Acute im-mobilisation test and Reproduction Test

3. OECD Guideline for testing of chemicals, Paris (1992). Guideline 203: Fish, Acute Toxicity Test

4. OECD Guideline for testing of chemicals, Paris (1992). Guideline 204: Fish, Prolonged Toxicity Test: 14- Day study [3]

5. OECD Guideline for testing of chemicals, Paris (1992). Guideline 210: Fish, Early-Life Stage Toxicity Test

6. International standard ISO 6341 (1989 (E)). Determination of the inhibition of the mobility of Daphnia magna Straus (Cladocera, Crustacea)

---

[1] *LISEC, Craenevenne 140, 3600 Genk, Belgium.*

[2] *CANMET, Natural Resources Canada, 555 Booth St., Ottawa, Canada K1A 0G1.*

[3] *This Test Guideline has been cancelled but may continue to be used until 2 April 2014.*